THE
HANDY
RELIGION
ANSWER
BOOK

THE HANDY RELIGION ANSWER BOOK

JOHN RENARD

Detroit

The Handy Religion Answer Book

COPYRIGHT © 2002 BY VISIBLE INK PRESS®

Visible Ink Press®
43311 Joy Rd. #414
Canton, MI 48187-2075

Visible Ink Press and The Handy Religion Answer Book are trademarks of Visible Ink Press LLC.

Most Visible Ink Press books are available at special quantity discounts when purchased in bulk by corporations, organizations, or groups. Customized printings, special imprints, messages, and excerpts can be produced to meet your needs. For more information, contact Special Markets Director, Visible Ink Press, at www.visibleink.com

Art Director: Mary Claire Krzewinski
Typesetting: Graphix Group

Library of Congress Cataloging-in-Publication Data

Renard, John, 1944-
  The handy religion answer book / John Renard.
    p. cm.
  ISBN 0-681-04716-x (pbk.)
    1. Religions--Miscellanea. I. Title.
  BL80.2 .R46   2001
  291--dc21   2001004052
                                                     CIP

Printed in the United States of America
All rights reserved
10 9 8 7 6 5

Contents

GENERAL BACKGROUND

RELIGIOUS TRADITIONS OF MIDDLE EASTERN ORIGIN

RELIGIOUS TRADITIONS
OF SOUTH ASIAN ORIGIN

RELIGIOUS TRADITIONS OF EAST ASIAN ORIGIN

Introduction

Religion is one of the most powerful and pervasive forces in our world. To dismiss religion as so much superstition and delusional thinking is to brush aside one of the most important features of the human condition: what people believe—and why they believe it—profoundly influence the way they act. Religious beliefs and cultural assumptions are often so intimately intertwined that it is rarely, if ever, possible to disentangle them. It is possible, for the sake of clarity and to promote further discussion, to provide a general outline of major themes in history, belief, structure, and practice. But it is essential to keep in mind that any study of a phenomenon so complex and broad begins from a particular point of view, makes certain working assumptions, and must inevitably indulge in the luxury of sweeping generalizations.

First, a word about my own perspective on the practice and study of religion. Raised in the Roman Catholic tradition, I began my professional study of religion after completing undergraduate work in philosophy and classical languages. Graduate study toward an M.A. in biblical languages and literature focused on the critical examination of the Hebrew and Christian scriptures. Since finishing a Ph.D. in Islamic studies in 1978, I have been teaching courses on Islam and other non-Christian religious traditions to undergraduate and graduate students. I remain an adherent of Roman Catholicism, but I work from the conviction that it is my professional responsibility to ask critical questions about the nature and function of religion—beginning with my own. One might legitimately ask whether my Roman Catholic background might lead me to compare other traditions using my own as some sort of standard. My answer is that I have sought to set up categories of comparability that privilege no tradition in particular, drawing from a broad spectrum of concepts, and in no instance do I engage in the comparative evaluation of truth claims.

Another personal conviction, based on over thirty years of studying and teaching the history of religions, has had a particularly formative influence on my approach to the subject at hand. It is this: I am persuaded that, as the great traditions teach in so many ways, there is an absolute truth that is somehow accessible to human beings honestly in quest of it. But I am equally convinced that human beings are by definition incapable of possessing that truth either exhaustively, so that any person or group can claim to have it fully; or exclusively, so that the world divides itself neatly between the "we" who own the truth and the "they" who are simply out of luck. Any such view both inflates human capabilities and reduces transcendent realities to pocket-size trinkets. This does not mean that I am one of those intellectually indecisive people called relativists who believe either that all religious traditions are the same or that one is as good as another. I do believe, however, that God, or Ultimate Reality, is far too great for any religious tradition, or all of them put together, to master or dispense; and that each individual who seeks with a sincere heart the center and goal of his or her life will be led to it. Meanwhile, one of the noblest and most useful tasks to which we can commit ourselves is a greater understanding of how and why people believe as they do. I believe, perhaps naively but nonetheless firmly, that the world is richer for its religious pluralism, and that it would also be safer if the quest for mutual understanding of that diversity were a higher priority.

I begin with a number of assumptions about religion—that is, aspects of the subject that a book like this will not and could not, without expanding to many volumes, begin to address. In addition to the assertions with which I opened this preface, here are several other "givens," naturally arguable and open to debate, on which this book builds. One is that it can be misleading to try to reduce any of the world's major religious traditions to a handful of questions and answers. But it can also be very helpful to do so occasionally, so long as one keeps in mind that these tidbits of information are offered as an invitation to dig deeper. Another assumption is that because religion is so susceptible to misunderstanding and caricature, specialists in religious studies have a responsibility to devise balanced approaches to the subject. It is my hope that foregrounding my own biases and limitations will assist the reader in evaluating the approaches in these pages. Misinformation about religious beliefs and practices, especially those of "other" people, abounds and has a way of perpetuating itself. This broad survey attempts to provide solid, basic information in the hope that readers will be encouraged to pursue particular aspects of this enormous subject and fill in for themselves the kind of historical context a book this size cannot afford.

Finally, I have opted for a bias toward the larger, more organized, and lettered or so-called world religious traditions. In doing so I have deliberately left out any direct consideration of the archaic traditions, such as Graeco-Roman and Egyptian; indigenous or tribal traditions, such as Native American or Oceanic; or nature-oriented traditions, such as Wicca. That is due in part to the practical constraints of size and in part to my own professional limitations. Of at least two of the traditions treated here, Buddhism and Confucianism, one might legitimately suggest that they fit more appropriately in the category of ethical system than religion. I believe, however, that in both instances there is more than ample reason for setting them alongside the

other religious traditions.

The Handy Religion Answer Book is organized in four parts. Part One lays out the ground plan to be followed through the eight chapters dealing with major traditions. In its eight subsections, the general introduction provides the reader with the fundamental working concepts needed to get a good start in religious studies. Part Two devotes a chapter each to the three traditions of Middle Eastern origin, namely, Judaism, Christianity, and Islam. Part Three covers the two largest traditions of South Asian origin, Hinduism and Buddhism; and Part Four deals with three traditions of East Asian origin, Chinese Confucianism and Taoism, and Japanese Shinto. Each of the chapters organizes the material in eight subsections: history and sources; religious beliefs; signs and symbols; membership, community, and diversity; leadership, authority, and organization; personalities and powers; holidays and regular observances; and customs and rituals. In order to facilitate comparison, many of the questions are phrased generically rather than specifically, so that readers will hear echoes of questions posed in other sections. Other questions are concept-specific, especially where the issues at hand already are mentioned in popular media and thus readily recognizable. A global chronology of religious history offers an overview that blends material from all the chapters.

One final note: These religious traditions represent vast and complex developments over many centuries and in countless cultural contexts. Reducing them, as I have here, to fifty or sixty pages apiece means barely scratching the surface to offer the merest hint of their richness. This volume's modest goal is to provide the kind of solid, basic information upon which interested readers might build a broader and deeper understanding of these world treasures through further investigation.

Acknowledgments

I am indebted to scholars too numerous to mention by name here, although the extensive bibliography will offer some idea of the throng of dedicated specialists on whose work I have relied. My deepest gratitude goes, as always, to my spouse, Mary Pat, for her unfailing good humor through the duration of the project. Special thanks go to David Vila of Saint Louis University for his advice on reading an early draft, to Darius Makuja for his research assistance early in the project, and to Elizabeth Staley for her editorial and research assistance in preparing the final draft.

Thank you also to publisher Martin Connors, editor Christa Brelin, proofreader Mary Ramsay, designer Mary Claire Krzewinski, photo coordinator Robert Huffman, and typesetter Marco Di Vita of the Graphix Group.

I also thank Michael Harter, S.J., Beata Grant of Washington University, and the St. Louis Art Museum for kindly providing illustrations, especially on Hinduism. Unless otherwise credited, all photographs are by the author.

The images on the pages listed below were provided to the Saint Louis Art Museum by the following sources: page 190, purchase, 1948; page 255, funds given by Merrill Trust Foundation, 1966; page 270, Friends Fund, 1962; page 273, funds given by William K. Bixby Asian Art Trust Fund, 1938; page 276, purchase, 1978; page 277, W. K. Bixby Oriental Art Purchase Fund, 1984; page 289, purchase, 1964; page 370, purchase, 1919; page 402, gift of Dr. and Mrs. Frederick O. Schwartz, 1977; page 441, bequest of Leona J. Beckmann, 1985.

Chronology
of Major Events

BCE

4000

The Vedic period begins; earliest Vedic hymns (Hinduism).

3500

Roots of the Semitic tradition.

2700–1500

Indus civilization flourishes as evidenced by archeological data from Harrapa and Mohenjo (Hinduism).

2697–2597

Huang Di, Yellow Emperor, one of the culture heroes in Chinese lore, was patron of ancient *fang shi* or shamans (Daoism).

2637

Reckoning of Chinese lunar calendar of twelve months of twenty-nine or thirty days.

c. 2000–1400

Patriarchal Age; Abraham, revered in Hebrew Bible as father of the Hebrew people, Isaac, Jacob, and Joseph; Ishmael, son of Abraham by Hagar; Muhammad considers Ishmael and Abraham as ancestors of Arabs, and associates them with the construction of the Ka'ba at Mecca.

1900

Age of *Ramayana* epic (Hinduism).

1994–1525

Xia dynasty instituted the principle of hereditary succession (Confucianism).

c. 1700
God's Covenant with Abraham (Judaism).

1500–1200
Traditional dating for Aryan Invasion of Indus Valley; now disputed (Hinduism).

1500–500
Major Upanishads composed (Hinduism).

1525–1028
Shang dynasty overthrows the last Xia tyrant (Confucianism).

c. 1400
Age of Krishna; Great Bharata War; early version of *Mahabharata* (Hinduism).

c. 1250–1050
Moses leads Exodus out of Egypt; development of Jewish community; conquest and subsequent settlement of Canaan; period of the Judges.

c. 1200–1000
Composition of the hymns of the Rigveda (Hinduism).

1028–222
Zhou dynasty: Yi Jing, Classic of Change, manual of divination (Confucianism).

c. 1020–1000
Kingship of Saul (Judaism).

c. 1000–973
Kingship of David over Israel (Judaism).

c. 970
Solomon, son of David, builds the First Temple in Jerusalem (Judaism).

922–722/1
Northern Kingdom of Israel (Judaism).

922–587/6
Southern Kingdom of Judah (Judaism).

835–765
Prophet Amos from Tekoa is the earliest of the Biblical prophets (Judaism).

c. 800–600
Shu Jing, *The Classic of History* (Confucianism).

c. 740–700
Isaiah prophesies (Judaism).

c. 732–725

Life of Prophet Hosea (Judaism).

722–481

Chun Qiu, *Annals of Spring and Autumn* (Confucianism).

722/1

Assyrians conquer Samaria; exile of ten northern tribes (Judaism).

660

Jimmu Tenno, first human emperor (Shinto).

c. 627–587

Life of Prophet Jeremiah (Judaism).

604

Traditional date of Lao Zi's birth (Daoism).

c. 593–571

Ezekiel, priest of Jerusalem, prophesies (Judaism).

587–6

Babylonians destroy Jerusalem Temple and exile Judeans to Babylon (Judaism).

563–483

Life of Siddhartha Gautama, the Buddha.

551–479

Life of Kong Zi (Confucianism).

539

Beginning of return from Babylion Exile to Zion (Judaism).

515

Jewish Temple rebuilt; emergence of classical Judaism.

c. 500–200

Bhagavad Gita composed (Hinduism).

468

Traditional death date of Vardhamana Mahavira, the twenty-fourth and last great "Ford-finder" of Jainism.

400

Confucius' sayings edited.

400–400 CE

Mahabharata epic composed (Hinduism).

400–200

Soferim class of scholars, forerunner of early Rabbinical Judaism.

389–286

Zhuang Zi, Daoist philosopher.

383

Second Buddhist Council.

c. 372–289

Meng Zi or Mencius and Xun Zi codified the teachings of Confucius into the foundations of a political philosophy.

c. 350–300

Dao De Jing composed (Daoism).

327–325

Alexander the Great invades northwest India.

322–185

Mauryan dynasty; Buddhism spreads throughout northern India.

300–600 CE

Buddhist missions expand beyond India to Central, East, and Southeast Asia.

c. 274–236

Maurya dynasty; Emperor Ashoka (c. 273–37) convert to Buddhism sends missionaries.

250

Third Council, official formulation of Tripitaka (Buddhism).

221–210

Emperor Qin Shi Huang Di tries to suppress Confucian texts, and transforms feudal China into centralized bureaucracy.

c.206–221 CE

Han dynasty; Confucianism official state philosophy.

c. 200

Rise of Mahayana Buddhism, distinction from Hinayana schools.

202–220 CE

Religious Daoism emerges.

220–280 CE

Three Kingdoms period: Wei (220–266); Shu Han (221–263); Wu (222–280).

200–200 CE

Rise of Mahayana; Buddhism spreads to Central Asia and China.

200–200 CE

Ramayana epic composed; period of increased Buddhist and Jain influence (Hinduism).

c. 200

Population shifts from northwest India to the Ganges plain (Hinduism).

200–30 CE

Class of Judaic scholars called Five Pairs of Teachers.

195

Early Imperial sacrifice at Confucius' tomb.

168

Maccabees revolt (Judaism).

165

Temple restored and purified (Judaism).

150–75 CE

Essenes live ascetical life at Qumran at northern end of Dead Sea (Judaism).

c. 140–87

Emperor Wu Di of Han dynasty makes Confucian system his official ideology.

135–104

John Hyracanus attempts to secure both religious and civil authority (Judaism).

100

Lotus Sutra (Buddhism).

103–76

Alexander Yannai restores the Pharisees to position of influence (Judaism).

100–100 CE

Rise of Hindu literature of bhakti (devotion).

63

Rise of Roman rule; conquest of Palestine (Judaism).

c. 50–30 CE

Life of Hillel the Elder, influential Jewish teacher.

37–4 CE

Herod of the Great, Idumaean king of Judea.

CE

1

Emperor Ping proclaims Confucius the "Exalted Mt. Ni Duke of the Highest Perfection."

4 BCE–29

Life of Jesus of Nazareth; ministry (26–29); Crucifixion (29) (Christianity).

30–200

Tanna'im School lays foundation of the Mishna (Judaism).

34–156

Zhang Dao Ling, cited as the founder of the first Daoist religious movement, the Celestial Masters School.

c. 50–135

Martyr Rabbi Akiva (Judaism).

c. 65

Death of Apostle Paul (Christianity).

66

Massacre of Jews at Alexandria.

70

Fall of second Temple to Romans (Judaism).

Rabbi Yochanan ben Zakkai founds center for legal study and administrative rule in Yavneh; canonization of biblical literature at Yavneh (Judaism).

c. 100

Li Ji, Classic of Rites (Confucianism).

c. 100–552

Primitive Shinto shrines dedicated to clan deities *Ujigami* appeared.

c. 100–165

Life of Justin Martyr (Christianity).

110

Martyrdom of Ignatius of Antioch (Christianity).

c. 120–162

King Kanishka of Kushan dynasty continues spread of Buddhism.

c. 120–220
Apologetic Writing (Christianity).

c. 150
Fourth Buddhist Council.

c. 150–250
Nagarjuna, Buddhist thinker.

c. 160–220
Life of Tertullian, Christian apologist.

166
Han Chinese Emperor sacrifices to Lao Zi and Buddha.

184
Rebellion of Yellow Turbans behind a military force (Daoism).

c. 185–254
Life of Origen (Christianity).

200–500
Jewish class of rabbi-scholars called Amoraim (Speakers) in Babylonian academies.

203
Martyrdom of Perpetua and Felicitas (Christianity).

220–552
Buddhist missionaries to Vietnam, Burma, China, Korea, Japan, Indonesia.

249–51
Decian Persecution of Christians.

c. 250–356
Life of Anthony of Egypt, "father of monasticism" (Christianity).

c. 250–336
Life of Arius, propagator of Arian heresy (Christianity).

251–334
Wei Hua Cun, famous woman Libationer (Daoism).

284–305
Emperor Diocletian's persecution of Christians.

290–347
Life of Pachomius of Egypt, founder of first monastic community (Christianity).

c. 296–373

Life of Athanasius of Alexandria, Church Father (Christianity).

300–500

Early Puranas: Markandeya, Matsya, Vaya, Narashimha, Vishnu, Devi (Hinduism).

c. 300

Lie Zi composes *The True Classic of Expanding Emptiness* (Daoism).

c. 300

Daoist sect, Sacred Jewel, introduces influential rituals.

305–311

Emperor Galerius persecutes Christians in the eastern empire.

306–373

Life of Ephrem of Syria, church father (Christianity).

312

Constantine, patron of Christianity, assumes control of Roman Empire.

c. 320–550

Gupta dynasty; India's Golden Age (Hinduism).

325

Council of Nicea (Christianity).

327–379

Life of Macrina, sister of Basil and Gregory of Nyssa (Christianity).

c. 329–389

Life of Greek Father, Gregory of Nazianzus (Christianity).

c. 330–379

Life of Greek Father, Basil (Christianity).

c. 330–395

Life of Greek Father, Gregory of Nyssa (Christianity).

354–430

Life of Augustine of Hippo (Christianity).

364–370

Highest Purity (Mao Shan) Sect emphasizes meditation (Daoism).

c. 390

Jerusalem Talmud is completed (Judaism).

c. 390

Simeon, Syrian ascetic (Christianity).

399

Buddhism is introduced to Korea from China.

c. 400

Confucianism is introduced to Japan from Korea.

fl. c. 430

Buddhist philosopher Buddhaghosa.

c. 406–477

Li Xiu Jing compiles earliest Doaist canon.

450

The Northern Transmission: Buddhism enters northern and eastern Asia.

451

Council of Chalcedon (Christianity).

c. 480–547

Life of Benedict of Nursia, founder of western monasticism (Christianity).

c. 499

Completion of Babylonian Talmud (Judaism).

c. 500–1000

Geonim ("Eminences") dominate Jewish scholarship in Babylonian academies.

500–1800

Medieval Period, devotional theism develops through the narrative theology of the Puranas (Hinduism).

c. 552

Korean monarch sends an image of Buddha as a gift to the Japanese emperor.

570–632

Life of Muhammad; marriage to Khadija (595) (Islam).

594

Buddhism proclaimed state creed in Japan.

610–622

Muhammad prophesies; Meccan Suras of the Quran are composed (Islam).

618–906

Tang dynasty; Daoism enjoys favor in high places.

700

He Xian Gu, patron of musicians, is noted for her asceticism and kindness (Daoism).

710–784

First permanent capital established at Nara; introduction of Confucianism, religious Daoism, and Buddhism; Shinto formally organized as all religions interact (Shinto).

711

Muslim armies cross North Africa into Spain.

715

Shinto shrine annexes a Buddhist temple to itself.

720

Nihongi and Nihon Shoki, Chronicles of Japan, Shinto's main "scriptures."

725–755

Antal, poet-saint of the Alvars (Hinduism).

726–843

Iconoclast controversy (Christianity).

732

King Charles Martel defeats Muslims at Poitiers.

737

Shinto shrines number three thousand.

739

Monastic Daoism flourishes during the Tang period.

740–747

Reform of Frankish Church under Boniface (Christianity).

742–814

Life of Charlemagne (Christianity).

748

Celestial Master recognized (Daoism).

749

First Buddhist monastery in Tibet.

750

Fall of Umayyads; rise of Abbasid dynasty; flowering of classical Islamic Civilization at new capital Baghdad.

750

An image of the Shinto war kami Hachiman is transported from the Shrine at Usa to Todaiji, in Nara.

760–1142

The Pala dynasty in Bengal supports a brand of Mahayana Buddhism that retains esoteric elements from Hinduism.

762–767

Anan ben David, Karaite leader, elected counter-exilarch of the Jewish communities in Iraq.

778–820

Life of major Hindu theologian Shankara.

778–864

The Shailendra dynasty in Java profess a type of Mahayana Buddhism.

794–1185

Heian period in Japan, Shinto's fortunes intimately bound up with the developments in Buddhism; foundation of Shingon and Tendai sects of Buddhism.

800

Charlemagne is crowned Holy Roman Emperor.

801

Rabi`a dies, a woman from Baghdad, first Muslim mystic.

845

Buddhists persecuted by a Daoist Chinese emperor.

845–903

Sugawara Michizane, poet-calligrapher, becomes a kami (Shinto).

850

Benjamin of Nehavand develops Karaite School of Thought (Judaism).

882–942

Life of Saadia, Gaon of the Iraqi communities who led counter attack against the Karaites (Judaism).

c. 900

Daniel ben Moshe systematizes Karaites, leads proto-Zionist movement in Jerusalem (Judaism).

900

According to the Sunni Tradition, the "door of independent investigation" closed for Islamic religious law.

901–923

Engi-shiki or Institutes of the Engi Era promulgated (Shinto).

916–1234

Northern Conquest dynasties; reunification of China; Chan is major form of monastic Buddhism.

918–1392

Koryo dynasty in Korea (Confucianism).

d. 922

Mystic Hallaj condemned and executed for blasphemy (Islam).

c. 950

Siddha Siddhanta School, blends theism and monism whereby all individual things are eventually re-absorbed into Shiva (Hinduism).

c. 960–1279

Song dynasty; Neo-Confucian revival; Canon of the Five Classics and Fours Books finalized by scholars.

960–1040

Life of Gershom ben Judah, Jewish scripture scholar.

c. 1000–1200

Five enormous collections of the Daoist Canon appear.

c. 1016

Initial printing of Daoist Canon.

1033–1107

Cheng Yi, his brother Cheng Hao (1032–1085), and Zhu Xi (1130–1200), establish "Cheng Zhu School," the School of Principle (*li xue*) (Confucianism).

1038

Death of Ibn Sina (Avicenna), the Muslim philosopher.

1040–1077

King Anawartha makes Burma entirely Buddhist.

1049–1054

Life of Pope Leo IX, excommunicates the Eastern Patriarch of Constantinople (Christianity).

1050

Christian persecution and massacre of the Jews in the Rhineland.

1054

Schism between East and West Christendom.

1056–1137

Traditional dates for Ramanuja, Vaishnava theologian (Hinduism).

1071

Seljuk Turkish victory over Byzantines at Manzikert (Islam).

1090–1153

Life of Bernard of Clairvaux, mystic (Christianity).

1095–1099

First Christian Crusade to regain control of Jerusalem.

1096–1141

Life of Hugh of St. Victor; leader of Victorine School in Paris (Christianity).

1098–1179

Life of Hildegard of Bingen, woman visionary (Christianity).

1099

Crusaders conquer Jerusalem (Christianity).

1105–1167

Basavanna, poet and influential source of qualified dualistic theism (Hinduism).

1111

Death of Ghazali, Muslim theologian and philosopher.

1119–1182

Sun Bu Er, female ritualist in the Perfect Realization order (Daoism).

1123–1170

Life of Wang Zhe, founded the "Perfect Realization School," or Chuan Zhen (Daoism).

1133–1212

Life of Tendai monk Honen establishes the Pure Land School in Japan (Buddhism).

1133–1568

The Muromachi/Ashikaga period in Japan; Shinto grows as a popular religion.

1134–1204
Life of Moses Maimonides, Jewish theologian.

1138–1193
Life of Saladin, the Kurdish Muslim leader of anti-Crusade.

1141–1215
Life of Eisai, founder of Rinzai Zen sect (Buddhism).

1147
Second Crusade undertaken (Christianity).

1170–1221
Life of Dominic, founder of the Dominican Order (Christianity).

1179
Third Lateran Council restricts Jewish residences (Christianity).

1181–1226
Life of Francis of Assisi, founder of Franciscan Order (Christianity).

1185–1333
Buddhist and Shinto theologians devise theories designed to blend the two belief systems, thus inventing "dual Shinto."

1187
Saladin reconquers Jerusalem at Battle of Hattin (Islam).

1190
Persecution and massacre of Jews at York, England.

1192
Richard I "Lionhearted," makes truce with Saladin (Christianity).

c. 1197–1276
Life of Madhvacarya, Hindui bhakti theologian.

1198
Death of Ibn Rushd, Averroes, Muslim theologian and philosopher.

1250–1517
Mamluk dynasty in Egypt (Islam).

1200–1253
Dogen, founder of Soto Zen lineage in Japan (Buddhism).

1207–1273
Life of Jalal ad-Din Rumi, Muslim mystic and original "whirling dervish."

1210–1526

Delhi Sultanates, powerful Muslim presence in India.

1215

Fourth Lateran Council (Christianity).

1222–82

Life of Nichiren, Japanese reformer, honors Lotus of the Good Law Sutra (Buddhism).

1224–1274

Life of Thomas Aquinas (Christianity).

1229–1244

Crusaders control Jerusalem.

1228

Eliezer ben Judah and Samuel the Pius foster Hasidic Spirituality at Worms and Speyer, respectively (Judaism).

1240–1292

Abraham ben Samuel Abulafia in Sarragossa, Spain, advocates spiritual freedom (Judaism).

1240–1305

Moses ben Shem Tov of Leon composes the *Zohar,* the Book of Splendor (Judaism).

1244

Ritual burning of the Talmud by Christians in Paris (Judaism).

1256–1302

Life of Gertrude, Christian mystic.

1258

The Mongols destroy Baghdad (Islam).

1260–1327

Life of Meister Eckhart, German Dominican and mystic (Christianity).

1260–1368

Yuan or Mongol dynasty in China favors Tibetan style Buddhism, Daoists lose monasteries and libraries in court debates.

1281

Emperor Kublai Khan burns Daoist Canon.

1290

Jews expelled from England.

1293–1381

Life of Jan van Ruysbroeck, mystic (Christianity).

1300–1921

The Ottoman Turkish dynasty (Islam).

1305

Jews expelled from France.

1328

Persecution and massacre of the Jews at Navarre.

c. 1329–1384

Life of John Wycliffe, Christian reformer.

1333–1568

Muromachi period in Japan; Shinto grows as popular religion.

1336–1565

Vijayanagara kingdom, major Hindu empire in India.

c. 1340–1380

Life of Catherine of Sienna (Christianity).

c. 1342–1423

Life of Julian of Norwich, English mystic (Christianity).

1360

Buddhism becomes state religion in Thailand.

1368–1644

Ming dynasty; late Medieval Daoism gains strength; Roman Catholic missionaries in China.

c. 1369–1415

Life of John Hus, Christian reformer.

1391

The first Dalai Lama is born in central Tibet (Buddhism).

1391

Persecution of Jews in Spain.

1392–1910

Yi dynasty; Korean Confucianism reaches its zenith.

1403–1424

Yong Le, third emperor of Ming dynasty (1368–1644), founds the Forbidden City in Beijing (Confucianism).

c. 1440–1518

Kabir, a Hindu saint, influences Guru Nanak (1469–1539) and the founding of the Shikh movement.

1444

Anthology of separate Five Daoist texts is published.

1453

Ottoman Turks conquer Constantinople (Islam).

1469–1538

Life of Guru Nanak, founder of Sikhism.

1472–1529

Life of Wang Yang Ming, leads School of Mind (*xin xie*) (Confucianism).

c.1475–1531

Life of Vallabha, bhakti theologian (Hinduism).

1479

Ferdinand and Isabella establish Spanish Inquisition (Christianity).

1483–1546

Life of Martin Luther, leader of German Reformation (Christianity).

1484–1531

Life of Ulrich Zwingli, Swiss Protestant Reformer (Christianity).

1485–1533

Life of Chaitanya, Bengali mystic and devotee of Krishna (Hinduism).

1491–1547

Life of King Henry VIII of England (Christianity).

1491–1556

Life of Ignatius of Loyola, founder of the Society of Jesus (Christianity).

1492

Ferdinand and Isabella take Alhambra in Granada; expel Jews and Muslims from Spain; Columbus reaches West Indian islands (Christianity).

1450–1547

Life of Mirabai, Hindu holy woman and ardent devotee of Krishna.

1501–1722

The Safavid dynasty replaces descendants of Genghis Khan in Iran, and establishes Shi'ite Islam as state creed.

1502–1757

Mughal dynasty establishes Islamic rule in much of South Asia.

1509–1564

Life of John Calvin, Christian reformer in Geneva.

1513–1572

Life of John Knox, Scottish reformer (Christianity).

1515–1582

Life of Teresa of Avila, Christian mystic.

1516

First Jewish "ghetto" opens in Venice.

1516–1555

Life of Yang Ji Shang, Confucian Literati, martyred.

1517

Luther's *Ninety-five Theses* are published in Wittenberg (Christianity).

1520–1523

Printed edition of the Talmud produced in Venice (Judaism).

c. 1526–1757

Moghul rule in India; destruction of Hindu temples in north and central India.

1530

CIT hierarchical structure is replaced with titles (Confucianism).

1540

The Society of Jesus is founded by Ignatius of Loyola (Christianity).

c. 1542

Francis Xavier, Jesuit missionary, lands in Goa (Christianity).

1542–1591

Life of John of the Cross, Spanish mystic (Christianity).

1545–1563

Council of Trent (Christianity).

1552–1610

Matteo Ricci, Jesuit missionary to China, steep himself in Classical Confucian learning (Christianity).

1578

Original Dalai Lama, head of the Gelug-pa lineage (Buddhism).

1580

Religious discussions take place between Akbar the Great and Jesuit missionaries.

1582

Pope Gregory XIII shortens the Julian Calendar.

1594

General Guan Di/Wu Di is deified by imperial decree (Daoism).

1600–1868

Tokugawa period in Japan; Confucianism gains influence in the Japanese Imperial government.

1619

First Black African Muslim slaves sold in Americas.

1622–1685

Yamaga Soko, Japanese Confucian scholar and military theorist, originator of the way of the warrior, *bushi-do* (Shinto).

1632–1677

Life of Baruch Spinoza, Jewish philosopher.

1644–1912

Ching (Manchu) dynasty in China; religious Daoism struggles to survive.

1649–1660

Puritan Revolution in England (Christianity).

1666–1708

Life of Gobind Singh, the tenth and final Sikh Guru.

1669–1736

Life of Kada no Azumamaro, considered the founder of the school of National Learning or *Kokugaku* (Shinto).

1697–1769

Life of Kamo no Mabuchi, applies philological methods to classical Japanese prayer.

1700

Last of the major Hindu Puranas composed.

1700–1760

Life of Baal Shem Tov, master of the Good Name Movement organized by Israel ben Eliezer in Eastern Europe (Judaism).

1703–1791

Life of John Wesley, founder of Methodism (Christianity).

1728–1786

Life of Moses Mendelsohn; Enlightenment ideas promoted, movement called *Haskalah* (Judaism).

1730–1801

Life of Motoori Morinaga, regarded Shinto's best scholarly mind.

c. 1740–1760

First Great Awakening in America (Christianity).

1756–1834

Life of David Friedlander, replaces Hebrew prayers with German.

1763–1843

Life of Hirata Atsutane, influential exponent of Kokugaku (Shinto).

1772–1833

Life of Ram Mohan Roy, founds Brahmo Samaj (1828) (Hinduism).

1780–1842

Life of William Ellery Channing, Unitarian reformer (Christianity).

1803–1882

Life of Ralph Waldo Emerson, American Transcendentalist (Christianity), popularizes Bhagavad Gita and Upanishads in America.

1805–1844

Life of Joseph Smith Jr., founder of Church of Jesus Christ of Latter-day Saints (Christianity).

1806–1860

Life of Samuel Holdheim, initiated liturgical reforms in Berlin (Judaism).

1810–1874

Life of Abraham Geiger; dramatic liturgical changes; leads a gathering of rabbis and argues for a reduced authority for both Bible and Talmud (1837) (Judaism).

1817–1892

Lifetime of Baha'u'llah, founder of Baha'i faith, which developed out of Shi'ite Islam.

1823–1897

Life of Sabato Moais, founded Jewish Theological Seminary of America.

1830

Church of Jesus Christ of Latter-day Saints founded.

1834–1886

Life of Ramakrishna Paramahamsa (Hinduism).

1835–1908

Mirza Ghulam Ahmad claims to be both the Mahdi and Jesus' Second Coming (Islam).

1836–1886

Life of Ramakrishna, Bengali mystic (Hinduism).

1849–1905

Muhammad Abduh promotes reason as source of knowledge (Islam).

1850

Rig Veda first translated into English (Hinduism).

1850–1864

Tai Ping "Highest Peace" rebellion (Daoism).

1852–1966

Life of Charles Taze Russell, founder of Jehovah's Witnesses in the USA (Christianity).

1852–1932

Life of Liao Ping, considers himself Confucius' prophet.

1856–57

Fifth Buddhist monastic council.

1863–1902

Life of Vivekananda; founds Ramakrishna Mission (Hinduism).

1868

Dual Shinto becomes dominant form of Shinto.

1868

Japanese impose a system of devotion to the emperor, a kind of State Creed (Shinto).

1868–71

Japanese persecution of Buddhists by Meiji emperor.

1868–1945

Confucians play important role in the Meiji Reform: restoration of the emperor's divine status (Shinto).

1869–1948

Life of Mohandas Karmachand Gandhi, received the title Mahatma "Great-Souled One" (Hinduism).

1869

Founding of Tokyo's Yasukuni Shrine (Shinto).

1873

Union of American Hebrew Congregations founded (Judaism).

1874–1952

Life of Chain Weitzmann, influential Zionist leader (Judaism).

1875

Arya Samaj founded by Swami Dayananda Sarasvati (Hinduism).

1879

Church of Christ, Scientist founded.

1881–1983

Life of Mordecai Kaplan, leads a movement and teaches that Jews were a civilization in process.

1881–present

Revival of Jewish nationalism, called Zionism.

1885

Pittsburgh Reform Platform (Judaism).

1890

Nathan Birnbaum coins the word "Zionism."

1892

Death of Baha'Allah, who claimed to be a prophet (Islam).

1896

Theodore Herzl organized Zionist political movement.

1896–1977

Life of A. C. Bhaktivedanta became a *sannyasi* in 1959 (Hinduism), leading figure of International Society of Krishna Consciousness.

1896–1982

Life of Nirmala Sundari (Hinduism).

1897

Theodore Herzl convened first Zionist Congress at Basle.

1900

Shrine Shinto no longer considered a religion, but a universally binding attitude of reverence for the emperor.

1900s

British Mandate Rule over the Holy Land of Palestine.

1911

Foundation of Chinese Republic. Confucius and sages held in the highest reverence.

1912

Abdication of the last Chinese emperor.

1917

Balfour Declaration (Judaism).

1917

Bolshevik Revolution.

1924

Rabbinical Assembly of America became Conservative Judaism's Institutional anchor.

1924–29

Buddhist scriptural canon published in Tokyo.

1933

The Shoah Holocaust begins (Judaism).

1933

The thirteenth Dalai Lama dies (Buddhism).

1942

Jews begin to return in large numbers to Israel.

1947

The State of Israel is formed.

1947

The partition of India and the creation of the Indian Union and Pakistan as independent and separatist Hindu and Muslim nations.

1948

Maoist Revolution; destruction of Confucian institutions; Daoism diminishes.

1945

Supreme Commander of Allied Powers, General Douglas McArthur, issues the Shinto Directive; Emperor no longer considered divine.

1949

Discovery of the Dead Sea Scrolls by a Bedouin shepherd near the Dead Sea (Judaism).

1949

The Republican Nationalist movement insists that Confucianism represent all genuine Chinese values.

1949

Indian constitution outlaws caste system's social discrimination.

1950

China invades Tibet; Dalai Lama flees to India in 1959.

1954–56

Sixth Buddhist Council in Rangoon, Burma (now called Myanmar).

1956

Buddhism celebrates 2,500 years of existence; B. R. Ambedkar leads revival in India.

1960s

Maharishi Mahesh Yogi and other popular teachers spread Hinduism beyond India and into Europe and Americas.

1962–1965

Second Vatican Council (Christianity).

1966–76

Chinese Cultural Revolution; disastrous losses for Daoism.

1967

Six Days War is fought between Israel and Egypt.

1971

Pakistan is divided into Pakistan and Bangladesh.

1976

Chairman Mao Zi Dong dies, fortunes of Buddhists and Daoists in China begin to improve.

1979

In Mecca, a claimant to status of Mahdi seeks to grab political power, trying to seize control of Muslim central shrine, the Ka`ba.

1979

Shi'ite Iranian students take over the U.S. embassy in Tehran; Islamic Republic of Iran proclaimed.

1980s

Daoism regains favor in China, monasteries reopen.

1989

Tian An Men Square massacre: symbol of young Chinese struggle for democracy.

1989

Death of Emperor Hirohito of Japan dies, ending the Showa era (Shinto).

1992

Li Hongzi founds Fa Lun Gong (Daoism).

1992

Destruction of Babri-Masjid and rioting in many Indian cities due to Hindu agitation concerning Rama's presumed birthplace in Ayodhya.

1993

Parliament of World Religions, Chicago, marks centenary of original Parliament called by Vivekananda.

1999

Chinese authorities attempt to suppress the sect called Fa Lun Gong (Daoism).

2001

World population surges past six billion, with India and China comprising over one-third of the human race.

THE
HANDY
RELIGION
ANSWER
BOOK

GENERAL
BACKGROUND

DEFINITIONS AND METHOD

HISTORY AND SOURCES

What is **religion**?

In its broadest sense, the term "religion" means adherence to a set of beliefs or teachings about the deepest and most elusive of life's mysteries. The word comes from an ancient Latin root (*religo*) that means "to bind" or "to obligate." Religious persons join together in a shared quest to understand a host of perplexing questions. What is the origin of life? What does it mean to be human? Are there greater-than-human forces responsible for the shape of things? How should a person of good will behave? Is life as we know it all there is, or are we destined for an adventure that goes well beyond an earthly life-expectancy? But the search for ultimate answers is a complex process requiring a balanced assessment of input from three critical sources: culture, tradition, and personal experience.

When we allow cultural norms to dominate our quest, the result can be satisfaction with the status quo in which, for example, the "American way of life" is itself the answer. Religion and culture always influence each other, but if we become too satisfied with the status quo, the result can be a sterile kind of "civil religion." Another important ingredient in the quest is "tradition," the rich treasury of practical wisdom preserved everywhere in families and local communities. Put too much stock in those time-honored solutions, complacently accept without question the "way we've always done things," and the result will be stifled conformity. But where is the individual in all of this? If I do not actively sort out my personal experience, with help from both culture and tradition, I will not advance in my search. But if I simply strike off on my own, rejecting other sources of input and relying only on my wits, my approach to life will be warped and totally subjective. Religion is very often life-affirming. It can also lull people into lethargy. Religion means being committed to a quest for answers that

3

transcend the appearances of things, but the quality of the quest has everything to do with the effort seekers are willing to invest.

What is a **religious tradition**?

"Religious tradition," as the term will be used throughout this book, refers to the various systems of belief and values around which communities of religious believers have formed throughout history and across the globe. Most readers are generally familiar with the names of many major religious traditions: Judaism, Christianity, Islam, Hinduism, Buddhism, Confucianism, Taoism, and Shinto, to list only the largest. It's tempting to imagine that the members of each of those traditions believe nearly the same things, but that is so only in a very general way. Each of those "super-traditions" in turn is really a cluster or family of traditions. There are many different flavors or styles within each, from the dozens of Christian "churches," to Islam's Sunni and Shi'i branches, to Buddhism's Theravada and Mahayana sub-communities. It would require a whole library of books to describe in detail the similarities and differences between the various communities of faith represented by the major traditions. This survey will hit the high points, but it will be helpful to keep in mind that it barely scratches the surface of an immensely complex reality. We will look only at some of the traditions that have left written records, and for practical reasons we cannot include the many traditions, such as the Native American, that have preserved their heritages orally.

Why is **archaeology** important in the study of religion?

Archaeology is the study of material evidence of cultures and civilizations past. It offers us a vast reservoir of data from which to reconstruct, tentatively at least, the stories of how our ancestors lived and what they believed. Armed with trowels and teaspoons, whisk brooms and toothbrushes, archaeologists painstakingly unearth layer upon layer of dwellings, cities, libraries, and places of worship. Without the hard data of archaeology, much of our knowledge of the story of religion would be sheer speculation. Unfortunately, because human beings have so often made their homes right on top of earlier settlements, much of that data will remain buried forever. Still, there is no danger archaeologists will run out of work, since hundreds of thousands of accessible major sites await a chance to unfold whole new chapters of the story.

What does **anthropology** have to contribute to the study of religion?

Working closely with archaeologists, physical and cultural anthropologists suggest interpretations of ancestral practices, belief systems, and social structures. Much of what they investigate contributes to our ongoing reconstruction of the remote past of religion all over the globe. Anthropologists also draw volumes of data about contemporary communities from ethnographic studies. Living among traditional societies whose roots reach back uninterruptedly for as many as several thousand years, ethnographers provide continuity to the history of religion. They study behavior and seek to discern in rituals of death and grieving, magic and taboo, pilgrimage and sacrifice, hints as to what people believe about the meaning of life. Most of the societies anthropologists explore are still predominantly oral cultures, so they gather a great deal of their data by immersing themselves as much as possible in the daily routines of local communities. Interviews and informal conversations yield a great volume of lore in the form of stories that are, in effect, living myth, the spiritual lifeblood of traditional societies. Cultural anthropologists sometimes work with texts, but they generally approach them as artifacts that function in the broader context of community life rather than as literary works.

What are some other **key sources for the history of religion**?

We learn about the history of all the many rich and varied religious traditions thanks to the accomplishments of generations of dedicated investigators in a wide range of academic disciplines. Specialists in literature have catalogued, analyzed, and translated thousands of volumes of religious writing that fill the libraries of the great traditions. Historians have unraveled and retold the complex stories of how the various communities of faith have evolved, spread, and interacted. Art history shows how religious art and architecture offer insights into religious practice and teaching that textual sources cannot explain by themselves. Until very recent times, the vast majority of visual art and architecture human beings have produced has served religious purposes. Ethnomusicology, as specialized and arcane as it sounds, can also provide important clues about the feel and shape of a religious tradition, since, as with art and architecture, so much traditional music and dance is overflowing with religious imagery.

What is **comparative religion**?

Comparative religion draws on the information supplied by all available sources for the history of religion. Scholars look for possible parallels between one tradition and another in the belief that common themes can offer insights into how the traditions developed and how their teachings differ or reinforce one other. We can talk, for example, about what kinds of beliefs and practices are characteristic of a tradition, how various communities of faith are organized, what sorts of signs and symbols a tradition uses to express its central teachings, and what kinds of special calendars different traditions follow. Comparative religion is not just about looking for similarities. Differences are every bit as important. And in the end, what we're seeking is greater insight built on an overall picture that is as fair and balanced as good scholarship can provide.

What is a **sacred text** or **scripture**?

All of the traditions surveyed in this book possess extensive sacred literatures. These sacred texts are commonly called scriptures—literally, writings. Some traditions

5

Archaeology and Religion: The Dead Sea Scrolls

In the spring of 1947, a young Bedouin shepherd, Muhammad adh-Dhib, discovered eleven ancient leather scrolls in a cave located in the cliffs above the northeastern corner of the Dead Sea. The eleven so-called Dead Sea Scrolls comprise seven distinct manuscripts. Through the work of E. L. Sukenik and other authorities, the eleven scrolls have been authenticated as genuine documents of roughly the second century BCE to the time of the unsuccessful Jewish revolt against Rome (CE 66–70). The manuscripts were written variously in Hebrew and Aramaic. They include portions of several of the books of the Old Testament, Apocrypha, prayers, hymns, commentaries, and rules; the most important set is "The Manual of Discipline."

Between 1949 and 1956, archaeological exploration of the area west of the Dead Sea was carried out by G. Lankester Harding and Father Roland De Vaux. The two men explored the original cave and more than two hundred others, finding numerous additional fragments of scrolls and other evidence of human occupancy. Most of these caves are located in the vicinity of Khirbet (Arabic for "ruin") Qumran, itself less than a mile south of the original cave, and in the ravine of Wadi Murabbaat some ten miles farther south. The manuscripts discovered at Wadi Murabbaat are very important in that, unlike those at Khirbet Qumran, they indicate that the Hebrew Bible had reached its final form by about 140 CE. The older Khirbet Qumran biblical manuscripts reveal a scriptural text that was still evolving.

The discoveries of the Dead Sea Scrolls stand among the greatest finds in the history of modern archaeology. The scrolls shed much light on the religious and political life of the Jewish people in the centuries just before and after the time of Christ. In addition, the documents are of great importance for the understanding of early Christianity. The biblical scrolls antedate the earliest extant Hebrew text by about a thousand years. Fragments of the Isaiah text discovered at Wadi Murabbaat are in complete agreement with the current biblical text, thus confirming the authenticity of later Hebrew texts.

revolve around a single scripture, a book composed over a relatively short period of time and perhaps associated with only a single human figure; Islam's Qur'an is such a text. Others have generated their sacred writings in stages lasting many centuries, resulting in scriptures that are more like anthologies of smaller books bound together in a single larger volume; the Hebrew scriptures, what many Christians call the Old Testament, are an example. Still other traditions revolve around the equivalent of whole libraries of sacred texts that came into being over as much as two millennia, as in the case of the greater Hinduism's vast patrimony. In addition to the primary sacred texts, many traditions have large collections of secondary texts, still considered essential but of slightly lesser authority. Islam has its Sayings of Muhammad (*hadith*), for example. In addition, the primary and secondary scriptures themselves often give rise to still further development of highly authoritative literature that takes the form of commentary on the scriptures. Rabbinical Judaism is enshrined in hundreds of volumes of this kind.

What is the relationship between **scripture and "oral tradition"**?

Numerous traditions preserve their teachings only in oral form or in ritual performance. Several dozen Native American and African traditions, for example, keep their heritages alive in the recitation of tribal storytellers and in the ritual reenactment of myth in the form of narrative dance. Some communities of believers have found it necessary to commit their heritage to writing in order to prevent it from being lost, given the advanced age of those entrusted with preserving it. Even then, the written version remains somehow less than the "real" tradition and the ideal remains oral and performative communication of the teaching, since committing it to writing was a last-ditch concession to the frailty of human memory. It is interesting to note that even in some of the religious traditions that boast the most voluminous sacred literatures, scripture began—and in some cases remained for many years—as oral communication. In many of those traditions the written text came to occupy a place of authority nearly equal to that of the recited text. In some traditions, reliance on "The Book" has rendered oral tradition virtually irrelevant.

How many **different kinds of scriptural writings** are there?

Sacred literature has taken virtually every form imaginable. The most ancient texts in many traditions are poetic, hymns of praise, songs of thanksgiving for victory, or prayers of petition for a favorable harvest. Early poetic texts are typically associated with liturgical rituals. Related to these are modified types of poetry adapted to specialized purposes such as prophecies or soothsaying or incantations meant to give power to the one who utters them. Wisdom sayings in the form of easy-to-remember proverbs are part of nearly every tradition. Narrative accounts in prose play several essential roles. One is to recount the deeds of the spiritual powers that brought the community into being (the "gods")—these are typically called "myth." Another is to preserve the history of the community or the biography of a foundational figure. Narratives also illustrate the central tenets of the tradition by way of vivid example, as in "just as our ancestor in faith...did when...."

Prophetic texts can be either poetry or prose, but either way, their main purpose is not generally to foretell the future, as is commonly assumed. Prophets "speak on behalf of" an ultimate spiritual power and their focus is typically on the need for change here and now. Another important type of religious text is called "apocalyptic"

7

Bantu Religion in Ancient Africa

The Bantu were among the most prominent peoples of ancient Africa. Originating in west central Africa, between the savanna and the forest, the Bantu began migrating south and east around 1200 BCE, ultimately spreading along the east coast. By 1000 CE they had reached central Natal, in what is now the country of South Africa.

Religion touched every phase of human experience in ancient sub-Sahara Africa. Specific beliefs varied from tribe to tribe, but some general tenets were common to all. Most Bantu-speaking people believed that the dead continued to influence the lives of the survivors. Ancestors were believed to remain in spirit, deserving respect and concern from the living, who might welcome them at meals or soothe them when they were angry. Sub-Saharan Africans also recognized many spirits identified with natural forces, both kind and dangerous. Most of these societies also believed in a supreme being as the highest power, the source of all excellence and virtue, but far removed from human understanding.

(from a Greek term meaning "revelatory"). Apocalyptic literature often uses highly figurative language, describing in detail events that the author has "seen" in visions or dreams and that will soon come to pass. Such dramatic texts are often taken as direct predictions of how the end of time will come about. Finally, many scriptures include rules or laws in the form of commands and prohibitions, but only a few sacred texts are entirely legal.

What **special qualities** do religious believers attribute to their **scriptures**?

Four important attributes of scriptures are literal and direct revelation, eternity, inerrancy, and inspiration. Some communities of faith regard their sacred texts as the literal, direct, unmediated divine word. Though that word has been delivered through a particular human being, tradition maintains that the messenger had no part in actually shaping the message. Naturally every scripture is communicated in some recognizable human language, a tongue in which the divine speaker chooses to be heard. Scriptures also unfold in time, sometimes evolving over relatively extended periods of history. Even so, some traditions teach that this sacred word is eternal, existing always in the divine mind and entering into the physical world of sound (and eventually writing) only at the moment the revealer deems proper. Another common teaching is that divine communication must surely be perfect in every detail since it comes from a perfect source. Insistence on this quality of "inerrancy" raises all sorts of practical problems for interpreters, who sometimes find themselves scrambling to explain away blatant inconsistencies in factual data such as chronology or geography.

Some communities of faith acknowledge that individual persons functioned from the very outset as human "authors" of sacred texts. Here the quality of "inspiration" explains that the divine speaker remains the actual author who entrusts the communication to a human writer.

How do **religious traditions** settle on the **contents of their scriptures**?

Scripture-centered traditions sometimes take centuries to decide definitively the question of which important texts to include in the category of scripture and which to exclude. The overall process is called the formation of a "canon." Sacred texts eventually proclaimed "canonical" carry considerably greater authority than those excluded from the scriptural canon. In some cases we know relatively little about the process itself, and in many instances we are not entirely certain when a given tradition fixed its canon. For the majority of the larger traditions the process of canon formation seems to stretch across many generations. In the case of Islamic scripture, which developed over a fairly short time and is traditionally associated with only one person, the process appears at first to have been rather straightforward. But even there, recent scholarship has begun to uncover details that suggest a different picture. What happens to texts not judged worthy of inclusion in the primary canon? Judaism and Christianity, for example, characterize works of secondary value as *apocrypha* ("hidden" because originally associated with esoteric groups) or *pseudepigrapha* ("works written under assumed names"). Study of canon formation is very instructive in the history of religion, since it reveals a great deal about how certain beliefs and teachings came to be regarded as central to a tradition.

What do the terms **"exegesis"** and **"hermeneutics"** mean?

"Exegesis" is from a pair of Greek words meaning "to draw out" (*ex*=out, *hegeomaii*=to lead or draw—also the root of the word "hegemony"). It refers to the processes of reflection and study that allow us to interpret a text. "Hermeneutics" comes from the Greek word that means "principles or theories of interpretation" (*hermeneutike*). Whenever scholars probe a text—the U.S. Constitution, for example—they engage in exegesis that uses certain hermeneutical principles. A Supreme Court Justice who prefers a more conservative approach, for example, might use a "strict constructionist" hermeneutics to interpret the Constitution. The idea is to implement the Constitution here and now without violating the spirit of the eighteenth-century document. You might think of hermeneutics as a set of lenses or filters—put them on and you will see things differently than you would with the naked eye. The glasses you put on bring out certain features of a text, but they also prevent you from seeing other features. That's the nature of all textual interpretation—we always start from a particular point of view. The more clearly we are aware of the presuppositions we bring to the text, the more honestly we can interpret it.

How many **different kinds of scriptural interpretation** are there?

One of the most interesting—and volatile—areas in the study of religion involves the many ways the different religious traditions "read" their sacred texts. Virtually every tradition has developed a range of approaches, often applying several to the same text to bring out its various "levels" of meaning. Every credible interpreter starts from a basic hermeneutical principle: if you want to be true to the text, you must first know what *kind* of text it is. What was its original purpose? What is its point of view and what kind of information is it trying to communicate? Nobody reads the sports page looking for tasty recipes. First concern is to determine what the text literally "says." But for any text to have a life expectancy greater than that of yesterday's sports page, it has to "mean" something beyond the bare facts. That's where religious interpreters begin to elaborate on the further significance of their sacred texts. Suppose that the "historical" meaning of a text is that "thus and so happened at a certain time and place." If that's all there is, the text is merely a museum piece. But religious exegesis looks deeper and draws out symbolic or allegorical meanings in which religious traditions find contemporary ethical implications. The dilemma in virtually all traditions is this: how to respect the historical reality of an ancient document while simultaneously explaining how its teachings are valid in every time and place. In more recent times scholars working both within and outside of major religious traditions have begun to ask different kinds of questions about how best to interpret sacred texts. The so-called "historical-critical method" attempts to show how a scripture can be both historically conditioned, and thus a product of a particular cultural context, and still claim substantial authority for all subsequent generations of believers.

Is **fundamentalism** the same as literal interpretation of a scripture?

Fundamentalism is an approach to religious teachings and values that emphasizes strict and direct reliance on a tradition's most ancient sources. That often means interpreting sacred texts quite literally, but even among fundamentalists extreme literalism remains the exception rather than the rule. Fundamentalist exegesis is found in many religious traditions. A major hermeneutical principle seems to be this: take the text literally, even if its literal meaning seems quite impossible in human terms, but interpret figuratively where a literal reading is clearly absurd. If the Book of Joshua says the sun stood still, take it as an actual divine intervention. But when Jesus says "I am the Vine, you the branches," it should be obvious to all that he is using a figure of speech. Alas, such things are not always so obvious. In general a fundamentalist approach seeks to interpret a sacred text by means of the sacred text itself rather than appeal to the intervening history of interpretation that comprises the community's repository of tradition.

RELIGIOUS BELIEFS

What is a **creed**?

As a general concept, "creed" refers to the totality of what members of a religious tradition believe. As a technical term, creed means a formal statement that sums up the key points in a belief system. Creedal statements are typically short enough to memorize, but can be long enough to take two or three minutes to recite. Members of many religious traditions engage in ritual recitation of their creeds as a way of reaffirming their assent to core beliefs. Creedal statements are occasionally direct quotations from a scripture. More often than not they are a later development, refined by generations of reflection. More elaborate creedal formulas typically evolve only when diversity of views begins to divide a community of faith so that the majority feel a need to define themselves against the unacceptable tenets of an emerging minority. Some religious traditions see no need for creedal formulas.

Is **belief** the same as **faith**?

There is a distinction between belief and faith. Belief, understood either generally or as a reference to a particular tenet, refers to the content of a tradition's central teaching. When believers recite a creed, for example, they affirm that they share a certain set of beliefs. Faith is the act or process of relying on or assenting to realities that one might not be able to prove as easily as one might like. People talk about "acts" of faith and often describe faith as a "leap" into the unknown, or as a kind of fundamental trust. Not every belief or act of faith is necessarily religious. Beliefs of every description rule our daily lives—they're all the millions of things we take for granted, like gravity and sunrise. And no one could get past breakfast without a basic level of trust. Religious belief and faith can seem riskier, because their objects are often not subject to the validation of actual experience. But what finally distinguishes religious belief and faith from their more mundane counterparts is that religious believers are willing to live without conclusive proof indefinitely.

What does the term **revelation** mean?

Revelation means "drawing back the veil" that covers the deepest mysteries of life, thus disclosing their inner meaning. Religious traditions that explain their origins in terms of direct divine revelation generally teach that human beings are incapable of attaining ultimate truths on their own and therefore need a supernatural intervention to gain access to saving realities. This is especially true of the so-called Abrahamic traditions, Judaism, Christianity, and Islam. Some sub-communities within those traditions are quite proprietary about their privileged and exclusive treasure, insisting that only a select few among the masses of humanity are chosen to benefit from the saving

11

Mortuary temple of female pharaoh Queen Hatshepsut, at Thebes, the former capital of the New Kingdom, near present-day Deir el-Bahri not far from the Valley of the Kings, on the west bank of the Nile across from Luxor, Egypt, c. 1480 BCE.

power of the divine self-disclosure. They emphasize to the highest degree the uniqueness of their elect status and seem little troubled by the notion that their convictions consign virtually the entire human race to damnation. Other sub-communities make more ample accommodation for the generality of humankind, leaving open some possibility that others not of the fold might still share in the revelation, however indirectly and secondarily. Some theologians talk of God's "special" revelation to their own traditions, with a broader or "general" revelation available to others. Alternatively, they might talk of particular and universal revelation. These concessions presuppose that those outside the fold have missed out on the core revelation through no fault of their own and are in no way actively refusing to be illuminated by it. Revelation-based traditions typically envision the divine disclosure as mediated by a series of messengers called prophets, each sent to particular peoples to reaffirm various aspects of the original message at critical junctures of history.

What do **traditions not focused on a "revelation"** say about the **source of religious truths**?

Revealed traditions suggest that the truth is sent down from on high and "received" by specially chosen persons. That is sometimes called the "prophetic" model. Other traditions have a rather different understanding of the process. From their perspective, eternal truth suffuses all things, filling the air with its creative sound and virtually

Religion in Ancient Egypt

Religion was the very core of ancient Egyptian culture (3500 BCE–950 BCE). It permeated every aspect of life, including art, medicine, and science. Egyptians believed that the gods had created Egypt as an oasis of order and inherent good amidst the forces of chaos that constantly threatened to overwhelm them. Justice, morality, and beauty—called Ma'at by the Egyptians—consisted of behavior in accordance with that tradition.

The Egyptian religion featured many deities, some strange but with human features, others clearly non-human, but all responsible for every aspect of life, from birth to death. The king of the gods was Amon-Re; followed by Aton, the disc that symbolized the sun god; Osiris, the god of both the Nile and the realm of the dead; and Isis, the moon goddess, wife of Osiris, mother of the universe, and queen of the world. Each god was associated with a particular sacred animal—cat, bull, crocodile, or scarab (beetle)—and huge temples were dedicated to their worship. In these temples, which were run by priests, the gods and goddesses made contact with humans through cult statues. Ordinary people prayed at the temple gates and were not normally allowed inside, though they were offered a peek at the Egyptian gods during great processions.

bubbling up from the earth itself. Certain individuals specially endowed with unique sensitivities "discover," "hear," or "tune in" to this pervasive and timeless wisdom. The greater Hindu tradition exemplifies this understanding in various ways, teaching that the divine truth has been passed along since time immemorial by "seers" and "hearers." In China's major indigenous traditions, sages and rulers reflecting deeply on the signs all around them seek an awareness of the all-encompassing "mandate of heaven." Japan's Shinto tradition offers another variation on the theme, drawing on the ageless well-springs of nature's wisdom for guidance in everyday life. As a general characterization, one could say that whereas the "prophetic" traditions understand revelation as a somewhat more restricted and privileged access to ultimate truths, the "wisdom" traditions regard the fundamental truths as more pervasive and available provided one is genuinely open to discovering them.

Are **"doctrine"** and **"dogma"** the same thing?

"Doctrine" in its general sense means "teaching" or "instruction" (from the Latin *doctrina*), both as an activity and as collection of specific beliefs or principles. It is sometimes used in a non-religious sense, as in the geo-political posture called the Monroe Doctrine (a warning that other governments that exert undue influence in the Americas should not be surprised if the United States pushes back). As a religious concept,

13

Massive lotus columns with hieroglyphics in the Temple of Amon, god of the Sun, at Karnak near the town of Luxor, Egypt, on the east bank of the Nile across from the Valley of the Kings, c. 1500 BCE.

doctrine means specifically all the individual teachings that a tradition identifies as essential. But why formulate a body of doctrine at all? Some traditions equate religious community with conformity of belief. Doctrine arises out of a desire to hold it all together and keep the tradition's inaugural insight as pure as possible. Doctrine is a measure of the role of authority in a religious tradition and provides a framework within which to pass along the content of the faith and to protect practices of ritual and worship from losing their distinctive character.

"Dogma" (from the Greek verb *dokein,* to think or to seem good) can also refer generally to a belief or opinion. But in religious studies dogma refers to a further specification of the category of doctrine. In some religious traditions, a teaching body or authority may deem it necessary under certain historical circumstances to clarify a particular doctrine. For example, suppose that the Buddhist monks in a certain region have gradually modified their interpretation of older ways of living the monastic life. Members of the larger Buddhist tradition might determine that they need to convene a "council" for the purpose of reaffirming and reinstating ancient practice. One can imagine other scenarios as well. When a tradition's core teachings come under attack, whether from within or without, or when changing times put undue pressure on traditional mores, those in leadership may decide corrective action is necessary. The result of the action is called dogma.

Finally, there is another important point to keep in mind: just as not all traditions possess specific creedal formulations, not all traditions have elaborated distinctive bodies of doctrine. Of those that do so, only some take the further, more elaborate step of "defining" particular doctrines as dogma. In other words, non-creedal, non-theological traditions generally do not develop systems of beliefs that might function as "litmus test" indicators of a believer's compliance with mainstream views.

What is **theology** and **what kinds of questions does it seek to answer**?

Theology is talk or thinking (*logos*) about God (*theos*). A wide variety of religious traditions naturally engage in some kinds of theology as it is understood in this general sense. Myth at its best is a type of "narrative theology," reflections on the nature of the supreme reality that give rise to story and re-enactment of myth in ritual. Some traditions develop the formal discipline of theology much more fully. In those traditions theology generally does three things. First, it involves a *systematic reflection* on the basic data, including scripture and/or the teachings of a foundational figure. Theologians sort out and organize the major themes, commenting on the original sources with a view to highlighting main ideas about the ultimate reality (or God), humanity, and the material world. In so doing they effectively help earlier generations of believers to shape the community's "master narrative," the guiding account by which believers begin to make sense of their lives. (For Jews, it is the story of God's delivering his people from slavery and bringing them to a promised land; for Christians, it is the life, death, and resurrection of Jesus in which they see victory over suffering and death, for example.) Second, theologians begin to *formulate* a distinctive way of talking about the tradition's central teachings. At this stage theological language grows more technical and idiosyncratic. Theology is now using a set of symbols that require some specialized training in the particular tradition to appreciate what the theologians are saying. Finally, theologians *articulate* those distinctive symbols into a unique *system* of thought.

What are some of the **main themes in religious belief** generally?

Statements of belief typically begin with basic statements defining the tradition's supreme being and the principal deeds of that being on behalf of the community of faith. Descriptions of deity and of other spiritual powers figure prominently in many traditions, often in the form of extended narratives that can be extremely elaborate and detailed. Believers in most traditions are taught the array of benefits they can expect from the supreme being if only they make appropriate petition. The ways believers ought to respond to the supreme being's actions are often paralleled by fundamental ethical considerations governing human relationships. Some traditions place great emphasis on the role of intermediaries or foundational figures, especially concerning their function of delivering a revelation to humankind. Those figures sometimes symbolize the whole history of the supreme being's dealings with his or her people. A major theme focuses on notions of the afterlife, and on how to achieve the best of rewards and avoid the direst of punishments.

What is **"myth"** and why is it so **important in the study of religion**?

Enduring myth and great poetry have one very important thing in common: both tell the truth without fail. That may come as a shock to readers accustomed to thinking of "myth" as a synonym for "just a story" at best, and "outright lie" at worst. Read a favorite poem aloud. Chances are you won't catch yourself saying, "Nice story, but did it *really happen*?" Yet that is exactly how many people respond to ancient mythic narratives. Either it happened just that way or it's the product of some overworked imagination. Once again it helps to recall a fundamental principle in the study of classic texts—first determine how the text is trying to communicate. Myth and poetry share another key feature: they are far more about value and meaning, about why things are the way they are, than about fact. Police reports are about facts. It makes perfect sense to ask whether what is alleged there "really happened." Myth, on the other hand, arises out of profound reflection on the human condition and on the nature of the world. Myth invariably articulates a vision of the underlying spiritual causes of things, typically personifying those causes as superhuman powers. In technologically advanced societies the creative imagination can be too readily discredited, but it is virtually impossible to understand how religion works without a deep appreciation of the imagination. Finally, myth has the power to bring a most welcome element of humor into religious thinking. Thanks to myth at its best, religious people have hope of not taking themselves too seriously.

What does the word **"millennialism"** mean?

Millennialism (or millennarianism) refers to the general expectation that at a certain point in time human history will undergo a dramatic turnabout, resulting even in the very end of time itself and the beginning of another age. A millennium is literally a thousand year period, at the turning of which some communities of faith believe their historic expectation of a new dispensation will be realized. Naturally the marking of millennial events depends on when a given religious tradition marks its own beginnings. The year 2000 has little or no religious meaning for the great majority of the world's peoples. For the most part, it is only some groups among the world's Christians who attach special significance to this event. But even for Christians the event is ambiguous since, due to anomalies in calendar calculations long ago, it is widely understood that the actual 2000th anniversary of the birth of Jesus has already come and gone. There is, however, a curiously broad appeal of the notion of millennium. Many have attached a vague sense of foreboding to its imminent arrival—beyond concerns about the so-called Y2K computer bug. As we will see later, some traditions have a strong sense of the importance of historic expectation, even if that is not tied specifically to the turn of a true "thousand year" millennium.

What is **religious cosmology** and **what sorts of issues** does it address?

Virtually every religious tradition has developed distinctive interpretations of how the world came to be and what it means spiritually. Cosmology (talk or thinking about the

Ritual ball court as seen from the Hieroglyphic Staircase on the main pyramid of the Maya sacred site of Copan, Honduras, c. 500 CE.

cosmos) includes traditional views about time and space and what it means to be embodied. A common element in cosmology is cosmogony or notions of how the cosmos came into being. Creation from nothing is a characteristic theme in Abrahamic cosmogonies. Asian cosmogonies include a wide spectrum of stories, from the spontaneous evolution of the primal egg, to the orderly elaboration of each living species, to the playful creative dance of the deity, to the violent sacrifice or dismemberment of the deity itself. Variations on the ancient theory of "emanation" have made their way into a number of religious traditions, including the Mediterranean systems influenced by neo-Platonism. Cosmologies also typically take a position on the structure or order of the cosmos, offering views as to the origins of human societies and their rituals. This world can be real or illusory; positive or evil; a work of art or the result of haphazard evolution; a mistake even the supreme being would like to change or the outcome of careful divine planning; a place to stay forever or a living hell to be escaped at the earliest opportunity. Time and change also occupy cosmological thinking, with linear and cyclical models forming the major options for understanding where it's all heading.

What is religious **anthropology** and what questions does it ask?

Virtually all religious traditions develop in considerable detail views of what it means to be a human being. Two especially important themes stand out. First, there are questions about the origin and makeup of the human person. Stories of human beginnings muse over whether we should ascribe them to direct creation, a freak happen-

17

The Religion of the Maya

The Maya civilization of Mesoamerica grew out of a very early agrarian way of life, beginning around 2500 BCE in the tropical rain forest lowlands of northern Guatemala (the area now known as El Petén). Maya civilization has been divided into five periods, beginning with the Formative period around 1500 BCE and ending with the arrival of the Spaniards in the sixteenth century.

Religion was a major part of the everyday lives of the Maya. With more than one hundred sixty different gods, the Maya spent much time fasting, praying, and offering sacrifices to the deities in hopes that they would bring rain and good crops, good health, and good luck. The universal creative force was referred to as Hunab K'U, and the towering ceiba tree was called the axis mundi, or tree of life, which was thought to reside in all three levels of the cosmos: roots in the underworld (Xibalba), trunk in the middle world, and branches in the heavens. Trees were thought to represent the sustainer of life because of their role in rain cycles, and the Maya believed that when the last tree disappeared so would the people. The Maya had a corn god, a rain god, a sun god, and a moon goddess, among many others. Each god or goddess influenced a specific part of Maya life. For example, the goddess of the moon, Ix Chel, was said to control medicine and weaving.

In the great ceremonial centers, priests and priestesses were often involved in vision-producing rites that would supposedly allow them to communicate with the gods. Maya carvings and paintings show men and women ceremoniously piercing parts of their bodies to shed blood and induce higher states of consciousness. Women often pierced their tongues and men their penises, using stingray spines, flints, or thorns. Blood was dripped onto bark paper and the paper was burned as an offering to the gods. Humans, often captured enemy warriors, were ritually sacrificed to appease the gods. The victim would be held down upon an altar and a priest would slit his chest under the rib cage and tear out the heart. Stone carvings of a reclining figure known as the Chac Mool, which is pictured holding a bowl or platform for a bowl, were thought to be receptacles for sacrificed hearts or blood. Captives were also tortured, bled, and decapitated. Some sacrificial victims were tossed into deep natural water holes (*cenotes*) to plead with the rain god for water. When an important person or ruler died, his servants were often killed and buried with him.

stance, or a long process of evolution. What constitutes "a person"? Are we spirit as well as body? What happens when the body dies—is that all there is? Or does something of the individual survive death? Some traditions have elaborated amazingly detailed psychological analyses of the human person. Two very broad types of religious psychology stand out. First there are those that see at the core of each individual an eternal, indestructible faculty or element called a "soul" or "true self." Sometimes called "substantialist" psychologies, these approaches describe in great detail the capabilities and needs of the spiritual self. In answer to the question of what happens to the soul after death, two general views predominate. One holds that each individual passes through this world only once. At death the soul moves on to another level, undergoing a variety of new experiences, never to return. The other is based on the concept that an unimaginable but still limited number of "selves" are continuously embodied in various forms in this world. At death, each living being's soul is recycled, eventually becoming re-embodied in some other life form. This is called reincarnation or metempsychosis. An large percentage of human beings alive now are heavily influenced by this view. The second important type of religious psychology, represented especially by classical Buddhist thought, denies that there is a substantial self or soul at the core of the person. Individuality itself is a construct held together by the "glue" of inappropriate craving—desire so powerful that it can perpetuate the cycle of rebirth and suffering through faulty thinking.

Another important anthropological theme is what some would call religious ethics. Here crucial questions of human relationships arise. As for the human-divine relationship, are human beings slaves? Puppets? Beggars? Heirs of a wealthy parent? Ambassadors of the deity to those unfortunate "outsiders"? The notion of grace is important in this context. How much help do humans need and get from the supreme being, and what shape does that help take? As for how human beings relate to one another, religious traditions offer a range of explanations. People are siblings estranged and in need of reconciliation, natural enemies who can hope only for an uneasy truce, perhaps even neutral entities dodging one another like so many billiard balls. The intractable problem of human suffering occasions a similar range of explanations: suffering is humankind's just desert, the outcome of impersonal fate, the sadistic entertainment of evil cosmic powers, or perhaps a tough-love form of pedagogy designed to set human beings on the road to reform. What moral options are available as solutions—means to salvation, in other words? Everything from altruistic service to others to the pursuit of enlightened self-interest, from quiet contemplation to extroverted worship, and from active cultivation of good deeds to hopeful resignation in the face of a foreordained outcome.

What is **eschatology**?

"Eschatology" derives from two Greek words meaning the "study (*logos*) of the last things" (*eschata*). The so-called "four last things" include death, judgment, heaven, and hell, and the study of them is often called "individual eschatology." In addition, "cosmic" eschatology encompasses religious teaching concerning how history and the world as we know it will come to an end. Although use of the term *eschatology* has been especially characteristic of the study of the Abrahamic traditions, it can also be useful in describing important aspects of belief in the religious traditions of Asian ori-

19

gin. Religious traditions of Middle Eastern origin have generally developed linear views of history whereby time is said to have a beginning, a middle, and an end, never again to be repeated. Their eschatologies explore the final and definitive transformations that will befall both individuals and the universe. Traditions of Asian origin tend to favor cyclical views of time. Although each cycle of time is unimaginably long, it is only part of a vast unending potentiality for further variations. As a result, though Asian traditions do talk of various realms of reward and punishment hereafter, they generally do not consider any of those realms to be a truly final destination for the individual. There is always the possibility of yet another existence and another outcome. Many traditions talk of an accountability after death, often describing it as a meeting between the individual soul and a judge or council charged with meting out just desserts. Only a few traditions worldwide, such as Japan's Shinto, have weakly developed notions of afterlife.

What is the **philosophy of religion**?

Some philosophers make a specialty of inquiring into the reasonableness of religious belief systems. As far back as Thomas Aquinas (d. 1274) in Europe, Ghazali (d. 1111) and Ibn Rushd (d. 1198) among medieval Muslims, the Hindu Shankara (d. 820), and even back to the Buddhist Nagarjuna (c. 150–250) and earlier, religious thinkers have tackled questions of how much truth reason can grasp. Thomas Aquinas' classic "five proofs for the existence of God" are among the most famous inquiries of this type. Philosophers of religion provide a great service in their attempts to keep religious language and truth claims honest. Along with philosophical attempts to give a rational justification for religious beliefs, a sub-specialty in the philosophy of religion deals with the intricate analysis of various forms of religious expression. It analyzes religious language, ritual, and statements of belief as to their rationality. Virtually every major religious tradition, at some periods during its history, has developed alongside of philosophical schools that have acted as gadflies or devil's advocates.

What does the term **"natural theology"** mean?

Natural theology, sometimes referred to as "theodicy" (the study of divine justice—*theou dike*), is actually a branch of the philosophy of religion. It is called "natural" to indicate that reason, not revelation or some other mode of divine communication, is the source of the truths it can discover. This discipline's subject is the nature of the divine being as expressed in what are believed to be the effects of the deity's power in the world. It presupposes, in other words, that human beings can begin with the world as they know it and proceed to some knowledge of the one whose work they believe it to be. Questions about whether God is subject to change, or how a just deity could allow the existence of pervasive evil and suffering in the world, are an important part of the discipline. Natural theology also explores such aspects of the human soul as its ethical freedom and immortality. Forms of natural theology occur in a variety of religious traditions but appear more highly developed in connection with European philosophical traditions.

Why do **religious beliefs** so often seem to be **associated with intolerance**?

Human beings dislike shades of gray. We prefer to persuade ourselves that we can keep truth and falsehood neatly separated. There is "us" and there is "them," and we know who has the truth. Stereotyping and demonizing are natural next steps. Not only are "they" wrong religiously, they are somehow not quite up to our standards of humanity and thus to be pitied if not simply dismissed as irrelevant. Intolerance of religious diversity is a serious historical evil, a force that can easily be exploited by people of ill intent. And yet it costs so little to approach religious pluralism with an open mind. On the other hand, wars are seldom fought for purely religious reasons. Communities of faith often develop side-by-side in relative harmony. When problems arise, they are almost always initially political, economic, and social. Then, often enough, those who wish to keep the pot boiling invoke age-old religious differences as though they were the cause of every evil. They remind their constituents that if they really want to be loyal, they will not rest until some ancient slight to the faith has been set right. Underneath it all is the awareness that if you want to destroy a people's will, you must attack the most powerful symbols of their identity, some of which are bound to be religious. So, for example, in Bosnia during the 1990s, a major thrust of Serb policy was to obliterate as completely as possible all visible signs of Muslim presence, destroying especially ancient mosques and libraries and leaving paved parking lots in their place.

What is a **miracle**?

A miracle is broadly defined as an apparent breach in the laws of nature that so defies rational explanation as to suggest the possibility of divine intervention. Miracles or the working of wonders figure prominently in the sacred texts and lore of most major religious traditions, but they do not necessarily serve the same purpose from one tradition to another. In some cases miracles are believed to provide incontrovertible proof of the truth of a particular revelation by establishing beyond doubt the power of the agent. Miracles are not just a fancy "extra" tossed in to entertain the masses, but an integral part of some systems of belief. Sometimes miracles occur in the context of a controversy by way of a dramatic settlement in favor of the miracle worker. One characteristic of miracles that does appear to be a feature in many traditions is that those who choose obstinately not to believe do not necessarily change their minds in the presence of a miracle. In fact, they simply do not see what the believers standing next to them see. That seems to suggest that, in some traditions at least, wonders are in the eye of the beholder, so that a witness must be predisposed to see a miracle. Some traditions regard miracles as a gift from a divine source to certain special persons, whether prophets or saints, designed to establish their spiritual credentials. A miracle can revolve around some symbolic action that, even apart from the apparently miraculous result, contains the central message.

SIGNS AND SYMBOLS

What is the **difference between a sign and a symbol**?

In general terms a sign is any verbal or visual indicator that conveys some basic message. The capital letter P inside a circle, crossed out by a diagonal bar, has become a widely understood indicator for "No Parking." It conveys no additional meaning. In the language of religious studies, a sign is an object or an action that communicates a specific religious meaning. Members of any tradition grow up learning the language of their tradition's system of signs. Gestures and implements employed in ritual comprise one of the most common categories. A bow, a knee bent to touch the floor, a clap of the hands, a lighted candle, all can function as signs suggesting a certain mood or atmosphere. Objects and actions used this way do not necessarily carry complex meanings. Some objects and actions, however, do communicate more specialized and even arcane messages. A symbol is an object or act that represents some reality other than itself. Most religious traditions use symbols to remind believers of the central realities of the faith, sometimes because that reality is considered too sacred to depict and sometimes because it is simply easier to use the shorthand of symbolism. Symbolism can be economical in many ways since it can pack a great deal of meaning into a small, often inexpensive, item. Visual symbols are called an "aniconic" form of expression when they use a nonrepresentational image to refer to a sacred personage. So, for example, the fish symbolizes Christ, the empty throne or riderless horse the Buddha.

Where and **how do religious traditions employ signs and symbols**?

Everything from buildings to sacred books to substances like oil and incense play important roles in the everyday lives of religious practitioners. Primary ritual spaces are naturally the most prominent venues for the use of signs and symbols. Temples, synagogues, mosques, and shrines are often visual galleries filled with sensory input composed entirely of signs and symbols. Architectural style and structure incorporate forms characteristic of each tradition, including towers of various kinds, domes, courtyards, rooms for special functions, and gathering spaces designed to accommodate certain activities and groups of a certain size. Everything about a well-executed ritual space expresses the tradition's beliefs. In their homes, too, religious persons often use signs and symbols to remind themselves of their central spiritual values.

Some go so far as to set up elaborate household shrines or altars at which to conduct their private devotions. In certain societies one can still readily identify members of some religious traditions by the signs and symbols they wear. For the majority of people who so identify themselves, signs and symbols of faith are at least as much a reminder to themselves of their faith commitment as they are a signal to others that they hold certain things sacred.

What are **"semiotics"** and **"semantics"**? How do they help **interpret signs and symbols**?

Semiotics (from the Greek *semeion,* sign) and semantics (from the Greek *semainein,* to show, be significant) are tools scholars use to study how linguistic and visual signs and symbols convey meaning. Semiotics is actually a branch of logic that examines how we put together all the various elements of thought so that they communicate complex ideas. One way semiotics contributes to the understanding of signs and symbols is by classifying different types of visual communication. For example, major "classes" of visual signs and symbols include inscriptions (text in any language, often taken from a scripture), aniconic imagery (symbols that do not "represent" or "depict" what they stand for), iconic imagery (representations of a sacred person or object), and countless combinations of these three classes. Semantic analysis then determines what "fields" of meaning each of those "classes" of sign or symbol draws on for its content. In the study of religion, major "fields" of meaning are sacred scripture, theological formulation, allusion to a widely known cultural symbol, or nature. Together the study of semiotic classes and semantic fields can suggest characteristic ways that religious believers communicate non-verbally in a variety of cultural settings.

What are some of the **main sources of religious sign and symbol**?

Virtually any visual design or gesture can be used in religious contexts. Religious traditions draw on a limitless supply of natural and invented materials. From nature come a huge host of candidates from the animal kingdoms. Birds seem especially apt symbols, sometimes as images of the human spirit or soul, sometimes reminders of the utter freedom and beauty of the deity. Fish are also particularly evocative, dwelling as they do in a medium uncongenial to human beings and thus capable of suggesting the "otherness" of the holy. Powerful beasts of prey as well as animals known for their gentleness often stir the religious imagination. Trees, along with every imaginable kind of flower, find symbolic place in numerous traditions. Among inanimate natural things heavenly luminaries and constellations have numerous resonances with qualities often associated with the divine. Sometimes related to astronomical symbols are the myriad geometric forms found across the whole spectrum of traditions, with the same form playing very different roles from one to another.

23

What is the **religious meaning of the term "relic"**?

A relic is a physical reminder of the ongoing spiritual presence of some important religious figure. In that sense one could say a relic is a type of sign. The most important relics are generally portions of the bodily remains of the holy person, including bones or bone fragments, teeth, skulls, cremated ashes, or even fingernails. A secondary type of relic includes items believed to have belonged to the holy person, such as pieces of clothing, books, jewelry. Even items said merely to have been touched by the holy person often carry a special significance. Some traditions even put particular meaning in possessing footprints said to have been left by the holy person, even though in most instances the prints are clearly either highly stylized symbolic artifacts or impressions left in stone scarcely identifiable as footprints. The most important reliquaries are the actual tombs of holy persons, assuming the remains were never removed in the interest of creating multiple relics to be spread abroad. Sites that claim ownership of the relics of one, or sometimes very many, holy persons frequently become destinations for pilgrims. The idea of a cult of relics strikes many as a rather ghoulish practice, and the sight of a barely preserved waxen cadaver under glass can indeed evoke morbid thoughts. But the use of relics is so common that some appreciation of how they function is essential to the study of religion.

What's the difference between an **"amulet"** and a **"talisman"**?

Both are types of symbolic objects often used as an expression of popular beliefs that have acquired religious associations. They help their owners manage different kinds of spiritual power. Amulets protect a person from negative or malevolent forces, and talismans in effect attract positive energies. Believers in many traditions carry objects of this kind on their persons or affix them to their homes or vehicles. Four-leaf clovers and rabbit's feet are common non-religious talismans that promise good fortune, and images of a large "eye" are popular examples of non-religious amulets designed to protect the bearer from the "evil eye." Explicitly religious talismans use sacred texts or images, as when Catholics bury a statue of St. Joseph in the front yard in hopes of selling their house quickly. The Jewish *mezuzah* and Christian "scapular" medals are examples of objects that can have properties of both amulet and talisman. Both types of symbolism are of interest for the study of religion because they offer greater understanding of how religious belief and culturally inspired custom often reinforce each other.

MEMBERSHIP, COMMUNITY, DIVERSITY

What are **"parent"** and **"established"** and **"universal"** religious communities?

From the distant perspective of at least several centuries we can look back into history in search of the origins of major religious traditions. Though we will never be entirely sure in some cases when a given tradition actually began, or when it became distinct enough from its religious surroundings to be identifiable as a separate entity, we can develop some useful general notions. But it helps to keep in mind that most of our judgments in this regard are quite relative. For example, is Judaism the parent tradition of Christianity? Is Hinduism the parent tradition of Buddhism? If so, then perhaps we need to say that Judaism and Hinduism are also "grandparent" traditions, since so many further developments have come out of Christianity and Buddhism. Whichever set of terms we use, it is important to be aware of the intimate interconnections among so many of the major religious traditions. The lines between them are never so tidy and firm as we might like to think. Established traditions (sometimes identified by the term *ecclesia,* Latin for "assembly") are those that enjoy some degree of official sanction or approval within a modern nation-state. The Church of England and Buddhism in Thailand are two examples. Universal communities are those well established in many national and cultural contexts, as exemplified by Sunni Islam and Roman Catholicism.

What is a **schism**?

Schism comes from a Greek word (*schismos*) that means a "rupture, break, or tear." Though strictly speaking the term has been used technically to refer to events in the history of Christianity, it can also be useful in understanding similar changes in other traditions. A schism occurs when a faction within a larger religious community decides to break away and assert its independence from the main body. Impetus for a separation may also originate with the "parent" group censuring a minority and demanding that they either change their position or depart. The result can be the creation of more than two sub-groups. Reasons for schisms are often ostensibly doctrinal, one group insisting that it cannot affirm some religious claim that the main body has declared essential to membership. However, since all theological issues ultimately have social and political implications, such changes are seldom purely theological. Ethnic divisions have been responsible for a number of important schisms. Some schisms have resulted in the formation of whole new religious traditions—as, for example, Christianity's emergence from Judaism or Buddhism's development out of Hinduism. Other yield sub-traditions that continue to identify themselves as members of the larger religious community. But just as often the parent group wants nothing further to do with the schismatic group, and the feeling is frequently mutual.

What is a **denomination**?

The term denomination came into common use in religious studies in reference to the various Christian "churches" that came into being during the Protestant Reformation. But we can also make appropriate use of the term in reference to developments in other traditions. In general, denominations differ from one another primarily on organizational rather than doctrinal grounds. Members of one denomination therefore do not generally consider members of others as religiously wrong-headed. It is nevertheless not uncommon for denominations to develop distinctive features of religious practice and expression, so that over many centuries one comes to differ from another in more than just structure and governance. Some scholars also take the view that denominations are inspired by a spirit of thoroughgoing reform and are far more than mere organizational variants. In addition, some denominations have sometimes formed along the lines of ethnicity or socioeconomic stratification. Denominations nevertheless tend to remain somewhat more inclusive in their criteria for membership than sects, retaining some of the openness characteristic of the larger or parent organizations from which they originated.

How does one identify a **sect**?

"Sect" is a generic term denoting any group that acknowledges a common leadership and shares a common set of beliefs. The word comes from the Latin verb *sequi*, to follow, and it has often been used pejoratively by members of larger traditions to refer to troublesome or non-conformist groups within their midst. An important characteristic of sects is their tendency toward greater exclusivity in membership, based on the notion that "true" believers must measure up to a higher standard than the generality of people who call themselves religious. Sectarian movements are therefore often the result of attempts at reform within a religious tradition that some leader rising from the ranks perceives to have lost its original purpose. But if sects tend to up the ante for membership, they do not necessarily declare their distinctiveness on narrowly theological grounds. What they want is a morally committed membership for whom faith means a willingness to abide by stringent ethical standards. To gain entry to a sect, one has to demonstrate worthiness, but once accepted, all members participate on an equal footing. There are, of course, leadership structures, but governance tends to be communitarian rather than hierarchical. Sects often perceive themselves as taking a stand against the rising tide of secularization they see around them, faulting larger religious bodies for failing to direct a sufficiently challenging critique of the surrounding culture. Some sectarian movements have eventually moved back toward greater integration in society as a whole, and these are sometimes referred to as "established" or "institutionalized" sects.

Are **cults** different from **sects**? Are they authentically religious groups?

We've become accustomed in recent years to hearing about various "cults," both here and abroad, that claim religious inspiration and legitimacy. Think, for example, of the Branch Davidians of Waco, Texas, the Heaven's Gate group suicide in California, or the Japanese Aum Shinri-kyo, infamous for its nerve gas attacks on Tokyo's subway system. The term "cult" is sometimes used synonymously with "new religious movement," and

Religion on the Silver Screen

Ben-Hur (1959). The third film version of the Lew Wallace classic stars Charlton Heston in the role of a Palestinian Jew battling the Roman empire at the time of Christ. The breathtaking chariot race is spectacularly conceived and filmed.

The Bible...In the Beginning (1966). Brings to life the book of Genesis, including the stories of Adam and Eve, Cain and Abel, and Noah and the flood. All-star cast includes George C. Scott, Richard Harris, Stephen Boyd, Peter O'Toole, and Ava Gardner.

David and Bathsheba (1951). The Bible story comes alive in a lush and colorful production starring Gregory Peck and Susan Hayward.

El Cid (1961). Charts the life of Rodrigo Diaz de Bivar, known as El Cid, who was the legendary eleventh-century Christian hero who freed Spain from Moorish invaders.

A Man for All Seasons (1966). Heavily Oscar-honored biographical drama concerning the life and subsequent martyrdom of Sir Thomas More, sixteenth-century Chancellor of England. Paul Scofield's performance as More is considered one of the greatest ever of its kind.

The Ten Commandments (1956). Cecil B. DeMille's remake of his 1923 silent classic is a lavish epic about the life of Moses, who turned his back on a privileged life to lead his people out of bondage in Egypt. The sequence depicting the parting of the Red Sea is considered to rival any modern special effects.

although there are varying opinions on the subject, it is possible to point out a few salient features. First, both "cult" and "new religious movement" are historically relative terms. A movement whose novelty and exotic qualities were so obvious to observers, say a thousand years ago, might have turned out to be a major religious tradition by our time. Most recent "new" movements are not truly sectarian in the sense that they are not offshoots of larger religious communities. In addition, cults take the exclusivity that seems to characterize the sect as classically defined and separate themselves from society to a much greater degree than sects. Cults tend to be quite small, often having only one very localized community centered around a charismatic leader who exercises virtually absolute control over members. Cult leaders sometimes claim their authority on the basis of a direct new revelation or special new insight and interpretation of mainstream sources such as the Bible. The leader's direct orders are often the only organizational structure, and when a cult leader dies, the cult often dies with him or her. Some cults seem to be oriented toward an "end time" scenario and on occasion seem ready to do whatever they deem necessary to facilitate that end.

What is **excommunication** or **religious banishment**?

Excommunication is the process whereby an individual or group that refuses to give up certain unacceptable views or practices are cut off from the community of believers. Though the juridical procedure is typically associated with the Roman Catholic church, numerous other religious bodies employ similar practices. From the formal and often technical proceedings of official excommunication to the more informal custom known as "shunning," religious communities have always had their ways of removing the weeds and the bad apples. Sometimes religious banishment has served as an alternative to punishment by death, or as a lesser punishment as atonement for sin. Religious banishment in most cases is a reversible sanction, depending on the individual's willingness to recant and repent.

What is the connection between **orthodoxy and heresy**? And what is **"heterodoxy"**?

Orthodoxy (from the Greek *orthe doxe,* "correct opinion") is in a way the diametric opposite of heterodoxy (Greek, *hetere doxe,* "variant opinion"). Heterodoxy is a generic category used to refer to any and all doctrinal views at odds with mainstream thinking in a tradition. Heresy (from the Greek *haireo,* "to seize, choose, decide"—in other words, to take a position) is one of the more common ways of characterizing heterodox views. In general, heresy refers to the deliberate holding of a set of beliefs in direct opposition to a religious tradition's established and widely accepted authority. It is important to keep in mind that fully articulated conceptions of orthodoxy typically develop long after the earliest generations of a given tradition have come and gone. During their early decades—even centuries in some cases—many religious traditions have historically allowed for some diversity of views. But one or another of those views can become so extreme that a majority of believers perceive a threat to their cohesiveness as a community. To hold such a threat at bay, religious communities sometimes find it necessary to define the limits of acceptable divergence of beliefs. The term "heretical" has sometimes been used to describe certain sectarian movements that form in response to restrictive definitions of orthodoxy.

What is **apostasy**?

The term "apostasy" comes from the Greek compound *apo-stasis*—literally "standing away or apart from," hence "rebellion or secession." It differs from heresy in several important respects. Heresy involves refusal to accept one or more mainstream doctrinal positions, but those holding the heretical views do not necessarily mean to repudiate the religious tradition altogether. In other words, heresy means a kind of selective rejection of religious teachings, often in the sincere belief that a certain view is simply mistaken. Apostasy implies a blanket rejection of a faith tradition and a return to former views or to another tradition. So, for example, some early Christians reverted to paganism, and some seventh-century Bedouin Arabs who had become Muslims rejected Islam when Muhammad died, and fell back on their ancient tribal ways. Official punishments for both apostasy and heretical beliefs have often been severe, including death, and have depended a great deal on the degree to which religious authorities exercised political clout. In the time of Constantine, apostate Christians suffered very harsh forms of banishment and loss of legal rights.

What does the word **conversion** mean?

From the Latin *convertere,* meaning "to turn about," conversion is a process of dramatic change. Religious conversion can mean a transfer of allegiance or membership from one religious tradition to another. When a conversion is formal or official, it can involve a repudiation of one's former beliefs, but it often means an affirmation of membership in the convert's new group. Many converts change from having no particular religious affiliation to active engagement in a community of faith. Recognition of a convert's acceptance into a new community varies widely. Some traditions require elaborate and lengthy preparation, including indoctrination in the new belief system, culminating in special ceremonies of initiation. Other traditions require minimal preparation and may mark a new member's acceptance with a simple welcoming announcement to the gathered congregation. Some traditions actively seek converts while others are not at all aggressive in this respect.

Another kind of conversion is equally important. Great religious figures in many traditions talk of soul-shaking experiences that leave them searching for a new way of recommitting themselves spiritually. They often describe a dramatic change of heart that results not in their leaving one community of faith for another, but in a renewal and deeper understanding of their original faith commitments.

Do all religious traditions send out **missionaries**?

Attitudes toward proselytizing (making converts) vary tremendously from one tradition to another. Christianity, Islam, and Buddhism are the three great missionary traditions. But within each of these there are considerable differences in emphasis on missionary activity. Some Christian groups support enormous mission operations, at least indirectly through private donation, all over the world. Other, generally smaller, groups make no attempt to mobilize their limited resources in order to proselytize. In between are Christians who consider it the ordinary duty of every believer to "evangelize" simply by sharing the "Good News of Jesus Christ." Muslims have also had a history of vigorous missionary work. Most Muslims consider "inviting" (*da`wa*) others to the faith a fundamental duty. In more recent times, however, Muslims have engaged in less widespread organized and institutionally funded missionary activity. Buddhist missionary work, especially between about 300 BCE and 600 CE, led to the spread of

29

the faith from India throughout central, east, and southeast Asia. Today small-scale efforts continue, but are generally quite low key. A few Hindu groups, such as the International Society for Krishna Consciousness and the Vedanta Society, have dedicated themselves in modern times to spreading their word. But on the whole, major missionary efforts have not been significant in other traditions.

What does **geography** have to do with religion?

A separate subdiscipline of religious studies called the Geography of Religion investigates how and why religious communities start and spread as they do. Geographers of religion don't just provide us with detailed maps that illustrate spatially where the world's major religious groups are and what percentages of a regional population belong to what tradition. They also study how people attach religious meanings to the physical circumstances in which they live and move. Practically every religious tradition has its "sacred geography." Cartographers devise a number of different kinds of maps—physical, political, meteorological. Sacred geography results in what might be called spiritual maps. These spiritual maps exist first of all in the minds of religious believers and reflect the distinctive perspective of their traditions, but we can also plot on paper how various religious traditions map their world. Places that are especially sacred to a particular community of faith provide believers with a unique kind of orientation to the larger world. In many instances a special place functions as a spiritual "center" of the universe, so that everything revolves around it. That is not a measure of the place's actual importance, of course, for many sacred places are relatively insignificant politically and economically, and quite hard to reach physically. Many traditions eventually develop networks of holy places. Their holiness can derive from their association with events in the life of some sacred person, from the belief that some special event occurred there, or simply from the perception that a natural feature such as a tree or mountain or spring possesses unusual spiritual power. What is most important to keep in mind is that physical settings matter a great deal and that religious traditions "claim" pieces of this earth as sacred to themselves.

What is a **holy city** and how do cities become holy?

Dozens of cities, towns, and villages across the globe have become especially sacred. Some places actually start off sacred. People acknowledge a place as the site of a unique revelatory event (often called a theophany, or divine manifestation). Some people choose to settle around the sacred site. Since holiness is often associated with natural features conducive to human habitation (springs, rivers, fertile soil), settlements can develop and expand. Other sacred places begin unremarkably as centers of population and acquire their sacredness later, often because a holy person has lived there. Whatever the genesis of a city's sacred character, people often come to believe that the place has *always* been holy. Over a period of centuries, a holy city may take on more and more religious associations, so that eventually believers regard it as the place where virtually everything of religious significance has happened. The holy city thus becomes a spiritual world unto itself. In a similar way, if believers perceive their holy city not only as the place where it all began but the place it will all come to an end, the city also becomes a microcosm of history. All power and even time itself comes into focus in this one place, this center of the universe. Though it may seem an affront to logic, this kind of symbolic religious cosmology sometimes finds room for more than one "center." In other words, some traditions claim several sacred cities, often ranked hierarchically, but all uniquely sacred. This has its own logic: wherever believers gather, for whatever reason, there is the meeting place of heaven and earth.

What questions does the prospect of **interfaith marriage** raise?

Attitudes toward marriage between members of two religious traditions vary considerably. In some traditions interfaith unions raise relatively little concern. But many others typically either forbid them altogether or take serious "official" exception and place explicit restrictions on such marriages. Many Muslims and Catholics, for example, continue to hold that interfaith marriages are to be discouraged because of the problems that often arise in the religious education of children. In some communities it is assumed that the intended spouse from another tradition (most often the wife) will agree either to convert or to see that the children receive solid grounding in the spouse's tradition. In the long run, interfaith marriage holds the potential threat of one tradition's gradual assimilation and loss of identity in favor of a dominant tradition.

Why are **gender issues** important in understanding religion?

Gender roles are significant everywhere on planet earth, both religiously and socially. A common pattern is that gender roles deeply rooted in local custom gradually acquire religious justification. With the added weight of sacred authority, social change becomes considerably more traumatic and threatening, especially in ostensibly male-dominated societies. Gender roles, both social and religious, have a great deal to do with the exercise of power. Religious rhetoric invariably canonizes the social status quo in the interest of greater stability, arguing that time-honored gender-based divisions of labor are divinely ordained. To tamper with the balance in quest of gender equality is to court disaster, traditionalists argue. Sweeping change is never easy. When it seems to imply major shifts in the exercise of religious authority, it can be excruciating. Dramatic realignments are afoot now all over the world, yielding slow improvements in the social standing of women and children. Those changes will inevitably manifest themselves in the social structures of religious communities everywhere. It is likely that fifty years hence scholars will be adding important new chapters to the history of religion, chapters in which women's roles will be much more evident.

31

The United States of America by Denomination (in Millions)

59.0	Roman Catholic
15.3	Southern Baptist
10.0	Muslims
08.7	United Methodist
08.2	National Baptist USA
05.5	Church of God in Christ
05.2	Evangelical Lutheran USA
04.4	Mormon
03.7	Presbyterian Church USA
03.5	African Methodist Episcopal Church
02.6	Lutheran Church of Missouri
02.4	Episcopal Church
02.2	Assemblies of God
02.0	United Synagogue of America (Conservative Jews)
01.5	American Baptist
01.5	Baptist Bible Fellowship International
01.5	Greek Orthodox
01.3	United American Hebrew Congregation (Reform Jews)
01.2	African Methodist Episcopal Zion Church
01.0	United Orthodox Jewish Congregation of America (Orthodox Jews)
01.0	Disciples of Christ

Note: Numbers are estimates, and not all sources are in agreement. The margin of error is approximately 3 percent for the larger religions, and slightly larger for the religions counting fewer than five million members.

Are **racial and ethnic issues** a significant factor in religion?

Race is just as formative an element in the history of religion as gender. When religious traditions expand beyond their regions of origin they must adapt to new cultural, racial, and ethnic circumstances. If political power accompanies the tradition's expansion, the social balances in the new territory will very likely call for change in the expanding tradition as well as in the lives of the local populations. What one might call "religious colonialism" often goes hand in hand with cultural hegemony. When a religious tradition is heavily identified with a racial or ethnic group, converts to the tradition may find themselves still second-class citizens. Within the greater American Christian tradition, for example, Black churches formed because of *de facto* segregation, even though in theory all Christians enjoy equality in the sight of God.

How important are questions of **"assimilation"** and **"distinctiveness"** in religion?

Concerns over religious cohesiveness and identity vary with social and political circumstances. For example, in the former Yugoslavia, Croatian Catholics, Serbian Orthodox Christians, and Muslims managed a remarkably peaceful coexistence. When political disintegration followed the death of Marshal Tito, divisions along religious lines began to assume greater importance. That was not a direct result of differences in religious beliefs, but because age-old social divisions had occurred along religous lines centuries earlier. With the loss of political cohesiveness came the convenient demonizing of "the others" and subsequent "ethnic cleansing." Most of the people of Bosnia, for example, had made little noise about their Muslim identity until they found themselves with little else to call their own. Serb propaganda warned of the imminent danger of a theocratic, fundamentalist Islamic state in their midst—the farthest thing from the minds of most Bosnian Muslims. Ironically, the loss of political standing has left the Muslims little choice but to reassert their religious distinctiveness. In the United States, concern over the danger of assimilation has likewise been linked to social factors. When Roman Catholics were still a small minority and subject to discrimination in several areas, they sought to maintain not only their Catholic distinctiveness but their nation of origin identities as well. American Jewish communities run the gamut from highly distinctive orthodox and conservative to highly assimilated. New Muslim communities in the United States are now facing the same issues in a story yet to unfold.

What do the terms **"ecumenism"** and **"inter-religious dialogue"** mean?

Ecumenism includes all the ways in which members of the many Christian churches and denominations have sought to come together in dialogue for mutual understanding. It does not necessarily envision any eventual unification, though that has happened in some instances. Inter-religious dialogue refers to the wider arena of direct attempts by members and administrations of the larger faith traditions to come together in hopes of deeper appreciation of their common interests as well as of the issues that divide them. So, for example, there are Muslim-Christian, Buddhist-Christian, and other organizations to promote dialogue. Attempts at inter-religious dialogue are gradually developing independent institutions, such as the Elijah School in Jerusalem, which focus on the notion that all the world's traditions have great treasures of wisdom to share with each other. Many people fear dialogue because they think it implies the eventual loss of diversity. People being what they are, there is little danger of that. Pluralism is an obvious fact of life. Mutual understanding is no longer a luxury but an absolute prerequisite for peace in the world.

What does **"syncretism"** mean?

Syncretism is from a Greek root meaning "mixed together" and refers in general to the blending of doctrinal and ritual elements from two or more religious traditions to form

33

a new tradition or sub-tradition. When two or more traditions co-exist in a cultural context, they invariably rub elbows and influence each other to some extent. Though the main traditions typically retain their characteristic features, there are often pockets or areas in a region in which elements of the larger traditions coalesce to shape a recognizably new system of belief. The Druze communities of the Middle East, combining Islamic and Christian themes, and India's Sikh tradition, blending Hindu and Islamic elements, are examples. Syncretism can also describe to some extent the fact of change within major traditions themselves when over many centuries they develop in such a way that, say, a modern form of the tradition looks very different from much earlier stages. The histories of the greater Hindu and Buddhist traditions exemplify this type. Tibetan Buddhism, to be more specific, represents a remarkable blend of elements from indigenous Tibetan Bon shamanism, Tantric Hinduism, and Buddhism.

LEADERSHIP, AUTHORITY, ORGANIZATION

What are some of the **main types of religious officials or specialists**?

Most traditions develop distinctive roles for specialists in the practice and preservation of ritual, the interpretation and implementation of rules, the works of teaching and pastoral guidance, and internal services and social outreach. In some traditions a single individual sometimes plays multiple roles, depending on the size of the local community. Division of labor typically occurs in larger communities and often requires extensive financial support. Ritual specialists play a crucial role in most traditions, but particularly in those having elaborate liturgies or other ritual practices. Some traditions, such as Hinduism, Roman Catholicism, and Shinto, maintain full-time priestly staffs at their larger institutions whose task is to serve the community and see that the main rituals are handed down intact. Traditions that have their own internal systems of law often train legal specialists for extensive administrative duties. Communities that establish their own educational systems often train teachers, administrators, and directors of religious education for their schools. Members of some traditions also look to their specialists for pastoral guidance in time of difficulty. Some religious leaders take on the role of counselor or spiritual guide, helping individuals and families through crises such as grieving or loss of employment. Related to these services are a host of community-based activities that, in larger local communities, can require a full-time director or social worker.

What role does **authority** play in religion?

At its best, religious authority provides needed guidance for individuals and functions as a moral compass for the community. It also serves as a community's backbone and a powerfully cohesive force. At its worst, religious authority, like any other kind, can be abusive and manipulative, playing on members' guilt and lack of confidence in their own sense of justice. Major religious traditions have developed a wide variety of authority structures. Some have highly centralized administrative systems, as in Roman Catholicism, the Church of the Latter Day Saints (Mormons), and the main branch of Shi'i Islam. The chain of command begins with God and descends through various levels of scholars, specialists, and bureaucrats. Those at the upper levels make decisions on large questions and those down the line communicate the decisions to the people and implement them. Structures of this sort can tend toward either a monarchy or an oligarchy, depending on the relative dominance of the person and office at the top. The hallmark of centralized structures is that they strive to elicit conformity from all members. At the other extreme are traditions in which authority is entirely local, centered in the village (as in tribal traditions or village Hinduism) or in the individual community place of worship or gathering (such as the churches of the Society of Friends, also known as the Quakers).

Many traditions fall somewhere between these two extremes. They have no direct line of authority from top to bottom, but local communities can be affiliated by conventions or conferences, for example. Many Japanese Shinto shrines belong to national associations. Baptist churches often belong to national "conventions" that meet regularly to decide organization-wide policy. American Muslim community leaders have formed the national Councils of Imams. In most of these cases and dozens of others like them, the majority of decisions are made locally.

How do **religious communities** structure their **internal administrations**?

Structure and organization generally relate more or less directly to the role and shape of authority within a religious tradition. There are, for example, various levels of organization such as denominations and sects. Here one finds a variety of structures ranging from rigidly hierarchical to egalitarian. Hierarchically oriented traditions (such as Roman and English Catholicism, Twelver Shi'i Islam, or the Mormons) often feature a pyramid of power capped by a single figure who can wield enormous moral and juridical authority. Just below that leader there is sometimes a rank or two of administrators who hold jurisdiction over specified territories within the tradition's geographic expanse. In some cases those top administrators may form a deliberative body or council that advises the leader in matters of tradition-wide importance. On the next rung or two down toward the base of the pyramid there will typically be ranks of administrative and pastoral offices charged with the daily affairs of the smallest community units where most members gather. Smaller religious traditions enjoy the practical luxury of opting for more egalitarian structures with fewer administrative offices. Whether large or small, all traditions have to deal with the practicalities of how their administrations are chosen. In some hierarchical structures the top official is elected by the members of the highest deliberative body, whose members in turn are appointed by the head. In others, such as Shi`i Islam, the process by which both the head and those next in rank are chosen is more a matter of public acclaim. In still other traditions with prominent official classification, such as temple Hinduism and Shinto, the priesthood is often associated with family and heredity and is typically entered for life. In the most egalitarian communities, all administrators are chosen democratically, serving either for set terms of office or indefinitely at the pleasure of the local community.

What is the **shape and purpose of religious law?** Where does **"custom"** fit in?

In its most basic forms, religious law consists of whatever strictures and sanctions a tradition's sacred texts call for. Many traditions that have not developed centralized authority structures strive for the simplicity of this kind of normative scriptural orientation. Some of these, such as the greater Hindu tradition, eventually include in the general category of "sacred text" a variety of documents of a distinctly legal character. A large number of other religious communities develop the equivalent of charters, constitutions, or by-laws to which they can appeal for clarification in the event that the scriptural text either does not address a particular issue at all or offers only ambiguous answers. Some, such as Islam, Judaism, and Roman Catholicism, have developed elaborate systems of religious law. This has often resulted in tension between the community's internal law and the civil law of the surrounding society. Resolution of the tension depends a great deal on the relationship of the religious authority structure to the local and regional political regime at any given time.

Custom, the long-standing practice of local communities even before the emergence of a particular religious tradition, inevitably has a significant impact on the religious law of most traditions. Over the long haul, religious law may "sanctify" certain local practices not specifically mentioned in the sacred text at all. For example, in some cultures Muslim women cover their faces. And although the Qur'an does not explicitly demand it, many Muslims will insist that it is a religious requirement. Sometimes local custom simply replaces older, even scripturally based, practices. Roman Catholic women in the United States once covered their heads in church, following a specific scriptural text, but this is no longer customary.

What is **religious education**?

Much of a tradition's prospects for growth, even for survival, lie in its success in passing along its core beliefs. For the vast majority of the world's people, education in religious beliefs remains a relatively informal process. Children grow up hearing stories from their elders about important religious figures and about the tradition's characteristic sense of ultimate realities. Some traditions, such as Hinduism, still retain some elements of a "classical" system whereby a select (usually male) portion of the population is eligible for special tutelage in the core teachings. In such a case, religious education is built right into the overall social structure. In the Confucian tradition, education in all that one needs to become a cultivated humanist is the equivalent of religious instruction and is part of the very backbone of the tradition. In other cases, such as Islam in some regions and many Christian churches, separate systems of religiously sponsored private schools have grown up to parallel available public systems. Some traditions have no fully developed structures to replace the public or non-sectarian options, but use periods of special instruction on designated days to reach children and young adults.

What are **monks and nuns**?

A surprising number of religious traditions include several different options or styles of affiliation for their members. The vast majority of members in every tradition belong to the broad category often referred to as "lay" persons. Within the orbit of the larger communities there are generally numerous social organizations of an ostensibly religious orientation open to lay believers. But another, more restrictive, category of membership is available, for example, to virtually all Buddhists, many Christians and Hindus, and to Muslims in a number of regions where various Sufi groups thrive. These organizations are often called "orders" or "confraternities." The Buddhist Sangha is arguably the oldest continuously functioning order of its kind on earth, dating to the late sixth or early fifth century BCE. In some traditions, these orders have devised separate but parallel structures for men and women. Two very different lifestyles have been important in the history of monasticism. When members live together in community at all times, they are called "cenobites" (from the Greek *koinos + bios,* "common life"). Those who choose to live alone or as hermits are called "anchorites" (from the Greek *ana-chorein,* "to withdraw"). Many of the orders originate as small circles of devotees gathered around a charismatic figure (in the case of Buddhism, the foundational figure himself). Some eventually grow into complex organizations with elaborate hierarchical systems of succession to leadership and authority. Larger orders often split into sub-orders, with members breaking off and founding their own groups, either because of a disagreement over spirit or practice, or to simplify administration and governance. Orders typically develop a system of training, beginning with a period of apprenticeship in which the "novice" or "aspirant" learns the order's ways and demonstrates aptitude for the life. Attaining full membership, the monk or nun (or "brother" in some cases) assumes ordinary responsibilities and shares fully in the community life. Some are asked to perform internal administrative duties, and become part of the governance structure. Orders can be either local, with only one or a few houses in a city or region, or more widespread, with foundations worldwide governed from a central administrative office. Some traditions also have organizations that serve a population whose religious commitments place them somewhere between "lay" and "professionally religious." These are sometimes called "third orders."

Theology as a Concept in the Third-Century Mediterranean World

The term "theology" was generally used by the Greeks to describe the character of theogonies and to designate critical studies of Greek mythology. Plato in the *Republic,* Aristotle in his *Meteorology,* and Cicero in the *Nature of the Gods,* came to approximate the later historical use of the term. The Neoplatonists, however, seem to have been the first to consider theology as the science of God. The term is altogether missing in the New Testament and in the apostolic Fathers.

Early stirrings in the development of the concept of theology are to be found in the writings of Irenaeus of Lyons and Clement of Alexandria. The former was one of the first Christians to attempt to impose a rational economy upon God in his recapitulation theory, and the latter's *Stromata* was an early attempt to impose order upon divine revelation in general. The apologists, themselves educated as philosophers or lawyers, especially felt the need to present the educated pagan world with a philosophically coherent expression of faith. While Justin Martyr attempted judiciously to weave Platonism into the Christian scheme, Tertullian developed the technical terminology to be employed by subsequent theologians. Hippolytus, the first Christian to employ the word "theologian," was seriously concerned about launching an orderly investigation into the psychology and economy of God.

In the third century, Origen, molded in the concepts of Middle Platonism and to some extent of Stoicism, greatly influenced the emergence of theology as a sophisticated, philosophical pursuit. The apostles, he felt, left the grounds of their statements to be examined by those who had the charismata of the Spirit: knowledge of the divine world, wisdom, skill in technical tools, and holiness of life. His express aim was to erect a clearly stated connected body of truth based on illustration and argumentation and arrived at by the "correct method." Even the title of his great work, *On First Principles,* betrays his intention to deal intelligently with God and heavenly beings and with men, the material world, and free will and its consequences. Origen was forced to rely heavily on the use of allegory to resolve contradictions, explain difficult passages, and correct misstatements purporting to be facts.

Where do **religion and political power** come together?

Virtually every religious tradition has had to come to terms with its relationship to civil authority and power. As often as not, the relationship varies at least slightly from one political setting to another. Even in the Unites States, many traditions have shifted their positions historically. The standard and seemingly straightforward principle of separation of church and state has been reinterpreted in various ways, with prominent religious figures seeking and winning national elected office as high as the United States Senate. The situation has historically been still more complex where political rulers have declared one religious tradition the "state creed." That has often meant hard times for members of faith communities that have not enjoyed official patronage and protection. Popular perception nowadays tends to label Islam as the tradition most likely to take political shape, as if no other has ever done so. But ample data from the history of religion suggests that questions of the relationship of temporal to spiritual power have arisen for virtually every major tradition at some time or other.

What are some of the ways **religious groups engage society** at large?

Whether or not a particular faith tradition mounts major missionary efforts, it will invariably devise ways of reaching out to the larger community. Social agencies devoted to health care, disaster relief, feeding the hungry, and sheltering the homeless are an integral part of the institutional histories of most religious traditions. Though they may not be as well known—and certainly do not generally have the resources—as large international aid organizations, countless local Muslim, Hindu, Buddhist, Christian, Jewish and other communities have given social concern high priority. For example, the greater St. Louis Muslim community has extended its care to several thousand Bosnian refugees during the 1990s, tutoring the children and finding jobs for their parents. Study the history of important temples, synagogues, and mosques across the globe and you will encounter evidence of social outreach stretching back centuries.

PERSONALITIES AND POWERS

What does the term **"spirituality"** mean?

Spirituality is the experiential dimension of a religious tradition. Theologies and creeds communicate the content of a tradition; myths and rituals describe how believers should externalize those beliefs in action; religious ethics suggest norms by which to evaluate one's behavior. Spirituality presupposes all that and goes deeper. Spirituality is about what all those things have to do with the *relationship* between a believer — both as an individual and as a member of a community of faith—and the source and final goal of human existence. Every tradition offers help in understanding how that central relationship unfolds through one's entire life. In many traditions, the various types of personalities and powers are an integral part of spirituality. But beyond these personalities and powers, religious persons express their spiritualities in a wide range of manifestations, from literature to architecture, from the minutest details of ritual to the largest institutions and structures of authority.

What is a **priest**?

A socio-religious class called "priesthood" has ancient roots in various traditions. Some priestly classes have perpetuated themselves through heredity. Some have been intimately associated with the performance of sacrificial ritual (whether bloody or not) and are typically connected with temple or church institutions both large and small. In some traditions, priests have been celibate as a group, but in most marriage is a prerequisite for all priests. Most of all, the priest functions as the chief ritual specialist and is often considered a mediator of spiritual power, an indispensable connection between the divine and the human. Even in societies where a hereditary priesthood is the norm, some type of specialized training is generally expected and provided. More often than not priestly education aims to steep the trainee in the sacred text and its ritual uses, as well as in the ritual actions the priest can be expected to perform hundreds or even thousands of times a year. On the whole it is safe to say that priests in most traditions are trained less as professional theologians than as public servants commissioned to facilitate the devotional life of the community. Special rituals—called "ordination" in some traditions—designed to dedicate individuals to the priesthood often bring the time of training to its culmination. Priesthoods are typically restricted to male membership, though there are some exceptions.

Are **shamans** the same as **priests**?

Shamans belong to the large, general category of priest, which is in turn part of the still larger category of ritual specialist. Women seem to be better represented in the ranks of shamans, depending on the cultural setting, than in priesthoods. In some traditions shamans are called medicine men or women. A shaman's training tends to include more closely guarded secrets than that of a priest, with greater emphasis on esoteric and arcane practices. Whereas priests more often perform their services as part of larger public settings, the work of the shaman also includes a great deal of private communing with the world of spirits. Shamanistic rites typically involve trances or loss of control, and often include exorcism to expel undesirable spiritual forces. Shamans are key figures in many indigenous or tribal traditions. Even though shamans do not generally find an official place in the major religious traditions, they often appear around the fringes. And the more closely a tradition's beliefs and practices are tied to nature, the more likely will the tradition's ritual specialists share characteristics of the shaman. Some features of shamanistic lore, however, have made their way into the heritage of major traditions. For example, stories in which a prophet or other important personality journeys beyond this world on a trip that can include tours of the various levels of heaven and hell can suggest roots in a shamanistic past.

What are **mystics**?

Mystics are those who have special insight into the deepest of spiritual mysteries. They often report first-hand, direct experience of realities far beyond the ordinary. There are

Doric order temple of Poseidon, Greek god of the sea, at Cape Sounion, Greece, c. 500 BCE.

some apparent similarities in the accounts of mystics across traditions. In a number of traditions we find two principal types of mystical experience. One is a highly personal encounter between the human subject and the divine reality, in which there is no permanent loss of individuality. This type is sometimes called "theistic" or "dualistic" mysticism. Another describes the mystic as utterly absorbed, annihilated, lost in a largely impersonal cosmic reality. "Monistic" is the name often used to describe this second type. There are equally telling differences from one tradition to another, and it is misleading to conclude that all religious traditions come together in mysticism. Especially in instances of theistic mysticism we find that the subject invariably describes the object of the experience in terms distinctive of his or her tradition. Christians encounter Christ and Mary, Muslims receive guidance from Muhammad, and Hindus merge in loving union with Shiva, for example. There are surely points of important cross-over in the mysticisms of the various traditions. Still, the differences remain and must be acknowledged.

What is a **martyr**?

The word "martyr" comes from a Greek word that means "witness." Some traditions have made a special place for believers so committed to their faith that they have been willing to die, either in the active spread and defense of the faith or as a way of protesting forced conversion or apostasy. Most people will likely associate martyrdom with Christianity and Islam. But there are numerous examples of unconditional wit-

41

The Ancient Greek Gods and Myths

Between approximately 850 BCE and 500 BCE, there arose a new Greek religion based on the god Zeus and on eleven other gods who resided on Mount Olympus in Thessaly, in northeastern Greece. The Greek gods were adopted later by the Romans and given different names.

The twelve gods made up a family: Zeus (Jupiter to the Romans), the ruler; his brothers Poseidon (Neptune) and Hades (Pluto); their sister Hestia (Vesta), who later gave up her place to Zeus's son Dionysus (Bacchus); Zeus's wife Hera (Juno); their son Ares (Mars); Zeus's children Athena (Minerva), Apollo, Aphrodite (Venus), Hermes (Mercury), and Artemis (Diana); and Hera's son Hephaestus (Vulcan). These "Olympians" were concerned with and controlled the fate of humankind. Many minor gods were believed to reside on earth and to play a part in the drama of the Olympians and their interaction with the Greek mortals. Zeus sometimes fathered children by mortal women, and the sons became the heroes of Greek legend.

The Greeks worshiped their gods as a regular part of their everyday lives. They were careful to please the gods in their actions and were especially careful to avoid angering them. When disaster befell their cities or crops, or when sickness took the lives of loved ones, they believed the wrath of the gods was responsible. The Greek gods also had a humorous side, and the mortals were able to laugh at the gods' plots against one another and at their concealed love affairs.

The Greek and Roman myths concerning the activities of the Gods and mortals are considered some of the world's greatest literature. Outstanding examples include the *Iliad* and the *Odyssey* of Homer. These and other works presented the ideals of physical beauty and heroic deeds in a poetic form that has inspired civilization since their creation.

nessing of religious beliefs and values from a host of traditions. Some examples involve self-immolation or voluntary starvation. Many great religious leaders have engaged in fasting as protest even to death. Whether they die in battle or in protest, all martyrs give witness to values they believe are more important than life itself. Are "martyrs" simply crazy? Are they masochists? Some, perhaps. A few may not have been authentic witnesses for faith but may have been acting out serious personal problems or merely calling attention to themselves. And in some instances, social pressure is the operative force, making it impossible for certain people not to participate. That too can result in a grotesque distortion of the ideal of committed witnessing. Real martyrs don't necessarily *want* to die, much less are they possessed by a mania for death.

What is a **sage**?

Some religious figures are celebrated for their function as living repositories of wisdom. Popular lore may occasionally attribute a wondrous deed to a sage, but the emphasis is decidedly on the person's depth of understanding and insight. Sages are especially important in Jewish and Confucian tradition, for example. They are the people entrusted with preserving the ancient ways, not by mere rote, but also by injecting new meanings that allow adaptation to changing times. In some religious traditions, such as Islam and Hinduism, the religious scholar occupies a special place of honor. But these scholars function on a more practical level than the sages, and Confucian tradition even keeps the two categories more or less clearly separate.

What is an **ascetic**?

An ascetic is a person who engages in a demanding "exercise" (from the Greek *askesis*) in the interest of spiritual progress. One of the ascetic's chief goals is freedom from the encumbrances of material existence. Various forms of self-denial and increased attentiveness to inner movements of spirit are therefore at the heart of ascetic practice. Fasting, use of the simplest possible clothing and other material needs, and the cultivation of solitude are common themes in ascetic discipline. In many religious traditions ascetics are known for their observance of silence for long periods. Ascetics vigorously pursue detachment from all that is not conducive to realizing one's nothingness in the face of ultimate reality. These spiritual athletes often appear to others to be going to unhealthy extremes—and in relation to widespread societal norms of ordinary behavior, they can indeed be extremists. Some ascetics are known for such practices as sitting atop pillars for long periods, staring at a blank wall for years, or lowering themselves head-first into the depths of a well. But there is another important way of understanding asceticism. Every human being who works hard at living a good life practices asceticism at some level. The ordinary disciplines of dealing with life's predictable setbacks, of treating others with consistent kindness, and of shouldering all of one's responsibilities are forms of asceticism. Most religious people must make the most of the ordinary opportunities, allowing their tradition's "professional" ascetics to remind them occasionally of the need to look deeper in the quest for spiritual freedom.

What is a **saint**?

Individuals who embody to the highest degree a religious tradition's spiritual ideals function in a variety of ways. Some traditions, such as Sunni Islam and various Christian denominations, emphasize the importance of each individual's direct relationship with the supreme being. They teach that no human being has the power or authority to act as a mediator for anyone else. But the need for help in achieving the highest spiritual aspirations seems to run so deep that examples of "saintly" characters appear in the histories of virtually every religious tradition. The ability to perform miracles is a major feature in some traditions. Healing is perhaps the most common claim, but miracles can include everything from finding lost objects to raising the dead. Saints in some traditions become more powerful and active after death than during their lives, and devotees shower them with requests generation after generation. According to some traditions, such as Roman Catholicism, individuals reputed for their holiness in life must show their worthiness to be formally declared saints by having certified miracles attributed to them after death. Healings are the most common wonders needed to bring about the saint's "canonization." Special "cults" (in the sense, not of exclusive religious organizations, but of people who "cultivate" a particular devotion) of certain saints have developed in some communities. Believers sometimes claim a particular holy person as their "patron" saint, associating him or her with a particular place and with specific types of miracles. But saints can also develop a more universal following and have devotees wherever members of a particular tradition are to be found.

Are there **religious heroes**? How are they different from saints?

Every culture has its heroes and heroines. Sometimes these pillars of strength and unusual ability represent largely "secular" or natural virtues. But in many instances heroes and heroines whose life stories are not explicitly religious in origin gradually take on religious associations. One typical pattern is that a local heroic figure rises to prominence on a larger scale and becomes a sort of "national" hero. A religious tradition formerly unknown in the region moves in, perhaps arriving on the wake of military conquest and newly established political power, and eventually becomes the dominant religious influence in the area. Heroes and heroines who had formerly been characters in folk or royal epic tales begin to rub shoulders with the saints and other prominent religious personalities imported by the now-dominant religious tradition. Before long (in the grand scheme of things, at least—but still generations or even centuries) the local or national heroes begin to acquire the characteristics and virtues of their religious counterparts. They may never rise to the status of "saints," but they definitely qualify for the title of religious hero. By way of distinction, wonders attributed to a saint typically speak loudly of divine power. A religious hero's spectacular deeds, on the other hand, typically reflect a sort of natural perfection now understood as part of a divine dispensation even if not a direct result of divine intervention.

Do all traditions have **savior figures** or **redeemers**?

Virtually every tradition acknowledges that life is full of difficulties, but not all teach that someone else can rescue people from their problems. Theravada Buddhism, for example, emphasizes self-effort following the example of Buddha the Teacher. Sunni Islam teaches that only surrender to God can bring a person's life to a good end. Some saviors, such as Bodhisattvas in Mahayana Buddhism, effect salvation for humanity purely by extending their power so that individuals are lifted out of their suffering. In those instances,

> ## The World's Biggest Religions?
>
> **N**early one-third of the world's population is Christian, making Christianity easily the single largest religous group. Within the general designation of "Christian," Roman Catholics number nearly 1 billion; Protestants number about 425,000,000; Orthodox constitute approximately 175,000,000; Anglicans number approximately 75,000,000; and all other Christians total just over 200,000,000. Muslims are the next largest religious group, with approximately 1.2 billion adherents. Next in line, Hindus number about 800,000,000, followed by Buddhists at about 350,000,000. About 1 billion people are commonly described as "nonreligious," and nearly 300,000,000 are designated as Atheists. Tribal religionists total nearly 100,000,000.

the savior remains largely above human misery. Some, such as Jesus Christ, work their saving deeds by redeeming or "buying back" a lost humanity. The notion of redemption presupposes that a savior figure spends him or herself as a kind of ransom, identifying profoundly with the plight of humanity. This kind of redemptive suffering is relatively rare. Some traditions in which saints are prominent underscore the suffering of some holy persons, but they do not generally effect salvation through their pain.

What kind of **literature** is the **principal source for information on holy persons**?

"Hagiography" (from the Greek terms for "sacred writing," *hagie graphe*) forms an important literary source in nearly every major religious tradition. Hagiography as a traditional literary genre is quite different from the modern forms of history and biography to which most of us are accustomed. As with sacred scriptures, it is essential to know what kind of document a work of hagiography is. That means reading with different lenses than are appropriate for more contemporary forms of communication. In general, hagiographical writing underscores the amazing and often downright miraculous elements in the life story of an important holy person. More often than not special signs attend the birth of the individual, who goes on to have an extraordinary childhood. The spiritually precocious youngster often seems to move directly into a religious maturity characterized by feats of towering personal endurance and asceticism. Alternatively, a holy person may spend many years wallowing in immorality and ignorance of the religious tradition's truth, then go through an astounding conversion. Many traditions have produced whole libraries of hagiography that include women's stories, but usually in notably smaller numbers than men's.

45

What is a **prophet**?

Especially important in the traditions of Middle Eastern origin, prophets play two indispensable roles. First, prophets are intermediaries in the divine communication to humankind. In the Abrahamic traditions, prophets speak on behalf of God, sometimes delivering a sacred scripture to the people to whom they are sent. In this capacity prophets appear often through history, whenever the divine revealer determines that the original message has been lost or has become so diluted as to need restatement. In addition, prophets function as critics of the ethical and religious status quo. They confront the powerful with a mandate to establish justice for all their subjects. They challenge the wealthy to account for their responsibilities in societies where the gap between the haves and the have-nots grows ever wider. They remind ordinary people of the need to render thanks to the divine source of life and giver of all gifts.

Are **"apostles"** the same as **"disciples"**?

An apostle is literally "one who is sent out" (from the Greek *apo-stellein*). Readers may associate the term mostly with Jesus' early community of twelve elect followers, but Muslim tradition also uses it to refer to an important sub-category of the group known as prophets. Apostles (*mursalun* in Arabic) are those special prophets who are given a scripture and a mission to all peoples. The other prophets are sent to a specific people only and do not bring a distinct sacred book. Disciples are literally "those who learn from" a master. Christian tradition numbers Jesus' formally commissioned disciples at seventy. According to Buddhist tradition, the Buddha gathered five hundred primary disciples around himself, with a handful of them eventually gaining special recognition for expertise in one or another aspect of Buddhist teaching.

Is a **reformer** anything like a **prophet**?

Reformers can share important characteristics of prophets, such as their scathing critique of the status quo. But there are also notable differences. First, reformers appear in virtually every tradition whereas prophets do not. Not all traditions teach that their sacred truths are delivered through intermediaries or spokespersons for the divine source. Second, reformers typically do not bring new revelations at all, nor do they claim an authority that simply abrogates all that has gone before them. Instead reformers try to awaken in their people an awareness that it is time to change, to renew, to recapture the original spirit that gave birth to the tradition. They do not necessarily advocate jettisoning the tradition's historical heritage to return to the sources, though that can be a feature in some fundamentalist reforms. Some reformers do, however, reevaluate religious teachings that they believe have become distorted or diluted and lay the axe to the root of institutions they believe have usurped unwarranted authority. The power of the Papacy, for example, was a major target of Christianity's sixteenth-century reformers. There have been rare instances in which

Major Shifts in Religion during the Twentieth Century

During the twentieth century, followers of Christianity grew from about 500,000,000 to nearly two billion, yet they remained at approximately the same percentage of world population as in 1900: 34%. Followers of the other major world religions grew at a faster pace. Islam, for example, grew from just over 12% of the world population in the late nineteenth century to about 18.5% today. By some accounts Islam is currently growing at an annual rate of of 6.5%, with cumulative growth of 225% in the last fifty years. By comparison, Hinduism has grown by about 115% during the same period, and Buddhism has grown by slightly less than 65%. Perhaps most notable is the spread of all faiths from their homelands, creating world religions where once there had been essentially "national" or "regional" ones.

important religious figures functioned as reformers while they lived but were elevated after death to the status of prophets. In those cases it appears that some members of the reformer's tradition chose to break away from the parent tradition so dramatically that they required the added authority of prophet-hood to legitimize their claim to independence as a new religious entity.

What is a **fakir**?

"Fakir" has become a widely used term generally disconnected from its original meaning. It comes from the Arabic word *faqir,* meaning poor person or beggar—in other words, someone who chooses spiritual and sometimes also material poverty. By extension, "fakir" has come to refer to a class of individuals, especially in western and southern Asia, who engage in shocking and apparently painful physical actions without suffering disastrous consequences. Fakirs capture attention precisely by their ability to come away seemingly unscathed by lying on beds of nails, walking on live coals, eating glass, piercing parts of the body without drawing blood, and similar bizarre actions. In India the term can also be a reference to perfectly credible and authentic renunciants called *sannyasis* who show no penchant for outlandish display. But the shift of meaning from Sufi mendicant to wonder-working oddity may have resulted from the claims of some Sufi saints and their followers to miraculous powers.

What are **angels**? Do they have a role in many traditions?

Angels and similar celestial beings appear in numerous traditions all over the world. The classic image of the angel, a winged ethereal body with human features, may have originated in the Middle East. The ancient prophetic tradition called Zoroastrianism

47

had a highly developed cosmology in which angel-like beings called *amesha spentas* were attendants at the heavenly court of Ahura Mazda. Even in the early books of the Hebrew Bible we find mention of heavenly emissaries who deliver divine messages to people. The name "angel" comes from the Greek word for messenger and became associated with the mysterious figures because of what appears to be their principal function. But angels play many other roles as well, including that of warrior, guardian and protector, heavenly councillor, winged mount, celestial guide or escort, to name but a few. Angels play prominent roles in Christian and Islamic, as well as biblical Jewish, lore and spirituality. On the whole they act as intermediaries between the realms of the divine and the human. Ancient Indian, especially Buddhist, tradition includes luminous beings called *apsaras*. Though not depicted as winged, these lovely beings usually float through the air in scenes decorating Buddhist temples all over Asia. They often function as dancers and musicians.

Architectural pier, originally part of a monumental portal, at the capital of the ancient Persian Achaemenid dynasty at Persepolis, in southwestern Iran, depicting a royal-religious ceremony under the protection of the winged god, Ahura Mazda, chief deity of the imperial religion of Zoroastrianism, sixth century BCE.

What are **devils and demons**? Are they all called **Satan**?

According to ancient Middle Eastern mythology, devils are angels gone bad. As with angels, the history of the development of devils is complex. Much depends on the ways various traditions conceive of the supreme deity. In many there has been a need to

48

name evil forces, since even if a tradition teaches that a supreme being has created all things including evil, it will not likely allow that the same being incites people to evil acts. The term "devil" typically refers to a single malevolent being of sufficient power that it may even appear to compete with the supreme being. The name *Satan* comes from a Hebrew root meaning "accused" or "adversary," and first appears in the Book of Job. Islamic tradition carried on the name, referring to the Devil as both Shaytan and Iblis (related to the Greek word *diabolos*). In the Abrahamic traditions, demons are generally lesser evil forces who act as Satan's minions. Satan sends his nasty foot soldiers out to tempt whom they may. Hindu myth tells numerous stories of struggles between gods and demons, originally distinguished not as good and evil, but as clever and not so clever. Eventually the demons came to acquire the characteristics

Rock-cut tomb of an Achaemenid dynasty Zoroastrian Persian ruler, Naqsh-i Rustam, near Persepolis in southwestern Iran, sixth century BCE.

of malevolence and ability to deceive. Countless demonic forces inhabit Buddhist hells. They are capable of assuming virtually any human or animal form and often appear in folk tales.

Are any other **denizens of the upper and lower worlds** important religiously?

Several of the major religious traditions have populated every level of their universes with spiritual powers and presences assigned to countless specific tasks. Angels and devils are only the beginning and the most widely known. One of their most important, and unsung, functions is that of guarding the sacred cosmos as a whole as well as individual holy places. Directional guardians hold sway over all of space, beginning with the four cardinal directions and the four intermediate directions. They occupy the power-niches filled by angels in some traditions, but expand the role of guardian considerably. Thousands of temples all over Asia sport multiple images of fierce, no-nonsense bouncers with orders to warn off the unworthy and offer the good-hearted a feeling of protection. Another personification of power are the characters, often styled "kings," who rule the various levels of the netherworld. Certain kinds of devils or demons occupy a similar place in some traditions, but the "kings" project a still larger impression of potency.

Are there any links between **dreams** or **visions** and personifications of holiness and power?

Dreams and visions serve a number of important functions in religious traditions. Accounts of dreams and visions often describe an important figure's meeting with a still more important figure, including even the supreme being. The experience described is often that of the dreamer or visionary receiving some special teaching or revelation. Dreams naturally tend to be more private, though famous religious figures have sometimes published extensive records of their dreaming states. Visions, on the other hand, occasionally become a rallying point for large numbers of believers. The visionary lets it be known that he or she has been privileged to encounter some important spiritual presence at a certain place or under certain circumstances. In some cases, the visionary claims assurance that further visions will occur on a timetable that has been revealed. Devotees may thereafter begin to gather in hopes of sharing the visions. For some people, the prospect of visionary experience assumes enormous importance, almost as if visions constitute the only credible form of religious experience. Visions and dreams can also function as vehicles of legitimation or induction of the subject into the ranks of some spiritual confraternity. These experiences amount to a kind of ultimate endorsement, with the dreamer or visionary now able to assert a higher level of authority on the basis of an exchange with some holy person.

HOLIDAYS AND REGULAR OBSERVANCES

What is **sacred time**?

Most traditions attach special meanings to history as a whole, to specific moments in the lifetime of an individual, and to various times in the ordinary cycles of days, months, and years. Ordinary time in human experience is inextricably linked to change, that most troublesome of all realities. Religious traditions offer a partial remedy to the perplexities of change with the notion that reliving or reenacting events of cosmic significance offers a brief respite, an opportunity to stop time or perhaps step out of ordinary time for a moment. From the perspective of a tradition's ritual life, sacred time is the time of ritual encounter with the divine. But in addition, religious believers also seek to hallow decisive life experiences with rites of passage.

What is a **religious calendar**?

Since anchoring sacredness in time is so fundamental, most religious traditions have developed ways of keeping precise track of their distinctive ways of hallowing the days and years. Religious (sometimes called "liturgical") calendars establish a definitive pattern of moments meant to recall specific events in the life of a divine or foundational figure. Each year thus becomes a replay of the sacred person's life in miniature. An annual calendar can also symbolically recapitulate the whole expanse of a tradition's sacred history by laying out essential events in sequence on a time line. With every year, then, the community celebrates a renewal in faith, confident that each new cycle brings with it sufficient spiritual aid to carry on. The religious calendar functions as a kind of map of time that highlights certain seasons. Even the times between the high festivities thus take on special meanings as periods of waiting or expectation. In traditions that view time as linear, the religious calendar seems to have a forward motion, rising to a peak and moving toward a symbolic end of history. For traditions with a more cyclic understanding of history, the calendar year is just another in an endless series of cycles, with its own high and low points marked by feasts or religious holidays.

How many **different kinds of religious calendars** are there?

All calendars naturally have intimate connections to some sort of astronomical calculation but there are various ways of determining the particulars. There are solar and lunar calendars, seasonal and non-seasonal. Seasonal calendars are generally solar. Major annual observances reflect regional agricultural cycles. Some festivities are associated with planting, others with harvest, still others with the fallow season of winter. Such calendars often place special emphasis on the winter and summer solstices (respectively the shortest and longest days of the year), and on the vernal and autumnal equinoxes (the days in spring and fall when daylight and nighttime hours are equal). Lunar calendars can be either seasonal or non-seasonal, depending on whether and how the system inserts days or months to compensate for the fact that the lunar year rotates backwards against the solar. Each lunar year begins approximately eleven days earlier each solar year. If the first day of a lunar calendar corresponds with the first day of this year's solar calendar, then the next year the lunar calendar will begin on the equivalent of December 20 or 21. A lunar calendar that inserts an extra month every few solar years can both maintain its observance of the shorter lunar months and keep each festivity connected to the appropriate part of the agricultural cycle. Non-seasonal calendars, generally lunar, do not compensate for the discrepancy between the religious year and the agricultural seasons. As a result, major annual observances coincide with the solar calendar in cycles of approximately thirty-three years.

What is the connection between **regular observances** and **sacred history**?

A fascinating variant in the ways different traditions arrange their calendars is how they determine the beginning of their reckoning of religious time or sacred history. Sacred history can begin with the creation itself (Judaism), with the birth of a foundational figure (Christianity), with a signal event in the early history of the community (Islam), or with a major political event or era (India and Japan). Some traditions regard the primordial event as a kind of mid-point in all of human history, a fullness of time. Others, especially those with cyclical notions of time, place considerably less emphasis on any particular event.

CUSTOMS AND RITUALS

What is the difference between a **custom** and a **ritual**?

Custom includes a whole range of activities that people in a particular time and cultural setting become so used to doing that they rarely examine their reasons for acting that way. Custom is "the way we've always done" things. It includes everything from social expectations and etiquette to the specific kinds of food people serve for special occasions. "Common law" is a type of customary social norm; its practices have been in use so long that they have assumed legal status and authority. Custom operates at various levels, from that of a society at large to that of the local community and family. Rituals are typically part of the larger category of custom, but ritual practices tend to follow a rigid sequence in the interest of insuring that the action is "correct." For example, it is customary in certain cultures for participants in a wedding to wear certain kinds of clothes. But wedding rituals mandate specific actions in a set order, even when the principal participants opt for non-customary fashions.

What is the **purpose of religious rituals**?

Religious rituals function primarily to help believers establish relationships of presence, imagination, or memory with the spiritual. There is naturally some over-

Religious Sects in America in the 1970s

In the open cultural climate of the 1960s and 1970s, a variety of religions new to the United States, or previously unnoticed, attracted attention from the press and the general public. Some of these organizations engaged their converts in beliefs and activities that seemed strange by traditional standards. Detractors labeled them cults and warned of their dangers, particularly to the young. Among the best-known of these are the following:

Hare Krishna: Some of these groups came from India, such as the International Society for Krishna Consciousness, which incorporated itself in the United States in 1966. The organization attracted increasing numbers of young people, who were called Hare Krishnas by outsiders. In cities with large numbers of hippies, passers-by encountered Hare Krishnas, dressed in saffron robes with distinctive hair cuts, performing on the streets. Even more visible were the Hare Krishnas soliciting contributions in airport terminals and other public places.

TM: Another popular Indian guru was Maharishi Mahesh Yogi, of Transcendental Meditation. In the early 1970s, large numbers of people went to one of 350 training centers where they were given a personal mantra, a word they were to use for engaging in meditation. TM, as it was sometimes called, attracted attention from physicians and psychologists investigating the psychic values of meditation. In 1974 the Yogi bought Parsons College in Fairfield, Iowa, and renamed it Maharishi International University. When the Yogi's followers began to claim that they could levitate and that their meditation could alter world affairs, the movement went into a decline.

Moses David: A group that started as a Christian mission to young people in the California counter-culture in the late 1960s took on cult-like qualities when David Berg, the founder of Teens for Christ, began to see himself as the Messiah. He changed his name to Moses David. While the group's name changed several times, it was best known as the Children of God. Berg and his followers established communes on the west coast and in Texas. Berg himself went to Great Britain, and his movement proselytized around the world. Moses communicated with his followers in letters, called the "Mo Letters", that spelled out the terms of his developing set of beliefs. In the course of a decade over 900 of the "Mo Letters" were published, delivering doctrines that departed increasingly from main stream Christianity.

lap among these three goals of ritual. Some rituals effect or mediate a connection between participants and a divine or spiritual presence. An important feature in this and other rituals is the emotion or feeling, such as dread or longing or joy, that it fosters in the participants. Other rituals engage the imagination and intellect primarily, allowing participants to enter into another level of experience through meditation or contemplation, for example. Still other rituals help believers connect in memory with persons now departed or with past formative spiritual experiences they want to recall.

What makes **important** religious practices **"rituals"** and ensures that they work?

In addition to the various primary ritual functions are a host of lesser or secondary ritual acts that help participants establish a proper ritual setting and ensure that the actions are maximally efficacious. The setting includes the space, time, and feeling that make a ritual "work." Many rituals occur in spaces designated for that purpose. But in some instances separate preparatory rituals are used to mark the boundaries of a ritual space. They can include sub-rituals, such as processions or purification ceremonies. Other sub-rituals establish the boundaries of sacred time. Bell, drums, or calls to prayer may mark the opening and closing of a ritual. Still other rituals enhance a feeling or mood by appealing to the senses. The use of incense burners is an example of a widespread practice. Finally, some traditions assure continuity and purity of rituals with precise instructions on how they are performed. These instructions are often called "rubrics," because they are sometimes printed in red (Latin *ruber*) to mark them as directions.

What is **sacred space**?

Many religious rituals call for a particular physical setting for their proper and effective performance. Nearly every major religious tradition has developed primary ritual sites dedicated in varying degrees to their chief rituals. Mosques, temples, shrines, synagogues and churches provide the most important communal sacred spaces. But the degree to which the primary ritual sites are dedicated and restricted to specific ritual actions varies. Some ritual spaces are in effect multi-purpose facilities, and some traditions' rituals simply require no special kind of space. But when local communities of most traditions have grown enough to have bank accounts, plans for dedicated facilities are rarely far behind. Individuals and families in some traditions (such as Hinduism, Buddhism, and Shinto) also perform sacred rituals at home. In those instances believers often establish a small corner of the house as a sacred space or shrine. Some rituals (such as Islamic daily prayer) believers can perform wherever they happen to be. They simply make that place sacred for the duration of the ritual action by intending it to be so. At the other end of the space spectrum are the holy places associated with particular geographical locations such as holy cities and pilgrimage goals. Some traditions establish perimeters around those places, marking them off as sacred and inviolable, sometimes limiting access to believers only.

Is there any difference between **"meditation"** and **"contemplation"**?

Meditation and contemplation are important practices in many religious traditions. The two terms are often used synonymously to refer to a prayerful focus on inner spiritual realities. There are, however, some important differences in the methods used for that focusing. It is helpful to keep in mind that there are variations in both theory and practice among the major religious traditions. In general, meditation involves a nondiscursive concentration on some object, either verbal or visual. The idea is not to engage in "thinking" about the object of focus, but merely to allow it to function as a kind of controlled distraction. By targeting the focal object exclusively, the meditator frees up the mind and spirit to achieve a deeper level of simple awareness. Many traditions follow the practice of having a preceptor or spiritual guide assign a specific symbol to each meditator. That symbol can be a word or a phrase, sometimes called a *mantra*, repeated slowly and deliberately. It can also be an object upon which the meditator concentrates visually, such as a candle flame or a flower. When a meditator becomes aware that the mind is wandering, the solution is to observe "My mind is wandering" or something similar, and return to concentration. Gradually the number and intensity of distractions dwindle. Some traditions allow that there is important intellectual content in meditation, such as a point of doctrine on which the meditator reflects for deeper insight.

Contemplation involves a different method. Here the immediate goal is to enter imaginatively into a spiritual reality, and ultimately to be united with that reality. As its Latin root words suggest, the contemplator seeks to become one with or abide in a sacred place (*cum*, with, and *templum*, temple). Some traditions hold that contemplation is a state of pure intuition beyond any mental content. Others include in their understanding of contemplation the active imaginative entry into an important "scene," as if the contemplator were there with the players in some sacred action. Whatever the precise definition or method used in a particular tradition, it is fair to suggest that meditation precedes and prepares for contemplation.

Is **sacrifice** an important feature in many religious traditions?

Sacrifice can take a number of forms, from the actual slaughtering of a living being to a more symbolic "offering up" of something dear to the sacrificer. The Latin root, *sacrum* ("holy") and *facere* ("to make"), suggests that the object sacrificed and the one(s) performing the action become holy or sacred. Some traditions (such as Islam and Hinduism) continue ancient rites of bloody sacrifice by killing animals, either to commemorate some similar act attributed to an important holy person of the past or because a certain deity requires it. In other traditions ancient sacrificial rituals have

Mayan sacrificial altar at the temple city of Copan, Honduras, c. 500 CE.

been either abrogated altogether (since the destruction of Judaism's temple) or symbolically transformed into an un-bloody substitute (as in Christian re-enactments of the Lord's Supper).

What does the term **liturgy** mean?

The Greek word *leitourgia* (from *ergon,* work, performed for the *laitos,* people) originally referred to various forms of public service and eventually came to be associated with priestly service of the gods. Because of the word's use in early Christian sources, it has become part of the religious studies lexicon. Liturgy now generally means any system of rituals mandated for public re-enactment by members of a religious tradition. Its public nature separates liturgical action from private or devotional ritual. And since liturgical ritual is by definition required, it is further distinguished from the optional rituals associated with the individual expression of faith. Since liturgy is both communal and required, its performance presupposes some sort of scheduled predictability as well as facilities large enough to accommodate a whole community or segment thereof. Liturgical ritual is central to various Christian communities, Islam generally, and Judaism. Not every tradition's ritual life revolves around liturgy strictly so called. For some communities a more piecemeal practice of individual or small group worship forms the dominant ritual theme, with larger communal events functioning as annual or occasional variations. Hindus, many Buddhists, and practitioners of Shinto gather for the equivalent of liturgical participation for special festivities, but they typically per-

Freedom of Religion in the Twentieth Century

In March of 1981, after more than thirty years of failed attempts, the United Nations Commission on Human Rights completed a Draft Declaration on the Elimination of All Forms of Intolerance and of Discrimination Based on Religion or Belief. After approval by the Economic and Social Council (ECOSOC), the declaration was adopted by the General Assembly on November 25, 1981. The declaration is a short document with eight articles. It states that no one should be subject to discrimination on the grounds of religion or belief, that such discrimination should be condemned as a human rights violation, that states should act to prevent and eliminate such discrimination, and that the parents or legal guardians of a child have the right to organize life within the family in accordance with their religion or belief. Although religious liberty was deemed to be better protected by under-specification than by over-specification, the declaration does enumerate nine freedoms. Article 6 describes the right to freedom of thought, conscience, religion, or belief as including, but not limited to, the following freedoms: to worship or assemble in connection with a religion or belief and to establish and maintain places for these purposes; to establish and maintain appropriate charitable or humanitarian institutions; to make, acquire, and use to an adequate extent the necessary articles and materials related to the rites or customs of a religion or belief; to write, issue, and disseminate relevant publications in these areas; to teach a religion or belief in places suitable for these purposes; to solicit and receive voluntary financial and other contributions from individuals and institutions; to train, appoint, elect, or designate by succession appropriate leaders called for by the requirements and standards of any religion or belief; to observe days of rest and to celebrate holidays and ceremonies in accordance with the precepts of one's religion or belief; and to establish and maintain communications with individuals and communities in matters of religion or belief at the national and international levels.

form daily or otherwise regular rituals individually or in small groups at various times during the day. One practical result is that their staffs of ritual specialists may perform the same or very similar services many times a day throughout the year.

What is a **rite of passage**?

In the life of every individual certain times naturally stand out as particularly significant. Birth, the transition from childhood to adulthood (or puberty), the assumption of a new state in life (as in a marriage), and death are especially critical times. Religious traditions generally acknowledge these and other formative experiences by developing

57

Votive offerings left by Christian pilgrims in search of healings and other blessings, at the shrine Sanctuary of Chimayo, New Mexico. Just to the right rear is the small outer room where pilgrims scoop sacred dust from the dirt floor as a religious memento.

rituals designed to help people cope with the changes they bring. Sheer difficulty and challenge can sometimes be the distinguishing features of important moments or phases of a life. Confusion, sense of loss and grief, even overwhelming joy or feelings of limitless possibility can be cause for recourse to the comfort and direction rites of passage can afford. Rituals of this kind help believers by allowing them to step out of ordinary time and space for a while to regain their bearings. They can then return to "real life" feeling renewed, spiritually refreshed, and strengthened for the challenges ahead.

What is a **ritual object** or **implement**?

Ritual objects include a large number of items both symbolic and practical that are the essential devices of religious practice. They may be as outwardly pedestrian as containers for the raw materials of religious offering—rice, salt, wine, bread—or the utensils needed to move those materials around. These tools often have no major symbolic meaning but are largely utilitarian, though they are generally regarded as sacred because of the context and are not to be used for non-ritual purposes. Many other ritual objects are more symbolic than practical in function. Every tradition has its symbols for the ultimate spiritual reality, for the various kinds of benefits and blessings believers seek from that reality, and for the gifts devotees bring as offerings. Among the most common are images or icons, books or scrolls of sacred text, lamps, musical instruments, weapons, and special vestments or garb for officiants and sometimes participants.

When Religion Becomes a Crime

The Russian Revolution of 1917 launched a wave of tremendous change in Russia, affecting all aspects and strata of society. When Vladimir Lenin, the principal leader of the Revolution, died in 1924, a struggle ensued for control of the party and, by extension, the country. Joseph Stalin emerged as the country's new dictator. By 1929, when longtime rival Leon Trotsky was exiled, Stalin was firmly in power. A ruthless dictator, he quickly set a course of isolationism and nationalism, policies that would effectively cut the USSR off from much of the rest of Western civilization. Stalin presided over a basic reorientation of Russian culture and society during the 1930s. He instituted severe policies in the realms of art, education, religion, and family life that had a tremendous impact on all Soviet citizens, from the poorest peasant to Moscow's leading intellectuals. This process came to be known as Stalinization.

In 1929 laws were passed under which the practice and spread of religion became a crime against the state. Churches were destroyed, priests were stripped of their civil rights, and their children were forced to renounce their fathers or risk death. Three years later a program for the total eradication of religion from the Soviet Union was announced: "the very notion of God will be expunged as a survival of the Middle Ages and an instrument for holding down the working masses," the official announcement proclaimed. The Communist party and the Soviet State subsequently established themselves in the place formerly occupied by religion.

The study of history, science, the arts, and other subjects also underwent significant change in the 1930s, as the government introduced new conservative standards designed to focus education efforts on increasing worker skills and productivity. Finally, Stalin insisted on a return to "traditional family values." Homosexual behavior and abortion were criminalized, divorces were made much more difficult to obtain, and the Marxist-inspired drive for women's emancipation fell into disrepair. To ensure that the masses heeded this new emphasis, it was understood that the state had an obligation to scrutinize all members of Russian society; thousands were found wanting and were punished severely.

What is a **votive offering**?

Votive offerings are directly associated with the making of vows (from the Latin *votum*, something promised) in connection with requests for special favors. When religious believers visit a special holy place, they often write their needs on some object and leave the object within the sacred precincts. They vow to perform certain devotional or chari-

59

Mural depicting aspects of the ancient Roman religious cult of the healing god Aesculapius, who had become incarnate as a serpent, in a private residence in the city of Pompeii, near Naples, Italy, which was destroyed by an eruption of nearby Mount Vesuvius in 79 BCE.

table acts if the deity will grant their request. Votive offerings include any of hundreds of ways in which people symbolize their willingness to repay the divine favor. Among the more common devotional acts are those associated with visiting holy places or making pilgrimages. The devotee promises, for example, to approach the place on his or her knees from a certain point, or to make a certain number of prostrations before a particular sacred image. One of the most widespread of votive practices is the lighting of small candles after making an offering to the holy place. In some instances the use of candles has become dissociated from making vows in the truest sense of that term, so that lighting a wick often merely symbolizes or accompanies a request for divine help. Larger places of worship in many traditions provide appropriate votive offerings for sale in small shops attached to the church, temple, or shrine. For a fee, considered part of the offering, devotees receive an object such as a small statue of a holy person associated with the place, a devotional card, or even a tiny replica of the holy place itself or some part thereof. For example, adherents of Shinto often hang miniature torii gates on racks designed to receive hundreds of them.

What is meant by the term **"divination"**?

Divination comprises a host of specific ritual practices meant to give practitioners a sense of control in the face of life's mystery. It occurs in association with most religious traditions, if only toward the popular fringe. Divination often involves some

Religion in Ancient Rome

Like the ancient Greeks, early Romans practiced a form of religion that recognized many gods. As Roman and Greek culture came into closer contact throughout the Classical period, Romans began to borrow many Greek religious beliefs, and more ancient Etruscan gods took on the characteristics of Greek gods. Thus, for instance, the Roman Jupiter, the king of gods, became associated with the Greek Zeus. Ceremonies and superstitions played a significant role in the daily lives of Romans. Omens from nature often influenced the actions of leaders, and priests divined the intent of gods by observing the organs of slaughtered animals or the flight of birds. As time passed, Roman religion began to lose favor among the people. As Roman society became more decadent, there arose the need for a religion that offered greater moral and spiritual assurances. A new religion, Christianity, gained in popularity and eventually became the primary faith of Rome. In addition to Greek culture influencing religion in Rome, other facets of Roman culture were also affected by the Greeks. The Romans held significant esteem for Greek life and adopted certain elements from it, ranging from sculpture to libraries, architecture to philosophy, while preserving some of their own valuable strengths. The result of this merging of ideas is known as Greco-Roman culture.

form of question and answer exchange. Not unlike the oracles of classical Greek and Roman cultures, divination often results in ambiguous or enigmatic responses to questions such as "Will I get the job for which I'm about to interview?" or "Will my daughter's child be a boy or girl?" Common forms involve the use of objects or substances that when dropped, tossed, or heated form revelatory patterns or shapes. Alternatively, one might do something equivalent to drawing lots, then interpret the outcome with the help of a guidebook or expert. In Hellenistic religious traditions devotees could also seek an omen through "incubation," going to sleep in a holy place in hopes of having a revelatory dream. In addition to the practice of asking specific questions in hope of direct answers, divination includes the discerning of omens or signs in nature or otherwise ordinary circumstances. Some astrological beliefs and practices fall into this category. Specialists in reading everything from the stars to palms to tea leaves to the still-warm entrails of sacrificial animals have been part of popular religious practice in nearly every time and place.

Are **music and dance** important in religious ritual?

Sacred dance is one of the oldest forms of religious ritual known. Many liturgical traditions have developed out of classical religious dance, which often arose in turn as a medium in which to reenact central mythic narratives. Dance can assume various forms, from performance by ritual specialists alone, to visual display by a highly trained and richly decked-out troupe, to whole congregations performing relatively simple repetitive movements. This is where the use of ritual costume sometimes extends beyond the clergy or central ritual specialists. Some traditions, such as Shinto and other indigenous communities of faith, use dance at various levels of sacrality. Special rites might occur at or near the holiest part of a place of worship, while dance of a more entertaining and less esoteric sort might be available on separate small stages elsewhere on the grounds. Most sacred are re-enactments of central mythic stories. More popular performances often teach some moral point humorously. Musical accompaniment to religious ritual takes many forms and is generally more widespread than dance. Religious traditions run the gamut, from those that use no instrumental or vocal music at all to those whose rituals are almost entirely musical. Some traditions favor very arcane music, played on ancient instruments, to establish a mood of solemnity by creating the kind of sounds one would hear only in a particular ritual setting. This kind of music can be difficult to listen to, but its purpose is to mark the occasion as genuinely out of the ordinary. Others use music designed to encourage maximum participation rather than to establish distance. The latter typically develop extensive hymnographies.

RELIGIOUS TRADITIONS OF MIDDLE EASTERN ORIGIN

JUDAISM

HISTORY AND SOURCES

When and where did **Judaism** begin? **Was it "founded" by an individual person**?

Jewish tradition traces its beginnings back nearly four thousand years. Abraham is the key figure here, not as a founder but as the first "Hebrew" to receive a revelation from God. Genesis 11–25 contain the bulk of our scriptural information about Abraham. According to tradition, God told Abraham to leave his homeland in Mesopotamia (present-day Iraq). Trusting completely in God, the patriarch was to travel where God would lead him. As Abraham journeyed across the central Middle East from Mesopotamia to Egypt and back to what is now southern Israel, he and his son Isaac lay the foundations of a monotheistic tradition. Abraham's grandson Jacob sired the twelve sons who would bestow their names on the original twelve tribes. The second half of Genesis recounts their stories. But the appearance of Moses, beginning with the story of his being adopted by Pharaoh, marks another major turning point. Moses lived probably toward the end of the third quarter of the second millennium BCE (about 1300 BCE). His story occupies a larger portion of the Jewish scriptures than any other single figure, stretching from the beginning of Exodus to the end of Deuteronomy. From his inaugural revelation at the Burning Bush to his leading the people called Israel (the special name divinely given to the patriarch Jacob) at last to the banks of the Jordan, Moses' story is that of the formation of a community of faith. At the center of that formative epoch is the pivotal revelation of the Law at Sinai at about the mid-point of that journey. Sources do not record use of the word "Jew" (from the Hebrew *yehudi*) until many centuries after Moses' time. Then the word referred to a member of the tribe of Judah, which in turn had given its name to the region called Judaea.

Synagogue, upper floor of a residential building, in the old Jewish Ghetto in Venice, Italy. The five windows symbolize the five books of the Torah, and the small dome-crowned apse at the right marks the place of the Ark inside, where the Torah scrolls were kept while the synagogue remained in use. Sixteenth century.

What are Judaism's principal **sacred writings**?

The Hebrew Bible is a collection of some thirty-nine shorter works composed and edited over nearly a thousand years and gathered in three large literary/theological categories. The foundational texts are known variously as the Torah, the Pentateuch, or the Five Books of Moses. They are Genesis, Exodus, Leviticus, Numbers, and Deuteronomy. A second grouping is called the Prophets, and that in turn is divided into the "former" and "latter" prophets. The Former Prophets include the historical books of Joshua, Judges, I and II Samuel, and I and II Kings. Among the Latter Prophets are the three major prophetic books, Isaiah, Jeremiah, and Ezekiel; and the so-called Twelve Minor Prophets, Hosea (or Osee), Joel, Amos, Obadiah, Jonah, Micah, Nahum, Habakkuk, Zephaniah, Haggai, Zechariah, and Malachi. Finally, a category of texts collectively known as the Writings includes a fascinating selection of wisdom and prophetic literature and historical documents. The lone prophetic text here is the book of Daniel. A set of wisdom books, some traditionally attributed to David and his son Solomon, include Psalms, Proverbs, Job, and a mini-anthology called the Five Scrolls (or *megillot*). These include the Song of Songs, Ruth, Lamentations, Ecclesiastes, and Esther. Four important historical books complete the category of the Writings: Ezra, Nehemiah, and I and II Chronicles. Taken together these sacred writings go by the acronym *Tanakh*, which is made up of the initial letters in the words **T**orah, **N**evi'im (Prophets), and **Kh**etuvim (Writings).

What is the meaning of **Torah**? Do Jews believe **Moses** wrote it all? What about "oral" **Torah**?

Torah is a Hebrew word generally translated "teaching" or "instruction." In reference to the Hebrew scriptures, Torah means the first five books, Genesis through Deuteronomy. According to tradition, Moses himself composed the whole of the Torah under divine inspiration. This ancient attribution has the benefit of lending maximum authority to the earliest sacred texts by association with the man most identified with the divine revelation that shaped the faith community known as Judaism. Modern scholarship has demonstrated convincingly the historical improbability of the traditional attribution. In its most general sense, Torah means revealed or divine Law—all that God requires of Jews. But as the Jewish community has grown and spread, moving into new lands and cultural settings, interpreting the scriptural Torah in practical terms has presented challenges. When Ezra led a group of Jews back to Israel from exile in Babylon in the late sixth century BCE, he confronted a problem: many Jews no longer knew Hebrew. In order to teach them the Torah, Ezra commissioned scholars who could translate the Torah into Aramaic as it was being read aloud to the people. That translation, or paraphrase, was itself a kind of commentary on the sacred text. Thus began the phenomenon called "oral" Torah. From the fifth century BCE on, classes of special scholars would oversee its elaboration. One generation would pass oral tradition down to the next until it became so extensive that it had to be written down to be preserved. Then a new class of scholars would initiate commentary on the now written "oral" law, extending the process further, until once again the burgeoning oral tradition had to be committed to writing or be lost forever.

How do Jews **interpret their scriptures**?

Biblical interpretation began within the Hebrew scriptures themselves, with later authors referring to the earlier texts and thus at least implicitly commenting on their meaning in new contexts. By the time the latest texts were written, new historical circumstances had inevitably led to interpretations of events long past that earlier authors could scarcely have imagined. According to tradition, one of the earliest rabbis to devise a systematic foundation for biblical exegesis was Hillel the Elder (c. 50 BCE–30 CE). His "seven principles" (*middot*) of exegesis taught generations of scholars how to approach the sacred text rationally and consistently. One example of an important principle is that called the "Light and Heavy" (*kal va homer*). According to this principle, if the scripture allows or prohibits a certain action in a minor matter, one is justified in assuming the same allowance or prohibition applies in a more serious case. If the Law allows you to rescue an animal from a ditch on Sabbath, surely it will also permit alleviating a human being's suffering. Later rabbinical scholars devised still more comprehensive and elaborate exegetical frameworks. Perhaps the most famous is summed up in the acronym *PaRDeS* (an ancient Persian term meaning "Paradise"). Each of the upper case consonants stands for a Hebrew term referring to one of the four principal levels or methods of exegesis. *Peshat* is the literal sense and the kind of interpretation prevalent in oral Torah; *remez* looks for the allegorical meaning; *derash* ("study") derives the homiletical or ethical significance; and *sod* ("more") unveils the mystical significance of a text. Jewish exegesis has devised highly sophisticated methods of drawing out the various meanings of the sacred text and has preserved the results in an enormous library known as rabbinical literature.

Do Jews call their scriptures the **"Old Testament"**?

"Old Testament" is a term originally used by Christians as a convenient way of characterizing the relationship of the Hebrew scriptures to the Christian or Greek testament. Although one might hear the term as a pejorative reference to a revelation once valid but now abrogated and rendered superfluous, some Jews still speak of the Old Testament as a concession to common usage. Christians generally regard the Hebrew scriptures as integral to their faith tradition but of secondary authority whenever it is necessary to resolve an apparent conflict or contradiction between the testaments. For Jews, Tanakh is the *only* testament.

What's the difference between **"prophetic"** and **"apocalyptic"** literature?

It is not always possible to apply the distinction neatly to important texts in the Hebrew Bible, but it is useful to keep the following important differences in mind. First, prophets and apocalypticists have different missions. Prophets tend to be action-oriented, passing critical judgment on individual events as they unfold in the political and religious development of Israel, which is under both divine and Davidic sovereignty. Apocalyptic works are products of people dedicated to the written word as a vehicle for passing judgment on the whole of history, not just that of Israel and its monarchy. Second, the content of the biblical works they have produced differs markedly. Prophets describe specific examples of injustice seen in the context of an ethical struggle within Israel, which God's judgment over his people will resolve on the coming "Day of the Lord." Writers of apocalyptic works offer more generalized and highly symbolic visions of the reign of evil, visions that only a divinely commissioned "angel" can interpret. God's judgment will be manifest in a final cosmic cataclysm, a final battle (sometimes called Armageddon) between the forces of Good and Evil. Finally, prophetic texts generally claim authorship by name while apocalyptic texts typically use a pseudonym, either to add credibility to their visions of the "future" or to avoid retaliation from the authorities of their own day.

Did Jews develop any **post-Biblical sacred texts**?

Jewish extra-biblical literature is vast and expansive. Two large bodies of literature are generally known as Talmud and Midrash. Talmud consists of the systematization of suc-

The Ten Commandments

Also known as the Decalogue, the so-called "Ten Commandments" are based on Exodus 20:1–17, in which God speaks to Moses at Mount Sinai and reveals his "Ten Words" on inscribed tablets. There is no single, definitive text of the Ten Commandments. Rather, various denominations of Jews and Christians alike have boiled down a relatively lengthy message into their own renderings of ten brief and direct statements. For the most part, they embody the following ten directives:

1) You shall have no other gods before me.
2) You shall not make unto yourself any graven image.
3) You shall not take the name of the Lord your God in vain.
4) Remember the Sabbath day, to keep it holy.
5) Honor your father and your mother.
6) You shall not kill.
7) You shall not commit adultery.
8) You shall not steal.
9) You shall not bear false witness against your neighbor.
10) You shall not covet anything that belongs to your neighbor.

cessive waves of originally oral commentary by religious scholars on sacred scripture. First, views of earlier generations of rabbis were codified in the Mishnah. Subsequent generations further commented on the Mishnaic material, and that was brought together in the Gemara. Then the Mishna and Gemara were combined in the Talmud, which was produced in two versions, the Jerusalem or Palestinian Talmud and the considerably larger Babylonian Talmud. Much of the content of the Talmud is described by the term *halakhah,* a word that means literally "proceeding, walking." It refers to the bulk of Talmud and more generally to the literature interpreting the specific rules and legislation found in the scripture. The plural of the term, *halakhot,* came to mean all the specific laws derived through exegesis, even if not explicitly mentioned in scripture. Halakhic literature peers into every conceivable nook and cranny of Jewish daily life, prescribing in minutest detail how the Torah should be used as a guide here and now. The term *midrash* means "study, commentary, amplification" and originally meant the method used by all scholars of sacred scripture. Hence, much Talmudic material is midrashic, for example. But eventually *midrash* came to be more popularly identified with the non-halakhic material in the Talmud and with another type of literature called *aggadah* (or *haggadah,* meaning "narrative"). Works of aggadic midrash, like halakhic works, primarily comment on scripture. But unlike *halakhah, aggadah* is more concerned with reading between the lines. Aggadic works tell the story behind the story and say little about specific legal implications. As such, *aggadah* is generally much more appealing and entertaining, offering interpretations that are frequently very moving, charming, and droll.

Were Jews ever ruled by a **monarchy**?

The thorny issue of monarchy arose during the later years of the Judges (c. 1200–1000 BCE), who ruled Israel after Joshua had led the establishment of the people in the newly reached Promised Land of Canaan. Some argued that Israel should be like all the surrounding lands, each ruled by its own king. They saw no other solution to the lawlessness they believed had overcome their land. Others held on to the conviction that embracing the institution of monarchy would amount to a betrayal of God's sovereignty. Saul was the first king (r. 1020–1000). From his capital at Gilgal he succeeded in uniting the tribes against the common enemy, the Philistines. David (r. 1000–961) established himself first at Hebron, but after taking Jerusalem from the Jebusites declared that city his capital. He sought to unify Jewish religious life and instituted the office of court prophet. David's son Solomon (r. 961–922) further centralized Jewish ritual in his newly built Jerusalem temple. But when Solomon died his sons divided the realm into the northern Kingdom of Israel (922–721 BCE) and the southern Kingdom of Judah (922–586 BCE). Two hundred years later the northern capital of Samaria fell to the Assyrians, never to be recovered. The southern kingdom carried on for over a century, with moments of greatness, and even major religious reform in the late seventh century BCE. Many of Israel's principal prophets lived and worked under the Kingdom of Judah. But Babylon was putting the squeeze on the small kingdom, and in 586 BCE Jerusalem and its temple fell to invading forces. Over a thousand years later, Jews founded the Khazar kingdom in the Caucasus, a small-scale experiment in monarchy that survived from about 700 to 1000.

What does the term **Babylonian Exile** (or Captivity) refer to?

The Kingdom of Judah had come under military and political pressure in the late 700s BCE, around the time of the fall of the northern kingdom. Some southern kings even paid tribute as vassals to Assyria. In the year 597 BCE the Babylonians, successors to the Assyrians as the major regional power, were closing in on Jerusalem. Though the city would hold out for another ten years, the invaders captured and deported to Mesopotamia a number of leading Jews. In 587/6 BCE, the Babylonians laid final siege to Jerusalem, destroying the temple. They and other Middle Eastern powers had found it useful to take important Jews into exile, the better to demoralize the subject peoples and insure the success of the conquering regime. Exact numbers are impossible to reconstruct, but the total deportation seems to have uprooted as many as twenty thousand people. Since only the poorest and least educated were left behind, the Exile amounted to a virtually total elimination of Jewish presence in Jerusalem and its environs. The good news was that the community would realize the possibility of taking root in a new

The Achievements of the Prophet Moses

Moses (born circa 1390 BCE) was the son of a Hebrew from the tribe of Levi. His mother was Jochebed. When Moses was just three months old, his mother set him adrift in a basket on the Nile to save him from the pharaonic decree that all Hebrew male babies were to be slaughtered in their infancy. A daughter of Pharaoh found the infant Moses and raised him in her household. As a foster son of Pharaoh's daughter, Moses would have been well educated in political, religious, and military affairs, and he would have been given important responsibilities in government upon reaching maturity. Although he could have enjoyed prosperity, power, and respect in his adopted Egypt, he chose instead to associate himself with his downtrodden people. Regarded as a prophet by Judaism, Christianity, and Islam, Moses led the people of Israel out of slavery in Egypt and through their desert wanderings; delivered to them their Law and liturgy—which remain to this day; and helped them form their nation. He supervised the construction of the Ark, a symbol of God's presence with Israel, and oversaw the construction of the tabernacle, a tent-shrine that was the focal point of the nation's worship. The celebration of Passover was begun in commemoration of the night God spared the lives of the Jewish firstborn sons and slew only the sons of the Egyptians.

land. Prophets preached a message of encouragement and survival, devising a whole new "exilic" theology built around the hope of restoration and return. Enter the Achaemenid Persian empire stage left, exit Babylon stage right. Jewish fortunes changed under the new sovereigns of the central Middle East. In 539 BCE, Persian monarch Cyrus the Great decided to release the captives and allow them to return to Jerusalem.

How does Jewish tradition interpret **history**?

Large portions of the Hebrew scriptures are some of the finest ancient historical writing. Authors of historical texts in the Bible do not merely catalogue events chronologically. They evaluate their data and pass judgment on the main characters from a particular perspective that views all happenings as part of a greater divine plan. They discern patterns in human behavior and in God's ways of dealing with people. So, for example, the author of the Book of Judges observes how, when the people do evil in the sight of God, God allows them to suffer the consequences. Once they've had enough chaos, they cry out to God for help. God then raises up a Judge to rule the people, and justice reigns for forty or eighty years. But when the strong ruler dies, the people again go astray, and the cycle starts again (Judges 2:16–23). History begins when God creates time and space, moves through many generations of human beings

Near the end of the nineteenth century, many Jews in eastern Europe began to view Israel as more than just a place for pilgrimages or for occasional settlement by strong believers. Encouraged by the rise of nationalism in Europe, certain Jews sought to return to the land of their ancestors and to make their homes there. This impulse gave rise to the political movement known as Zionism. (The expression comes from the word "Zion," which is a poetic term for the Holy Land.) Zionists see Jews as more than a loosely bound group of religious believers. Politically, Zionists argue that Jews are bound to the land—to Israel—and that they were chosen for a role that is inextricably connected with Abraham. During the 1930s, with the rise of Nazism, this view became more urgent and provoked heated debate about the nature of Judaism. Must a Jew live in Israel? Similarly, what is the role and importance of a Jewish state, of a concentration of Jews in a secular nation? The establishment of the State of Israel in the wake of World War II renewed and shifted the debate. Today, the autonomy of Israel is accepted by many nations, but the debate concerning the rights of Arab settlers in Israel rages on.

struggling with and for each other, and will come to an apocalyptic conclusion at a time known only to God. Above all, history is the arena in which God deals actively with humankind as a whole, but directs both special attention and expectation to the Children of Israel.

What did the **Jerusalem Temple** look like?

Solomon built the first Temple around 950 BCE. After that was destroyed in 587/6 BCE, it was replaced by the Second Temple in about 516 BCE. That in turn was modified many times over the subsequent five centuries, most recently by King Herod. Though the Second Temple was destroyed in 70 CE, parts of Herod's construction are still visible as the Western, so-called "Wailing," Wall. Biblical accounts offer detailed descriptions of various components of the Temple, filling in some of the information archaeology has yet to unearth. Solomon's Temple was in a way a permanent version of the Tabernacle described in the Torah. A rectangle about two hundred feet long by forty wide, the Temple consisted of three chambers. Up a few steps flanked by the two columns symbolic of the monarchs, Jachin and Boaz, and just through the east-facing main door was the vestibule. Beyond that was a large windowed room (the *heikhal*, "great hall") where most rituals occurred, and the dark Holy of Holies (*devir*, "shrine"), elevated five or six steps, which only the priestly staff could enter and where the Ark was kept. Surrounding the central building was a huge courtyard with three gates on each of its four sides. In the Second Temple the central building was larger and set in the grander context of a series of courtyards. Along the walls of the court immediately enclosing the Temple proper were chambers for the sacrificial materials. Directly in front of the Temple porch, in the Court of the Priests, was a large altar for burnt offerings and a small slaughterhouse. Directly east of that, through a gate and down six or eight steps, was the large Women's Court with corner chambers for lepers, Nazirites, oil, and wood. The Second Temple's shrine held no Ark of the Covenant. Surrounding the entire high platform was an immense wall, some of which remains today.

How did **other Jewish communities** develop outside of Israel?

Small pockets of Jews had grown up in various places in the Middle East since at least the early days of the monarchy. Foreign alliances allowed Jewish kings to bargain for

Model of the Second Temple, Herodian renovation, showing the forecourts and the main structure that contained the Holy of Holies.

power and influence and opened economic doors. With the trade routes came traveling merchants, some of whom decided to relocate. The first major Jewish communities outside of Israel and Judah were the result of the various mass deportations. By the time Cyrus had made a return possible, Mesopotamian communities had been established for over two generations. With the threat of imminent persecution lifted by a tolerant ruler, many Jews simply stayed in Iraq. There they founded thriving cultural and religious institutions, including the academies that went on to produce some of Judaism's most important legal and theological works. Under successive political regimes with varying policies toward religious pluralism, Iraqi Jews experienced

Orthodox Jew praying at the Western ("Wailing") Wall, Jerusalem. Note his characteristic long black coat and circular hat, and the small wadded-up paper notes stuffed into the chinks of the masonry, petitions and other prayers left by worshipers.

uneven fortunes, but on the whole did much better than merely survive. During the first several centuries of Islamic rule from the capital cities Damascus and Baghdad, Jews enjoyed considerable autonomy and even held high government office. But after the invasion of the newly Islamized Saljuqid Turks from Central Asia, Jewish life in the Middle East changed dramatically. The Saljuqid Sultan effectively abolished the offices of Exilarchate and Gaonate, which had been the backbone of Jewish autonomy. Meanwhile Jewish communities had grown in Europe since Roman times and had begun to thrive in Germany under Charlemagne. Now many Middle Eastern Jews would look to Europe in hopes of another new start. From the eleventh century until at least the late nineteenth, the center of Judaism would shift from the eastern Mediterranean to central and eastern Europe.

What was the genesis of **"rabbinical" Judaism**?

It may be helpful to think of rabbinical Judaism as evolving in a long history of classes of religious scholars. The earliest were the Soferim, or Scribes, scholars of the Second Temple period (400–200 BCE) who emerged with Ezra's attempts to restore Torah to the center of Jewish life. From 200 BCE–30 CE, the period of the Five Pairs of Teachers (or *Zugot*) ended with Hillel and Shammai. A school called the Tanna'im ("repeaters," 30–200) lay the foundations of the *Mishna*. That would become the first major written systematization of oral Torah. They also initiated a branch of oral Torah

The "Final Solution"

On January 20, 1942, fifteen Nazi bureaucrats met in the Berlin suburb of Grossen-Wannsee to discuss what they euphemistically termed the "final solution to the Jewish question." The meeting was headed by SS Obergruppen-führer Reinhard Heidrich and included Adolf Eichmann among its attendees. A decision was made to evacuate every Jew in occupied Europe to camps in the East. There, they would be "treated accordingly." The intention was to exterminate most Jews immediately upon arrival at the camps but to identify some Jews for placement in organized labor battalions. Death would soon come to the laborers through starvation and overwork. The "Final Solution" was implemented ruthlessly and with great efficiency. Death camps were established throughout the East, with Poland as the principal center. The names of the camps— Auschwitz, Birkenau, Treblinka, Chelmno, Majdanek, Sobibor, Belzec, and many others—are today instantly recognized for their connection with one of the darkest periods in human history.

commentary called the *Tosefta* ("additions"), collections of statements of Tanna'im not found in the Mishna (called *beraitot*, meaning "outside") arranged according to Mishnaic order. From 200–500, the *Amora'im* ("spokesmen, interpreters") communicated lessons of the great rabbis to pupils and later scholars who taught in Babylon (Iraq) in rabbinical academies established after the Babylonian Exile. Their work eventually comprised the *Gemara* ("completion") of the Jerusalem Talmud, completed around 390. From 500 to about 589 a class called the *Savora'im* ("reflecters") completed the writing of the Babylonian Talmud but left no independent work. The *Geonim* ("eminences," heads of the academies of Sura and Pumbedita in Iraq) dominated Jewish scholarship from about 589 to 1000, providing their answers to queries on the Torah from all over the diaspora in a body of literature called *Responsa* ("responses"). From 1000 to 1400, the *Meforashim* and *Poseqim* elaborated on the practical implications of *Halakhah* (rules and regulations); and the *Tosafists* ("those who added on") produced collections of comments on Talmud arranged according to the order of the Talmud's sections or tractates. They based their writings on comments of earlier authorities, especially the twelfth- to fourteenth-century school of Rashi in Germany and France. This ongoing layering of tradition turns out to be the complex and multi-faceted foundation of what we know as Rabbinical Judaism.

What was the **Holocaust**?

The term "Holocaust" derives from a pair of Greek words that mean "whole burnt offering." The term originally referred to a kind of sacrifice performed in the Jewish temple

How many Jews were killed in the Holocaust?

It is impossible to establish precisely how many Jews were killed by the Nazis during the Holocaust period. Credible estimates range from a low of about three million to a high of about ten million, with most historians accepting a number in the range of six million. Estimates are generally based on several factors: train records indicating the transport of Jews to Nazi death camps; assessments based on the number of Jews in Europe before and after the Holocaust, with allowances made for migration; the rare surviving records of certain death camps; detailed accounts of life and death in Jewish ghettos; and much physical evidence in the form of human remains, blueprints for high-capacity gas chambers and crematoria, and the physical remains of the death camps themselves. Among the most compelling and moving evidence is the eyewitness testimony of survivors of the camps.

in Jerusalem. In more common contemporary usage, however, Holocaust refers to the suffering and death of as many as six million Jews during World War II as a result of Adolph Hitler's "Final Solution." Jews all over Europe were systematically targeted by Nazi propaganda and police action. The *Sho'ah,* as it is called in Hebrew, began in 1933 and escalated dramatically after Kristallnacht (the night of shattered glass, November 9–10, 1938). According to the Nazi view, only a return to Aryan racial purity could save the human race. With their Semitic blood, Jews were a source of racial pollution and needed to be exterminated. Throughout the late 1930s and early 1940s, Hitler and his collaborators, led by the Gestapo *(Geheime Staats-polizei,* or state secret police) and the feared black-shirted S.S. *(Schutz-staffel),* rounded up hundreds of thousands of Jews and herded them into boxcars for transport to concentration camps scattered through central and eastern Europe. Many prisoners too small or too weak to work were immediately taken to the gas chambers—often disguised as showers—where they were killed with Zyklon-B gas. The Holocaust represents one of history's most extraordinary and horrifying examples of both genocide and scapegoating.

RELIGIOUS BELIEFS

Is there a Jewish **creed**?

Several important creedal formulations have appeared at different times in Jewish history, but a good starting point is the single sentence from Deuteronomy 6:4. It is called

Model of the Second Temple, Herodian renovation, showing the forecourts and the main structure that contained the Holy of Holies.

simply "the *Shema.*" Devout Jews recite these few words more often than almost any other phrase. "Hear, O Israel: the Lord our God, the Lord is One" (or the Lord our God is one Lord). Two essential ingredients in Jewish belief are enshrined here in elegant simplicity. First, the notion that the people constitute a community of faith, and second, the affirmation of the absolute unity of God. In the next verse, Jews are enjoined to love the Lord with all their heart, soul, and strength. Another very ancient text that functions like a creedal statement appears in Deuteronomy 26:5–10. In his final instruction to the people, Moses tells them that when they come into their newly God-given land they are to make an offering and recite a short historical summary of all that God has done for them. "A wandering Aramaean was my father," it begins, referring to Jacob, father of the twelve tribes. The text goes on to recount in brief how God rescued the people from slavery in Egypt and gave them a land in which to dwell. Apart from these two biblical texts, the anonymous fifteenth-century "I Believe" based on the "Thirteen Articles of Faith" of Maimonides (d. 1204) is the best known creedal statement. Each of thirteen affirmations begins "I believe with an unwavering faith." Articles one through five affirm that God is omnipotent and one, beyond all things material, master of time and space, and the sole object of prayer and devotion. Moses' prophetic authority (along with that of the other prophets as well), scripture's authenticity and truth, and the finality of the divine Law are the subjects of articles six through nine. All the remaining four articles speak of the ethical demands of adherence to the revealed law, of the final consequences of human choices in the form of reward or punishment, of the Messiah's eventual coming, and of the ultimate resurrection of the dead.

What does the term **revelation** mean in Jewish tradition?

Multiple descriptions of revelation appear in the Hebrew scriptures. Earlier books depict a strikingly direct relationship between individual people and the Creator. Beginning with Adam and Eve and continuing through the stories of the great patriarchs, we hear of God's forthright communication and self-disclosure. God is depicted as dealing directly with Noah and Abraham. Moses' encounter with the divine presence at the Burning Bush and on Mt. Sinai are definitive events in the unfolding revelation. The tone and manner of revelation changes somewhat in the historical chronicles of the various kings (see especially I and II Samuel, I and II Kings), for "visions were rare in those days." The sources suggest that God now reveals less through fantastic events and more through the agency of prophets sent to deliver a message, beginning with the court prophets of the early monarchy. Now the prophets hear the divine word not in storm or earthquake or fire, but in "a still small voice" (I Kings 19:9–12). When the great writing prophets (such as Isaiah and Jeremiah) deliver the message, they simply preface it with the words "Thus says the Lord...." Even there, God appears as one who speaks clearly and intimately with select individuals. The Hebrew scriptures are as rich in this kind of imagery as any sacred text on earth. But the most important issue here is not the imagery with which the scripture describes divine self-disclosure, but the content of the message. Revelation runs the gamut from sanction to solace, from unquenchable wrath to unfathomable mercy.

Are **"doctrine"** and **"dogma"** important to Jews?

Jewish tradition is generally more concerned with orthopraxy (correct practice) than with orthodoxy (correct opinion). Creedal statements such as the "Thirteen Articles" offer a convenient distillation of the heart of Jewish belief. But there have been few historical instances of prominent attempts to use adherence to a body of doctrine as a measure of membership. Even now, with ultra-Orthodox groups in Israel pressing the question of who has the right to call him or herself a Jew, the issue turns more on behavior than on belief. The most conservative elements claim that only religiously engaged Jews are truly Jews, but practical adherence to the *halakhah* is the crux of the matter. There have been no major cases of Jewish "Inquisitions" targeting false teachings.

Are there **"mythic"** elements in Jewish tradition?

Many texts in the Hebrew Bible suggest associations with ancient mythic narrative, not so much in what they discuss as in the way they express it. The paired creation stories in Genesis preserve mythic elements in their description of the watery "chaos" that existed prior to God's imposing upon it the order of a "cosmos." These texts probe the mysteries of the origins of all things. Similarly blended twin accounts of destruction by a universal Flood in Genesis also hint at mythic underpinnings. The Book of

Jewish State Declared on May 14, 1948

In the 1930s the world's Jews could see that the survival of European Jews depended on mass immigration to Palestine and to friendly states. This humanitarian imperative, however, was rejected by Britain and by those countries, like the United States, where Jews might conceivably have found a home. Faced with Hitler's hatred on the one hand, and world indifference on the other, the world's Jews realized the absolute need for a Jewish homeland, a sovereign state where Judaism was not only a religion, but a nationality. With the Proclamation of an Independent Jewish State on May 14, 1948, for the first time since the destruction of the Temple and the dispersion of the Jews, Jewishness became a national as well as a religious identity. By the law of return every Jew had a right to Israeli citizenship. Thus the State of Israel had become a solution to the problem of the Jews whose history since the dispersion had been one of trauma and tragedy. In medieval England the Jews had been expelled; in fifteenth century Spain they had endured the same fate. In most cases, Jews could not achieve political equality in the lands where they settled, and they lacked a land they could call their own and to which they could return. The proclamation of an independent Israel was the signal for a combined attack by the Arab states. After initial setbacks and mixed success, the Israelis were able to create a national army and to arm it, to an extent, with modern weapons. As a result of these efforts, the tide of battle gradually turned, and, by the end of 1948, Israeli forces led a campaign through Southern Palestine and even into Egypt itself. In a later thrust, an Israeli column drove down to the Red Sea, securing the port of Eilat. During one of several cease fires, Count Folke Bernadotte Af Wisborg, the United Nations mediator, was assassinated by Zionist terrorists. Finally, by July, 1949, armistice agreements were signed with the Arab states.

Job's grand panorama of the divine work uses analogous imagery and conveys an unmistakable note of majesty and splendor. At the other end of the timeline of creation are the apocalyptic texts (in books such as Ezekiel and Daniel, for example) that describe the inevitable cataclysmic events that will herald the completion of history. To describe the biblical text as sharing important features with myth in no way impugns or discredits the scripture. It is merely a way of characterizing how the Hebrew Bible communicates in several key accounts.

What do Jews believe about **God**?

God is both utterly transcendent and strikingly accessible, both awe-commanding and irresistible. As the ultimate majestic power, the merest hint of divine nearness brings all creation to its knees. This God is the Holy One of Israel into whose presence only a fool would enter nonchalantly. Any person of sense knows instinctively that to approach God is to be filled with dread. That's what "holy" means—forbidden, off-limits, wholly other. Dread is not always a bad thing. Here it is clearly an appropriate response. This does not mean that God is cruel or despotic, although some scriptural accounts might seem to convey that impression. Recall the story of the men assigned to carry the Ark of the Covenant to its new abode. When their ox stumbled, one man lunged for the Ark to keep it from slipping from the cart and was instantly struck dead. The point of the story is that "God" means "danger." And when God claims allegiance, there is no room for the tentative. Abraham was ready to sacrifice his son Isaac. Israel's kings and military commanders were ordered to commit "total war," sparing nothing, so jealous was God for complete dedication. At the same time Jewish images of God convey a divine intimacy and immediacy. God creates all things by the unimaginable power of divine speech. Every divine word is immediately embodied in some undeniable event. God walks with Adam in the cool of the evening and delivers through the prophets a message of absolute tenderness. Most of all, the God of the Hebrew Bible is unfailingly devoted to his people. This God acts in all the events of human history.

What do Jews call **God**?

Various important terms appear through the Hebrew Bible. Torah uses the words *Elohim,* a kind of plural form related to the same Semitic root (*el*) from which the Islamic name for God, Allah, derives. But the word Yahweh is a still more central term. Sometimes translated as "He Who Is," in connection with God's identifying himself to Moses through the Burning Bush as "I am Who am" or "I will be Who I will be" (*ehyeh asher ehyeh*). Many Jews choose not to pronounce this most sacred name of God. When reading scripture they prefer to substitute the Hebrew *ha-shem,* "the Name," every time the word Yahweh appears. Similarly, many Jewish publications in English print simply G-d in place of God, out of reverence for the sacred word. Another term, *adonai* ("my Lord") is also significant here. Some people combine the vowels from *adonai* with the consonants of *yahweh* to get Jehovah. This linguistic compromise allows people to both say and not say the sacred name of God.

What is meant by the term **"covenant"**?

Covenant (*berith* in Hebrew) describes better than perhaps any other single notion the essential quality of God's relationship to humankind. Discussion of divine initiatives that result in the sealing of a covenantal bond appears early in the Torah and continues through the prophetic books. Covenants were a crucial social cement in many ancient Near Eastern societies, including Israel. Partners in a covenant need not be equal in status and power. Many covenants described between human partners in the Bible are between a lord or ruler and his vassals. A more or less common formula for these lord-vassal relationships evolved. This "covenant treaty" form typically began with a section in which the lord names himself in relation to the vassal or subject. A brief historical summary recalls all the good things the lord has provided. That is followed by a list of blessings that will accrue to the subject who is faithful, and the curses that will befall one who is lax or breaks the covenant. Some elements of the treaty form, as well as of the treaty "lawsuit" the lord might bring against one who violated the agreement, appear here and there in the Hebrew Bible. Accounts of major covenants between God and his people include those with Noah (Genesis 6 and 9), marked by the appearance of the rainbow and the cessation of destruction by flood; Abraham (Genesis 15–17), sealed by the sign of circumcision; and Moses at Sinai (Exodus 19–24), embodied in the revealed Law. At various points in the historical and prophetic books we hear of covenant renewals. A leader, such as Joshua, calls the people to account for their past behavior and challenges them to reaffirm their allegiance to God, the sovereign. Joshua 24 is a fascinating example of how some elements of the ancient treaty formula apparently survived in the practice of Israel. King David's rule is also marked by a covenant renewal led by the court prophet Nathan (II Samuel 7). Prophets, such as Jeremiah, spiritualize the notion of covenant, saying that God wishes to inscribe the special relationship on the tablets of their hearts (Jeremiah 33).

What are the "Ten Commandments"?

Also known as the Decalogue, the Ten Commandments as they are most widely known from Exodus 20:1–17 are actually an abbreviated version of the Law revealed to Moses at Sinai. The first three concern Israel's relationship to God. They forbid idolatry—the worship of gods other than God—along with making images of God, and prohibit taking the name of God in vain. Believers are commanded to keep the sabbath holy as God did after the labor of Creation. Commandments four through ten have to do with proper behavior toward fellow human beings. They begin with the need to honor one's parents. They then enjoin against a series of five evils: murder, adultery, theft, lying and defaming another, and coveting anything that belongs to a neighbor, including members of his family. The Decalogue is followed by scores of more specific regulations concerning every conceivable area of ordinary life that further interpret the details implied in the Ten Commandments. Thus the Ten function as a kind of minimum ethical standard. Following them carefully even in a general way is challenging enough, but to observe them in the full detail given in scripture is another matter altogether.

Do Jews believe in miracles?

Belief in miracles depends a great deal on what people think are the ordinary limits of nature, since a commonly accepted conception is that miracles presuppose some divine intervention in the order of nature. The Hebrew Bible tells of dozens of events, great and small, that appear to fit that broad definition. But what people took for the ordinary limits of nature were in all likelihood significantly narrower in biblical times than they are now. In fact, ancient Middle Eastern societies do not seem to have considered the natural world as a coherent, integral system. Virtually all unusual events were to some degree attributed directly to a divine power simply because by definition the deity had all power. In that world, secondary causes were practically negligible. Everything is cause for wonder. Hebrew scripture calls important events signs, wonders or portents of the future, or simply prodigies or unexpected phenomena. The category of signs includes, for example, the plagues visited upon the Egyptians and the appearance of the rainbow as a sign of Noah's covenant with God. Wonders or portents include the unusual works of a false prophet. And such things as God's creative and redemptive deeds the scripture calls extraordinary events. On some curious happenings, such as the bodily "ascensions" of figures like Enoch (Genesis 5:24) and Elijah (II Kings 2:11), the scripture makes no evaluative comment, merely describing the occurrence briefly. Reference works on Judaism provide few entries on "miracles." But numerous religious figures, particularly rabbis and mystics, in Jewish history and lore are said to have occasioned or mediated marvels of all kinds.

What are the main Jewish notions of **afterlife**?

Surprisingly little detailed information on the afterlife is given in the Hebrew scriptures, and mostly in the very latest material at that. We find a few vague references to a nondescript region called Sheol, a gray, dreary warehouse of souls. Not a place of absolute suffering, Sheol is little more than a synonym for death itself. Toward the latter centuries of the first millennium BCE more concrete notions of afterlife begin to emerge. Propelling the development were questions of justice such as those that the Book of Job raised. If a just man like Job suffers so much in this life, and so many wicked people seem to flourish, perhaps retribution for one's deeds will be deferred until after death. If not, how can one say that God is just? Sheol becomes identified more as recompense for an evil life, but is gradually replaced by the concept of Gehenna. Just south of Jerusalem lies a small valley that may at one time have belonged to a man named Hinnom, hence *ge-hinnom,* the valley of Hinnom. It must have been a most unpleasant place. Longstanding tradition associates it with fiery punishment, possibly because it had been a place for incinerating refuse in ancient times. As a parallel to this abode of deserved misery there must surely be a place where the good are rewarded, perhaps near the dwelling of God himself. Generic notions of "the heavens" as a place above earth appear very early in biblical thought. Gradual spiritualization of the idea of "heaven" went along with the notion that there are multiple levels, the third of which is a Paradise for the just. All of this is linked to the idea of resurrection of the body, taught by the Pharisees and accepted as a rule in post-biblical rabbinical tradition.

What role do views of **life on earth** play in Jewish tradition?

Although many Jews prefer not to speculate about whether some version of a "next" world may exist, many others believe there will be some form of reward or punishment after death. Nevertheless, life as we know it deserves far more attention than any possible hereafter. Jewish tradition would agree with the poet Robert Frost's observation that earth is the right place for loving. As a result, a major emphasis in Jewish tradition is the commitment to bettering the lot of humankind here and now. All of life is a gift worth receiving gladly and sharing with others. The well-known Jewish toast in Hebrew, *le-chayim*—"To Life!"—sums it up. Wealth, success, the influence one can wield through involvement in community affairs—all are an integral part of Jewish spirituality. To such things guilt is not an appropriate response.

Is there a distinctively Jewish **"ethic"**?

Every major religious tradition has its equivalent of the "golden rule"—treat others as you would like them to treat you. One classic Jewish version says, "Do not do to others what you would not want others to do to you." As a humanistic guide, it is very important, and pretty obvious on the face of it. But no religious tradition has ever just left the matter there, hoping their members would work out the details. Most readers will be familiar with the expression "Judaeo-Christian ethic." Politicians and preachers alike are fond of using the phrase as a handy, if rather vague, summary of values espoused by large populations like those of the United States. The term does not suggest that there are no significant differences between Judaism and Christianity as communities of faith, but it clearly implies that Jews and Christians generally agree on basic ethical principles. Most people would instinctively identify the "Ten Commandments" as that shared foundation of morals. But since for Christians as well as for Jews, the Decalogue functions as an ethical minimum, there is much more to both approaches to morality than one can squeeze into a handful of commands and prohibitions. This is where religious motivation enters the mix, making each tradition of religious ethics distinctive. Jews strive for a moral life because, in addition to the need for basic mutual respect (Golden Rule) and for broad guidelines meant to prevent social chaos (the Decalogue), the revealing God demands nothing less of believers. Some Jews also draw motivation from the prospect of reward or punishment in the next life. Many find it sufficient that God has given all good things and wants people to share them so that more people can enjoy the gift of life. Since life's gifts don't always simply fall into one's lap and take care of themselves, believers need to work toward worthy goals and care the gifts attained.

Is there such a thing as Jewish **fundamentalism**?

Fundamentalist approaches to scriptural interpretation and to the conduct of life in general have been an on-going reality in Jewish tradition and history. As far back as the last few centuries BCE, groups like the Sadducees and Karaites had rejected any traditional developments beyond the written scripture, going so far as to reject even scriptural texts apart from the Torah. In more recent times, a number of arch-conservative groups have asserted themselves, especially in Israel. The *Gush Emunim* or "Bloc of the Faithful," for example, represent the concerns of a number of Israelis who have settled in the occupied West Bank, which is now part of negotiations with the Palestinian Authority. Jewish fundamentalism in this and other cases turns largely on a given group's literal insistence that the Land is a divine and irrevocable gift, and must therefore be reclaimed and occupied by whatever means necessary.

SIGNS AND SYMBOLS

What **signs** or **symbols** might identify an individual as Jewish?

One of the most common and easily visible signs of Jewishness is the small circular skullcap called the *yarmulke* or *kippah*. Worn by many Jewish men and boys as an ordinary item of clothing, the yarmulke is especially significant in ritual contexts. In some congregations, women rabbis now wear the head-covering as well. Men of very conservative and Orthodox communities often wear a plain black fedora or Homburg hat over the yarmulke. On special occasions, Orthodox men wear a round hat trimmed in beaver fur. Orthodox men also often dress all in black, with long overcoats, sometimes substituting a differently colored outer garment for special occasions. Special items of clothing include several for ritual purposes only, such as the larger woolen, cotton, or silk prayer shawl *(tallit)* with corner fringes *(tzitzit)* worn as an outer garment during morning prayer and all day on Yom Kippur. The *tallit katan* (smaller prayer garment) is a cotton undergarment, worn at all times, with fringes bearing 613 knots (the total number of commands [248] and prohibitions [365] in Torah) that hang out at the belt line as stipulated in Numbers 15:37–38. Some Jewish men don phylacteries *(tefillin)* on the left arm and forehead. These small leather boxes bound with leather thongs contain texts of scripture (Exodus 13:1–9, 11–16; Deuteronomy 6:4–9, 11:13–21) and are worn by Orthodox and some Conservative Jews for daily morning prayer both privately and in synagogue. Another symbolic practice involving the body itself is the growth of sidelocks *(pe'ot)*. Men and boys do not cut their forelocks, and when they are long enough, they curl them so that they look like coiled springs. This is in response to the biblical injunction of Leviticus 19:27, "You shall not trim the hair on your temples...." Smaller items often worn by both men and women, whatever their communal affiliation, include rings or necklaces with the six-pointed Star of David or the two Hebrew letters that spell out a name of God, *"chayy"* ("Living One").

What **signs** or **symbols** distinguish **ritual specialists** in Judaism?

Since the Temple was destroyed by the Romans in 70, there has been no formal Jewish priesthood. With the priesthood several other special ranks of ritual specialists disappeared. What replaced the priesthood was a more egalitarian system of rabbinical leadership. Nowadays, when Jews worship together, the community leader is not nearly so visually distinctive as in days of old. Since the nature of post-Temple worship is radically different, leaders in worship are visually distinguishable largely by their being in front on the congregation, often on a raised stage. Temple priests once wore easily recognizable garb. In addition to the simpler vesture of the ordinary priests, with a full length cloak and sash or girdle, the High Priest's cloak had a hem fringed with gold bells and woolen pomegranates. He also wore a tall miter with a blue band at the top and a gold head band. An elaborately decorated vestment called the *ephod* was worn over the cloak. Over that the High Priest wore the "breastplate" suspended from the shoulders like a large pendant on a necklace hung down the front from epaulette-like onyx stones, on each of which were

Ritual objects for personal devotion and domestic worship, in a Jewish religious goods store, the Jewish ghetto of Venice. In addition to the Menorah and Star of David, there are miscellaneous small items such as the protective hand-shaped amulet.

written the names of six of the twelve tribes. Attached to the breastplate were twelve semi-precious stones symbolizing the tribes. And inside the breastplate pocket were the *urim* and *thummim,* mysterious devices used for divination.

Why do some Jews touch their **door frames** when they enter their homes?

Jewish households often display a *mezuzah* ("doorpost") at the front door and sometimes at interior doorways as well. Upon entering the house, they reverently touch this small container of scriptural texts from Deuteronomy 6:4–9 and 11:13–21. The first of

Monumental Menorah engraved with low-relief biblical scenes, standing opposite the Israeli parliament, the Kenesset. Twentieth century.

these texts includes the *Shema,* the brief creedal formula. Part of that text (6:9) also instructs Jews to write the words of scripture on their doorposts and gates.

What is a *menorah*?

Menorah means "an object that emits light," hence a candle holder. A seven-candle menorah was used in the ancient temple and has continued to be perhaps the most widely known and used Jewish symbol. When the Romans despoiled the Jerusalem Temple in 70, they carted away all the temple's riches. They regarded the menorah as such an important emblem of their conquest that the Emperor Titus had it depicted on his triumphal arch in the Roman Forum. Some scholars suggest the menorah is a variation on the symbolic "tree of life" that grew at the center of the original Paradise garden, versions of which are widely used in many cultures and religious traditions. An eight-branched candle-stick, now also called a menorah, features prominently in the eight-day observance of Hanukkah.

Do Jews mark their **sacred spaces** with any distinctive signs and symbols?

In many parts of the world, Jewish places of worship have developed architecturally in the context of the local culture. The one architectural feature that sometimes distinguishes synagogues from nearby religious structures is that synagogues often have a central dome. Many mosques and churches have domes as well, but domed churches typically also have some sort of tower or spire and mosques have a minaret or two. Synagogues with central domes rarely have prominent flanking towers. A common decorative item that can mark synagogues externally is the twin tablets of the Law, a reminder of Moses' reception of the revelation at Sinai. A large Star of David often graces the facade or windows. Synagogues of more contemporary style often place a menorah of monumental scale, and sometimes even very abstract design, in front. One small but remarkable synagogue, that of Jerusalem's Hadassah Medical Center, boasts a striking array of symbolic decor. Famed artist Marc Chagall designed a series of twelve windows to adorn the upper walls of all four sides of the room. Each of the windows recalls one of the twelve tribes. Coordinating each window's colors with the intensity of natural light available through the day on the various sides of the space, Chagall arranged the windows roughly in order of the age of the patriarch from whom

The Star of David

Known in Hebrew as *Magen David* ("Shield of David"), this important Jewish symbol is composed of two superimposed equilateral triangles forming a hexagram. The symbol was common in many ancient civilizations and cultures, where it served variously for decoration and for the practice of magic. The Star was not associated specifically with Judaism during biblical or Talmudic times. It appeared as early as the tenth century as a lucky sign in *mezuzah,* and later—around the seventeenth century—it began appearing on Jewish tombstones and as decoration in synagogues. In the nineteenth century, the appearance of the Star became widespread when it was adopted by central European Jews as a symbol to represent Judaism, much as the cross represents Christianity. The symbol spread quickly and was in use in most synagogues by the early years of the twentieth century. In 1897 the First Zionist Congress adopted the Star; later, it was utilized as the central image of the flag of the State of Israel. During the Nazi period, Jews in Europe were forced to wear a Magen David as an identifying badge.

each took its name. As the sun makes its round, it illumines each in turn. Chagall placed Ruben, the oldest, on the east, and Joseph and Benjamin, the youngest, at the other end of the sun's circuit. Each window is bursting with Chagall's own unique choice of symbolic reminders of the stories of each tribe.

What should I expect to see upon entering a **synagogue**?

Synagogues of the various different Jewish communities use their interior spaces in different ways, but the one thing you will invariably see is the Ark. Almost as soon as you enter your eye will be drawn to the back wall. There, a pair of small doors, or perhaps a beautifully embroidered or brocaded cloth, mark the place in which the Torah scrolls are kept. This is the post-Temple version of the Ark of the Covenant. Should you visit during worship ceremonies, you will also see the Torah scroll itself, often cloaked in a beautiful cloth (sometimes tooled silver). Some Torah scrolls are topped with a crown (*keter*) as a reminder of the kingly, royal status of the divine source. Inside the cloth a binder (*mappa*) might further protect the scrolls from damage. Many Ashkenazic synagogues in central and eastern Europe also adorn the scroll with a Torah shield (*tas*). Wealthier synagogues often possess many sets of Torah scrolls, used in rotation for different occasions. In order to keep track of the point in the text at which a given scroll was open, the elaborately tooled silver Torah shield might have interchangeable plates with the word "Sabbath" or the name of a particular holy day. Many synagogues will have a *bimah* ("high place," also called *almemar*), a platform on which there is a desk to hold the Torah scrolls for reading. Traditional communities

Main synagogue of Florence, Italy (1882), showing the central dome that has historically been a feature of countless synagogues.

place the bimah, which symbolically replaces the Temple altar, in the center of the space facing the Ark. Reform synagogues move it nearer the Ark, elevated on a stage and facing the congregation. A sanctuary lamp is also symbolic of the sacred presence and is usually located near the Ark. One feature that often distinguishes Orthodox synagogues is the provision of separate sections for men and women, with men typically in front and women behind or to the side, either on the main floor or in a gallery above. Like many contemporary mosques, some synagogues separate genders with a partition running front to back down the center of the main floor.

Do Jews use **special symbolism** in personal, private, or non-liturgical rituals?

In addition to the ritual articles mentioned earlier, Jews use a number of important symbols while praying at home or for occasions such as weddings. During the observance of Passover, the *Kiddush* (or blessing) cup is an important item. Some ritual sets designed for the *Seder* ("order," ritual for Passover) ceremony include a special "Elijah cup" set aside for the special guest, the prophet who may appear at any time. Some families are fortunate enough to own heirloom silver cups. Similar goblets are used in wedding ceremonies and in the ceremony that marks the "separation" (*havdalah*) of holy sabbath time from the rest of the week. The *havdalah* occurs Saturday evening at sundown to mark the end of the twenty-four hour period begun Friday at sundown. (Jewish tradition measures all days this way.) Also used in the latter is a small symbol called the "spice tower" that recalls a reference in Song of Songs to the safekeeping of precious spices. Traditional Jewish communities have produced magnificent illuminated pages called *ketubbah* to recognize marriage vows. Typical decorations there include allusions to the Temple and its implements in addition to scenes of domestic life. Amulets worn around the neck or suspended over an infant's cradle have been popular throughout Jewish history. Many are made of silver. A more elaborate and expensive amulet might include the tablets of the Law along with a number of symbols of the Temple, such as the menorah, incense burner, and ritual headdress of the High Priest. A stylized hand in outline, used as a pendant or on a keychain, symbolizes divine protection and functions as an amulet.

Are **number and letter symbolism** important in Jewish tradition?

Rabbinical interpreters of the sacred text have always loved to play with words. That is not so surprising in a tradition that teaches that words are so powerful that to speak a word is to bring its meaning into being as an event. Writers of *aggadah*—learned narrative intended to entertain as well as teach—analyzed words or clusters of words in the text at hand, looking for hidden meanings. Every letter of the Hebrew alphabet has a numerical value, and the interpreters would, for example, count up the total numerical value of certain words in order to decide where to place their emphasis in interpreting a passage. This type of interpretation is based on a system called *Gemetria* (from the Greek word for "geometry") and was especially associated with a kind of often arcane Jewish mysticism called Kabbalah. Other kinds of letter symbolism have to do with which words they begin. A charming bit of lore called the Alphabet of Creation tells how the letters of the Hebrew alphabet debated among themselves which one should go first. They each made their case, responding to the others in turn, not hesitating to poke fun at some of the funnier looking letters. In the end it was the humble letter aleph that God judged worthy of going first, because with aleph the name of God, Elohim, begins.

What about **animals** or other **natural objects**?

Pomegranates (*rimmonim*) are a very commonly used symbol. They appear on all sorts of objects, most importantly perhaps on the tops of the two spindles that hold the Torah scrolls in many synagogue. Bursting with countless seeds, the pomegranate is a reminder of the innumerable meanings one can find in the divinely revealed scripture. As this single fruit contains so many parts, so is all of our world's perplexing multiplicity contained in ultimate unity. The only object that apparently has survived from Solomon's Temple is a tiny pomegranate carved of ivory and bearing the inscription, "Belonging to the Temple of the Lord, holy to the Priests." Some Torah scroll finials further decorate the pomegranate with small bell towers. Imagery of the twelve tribes is often associated with animal symbolism.

Do Jews use **statues** or other similar imagery in worship?

Along with Islam, Judaism has traditionally avoided three-dimensional figural art altogether in its ritual life. The prohibition against setting up any "graven images" that is part of the Decalogue may have arisen as a way of establishing a clear distinction between Israel and its pagan neighbors, whose polytheistic beliefs were so vividly portrayed in the images they seemed to worship. The need to prevent believers from backsliding into pagan cultic practices was so strong that the prohibition of representational images in three dimensions was virtually absolute. There are minor exceptions. Some smaller ritual objects, such as Torah shields, depict human beings and animals in high relief. Surprisingly, some of these images even include sacred figures like

Moses and Abraham, but these are extremely rare. A number of prominent sculptors have been Jewish, but they have typically not produced their work for explicitly ritual settings, even when the subject matter is expressly religious. Ancient mural and mosaic arts, as well as more recent (especially medieval) manuscript art, are another story. Illuminated texts, even some of the Bible, contain figural images of human beings and animals, but these are generally not done in very realistic fashion.

What is the **Ark of the Covenant**?

Part of the revelation Moses received at Sinai included specific instructions from God about how to prepare a holy place in which the people could come to be in the presence of God. First they were to fashion a special tent, called the tabernacle, then the Ark in which the tablets of the Law would be kept. The Ark was to be a gold-clad box of acacia wood of specific dimensions. It was to have two rings on either side to accommodate poles for carrying it, since the Ark had to be portable—the people were still on the move. On top there was to be a "mercy seat" made of gold in the shape of two cherubs facing each other, whose wings would spread over the mercy seat. Ironically, this feature of the most sacred of all ritual objects must have been one of the rare examples of three-dimensional figural art in the history of Judaism. The mercy seat was to be a symbol of the place to which God would descend to meet Moses. Inside the tabernacle a large veil was to separate the larger part of the space from a space called the Holy of Holies, in which the Ark would be kept. From then on, the Ark would travel with Israel, resting only temporarily in any given location, until Solomon built the first temple in Jerusalem. In the temple the Ark was to reside permanently in the innermost part, also called the Holy of Holies.

Have Jews used **symbolism** to remind them of the **Temple** since its destruction in 70 CE?

Many illuminated manuscripts of the Bible and other important Hebrew texts have included a one- or two-page spread depicting the various implements or ritual objects once used in the Temple. These pages show all of the more portable items mentioned in the text of Exodus 25–30. They include, among other things, the tablets of the Law, the menorah, the table supporting the containers of the twelve loaves of sacred bread, a bronze "laver" used for ceremonial purification, the ram's horn (*shofar*), and the incense burner. Decorative panels or hangings, called *mizrach* or "east" since they are hung on a home's eastern wall toward Jerusalem, also frequently depict a building meant to be the Jerusalem Temple. Sometimes these hangings show Temple implements rather than the building itself. The mizrach is a reminder not only of the ancient Temple, but of the holy city of Jerusalem, toward which Jews turn when they pray. Another ritual object that often uses imagery of the Temple is the Hanukkah lamp. Though some lamps look very much like the standard seven-branch menorah, many take the form of a small architectural design that can be either hung on the wall or set on a table. The architectural imagery sometimes depicts the back interior wall of a synagogue, with its Ark flanked by two pillars meant to recall the two pillars of the Temple representing Boaz and Jachin. Sometimes the Hanukkah lamp bears an elaborate architectural facade, the metalsmith's version of what the Temple looked like.

Have **relics** ever been important in Judaism?

Relics have generally not formed an significant part of popular Jewish practice. Reverence for the burial places of holy persons, however, does play a role. After the site of the former Temple, tombs of the patriarchs and their wives have highest priority in the hierarchy of holy places. In the town of Hebron, not far south of Jerusalem and David's first capital, a mosque stands on what tradition identifies as the cave of Machpelah. Accounts in the Hebrew Bible tell how Abraham bought the property as a burial place, and how generations of patriarchs (Abraham, Isaac, and Jacob) and their wives (Sarah, Rebekah, and Leah) were laid to rest there. Rachel's tomb, not far from Bethlehem, has attracted pilgrims for over fifteen hundred years. She was Jacob's favorite wife and the mother of his two youngest sons, Joseph and Benjamin.

MEMBERSHIP, COMMUNITY, DIVERSITY

What do the terms **"diaspora"** and **"aliyah"** mean?

Diaspora is Greek for scattering or dispersion. It refers to the growth of Jewish communities, at first throughout the Middle East, and eventually throughout the Mediterranean and the world at large. Some diaspora communities were the indirect result of the persecution and exile of Jews, not only from the eastern Mediterranean, but from numerous sites throughout the greater Mediterranean basin. In other words, Jews have experienced dispersion after dispersion. *Aliyah* means "going up" in Hebrew. Originally associated with travel to Jerusalem, which is a high point in the regional topography, the term came to mean especially the modern day return of Jews to Israel. It is thus the opposite of *diaspora,* but much of the impetus for *aliyah* continues to come from the very kind of intolerance and persecution that gave rise to many diaspora communities in the first place. In other words, global migration patterns in the history of Judaism have been cyclical.

What is meant by the term **Zionism**?

In general Zionism means the modern movement of Jewish return to the holy mountain of Zion in the hope of reclaiming it as the heart of the biblical Promised Land.

> **Why is the land of Israel so important
> in the history of the Jewish people?**
>
> Israel is the homeland of the Chosen, or Covenant, people. It is the land to
> which God led Abraham. God chose the people of Israel "in love" for a mutual-
> ly binding agreement. The obligations of the Covenant were formalized in Torah,
> with Israel bound in obedience. Today, Israel remains the focus—the land of des-
> tiny—for many Jews, thanks especially to God's own statement that he chose the
> people of Israel as his "treasured people" and consecrated them to himself. The
> land of Israel therefore holds a special place for Jews as both a gift from God and
> as an enduring and tangible sign of the Covenant.

Nathan Birnbaum coined the usage in 1890. In 1896 Theodor Herzl organized the political movement that has borne the name ever since. Herzl convened the first of many Zionist Congresses at Basel in 1897. Chaim Weitzmann (1874–1952) was one of the most influential leaders of the movement. He was a powerful presence from the negotiation of the Balfour Declaration of 1917, a watershed document that ultimately made serious talk of a Jewish state possible, right through negotiations for Israeli statehood in 1947. Weitzmann also served as Israel's first President. Zionism has, to be sure, been a bone of contention because of the political and social implications of so dramatic a reshaping of what had formerly been called Palestine.

Where do Jews live today? Any estimates of numbers available?

Few nations of the world were without significant Jewish communities in early modern times. Many of those diaspora communities have dwindled considerably since the formation of the State of Israel and the open invitation to Jews to "return" to the homeland. Several million Jews now live in Israel, but by far the single largest concentration of local Jewish communities is in the United States. Jews have thrived throughout the Americas. European Jewry suffered dramatic losses as a result of the Nazi-led Holocaust, but since World War II Jewish communities have begun to reestablish themselves in many major European cities. Jews number some fourteen to fifteen million worldwide. In the United States a Jewish population of around four to four and a half million is associated through over 2000 synagogues and "temples."

What is a Jewish "ghetto"?

Some say that the word ghetto comes from the Italian word for "foundry" and that it came to mean a closed or restricted neighborhood because a Jewish community near a foundry in Venice was declared the only area open to Jews in 1516. The actual practice of restricting Jewish residences to a certain quarter of town is very ancient, even gaining official religious sanction, for example, from the Christian Third Lateran Council in 1179 in Rome. Jews have been forced to live in ghettos in many times and places. Most recently, Adolph Hitler used the practice fairly early in his career as a way of controlling Jewish residents. Nazis in effect turned these ghettos into urban concentration camps. The Yiddish term *shtetl* was the common European Jewish term for the local community, but it did not carry the often gruesome connotations now borne by the word ghetto.

Do all Jews belong to the same large **group**?

Jews have formed a number of important sub-communities throughout their history, though there are generally fewer formally constituted denominations, sects, or other subgroups in Judaism than in most other major traditions. That is quite remarkable, considering the relatively small global population of Jews and the enormous diversity of cultures in which Jews now live. Major differences among Jewish communities appear most frequently in the relative strictness of ritual observance. Variations in theological views are also noteworthy in some cases, but they are less critical. Strictest in observance are Orthodox Jews, with Conservative communities somewhat less strict. Further removed from the nearly all-inclusive adherence to biblical and traditional practices stands Reform Judaism. And most flexible of all, both doctrinally and ritually, are the Reconstructionists.

What is distinctive about **Orthodox Judaism**?

Emphasis on the direct, verbatim revelation of the Torah to Moses is the foundation of Orthodox Jewish tradition. Rabbinical interpretation of Torah serves the purpose of drawing out the meanings of scripture so that every situation in life is anchored in divine revelation. If scripture does not address an issue directly, the rabbi employs traditional principles of exegesis to make what limited adaptations are deemed necessary. Strict observance of the 613 commands and prohibitions contained in the Torah is perhaps the most significant feature of Orthodoxy. As an increasingly distinctive approach, Orthodoxy began to emerge in eighteenth-century Europe in response to the perception that Jews were being assimilated too rapidly into society at large. Reform attempts to adapt ritual observance in early nineteenth- century Europe elicited a strong reaction on the part of those who refused to acknowledge a need for more than the most minimal adaptation. Orthodox Jews consider their communities a last bastion of tradition in an increasingly secularized world. Just over one American Jew out of ten belongs to an Orthodox synagogue.

What problems did **Reform Judaism** attempt to solve?

Many German Jews of the early 1800s began to feel that the tradition-bound approach of Orthodox Judaism was losing touch with life in rapidly changing societies. Reform (alternatively called Liberal or Progressive) leaders began by seeking to adapt prayer and liturgy to the needs of people less able to follow them meaningfully in Hebrew. Ideas from the Enlightenment (*Haskalah*) that informed further developments were Moses Mendelsohn's (1728–86) principles of rational religion: the existence of God, divine providence, and the immortality of the soul. Reform was a grass-roots movement initiated by lay people and only later enjoying rabbinical support. A student of Mendelsohn, David Friedlander (1756–1834) launched the movement by replacing Hebrew prayers with German and replaced the Jews' plea for the restoration of Israel with hope for global renewal. Samuel Holdheim (1806–60) took liturgical reforms further in Berlin, and, with Abraham Geiger (1810–74), instituted dramatic changes. Sabbath worship moved to Sunday, with no gender separation, kippah, prayer shawl, or shofar. Their radical program of assimilation also rejected dietary laws and circumcision. Geiger led a gathering of rabbis in 1837, arguing for a much-reduced authority for both Bible and Talmud. He believed Judaism was a world community rather than an ethnically based "nation." The World Union for Progressive Judaism is the movement's international umbrella organization. Several important developments have marked Reform Judaism in the United States. Reform theology regards scripture as divinely inspired (rather than directly revealed verbatim) and subject to the interpretation of each individual. In 1885 the Pittsburgh Platform altered ritual practice by doing away with strict dietary regulations and ancient codes of priestly purity. Reform Jews believe in the immortality of the soul, but not in bodily resurrection. Numbering about two million, they are the largest Jewish community in the United States, gathering in some nine hundred synagogues or temples.

How did **Conservative Judaism** get its name?

Many twentieth-century European and American Jews have agreed that Orthodoxy must adapt to changing times, but have found some modifications introduced by leaders of Reform Judaism too dramatic. Conservatives have thus become Judaism's midground. Responding to the Reformers' Pittsburgh Platform of 1885, Sabato Morais (1823–1897) joined other Reform rabbis to found the Jewish Theological Seminary of America as a way of promoting a middle path between Orthodoxy and Reform. They stressed the progressive nature of the faith while retaining traditional practices. Like the Reformers, Conservatives allowed some English prayers as well as organ music, and did not separate the sexes, and they taught immortality of the soul but not resurrection of the body. In 1924 the Rabbinical Assembly of America became Conservative Judaism's institutional anchor in this country. Conservatives retain the Orthodox emphasis on Scripture as normative, along with the bulk of its traditional interpretation. They do, however, make allowances for adaptation to modern needs, such as driving to synagogue on Sabbath. But while traditionalists among them insist that the revelation of Sinai was complete and definitive in itself, more liberal Conservatives lean toward the idea that divine revelation is an unfolding process. Conservatives make up the second largest body of American Jews, numbering over one and a half million with about eight hundred synagogues. Zionism has had many staunch supporters among Conservative Jews.

Shrine of the Book, Jerusalem, a museum housing priceless archaeological remains, most importantly the manuscripts discovered at the ancient Essene monastery of Qumran overlooking the Dead Sea.

What distinguishes **Reconstructionist** Jews from others?

Reconstructionists have sought to reorient Jewish belief from its generally otherworldly focus to greater attentiveness to the here and now. Mordecai Kaplan (1881–1983) led the movement and taught that Jews must understand themselves as a civilization in process. Jewish life depended on so much more than unchanging religious practice, and he introduced dramatic changes into the religious understanding of Judaism. He chose to refer to the "divinity" rather than to God, seeking to purge the object of prayer of its anthropomorphic overtones. Thus God is more of a cosmic process than a personal creator and sustainer of all that is. Kaplan was most influential in expanding the function of the typical synagogue to include much more than regular liturgical worship. Reconstructionism is by far the smallest of the sub-communities of Judaism, with only about a hundred thousand in the United States, since many Reform and Conservative Jews have come to accept much of what Kaplan taught. In general, Reconstructionist congregations retain more traditional practices, such as wearing the prayer shawl, than do Reformers.

Who were the **Essenes**?

One day in 1949 a young Bedouin herded his flock in the Wilderness of Judaea near the northwestern end of the Dead Sea, at a place called Wadi Qumran. He amused himself, the story goes, by tossing stones into some of the many caves nearby. After

95

one toss he heard the sound of something breaking deep in a cave. Inside he found a cache of covered clay jars containing very old manuscripts. Fortunately for us all, the shepherd gave most of them to people who might be able to make sense of them. The treasure, now known as the Dead Sea Scrolls, has proved a gold mine of information about a strange and little-known religious community that had lived at Qumran. It appears that the Essenes lived an ascetic, semi-monastic life in communities that flourished from around 150 BCE to 75 CE. Numbering about four thousand at one time, this small Jewish sect accepted only male adults to full membership, though some members were apparently married. The Essenes are perhaps the closest analogy to a form of monastic life in the Jewish tradition. As Jews they studied Torah and observed strict purity in ritual practice, but did not participate in Temple worship in Jerusalem. Belief in immortality of the soul and the eventual resurrection of the body were central to their theology.

Who were the **Karaites**?

Around the middle of the eighth century, Anan ben David (c. 762–67) was elected counter-exilarch of the Jewish communities in Iraq. Tradition has it that he laid the foundations of a school of thought that would come to be called the Karaites (from the Hebrew "to read, recite" scripture) because of their emphasis on scripture as the sole basis of Judaism. Like latter-day Sadducees, the Karaites rejected centuries of oral tradition as superfluous. Like the Maccabees of old, they proclaimed every individual his own rabbi, capable of interpreting scripture for himself. Benjamin of Nehavand (c. 850) is said to have further developed the thought of Anan during the ninth century. The principal systematizer of Karaite thought was Daniel ben Moshe (c. 900), who led a kind of proto-Zionist movement in Jerusalem. Karaite rejection of Talmudic learning gave rise to their preaching a need to return to the Holy Land. Talmud and later oral tradition had, they argued, generally developed as a way of adapting the Law to Jewish communities in exile. Return to the Land would imply a return to the original sources and hence obviate the need for adaptive interpretation. Saadia (882–942), the most famous Gaon of the Iraqi communities, led a vigorous counterattack against the Karaite position, insisting on the need to combine tradition with revelation and reason for a balanced approach. Small groups of intellectual descendants of the original Karaites survived into the twentieth century, but they have had little influence in recent times.

What are **Hasidic Jews**?

Some of the biblical prophets emphasized the notion of God's unconditional, absolutely faithful love, *chesed* in Hebrew. They taught that God would continue to seek out sinners and bring them back. Out of that emphasis grew an important theme in Jewish spirituality, a focus on the transforming power of divine compassion. Learning and moral righteousness were still worthy goals, of course, but not to such a degree that they should raise divisions in a community that amounted to religious class distinctions. Most important was the quest for individual salvation sought within community. A major movement organized around these emphases was begun in eastern Europe by Israel ben Eliezer (c. 1700–1760), known as the *Baal Shem Tov* (Master of the Good Name, that is that of God). He was a highly charismatic man with a reputation for working wonders, especially healing. He de-emphasized Talmudic scholarship in favor of devotional intensity. After his death the Hasidic movement became more formally organized as a closed society around the person of a charismatic leader called the *Tzaddik* (literally, righteous one). As the community grew, sub-groups developed and carried the spirit of the tradition abroad, most notably to Israel and New York. The Chabad branch moved more toward scholarship and education while other groups stayed focused

Hasidic Jews returning home after praying at the Western Wall in Jerusalem. One man wears the prayer shawl and both wear the decorative fur hat distinctive of Hasidic men's ritual fashions.

on emotional involvement in devotion. Hasidic groups have often been "excommunicated" even though none have formally broken away.

Who are the **Samaritans**?

After the northern kingdom's capital, Samaria, was overrun by the Assyrians in 721 BCE, many of the leading and best educated Jewish citizens were deported. The invaders imported significant numbers of colonists who gradually infiltrated the people of Israel. They came to trace their ancestry to the tribes of Manasseh and Ephraim, thus identifying themselves as Jewish at least genealogically, and intermarried with Jews. The Samar-

Hasidic Jewish children in Jerusalem. Note the sidelocks and skullcaps.

itans established their own temple on Mt. Gerizim. As a result of a falling out with Nehemiah in the fifth century, the Samaritans split off from Judaism more or less definitively and came to think of themselves as a separate people. Now very few in numbers, the Samaritans still have their own version of the Torah and distinctive codes of religious law. At Passover they still sacrifice a lamb on Mt. Gerizim. Only a small community of Samaritans, well under a thousand, survive. Plagued by health problems as a result of inbreeding, most Samaritans live around the city of Nablus in the West Bank.

What's the difference between Sephardic and Ashkenazic Jews?

Prior to 1492 there were large Jewish communities on the Iberian peninsula, modern-day Spain and Portugal. During the final phases of the Catholic reconquest of Spain, Jews were given the option of converting or going into exile. Many of those who chose to leave migrated all over the Mediterranean basin, including North Africa and the Middle East, to found new communities. These descendants of Iberian Jewry are called Sephardic Jews. They comprise a small minority, perhaps 20 percent or less, of the global Jewish population. Sephardic Jews retain a number of distinctive ritual and legal interpretations, and in some places managed to preserve the Ladino language of their ancestral Iberia and maintain separate educational institutions. By far the majority of Jews are Askenazim. Their name derives from the medieval Hebrew designation of central Europe as Ashkenaz. Descendants of the early Jewish settlers in central and eastern Europe preserve Ashkenazic traditions all over the world. Most Jewish immigrants to the United States have been Askhenazim, although the majority of the earliest, in colonial times, were Sephardim. In general, Jews in the Americas have not maintained a serious distinction between Sephardic and Ashkenazic customs and practices, and few synagogues nowadays restrict membership one way or the other.

Have Jews traditionally sent out missionaries to convert others?

Unlike Buddhism, Christianity, and Islam, Judaism has never been connected with major missionary movements. There are several important reasons for that. One is that the Land God promised and delivered to the people of Israel is so central to the tradition that deliberate attempts to send representatives abroad in search of more members simply don't fit the picture of a people so identified with geography. Another is that while many Jewish communities gladly receive converts from other traditions, most Jews believe there is more to "Jewishness" than the profession of a set of religious beliefs.

Why is Jerusalem **Judaism's holiest city**? Are any others especially important?

Jerusalem was the last of several places that functioned as seats of power during the early years of Judaism's monarchy. Around the year 1000 BCE, King David captured the hilltop stronghold from a Canaanite tribe called the Jebusites. David's choice of location may well have been motivated by a desire to establish himself politically in a city that had

Statue of the great medieval Iberian rabbi Moses Maimonides (1135–1204) in the old Jewish quarter of his hometown, Cordoba, Spain.

few links to pre-monarchical Jewish factions. Jerusalem, also called the Hill of Zion, promised David a fresh start. Situated on the highest point in the region (some 2500 feet above sea level), and more or less in the center of tribal territories, the city already had great physical and topographical potential for acquiring symbolic power. But it would be Solomon's Temple, not David's royal headquarters, that would confer on Jerusalem the mantle of great holiness. Within a few generations after David, the city had become the focal point not only of major Jewish ritual and pilgrimage, but the very throne of God. Messianic hopes and expectations came to be attached to Jerusalem. After the Babylonian Exile the prospect of restoring the city to its former glory gave rise to a new theological interpretation. No longer a mere earthly city, Jerusalem was

Rolling stone door at the rock-cut burial place popularly known as the Tomb of Herod's Family just west of the Old City of Jerusalem. First century CE.

also—and even more importantly—a heavenly reality mirrored in a terrestrial one. For many centuries after the Romans destroyed the Second Temple in 70 CE, Jerusalem was a source of longing for Jews scattered across the globe. As Jews began to return in significant numbers, especially after 1492, Jerusalem's importance regained some of its earlier concreteness. The proclamation of the State of Israel in 1948 raised hopes further, and with Israel's recapture of the city in the Six Day War of 1967, many Jews revived plans for a full restoration of Jerusalem. For some now that means plans to rebuild the Temple, but the political implications are so enormous as to make that a most unlikely eventuality. Virtually every square foot of the "Holy Land" bears some special meaning. Places that had been especially holy in the days of the Patriarchs and Judges (prior to the Monarchy) have retained only a shadow of their pristine sacredness. Nothing compares with Jerusalem in that regard.

What is meant by the term **"Anti-Semitism"**?

Jews generally think of themselves as descended from Semitic racial or ethnic stock. Tradition says that the principal branches of the tree of humanity grew from Noah's male offspring, Shem, Ham, and Japheth. Descendants of Shem are called Semites. The earliest Semites spread all over what we call the central Middle East, from northern Syria and Iraq to the south of the Arabian peninsula, and from the Mediterranean eastward to what was once called Mesopotamia. Jews are ethnically one of several families of Semites. Beginning in Roman times, Jews all over the Mediterranean became the objects of hatred and intolerance because of their refusal to revere the Emperor. Through the history of the Middle Ages, especially in Europe, animosity toward Jews runs like a dark cultural and religious thread. Particularly in areas predominantly Christian, Jews suffered massive discrimination and segregation—largely because Jews generally preferred not to surrender their identity through assimilation and because so many Jews were sufficiently successful in their endeavors to arouse envy. Gradually there arose a popular notion that enmity for Jews had a rational basis in the racial inferiority of Semitic people. Only those of Aryan descent could claim racial purity. The earliest formal anti-Semitic organizations appeared in Austria in the late nineteenth century. After the Bolshevik Revolution in Russia in 1917, some Europeans sought to fuel the flames of hatred still further by claiming that Jews were in league with the Bolsheviks in promoting godless Communism. This was among the first of many global conspiracy theories that attributed virtually everything evil to Jews. It was a relatively short step from there to Adolph Hitler's attempts to rid the earth of racial "pollution" once and for all. Today the two most important Semitic groups are Arabs and Jews. Strictly speaking, the term "anti-Semitism" ought to include Arabs, but by common usage it has come to refer only to anti-Jewish sentiment.

Is there such a thing as a **non-religious Jew**?

Some people who consider themselves Jews are not actively involved in the practice of the religious tradition. It is equally true that some people who call themselves Muslims or Buddhists do not engage in any religious practices. In both cases one can speak of religious identification as a cultural phenomenon. People grow up in Buddhist or Muslim families and live where the vast majority so identify themselves as if by habit. But in the case of non-religious Jews, the racial or ethnic element is at least as important as the religious, and perhaps more so.

What questions does the prospect of **interfaith marriage** raise for Jews?

Attitudes to interfaith marriages vary a great deal among Jews. It is probably fair to say that the preference of most would be that their sons and daughters marry other Jews. But resistance to interfaith marriage is certainly stronger among Orthodox and Conservative Jews than among Reform. Virtually complete prohibition of interfaith marriages in some Jewish communities arises less out of concern for ethnic purity as such than out of a desire to prevent the faith tradition from being irreversibly diluted. Experience has shown that families in which the parents are not both Jewish are less likely to educate their children in the Jewish tradition. Tradition lost is extremely difficult to recover, especially in cultures and societies that seem to value the "new" much more highly than anything with deep historical roots. Even the musical "Fiddler on the Roof" goes a long way toward helping non-Jews to appreciate the beauty and centrality of "Tradition! Tradition!" for Jews. Families are the first line of defense against the permanent loss, not just of a collection of ritual deeds performed mechanically, but of the meaning of life itself as interpreted from a Jewish perspective.

What happens when a non-Jew wishes to **convert** to Judaism?

Prospective converts who present themselves with appropriate motivation for the change undergo a period of special instruction in the faith and its main practices. They meet regularly with a rabbi or learned lay person to discuss key texts of scripture and major features of tradition. The precise details of instruction may vary somewhat from one branch of Judaism to another, but in general the emphasis is on the religious obligations the convert is about to accept. Candidates then have a brief examination before the modern-day equivalent of the ancient "House of Judgment" (*Bet Din*), usually three people active in the faith, including but not limited to rabbis. A ceremonial purifying bath in a pool called a *mikvah* comes next. Men must be circumcised, and those already circumcised go through a ceremony called "circumcision for drawing blood" to remove only a token drop of blood. Finally, the convert is welcomed into the community of believers.

What **gender-related issues** are important for religious Jews?

Concern for ritual purity has occupied a central place in much of Jewish tradition. Beginning with the Torah's laws of holiness and continuing in the observance of the stricter branches of Judaism, matters related to female fertility, menstruation, and child-bearing, for example, have received a great deal of attention. According to scripture, menstruation renders a woman ritually unclean, as does the birth of a child (for seven days if a boy, fourteen if a girl). Gender has had significant implications in religious as well as social roles, especially in Orthodox and Conservative communities. In modern times the question of whether women should become rabbis has arisen. Reform and Reconstructionist communities do have increasing numbers of female rabbis, and the Conservative Jewish Theological Seminary of America began accepting female candidates not long ago. Orthodox communities still sponsor only men as candidates for the rabbinate.

Do Jewish communities practice **excommunication** or **banishment** for religious reasons?

Concern for purity led to the expulsion of lepers, those impure because of contact with the dead, and those "suffering from a discharge" of bodily fluids, from the camp of the Israelites as described in Book of Numbers 5:1–4. Lepers especially were considered not only unhealthy but ritually and ethically unclean, due to the prevalent belief that such an affliction implied some moral guilt on the part of either the individual or the leper's parents. Elsewhere in the Hebrew scripture we hear of the practice of *herem*, placing a "ban" on certain things, such as the spoils of war or the results of ritual sacrifice. In biblical usage, to ban an item was to dedicate it totally to the Lord. Later Jewish tradition used the term *herem* to apply to a kind of excommunication. When authenticated instances of heretical views came to the attention of rabbinical authorities, they could banish the culprit from the community. The philosopher Baruch Spinoza (1632–1677), for example, was excommunicated from the Sephardic community for his insistence on the primacy of reason and for views judged to be pantheistic. Earlier a Portuguese Jew named Uriel da Costa (1585–1640) underwent formal excommunication twice and endured public humiliation for his unacceptable views. Some interpret both Spinoza and da Costa as examples of a clash between Enlightenment views and traditional Jewish beliefs.

What is a **scapegoat**?

We use the term "scapegoating" to refer to any attempt to shift blame onto some person or group in order to escape consequences for oneself. In religious studies the term applies to the ritual transference of guilt or evil intent, and it implies that those effecting the transfer are aware of their complicity in the performance or furtherance of some evil act or condition. Chapter sixteen of the Book of Leviticus describes perhaps the best-known example of the ritual use of a scapegoat. God instructs Moses as to how his brother, Aaron the priest, is to perform the ritual of atonement for sin. He must take two goats and cast lots to decide which will be sacrificed. After sacrificing the one, he must lay his hands on the live goat, confess all the people's sins upon the animal's head, and send the goat out into the wilderness. Through this ritual transferral the guilt of the whole community, once acknowledged, is purified from its midst. Ironically, Jews themselves have often been the victims of a more tragic scapegoating through history. Scapegoating now typically involves projection of evil and ill-intent onto a hapless but convenient "other," sad confirmation of the adage that we hate most in others the very things we cannot face in ourselves.

How do Jews view Judaism's relationships to **other traditions**?

Even the earliest biblical texts that describe the formative years of Judaism as a faith tradition show a vivid, if largely disapproving, awareness of the religious practices and beliefs of other peoples. Jews were to be a people of faith who would distinguish themselves by their faithful response to divine initiative. Biblical Judaism defined itself in the context of various Canaanite pagan cults, which often exercised an unholy fascination on Jews of wavering faith. Most Jews are, of course, keenly aware of their tradition's complex relationship to Christianity, which claims to be a fulfillment of an ancient messianic expectation. From the Jewish perspective, Christianity was just another of many false movements of its kind. Many have also been puzzled and hurt by ongoing Christian condemnations of Jews as "Christ-killers," a hateful epithet only

recently repudiated by the Pope. Throughout medieval times in Europe, Jews often suffered cruelly as a result of severely prejudicial Christian decrees as to how Jews should live and even what they should wear in public. Most of all, many Jews simply do not understand why so many Christians have harbored such a virulent animosity toward Jews. Judaism has also had an important connection to Islam over the centuries. Jews have generally fared better under Muslim regimes throughout the Middle East, North Africa, and Spain than under Christian authority. From a strictly religious perspective, however, Judaism is strikingly close to Islam in many respects, both in practice and belief, from an uncompromising monotheism to dietary concerns to an egalitarian style of worship and view of authority.

Medieval synagogue of Joseph ibn Shushan (twelfth century), which was later turned into the church of Santa Maria La Blanca, Toledo, Spain (early 1400s). The "horseshoe" arches were typical of an architectural decorative style brought to Spain by Muslims of North Africa.

LEADERSHIP, AUTHORITY, ORGANIZATION

How and where do members of local **Jewish communities** come together?

The synagogue (from the Greek for "coming together"), sometimes referred to as the temple, is the principal venue of Jewish community life. More traditional synagogues have served very localized communities, especially for Jews who choose to observe Sabbath restrictions on the use of motor vehicles and prefer to walk to worship. It is more usual nowadays for Reform synagogues especially to draw members from much greater distances, shifting their scope from neighborhood to wider metropolitan area or even broader region. Many synagogues, especially those serving wealthier communities, are parts of extensive complexes. Some include libraries, auditoriums for plays and concerts, and even art galleries, in addition to worship space (some with both larger and smaller spaces), staff offices, and facilities for social functions.

What is a *minyan*?

When Jews gather for worship they need a minimum number in attendance, or quorum. Orthodox tradition excludes women from being counted toward the minimum of ten members over thirteen years of age. But both Reformed and Conservative traditions have in recent times voted to count women in the *minyan*. The accommodation presupposes that women in the local community have passed their *bat mitzvah,* a rite of passage not open to Orthodox women. The notion of a religious quorum seems to rest on a fairly clear distinction between private and public worship. Since public or communal worship is of a different order than private worship, tradition draws a clear line between them. So when there are not enough people to form a minyan, everyone returns home or prays privately in the synagogue.

Is there a **central teaching** or **legislative authority** for Jews?

During later biblical times, beginning around 200 BCE, a principal deliberative body of seventy-one members, called the Sanhedrin (Greek *synedrion*), handled all religious and secular matters of importance to Jewish life. Originally located in the Jerusalem Temple, the Sanhedrin remained active until around 425 CE. Membership consisted of three groups (at least during New Testament times): the Elders who represented the major tribal clans and families; the High Priests, including elders of the four priestly families as well as former high priests; and the Scribes, religious legal scholars belonging mostly to the sect known as the Pharisees. The High Priest (or *nasi*) was chosen from descendants of Moses' brother Aaron and governed the council. While the Sanhedrin did function as a court of law in exceptional cases, it was concerned mostly with larger administrative and juridical issues. Meanwhile, the *Bet Din* (literally, "House of Judgment") generally adjudicated legal questions, including both religious and civil matters affecting the Jewish community exclusively. Roman law allowed for a large measure of internal rule among Jewish subjects. The Bet Din required at least three (male) judges but handled criminal cases with as many as twenty-three judges. The class of religious scholars known as the "Five Pairs of Teachers" bore special responsibility for the two legal bodies. Hillel (*nasi*) and Shammai (*Av Bet Din,* Chief Justice of the Court) were the last of the Pairs. In this separation of civil and religious spheres, the High Priest generally retained final authority. Though the Sanhedrin did not survive into Late Antiquity, the Bet Din remained vital through the middle ages and still functions as arbiter of personal status law for Israeli Jews, with the Chief Rabbi presiding. During later Antiquity (c. 500–1000) the scholarly class called the *Geonim* ("Eminences") functioned as a major authority for Middle Eastern and European Jews by publishing their rulings in documents called *Responsa.* For Jewish communities in Iraq, land of the Exile, the position of Exilarch (*resh galuta,* "head of those in exile"), generally occupied by laymen, continued to wield some authority until about the mid–thirteenth century. For many generations, even up to early modern times, the *Qehillah,* or local Jewish community organization, was the principal decision making body.

Do Jews have a system of **religious law**?

Jewish religious law is among the most highly developed and extensive systems ever devised. This is not surprising in a tradition whose scripture begins with a large section, the Torah, for which "Law" is the chief synonym. Ever since the end of the Monarchy, Jewish communities have struggled with the problem of how to observe their own religious ordinances within the context of a larger secular or civil regime. In some circumstances the civil authorities allowed Jews considerable autonomy in administering their religious law, with the understanding that none of its provisions would run afoul of secular statutes. Legal scholars in late Antiquity and through the Middle Ages produced voluminous collections referred to generically as the "codes" of law. Ancient concern with ritual purity and precision persists in some branches of Judaism, especially among the Orthodox and many Conservatives. Rabbis function as legal scholars in those situations, interpreting the six hundred thirteen specific commands and prohibitions of the Torah. For Jews less attentive to the minute details of practice, the rabbi's role is more broadly pastoral.

Do Jewish communities run **private schools** for their children?

Educational institutions called *yeshivot* ("academies," plural of *yeshiva*) began to proliferate in Iraq, in communities that grew out of the Exile, and in Israel especially after the Temple was destroyed in 70 CE. Tradition credits Rabbi Yohannan ben Zakkai with founding the first academy at Jabneh in Israel. Since the Sanhedrin had been housed in the Temple, it found a home at the academy. Academies in Iraq began in the third century CE at Sura and Nehardea, and later at Pumbedita. As the center of Jewish life shifted from the Middle East to Europe during medieval times, academies arose in central and eastern Europe. Famous biblical scholars such as Gershom ben Judah (960–1040) and Rashi (Shlomo bar Ishaq, 1040–1105) founded major schools, in Mainz, Germany, and Troyes, France, respectively. The traditions, if not the actual structures, of these and other scholarly "dynasties" have continued into modern times. Many local Jewish communities maintain schools for younger students, emphasizing the study of Hebrew. Orthodox Jews typically refer to synagogue as *shul,* German/Yiddish for "school," emphasizing the study and discussion of scripture and Talmud. Rabbinical seminaries, such as Yeshiva University in New York, now offer advanced learning in Jewish tradition in the context of training for the ministry.

What are some of the main varieties of Jewish **religious officials** or **specialists**?

During biblical times the centralized cult of the Temple in Jerusalem required a large and elaborate system of specialists and functionaries. Special roles were assigned to tribes, and to certain clans and families within the tribes. Destruction of the Second Temple in 70 CE brought dramatic change in its wake, including a great simplification in ritual practice. The shift to local synagogue worship naturally required the development of a local officialdom whose duties would include presiding over much smaller-scale ritual and, at the same time, looking after the more comprehensive spiritual needs of a local community for whom the synagogue was now the focus of religious life. The rabbi (Hebrew for "my master") is the principal religious authority and community representative in contemporary Judaism as well as the primary leader of synagogue worship. The latter function seems to be a relatively modern development, with emphasis in earlier post-biblical eras on the rabbi as scholar and teacher. In some regions, rabbinical conferences or other organizations may elect or appoint one of their members to serve as "chief" rabbi. Most synagogues and local communities divide duties among several other offices. One of the more important is that of the cantor (*hazzan*), often a person of considerable musical ability and training whose duty is to chant sacred text and to sing special prayers for the various religious observances. The position has been especially necessary in communities whose members generally do not read Hebrew. In late antiquity the term *hazzan* referred to several community functions but later it was applied exclusively to the cantor (*sheliach zibbur*). Throughout Jewish history, many rabbis have served as cantors in their synagogues, but rabbi-cantors are now less common. In some congregations a lay person called the *gabbai* ("overseer," roughly) has the duty of commissioning Torah readers for each service.

How are Jewish **religious leaders** chosen and given authority?

In biblical times religious authorities and specialists came largely from hereditary lines within particular tribes that traced their sacred mandates back to the Mosaic revelation at Sinai. Post-biblical developments gradually moved away from hereditary models of religious leadership to a parallel model in which one leader passes on authority to a successor by laying on of hands (called *semikhah* in Hebrew). Thus did Moses "ordain" Joshua and the seventy elders (Numbers 11:16–25, 27:18–23). Members of the Sanhedrin were likewise ordained. But post-biblical communities in the Middle East eventually did away with formal ordination, preferring only to see to it that prospective rabbis were thoroughly versed in Talmudic and legal studies. A number of modern seminaries, or rabbinical colleges as some are called, have broadened their curricula to include non-traditional studies, the better to equip future rabbis to engage more broadly educated congregations. The rich, age-old ritual of *semikhah,* imposing hands, survives largely in the practice of Orthodox rabbinical academies.

Who were the **Pharisees**?

During the Maccabean (or Hasmonean) revolt in 164 BCE against the foreign rule of the Seleucids, a fascinating sect or school of thought called the Pharisees began to emerge from obscurity. They were called *Perushim* ("separatists, seceders, heretics") in Hebrew, but that may originally have been a pejorative term coined by their opponents, the Sadducees. At first the Pharisees supported the Maccabees, who initially packed their new Sanhedrin with members of the sect. But the Pharisees disapproved of the way ruler John Hyrcanus (135–104 BCE) attempted to secure both religious and civil authority for himself and so withdrew their support. In general the Pharisees enjoyed the favor of the masses for their stand on political issues. Meanwhile the new Hasmonean ruler Alexander Yannai (103–76 BCE) cultivated the support of the Sadducees, who tended to be aristocratic. When the Pharisees condemned Alexander's priestly conduct of sacred ritual as blasphemous, they paid with death or exile. But Alexander's wife, Alexandra, brought back the Pharisees after her husband's death, allowing them to restore both Sanhedrin and temple ritual. The Pharisees emphasized God's love for each person and taught the resurrection of the body. They stood against the priestly aristocracy in their teaching of the individual's personal relationship with God. After the Romans ended Hasmonean rule in 63 BCE, the Pharisees insisted that a separation of secular and sacred spheres would allow the Jewish people to tolerate foreign rule so long as the Romans left them their religious freedom. After 70 CE, the Pharisees disappeared as a distinct sect or party, but much of their spirit lived on in the growth of rabbinical Judaism.

Who were the **Sadducees** and are they still around?

Around the time the Pharisees became important players in Jewish history, the Sadducees (*Tseduqim*) also emerged. They held that only the Torah was authentic revelation, repudiating the Pharisaic emphasis on the full Bible as well as all subsequent oral tradition. They also denied the Pharisees' teaching of the soul's immortality and bodily resurrection. As the Pharisees presented themselves as the heirs of Moses and of his authority as lawgiver, the Sadducees anchored their authority in that of Moses' priestly brother Aaron. More specifically, the Sadducees may have gotten their name because of their claim to be directly descended from Zadok, the High Priest in Solomon's temple. The Sadducees had struck a compromise with the Hasmoneans, agreeing to support the rulers if they would officially nullify the Pharisaic teaching on the validity of the Oral Law. In exchange, the Sadducees would tolerate the Hasmonean claim to priestly authority—a stunning accommodation indicative of the enmity between Pharisees and Sadducees. When the Pharisees were restored to favor under the ruler Alexandra (76–67 BCE), they in turn struck a deal by which they would sanction the priesthood of the Sadducees in exchange for the Sadducees' acceptance of the binding force of Oral Torah. During the time of Jesus, the High Priest named Caiaphas was a Sadducee, but the sect disappeared along with the Temple.

PERSONALITIES AND POWERS

What is a **Messiah**?

Mashiach is a Hebrew word that means "anointed one" (*christos* is the Greek equivalent). Anointing is an ancient Jewish ritual first used to consecrate the priesthood and later to elevate Saul and David to kingly office. Expectation of the coming of a Messiah arose in Jewish tradition especially during and after the Babylonian Exile. Bereft of both Temple and monarchy, Jews longed for a restoration of their former estate under the guidance of a descendant of David. For the next several centuries various notions developed as to how one would recognize the Messiah when he appeared, but tradition did not arrive at a consensus. The Essene community evidently looked forward to two Messiahs, one with spiritual and the other with political power. Protracted Roman occupation of Israel two thousand years ago gave rise to renewed messianic expectation. One community of belief, now called Christianity, crystallized around Jesus, convinced that he had all the necessary qualifications. Even so, the New Testament gives evidence of mixed opinions as to how people would know with certainty that Jesus was the Messiah. For Jews, messianic expectation did not end with Jesus. A century later many Jews acclaimed Bar Kochba as Messiah and rallied in support of his revolt, but the Romans quelled the uprising in 135 when they laid siege to the famous Dead Sea stronghold called Masada. Several significant claimants to messiahship have appeared since then, especially under Muslim rule and in medieval Europe, including David Menachem Alroy (12th c., Kurdistan), David Reuveni (d. c. 1538), Solomon Molcho (1500–32), Shabbetai Zevi (1626–76), and his successor in the movement, Jacob Frank (1726–91). Some sub-communities of extremely Orthodox Jews have even more recently looked upon local leaders as Messiahs. For the majority of Jews today, messianic expectation remains a minor article of faith at most. Reform theology has spiritualized the concept, teaching that the advent of the Messiah is a purely personal event rather than one that will usher in a new age.

How have **prophets** figured in Jewish tradition?

Even in the Torah we find references to Abraham and Moses as prophets, and Moses is told that his brother Aaron will be his "prophet" when they confront Pharaoh. In those texts the term appears to be a still rather generic indicator of one who speaks for another rather than a reference to a figure of official or institutional status. Prophetic figures continue to appear during the days of the Judges. Deborah is a "prophetess," according to Judges 4:4; and Judges 6:8 says God sent an otherwise unnamed prophet to the people of Israel with a divine message. Prophets as an institutional class rose to prominence in connection with the Monarchy. Samuel, called as a youth to special religious service, was both the last of the Judges and a prototype of the court prophet. He served as critic and spiritual guide to King Saul, as the prophet Nathan would later be for David. Elijah and his successor Elisha are perhaps the most famous of the itinerant prophets of the early Monarchical years, best known for the wonders they worked. But it is the writing prophets, beginning with Amos, Hosea, Isaiah, and Jeremiah, who seem to exemplify the quintessence of Jewish prophetic office. They left amazing records both of their experience of the prophetic vocation and of the content of the message they believed God commissioned them to deliver. Prophets are, in short, a constant presence in the biblical record. Post-biblical Jewish tradition generally assumes that the age of prophecy is over for good.

Do Jews revere any persons as especially **gifted with wisdom**?

Wisdom has always had a special place in Jewish tradition. King Solomon, for all his faults, has occupied the place of honor in this respect. In the biblical story of how two women came to him, both claiming a child as theirs, Solomon responds by decreeing that the child be cut in half. At that the child's true mother offered to save the baby's life by letting the other woman have the infant. Solomon then gave the child to its mother. Tradition says Solomon wrote a number of the "wisdom" books in the Hebrew Bible, as well as few extra-canonical or apocryphal works. Since Solomon's time, the custodians of the tradition's treasures of wisdom have been known generically as Sages. They have included largely religious scholars and rabbis, such as Hillel and the legendary Rabbi Akiva (c. 50–135) and Yohannan ben Zakkai (c. 1–80 CE). According to legend, Moses went to heaven for a preview of the Torah and asked God whether his works would prosper. God showed Moses a vision of a future disciple named Akiva. His lecture was so profound that even Moses could not understand it! The centrality of the Sages in Jewish spirituality is indicative of the importance of practical wisdom in the tradition. Wisdom is the highest form of holiness.

Is there such a thing as a Jewish **saint**?

Jewish tradition tells of numerous individuals noted for their holiness and even for the ability to work marvels. But there has never been a formal process by which a man or woman was officially recognized as a paragon of sanctity. Embodiments of holiness fill the pages of the Bible, beginning with Abraham, Jacob, and Joseph and continuing with Moses and David. Numerous women of the Bible are revered for their virtues, including Sarah, Rebecca, Ruth, Esther, and Judith. But saintly figures are not lacking in post-biblical tradition. Some early rabbis, such as Simeon ben Yochai (circa 150),

David and Goliath

David, second King of the Israelites (born circa 1013 BCE), is one of the most vividly portrayed characters in the Hebrew Bible (Old Testament). He was a warrior, lawgiver, musician, and poet, loyal to his superiors, harsh in his judgments, ruthlessly cruel in war, but singled out by God for glory. He stands at the center of several crucial events in the history of the Israelites and has, accordingly, been a subject of exhaustive study among Jewish scholars for centuries. Christians have been almost equally fascinated with David, some seeing him as an Old Testament foreshadowing of Jesus, and others noting that Matthew's Gospel begins by tracing Jesus' lineage through the House of David. David is perhaps best remembered for his epic duel with the giant Goliath (begins I Samuel 17), a Philistine who was demoralizing the Hebrew army by offering single combat that no one dared accept. David, swearing that Yahweh would defend him, took up the challenge. He stepped forward, unarmed, and struck down the giant with a single stone from his slingshot. The Philistines panicked and fled, pursued and cut down by the Israelites. David is also known as the greatest of all Hebrew poets, having singlehandedly composed the biblical Book of Psalms.

continue to fascinate, most notably in mystically oriented sects such as the Hasidim. Founders of certain sects have also been canonized by popular acclaim. The figure of the *tsaddiq* has been especially important among mystically oriented groups, capable of performing wonders and possessed with esoteric knowledge. An important group of holy persons are the Jewish martyrs of various periods in history. When the Maccabeans revolted against the Seleucids, many of their number were martyred and acknowledged as heroes for the faith. During the Roman period, Jews were forbidden to teach Torah openly. According to much later traditional accounts a number of stalwart sages acted in defiance of the prohibition and were executed by Hadrian. They came to be called "The Ten Martyrs." One of the most famous of those killed by Hadrian was Rabbi Akiva (c. 50–135 CE), also celebrated for his profound wisdom.

What is the difference between a **Prophet** and a **Sage**?

Biblical prophets and sages arose from similar backgrounds and cultural circumstances, but had different ways of describing the relationship of the human and the divine. First, their overall purpose—call it strategy if you like—differed in several ways or strategy. Prophets spoke for God, focused on divine justice, and were motivated by the divine Word and by a conviction of God's presence. Sages spoke for humankind, addressed human reason, and were moved by social conscience. The prophets' rhetoric was fiery and animated, idealistic, and meant to engage people's emotions, while that of the Sages was cool and dispassionate, practical, and aimed at persuading listeners by the strength of the argument. Finally, Prophets and Sages directed their messages at different publics. Prophets struggled urgently to make God known to the rich and powerful in the hope that they would modify their ways of ruling others. Sages sought through steady pedagogy to help ordinary people apply knowledge to their daily lives.

Have there been important Jewish **mystics**?

Esoteric interpretation of certain texts of the Hebrew Bible has formed the basis of developments in Jewish mysticism. Visionary accounts in which the prophet Ezekiel, for example, describes seeing four wheels in the sky led to what is called *merkavah* (chariot or throne) mysticism. The *Sefer Yetzirah* (Book of Creation), an ancient cosmological treatise, eventually exercised great influence on mystical thinking. Traditional accounts trace the origins of mystical interpretation to twelfth-century Europe. There the originally Italian Kalonymus family, transplanted to the Rhine valley in Germany, became the nucleus of important developments. Samuel the Pious and son Judah began an important movement of Hasidic spirituality at Speyer, as did Eleazar ben Judah (d. 1228) at Worms. They were contemporary with similar developments among Christian Rhenish mystics, and devised a style of spiritual canticle called the *Din Shamayim* ("Law of the Heavens") with a type of prayer, called "Jacob's Ladder," that symbolized spiritual ascent. Further important developments occurred with a later generation of Iberian Jews. Abraham ben Samuel Abulafia (1240–1292) of Sarragossa wrote prolifically of the need to achieve spiritual freedom, liberating the soul through a combined discipline of contemplation, reflection on mystical meanings of Hebrew letters, and the cultivation of what was in effect a kind of Jewish "yoga." According to tradition, Abulafia's contemporary Moses ben Shem Tov of Leon (1240–1305) composed perhaps the single most influential mystical text, the *Zohar* (Book of Splendor). Based on a theory of emanation, the *Zohar* teaches that the divine presence becomes manifest in the material world through a series of ten *sefirot* or spheres that symbolize the increasingly tangible presence of divine energy (the *shekhinah*). As a movement, Jewish mysticism generally goes by the name *Kabbalah* ("reception"). It was revived in the sixteenth century in Israel by Solomon Alkabez (1505–84) and Isaac Luria (1534–73).

What is a **Golem**?

A Golem is a creature of legend and folklore that is also mentioned in the Talmud and in the Kabbalistic text called *Sefer Yetzirah* (Book of Creation). According to tradition, a specialist in the use of sacred words with magical power can cause a figure of clay to come to life by inscribing on its forehead the Hebrew word for "truth," *emeth*. Stories from Prague's Rabbi Judah Loew describe the Golem as a helpful house servant at first, but it must be kept under control and not allowed to leave the house. Since the

Golem gradually grows larger and more powerful, it can be a frightening and destructive creature, rather like a Frankenstein monster. To end a Golem's active life, one has to erase the letter *aleph,* the beginning of the word *emeth.* Without its initial *aleph,* "truth" becomes "dead," *meth.* Stories of the Golem were especially popular in the Jewish ghettos of central and eastern Europe. One especially grim tale relates how one Golem's owner reached up to erase the letter *aleph* and immobilize the creature. He succeeded, but died when the small mountain of clay fell on top of him. A few years ago an episode of the television show "The X Files" was based on the lore of the Golem and told of a deceased Jew who returned from the grave in order to avenge a social injustice associated with his family.

Do Jews believe in **angels**? What about the **devil**?

A number of important biblical narratives seem to describe encounters between divine emissaries or messengers and major religious figures. Three "visitors" tell Abraham that he and his barren wife will have a son in their old age (Genesis 18:1–15). Jacob dreams of a ladder to heaven on which "messengers" ascend and descend (Genesis 28:10–22) and later wrestles with a mysterious "man" (Genesis 32:22–32). Tradition has often interpreted these and dozens of other texts in the Hebrew Bible as referring to angels. The texts are often quite ambiguous and do not describe the mysterious actors as winged beings of light or in ways that many people today would recognize as characteristic of angels. These figures are generally understood as messengers from God, and only much later did they acquire the features now commonly associated with angels. Demonic or diabolical presences also appear in the Hebrew scriptures. Tradition has sometimes identified the wily serpent in Genesis as Satan or the Devil, but not until the very latest books of the Bible, such as Job and Zechariah, do we find malevolent forces specifically called Satan. Post-biblical Jewish tradition often identifies Satan with the angel of death or with the innate human inclination to evil.

What is a *Dibbuk*?

Kabbalistic thought included a feature quite foreign to Jewish tradition generally, namely, belief in reincarnation *(gilgul).* The idea developed during the Middle Ages as a proof of God's perfect mercy. Even a seriously sinful person who died unrepentant might have another chance to make things right. Since the idea did not fit neatly with the concept of a permanent afterlife of punishment in Gehenna, the Kabbalists gradually modified the idea of transmigration of souls into that of a generalized cosmic flux. Some of the greatest people who died in sin, such as Adam and Eve or Cain and Abel, were said to have returned in a later age, in these cases as David and Bathsheba or Moses and Jethro, with a second chance to make good. Eventually the term *dibbuk* ("adhesion"), at first a common term for "devil," came to refer to the homeless souls of the unforgiven who roamed the cosmos in search of people to possess.

113

How important are **dreams** and **visions** in Jewish communication with the spiritual realm?

Numerous intriguing biblical accounts tell of a major religious figure encountering spiritual beings or receiving messages beyond the ordinary. Two of the most important and well-known are from the Book of Genesis. Jacob wrestled with an "angel," after which Jacob received the name Israel (said there to mean "He who has striven with God)." Joseph dreamed that the stars, sun, and moon paid him homage; eventually he realized that the heavenly lights symbolized his family members, who would come to acknowledge his position of authority in Egypt. In Exodus, Moses encountered God at the Burning Bush and as a result accepted his commission to confront Pharaoh on behalf of the Israelites. Several other major biblical figures among the Patriarchs and during the time of the Judges and early Monarchy experienced dreams or visions. The great writing prophets often describe in auditory terms their reception of the message they are to speak—"Thus says the Lord...." But some of them also record impressive visual experiences. Isaiah characterizes many of his revelations as visionary, as does Jeremiah, though less frequently. Ezekiel in particular uses strikingly vivid images of visionary experience, from the "four living creatures" to the "valley of the dry bones" to the highly detailed vision of the heavenly temple and the new Israel (chapters 1, 37, and 40–48).

HOLIDAYS AND
REGULAR OBSERVANCES

What kind of **religious calendar** do Jews observe?

The Jewish liturgical calendar combines elements of both lunar and solar reckoning. Lunar months are 29 or 30 days long, and the first month of the year is that in which the Exodus began. But tradition dictates that certain feasts must occur during certain seasons, so the calendar has to be adjusted every so often to prevent the lunar months from straying too far from the agricultural, or solar, cycle. To make it work, an extra month, called *Adar sheni* (second Adar), is added during seven out of every nineteen years. The Jewish lunar months are called Tishri (September/October), Cheshvan (October/November), Kislev (November/December), Tevet (December/January), Shevat (January/February), Adar (February/March), Adar Sheni (Second Adar, inserted only in "leap years"), Nisan (March/April), Iyyar (April/May), Sivan (May/June), Tammuz (June/July), Av (July/August), and Elul (August/September). With the leap year provision, the lunar months slide back or forward but remain within the solar months indicated in parentheses.

What are the **High Holy Days**?

The autumnal holy days begin with *Rosh Hashanah* ("Beginning of the Year") on the first and second days of Tishri, ushered in with the sound of the ram's horn (*shofar*) as a symbol of divine sovereignty over the universe. This begins a period in which people make an accounting of how they have cared for creation entrusted to them. On the third day of Tishri comes the "Fast of Gedaliah" (*Tsom Gedalyah*), on which Jews recall the end of the first Jewish commonwealth (II Kings 25:25). But the culmination of the period occurs on the tenth day of Tishri in a major fast observing the Day of Atonement (*Yom Kippur*). This day features five worship services and includes a communal confession. On the evening before, a cantor prays the very moving *Kol nidrei* ("All the vows") which annuls all rashly made promises of the previous year. Emphasis is on forgiveness of all wrongdoing. Regular morning prayer begins the next day, followed by additional prayers later in the morning focused specially on this feast. Afternoon prayer is followed by a service that recalls the closing of the Temple gate in olden days and includes the *Amidah,* a litany called "Our Father, our King," the *Shema,* and a concluding sound of the ram's horn. The five services virtually flow from one to the next, making for a very full day of prayer.

How and when do Jews celebrate **Passover** (*Pesach*)?

Celebrated Nisan 15–22 (a day longer outside of Israel), Passover (*Pesach*) is a spring festival commemorating God's deliverance of Israel from Egypt. The rebirth of nature recalls the birth of Israel as a people. Specifically its imagery derives from the belief that God instructed the Israelites to mark their doorposts with the blood of the sacrificial lamb. When God sent an angel to strike dead the firstborn of all the Egyptians, the angel would "pass over" the houses of the Israelites. The biblical account appears in

Exodus 11–12. During the observance of the Passover *Seder* ("order of service") participants recount the story in the *Haggadah shel Pesach.* Celebrating with unleavened bread and wine, participants begin by blessing the the wine and washing their hands. They then dip a vegetable into salt water and eat it, recalling the Red Sea. They then break the second of three pieces of bread (*mazzah*) and hide it for the children to search out later, in recollection of hunger and divine manna in the desert. After recounting the story of the Exodus, they drink a second cup of wine and wash their hands again. Blessing the bread, they eat the first piece and what remains of the second piece. They eat some bitter herbs, recalling the suffering of the slaves in Egypt, then dip some herbs into *charoset,* a paste of spices, wine, *mazzah,* and fruit, symbolizing the mortar the former slaves made for Pharaoh. The main meal is followed by eating the hidden part of the second *mazzah,* and by a final blessing and a third cup of wine. The celebration closes with a psalm of praise and another cup of wine.

What are the other great feasts of **pilgrimage** and **remembrance**?

The feast of *Shavuot* ("Weeks") begins seven weeks after Passover. Originally coinciding with the wheat harvest, the Feast of Weeks recalls Israel's spiritual harvest of the divine Law at Sinai. The feast occurs on Sivan 6 the (a day longer outside Israel), the fiftieth day (*pentecost* in Greek) after Passover, marking the end of the "days of the *omer*" ("sheaf") in reference to the ancient practice of bringing the first sheaves of barley as Temple offering. The third of the great holidays is *Sukkot,* the Feast of Booths, or Tabernacles. Five days after the Day of Atonement, from Tishri 15–23 (a day longer outside Israel except in Reform congregations) Jews celebrate this harvest festival marking the end of the vintage season. Many families construct small symbolic structures in the back yard, recalling as they take their meals there how God sheltered the people through the wilderness of the Exodus. Along with Passover and Weeks, this was a pilgrimage feast before the destruction of the Temple, when many traveled to Jerusalem to celebrate. Families bless four plants as symbols of unity in diversity. Holding in the left hand a citrus called the *ethrog,* and in the right a bound cluster of one palm, two willow, and three myrtle branches (together called the *lulav*), they make gestures of blessing and sing "Hosanna," "Save us."

What are **Hanukkah** and **Purim**?

An observance perhaps best known to non-Jews is the late autumn Feast of Dedication called Hanukkah, which begins on Kislev 25 and continues for eight days. The nine-branch candlestick recalls how, during the Maccabean revolt against the Seleucid profanation of the Temple, a one day supply of oil miraculously lasted all eight days of the rededication of the holy place. Each evening families light an additional candle from the central flame, sing devotional songs, and exchange small presents. Another remembrance of a similar Jewish victory against great odds is the feast of *Purim.* A

Sacred and Notable Days of the Jewish Religious Year

Tishri (September–October)
1, 2	Rosh Hashana (New Year)
3	Tzom Gedaliahu (Fast of Gedaliah)
10	Yom Kippur (Day of Atonement)
15–21	Sukkot (Tabernacles)
22	Shemini Atzeret (Eighth Day of the Solemn Assembly)
23	Simhat Torah (Rejoicing of the Law)

Cheshvan, or Marcheshvan (October–November)

Kislev (November–December)
25	Hanukkah (Feast of Dedication) begins

Tevet (December–January)
2–3	Hanukkah ends
10	Asara be-Tevet (Fast of Tevet)

Shevat (January–February)
15	Tu bi-Shevat (Fifteenth of Shevat: New Year for Trees)

Adar (February–March)
13	Ta'anit Esther (Fast of Esther)
14, 15	Purim (Feast of Lots)

Nisan (March–April)
15–22	Pesah (Passover)

Iyyar (April–May)
18	Lag ba-Omer (33d Day of the Omer Counting)

Sivan (May–June)
6, 7	Shavuot (Feast of Weeks, or Pentecost)

Tammuz (June–July)
17	Shiva' 'Asar be-Tammuz (Fast of Tammuz)

Av (July–August)
9	Tisha be-Av (Fast of Av)

Elul (August–September)

Additionally, many Jewish calendars now list Iyyar 5—Israel Independence Day—among the Jewish holidays.

Western Wall of the Jewish Temple, popularly known as the "Wailing Wall" because of its association with annual lamentation on the Ninth of Av over the destruction of the Temple. The lower courses of masonry are from Herod's time, identifiable as Herodian by the trimmed outer margin of each stone.

month before Passover, after a day-long preparatory fast, the feast of "lots" on the 14th of Adar commemorates how the evil Persian Haman tried to wipe Israel out by casting lots. The Book of Esther (one of the five *Megillot*) tells the story of one of Judaism's most redoubtable heroines. The day before Purim recalls the Fast of Esther (*Ta'anit Ester*), and the day after, called *Shushan Purim,* observes the memory of how Esther's deeds gave cause for joy among the Jews of Shushan. Purim has an almost carnival atmosphere, complete with costumes and the giving of gifts.

Are any other **regular observances** significant in the Jewish ritual year?

Three days of fasting and mourning, two in summer and one in winter, are connected to remembrance of the First and Second Temples. Tesha b'Av (the Ninth of Av) is a day of lamentation for the destruction of Solomon's Temple in 586 BCE. Israeli Jews and pilgrims gather at the Western Wall of the Herodian Temple to grieve over the loss. The short biblical book called Lamentations is a traditional reading for the occasion. Associated rituals have given the remains of the Temple the popular name the "Wailing Wall." Eight days after Hanukkah, on the 10th of Tevet, another fast commemorates the Babylonian king Nebuchadnezzar's initial siege of Jerusalem in 587 BCE. In more recent times the occasion has become associated with mourning for victims of the Holocaust. On the 17th of Tammuz, a less popular occasion, some Jews fast to recall the times when the armies of Nebuchadnezzar and Titus first broke through the walls of the Temple in 587/6 BCE and 70 CE, respectively. Finally, there are two other minor observances. One is the 15th of Shevat, the New Year for Trees (*Rosh ha-Shanah le-Ilanot*), a day of thanks to God for the bounty of the earth. The other is called *Simchat Torah* ("Rejoicing in the Torah"). The day after the Feast of Booths, Jews celebrate the end of the annual cycle of liturgical readings with processions in which the scrolls are carried around the synagogue with children leading the crowd.

CUSTOMS AND RITUALS

What kinds of **rituals** do Jews engage in privately or alone?

Home remains the principal place for Jewish prayer and religious observance. Traditional prayer includes the thrice-daily *Amidah* ("standing") prayer in morning, afternoon, and evening. The morning and evening prayers begin with benedictions that praise God's love of Israel as manifested in the creation of light and in the ordering of day and night. The *Shema* follows, acknowledging the one God's redemption of the people. At the center of all three prayers is the *Shimoneh esreh,* or "Eighteen" blessings. Prayer ends with the *Aleinu,* "Upon us praise is encumbent...." Afternoon prayer usually adds Psalm 145. According to the Talmud, all Jews should pray a hundred benedictions (*berakhot*) every day, in recognition of all things enjoyable, to give thanks, and prior to all other religious duties, in addition to the blessings that are part of daily prayers.

How do Jews conduct their regular **communal liturgical worship**?

A feature of ritual practice common to all Jewish congregations is the reading of scripture. Ancient Palestinian custom used a cycle in which Sabbath readings completed the whole Torah in a three-year cycle. Some Reform and Conservative communities have reinstituted that practice in recent times. Orthodox and Reconstructionist congregations continue to use the ancient Babylonian custom of a one-year cycle of fifty-four *sedarim.* On Mondays, Thursdays, and Sabbath mornings and afternoons, as well as on new moons and special religious festivals, Jews read Torah in the synagogue. Regular Sabbath readings follow the Torah in order, continuously, from Genesis through Deuteronomy. Readings for the various feasts and fasts are chosen specially for the occasion and do not follow a continuous cycle. In addition, texts from the Former and Latter Prophets (but not from the Writings) are selected as a kind of parallel or commentary on the day's Torah texts. These supplementary readings, used on Sab-

119

baths, fasts, and feasts, are called *Haftarah*. Some theorize that the practice of parallel readings originated during Seleucid times when persecution included a ban on Torah reading. Communal prayer adds to the regular prayers of the privately performed *Amidah* the *Kedushah* (triple "Holy") at the end of the third benediction in morning and afternoon, as well as the *Kaddish* ("Holy" in Aramaic) to mark the end of the various segments of the communal prayer and to bring it to a close. The standard prayerbook for synagogue worship is called the *Siddur* ("order"), which is based on the Psalter. The first formal edition dates back to about the ninth century CE.

Do Jews practice **rituals of divination**?

In biblical times one of the roles of the Temple's high priest was to serve as a medium for oracles. Part of the priestly paraphernalia was a mysterious pair of objects called the Urim and Thummim, which were a form of lot carried in a pocket called the "breastplate" and suspended from the shoulders. The Urim and Thummim, a pair of flat stones, are mentioned a number of times in the Hebrew Bible, suggesting that this form of divination was of some importance, even though others were explicitly forbidden. Thummim may derive from a word that meant "perfect," hence of positive value. Scholars surmise that Urim probably carried a negative meaning. They may thus have been read as "yes" or "no," "guilty" or "innocent," for example, in determining the answer to a question. Even the word "Torah" apparently comes from a root that means to "cast lots" in order to obtain an oracle. The High Priest would toss the Urim and Thummim, one meaning "yes" and the other "no," in order to determine God's will in a given instance. King Saul was so chosen to rule Israel, as were priests in outlying areas selected to work in the Temple. Divination has found no significant place in post-biblical Jewish tradition.

Has **pilgrimage** ever figured prominently in Jewish practice?

In biblical times Jewish males were expected to make pilgrimages to Jerusalem for three occasions, the feasts of Passover, Booths, and Weeks. Special ritual requirements attended each of the three pilgrimage feasts. But since all were tied to the existence of the Temple, pilgrimage as a specific religious duty lapsed during the Exile and again when the Second Temple was destroyed in 70 CE. Throughout post-biblical Jewish history, Jews in the diaspora have continued to pray about Jerusalem and have longed to return to it. Since the Six Day War of 1967, many have realized the dream of one day visiting the site of the Temple and praying at the Western Wall. Strictly speaking, modern-day Jewish pilgrims are not fulfilling a biblical injunction, since the Temple remains only a memory. But pilgrimage has in effect assumed a new form for many Jews. For most it is a journey of remembrance of a former dispensation and a chance to connect with deep roots. Some journey in the hope that they may live to see the glory of the Temple and its associated ritual practices restored.

What is the significance of **"keeping kosher"**?

Kashrut is the Hebrew term for the use of "ritually pure" (*kasher*) food. It refers to the way food is prepared as well as to certain types of food. With respect to manner of preparation, the opposite of *kasher* is *terefah,* "torn" by a predator, rather than properly butchered. The basic principle here is that an animal's death by predator constitutes a defect in the animal product. Proper butchering (called *shehitah*) involves using only perfectly smooth blades to slit the animal's throat and windpipe, draining the blood, and inspecting for blemishes. With respect to types of food, Jews make a number of major distinctions between what is clean and what is unclean. Clean animals include cattle, sheep, and other ruminants with fully cloven hooves (but not non-ruminant mammals or those with solid or only partly cloven hooves, such as dogs or horses). Clean birds include pigeons, doves, chickens, pheasant, and domestically raised geese and ducks (but not birds of prey, wild water fowl, or most other common wild birds). All reptiles and amphibians are unclean, but fish with scales and internal bones (as opposed to cartilage, as with shark) are acceptable. In addition, expanding on the biblical prohibition of "cooking a kid in its mother's milk" (Exodus 34:26), dairy and meat products may not be combined in any way. Strict observers of *kashrut* keep separate sets of kitchen tools—some even totally separate kitchens—for meats and dairy products. Kosher practice is an excellent example of the distinction between custom and ritual. Observance of dietary laws often involves, or presupposes, precise ritual action, such as in the *kosher* method of slaughtering an animal or the care taken not to contaminate utensils. But in general it means simply a customary way of handling food that has religious implications.

What are the principal Jewish **rites of passage**?

Circumcision, giving a name, and redemption of the first-born son are important early rites. To welcome older youngsters into full membership in the community, the most prominent rites are puberty or coming-of-age rituals. At that time a young boy becomes a "Son of the Commandment" (*bar mitzvah*). In a similar ritual a young girl becomes a "Daughter of the Commandment" (*bat mitzvah*), except in the Orthodox tradition. "Confirmation" still often acknowledges an older teenager's full maturity. Marriage rites continue to be important traditional practices, as do specific rites of departure from this life.

How do Jews celebrate **birth**?

When God made a covenant with Abraham (Genesis 17), the removal of the foreskin of the penis was to be the sign of its ratification. Circumcision of baby boys generally occurs on the eighth day, performed by a specialist called a *mohel,* who is often a rabbi, in the baby's home. After the surgical procedure and accompanying prayers are completed, participants bless a cup of wine. Parents then declare the child's name.

Synagogue of Capernaum, Galilee, northern Israel, c. 200 CE, showing Hellenistic influence in its columns and plan.

Reform communities now have a parallel home ritual to welcome baby girls, including all but the surgery. Other congregations still generally perform the naming ritual for girls in the synagogue. Some still give children two names, one religious, in Hebrew or Yiddish, and one secular. In addition to these early rituals, a ritual of "redemption" of a first-born son also occurs on the thirty-first day of his life. The practice arose from the biblical teaching that each first-born son belongs to God but can be "bought back" (Numbers 18:15–16). In general the ritual is tied to the residual importance of the hereditary priesthood, for it requires a *kohen,* or descendant of the biblical priesthood, to perform it.

What happens at a **Jewish initiation (bar/bat mitzvah) ceremony**?

Jewish boys of thirteen and girls of twelve are formally recognized as religiously mature. They become sons and daughters of the commandment (*bar* or *bat mitzvah*) in rituals that acknowledge that they are now responsible for fulfilling the prescriptions of the divine Law. Most communities, other than the Orthodox, celebrate this coming-of-age for both genders publicly in the synagogue. A central feature of the ritual involves the initiate's reading from the Torah scroll in Hebrew. Other features can extend to a much broader participation in the service, including carrying the scroll to the reading table and reciting other prayers. In some communities, a joint confirmation ceremony for sixteen- or seventeen-year-old boys and girls occurs in conjunction with the Feast of Weeks, since that observance commemorates the original reception

Ritual Details of Circumcision

Circumcision—the removal of the foreskin of the penis—is performed on all male Jewish children on the eighth day after their birth. It is also performed on male converts to Judaism. The operation is called for in Genesis 17 and is considered the strongest required sign of adherence to Judaism. It is also a powerful symbol of the Covenant of Abraham. As implied by the Talmudic tractate Nedarim 31b, circumcision was originally performed because the foreskin was considered to be a blemish. To attain a state of perfection, the foreskin had to be removed. During ancient times, some Hellenistic Jews—especially those whose loins would be exposed in the course of athletics or public bathing—had an operation performed to conceal their circumcisions. Later, in order to prevent Jewish men from hiding their circumcisions, rabbis added the requirement that the entire foreskin—not just the end portion—be excised completely. This is known as *peri'ah*, the laying bare of the glans. An additional requirement was added at a later period directing that the circumciser apply his lips to the penis in order to draw the blood that flowed from the incision. For hygienic reasons, this practice was modified to allow the blood to be drawn by an absorbent material like cotton. For a baby boy, the circumcision must take place on the eighth day after birth, unless medical reasons prevent it. Only one exception is allowed to the universal requirement that Jewish infant boys be circumcised. If two previous sons have died as a result of the operation, thereby implying hereditary hemophilia, the third and all subsequent sons are exempted from circumcision. The day of circumcision for an infant boy is considered a time of celebration for the entire community. Customarily, the father of the boy hands his son to the circumciser, who recites appropriate prayers and typically invokes Elijah. The ceremony is often followed by a religious meal of celebration.

of the Torah at Sinai. Confirmation replaced the puberty rite in some European communities. Now some Reform, Conservative, and Reconstructionist congregations practice both confirmation and *bar/bat mitzvah*.

Is there a Jewish ritual of **marriage**?

Many readers will be familiar with the Jewish custom of having the groom, standing with the bride under a canopy (the *huppah*), shatter a wine glass with his foot at the conclusion of wedding ceremonies. The symbolic act is meant to help people keep in mind the seriousness of marriage, and perhaps even to recall the destruction of the Temple. The whole ceremony is called *kiddushin,* the sanctification. Taking place in almost any kind of public space, including a synagogue, it begins with a procession.

The ritual is largely up to the couple and their families, along with the rabbi presiding, and is not dictated by traditional text or established rubrics. A reception typically follows, often with a blessing before and after the meal.

How do Jews deal ritually with **death**?

Most Jews do not observe the custom of the wake, either at the mortuary or in the private home, since embalming is not customary. Cremation is not ordinarily done. Family members prepare the body and burial ideally occurs within a day of death. Sitting Shivah refers to a seven (*shivah*) day period of mourning for a family member. Friends and relatives visit the home of the deceased to extend their sympathy and pray with the family. Every period of seven days naturally includes a Sabbath, but on that day mourners refrain from manifesting their grief outwardly. Among Ashkenazic Jews in some countries, groups called *Hevra Kaddisha* ("holy brotherhood") may be available to provide burial services for the needy. The custom of observing the anniversary or *Yahrzeit* of a relative's death involves visiting the grave and reciting the mourners' *Kaddish,* a prayer in praise of the Holy One whose dominion is everlasting.

CHRISTIANITY

HISTORY AND SOURCES

When and where did **Christianity** begin?

People who professed themselves to be followers of Jesus were first called "Christianoi" in the Syrian town of Antioch perhaps twenty or thirty years after the death of Jesus of Nazareth. But as with other traditions, it is difficult, if not impossible, to assign a precise date to the origins of Christianity. Reasonably sound historical information, however, supports a number of general conclusions about the matter. Most of the earliest followers of Jesus were Jews who believed that this man from Galilee, a northern sector of the Roman province known as Palestine and administered by the Herodian dynasty of Jewish kings, fulfilled enough of the traditional criteria to be proclaimed Messiah or, to use the Greek equivalent, "Christ." Jesus seems to have formed a core community of supporters among Galileans and other Jews who, according to the Greek or New Testament, accepted his invitation to follow him on his itinerant mission to preach the coming of the Kingdom of God. During his lifetime, Jesus apparently sent out his seventy disciples, among whom were the twelve Apostles, to announce the Kingdom, to heal the sick, and to forgive sins. Jesus' death around 30 CE was a severe blow to his followers' sense of identity. But, reinvigorated by their belief that Jesus had risen from the dead, they regrouped and organized themselves as a missionary movement, some preaching to Jews and some to Gentiles (all non-Jews). They fanned out over much of the eastern Mediterranean basin, and within a generation after Jesus' death, numerous small religious communities had begun to call themselves Christians. At first the Christians met in "house churches" under the local leadership of elders or "presbyters," later to be called priests. Deacons and deaconesses served special needs of the local community, and the communities in a given region looked to the leadership of "overseers" (from the Greek *episkopoi*) or "bishops."

Did Jesus "found" Christianity as a **distinct religious tradition**?

Jesus and the Buddha had this in common: they were both primarily teachers who offered what were judged to be non-traditional interpretations of already ancient traditions. Neither seems to have set out deliberately to "found" a new religious community, though they both gathered about themselves the nucleus of what would eventually become distinct institutional structures. As such, Jesus and the Buddha were foundational figures rather than founders. Leaders among their immediate communities inherited the task of working out the organizational details. A number of able leaders emerged from the early followers of Jesus. They included in particular Peter, one of the original twelve Apostles, and Paul, a Pharisee from Asia Minor who had experienced a dramatic change of religious orientation. They and other members of the first generation followers of Jesus disagreed about precisely what traditional Jewish practices they should retain and how they should set about establishing their own distinct religious identity: Should Christians keep the Mosaic Law? How much of it? Did that include circumcision? Should they continue to go to the Temple in sage of Jesus to all people. The story adds that he was blinded and forced to fast for three days until a Christian named Ananias laid hands on him and restored his sight, after which he was baptized. The usual date assigned to this event is between 34 and 36 CE.

During the next 15 years Paul undertook three extensive journeys in the eastern Mediterranean region, preaching to the Gentiles particularly. Between the beginning of these missionary journeys and his marytrdom in Rome in 66 or 67 CE, he wrote a number of letters that became part of the Christian New Testament. Paul's teaching rested on three main principles: Jesus is the Son of God and the Messiah foretold by the prophets of Israel; by his death, Jesus atoned for the sins of all and opened heaven for humanity; the Mosaic law had, by the fact of Jesus' death and resurrection, been abrogated and replaced by the Law of Jesus. There was, therefore, no longer any distinction between Jew and Gentile. Paul frequently used texts from the Old Testament to argue his points, interpreting them according to the rabbinic method of exegesis that he had learned in Jerusalem.

As the first systematic theologian and writer of the Christian faith, Paul wielded great influence on such medieval theologians as St. Albertus Magnus, St. Anselm and St. Thomas Aquinas. Paul's writings also provided the sixteenth-century reformers with their basic ideas. These religious thinkers preferred to return to Paul's text rather than to adhere to the metaphysical speculations that had developed in Christianity throughout 1,500 years.

Jerusalem? Leaders convened a council or conference in Jerusalem around the year 48 CE to work out the most vexing of these problems (Acts of the Apostles 15). A group of Pharisees among them insisted on imposing Jewish Law and custom intact, but the majority opted to retain only basic dietary, ritual, and ethical constraints. A majority resolved to preach the Gospel to non-Jews, arguing that the Hebrew scriptures enjoin such universality. The "founding" of Christianity was far less the result of a clear one-time decision than the gradual evolution of a set of views and practices that the leaders representing the various local communities judged consistent with their emerging identity.

What are the **earliest Christian sacred writings**?

Two broad types of literature comprise the bulk of the Christian scripture. Among the earliest documents are the letters of Paul. Tradition attributes fourteen of the New Testament's twenty-seven "books" or epistles to Paul, but it seems likely that several were penned under a pseudonym. The largest and most important of the texts are addressed to local Christian communities collectively (Romans, I and II Corinthians, Galatians, Ephesians, Colossians, I and II Thessalonians). Four are addressed to individual Christian leaders with whom Paul worked (I and II Timothy, Titus, Philemon). The addressees of the Letter to the Hebrews, almost certainly not written by Paul, are curiously diffuse and not geographically identifiable as are the local churches. These epistles provide a great deal of information about the spread and organization of the early Church, and, to a lesser degree, about the personality of this man of prodigious energy called Paul, a man some regard as the true "founder" of Christianity. Seven other letters, two attributed to Peter, three to John, one to James, and one to Jude, afford small glimpses into the variety of theological and practical issues facing the Christian "diaspora," the communities developing beyond the central Middle East. At the heart of the Christian scriptures are four remarkable documents called "gospels" ("good news"). Mark's gospel, likely the earliest, is also the shortest of the four. Matthew's is addressed largely to those of Jewish background, and Luke's followed within the next twenty to thirty years. Luke's also has the distinction of being part of the only consciously crafted two-volume work in the New Testament, completed by Luke's account of the post-Jesus church in the Acts of the Apostles. Because of their similarity of perspective and emphases, the Gospels of Matthew, Mark, and Luke are called the "synoptic" Gospels. John's Gospel, often referred to as the most theological of the four, almost certainly came last, around the end of the first century CE. Last but not least is the Book of Revelation, also called the Apocalypse. Tradition attributes the work to John the Evangelist, since the work seems to date from around the same time as the fourth gospel.

How did the early Christians regard the **Jewish scriptures**?

From the very beginning, the emergence of Christianity as a distinct tradition depended on the young community's exegesis of the Hebrew scriptures. Since the majority of the earliest Christians were Jewish by birth and education, they naturally regarded the Hebrew Bible as their own and as authoritative divine revelation. But the tradition of messianic expectation that had evolved especially in the later writings evoked continual scrutiny and re-examination among Jews everywhere: When would the Messiah come? And how was one to identify Him? Largely on the basis of their reading of scripture, the early followers of Jesus found the answers in Jesus. By a process that would come to be known as "typological exegesis," early Christians saw in numerous Old Testament personages anticipations or "types" of Christ. Abraham, for example, was a type of God the Father in his willingness to sacrifice his only son, Isaac, who was in turn a type of Christ. Jonah, who emerged alive after three days in the belly of the whale, was a type of Christ's resurrection after three days in the grave. A variation on the theme of typology saw in Jesus the perfection of realities only adumbrated in the Hebrew scriptures. Aaron's priesthood, for example, was merely temporary (as evidenced by the destruction

Medieval Gothic style Cathedral of Notre Dame, Paris. The flying buttresses allow extensive wall space for stained glass, and the huge mandala-like "rose window" over the south transept is rich with Biblical symbolism.

of the Temple), but that of Christ was eternal (Hebrews 7). In addition to discerning these and other typological antecedents of Christ, interpreters saw in many prophetic writings veiled allusions to the Christ who was to come. In the so-called "suffering servant" texts of Second Isaiah, for example, early Christians detected such striking parallels to what they believed were the very essence of the life and death of Jesus that the prophet could only have been referring to this Messiah. In the Greek Testament, Jesus suggests a parallel between the works he now performs and Isaiah's references to a Spirit-filled anointed one who preaches good news to the poor, frees the imprisoned, and heals the blind, and likens himself to Elijah and Elisha (Luke 4:16–30). These are only a few of the ways in which early Christians found legitimation for their views in Jewish tradition.

How do the **Christian scriptures describe Jesus**?

Weaving together historical fact, interpretation of pre-Christian sources, and an emerging understanding of the circumstances in which the earliest Christians found themselves, the Gospels provide insights of various kinds into the life and identity of Jesus. The four Gospels are not historical biography in the modern sense of that term. Behind each of the Gospels is a particular theological view about who Jesus is. A concrete example will make this clear. Matthew and Luke both include genealogies of Jesus. Not only are the figures mentioned not identical, but the two authors approach

129

the matter quite differently. Matthew opens his Gospel with the genealogy, tracing Jesus from Abraham forward through David and the Babylonian Exile, emphasizing his Jewish lineage and explicitly calling him "the Christ," the Messiah (Matthew 1:1–17). Luke inserts his genealogy just after John baptizes Jesus, a scene that ends with the voice of God declaring Jesus his "beloved son." Luke then traces the line backwards through history all the way to Adam, "the son of God" (Luke 3:23–38), emphasizing the universality of Jesus in our shared humanity.

Taken together the Gospels give this general picture. Jesus was born in Bethlehem and raised in Galilee by devout Jewish parents. He was well educated—he quotes scripture liberally and reads in the synagogue—and his belief in immortality of the soul and resurrection of the body suggests that he had more in common theologically with the Pharisees than one might at first suspect. After perhaps thirty years of relative anonymity, Jesus' "public life" began with his baptism in the Jordan. After his initial desert experience, recalling the Exodus, he worked in Galilee, gathered followers, and turned toward Jerusalem for Passover (John says little about the Galilean period and has Jesus attending three Passovers in Jerusalem). After cleansing the Temple, Jesus gathers the Twelve for the "Last Supper," after which he is arrested, tried, executed, and rises from the dead. Luke's Acts of the Apostles picks up at that point and describes the post-resurrection appearances and Jesus' ascension into heaven forty days later.

How do Christians **interpret the scriptures** they consider uniquely theirs?

Christians believe the sacred texts collectively called the New Testament are divinely inspired, but composed by the human authors to whom tradition attributes them. Some take that a step further, insisting that divine inspiration consisted of a literal transmission from God through the author who communicated the message unaltered. As the previous question suggests, early Christian exegesis of the Hebrew scriptures had already moved beyond merely literal interpretation. Though the literal meaning of the sacred text naturally remained the bedrock of exegesis, typological understandings of Jewish tradition soon developed into more specific varieties of figurative exegesis to be applied to the Greek as well as the Hebrew scriptures. Within a few generations of the death of the last people who actually lived during the time of Jesus, Christian literature gives evidence of what would eventually develop into the "four senses" of scripture. These four are the literal sense (*historia*); the symbolic or figurative meaning (*allegoria*); the moral or ethical implication (*tropologia*); and the eschatological parallels—that is, what the text suggests about the goal of human life (*anagogia*). A simple but useful rhyme helps keep the four levels of meaning straight: what our forebears did (history), where our faith is hid (allegory), rules for daily life (tropology), where we end our strife (anagogy). A good example of how major early Christian interpreters applied the four senses might be the four rivers of Paradise mentioned in Genesis 2:10–14. Their literal meaning is simply that of historical identity—the Pishon, Gihon, Tigris, and Euphrates rivers. On the figurative level, the rivers might symbolize the four Gospels, the divine revelation fanning out to all the world's four directions. In addition, one might understand these four streams as the four cardinal virtues, prudence, justice, fortitude and temperance. And finally, the earthly rivers have their heavenly counterparts in the Paradise awaiting true believers.

Why do Christians call their scriptures the **New Testament**?

Everything hinges on the ancient theological meaning of "testament." Most readers are familiar with the common expression "last will and testament" as a legal description of an individual's final disposition of whatever earthly goods remain at his or her death. In this context, testament means "covenant," a unique relationship between God and believers described in various ways by Jewish, Christian, and Muslim sources. For Jews, a universal covenant relationship of divine protection, promise, and fulfillment began with Noah, then was further specified to include Jews as the uniquely chosen people. Terms of the relationship were made still more specific in the revelation of the Law to Moses at Sinai. For Christians, the terms of the Jewish covenant with God have been superseded, or perhaps even abrogated, by a radically new divine-human relationship embodied in Jesus Christ. No longer bound by the ancient Law, Christian tradition teaches that a balance of grace and actions bind believers to God in Christ. Hence the name "New Testament."

What does the term **historical-critical method** mean?

When Christians study their scriptures they can take any of a number of approaches, as already suggested. A common pastoral approach nowadays reads the scriptures almost entirely as if they are addressed to twentieth-century Christians and are thus in a way "timeless" and not subject to historical conditions. Another approach tries to get behind the words as much as possible to understand their meaning in their original context. This second approach by no means disregards the personal, pastoral, and deeply spiritual implications of the sacred text. But it begins with the assumption that one cannot know those deeper meanings without first understanding how and why the inspired authors wrote as they did. Historical-critical scholarship looks, for example, at the differences in how even texts as generally concordant as the synoptic Gospels show divergences in vocabulary, major themes, order of events in the life of Jesus, and points of view tailored to different audiences. It notes how the inspired authors, as much editors as original writers, interwove Jesus' words and actions, telescoping time and space. As skilled literary communicators, the inspired writers also made use of stylized scenes that followed predictable patterns in their description of the main actors, actions, and crowd responses. Combining analyses of the literary, linguistic, and historical elements, the historical-critical method seeks insight into how these documents, two millennia and many layers of culture removed from us, appear to speak in so many distinct voices about the same great spiritual reality. Underlying it

131

Saint Mark's Square, Venice, showing the 300-foot bell tower and several of the church's domes beyond the Doge's Palace on the right.

all, the method suggests, are the unique theological insights granted to each of the sacred authors. Each offers a characteristic reflection on the deeper meaning of the "good news" and of Jesus the Christ. For Mark, Jesus was most of all the Suffering Servant; for Matthew, the Messiah; for Luke, the Savior whose ongoing presence is the Holy Spirit; and for John, the Divine Son. These are not exclusive, but complementary insights. Unlike the predominantly spiritualized or pastoral method of interpretation, whose immediate concern is to deal with apparent inconsistencies among the sacred authors by "harmonizing" them into a seamless reconstruction, the historical-critical method seeks a unity of scriptural revelation through the uniqueness and diversity of the evidence.

What other **early texts** are especially important for Christians?

In addition to the twenty-seven books of the New Testament, early Christian authors produced a number of other important works. It is important to keep in mind that the formal Canon of the New Testament was not finalized until around 198 CE. Previous generations of Christians may well have been in general agreement about what constituted the core of their scripture, but until the late second century, some factions continued to claim the status of divine inspiration for a number of texts eventually judged to be apocryphal and thus not part of the Canon. Most prominent among those apocryphal writings are a sizeable group calling themselves Gospels. Some (such as the

Gospels of Thomas and Philip) were an attempt to support the views of tendentious or heretical factions, while others (such as Gospels of Nicodemus and of the Childhood of Jesus) purport to fill in the gaps of Canonical texts with legend and lore. Apocryphal works called "Acts" and identified with one or another of the Apostles generally, but not necessarily, reflect heretical views. Writings by a group of post-biblical authors known as the Apostolic Fathers, mostly of the late first or early to mid–second century, provide important information on the concerns and theological themes of bishops and their communities throughout the Mediterranean basin. A third significant corpus of writings dating from about 120 to 220 CE are those of authors known collectively as the Apologists. Major figures like Justin Martyr (c. 100–165 CE), who founded a Christian school in Rome, and Tertullian (c. 160–220 CE) of Carthage in present-day Tunisia and later

Medieval reliquaries in the shape of the body part they were designed to contain, arm and hand bones of holy persons.

Rome, wrote in defense of Christian views when outsiders mounted theoretical or political attacks against them.

Were **early Christians persecuted** by Rome? How long did that go on?

As Christianity became more clearly separated from its Jewish roots, Roman authorities all over the Mediterranean became more wary of Christianity's potential threat to Rome's authority. Many Christians refused to burn incense to the emperor and paid with their lives, but executions remained largely a matter of local jurisdiction until about the middle of the third century. Several Roman emperors, such as Nero and

Marcus Aurelius, were known for their personal antipathy to Christians. But it was Decius who in 250 CE issued the first general order requiring all in the realm to worship the gods of Rome. Thousands of Christians were executed and many more renounced the faith, at least publicly. Diocletian (284–305 CE) began his reign with greater tolerance, but toward the end sanctioned the razing of churches, the burning of scriptures, and wholesale executions. The reign of terror continued until 311 CE, when Emperor Galerius proclaimed a renewal of official toleration of Christians.

Why was the **Emperor Constantine** important in Christian history?

After learning the protocols of the Roman court by serving under Diocletian, Constantine (c. 274–337) consolidated his power in the eastern empire around 312 CE. Tradition says Constantine underwent a dramatic conversion to Christianity around that time. The following year he met with his western counterpart, Emperor Licinius, at Milan and the two concurred on a formula for what would become Christianity's political enfranchisement. In a dramatic about-face in the fortunes of its adherents all over the empire, Christianity now had power on its side. Thenceforth, whenever dissension within the ranks of Christians led to violence, the mainstream could enforce its views by appeal to the Emperor. Under Constantine, Sunday officially became a religious holiday for Christians. Constantine has the further considerable distinction of having convened the first of many "ecumenical councils," that of Nicea in 325. Though he was as yet unbaptized, the Emperor presided over the debates concerning a claim by Arius (c. 250–336 CE) that Jesus was a human creature, not eternal and divine. Bishop Athanasius (c. 296–373) made the case for the orthodox response to Arius' heretical views. Five years later, Constantine tightened his grip on the empire, established his capital at Byzantium, newly renamed Constantinople ("City of Constantine"), and went on to become known among Orthodox Christians as the "thirteenth apostle."

Who are the **Fathers of the Church** and why are they important?

Some of Christianity's most important religious and theological literature dates from the fourth to the eighth centuries CE. During the Patristic Age, or "late antiquity," dozens of influential authors from North Africa, through the central Middle East and Anatolia (now called Turkey), to Rome and westward even to Spain, wrote major works in Latin, Greek, and Syriac. Patristic literature includes virtually every type, from extensive biblical commentaries to sermons to theological treatises. Among the most important Latin Fathers are Augustine (354–430), Bishop of Hippo in North Africa and author of the monumental *City of God* and one of the best known spiritual autobiographies, *The Confessions*. Tradition credits Augustine with a monastic rule that has influenced religious orders such as the Dominicans and Servites, as well as Ursuline and Visitation nuns. Major Greek Fathers include the three Cappadocians, so called because they lived and worked in the province of Cappadocia in Asia Minor (now in east-central Turkey). More famous were Basil (c 330–379) and his brother Gregory of Nyssa (c. 330–395). Gregory of Nazianzus (329–389), like the other Gregory, was an outspoken bishop much involved in the theological controversies of the day. All three made critical contributions to the clarification of Christian doctrines about Christ and the Trinity. Less famous but very important in the early Christian history in the eastern Mediterranean are the Syriac Fathers. They wrote in a Semitic language related to the Aramaic commonly spoken in the time of Jesus. Ephrem of Syria (306–373) authored dozens of works, almost all in verse and including many hymns that are still sung in worship rituals.

Were there any **Mothers of the Church**?

There were many important "Church Mothers," women of great influence in the early Church. They have been less famous because they rarely wrote and published as did their male counterparts. Unfortunately, we know little of many of these women apart from often scanty or anonymous references in the writings of the Fathers and in early histories of Christianity. The historian Eusebius, for example, mentions some fifty-five women as making important contributions. Recent research has begun to give some of these outstanding women names and "faces." Some of the first well-known women were martyrs such as Blandina (d. 177) and Perpetua and Felicitas who died in 203. Along with the so-called Desert Fathers credited with the beginnings of monasticism were a number of Desert Mothers. Macrina (c. 327–379), sister of Basil and Gregory of Nyssa, was also a prominent churchwoman. We know from the testimony of other authors that she was a respected theologian.

What were the **Crusades** and why are they important?

Beginning in 1096 and continuing intermittently for the next two centuries, the Crusades were wars fought over possession of the "Holy Land" and its chief sacred place, Jerusalem. Muslims had been in control of Jerusalem since around 636, but the Christian powers of central and eastern Europe mobilized only after a Turkish force vanquished a Byzantine army in eastern Asia Minor in 1071. The Byzantine emperor sought help from the pope in Rome and the first Crusade began twenty-five years later. From the Christian perspective the first was the only genuinely successful Crusade, resulting in the establishment of the Latin Kingdom of Jerusalem. An ill-fated second Crusade was launched in 1147 in hopes of expanding Christian control. From 1099 till 1187, Crusaders held the holy city and surrounding regions. Then, under the famous hero Saladin, Muslim armies brought the Latin Kingdom down and reclaimed Jerusalem, and in the following year Christians organized the third Crusade. The English king Richard I "The Lionhearted" managed a truce with Saladin in 1192, securing little more than a token visit to the Church of the Holy Sepulcher. One of the truly grim episodes in Crusading history occurred during the fourth Crusade. Western

Christian troops overthrew the Byzantine emperor, vented their wrath on their Eastern Christian cousins, and never made it to the Middle East. Four more major Crusades and several minor ones followed during the thirteenth century. Only one was a qualified success, securing control over Jerusalem for fifteen years (1229–1244). Muslim authorities retained primary custody of the holy places for nearly the next seven centuries, finally yielding to the British mandate in the early 1900s. Christian sources often glorify the Crusades as examples of heroism, but in fact those who suffered most from their consequences were the Christian communities of the Middle East.

RELIGIOUS BELIEFS

Is there a **Christian creed**?

A number of New Testament texts suggest early forms of creedal statements. For example, the Letter to the Philippians 2:1–11 describes how Jesus "emptied himself" of all divine prerogatives, even to the point of becoming a slave and dying on the cross. The passage ends by saying that all should bend the knee at the name of Jesus and that "every tongue should confess that Jesus Christ is Lord, to the glory of the Father." The Gospel of Matthew 28:19 records Jesus sending his followers to baptize "In the name of the Father and of the Son and of the Holy Spirit," an early expression of the notion of the Holy Trinity. But the first important formal creedal statements did not gain wide currency until the early fourth century. An important outcome of the Council of Nicea, in 325, was the Nicene Creed. As has so often been the case in the history of religion, Christians first formulated a comprehensive statement of "orthodox" or "right" belief in response to serious challenges that threatened to distort ancient traditional beliefs. In other words, the Nicene Creed does not represent the first expression of these beliefs, but rather the first comprehensive clarification of points that had come under attack by factions now considered "heretical." Christians all over the world now recite in their liturgies a later and somewhat longer version of the Nicene statement, with sections devoted to the Father, Son, and Holy Spirit, and concluding with affirmations of belief in the church, baptism, forgiveness, and the resurrection of the dead in the next life. The liturgical formula does not include the "anathemas" or condemnations of unacceptable views contained in the Council's original document. Subsequent Church councils have published other creedal statements, but the only other creed in common use (outside of the Eastern Christian churches) is the briefer so-called "Apostles' Creed," earlier versions of which seem to have come into common use around the fourth century.

What does the term **revelation** mean in Christian tradition?

Christianity's central teaching on divine revelation is that God has become fully manifest in the Person of Jesus Christ through the Incarnation. Jesus himself is the eternal Word of God and Son, who took on human nature and lived among humankind. Tradition situates this humanly embodied revelation within the broader context of God's progressive and ongoing self-disclosure in a wide variety of ways. Most prominently, Christians believe God has revealed divine truths through the Hebrew and Greek Testaments, for both scriptures point to the Christ. Through the Holy Spirit Christians discern the continued revealing, clarifying presence of God in the days since Jesus departed this world.

Are **doctrine** and **dogma** important to Christians?

Clarity about the content of Christian beliefs has been a significant concern since at least the late first century CE. Within a few generations after the death of Jesus, Christians had begun to debate doctrinal issues that went beyond the questions of ritual and practice that had preoccupied the earliest Christians. Emphasis shifted from the traditional Judaic orthopraxy to the gradual articulation of an increasingly distinctive

The Nicene Creed

I believe in one God, the Father almighty, creator of heaven and earth, of all things visible and invisible.

And in one Lord Jesus Christ, Son of God, the only-begotten, born of the Father before all ages. Light of light, true God of true God, begotten, not made, of one substance with the Father through Whom all things were made. Who for us men and for our salvation, came down from heaven, and was incarnate of the Holy Spirit and Mary the Virgin, and became man. He was also crucified for us under Pontius Pilate, and suffered, and was buried. And He rose again on the third day according to the scriptures. And He ascended into heaven, and sits at the right hand of the Father. And He will come again with glory to judge the living and the dead, and of His kingdom there will be no end.

And in the Holy Spirit, the Lord and Giver of Life, who proceeds from the Father, Who together with the Father and the Son is worshiped and glorified, Who spoke through the prophets.

In one, holy, catholic, and apostolic Church. I profess one baptism for the remission of sins. I expect the resurrection of the dead, and the life of the world to come. Amen.

body of Christian teaching about God, Jesus, and the ongoing divine presence called the Holy Spirit. Specific issues in the first of these categories included the concept of the Trinity and the relationship between divine grace and human initiative. Christian teaching about Jesus sought to express the perfect blend of divinity and humanity in Christ and to understand how Christ is present in the sacrament or mystery called the Eucharist. Doctrine concerning the Holy Spirit evoked questions as to the nature of revelation and of membership in the Christian community. The more these and other issues generated an increasing variety of views through the second and third centuries, the greater the need to set clear standards as to which were acceptable and which were potentially destructive. Beginning with the Council of Nicea in 325 CE, mainstream Christian doctrine would take the shape of formal dogmatic expression. And since not all Christians would concur on a given formulation, differences of opinion on dogma would soon come to distinguish various churches from each other.

What do **Christians believe about God**?

God is first of all creator and sustainer of all that is. Lord of time as well as eternity, this Supreme Being is ceaselessly active in human history. Beginning with the divine

What is the central mystery of the Christian faith?

The doctrine of the Trinity is the central Christian teaching about God. Christians believe that there is only one God, but in that one God are three distinct divine Persons, the Father, the Son (Jesus Christ), and the Holy Spirit, who possess equally and eternally the same divine nature. The early ecumenical councils took care to define the mystery of the Trinity with great preciseness because the mystery of God, obviously, is the most important of the mysteries of faith. During the early centuries of the Church's life, many individuals denied elements of what Christians believed concerning the Trinity. Some claimed that Jesus was not really God; others rejected the divinity of the Holy Spirit; and some presented a very faulty understanding of God the Father. Belief in the Trinity is what distinguishes Christians from their Jewish and Muslim brethren.

labor of fashioning the universe, God has provided ongoing guidance and deliverance for all who believe in providence. Christians, like so many other religious people across the globe, sometimes have difficulty reconciling their belief in a God who is good and just with the undeniable evidence of cosmic evil and injustice. In general, Christians believe that God creates all possibilities, good and evil alike, but allows, rather than actively causes, evil actions. At the center of Christian theology is the doctrine of the Incarnation, according to which God the Son (Jesus Christ) came into the world, fully immersed in suffering and evil, in order to redeem humankind from sin by dying on the cross and rising from the dead. In the most vexing kind of paradox, the God-made-man Jesus Christ suffers and dies for human beings, who are in turn his murderers. According to Christian belief, God is "triune," three equal Persons in one deity—Father, Son, and Holy Spirit—and the Son is at once wholly human and wholly divine. The Holy Trinity represents perfect transcendence and perfect immanence. In other words, God is both infinitely beyond the realm of human experience and immediately accessible to all who seek divine aid.

What is **original sin**?

According to mainstream Christian tradition, the story Adam and Eve is critical to an understanding of the relationship between human beings and their Creator. According to Genesis 2: 16–17 and 3:1–24, God commanded these first human beings not to eat of the Tree of the Knowledge of Good and Evil. A tempter tried to persuade them that God was merely defending his own turf in order to prevent Adam and Eve from becoming like Himself. Once the primordial couple succumbed to the lure of such dangerous knowledge, they became aware of their potential for disobedience and lost their pristine innocence. Christian theologians have interpreted this critical moment in human history, known as the Fall, in various ways. From the time of the early Church Fathers on through the Middle Ages, theologians have discussed how the descendants of Adam and Eve inherited both their guilt and their inherent moral weakness. Protestant reformers stimulated further debate in the context of their discussion of faith and works. To what extent, they asked, can human beings remedy the situation by well-intentioned action? And what is the role of faith, utter abandonment to divine grace, in remedying the situation? Many interpreters associated the primal sin with sexuality and lust, but disagreed as to whether the descendants of Adam and Eve are merely deprived of original virtue or positively depraved and thus wilfully wicked. More recently exegetes and theologians have read the story of the Fall as a metaphor for the dawning of moral consciousness.

What do the terms **salvation** and **redemption** mean for Christians?

All of the major religious traditions hold out the prospect that human beings can find a way out of the suffering, confusion, and alienation that are part of everyone's life. Some traditions emphasize that only steadfast adherence to a core of ethical doctrine can effect the ultimate transformation of the human condition. Others teach that even the strongest, best motivated and most determined individuals need assistance from a greater than human power. "Grace" is a widely used term for that superhuman or divine aid, and it is the power of salvation. Some traditions go so far as to say that grace alone, apart from any human action, has the power to save. Religious doctrine about the source, nature and function of such saving power is called *soteriology* (from the Greek *soter,* savior). Christianity and Buddhism, and to a slightly lesser extend, Hinduism, have developed the most elaborate soteriologies. For Christians generally, God's sending Jesus Christ to die and rise from the dead for humankind brings about salvation through victory over evil and death. But in addition to rescuing believers, Christ also redeems (from the Latin meaning "to buy back") them from their former condition. According to some Christian thinkers this means a restoration to the condition of original innocence that human beings enjoyed prior to the Fall. Strictly speaking Buddhist and Hindu notions of salvation are about release from the status quo and do not include this element of reinstatement. Christian soteriology is about both salvation and redemption.

Do Christians believe in **miracles**?

Events that seem to defy scientific or commonsense explanation have been part of Christian tradition since biblical times. The Gospel of John refers to seven such marvels as signs of God's power and glory as manifested in Jesus. Beginning with his changing water into wine at the wedding feast at Cana (John 2:1–11) and ending with the raising of Lazarus from the dead (John 11), the fourth Gospel emphasizes the connection between faith and the recognition of signs. At the end of his work the evange-

> ## What is meant by the phrase "resurrection of the body"?
>
> Christians believe that all who have died will rise again when Jesus Christ comes in glory at the end of the world. Humanity's rising will be patterned on the resurrection of Jesus: "He who raised the Lord Jesus will raise us also with Jesus and bring us with you into His presence" (II Corinthians 4:14). Christians believe that human beings are called not to be simply souls or spirits, but to be fully alive, in body and in soul. Thus, the entire human person—body and soul—is destined to share eternal life with God in heaven.

list refers to Jesus' post-resurrection appearances as signs as well, and says that Jesus worked many others not recorded in his Gospel, all so that people might believe in the name of Jesus Christ (John 20:30–31). The other Gospels likewise use the language of signs so as to underscore two important aspects of miracles. First, miracles are in the mind of the believer. On numerous occasions Jesus performs a deed before large crowds. Some see the deed and believe; others see it and ask Jesus when he will work a "real" sign. Second, in the absence of faith on the part of those present, Jesus cannot or chooses not to effect his wondrous actions (Mark 6:5–6). In other words, miracles are not merely a gimmick for changing people's minds. Post-biblical Christian tradition has attributed numerous miraculous deeds to the mediation of holy persons as well as to direct divine intervention. Most common are reports of healings and apparitions, but accounts of paranormal events such as levitation or bleeding wounds on hands and feet (known as *stigmata*) are also well known.

What are the main Christian notions of **afterlife**?

Christian eschatology focuses on distinctive understandings of death, judgment, and consequential experiences called purgatory, heaven and hell. First of all, death is not the end of life, but the beginning of a different mode of existence. Death is the doorway to a world beyond this. But since each person is responsible for his or her choices in life, there will be an accounting called Judgment. Immediately after death comes the Particular Judgment, of significance especially in Catholic theology. At that moment the individual becomes aware with utter clarity where he or she stands with God. Depending on the situation, the state of the individual soul then changes to an experience of either damnation, purification, or bliss. Individuals who have consistently chosen separation from God (a state called "mortal sin") will then be granted their wish permanently, in hell. Those whose lifelong choices have been tainted with self-will and ill intent (called "venial sin") may need to experience a long but limited period of purification called purgatory. Once cleansed of the last vestiges of self-absorption, these individuals will experience a change and be ready to enjoy the eternal presence of God.

Hell depicted in the form of a giant serpent, as demons eagerly stuff the damned into its gaping maw, a portal sculpture on the Gothic-style Cathedral of Chartres, France, twelfth century.

Those whom the Particular Judgment reveals to be in a "state of grace" are believed to move directly to the experience of the beatific vision, or heaven, a state of eternal delight enveloped in divine love. All Christian theologies speak of a General Judgment, which will occur at the end of time at the Resurrection of the Dead. Then God will call all humanity to account and seal its fate for eternity. Protestant reformers rejected both the notion of Particular Judgment and the intermediate state of purgatory, teaching that only two possibilities, heaven or hell, awaited at the General Judgment. A further state known as limbo is reserved in some traditions for the unbaptized. Limbo is a rather neutral condition, lacking either suffering or supernal bliss, for all the righteous who lived before Christ, as well as for all infants who die without baptism.

How does Christian tradition interpret **history**? What is **millennialism**?

Christian tradition, like the Jewish and Islamic traditions, views history generally as a linear process with a beginning, middle, and end. Christian and Islamic views are different from the Jewish in that both later traditions regard the ages of their central figures, Jesus and Muhammad, as the high points of history. Christians believe Jesus the Christ entered the world at the "fullness of time," establishing a new dispensation and initiating a sense of expectation of the eventual end of time. All that went before Jesus pointed to him and all that will happen since his life on earth moves inexorably toward a final resolution over which Jesus Christ will preside. Christian expectation of the "end times" is an ancient theme with roots in Jewish tradition and in the New Testa-

What is a beatitude?

A beatitude is a blessing proclaimed by Jesus in the New Testament (Matthew 5:3–11; Luke 6:20–23), commending a characteristic of life that is most precious and dear to God. Jesus pronounced the beatitudes at the very beginning of his public ministry:

Blessed are the poor in spirit, for theirs is the kingdom of heaven.
Blessed are those who mourn, for they shall be comforted.
Blessed are the meek, for they shall inherit the land.
Blessed are they who hunger and thirst for righteousness, for they shall be satisfied.
Blessed are the merciful, for they shall obtain mercy.
Blessed are the pure of heart, for they shall see God.
Blessed are the peacemakers, for they shall be called children of God.
Blessed are those persecuted for righteousness' sake, for theirs is the kingdom of heaven.

ment. Just as the identification of Jesus as the Christ fulfilled the hopes of some Jews for a Messiah, Jesus' own preaching seems to have fueled further anticipation of history's grand finale. Many early Christians apparently thought the end was imminent, for we find important writers backtracking and suggesting that no one can know when the "Day of the Lord" will come (e.g. I Thessalonians 5:1–11). Eventually the idea emerged that Jesus would come again after a millennium, a thousand years, and rule for another thousand before bringing time to an end.

What is the **harrowing of hell**?

According to ancient Christian creeds, Jesus Christ descended into hell after his death on the cross. Some traditions associate this curious visit to the abyss or nether world with Christ's ultimate victory over evil as well as death. But the majority opinion is that Christ descended not into hell, the place or state of eternal torment and punishment, but to that intermediate realm in which all just persons who had died previously awaited the coming of Christ. According to that view, Christ descended in order to lead those righteous souls heavenward.

What is Christian **fundamentalism**?

Christian fundamentalism as a specific movement began in the early 1900s, following the tragic events of World War I. Central to the movement's teaching are the notions of biblical inerrancy and verbatim divine revelation. Inerrancy means that any contradictions apparent in the Bible result from human misunderstanding alone. The so-called "Scopes Monkey Trial"of 1925 brought fundamentalist concerns great notoriety with its public debate over the question of evolution. The prosecution argued that science teacher J. T. Scopes was in violation of Tennessee law for exposing students to a doctrine clearly at odds with a type of biblical interpretation now widely known as "Creationism." According to that view, God created the universe in seven twenty-four hour days—including a final day of rest—exactly as written in the Bible. Scopes was convicted, but the fundamentalist movement failed to make as much progress in purging American Christianity of traces of "modernism" as its leaders had anticipated. A principal teaching is a type of biblical interpretation called Dispensationalism, which divides history into seven eras or dispensations that vary according to the quality of humanity's relationship with God. Believers await the seventh, the millennium, by cultivating a strict code of conduct designed to avoid contamination by such worldly behavior as smoking, dancing, gambling, and ostentatious dress. These and other beliefs and practices form the Fundamental Articles. Fundamentalists generally have avoided political involvement until recently, but groups like the Moral Majority (founded in 1979) have changed dramatically the public face of the movement.

SIGNS AND SYMBOLS

What **signs or symbols** might identify an individual as Christian?

Except in a few rare traditional societies in which ordinary garb can still distinguish members of different religious traditions, ordinary Christians typically display few obvious signs of their religious affiliations. The most common symbols are small items of jewelry, such as rings or necklaces, displaying the symbol of the cross. Another decorative symbol is the stylized outline of a fish, with or without an enclosed text. Sometimes the fish has the word Jesus written within it, sometimes the Greek word for "fish" (*ichthus*). The symbolism of that Greek word derives from an ancient acronym meaning "Jesus Christ, Son of God, Savior" (**I**esous **Ch**ristos **Th**eou **U**ios **S**oter). Fish symbols often take the form of metal automobile decorations or bumper stickers. Individuals wearing or displaying either the cross or the fish symbol might belong to any of a number of Christian denominations or communities. Angels have become extraordinarily popular in recent years among Christians of all persuasions and can be seen on such objects as lapel pins or dashboard magnets. Other small identifying items are distinctively Roman Catholic. Various kinds of medals hung around the neck, or rings, might depict Jesus, his mother Mary, a patron saint, or an angel. Catholics sometimes use a variation on the more generic and plain Christian cross, called the crucifix, which depicts the body of the suffering Christ. In addition, Catholics and Orthodox Christians may make the "sign of the cross" in public, asking a blessing on the activity at hand.

The Sign of the Cross

The sign of the cross is a simple and profound prayer. In part it is an action or gesture. A Christian marks himself with the cross to show faith in Christ's saving work. A cross is described on the body by the right hand moving from the forehead to the breast, and then from shoulder to shoulder. In the Eastern church the cross stroke is made from right to left; in the Western church from left to right. While tracing the sign of the cross, the Christian says: "In the name of the Father, and of the Son, and of the Holy Spirit." This formula, which recalls the words of Christ sending his apostles to teach and baptize (see Matt. 28:19), expresses an act of the faith in the Trinity.

What signs or symbols distinguish **Christian ritual specialists** or **religious officials**?

A number of Christian communities expect their officials to wear distinctive clothing in public. Roman Catholics and Anglicans, especially, but increasingly clergy of other groups as well, wear dark or black suits with a clerical or "Roman" collar. A small square of white appears at the front-center of the shirt collar. Clerical shirts have become more colorful of late, so that one can expect to see clerical collars with white, gray, or any other shade of shirt. Many Protestant ministers prefer to dress in coat and tie. But when Christian officials lead their communities in worship they almost all wear special garments or "vestments." Among the most elaborate are those of the Eastern churches—both Orthodox and Catholic—usually including richly brocaded copes and even regal crowns, especially for bishops and patriarchs. Roman and Anglo-Catholic liturgical garb ordinarily features a plain white undergarment called an alb, with a neck band, called the stole, hanging down in front, and perhaps an outer vestment, color-coordinated to the liturgical feast or season, called the chasuble. Ministers in some denominations wear an academic style robe to preach and lead worship. Ethnically based Christian communities often supplement their ritual garb with distinctive colors or items of clothing, such as head gear or sashes.

Do Christians mark their **sacred spaces** with any distinctive signs and symbols?

Christian places of worship, generally called churches, almost always have one immediately identifiable feature—namely, a cross. Eastern churches often display a cross with distinctive short (sometimes slanted) bars above and below the main horizontal crossbar. Many also have one or more spires that have traditionally held the church's bells. Although the bells of most churches rarely mark all the hours of the day as they once did, some communities still mark the beginning of services by tolling them. Church designs today are remarkably varied. Some employ medieval or classical models, some favor the simplicity of early American colonial models, and some represent the latest in avant garde architecture. One symbolic feature of many traditional and contemporary designs alike is the arrangement of the interior space in the form of a cross. A metaphorical shape that has been fairly popular in modern churches is that of a ship, recalling ancient images of the church as "Peter's Barque." A feature of many churches is an ante-chamber or vestibule that marks a transition between outer and inner worlds, a brief passage that might allow worshipers to shift mental and spiritual gears. Interior features vary from one denomination to another. Catholic and Episcopalian churches, among others, typically have an altar table near the back wall. Almost all have one or more podiums, possibly well elevated. One of them will be called the pulpit, from which the preacher delivers the sermon or homily. Christian churches generally arrange their spaces for open visual communication between the sanctuary and the body or congregational area. Orthodox (such as Russian, Greek, Armenian, and Serbian) and some other Eastern churches often lack the benches or pews found in most other churches. They also typically have a high screen, called the "iconostasis," that hides the congregation's view of actions that take place at the altar behind it, emphasizing the mysterious nature of the ritual.

Do Christians use **statues** or other similar **imagery** in worship?

Christian communities evidence a wide range of attitudes toward the use of visual imagery in the context of religious ritual or personal devotion. Some avoid it altogether, preferring all-white church decor and clear glass windows. At the other end of the spectrum are churches decorated with everything from stained glass to veritable galleries of statuary. Still others ornament their ritual spaces heavily, but use only two-dimensional images and no sculpture. Some of the earliest evidence comes from the second- and third-century catacombs in which worshipers sought refuge from their Roman persecutors. Early Christians at first seemed to limit their sacred imagery, using human figures for sacred personages other than Christ. Perhaps they felt Christ was too sacred to depict directly or that representation violated the Jewish prohibition against graven images. In any case they often used symbols such as the fish, or loaves of bread, or an empty cross. By the middle ages Christians had developed extensive iconographic repertoires with which to depict an enormous array of holy personages. Elaborate programs in sculpture and stained glass depicted biblical figures, from patriarchs to kings to prophets, and saints, in addition to Jesus and Mary. Many sacred personages became associated with specific symbols as their identifying marks, such as St. Clement's anchor (he was martyred by drowning tied to one), the crutch of the ascetic hermit Antony, and St. Ambrose's beehive (for his words were sweeter than honey). Some Protestant reformers vigorously opposed the use of images because of abuses associated with them (especially miracle-monger-

Statues of patron saints known popularly as "santos," lined up along a wall in the small Mayan village church of Santiago Atitlan, on the shores of Lake Atitlan in Guatemala. Devotees regularly visit, place candles, and engage in animated conversations with their patrons or saintly figures known for certain healing or other special powers.

ing), and as a result this imagery is generally less common in Protestant churches today.

What are **santos**?

Walk into virtually any small neighborhood or village church anywhere in Latin America and you will find *santos*. *Santos* (Spanish for "saints") are small carved, painted statues of holy persons specially revered because of their spiritual power and presence. You will generally see them lined up on shelves along the side walls of the church or occupying small side altars flanking the main altar. All who come to the church regularly are likely to have a particular favorite among the diminutive saints. Devotees are not shy about expressing their needs to their patrons and these little churches are often alive with voices communicating in loud whispers every conceivable physical and spiritual need. People often light candles, soften the wax on the bottoms so that they will stick to the floor, and proceed to harangue their *santos* with animated gestures, humbly demanding rain for the crops or asking why a sick child has not yet been healed. *Santos* are an important form of folk religious art that reveals a great deal about popular Christianity in the Americas. Cathedrals and wealthier churches have their equivalent of *santos* in their multiple side altars and shrines, but there the conversations are quieter, the candles mounted on racks, and the saints often protected behind glass.

147

What is an **icon**?

"Icon" comes from the Greek word *eikon,* meaning image or likeness. From around the 400s on, the use of colorful two-dimensional images of Christ, Mary and the saints became an essential part of Byzantine liturgical and devotional prayer. Most icons depict the sacred figure frontally, often displaying a very stylized face that directs a striking gaze at the viewer. Some have described the devotional act of venerating an icon as a process of seeing and being seen, almost as if the image had a life of its own. Artists who create icons are called iconographers, people who "write with pictures." They undergo a long and very traditional course of training steeped in spiritual practices of prayer and asceticism. They employ only natural materials in their art and follow strict canons concerning characteristic ways of depicting certain figures and specific prescriptions about size and proportions of the sacred figure's form. Many icons use gold leaf for the sky around the holy figure, an immediate clue that the world into which the artist invites the viewer is not that of everyday life, but a spiritual realm beyond this. In Orthodox and other Eastern Catholic churches a screen called the *iconostasis* (place of the icons) stands between worshipers and the sacred action occurring on the altar beyond. In addition to individual icons placed on stands in various parts of the church, further mural-like images are displayed across the iconostasis.

What was the movement know as **Iconoclasm** and why was it important?

The Iconoclastic (from the Greek for "image-breaker") controversy arose in the early eighth century CE and lasted until 842 CE. For centuries Byzantine Christianity had used sacred icons, but Emperor Leo III called the practice into question on the grounds that it prevented Muslims and Jews from converting. Leo's order that all icons be destroyed provoked turmoil throughout the church, both politically and theologically, with monks and their monasteries taking most of the punishment for refusing to submit. Sixty years after Leo began the controversy, the Second Council of Nicea in 787 reversed his decrees. But within less than thirty years another Leo (the Fifth) returned to his namesake's policies with a vengeance, severely persecuting iconodules (those who supported the use of icons). The theological sore point was the argument that people who venerated icons were ever on the brink of idolatry. Their counter-argument was that icons were merely symbolic of the sacred realities beyond them. Though the controversy did considerable damage and cost a surprising number of lives and careers, the Eastern church recovered from it rapidly and has suffered no challenge of its kind since.

What is **holy water** and how do some Christians use it?

Roman and Anglo-Catholics especially are accustomed to blessing themselves when they enter church. They dip their right hand into a font filled with holy water and make the sign of the cross on themselves. Water is also a medium of blessing for a congregation. The celebrant takes a branch (or uses a small sprinkler with a handle) dipped in water and scatters a few drops over the crowd. Water from pilgrimage sites has long been a favorite religious souvenir, sometimes brought home to be given away as gifts or used for its healing properties. For many Christians, this is all an extension of the use of water for the rite of baptism, which in turn recalls how God brought the Israelites safely through the waters of the Red Sea and the Jordan River, and how Jesus was blessed by his cousin John the Baptist.

Have **relics** ever been important for Christians?

Since very early times, Christians have cultivated a sense of the sanctity of the remains and memorabilia of holy persons. Since Christians believed early on that Jesus had resurrected bodily from his tomb, they began to focus (by around the third or fourth century) on other reminders of Jesus' earthly life. People sought, and sometimes believed they had found, the cross on which Jesus was crucified, the nails that fastened him to it, or the crown of thorns he had worn. According to ancient tradition, St. Helena, mother of the Emperor Constantine, discovered the "true" cross of Christ during excavations for her son's new basilica of the Holy Sepulcher in Jerusalem. The resulting devotional ritual of venerating the sacred relics there may have been among the first of its kind and the beginning of a much expanded practice. During late medieval times the Holy Shroud, thought to be the winding-cloth in which Christ had been buried, became a center of widespread devotion in Europe. A veil, said to be the one with which St. Veronica wiped Jesus' face during his march to Calvary, and to which an image of Jesus' face was transferred, was venerated at St. Peter's in Rome from the thirteenth century on. Far more numerous, of course, are the relics of martyrs and saints, some dating back to early Roman persecutions of Christians. Sacred remnants can be anything from entire bodies, skeletal remains, to intact or fragmentary bones and skulls, to items once owned or touched by the holy person. Claims to possession of certain sacred relics have often conflicted—there are several heads of John the Baptist, for example. Famous relics conferred a great deal more than religious prestige on the churches, monasteries, and shrines that owned them, for the more renowned and powerful the relic, the greater the traffic of pilgrims to the holy place. Relics generally have been more significant for Catholic and Orthodox Christians.

What is the **Tree of Jesse**?

According to ancient tradition, Jesus was a direct descendant of King David, who was the son of a successful farmer named Jesse. Beginning in the Middle Ages, the Tree of Jesse became a very widespread visual symbol displayed especially in the stained glass windows of Europe's great Gothic cathedrals and in illustrated manuscripts of the Bible. Depictions of the Tree typically show an aged Jesse sitting or lying down, with a large tree growing from his upper body or from the middle of his back. On the lower

branches and trunk are shown the faces of David and Solomon and their royal descendants, along with other important figures in the genealogy of Jesus. An image of Mary holding the child Jesus typically appears at the apex of the tree. The symbolism emphasizes both Jesus' royal legitimacy and Mary's restitution for the evil originally caused by Eve eating from the Tree of Knowledge.

(Jewish King) David by Michelangelo, sixteenth century, a copy of the original (which is on view in the Accademia Nazzionale in Florence) in the courtyard of the Palazzo Nazzionale in Florence.

MEMBERSHIP, COMMUNITY, DIVERSITY

Where do **Christians live** today? What are their estimated numbers?

Members of the several dozen major Christian churches and denominations live in virtually every country on the planet. As the largest single group of religious communities, people who identify themselves at least nominally as Christians number just under two billion. Christianity's numbers are expanding at a rate somewhat slower than that of the global Muslim community. Catholicism is the single largest Christian church, with around one billion members. Protestants combined number about a third of a billion, with Orthodox believers just under a quarter-billion, with Russia's church the largest single body. The smallest Christian communities in major countries are those in Japan and China.

Have Christians traditionally sent out **missionaries** to convert others?

Christianity has historically been one of the three great missionary traditions, along with Islam and Buddhism. According to the Gospels, Jesus commissioned his followers to fan out into all the world and preach the Good News, baptizing as they went. Most famous among the early missionaries were Jesus' twelve Apostles. Tradition soon associated Christian communities all over the Middle East, and points farther flung, with individual Apostles. Along India's southwestern Malabar coast, for example, members of families that converted centuries ago still call themselves "Thomas Chris-

150

tians," in honor of Thomas the Apostle who is said to have brought the Gospel there shortly after the death of Jesus. Missionary activity on a global scale naturally increased dramatically with the Age of Discovery, in the sixteenth and later centuries. Orders such as the Franciscans, Dominicans, and Jesuits sent their most talented people abroad, hoping to penetrate the exotic cultures of India, China, and the Middle East. In modern times Roman Catholic orders and Protestant organizations dedicated solely to missionary work have multiplied throughout the world. Today Christians generally take a different approach to sharing their Good News with others, balancing missionary outreach with inter-religious dialogue.

Do Christians have a **holy city**?

Members of various individual churches have come to associate sanctity with a number of places uniquely important for their traditions. For Mormons, several sites along the church's difficult path from New York to Nevada are holy in retrospect, as well as nostalgically sad, because they represent places from which Mormons were expelled or where they were persecuted. Above all stands Salt Lake City, founded by Brigham Young, and seat of the church. Geneva remains a city with overtones of sanctity for Christians of Calvinist traditions. For Western Catholics, Rome is especially holy because of its place at the center of the church's entire history and because it is Catholicism's administrative home. But perhaps the majority of Christians consider Jerusalem the only genuinely holy city, and regard the surrounding territory as the Holy Land. Jerusalem, Bethlehem, Nazareth, and the hundreds of lesser sites associated with the life and death of Jesus remain for many a source of spiritual strength and hope.

How did so many **different Christian churches** come into being?

Three major points of division mark the history of Christianity, and nearly all of the tradition's diverse branches derive from those critical events. Intense controversy over the theological identity of Jesus culminated in the Council of Chalcedon (in present-day Turkey) in 451. Decrees of the Council taught definitively that Jesus was one person possessing both human and divine natures. In so doing, Chalcedon ruled against both the Nestorian heresy and the various Monophysite Christians. The former taught that Jesus was two distinct persons in one; modern day Nestorians call themselves Assyrian Christians. According to the latter, Christ was not human at all. Today the many originally Monophysite churches include Copticand Abyssinian groups in Egypt and Ethiopia, Syrian Jacobites, and the Armenian Orthodox Church. Even though the majority of these groups eventually came to accept Chalcedon's formulation, the initial effect of the Council was to separate what have come to be the indigenous Middle Eastern churches from the rest of Mediterranean Christendom. A second point of division came officially in 1054, the culmination of centuries of disagreement, both theological and political, between the Rome-based Western church and the Constantinople-based Eastern

Classic Baroque altar, seventeenth century, in the Jesuit church of Lucerne, Switzerland.

church. Pope Leo IX (1049–54) sent emissaries to excommunicate the Eastern patriarch on the basis of his refusal to accept changes in the language of the Nicene Creed. Finally, the largest of all the divisions was set in motion by several fourteenth–fifteenth century Christian reformers, including John Wycliffe (c. 1329–84) and John Huss (c. 1369–1415), and culminating in the work of Martin Luther (1483–1546), John Calvin (1509–1564), and Henry VIII (1491–1547) of England.

Who are **Roman Catholics**?

As early as the fourth century, Christendom experienced political and religious tensions between Western (Latin) and Eastern (Greek) styles of theology and governance. These differences were magnified by the East-West division officially declared in 1054, with many Eastern communities (Orthodox or "right-believing" Christians) proclaiming themselves formally independent of Rome. But the use of the term "Roman Catholic" came into common use after the sixteenth century Protestant Reformation. Papal authority, an often contested issue during the previous millennium or longer, again became a critical question. The reformers protested against the Church's rigidly hierarchical structure, officially a kind of oligarchy but often in effect a monarchy in which the Pope enjoyed greater power than the College of Cardinals. The theological counterpart to the hierarchical system of internal governance were distinctively Roman teachings on the seven sacraments and on a vast multi-tiered celestial realm populated by saints and angels. Against these and other symbols of authority and mediated spiritual power, the reformers emphasized the priesthood of the faithful and the

152

unmediated relationship of each believer to God. In response, Roman Catholicism further defined itself through the decrees of the Councilof Trent (1545–63) and the Counter-Reformation, spearheaded by the newly founded Society of Jesus or Jesuits (1540), among other emerging religious orders. Today Roman Catholics constitute about half the number of Christians worldwide.

What are some of the main **Protestant communities** that arose out of the Reformation?

As a result of the Reformation and associated movements in late medieval Christendom, four large families of Christian communities began to develop. Among the earliest were those identified with the reformer Martin Luther. Today a number of structurally distinct churches, all calling themselves Lutheran, have local branches all over Europe and the United States especially. Out of the reformist teachings of John Calvin have grown a variety of ecclesial bodies. Most notable are the half-dozen or more Presbyterian churches, which trace themselves directly to John Knox (c. 1513–72), a Scottish reformer much influenced by Calvin's thought. The second group are known as the Reformed (including the Evangelical and Reformed) churches. A still more varied group of churches developed out of the so-called Radical Reform. From the Anabaptist wing of that movement came the numerous different Baptist churches as well as the Mennonites. From the Congregationalist wing arose the several Congregational churches, from which the United States organizations called the Unitarians and Jehovah's Witnesses split during the nineteenth century. While the reformers in Europe organized their various communities, King Henry VIII proclaimed himself head of the Church of England, now no longer obedient to the Bishop of Rome. From that original movement, also known as Anglicanism, have emerged the Protestant Episcopal and Methodist churches, the latter begining with the teaching of the once-Anglican John Wesley (1703–91).

Why are some **Eastern Christian groups** called Orthodox and others Catholic?

As early as the fifth century, Eastern Christians identified themselves as "orthodox" in distinction to the various heretical factions whose views the Council of Chalcedon had condemned in 451. When the Iconoclastic Controversy ended in 842, Eastern Christian authorities declared the first Feast of Orthodoxy. At that time, the term distinguished the "right belief" of all supporters of image veneration from all who opposed that essential part of liturgy and devotion. Since the definitive disconnection of several major Eastern churches from Papal authority, the term has generally distinguished them from the "Uniat," or Eastern Catholic communities that retained or renewed ties to Rome. Eastern Catholic churches include members of the Antiochene, Chaldean, Alexandrine, and Byzantine traditions. Individual bodies are the Ukrainian, Maronite, Armenian, Coptic, Ethiopian, Ruthenian, and Melkite, several of which also have their Orthodox counterparts.

Are **Mormons** Christians?

Members of the Church of Jesus Christ of Latter-day Saints consider the Bible a critical sacred text, and, as their official name suggests, consider themselves Christians. Anyone who visited the new Mormon Temple in St. Louis prior to its dedication in 1997 would have been impressed by the prominence of a huge statue of Jesus in the entrance tent. But one of Mormonism's central tenets presents a major problem for mainstream Christian tradition. That tenet is the belief in a prophet after Jesus, with its implication that the revelation of Jesus was not final and definitive. Mormon tradition regards the work of founder and prophet Joseph Smith, Jr. (1805–44) as a necessary corrective to centuries of corruption of the true Christian teaching of Jesus. Smith himself believed the scripture revealed to him, The Book of Mormon (origin of the popular name of the Church), did not replace the Bible but merely supplemented it. Today the majority of Mormons live in Utah, while most members of a branch called the Reorganized Church are headquartered in western Missouri.

Are **Unitarians** Christians? How about **Jehovah's Witnesses**?

Unitarians, by definition, profess belief in a non-Trinitarian deity, denying the divinity of Jesus. Insistence on the "unipersonality" of God finds ancient echoes in teachings declared heretical by early church councils. Jesus' role is that of an important prophet, teacher and ethical model, but no more than an especially favored human being. Unitarianism began as an offshoot of Radical Reformation groups and in modern times was significantly reinterpreted by American thinkers William Ellery Channing (1780–1842) and Transcendentalist Ralph Waldo Emerson (1803–82). Many Unitarians consider themselves part of the larger Christian community, but generally prefer the identity of an open community not defined by assent to a particular body of doctrine. Jehovah's Witnesses was founded in the United States by Charles Taze Russell (1852–1916). He emphasized Messianic expectation based on an Old Testament concept of theocracy. Jehovah's Witnesses publications have generally maintained a consistently critical attitude to mainstream Christian beliefs.

What questions does the prospect of **interfaith marriage** raise for Christians?

Attitudes toward inter-marriage vary from one church to another. It is safe to say that on the whole, Christian parents tend to prefer that their children marry other Christians, and that Christian pastors tend to offer similar advice. There are two large issues at stake here. One is that when both spouses worship together, they may have a better chance at a durable marriage. The other has to do with raising children. Without question, parents from two traditions often need to work much harder to arrive at a mutually satisfactory answer to the question, "What religious values, if any, do we want to inculcate in our children?" Even when neither parent has been particularly active in any religious tradition, raising children often moves one or the other, or

What is ecumenism?

Ecumenism is the movement supported by many groups of Christians to heal the divisions among Christians and to promote unity among all who believe in Jesus Christ.

both, to reconsider the merits of some basic religious education. Some churches have historically done more than merely discourage inter-faith unions. Catholics still cannot have their nuptials officially witnessed by a priest unless the Catholic spouse has agreed—and the non-Catholic spouse has not disagreed—to raise the children Catholic. Several other traditions have taken similar positions, and some have relaxed their position on intermarraige considerably in recent years.

What **gender-related issues** are important for Christians?

According to the New Testament, women played important roles in the life of the early church, including that of deaconess dedicated especially to ministering to women. Women in the categories of "virgins and widows" also occupied a special place in church society. The ordained office of deaconess was revived by the Church of England, and slightly later in Methodism, during the nineteenth century. Nowadays, opportunities for women to exercise leadership varies a great deal among Christian communities. Catholicism is well known for its refusal even to discuss the possibility that women might be ordained to the priesthood. But the Catholic Church is not alone in its stance on gender-exclusiveness for positions of official service and authority. Though many churches have never issued formal statements on the matter, the dominant social culture of the groups is such that an exclusively male officialdom is simply presumed. At the other end of the spectrum, Anglican churches in the United States have recently ordained women to the priesthood. Some Pentecostal and Holiness churches are entirely comfortable with women ministers and preachers, and in some cases have women as bishops.

Do Christian communities ever practice **excommunication** or banishment for religious reasons?

Various kinds of excommunication have played a role in a number of Christian organizations. In the Letter to the Galatians (1:8) Paul uses the word *anathema* (meaning literally "suspended or set above") in the sense of "cursed, cut off" in reference to individuals who preached an unacceptable interpretation of the Gospel. Early church councils as well as official documents from later times have often applied the term *anathema* to any beliefs deemed inadequate or simply mistaken as well as to those who held such

155

The Relationship between Judaism and Christianity

Of all the non-Christian religions, Judaism holds a unique place in the history of salvation. The Old Testament records the history of the Jews, and it shows how God chose them in a special way and revealed Himself to them. God entered into a covenant with Abraham and, through Moses, with the people of Israel. He taught them to acknowledge Him as the one living and true God. When Jesus Christ came among humanity he came as a Jew. Those Jesus chose as apostles were Jews. Most of the early disciples were Jews. Thus the beginnings of the Christian faith were already found among the Jewish patriarchs, Moses, and the prophets. There is a spiritual bond, then, that links Christians with Jews.

beliefs. Until the sixth century to be pronounced anathema was equivalent to excommunication, but thereafter canon law introduced an important distinction. Anathema meant total exclusion from the life of the church, while excommunication meant only an inability to participate in the full sacramental life of the community. These two degrees came to be known as Greater and Lesser Excommunication. In more recent times, the Roman Catholic practice has introduced the distinction between excommunicates who are "to be avoided entirely," a status now limited to persons who physically threaten the pope, and those who are "tolerated," allowed to attend certain services but not to receive communion. Excommunication is one of three types of official "censure" in canon law, all of which are very rarely invoked nowadays. "Suspension" means that a cleric cannot perform certain ritual actions. "Interdict," denial of the right to celebrate some or all of the sacraments, can be imposed on individuals or groups, clergy or lay alike, in response to a cause for scandal. Roman and Anglo-Catholic traditions have by far the most elaborate juridical language, but many Christian churches have historically practiced varieties of excommunication. "Shunning," for example, forbids members in good standing to associate in any way with those under the ban, even if they are family members. The practice is rare except among Radical Reform groups such as the Mennonite and Amish.

How does a non-Christian go about **converting to Christianity**? How about changing **Christian membership** from one church to another?

Prospective converts to Christianity generally begin with a period of instruction in the essentials of Christian doctrine. In some communities a sponsor presents the interested party to the appropriate representatives of the church and accompanies the candidate through the process of preparation. Instruction can occur either individually or in groups. In some cases the teacher is a lay specialist in religious education, while in others a priest, minister, or deacon assumes that role. Some churches coordinate the formal reception of converts with the liturgical cycle, so that members are officially received into full communion on a special occasion, such as the Holy Saturday Easter Vigil service. Baptism is the primary rite by which new members are incorporated into their chosen communities. When the individual is converting from a non-Christian tradition, baptism is invariably conferred. But what about conversion from one Christian group to another? In those cases practice concerning baptism varies. Some churches re-administer the ritual in the belief that the convert's former community was not authentically Christian. Others consider all Christian baptism valid and binding. Since it is unnecessary to repeat the ceremony, they might substitute for it another religious ritual of welcome into the new community of believers.

How do Christians view **Christianity's relationship to other traditions**?

Three major issues are especially important here. First is the notion that Christianity completes, supersedes, or abrogates Judaism. Ancient Messianic expectation found its mark in Jesus, Christians believe, thereby rendering Judaism historically irrelevant. Second, Christians believe that in Jesus God has granted the final and definitive revelation. Any post-Christian claims to prophetic authority are therefore unacceptable and not to be believed. Islam is the most obvious example of a claim to prophetic revelation after Jesus, so it is not surprising that the history of Christian-Muslim relations has often been stormy. Third, personal assent to the divine revelation embodied in Jesus is essential to salvation, so that only those who so believe can hope to be rewarded in the hereafter. For many Christians, it simply does not matter that most human beings through the course of history have never heard of Jesus. In this instance many Christians have in mind not only the 80 percent of humanity that are not Christian, but even some of their fellow Christians whose beliefs they consider flawed or incomplete. Such exclusive views are hardly unique to Christianity. But many Christian groups recently have begun to respond to the reality of the world as it is, with all its religious wealth, by understanding that very diversity as an essential ingredient in the divine plan. From this perspective it is no longer possible to assert simply and categorically that one segment of humanity is assured of salvation while another segment is lost virtually by an accident of birth.

Are the teachings of **racial-supremacist groups** consistent with Christian tradition?

Members of a number of white-supremacist groups, such as the Aryan Nations and the Ku Klux Klan, frequently display ostensibly Christian imagery and quote the Bible as part of their inflammatory racist rhetoric. Some of the leaders of these groups present themselves as ministers or leaders of small dissenting churches, providing haven for people disillusioned with American society and looking for religious justification for their views. Preachers and leaders of these groups often present their message as if it

157

were bibically sanctioned, citing passages from both the Old and New Testament that might be interpreted as indicators of divine preference for one race over another.

LEADERSHIP, AUTHORITY, ORGANIZATION

How and where do members of local Christian communities come together?

Christians generally gather for worship in buildings called churches, although numerous smaller groups meet in homes or places not set apart exclusively for religious functions. (Some Pentecostal and holiness communities called their gathering places "temples.") Attached to many churches may be a variety of facilities such as schools, kitchens for catering community celebrations, auditoriums, social service offices, pastoral residences, monasteries and convents, libraries, shelters for the homeless and for battered women, soup kitchens, and cemeteries. In general, the larger the community attached to a particular institutional framework, the greater the diversity of facilities and the broader the social outreach is likely to be.

Is there a central teaching authority for Christians? What is a pope?

Not since very early in Christian history have all (or at least the vast majority of) Christians acknowledged a central temporal authority. The role of the papacy through the centuries has been central to the story of pre-Reformation Christendom especially, and even churches that eventually repudiated papal authority were indirectly acknowledged the importance of the institution. Roman Catholic tradition is structured around the institution of the papacy. Popes have exercised varying degrees of independence in their governance, depending on the will and vigor of the church's bishops in any given period. Eastern Orthodox churches have had their unique authority structures in the form of a federation of fourteen independent autocephalies (four of which are the patriarchates of early Christian times) each further divided into eparchies (or dioceses). Since the Reformation, proliferation of Christian churches and denominations has spurred the development of a variety of governance styles and systems. Within individual denominations (such as the Baptist) and even their sub-denominations (such as the Southern Baptist Convention), governing bodies do not always exercise overall prescriptive control. Their central authority is in many cases largely advisory, since local church com-

Byzantine Emperor Justinian's basilica Hagia Sofia (525 CE), Istanbul, Turkey. The enormous central dome is one of the world's widest, and the four minarets were added after the Ottoman conquest of Constantinople in 1453, converting the church into a mosque.

munities in many denominations enjoy considerable autonomy, both structurally and financially.

Do Christians have a system of **religious law**?

For over a millennium, Church law grew from the earliest ad hoc responses to particular problems of practice and discipline to an elaborate system called canon law. Early ecumenical councils promulgated their decisions in the form of "canons," or laws. Meanwhile, many major decrees from powerful bishops and formal opinions from important theologians added to the increasing body of legislation. Influenced by the codes of civil law of the Emperor Justinian and others, medieval authorities began to systematize the massive and still expanding body of legal tradition. Gratian (d. c. 1179) first began to impose order on the chaos and remained an important authority in Roman Catholicism until his work was thoroughly revised in 1917. Meanwhile, the Protestant Reformation brought about major changes in the new church bodies. Nearly all of the larger church organizations have developed legal structures of some kind to serve the concerns of what is called "church polity." Often taking the form of articles, charters or conventions, the legal formulations of the various ecclesiastical bodies typically claim authority only within a particular family of churches. For example, the Southern Baptist, Northern Baptist, and National Baptist Conventions have all developed distinctive legislative and procedural frameworks within which to handle matters of policy and discipline.

159

What does the term "**hierarchy**" mean? Which Christian groups are the most hierarchically structured? Which are the least?

"Hierarchy" comes from the Greek words for "sacred leadership." Church organizations vary from predominantly egalitarian and democratic to highly structured and institutionalized. Even the most egalitarian tend to feature some sort of division of labor within their leadership, but they typically choose leaders from among the rank and file members. Roman Catholicism is perhaps the most hierarchically structured of the churches. A leader, called the pope or Holy Father, has been elected, since the Middle Ages, by a body called the College of Cardinals. The pope is the ecclesiastical descendant of Peter and the custodian of apostolic tradition. Cardinals are specially appointed by the pope from among the bishops and archbishops. Another rank of clerics have the honorific title of monsignor, a designation until recently further divided into those called "right reverend" and a lower rank called "very reverend." The office of priest, from which the upper levels of the hierarchy are taken, consists of men responsible for the day-to-day life of the church in its thousands of parishes. Another office, that of deacon, is just below that of priest. Men studying for the priesthood are ordained as temporary deacons, but more recently the office of permanent deacon has been made up of laymen chosen and trained for the work of assisting parish priests. Several other churches retain a highly structured organization, but generally on a smaller scale. For example, many have archbishops and bishops as main administrators. Many of the Eastern Orthodox churches are governed by patriarchs, to whom archbishops (or metropolitans) and bishops report.

What is a **bishop**? Do all Christian churches have them?

"Bishop" means "overseer" (from the Greek *episkopos*). Many churches use the episcopal system as their principal administrative structure. Among the churches for which episcopal succession represents an unbroken connection back to the apostles, the first bishops, are the Catholic, the Orthodox, and the Anglican. Catholic bishops confer as a global body by sending representatives to occasional synods in Rome, and in many countries are organized into national conferences. Orthodox bishops also convene in synods, but usually on a nation-by-nation basis. Anglican bishops meet at the Lambeth Conference every ten years, but the results of their deliberations are not juridically binding. Many of the Methodist churches also have bishops, and there are Lutheran bishops as well. Some smaller churches, such as those in Holiness or Assembly of God traditions, sometimes refer to their founder as a bishop, but the latter are not linked with any larger episcopal governing body. Alternative forms of governance are the presbyteral and the congregational. Presbyterian churches are governed by a body called the "session," elected by the congregation and consisting of ordained clerical and lay presbyters or elders. Local churches join together in a presbytery, and regional presbyteries (never fewer than three) in turn form a synod. Presbyteries also elect members of an overall body called the General Assembly. The congregational structure maintains the complete independence of each local community, but most churches that employ the structure nevertheless come together in national conventions or synods. Baptist churches and those forming the United Church of Christ use this general structure of governance.

Are there characteristically Christian views about **religion and political power**?

Views about Church-state relations have varied over the centuries among Christian groups. Bearing in mind that the following is an oversimplification of a very complicated issue, it is possible to characterize four principal positions on this issue. At some times and in some places, Christians have thought of the state as virtually synonymous with the church. The early years of the Church of England as proclaimed by Henry VIII, and the Byzantine church under Constantine are examples. Some traditions have accorded the state enormous power over the church, as with early Lutheranism in northern Europe. Reversing the situation, the church has sometimes dominated the state, as during the heyday of Calvinism in Switzerland. Finally, certain communities of the "radical reformation" proclaimed a total separation of church and state, insisting on their right to reject some aspects of ordinary corrupt society altogether. Some descendants of those communities continue to practice conscientious objection with respect to compulsory military service, for example. Throughout history prior to the Reformation, popes often had stormy relationships with the monarchs of the Mediterranean world. The result was a variety of official church positions ranging from supremacy over temporal power, to an attempt at equal balance between the spiritual and the temporal, to *de facto* admission that the civil authority held supremacy.

Do Christian communities run **private schools** for their children?

Private or parochial education continues to be a concern for many Christians. In addition to the thousands of Catholic schools attached to parishes in the United States, for example, other denominations maintain hundreds of schools and Christian academies throughout the country. By far the most numerous are primary schools, but secondary schools and colleges also offer the possibility of more advanced learning in a Christian setting. The majority of non-state institutions of higher education in the United States historically have been founded in connection with religious traditions. For various reasons, including difficulty in securing government funding, large numbers of them no longer retain their original religious affiliation. A notable exception are the clusters of Catholic high schools, colleges, and universities that still identify themselves with that religious sponsorship.

How are **Christian religious leaders** chosen, educated, and given authority?

Candidates for ministry and governance in most churches simply present themselves for admission to the appropriate educational branches of their organizations. Seminaries oversee the special ministerial training of church members. Many refer to the

161

Orthodox Christian monastery clings to the side of a cliff overlooking ancient Jericho, the West Bank, Palestine. Its placement in the Judaean wilderness reflects longstanding tradition of preference for austere environs for monastic asceticism.

desire to enter the ministry as a "vocation" or a calling from God. In some cases members of many denominations take their ministerial theological education at non- or multi-denominational seminaries or schools of divinity, generally emerging after three or four years with a Master of Divinity (M.Div.) degree or its equivalent. Some students may pursue further studies toward a Doctor of Ministry (D.Min.) degree or a Ph.D., hence the common appellation "Reverend Doctor." Protestant ministers more often than not obtain their pastoral appointments at local churches of their denominations through the mechanism of the "call," whereby a congregation interviews prospective pastors and then invites its first choice. Catholic bishops generally appoint priests of their dioceses to specific parishes without consulting the local congregations. Orthodox and other Eastern church administrators sometimes exercise a similar appointive authority.

Has **monasticism** played a significant role in Christianity?

Since about the third century, small numbers of Christian men and women have sought ways of dedicating themselves entirely to an intensified spiritual quest. At first that quest typically took the form of a highly ascetic withdrawal from society. One of the earliest, and eventually most influential, of these hermits was St. Antony of Egypt (c. 250–350). Early in the fourth century he decided to organize a community of fellow hermits. Later monastic founders also developed rules of common life. Pachomius (c. 290–346), also of Egypt, is known as the true founder of communal or cenobitic monasticism. During his lifetime, there were nine male and two female monasteries. Other important developments were the work of Benedict of Nursia (c. 480–550), whose Rule became the basis of the worldwide order called the Benedictines, now including a number of women's orders as well as monks. Benedict himself was not an ordained priest, although nowadays the majority of Benedictine monks study for the priesthood. Other important monastic orders have been founded since, especially in medieval times. Major orders are the Franciscans, founded by Francis of Assisi (1181–1226), with various sub-branches, and the Dominicans, founded by Dominic (1170–1221). They are known as "mendicant" orders, since they were historically dependent on alms for monetary support. The Church of England also still sponsors several small monastic orders, such as the Monks of St. John the Divine, and distinctive monastic communities, such as the Order of St. Basil the Great, continue to make important contributions to several of the Eastern churches.

What kinds of **smaller religious organizations** do Christians belong to?

In addition to the various monastic orders that are still an integral part of religious life in the Anglo and Roman Catholic as well as Eastern communities, a number of non-monastic religious and lay organizations have also made significant contributions. There are several types of organizations for men and women fully committed to various kinds of religious life. Members of those formally known as "orders" (such as the Society of Jesus, or the Jesuits) take solemn vows of perpetual poverty, chastity, and obedience. Members of "congregations" take simple vows that can be either perpetual or renewable at set intervals. Most religious organizations belong in this category. "Lay institutes" are like congregations, except that most or all members of the former are not ordained to the priesthood, as with the Daughters or Charity or Christian Brothers. In addition, a number of the "orders" strictly so-called (such as the Dominicans and Franciscans) have "second" orders (for female members) and "third" orders (also called Tertiaries) for lay affiliates. Although the Roman Catholic tradition is more structured in this respect than most others, almost all Christian churches provide multiple organizational opportunities designed to allow members fuller participation in the life of the community. These groups typically revolve around some specific socio-religious focus, such as church maintenance, social outreach, or the interface of religion and politics.

PERSONALITIES AND POWERS

Is there such a thing as a **Christian saint**?

Paragons of holiness and virtue have always played an important role in Christian tradition. The Old and New Testaments describe hundreds of outstanding models of the life

The Virgin Mary

Mary, the mother of Jesus, occupies a pre-eminent position in the theology of the traditional Eastern and Western churches. Information about her life is extremely limited (Matthew 1 and 2; Luke 1 and 2). It is clear that Matthew and Luke believed that Mary's conception of Jesus was miraculous, involving no human paternity, and that her son was the Messiah expected by Israel. Mary belonged to the house of David (Luke 1:26), was engaged to man called Joseph (Matthew 1:18), and lived in Nazareth in lower Galilee (Luke 1:26). The Gospel of Luke relates that an angel of God announced that she, although a virgin, would conceive the son of the "Most High," to be named Jesus, and that he would found a new Davidic kingdom (Luke 1:31–33). Mary consented. When Joseph discovered that Mary was with child, he wished to dissolve the engagement quietly. In a dream, however, God's angel admonished him to marry Mary because the son she would bear was the result of divine intervention (Matthew 1:19–21).

The dates of Mary's life can only be surmised. Researchers place the birth of Jesus between 7 and 4 BCE. Granting Mary a minimal age of 16 to 18 years at the time of Jesus' birth, this would place her birth at sometime between 20–22 BCE. There is no precise information as to her death. At the Council of Ephesus in 431, Mary was proclaimed the "Theotokos" (God-bearer), or mother of God. Her position was further defined in the Roman Catholic Church, which in 1854 stated as an article of faith that Mary had been conceived without the original sin that affects all humanity. In 1950, Pius XII declared that at her death Mary's body had not corrupted in the grave but that God had taken both her body and soul into heaven.

of faith. Different churches have had various ways of acknowledging sanctity in historical individuals. Roman Catholic, Orthodox, and other Eastern traditions have placed the greatest emphasis on the role of saints in piety and devotion. All share a reverence for the great Greek Fathers of the Church, for example. All mention the names of saints as part of their liturgical prayer, and Eastern Christians venerate icons of saints much as Catholics incorporate various types of saints' images in their devotional life. Holy persons are especially important as mediators, embodiments of holiness popularly thought to be immediately accessible to ordinary people. Saints hear the needs and aspirations of those who beseech them, and present these prayers to God. Protestant tradition has generally denied any such mediatorial role, as well as the human mediation implied in priesthood. Many Protestant reformers regarded devotion to the saints as an unacceptable dilution of Christian piety, an unnecessary detour on a direct road to God. Catholics and Orthodox continue to identify extraordinary individuals as worthy of sainthood, and the Catholic Church particularly maintains an elaborate mechanism for assessing the merits of individual claims. Advocates for a potential saint present the case to the local bishop, perhaps including claims of miracles and authentication of relics. The bishop may then forward the case to the Sacred Congregation for the Causes of Saints. A church official known popularly as a "devil's advocate" raises objections to the cause so as to expose any weaknesses in the argument. Once sufficient evidence of two authentic miracles has been advanced, the pope may declare the person "blessed" in what is called a "beatification" ceremony. Before the final declaration of sainthood, or "canonization," proof of two further miracles is required.

Have **prophets and prophecy** figured prominently in Christian tradition?

Christianity grew at least initially out of Jewish tradition, in which the prophets of the Old Testament played a central role. A prophetess named Anna was in the Temple when Mary and Joseph presented their child there to fulfill the Law, and proclaimed Jesus the salvation of Jerusalem (Luke 2:36–38). Jesus himself was very much a part of that prophetic heritage. He and his contemporaries wondered about the spiritual identity of Jesus' cousin John (the Baptist). Many considered John a prophet (Mark 11:32), and Jesus told his followers that John was indeed a prophet, but even more, he was the very Elijah whose return had been foretold (Matthew 11:11–15). The Gospels report that many identified Jesus, too, as the expected prophet, and that Jesus even hinted that they were correct (see e.g. Matthew 10:41, 13:57, 21:11). Pauline letters list prophets as belonging to a rank or office second only to that of apostle, suggesting that prophecy continued to play an important role after Jesus' death (e.g. I Corinthians 12:28, Ephesians 4:11). It is not clear in those cases how these prophets functioned. Long after the age of biblical prophecy, some Christians have identified modern "saints" as prophets who have raised their voices in opposition to oppression and injustice. Such courageous people are, therefore, spokespersons for God in our time, thus fulfilling the role of prophets of old. Many are tempted to regard prophecy as a synonym for foretelling the future, but that has never been the primary role of prophets.

Have there been important **Christian mystics**?

Since late antiquity many Christian men and women have been known for their profound experiential insight into the divine mystery. Some of these mystics have been theologians, authors of important treatises on various aspects of the Christian faith. But more importantly, theirs is a legacy of wonder and even bewilderment at the ways God relates to attentive human beings. Some of the best-known Christian women have been mystics. Accounts of Christian mysticism typically begin with the sixth century Dionysius the Pseudo-Areopagite, whose Greek writings laid the foundations of mystical thinking and provided a lexicon that subsequent authors would use for many centuries. Most of the great mystics lived during the high and late Middle Ages, though a number lived during Renaissance and early modern times as well. Hugh (c. 1096–1141) and Richard (d. 1173) of St. Victor, leaders of the Victorine School of Paris, believed that creation manifested the mind of God and was thus the beginning of a path to contemplation. Hildegard of Bingen (1098–1179) was a visionary Benedictine nun whose extensive writings and musical compositions have enjoyed remarkable popularity of late, thanks to fine new translations and CD recordings. Mechtild of Magdeburg (c. 1210–80), a member of a lay sisterhood called the Beguines, recorded her revelatory visions of the Sacred Heart of Jesus, as did her younger contemporary Gertrude (1256–1302). Meister Eckhart (c. 1260–1327) was a German Dominican whose teaching on divine-human intimacy evoked accusations of pantheism and heresy. His spiritual descendants Henry Suso (c. 1295–1366) and Johann Tauler (c. 1300–61) sought to clarify Eckhart by connecting him to the officially acceptable thought of Thomas Aquinas (d. 1274). Other famous mystics, far too numerous to mention individually even briefly, included Catherine of Siena (c. 1340–80), Jan van Ruysbroeck (1293–1381), Juliana of Norwich (c. 1342–1413), Ignatius Loyola (1491–1556), Teresa of Avila (1515–82), and John of the Cross (1542–91).

Has **martyrdom** ever been important in Christian history?

According to Christian tradition, Stephen was the first person to die for his commitment to faith in Jesus Christ (Acts 6–7). Paul, one of those among the crowd that stoned Stephen to death, would later become a martyr himself, as would Peter and many others among the earliest Christians. In Christian prayer, martyrs have enjoyed an honor above that of all other saints. Most of the martyrs whose stories are told in a literary form called "martyrology" lived during the first three centuries, the time of direst persecution by Roman authorities. But martyrs more recently have also been celebrated for their witness to the faith as missionaries in far-flung lands. The high age of missionary martyrs coincided roughly with the opening of new maritime routes around the globe. Even more recently a young woman shot to death in a Colorado school massacre has been hailed as a martyr, for when her assailant asked her if she believed in God, she bravely said "Yes" and died moments later. Martyrs are those who witness to their faith regardless of the threat of dire consequences to themselves.

What is a **Doctor of the Church**?

Since the Middle Ages, the Catholic Church has recognized individuals known for their theological learning and spiritual wisdom with the formal title "Doctor of the Church." At first the title applied only to four of the Latin Fathers of the Church, Jerome, Ambrose, Augustine, and Gregory the Great. Before long, to balance things off, four Greek Fathers were named: Athanasius, Basil, Gregory of Nazianzus, and Gregory of Nyssa. But since the mid–sixteenth century, another two dozen have had the title officially conferred upon them. These include, for example, Church Fathers (Venerable Bede, Cyril of Alexandria, John of Damascus, and Ephrem of Syria); medieval theologians (Anselm of Canterbury, Albert the Great, Thomas Aquinas, and Bonaventure); and mystics (John of the Cross, Francis de Sales, and the only two female Doctors, Catherine of Siena and Teresa of Avila).

Have there been any major **ascetics** in the history of Christian spirituality?

Asceticism is an intensely focused spiritual striving that emphasizes various forms of self-discipline. According to the New Testament, Jesus himself led a simple life and taught his followers that it was preferable to possess only the basic necessities. He counseled followers to deny themselves luxuries if they wished to follow him. Jesus did not recommend extreme forms of self-denial as such. Nevertheless, individuals and small groups throughout Christian history often have interpreted the Gospel preference for simplicity and non-attachment in dramatic ways. Some Christians have engaged in strict fasts, arduous penances, and occasionally even self-mutilation. Several early Christians sat atop pillars (some had tiny huts, somewhat like treehouses) for lengthy periods. These "stylites" took their cue from a Syrian, Simeon (c. 390–459), to whose pillar many pilgrims came to pray and to send up a few supplies. Pillar ascetics were not uncommon in the Middle East for about five hundred years. The ideals of the "Desert Fathers," who began the monastic movement and called their followers to a life of voluntary poverty and solitude, are still emphasized by such strict religious orders as the Trappists.

Who was the "Grand Inquisitor" and what was the **Inquisition**?

Since the second or third centuries, Christians have used "inquisitions" (with a small "i") to root out unacceptable theological views called heresies. During the thirteenth century, Emperor Frederick II made heresy-hunting the responsibility of the state. In response, Pope Gregory IX thought it best to claim that prerogative for the Church. He set up a court of inquisitors from the Dominican and Franciscan orders, charging them to identify wayward persons. Those accused of heresy had a month to recant before undergoing a formal trial with at least two witnesses. Unrepentant persons found guilty could be jailed and tortured. The most serious offenders could be turned over to civil authorities and executed, typically by being burned at the stake. Spanish monarchs Ferdinand and Isabella established their own version of the Inquisition in 1479. Jews and Muslims who had converted to Christianity were their initial targets, but they eventually sent their Grand Inquisitor, Torquemada, after Protestants as well. Even people who are now famous saints, such as Ignatius Loyola, were occasionally required to give an account of themselves. The Spanish Inquisition lasted until the early nineteenth century.

Who is the **Antichrist**?

Antichrist is the generic title given to an individual, organization, or principle of evil believed to represent all that runs counter to the values of Jesus Christ. Only the two Letters of John use the term, referring to people who refuse to believe in the Incarnation. Some early Christians labeled Roman emperors "Antichrists" because of their opposition to the faith. Some Protestant groups occasionally have dubbed the pope the Antichrist; similarly, some Muslims today characterize any external enemy as "The Great Satan." Christians throughout history have identified as the Antichrist the various evil forces of which the Book of Revelation speaks, including Rome and the "beasts" whose appearance will signal the apocalypse. Perhaps the most common and persistent view is that at the end of time, Jesus (in his "Second Coming") will confront and vanquish an impostor who claims to be Christ (i.e., the Antichrist), but not before the impostor has managed to lure many believers from the faith.

What role do **angels** play in Christian belief?

Angels are spiritual beings with intuitive, though still partial, access to the ultimate truths. Roaming the universe at God's command, angels can make their presence known in countless ways. As messengers of the unseen world, angels represent God's ongoing communication with individuals on earth. Tradition divides angelic beings into three ranks or orders, each comprising three further "choirs." In descending order, the first rank includes the Seraphim, Cherubim, and Thrones. Second in rank are the Dominations, Principalities, and Powers. Virtues, Archangels, and Angels fill the lowest three orders. Apart from Archangels and Angels, none of the angelic ranks descend to the human world, and the so-called guardian angels belong to the lowest rank. Michael, Raphael, and Gabriel are the only angels commonly named in Christian tradition. Many Christians consider themselves blessed and guarded by the presence of an angelic guardian, as the dramatic increase in colloquial American references to angels in recent times will attest. Even Christians whose traditions avoid talk of saints because their mediatorial role is deemed unnecessary now commonly talk of angelic intervention. Some perceive angels as kind strangers or as invisible forces that prevent accidents, for example.

How is the **devil** significant for Christians?

The English word "devil" comes from the Greek *diabolos,* meaning "one who throws something against"—in short, a disruptive power or presence. In the Gospels, Jesus deals with many such presences. Sometimes the presence is associated with a physical disease, sometimes with what seems to be a form of psychosis. There is a subtle distinction between a devil and an evil spirit, the latter being a soul gone awry under the influence of the former. According to tradition, the only difference between an angel and a devil is that a devil has made a choice that caused the loss of divine grace.

Lucifer, "Bearer of Light," is the name of the angel who first separated himself definitively from God and got the name Satan or "adversary." Others are said to have followed his example and joined an army of malevolence under Satan's lead. In one of the few remaining mythological elements in Christian tradition, Satan does battle against the forces of good represented by the Holy Spirit. At the end of time, Satan and his minions will suffer crushing defeat. Homage to the devil remains a feature of folk traditions among Christians in many parts of the world. In a mountainside cave in Guatemala overlooking Lake Atitlan, for example, locals still show interested visitors the remnants of chickens sacrificed to "the Prince of the World" represented oddly by a stone cross on the wall. This is not the same as Satanism or devil worship as such, but an acknowledgment of the continuing presence of evil in the world. Popular lore has cloaked the devil in red, given him horns, a pointed tail, and a pitchfork, but imagery of that sort does not have biblical roots.

What is a **patron saint**?

Patron saints function in some Christian communities as a human counterpart to guardian angels. There are two general types of patron saint. It was once common for some Christians to name their children after holy men and women, thus attaching the youngsters to "patrons" who would look after their spiritual needs. More often, saints are identified with groups of people, such as members of a profession (carpenters, musicians, mariners), or with special circumstances, such as affliction with a particular illness or a challenge. People pray to St. Jude, patron of lost causes, for relief from apparently incurable diseases. Some beseech St. Anthony for help in finding what has been lost.

Are **dreams and visions** important in Christian spirituality?

Some New Testament accounts describe dreams as a way God communicates warnings or courses of action to the dreamer. An angel tells Joseph to take Mary as his wife and to flee to Egypt (Matthew 1:20, 2:13). A dreams warns the Magi not to return to Herod (Matthew 2:12), and as a result of a dream Pilate's wife counsels her husband to release Jesus (Matthew 27:19). The Acts of the Apostles records a number of instances in which visions supplied needed insights to Peter and Paul (Acts 11:5, 16:19, 18:5, 26:19). Throughout Christian history individuals have reported special access to divine truth through both dreams and visions. Mystical insight is often described in visionary terms. The claim is not primarily one of optical vision, but of spiritual encounter. More prominent in recent times have been claims concerning apparitions, particularly of the Virgin Mary and Jesus. Individuals who claim to receive special revelations typically communicate the need for peace or repentance and preparation for the coming apocalypse.

What happens when a person is **"slain in the spirit"**?

In their worship services Pentecostal and other Charismatic churches include segments during which the leader walks among the crowd or invites individuals to come forward so that he or she might pray over them. Many ask to be healed of specific ailments. The prayer leader often places one or both hands on the person's head or shoulders, sometimes raising one hand high in a gesture of blessing or petition. While the preacher or healer prays with increasing intensity, the individual may become very agitated and then seem suddenly to lose consciousness, perhaps falling back into the arms of fellow worshipers ready to break the fall. Such a worshiper is said to be slain in the Spirit, or baptized in the Holy Spirit. Sometimes the one praying appears to signal that the moment has come, by giving an extra squeeze or a slight push. Dozens or even scores of worshipers may report having this experience in the course of a service.

What is meant by the term **"the Rapture"**?

Some millenarian sects hold that at the Second Coming of Christ all believers will be taken up (rapt) into heaven. Only those deemed to be "saved" will enjoy the benefit of the experience. Numbers of the saved and the criteria by which to determine one's own or others' membership in that group vary. Some churches adhere to a literal reading of the scriptural text, according to which one hundred and forty-four thousand, equal numbers from each of the twelve tribes of Israel, will be "sealed" on their foreheads (Revelation 7:1–8). Strict interpretations limit to that number those who will survive the "great tribulation" (Revelation 7:14) that will precede the Second Coming of Christ. Others allow that the number is symbolic, though the actual number of those saved will remain relatively small.

HOLIDAYS AND REGULAR OBSERVANCES

What kind of **religious calendar** do Christians observe?

Most of the world's Christians mark time on the solar Gregorian calendar, a late medieval correction of the much older Julian calendar. Julius Caesar had initiated the calendar named after him in 46 BCE, but it was based on some miscalculations. In 1582, Pope Gregory XIII shortened the Julian year by ten days and added a day to February every fourth or "leap" year. Some Eastern Christian churches still use the Julian calendar, so that their major feasts fall just less than two weeks later than those of the Western churches. Until the Gregorian reform, Christians considered March 25 the beginning of the year, since that was judged to be the day on which Gabriel announced to Mary that she would give birth to Jesus. March 25, which had in ancient times been

What is the "Parousia"?

According to the New Testament, Jesus promised his followers that he would come in glory at the end of the world as Lord and Judge. This coming of Christ in glory is called the "Parousia." The Greek word literally means presence or arrival. The ceremonial entry of a king or triumphant conqueror into a city was called a "parousia." In this final coming Christ will be recognized as Lord of all. Christians from the very start have looked forward with confident hope to the final coming of Christ in glory. The early Christians' prayer "Marana tha," Aramaic for "Our Lord, come!" (I Corinthians 16:22), was an expression of their eager desire to see the final triumph of Jesus' saving work.

mistakenly calculated as the spring equinox, the first day of Spring, remains the Feast of the Annunciation. For centuries Christians continued to observe the timing of traditional Jewish feasts, which were movable within limits of specific agricultural seasons (such as planting and harvest times). Using the Jewish seven-day week, Christians gradually added fixed feasts, such as those of saints and martyrs. The custom of designating Sunday as a day of special religious observance began during the first generation after Jesus' death and Emperor Constantine decreed it a day of rest in 321. Wednesdays and Fridays had anciently been days of fasting, a practice now surviving largely on the first day of Lent, Good Friday, and other Fridays during Lent. For most Christians the year consists of three liturgical seasons, Advent and Christmastide, Lent and an Eastertide that ends with Pentecost Sunday, and "Ordinary" time until the first Sunday of the following Advent. Some Christians in Egypt and Ethiopia still use the solar Coptic calendar, based on the ancient Egyptian reckoning. Recent recalculations suggest that Jesus was actually born closer to 4 BCE than to the year 1.

What is the season of **Advent**? Why is **Christmas** so important for Christians?

The Western Christian liturgical year begins with the first Sunday of Advent. Western churches set that Sunday as the one closest to the feast of St. Andrew (November 30), while Eastern Christians begin a period of fast in preparation for Christmas on the feast of St. Philip (November 14). For most Christians, four Sundays mark this season of waiting and expectation of the birth of Christ. Christmas, the celebration of Jesus' birth, was originally fixed on December 25 around the year 336. That was the date then calculated as the winter solstice on the Roman calendar, with its symbolic celebration of the rebirth of the sun after the year's darkest day. In the practice of the liturgical churches, purple vestments still recall the originally penitential spirit of the season, with its overtones of apocalyptic expectation of Christ's second coming. But on the third Sunday, called *Gaudete* ("Rejoice") Sunday, rose vestments introduce a note of relief. Christmas represents for all Christians the pivotal event in human history called the Incarnation, in which God took on human flesh and assumed all aspects of the human condition except sinfulness.

What is the meaning of the season of **Lent** or the **Great Fast**?

For at least three centuries, early Christians observed a two or three day fast in preparation for Easter. Canons of the Council of Nicea in 325 represent the first reference to the later observance of a forty-day fast recalling symbolically similar practices by Moses and Jesus. Lent now begins for Western Christians on Ash Wednesday, while Eastern Christians typically begin the "Great Fast" two days earlier. Until the seventh century, the season began on a Sunday, but since Sunday was exempted from fasting, the beginning was advanced so as to include a full forty days' fast. Ashes applied to the head are a reminder of human sinfulness and mortality and recall an earlier practice in which penitents appeared in public wearing sackcloth and ashes. For centuries Christians fasted for a significant portion of each day, Monday through Saturday, and generally abstained entirely from meat. Contemporary practice has generally limited a modified form of fasting and abstinence to the first day of Lent and Good Friday. For example, Catholic practice recommends taking smaller meals at breakfast and lunch, together equaling less than one takes at the main meal, with no food in between. That is a far cry from serious fasting, but still at least a reminder of the purpose of the season—namely, a heightened awareness of the need for spiritual conversion and dependence on God.

What do Christians commemorate on **Holy (Maundy) Thursday, Good Friday** and **Holy Saturday**?

The Easter Triduum (three-day period) begins with the commemoration of the evening on which Jesus gathered his apostles for the Last Supper. Maundy (from the Latin word *mandatum,* the new "commandment" of service Jesus gave his disciples then) or Holy Thursday is marked in several churches by special rituals, some of which include a symbolic "washing of the feet" of several attendees by the priest or bishop. Good Friday recalls the crucifixion and death of Jesus. What could be "good" about such a day? It represents the ultimate sacrifice by which God redeemed the world through the offering of the only Son. For Christians, this is at the heart of the mystery of salvation. Special services acknowledge the sanctity and somber nature of the occasion. Some churches feature an extended reading of one of the Gospel accounts of the Passion and Death of Jesus, while some perform classic musical settings; others commemerate the events of the day with a ritual called the Stations of the Cross, the "Three Hours" ritual recalling the time Jesus spent on the cross, or by reenacting Christ's deposition from the cross and burial . Pilgrims to Jerusalem on this day participate in a lengthy procession through the streets of the old city, retracing (at least in part) the steps of Jesus toward Calvary or Golgotha, the hill of the cru-

Christian pilgrims carrying the Cross in procession through the streets of Jerusalem en route to the Church of the Holy Sepulcher, recalling the last hours of Jesus' life.

cifixion. In liturgical Western churches, the day ends with the stripping of the altar, leaving a bare table and an empty tabernacle (where the consecrated bread is ordinarily kept) as symbols of mourning. Holy Saturday memorializes the day of waiting and uncertainty experienced by Jesus' followers, who hoped his predictions of a victory over death would prove true. Some churches celebrate a special ritual on Saturday at midnight or earlier in the evening in anticipation of Easter.

What is the Christian feast of **Easter** about?

Christ chose to suffer death on the cross to save humanity from its sin, and Christ's victory over death fulfilled the promise of redemption. As the name suggests, Easter celebrates the rising of the sun of life from the dark night of the grave. Christian tradition teaches that when a group of myrrh-bearing women and then the Apostles went to the tomb on the third day after the cruxification, they found the grave empty. Enemies of the early Christians argued that Jesus' followers had taken his body away to give credence to his predictions that he would rise from the dead. New Testament accounts in the Gospels and Acts of the Apostles narrate a number of post-Resurrection appearances in which Jesus visited his disciples and spoke with them. The Eastern Christian year is organized entirely around Easter in three segments: ten weeks prior to Easter, fifty days after Easter, and a more generic "remainder of the year." Western churches generally accord the Christmas season a liturgical and spiritual importance equal to that of Easter.

173

Why do Christians put special meaning on the **Ascension** and **Pentecost**?

Christ's Ascension into heaven is commemorated on a Thursday forty days after Easter. Tradition places the event on the Mount of Olives, to the east of Jerusalem. It was the culmination of a period of post-Resurrection appearances in which Jesus is said to have visited with his disciples. Christians have been observing the day since at least the end of the fourth century. Now, on the site traditionally connected with the event stands not a church but a small mosque. Ten days after the Ascension, the feast of Pentecost ("Fifty") recalls how Jesus promised his disciples he would soon send a "paraclete," or advocate, to continue guiding the young community in his stead. Tradition identifies the paraclete as the Holy Spirit. The Acts of the Apostles recounts how the disciples were gathered in an upper room when something like a storm enveloped them, and they experienced the power of the Spirit descending upon them in "tongues as of fire." Many Christians refer to this event as the birthday of the Church, since it gave the disciples the courage to emerge from hiding to preach the Gospel far and wide.

What are some of the **other religious days** Christians observe annually?

Numerous fixed feast days recall the lives of important saints as well as significant moments in the lives of Jesus and his mother Mary. Two significant events in the life of Jesus include the day his parents presented the infant in the Temple (February 2, The Presentation) and the Transfiguration in which he appeared in divine glory to several apostles (August 6). Jesus' baptism by his cousin John is, in the western liturgical tradition, a movable feast that always occurs within the first two weeks of January. Feasts honoring Mary include those commemorating her being conceived without sin (Immaculate Conception, December 8); her birth (September 8); her presentation in the Temple (November 21); Elizabeth's visitation with Mary (May 31); and her bodily ascension into heaven (Dormition/Assumption, August 15). In some churches well over half the days of the year are associated with holy persons, often commemorating the death date. A major saint such as John the Baptist might even merit an observance of both his birth (June 24) and his death (August 29).

CUSTOMS AND RITUALS

What **rites** do Christians practice in church?

Primary Christian communal rituals are as nearly varied as the communities that perform them. A broad distinction between liturgical and non-liturgical churches is use-

Russian Orthodox Church on the Mount of Olives in Jerusalem, opposite the site of the Dome of the Rock, also known as Temple Mount.

ful here. Liturgical churches feature a carefully regulated set of rituals, often of great antiquity. Only a handful of specialists, typically garbed in traditional vestments and sometimes using ancient liturgical languages for all or part of the ritual, may participate. In liturgical churches this spectator model emphasizes the performance of a sacred action with relatively limited participation by the congregation. In the middle of the spectrum, some churches follow what is called an "order of service," with the emphasis on preaching rather than on the sacred action of liturgical ritual as such. Leaders here often wear an academic-style robe and lead from a pulpit within a separate space called the sanctuary. Activities in entirely non-liturgical churches often tend to be more like a town meeting. Worship leaders sometimes a robe, but more often ordinary semi-formal street clothes. Services emphasize more inclusive participation during virtually all phases of the gathering, but preaching by the leader and sometimes by one or more others as well, remains a centerpiece.

Do Christians pray in any particular **language**?

Use of sacred liturgical languages goes back to early Christian times. Aramaic and Hebrew were the languages the first Christians inherited from Jewish tradition. But before long Latin and Greek would become the dominant liturgical languages of Mediterranean Christendom, along with such regional Middle Eastern tongues as Coptic, Arabic, Armenian, and Syriac. Latin became the sacred language of most of

175

> ## The Lord's Prayer
>
> The Lord's Prayer, or the "Our Father," is found in the gospels of Matthew (6:9–13) and Luke (11:2–4). Both gospels position the Lord's prayer as Jesus' response to his disciples request to teach them how to pray. Based on linguistic studies, most biblical scholars today agree that this prayer likely came from Jesus' own lips:
>
> > Our Father, who art in heaven,
> > hallowed be Thy name;
> > Thy kingdom come;
> > Thy will be done on earth as it is in heaven.
> > Give us this day our daily bread;
> > and forgive us our trespasses
> > as we forgive those who trespass against us;
> > and lead us not temptation,
> > but deliver us from evil. Amen.

Western Christendom until the Reformation, resulting in the use of Europe's vernaculars as standard practice of many Protestant churches. Greek continued as the language of the Byzantine rite, but among the Eastern churches the equivalent of vernacular usage eventually became more common. Russian Orthodoxy and related churches preferred Old Slavonic as their sacred liturgical tongue. Today, vernacular languages dominate Christian liturgical practice. Some churches retain the ancient tongues for the most sacred part of the liturgy, namely the Eucharistic Prayer in which the sacred species (bread and wine) are consecrated. A few very small Roman Catholic churches have sought to revive the use of Latin for the entire mass. Change to exclusive use of vernaculars in most communities has been designed to increase participation and intelligibility for the congregation, but some argue that this has emptied the sacred action of its sense of mystery.

What is the difference between a **sermon** and a **homily**?

In general, sermons tend to be longer and organized around a doctrinal or moral theme. Homilies may be lengthy, but they are generally situated in the context of a larger liturgical service, whereas sermons as often as not are the main focus of a worship gathering. Sermons frequently take as their subject a line or somewhat longer passage from scripture. The homily form seeks to comment on and elucidate a pair or set of scriptural texts precisely as scripture and not so much as a springboard for an ethical discourse. The preacher typically chooses the sermon's signature passage because of its theme, rather than because the text has come up in due course as part of a prearranged cycle of readings. Homilies are more often a way of helping the congregation appreciate how the selected readings fit together and comment on each other, and how they fit in the larger scheme of the liturgical cycle for the season at hand (such as Advent/Christmas, Lent/Easter, Ordinary time).

What is a **sacrament**?

"Sacrament" comes from a Latin root that originally referred to an oath by which soldiers swore their loyalty (Eastern Christians typically call a sacrament a holy "mystery"). Traditional Christian sources from a variety of churches generally define a sacrament as a visible sign of divine grace bequeathed by Christ himself. Since the Middle Ages, Catholics and Eastern Orthodox Christians have held that there are seven sacraments of equal spiritual significance: Baptism, Confirmation or Chrismation, the Eucharist, Penance, Holy Orders, Matrimony, and Final Anointing. Most Protestant communities have accorded a central place to Baptism and the Eucharist, usually called the Lord's Supper, regarding the other five as of lesser importance, but some churches have recently begun to pay greater attention to those five as well. Almost all Christian communities practice Baptism frequently, though in very different ways. As for the Eucharist or the Lord's Supper, frequency varies a great deal. Catholic and Orthodox churches, for example, give "holy communion" as part of nearly every liturgical worship service. In most Protestant communities, the Lord's Supper is much more occasional and a ritual set apart from the usual Sunday worship. The Society of Friends (Quakers) and the Salvation Army are the only larger groups that have no sacramental rituals at all.

Is **sacrifice** important in Christian ritual?

Christians generally believe that the death of Christ on the cross replaced the ancient Jewish ritual of animal sacrifice once integral to Temple worship. The "whole burnt offering" known as the "holocaust" was offered in atonement for sins, but Christ's death has redeemed humankind once and for all. Christians often speak of the Eucharist, Divine Liturgy, or Mass as an "unbloody sacrifice" in which worshipers reenact symbolically Jesus' cosmically efficacious offering of himself. Sacrifice as a symbolic act still plays a role in the personal spirituality of many Christians. For example, charitable giving, support of one's local religious community, and doing without food or other pleasures for a time, can be a form of metaphorical sacrifice meant to heighten awareness of deeper spiritual values.

What kinds of special **ritual objects** figure in Christian worship and prayer?

In addition to the cross or crucifix Christians use a variety of ritual objects, more commonly in liturgical communities than in non-liturgical ones. The more elaborate the

The Rosary

The rosary is a popular form of Roman Catholic prayer that combines meditation on the mysteries of faith with the recitation of vocal prayers. A "decade" of the rosary corresponds to each of the fifteen mysteries commemorated in the rosary. Ten Hail Marys are said for each decade; they are preceded by an Our Father and followed by a Glory Be to the Father. While reciting a decade of the rosary, one is to meditate on the particular mystery for that decade and on its meaning for life. The entire rosary is divided into three chaplets: the joyful, the sorrowful, and the glorious mysteries. To "say a rosary" commonly means to pray one such chaplet of five mysteries. Commonly a chaplet is preceded by the recitation of the Apostles' Creed and of an Our Father and three Hail Marys. The Roman Catholic Church has long recommended this form of prayer as a convenient and effective way of meditating on the Christian mysteries of salvation.

The Joyful Mysteries
    1. The Annunciation.
    2. The Visitation of Mary to her cousin Elizabeth.
    3. The Birth of Jesus Christ.
    4. The Presentation of Jesus in the Temple in Jerusalem.
    5. The Finding of the child Jesus in the Temple in Jerusalem.

The Sorrowful Mysteries
    1. The Agony of Jesus in the Garden of Gethsemane.
    2. The Scourging of Jesus at the Pillar.
    3. The Crowning with Thorns.
    4. The Carrying of the Cross.
    5. The Crucifixion.

The Glorious Mysteries
    1. The Resurrection of Jesus from the Dead.
    2. The Ascension of Jesus into Heaven.
    3. The Descent of the Holy Spirit upon the Apostles.
    4. The Assumption of Mary into Heaven.
    5. The Coronation of Mary as Queen of Heaven.

liturgical practice, in general, the more kinds of symbolic and practical implements are required. Most Christian churches have an altar on a raised platform in front of, or in the midst of, the congregation. Exceptions are Pentecostal and similar groups whose primary rituals revolve entirely around preaching, singing, and the ongoing interaction of the leaders with the congregation. Churches such as the Roman and Anglo-Catholic, most Eastern churches and some Lutheran groups, feature a ritual that includes some reenactment of the Eucharistic prayer. Their ritual leader typically wears special vestments and handles the sacred vessels. A large cup called the chalice, traditionally either made of or lined with precious metal, holds the wine (grape juice in some churches). A still larger vessel called the *ciborium* (Latin for "food container"), kept covered except during the prayers of consecration, holds the altar bread either in the form of small unleavened wafers or leavened cubes that can be dipped into the wine before dispensing to communicants. Another common implement used in more elaborate liturgies is the thurible or incense burner, a small spherical container with a lighted charcoal for igniting grains of incense, which is swung from a chain in gestures of benediction. Less common but worth mentioning if only because of its artistic beauty is the ostensorium or monstrance, a large ornate device shaped like a spectacular sunburst or a small Gothic cathedral used for displaying the consecrated host during special processions or for Western congregational adoration.

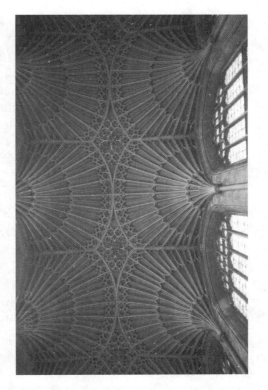

Fan vaulting in the Cathedral of Bath, England, twelfth century; one of many decorative treatments that developed along with advances in the sophistication of engineering for Gothic vaulting.

Are **music and dance** and dance important in Christian religious ritual?

Almost all Christian churches make music an important element in worship, and a few engage in various forms of prayer-related movement. In some non-liturgical churches, singing and dancing form the majority of congregational worship, even to the point of having music accompany the preaching. Individual hymns, some lasting ten to fifteen minutes or more, are the largest feature in those cases, punctuated by prayer and testimony from the assembled worshipers. In other words, songs and preaching make up most of the "order of service." Liturgical traditions use the hymn form, but also sing set pieces of the liturgical ritual itself. For example, the "Holy, Holy, Holy" announces the beginning of the Eucharistic Prayer, and the "Lamb of God" is sung just before communion in the Western liturgical tradition. Since the liturgical traditions strive for an atmosphere of greater solemnity, they tend to incorporate dancing less often, and then only of a rather restrained kind. In many non-liturgical churches the expression

179

of feeling is a major component, so that one can expect to find much more animated movement in such settings. More staid and stately liturgical traditions have historically preferred the majestic sonorities of the pipe organ, occasionally joined by brass, woodwinds, or classical strings. In other traditions, piano is the primary instrument, and even small congregations may feature bands with electric guitar and other keyboards, bass, and full drum kit. In most Eastern Christian traditions, however, liturgical services are chanted without any musical accompaniment. Christians communities all over the world naturally make use of distinctive ethnic and local musical styles and instruments.

What **special rituals** do Christians engage in **at home**?

In Jewish tradition the home continues to be the center of religious life and education. Many Christians tend to think of church as fulfilling that purpose. As a result, there are few Christian rituals universally associated with the home. Among the few common practices Christians report as important to them are shared reading of scripture and group prayer, whether in connection with meals or as a distinct activity. If there is one religious activity that qualifies as a regular ritual in the majority of Christian homes, it is probably the practice of bedtime prayer with the children of the house. This can be a powerful formative influence on young Christians, because they can learn to include others in the orbit of their religious concern. Praying "for" thus becomes a way of connecting spiritually with the rest of the world.

What distinguishes **"charismatic" Christians** from others?

Charismatic communities are those that emphasize the various manifestations of the "gifts of grace" (from the Greek *charismata)* that Paul enumerates in I Corinthians 12:8–11. They include healing, miracles, prophecy, discernment of spirits, speaking in tongues, and the interpretation of tongues. For the past couple of centuries, Pentecostal churches have been at the forefront of charismatic Christianity. More recently the Charismatic movement has become important to many Roman Catholics as well. The movement is centered around the belief that the outpouring of the Holy Spirit on Pentecost was an essential grace that allows Christians to give expression to their deepest experience of God in their daily lives. Charismatic ritual and spirituality give practitioners permission to feel their religious commitment by acknowledging that emotion is as important an ingredient as intellectual assent.

What does **"speaking in tongues"** involve?

"Speaking in tongues" or *glossolalia* (from the Greek *glossa* and *lalia,* "tongue talking") refers to the phenomenon of excited utterance apparently not identifiable as any known human language. Linguistically, therefore, speaking in tongues amounts to little more than a string of nonsense syllables. However, psycho-linguistic research has discovered similarities across cultural and traditional lines, suggesting that trance-like states induced under certain circumstances all over the world may bring about common neurophysiological changes with similar results regardless of religious affiliation. Christian tradition has often regarded the "gift of tongues" as a spontaneous behavior, but it appears in fact to be learned. Some Christian groups place so much emphasis on the practice that it has become an indicator of full membership. According to Acts of the Apostles 2:4, when Jesus' closest followers were filled with the Holy Spirit, they began to speak in various identifiable languages so that all the people present from whatever land clearly understood them. In I Corinthians 14:1–40, Paul cautions that the gift of interpreting is as important as speaking in tongues, and that without interpretation, there is a danger that speaking in tongues by itself can be divisive.

What does **"serpent handling"** have to do with Christianity?

Several small, mostly rural, churches in the United States have focused their worship life around the unusual and dangerous practice of handling poisonous snakes. They take their cue from Mark 16:18, according to which a sign of those who believe in Jesus is that they will "take up serpents." Worship gatherings in these churches involve intensely emotional prayer and increasingly agitated music and dancing. People toward the front of the church who feel so moved will remove a poisonous snake, or even two, from their containers, holding them up at face level while dancing around the room. Some say it is the music and motion that prevent the serpents from striking. Rattlesnakes seem to be the serpent of choice, perhaps because the noise they make with their tails adds to the drama and because the rattling might warn of an imminent strike. Copperheads and water moccasins are also sometimes used. Many worshipers have been bitten, some many times, and more than a few have died. But that in no way deters worshipers from continuing the practice, ever in search of perfect faith and trust in God.

Do Christians engage in **exorcism**?

Many readers will be at least vaguely familiar with a novel called *The Exorcist*, or with the movie based on it. The author based his story loosely on a now-legendary series of events said to have taken place in St. Louis, Missouri some fifty years ago. Exorcism has long been available to Roman Catholics as a ritual designed to free individuals thought to be possessed and tormented by evil spirits. Church authorities have very rarely given permission to perform exorcisms and only after extensive psychiatric and medical consultation. The local bishop appoints a priest known for his sanctity, sanity, and personal strength to act as the principal ritual specialist. That exorcist then prepares to use a set ritual and to subject himself to whatever spiritual discipline may be

181

necessary to withstand the rigors of the experience. Peculiar and frightening occurrences are said to accompany exorcisms. Father William Bowdern, the Jesuit priest who performed the St. Louis exorcism, refused ever to speak of the experience in public, except to affirm that he did indeed believe in the existence of the devil. According to the New Testament, Jesus and his Apostles performed a number of exorcisms, a practice not altogether rare among Jews and pagans of the time. His actions are the ultimate sanction for the practice in Roman Catholicism. During medieval and even into early modern times, some people were executed as witches because they proved impervious to exorcism. Until about thirty years ago, Roman Catholic practice continued to confer on candidates to the priesthood the "minor order" or office of exorcist. Exorcism remains relatively common among some Christian denominations, especially Pentecostal or Charismatic groups. Leaders of worship might perform an exorcism as one among many manifestations of the Spirit, by prayer and touch intended to free the one possessed. Here exorcism is generally a very brief part of the larger ritual. A much simplified form of exorcism remains a brief preliminary part of the ritual of Baptism in many churches.

Is **pilgrimage** an important part of Christian tradition?

By about the fourth century, pilgrimage to Jerusalem had become common enough that significant examples of a type of literature called the pilgrimage narrative have survived. Pilgrims talk of their burning desire to visit sites mentioned in the Old Testament as well as those associated with key events in the life of Christ. Emperor Constantine's renovation of many of the holy places also made the practice more popular. After the Muslim conquest of Jerusalem and surrounding lands in 638 CE, Christian access diminished somewhat, then improved for a while under the Crusaders' Latin Kingdom. But during the Middle Ages, other sacred sites associated with famous saints gradually replaced Jerusalem as the goal of choice for countless European pilgrims. The shrine of Santiago de Compostela in northwestern Spain was a major site, said to be built around the remains of St. James the Apostle. Compostela came to symbolize Christian efforts against the infidel Muslims in the Holy Land. In more recent times the practice of pilgrimage to Jerusalem and associated holy places has revived with increased ease of travel. Some Christians also flock to lesser shrines associated with saints or apparitions of the Virgin Mary. Pilgrimage was once occasionally prescribed for individuals as penance for sins but it has never been a central requirement for Christians as it has for Muslims.

How do Christians mark **formal entry** into their various faith communities?

Along with the Lord's Supper, Baptism is one of the two rituals the vast majority of Christians recognize as a sacrament. Its symbolism recalls the cleansing waters of the Flood and the crossing of the Red Sea and Jordan. Essential elements in Baptism are flowing water and the formula "I baptize you (or "The servant of God is baptized") in the name of

What is "negative mysticism"?

Certain Christians believe in the absolute unknowability of God. To them, even the Trinity fails substantially to capture or transmit the true nature of what they consider to be a God-Beyond-God, a mystical, indistinct presence. For such believers, God can be "known" only by following a "negative" path that treats God as a divine mystery, eternally dark and invisible to human beings. The closest we can come to knowing God is through the love and goodness that is revealed to humankind by God's own action. An early exponent of this belief was Pseudo-Dionysius, who envisioned a "super-essential Godhead" distinctive from all positive terms ascribed to God. Later, in the fourteenth century, the English author of *The Cloud of Unknowing* advocated a "negative path" to God. Today, the practice of negative mysticism is not widespread, but some Christians find it helpful to imagine what God is *not* in their quest to understand God as he is. Some refer to this as *apophatic* mysticism, to distinguish it from the *kataphatic* tradition in which proponents believe one can make more affirmative statements of mystical experience.

the Father, and of the Son, and of the Holy Spirit." Infant baptism was the norm until the Reformation. Catholic, Orthodox, Lutheran, Methodist, Presbyterian, and Congregational churches still baptize infants, while some churches defer the ritual until the candidate is a teenager or older. Baptism can be administered by total or partial immersion, with the candidate descending into a pool or with the officiant lowering the infant into a font, or by affusion, in which the officiant pours water over the candidate's head only.

Do Christians practice any other forms of **initiation ceremony**?

Confirmation, or Chrismationas it is called in the Eastern Churches, has historically been closely linked with baptism, in some cases even conferred immediately afterward. But in some churches confirmation represents the remnant of an ancient puberty rite, in which the baptized Christian receives a special strengthening with the Holy Spirit. To the baptismal use of water symbolism, confirmation adds anointing and laying on of hands as symbols of further sealing the candidate's full membership in the Christian community. In some Western churches a bishop administers confirmation, but priests can do so under some circumstances as well.

Are there Christian rituals of **marriage**?

Most Christian communities have developed some form of ritual, however brief or simple, to acknowledge and bless the union of two people in matrimony. Marriage cere-

Catholic cemetery outside New Orleans, Louisiana, where the dead are buried in mausolea above ground because of the area's susceptibility to flooding.

monies can occur in church, in the home, or in some place chosen for its beauty or romantic appeal, such as a garden. By custom, representatives of the church community who preside over the ceremonies typically function as the primary witnesses of the union and sign the marriage license that is then filed as a legal record of the marriage. In that capacity, ministers and priests are acting as representatives of the civil authorities as well, but the ceremony emphasizes the religious context and divine sanction of loving union. Religious weddings often include readings from scripture—perennial favorites are Genesis 2:18–25 on Adam and Eve, and Paul's splendid description of true love in I Corinthians 13—as well as brief homiletical reflections and exhortation to the new spouses. Catholics, and Eastern churches that call the ceremony the "Crowning," generally situate weddings in the context of the Eucharistic liturgy. Christians generally believe that the couple themselves effect the marriage and that the officials and assembled community are there to witness and support their union.

What do Christians believe about **divorce and remarriage**?

Whether or not the witnessing community regards matrimony as a sacrament, Christian groups universally teach that marriage is a permanent commitment. Unfortunately, there is often a large gap between ideals and realities. However common it has become in some societies, most Christian communities consider divorce a solution of last resort. Many churches train their ministers and priests in marriage and family

184

counseling so that they can assist their members when they find their relationships threatened for whatever reason. In the hope of obviating the eventual need for divorce, some churches recommend or even require pre-marital counseling and education, designed to impress on the couple the nature of the commitment they envision. Some churches do not recognize divorce as a religiously acceptable choice, teaching that marriage is an indissoluble bond. But those churches also acknowledge that in some cases the parties in a marriage may not have made the commitment with sufficient maturity, proper intent, or full consent. In those instances the marriage can be annulled, allowing both parties to seek legal divorce and remarry if they choose.

How do Christians deal ritually with **death and mourning**?

Death signals the final rite of passage, and most Christian communities have rituals designed specially to help mourners understand their loss from a religious perspective. A more or less formal period of mourning generally follows for a day or two. A few Christian groups do not permit embalming, preferring to bury the body on the day of death or shortly thereafter. American Christians generally prefer to have a "wake," usually at a mortuary but sometimes in a church or even in the home, during which mourners offer their condolences to the dead person's family. Wakes can last from several hours to several days. Some groups prefer a memorial service in the mortuary chapel following the wake. Many churches offer funeral rites in church, either as part of a special version of the regular liturgical prayer (as with the Roman and Anglo-Catholic mass) or as a distinct ceremony. Generally the body of the deceased is present in the casket, which is sometimes open for a final viewing and generally closed during the funeral ritual itself. When the deceased has willed his or her body to a medical school, or when an immediate cremation is judged necessary, a memorial service is held without the body. In the United States burial is still the most common means of dealing with human remains, but cremation is gaining acceptance even in churches traditionally opposed to the practice.

ISLAM

HISTORY AND SOURCES

When did **Islam begin**?

Five hundred years after the Roman destruction of the Temple in Jerusalem dramatically altered the history of Judaism, an equally momentous event occurred in the Arabian peninsula. According to tradition, Muhammad was born around 570 CE in the trading town of Mecca. When he was about twenty-five, Muhammad married a businesswoman named Khadija, fifteen years his senior. Muhammad developed the habit of seeking prayerful solitude in the hills and caves surrounding Mecca. One day around the year 610, he began to undergo some troubling auditory and visual experiences. Encouraged by Khadija not to dismiss the experiences, Muhammad came to understand them as divine revelations that he was meant to communicate to his fellow Meccans. He was to be a messenger of God, a prophet charged with delivering a message that would set straight misinterpretations of earlier revelations given through the prophets God had sent to the Jews and Christians.

What were some **critical events** in Islam's earliest years?

Over the next 23 years or so, Muhammad continued to preach the word God had spoken directly to him. At the heart of the message was the notion of "surrender" (the root meaning of the Arabic word *islam,* pronounced isLAAM) to the one true God. His early preaching called for social justice and equality and condemned oppression of the poor by the wealthy and powerful. Muhammad belonged to a powerful tribe called the Quraysh, who exercised considerable control over the lives of the Meccans generally. But Muhammad's family and the clan of which they were a part were among the poorer and less influential within the tribe. Muhammad's preaching did not endear him to the

Quraysh, who made life difficult for the small community of Muslims. In 622, Muhammad and his followers made the crucial decision to move north to the city of Yathrib, whose representatives had offered the young community sanctuary. This "emigration" or *Hijra* marked the official beginning of the Muslim calendar. Muhammad the prophet became a statesman as well, and Yathrib became known as Madinat an-Nabi, the City of the Prophet, or Medina for short. The Muslim community grew rapidly, doing battle with the Meccans and eventually regaining access to Mecca in 630.

What place does **Muhammad** occupy in Islamic tradition?

Muslims consider Muhammad the last in a line of prophets commissioned to act as God's spokesmen to humankind. Beginning with Adam and continuing down through Jesus, the pre-Islamic prophets preached the same fundamental message of belief in one sovereign transcendent God. But because successive generations invariably found the message difficult and inconvenient, people sometimes corrupted or diluted the revelation. Hence, God chose upright individuals to reassert the original revelation.

What **sort of person** do Muslims think **Muhammad** was?

Muhammad was a man singled out for his natural virtue and integrity to fulfill the role of final and definitive intermediary of the divine communication. As a human being, Muhammad naturally had his faults. But Muslims regard him as the finest our species has yet produced, the ideal family man and leader of humanity. Muhammad himself never claimed to be a wonder-worker. His sole miracle was the Qur'an (pronounced koRAAN and hereafter transliterated as Koran), the Muslim sacred scripture.

Popular tradition has nevertheless sometimes idealized Muhammad, expanding his powers and prerogatives to include various kinds of marvels. One special double experience, called the Night Journey and Ascension, stands out. According to tradition, God conveyed Muhammad by night from Mecca to Jerusalem, and from there through the various levels of heaven and hell. Popular lore has attributed other wonders to Muhammad, but it is most important to appreciate the enormous affection and reverence Muslims universally feel for their Prophet.

What is the **principal Muslim sacred text**?

In about the year 610, Muhammad began to deliver orally the messages he believed were of divine origin. His "recitation" (*qur'an*) of the revelation was initially held in memory by his followers, and, according to traditional accounts, was not

Congregational mosque (*Jami Masjid*), seventeenth century, Delhi, India. Note the large reflecting pool in front of the triple-domed prayer hall.

produced in full written form until some years after Muhammad's death in 632. What began as "an Arabic recitation" retained that name even after it was written down, and the resulting book is still known as "The Recitation" or Koran.

How big is **the Koran** and how is it organized?

The sacred scripture contains about 6000 verses, roughly equivalent in length to the New Testament, arranged in 114 sections called *suras* (pronounced SUrah). Muhammad's earliest revelations tend to be short, rhetorically potent utterances in an ancient form of rhymed prose used by pre-Islamic seers and soothsayers. Later suras tend to

189

Qur'an (Koran) page, eighth–ninth century, Middle East. *Courtesy the Saint Louis Art Museum.*

be lengthier and more prosaic, and often take up more practical concerns. Suras are arranged in more or less descending order of length, so that many of the earlier sections are actually in the latter part of the book now. The heading of each sura contains the title, number of verses, and an indication as to whether it was revealed at Mecca or Medina. Interpreters consider it very important to place each text historically, for the "circumstances of the revelation" are critical in unwrapping its original meaning. Tradition has identified the suras, or portions of them where it is clear that a single sura is actually a composite, as early, middle, or late Meccan (610–622), or Medinan (622–632). Muslims believe the Koran is the direct, literal word of God unmodified in any way by the Prophet who uttered them at God's bidding.

What was **pre-Islamic religion** like and did Islam retain any of its features?

Pre-Islamic Arabian tribes believed that the universe was animated by innumerable spirits, each inhabiting its own distinctive elements and natural features. They called each of these minor deities an *ilah,* "god," but tribespeople in many regions singled out one particular local power as the chief spiritual force. That power they called *the* god, *al-ilah,* or *allah* (pronounced alLAAH). Mecca was one of several major cultic sites over which such a chief deity ruled. There, a peculiar cubic shaped structure called the Ka'ba stood for perhaps centuries at the center of pilgrimage traffic associated with a lively caravan trade. Pre-Islamic beliefs also acknowledged the existence of numerous troublesome beings called *jinns,* as well as downright diabolical spiritual forces. Muhammad's ancestors emphasized the importance of following the moral code of tribal custom unquestioningly and did not believe in an afterlife. In his early preaching the Prophet focused on the need to behave morally and justly in light of the coming judgment. He taught that a divine will was more important than tribal custom, however ancient, and gradually increased his condemnation of the cult of many spiritual powers (called polydaemonism). The Ka'ba remained an important symbol, as did the practice of pilgrimage, but Muhammad appropriated those aspects of tradition by underscoring their association with Abraham and Ishmael especially.

What is **the Ka'ba** and why is it important?

According to tradition, Abraham and his son Ishmael built (or prehaps rebuilt) a simple cube-like structure in what came to be the center of the city of Mecca. During Muhammad's time the Ka'ba was a relatively small structure, about fifteen feet tall, with a black stone, the size of a bowling ball, of (perhaps) meteoric origin built into one of its corners. Rebuilt several times since Muhammad's day, the Ka'ba now stands about forty-three feet high, with irregular sides ranging from thirty-six to forty-three feet. During Muhammad's lifetime, the building is said to have housed some 360 idols. In 630, Muhammad cleansed the Ka'ba, and it has since remained empty except for some lamps. Its holiness as a symbol of divine presence derives largely from its associations with the lives of Abraham and Muhammad.

Are there any important links between the **Koran** and the **Bible**?

Since the Islamic interpretation of history overlaps in significant ways with those of Judaism and Christianity, one should not be surprised to find that some material in the Koran parallels some biblical material. Some narrative treatments of various biblical patriarchs and kings, whom the Koran identifies as prophets and messengers, immediately recall aspects of biblical accounts. But there are also interesting variations in the stories. Adam and Eve's fall, for example, is connected with eating from a forbidden tree (or an ear of wheat in one version). Sprinkled throughout the scripture are references to Abraham's near-sacrifice of his son (whom Islamic tradition takes to be Ishmael rather than Isaac), and to Moses' mission to Pharaoh, David's musical gifts, Solomon's royal grandeur, and others. Perhaps the single most important parallel is the story of Joseph. Sura 12 of the Koran retells the tale found in Genesis 39–50 with its own distinctive flavor and variations in detail. Only Joseph's story is told in its entirety, and all in a single sura dedicated entirely to it. Though many Jewish and Christian readers often conclude that Muhammad "borrowed" from the Bible, that is not necessarily the case. The way the Koran tells the stories, mostly in short excerpts and allusions, suggests that Muhammad's listeners must have been already familiar with at least the general drift of the narratives. There are also some accounts of non-biblical prophetic figures, called Hud, Salih, and Shuayb, in some ways unique to the

Why is the Koran important for Muslims?

Muslims believe the beautiful prose of the Koran to be the words of God Himself who spoke through Muhammad. Further, it is believed to be only a copy of an eternal book, which is kept by Allah. The Koran is also held up by Muslims as proof that Muhammad was indeed a prophet since no human is capable of composing such text. Among the most widely read texts today, the Koran is also taught orally so that even Muslims who are illiterate and do not speak Arabic might learn to recite the most important verses in Arabic.

Arabian peninsula. It is important to note that Muslim tradition has discerned in both the Old and New Testaments references to the coming of Islam's prophet. God promised to raise up for Israel a prophet like Moses (Deuteronomy 18:18)—Muhammad. The prophet Isaiah sees two riders approaching, one on a donkey and the other on a camel: Jesus and Muhammad. Jesus promised to send a *parakletos* ("advocate," John 14:16), but Muslim commentators argue that with the correct vowels, the Greek word is *periklutos,* meaning "highly praised," the exact meaning of *muhammad* in Arabic.

What other **early texts** are especially important for Muslims?

Second only to the Koran in both authority and antiquity is the large body of works containing sayings attributed to Muhammad, along with hundreds of anecdotes about him. This material is known collectively as *Hadith* (sayings or traditions, pronounced haDEETH). When Muhammad died, neither the scripture nor the Prophet's words and deeds had been formally committed to writing. And even long after the Koran had been carefully edited, Muslims hesitated to produce written versions of Muhammad's sayings. Custodians of these Prophetic Traditions kept them by heart, much as the earliest followers preserved the Koranic revelations. Not until over two centuries after Muhammad died did his community deem it necessary to gather and edit the Hadith. The impetus to do so came in part from legal scholars, who believed that the only way to interpret the spirit of the Koran faithfully in cases not explicitly treated in the scripture was to have a sound testimony of the Prophet's own views. Through much of the ninth century, Muslim religious scholars undertook the massive task of traveling widely and gathering and recording thousands of Hadiths from countless individuals known for their reliable memories. These scholars, often working independently and at some distance in time and space, then sifted through what they had gathered. Since the very existence of this treasure trove depended on its oral transmission from one generation to another, scholars looked first at the chains of transmission to see whether all individuals listed were trustworthy. If not, one likely could dismiss the

Hadith itself as not entirely reliable. By the end of the ninth century half a dozen authoritative collections, and many lesser ones as well, of Hadith were available, complete with scholarly evaluation as to the relative soundness of each saying and anecdote. Muslims traditionally consider the content of the Hadith to be divinely inspired, only expressed in Muhammad's own words, unlike the Koran, which is in God's own diction.

How do Muslims **interpret** their **sacred texts**?

Discussion of the Koran is a regular activity in most mosques, usually in connection with the Friday congregational prayer (and in the United States also held on Sundays). One or more discussion leaders might present a text and then open the floor to comments and questions. The first concern is generally to establish the "circumstances of the revelation." What was the specific occasion on which this particular text was revealed to Muhammad? Was it revealed in connection with any unusual or momentous event? Was it a direct response to some question or predicament that had arisen in the early Muslim community? Contemporary Muslims can dip into an enormous reservoir of traditional scholarship for help in interpreting the Koran. Exegetes began compiling detailed and extensive commentaries on the sacred scripture as early as the eighth century. They refined the tools of a specialty called *tafsir* (pronounced tafSEER, "explanation, elaboration"). Dozens of multi-volume works in Arabic (plus countless more in various other languages) of great antiquity and authority are still widely available from publishers of Islamic books, and many are now being translated into Western languages. Classical commentators and modern-day interpreters alike look first to the Hadith for help on obscure passages of the Koran, for Muhammad himself often responded to questions about specific texts. Careful study of Arabic grammar and a wide knowledge of other works of Arabic literature for purposes of comparison are also essential background for professional exegetes. In addition to elucidating the basic or literal meanings of a sacred text, Koran commentary can also probe into further levels of meaning. Muslim mystics especially have written allegorical or symbolic interpretations (called *ta'wil,* pronounced ta'WEEL) to uncover the deeper spiritual implications of the scripture.

Where does the word **Muslim** come from? Is it the same as **Moslem**?

Arabic is a Semitic language, as is its distant cousin Hebrew. Both languages are based on roots made up of three consonants. For example, many words can be derived from the root *S-L-M* (*Sh-L-M* in Hebrew). Keep your eye on the upper case letters to follow the root. A basic verb from that root, *SaLiMa,* means to be safe or whole. A related Arabic noun is *salaam,* meaning "peace" (like the Hebrew *ShaLoM*), is part of a standard greeting among Muslims. When Arabic speakers want to build further meanings on a particular root, they do so by modifying the root with either prefixes, infixes (modifying interior letters), or suffixes. For example, to convey the notion of "*causing* someone to be safe or at peace," one modifies the root *SaLiMa* so that it becomes *aSLaMa*. In religious terms, to bring about a state of safety, peace, and wholeness, one has to get one's relationship to God in perfect order. That means letting God be God, and giving up all pretense at trying to do what only God can do—in short, surrendering to the supreme power. That state of surrender is called *iSLaaM,* and a person who acts in such a way as to cause that state is called a *muslim.* One of the first major non-Semitic languages early Muslim conquerors encountered was Persian, in which the *u* was pronounced as an *o,* and the *i* as an *e.* Hence the variation so common today, *Moslem.* Both mean exactly the same thing; the variations are entirely due to differences in pronunciation.

What was happening in and around **Arabia** when Islam began?

In pre-Islamic times the Arabian peninsula had rarely been at the center of Middle Eastern events. An immense coastline made the land accessible to and from the Red Sea on the west, the Persian Gulf on the east, and the Indian Ocean on the south, but the real estate of that vast, inhospitable ocean of sand held little strategic interest for the regional powers. Local kingdoms had ruled to the north, in Syria, and to the southwest, in the Yemen. Although the Greeks and Romans knew about the place and liked its incense, they never set their sights on the territory. When Muhammad was growing up, an important trade route ran up and down the western coastal region, a highway for exchange from Abyssinia (Ethiopia) and the Yemen, to Syria and points north by way of Mecca. To the northwest of the peninsula, the Christian Byzantine empire ruled. To the northeast, in Persia, the Zoroastrian Sasanian empire had displaced the Parthians, a client state of Rome, in 226 CE. These two "confessional" (i.e. religiously connected) empires had been engaged in a protracted tug-of-war over the Fertile Crescent with its enormous river systems. Two Arab tribes in adjacent states did much of their fighting for them, namely the Monophysite Christian Ghassanids for Byzantium and the unchurched Lakhmids for Persia. As it turned out, their ongoing struggle would pave the way for the early expansion of Islam. By the time Muhammad died, Byzantium and Persia had all but spent themselves into bankruptcy and had so worn each other down that neither would mount serious resistance when the Muslim tribes advanced out of Arabia in a conquering mood.

How did **Islam spread** under Mohammad's immediate successors?

Muhammad's immediate successors, called *caliphs* (pronounced KAYliff), inherited an expanding but loose-knit social fabric. The Prophet had united the Bedouin tribes under the banner of Islam, but tribal loyalties cooled quickly when the leader died. When Muslim elders in Medina chose Muhammad's father-in-law Abu Bakr as the first caliph, the initial challenge was to regather the tribes already reverting to their pre-Islamic ways. Umar (634–44), the second caliph, then mobilized tribal forces to move northward into Syria and Mesopotamia (Iraq), westward into Egypt, and eastward into Persia. Next, Umar instituted important policies in the conquered lands, allowing the subjected peoples to retain their religion and law, and levied taxes often lower than what had paid previously to Byzantium and Persia. Muslim armies remained apart in garrisons that eventually became cities in their own right. Umar's successors, Uthman (644–656) and Ali (656–661), compassed the downfall of the last Sasanian emperor, but had to deal with disastrous internal strife as well.

What were the first great **Muslim dynasties**?

Relatives of Uthman, called the Umayyads, brought Ali down for his complicity in the murder of Uthman. They established a new seat of power in the ancient city of Damascus (Syria), thus inaugurating the first of a series of Muslim dynasties. Under the Umayyads the map of Islamdom expanded dramatically. By the year 711, Muslim armies had claimed ground across North Africa to Spain, and as far east as the Indus River in present-day Pakistan. Consolidation and some further expansion continued under the Abbasid dynasty, which ruled from its newly founded capital, Baghdad, after supplanting the Umayyads in 750. But the early plan for a single unified Islamic domain soon began to unravel. Increasingly aware that Baghdad could not continue to hold its far-flung empire together, regional governors and princes at the fringes began to declare independence. Although the Abbasid caliph would continue to claim nominal allegiance until 1258, the future belonged to countless successor states, from Spain to central and south Asia.

What were the most important early Islamic **sectarian movements**?

Immediately upon Muhammad's death Muslims had to face the question of succession to leadership of the community. One faction claimed that the Prophet had designated his cousin and son-in-law, Ali, as his successor. They were to become known as the Party or Faction (Shi'a) of Ali, and today their various subcommunities are called Shi'i Muslims or Shi'ites. But a majority held that Muhammad had made no such appointment and that it was up to the elders to choose from among themselves. They considered their course of action to be both in keeping with the example of Muhammad (called his *Sunna,* SUNnah) and in the spirit of the needs of the whole community (*jama'a,* jaMAA'ah) of Muslims. This majority group came to be known as the People of the Sunnah and the Assembly (*Ahl as-sunna wa-l'jama'ah*), or Sunni Muslims for short.

Were there any **other early sectarian** developments?

Several other sects made their views known early on. When Ali was doing battle with the Umayyads to claim his rights to the caliphate, a number of his troops seceded on

195

Why do Jews, Christians, and Muslims all claim the same Holy Land?

Palestine lies in southwest Asia at the eastern end of the Mediterranean Sea. It is the Holy Land of Jews, since it was here that Moses led the Israelites after he led them out of slavery in Egypt and where they subsequently established their homeland; of Christians, since it is where Jesus Christ was born, lived, and died; and of Muslims, since the Arab people conquered Palestine in the seventh century and, except for a brief period during the Crusades, it was ruled by various Muslim dynasties until 1516 (when it became part of the Ottoman Empire). Palestine, which covers an area of just over 10,000 square miles, is roughly the size of Maryland.

Palestine's capital, Jerusalem, is also claimed as a holy city by all three religions. Jews call it the City of David (or the City of the Great King) since it was made the capital of the ancient kingdom of Israel around 1000 BCE. Christians regard it as holy since Jesus traveled with his disciples to Jerusalem to observe the Passover. It is the site of the Last Supper, and just outside the city, at Golgotha, Jesus was crucified (c. 30). Muslim Arabs captured the city in 638 (just after Muhammad's death), and, like the rest of Palestine, it has a long history of Muslim Arab rule. Jerusalem, which is now part of the modern state of Israel, is home to numerous synagogues, churches, and mosques. It also has been the site of numerous religious conflicts throughout history.

the grounds that Ali was too lax in his appeal to religious principles in the conduct of battle. They judged Ali a serious sinner who was no longer worthy of the name Muslim. That group became known as the Kharijites (or Khawarij, "those who secede"), and a small remnant of their several factions live today largely in Oman on the Persian Gulf. Several other groups also expressed their opinions as to how far one might go in judging another person's suitability for true membership in the Muslim community. One of the more influential believed that only God could judge a person's soul, and that it was therefore best to postpone judgment on the matter. They were known as the Murji'ites or "Postponers."

Was Islam especially important in **medieval Spain**?

Not long after Arab troops began to occupy the Iberian peninsula, Muslim princes (called *amir*s, literally commanders, pronounced aMEER) established themselves in major cities. In 750 the Abbasids sought to put an end to their Umayyad rivals by assassinating all of the family's princes. One managed to escape and take refuge in Spain. This Abd ar-Rahman proclaimed himself Amir of Cordoba, still holding aloft the Umayyad standard. His successors eventually broke with Baghdad definitively by proclaiming the Umayyad Caliphate of Cordoba. A major step up from an Amirate, the Caliphate laid claim to the universal allegiance of all Muslims. For several centuries Cordoba would be a marvel of cultural splendor and inter-religious harmony. On the whole, Cordoba was an outstanding example of how Jews, Christians, and Muslims could live together in peace under Muslim rule. Islam's presence was highly visible in other Spanish cities as well. Seville became an important political and cultural center as Cordoba receded in importance in the mid–eleventh century. Christian reconquest of Spain gradually retook ground from Muslim rule, from Toledo to Cordoba to Seville. Granada would remain the last stronghold of Islam until the armies of Catholic monarchs Ferdinand and Isabella took the legendary Alhambra in 1492. Nearly eight centuries of Islamic presence in Spain left a rich religious and cultural heritage. Five hundred years

Taj Mahal, a seventeenth-century tomb constructed by Mughal Muslim ruler Shah Jahan as burial place of his favorite wife. It is located in Agra, north-central India.

after the fall of Granada, small communities of Muslims are once again taking root in Spain.

How did **Muslim history** unfold after the age of the first great Caliphal dynasties?

Among the numerous dynasties and political regimes that ruled throughout the Mediterranean and central and south Asia, several stand out. In Egypt, the Mamluk dynasty (1250–1517) presided over two and a half centuries of relative peace and prosperity throughout the central Middle East. They were patrons of the arts and architecture on a grand scale under whom Cairo especially grew into a worthy rival of any great Mediterranean city. The Ottoman Turks (1300–1921) supplanted the Mamluks as they expanded to conquer most of the former Byzantine empire and more. To the east, the Safavid dynasty (1501–1722) replaced the descendants of Genghis Khan, who had ruled Iraq and Iran for two hundred fifty years. Establishing Twelver Shi'i Islam the official creed of the realm, the Safavids created splendid art and architecture in cities such as Isfahan.

How did Islam become important in **southern Asia**?

Further east than Iraq and Iran, the Mughal dynasty (1502–1757) established Islamic rule over much of south Asia, from Afghanistan across at least the northern two-thirds of India. Great monarchs such as Akbar, Jahangir, and Shah Jahan turned cities like Delhi and Agra into architectural showpieces with works like the Taj Mahal. After about the mid–eighteenth century, European colonialism began to make inroads into lands formerly under Islamic regimes. Not until the mid–twentieth century did major colonial powers begin to withdraw, ceding political control back to indigenous populations. One dramatic example of that relatively recent change is the independence of India from Britain and the partition of India that created the Muslim state of Pakistan (1948), itself divided in 1971 into Pakistan and Bangladesh.

RELIGIOUS BELIEFS

Is there an **Islamic creed**?

One short, two-part statement sums up the essentials of Muslim belief. "I confess that there is no deity but God, and that Muhammad is the Messenger of God." In this "testimony" called the *shahada* ("confession or witnessing"), Muslims affirm the two foundational elements from which all other beliefs and practices flow. First, they assert that only the one, transcendent, supreme being called Allah in Arabic can claim the full allegiance of humankind. *Allah* means literally "the deity," or what ordinary English usage calls God "with a capital G." Allah is therefore not a distinct name for God as such, but the primary designation for the Absolute, the deity above all other powers both spiritual and worldly. Affirming God's absolute oneness is called *tawhid* (pronounced taw-HEED) Second, Muslims attest that human beings know of this Supreme Being through the agency of prophets, the last of whom was Muhammad. This profession of faith is the first of the "five pillars" of Islam (along with almsgiving, daily ritual prayer, fasting during Ramadan—pronounced RamaDAAN—and pilgrimage to Mecca, all of which will be discussed later in detail). Muslim religious scholars between about 750 and 950 formulated a number of other, more detailed creedal statements, but none has been as widely known as the Nicene Creed among Christians or

The Five Pillars of Faith

Muslims practice adherence to the Five Pillars of Faith: 1) profession of belief in Allah as the only God and Muhammad as his prophet; 2) ritual prayer five times daily—at dawn, at noon, in the afternoon, in the evening, and at nightfall; 3) giving alms to the poor; 4) fasting from dawn until dusk during the holy month of Ramadan; and 5) making the pilgrimage (hajj) to the holy city of Mecca at least once during their lifetime.

the "Thirteen Articles" among Jews. Those later Islamic creeds developed largely as correctives to theological positions that arose during Islam's early centuries, views that the creeds formally repudiated as unacceptable.

What does the term **revelation** mean in Islamic tradition?

Islam's scripture, the Koran, consistently refers to itself as the word that God has "sent down" (*tanzil,* pronounced tanZEEL)) to humankind through Muhammad. That which is "sent down" represents a manifestation of truths that have existed from all eternity in the heavenly archetype of the Koran known as the "Mother of the Book." God reveals by communicating in a language understandable to the intended audience. Both the Koran and subsequent Muslim tradition describe the actual process of revelation by a technical term (*wahy*) that distinguishes prophetic revelation from the kinds of "inspiration" that animate holy persons and artists, for example. The prophetic intermediary "hears" the message, not with physical ears but with the ears of the spirit and heart. Some descriptions of revelation suggest a visionary dimension as well, as when the angel Gabriel or another mysterious unnamed presence appears. According to both Koran and Hadith, Muhammad received revelations in a wide variety of circumstances. In some cases revelation is given in response to a particular question asked of the Prophet. In others, Muhammad is described as praying, preaching, eating, or even bathing. Muhammad is said to have experienced a variety of actual sensations when he received a revelation. He spoke of a sound like bees humming around his face, or a loud bell, the sound of which was physically painful. Sometimes he broke into a cold sweat or showed signs like those of a trance or seizure. All of the prophets are said to have experienced similar forms of revelation. What is most significant here is Muhammad's overwhelming sense of the divine presence at these moments.

Are **doctrine** and **dogma** important to Muslims?

Islamic tradition centers on the relatively compact body of beliefs summed up in the Shahada. Straightforward affirmation of God's unity and transcendence, and divine commu-

Plaque indicating the times for the five regular daily prayers plus one devotional time, at the Mosque of Lady Khadija, Kusadasi, Turkey.

nication through a succession of prophet-messengers, are the core of doctrine. Further basic elements that flow from these core doctrines include, especially, belief in God's use of angels as helpers and guides, resurrection of the body, personal accountability at judgment, and ultimate reward or punishment in heaven or hell in the next world. Since there is no central teaching authority, Muslims do not think in terms of official dogmatic formulations of their beliefs. Simplicity is the key. So long as one prefaces every act of faith with proper intention, one can be assured of pursuing the path God has revealed. In other words, Islamic tradition emphasizes *orthopraxy* over *orthodoxy*.

Is there such a thing as **heresy** in Islamic tradition?

Muslim tradition recognizes varying degrees of deviation from pure faith or *iman* (eeMAAN). Certain forms of departure from strict Koranic teaching and practices clearly identified as deriving from the Sunna of the Prophet have been labeled "innovation" (*bid'a,* BID'ah). Some things once considered innovations, such as attaching minarets to mosques, have long since become widely accepted. All but today's most traditionally minded Muslims give little consideration to this category. A daily danger for all human beings, one that Muslims seek to combat constantly, is called *shirk,* or associating partners with God. Any undue attention or attachment to that which is not God is thus a form of *shirk,* but while it is a natural tendency, it is not necessarily a permanent condition unless one chooses to make it so. A more serious problem,

200

Sultan's mosque in the city of Shah Alam, in Malaysia near the capital city of Kuala Lumpur. One of the world's largest mosques, its minarets are nearly 450 feet tall. Late twentieth century.

known technically as "deviation" (*ilhad,* ilHAAD), comes closer to what many understand by the term heresy. A *mulhid* is someone who deliberately strays from the broadly accepted tenets of the faith, introducing innovations to the extent that one can no longer readily recognize basic Islamic teachings in the new formulation. Farthest from adherence to true belief is the category of *kufr,* the kind of willful unbelief that leads to outright blasphemy.

What do Muslims believe about **God**?

God is one, transcendent, and wholly unlike anything in ordinary human experience. But such a barebones description of ultimate reality leaves little for the human heart to grasp. Muslim tradition speaks of God most of all through the "Ninety-Nine Beautiful Names." "Compassionate" and "Merciful" are by far the most important of these. They occur in the phrase "In the name of God, the Compassionate, the Merciful," with which all but one of the suras of the Koran begin. Whatever devout Muslims do, they dedicate with that phrase. God's names include about equally those that suggest divine power and majesty (*jalal,* pronounced jaLAAL) and those that speak of his beauty and infinite attractiveness (*jamal,* pronounced jaMAAL). God both brings to life and causes to die, gives freely and calls all creation to account. Non-Muslims often have the mistaken impression that the Islamic God is most of all a fearsome, even despotic, power before whom all must cower and cringe. To the contrary, while Muslims are

201

ever aware of God's uncontested sovereignty and dominion over all things, they believe as well that, as the Koran teaches, God is closer to individual persons than even their jugular vein. Muslim tradition reminds believers that, in the end, God's mercy outweighs his anger. Scores of Hadiths describe this God of mercy in such beautiful and moving terms that any outsider who studies them can readily understand why so many Muslims find devotion to such a deity so compelling.

Do Muslims believe in **miracles**?

Muhammad's early critics in Mecca sometimes taunted him for being so much like an ordinary human being: If he were really a prophet of God, surely he would entertain them with some sort of heavenly pyrotechnics. Muhammad regarded the Koran itself as his only miracle, a marvel of eloquence uttered by a man considered technically "unlettered." But the scripture does refer often to spectacular "signs" God brought about to vindicate earlier prophets. For example, Moses' staff became a dragon that devoured Pharaoh's magicians, and Moses' hand turned white with leprosy and was then restored to health (Koran 7:107–08). Within a generation or two of Muhammad's death, tradition had begun to attribute to the Prophet a number of extraordinary occurrences. He could fast for inordinately long periods, could see people behind him, heal various ailments, supply water where there was none, and stretch limited food sources as needed. Trees and stones saluted Muhammad, a pillar in his house mourned that the Prophet no longer leaned on it when he preached, and the Prophet split the moon in two to confound his critics. Throughout the history of Islam holy persons called "friends of God" have been famous for the ability to perform wondrous deeds. Many Muslims today regard accounts of such legend and lore of secondary importance. Classical Muslim theologians devised technical terms to distinguish between two levels of miracle. They called the works God did as proof of his prophets' truthfulness "evidentiary miracles" (*mu'jizat,* pronounced mu'jiZAAT), and those effected by Friends of God "marvels" (*karamat,* pronounced karaaMAAT). Theologians further called attention to key differences between works of sorcery and wonders performed authentically under divine power.

What are the main Islamic notions of the **afterlife**?

Muslim eschatology has much in common with most Christian and some Jewish traditions about the afterlife. Death is not the end of life, but a transition to another level of existence. Muslims believe human beings are accountable for all of their free moral decisions. People are not held similarly responsible for actions with negative consequences but done under duress or in the absence of intent to do evil. Numerous texts of the Koran warn of the coming Day of Judgment, the Day of Resurrection, the Hour in which the true quality of everyone's deeds will be revealed. On the basis of that accounting, individuals will go across a narrow passage of no return called the *barza-*

kh (pronounced BARzakh) to one of several destinations. Paradise is called the Garden (*janna,* pronouned JANnah), a verdant place of repose and delight, an oasis for the just. Heaven is not so much literally a place as a state of being whose principal feature is the vision of God. Koranic texts refer to several different levels or degrees of heavenly reward. Hell, known as the Fire or Gehenna (*jahannam,* pronounced jaHANnam), represents the state of refusal to acknowledge God's sovereignty. Some Muslim theologians have taught that hell is not necessarily a permanent state, since God can always forgive any sin except unrelenting denial of God's existence. Hell can thus function in a way similar to that of the state of purgatory in Christian tradition, though Islamic tradition does not have a separate term for that state of purification. Muslim tradition also hints at something like an intermediate state, perhaps similar to the Christian idea of limbo.

Do Muslims believe in **predestination** or fatalism?

A common misperception of Islamic tradition is that God exercises such minute and perfect control over all things that human actions have no bearing on the individual's ultimate destiny. When Muslims use the expression "God willing," they do not mean to suggest that human beings are mere marionettes dancing at the whim of the divine puppeteer. They are simply reminding themselves that God is ultimately in charge of everything, regardless of individual human preferences. True, the Koran often describes how God both guides and leads astray "whomever he chooses." But that does not suggest that God is capricious or spiteful, only that God is God and that lesser beings ought not to take God's sovereignty for granted even for a second. Equally often, the Koran reminds believers how God lays out his "signs" in creation and in the individual heart, adding "perhaps you will understand." Muslims believe in God's justice. The Koran insists that each person will be held accountable for his or her actions at judgment. But since God is just, Muslims conclude that human beings exercise a significant freedom of choice—otherwise accountability at the judgment would be a sham, a cruel hoax to which God hardly needs to resort. All in all, Muslim tradition seeks to maintain the delicate balance between belief in God's absolute power, and a limited, but more than adequate, human freedom to choose either good or evil.

Does anything like **millennialism** have a place in Islamic thinking?

Yes, so long as one understands "millennialism" broadly rather than as a precise reference to measures of a thousand years. Numerous Hadith, called Traditions of Discord, talk of various general features that mark a decidedly downward trend in human life. Honesty will be hard to find, fewer and fewer people will observe the religious law, and violence will rise. According to other ancient traditions, various explicit signs will herald the end of time itself. A resurgence of chaos symbolized by Gog and Magog will mark a radical turn for the worse, the beginning of the final chapter in the unraveling of history. A figure resembling the Prophet, called the Mahdi (Guided One), will usher in a temporary age of justice. Numerous individuals throughout the history of Islam have sought to gain political power by claiming to be the Mahdi, most recently in 1979, when armed bandits seized control of the sanctuary of the Ka'ba in Mecca. A one-eyed Antichrist figure (called the *Dajjal,* that's dajJAAL) will supplant the Mahdi, luring people away through magic masquerading as miracle. Jesus will eventually return to battle the Antichrist, overthrowing that false prophet and paving the way for the Day of Judgment. Shi'ite tradition features its own distinctive type of millenarianism. According to the Shi'ite interpretation of history, Muhammad's spiritual authority was passed along through a series of descendants called Imams. In the view of the "Twelvers," by far the majority of Shi'ites, the twelfth and last of these Imams (also called the Mahdi) went into "greater concealment" in 940. This Hidden Imam did not die but has remained in a mysterious state from which he will return to establish full justice. In the meantime, the Imam hears prayers and intercedes for believers.

What is **jihad**?

Jihad (pronounced jiHAAD) comes from an Arabic verb that means "to struggle or exert oneself." In recent years both Muslims and non-Muslims alike have bandied the term about so loosely that one has to do some digging to retrieve an accurate understanding of it. According to news reports, everyone from the scarcely devout Saddam Hussein to Usama bin Ladin and the Taliban has called for a jihad against somebody, usually "the West." Hence the virtually automatic translation of jihad as "holy war"—at best a misleading, and at worst a highly inflammatory, interpretation. Jihad does have a range of precisely defined meanings in Islamic tradition. Under prescribed circumstances jihad can include offensive military action where the free practice of Islam is under threat of constraint. Many scholars in recent times have held that one cannot justify an offensive jihad unless Muslims are being persecuted religiously. Even then, therefore, we are talking about a type of defensive action. Military jihad has always been subject to strict criteria and is in many ways parallel to the Christian notion of "just war." Very few, if any, recent calls for Jihad have actually satisfied the necessary criteria. Muslims also speak of various non-violent forms of jihad. One can battle injustice and evil through jihad of the pen or the tongue, for example. When someone asked Muhammad what the greatest jihad was, the Prophet replied that it was to speak a word of truth in the ear of a tyrant. An important theme in Islamic spirituality has been called the "Greater Jihad," as distinct from all the various forms of exterior, lesser jihads. Warriors of the spirit must take up the sword of self-knowledge against the fiercest enemy of all, their own inner tendencies to evil and idolatry.

Is there an **Islamic fundamentalism**?

Unfortunately, the term "fundamentalist" has become virtually synonymous with "Muslim" in contemporary American usage. This is unfortunate because, when applied to

Muslims, "fundamentalist" has been simultaneously linked to terrorism. It is fair to say that most devout Muslims interpret their scriptures conservatively and quite literally, as do the vast majority of devout adherents to many traditions. Islamic fundamentalism is not inherently more likely to be expressed in extreme behavior than any other brand of fundamentalism. One can of course point to examples of such behavior in virtually every tradition—including the assassination of abortion providers by American Christians and the burning of Christian villagers by angry Hindu mobs in India. Extreme and violent behavior that claims religious justification invariably has a great deal to do with predominant political and social climates in particular places and times. Non-Muslims often apply the epithet "fundamentalist" indiscriminately to widely diverse situations. For example, so-called militant fundamentalists in Algeria attempt to justify their activism on very different grounds than do, say, Shi'ite factions in southern Lebanon, the Palestinian organization called Hamas, and the revolutionary government of Iran. In other words, while the term fundamentalism has value in describing some religious phenomena, it has become so imprecise as to be virtually useless as a way of describing Muslims.

SIGNS AND SYMBOLS

Are there any **signs or symbols** that might identify an individual as a Muslim?

Muslim men and women sometimes wear items or styles of clothing that clearly set them apart from non-Muslims. Stop by the local mosque on Friday afternoon and you will invariably find men arriving for the congregational prayer wearing long flowing gowns and small knit or other fabric caps that cover most of the head, in honor of Muhammad's practice of covering his head during prayer. Men of southern Asian origin (India, Pakistan, Bangladesh) sometimes wear a kind of boat-shaped cap commonly worn back home. In some parts of the world men who have made the Hajj signify their status as *hajjis* by wearing a burgundy fez wrapped in a white cloth. The rimless fez became popular because it was practical for use during prostration in prayer, allowing easy contact of the forehead with the ground. More than likely the women attending a mosque will be wearing some form of head covering and an ankle-length dress or tunic with slacks. In many instances the choice of distinctive garb is related to an individual's personal devotion and desire to symbolize his or her commitment to Islamic religious and social values. Most items of clothing are best understood as traditional rather than inherently religious, since they carry no explicit and uniquely Islamic symbolism. However, many Muslim women and men wear various items of jewelry bearing Islamic symbols. Most common are rings, pendants, and bracelets containing religious words or phrases in Arabic. Some show a star within a crescent moon, a symbol some interpret as a reference to the astronomical signs that mark the onset of the month of Ramadan. Favorite texts include the word Allah, phrases such as *In sha'a 'Llah* (God Willing), the Shahada, names of Muhammad and the four Rightly Guided Caliphs (Abu Bakr, Umar, Uthman, and Ali). Muslim designers produce a wide range of religious adornment and market them through an increasing number of suppliers and boutiques that advertise in Muslim publications worldwide.

Are Muslim women required to **veil** their faces?

Use of the veil depends a great deal on cultural custom. The Koran does not explicitly require that women cover their faces. It calls for modest dress, but some have interpreted one ambiguous text—"they should draw their veils over their bosoms..." (Koran 24:31)—to mean that the head covering should continue down over the upper body. In some cultures, Muslim women wear various forms of facial covering, whether drawn across the lower face from side to side, or covering the head completely like a small tent. Those coverings also vary in texture from a fine gauze to a fairly heavy weave with slits cut at eye level. The majority of women who wear some form of special clothing, technically known as *hijab* (pronouned hiJAAB, veiling or covering), opt for a head scarf down to the mid-forehead so that it covers all the hair. Some wear a flowing gown (*jilbab,* pronounced jilBAAB) that extends to the ankles. Note that the emphasis is on modesty rather than on some specific style of covering. Muslim immigrants to Europe or the United States from the Middle East or southern Asia might choose to continue wearing styles common in their homelands. Where prevailing social norms allow greater latitude in choice of dress, Muslim women often report that they opt for fuller covering for two reasons: They seek an explicit symbolic connection with Islamic practice and they choose to make a statement of personal freedom from the general exploitation of women that they often experience in society at large.

What signs or symbols distinguish **Muslim ritual or religious specialists**?

There is no ordained Muslim clergy as such, but a category of specialists, known as religious scholars, sometimes wear distinctive garb. Style and color generally depend on variant traditions in the country of origin. Many religious scholars from many lands prefer the fez wrapped in the white cloth (signifying that the wearer has made Hajj). Some, from the Sudan for example, wear a white turban. Shi'ite mullahs and higher ranking scholars in Iran and Iraq often wear a black turban that identifies them as Sayyids, descendants of Muhammad through his daughter Fatima and her husband, Ali. Size, color, number of turns, and so forth, allow a practiced eye to distinguish national and sectarian connections. Members of Sufi orders often wear special clothing, particularly during their prayer gatherings. Various organizations have unique headgear, sometimes using colors or varied ways of wrapping the basic cap with windings to indicate rank or status within the order.

Mosque of the Islamic Foundation of St. Louis, Missouri. The minaret symbolizes the call to prayer—here in a suburban neighborhood the call does not emanate from the tower itself—and the five windows on front and left side symbolize the "Five Pillars" of Islam. The small house-like feature protruding from the front marks the place of the niche (*mihrab*) that indicates the direction of Mecca.

Do Muslims mark their **sacred spaces** with any distinctive signs and symbols?

Drive by the mosque nearest you—there is probably one not very far away—and you are likely to notice two distinctive features. Attached to, or alongside, the building you will see one or perhaps two slender towers called minarets. Originally designed to provide maximum broadcast of the call to prayer, the minaret eventually became a visual symbol of Islamic presence. Most structures designed as mosques feature a dome of some sort, typically spanning the central interior space called the prayer hall. Many synagogues and Eastern Christian churches also use central domes, but generally do not have towers that one might mistake for minarets. Atop some minarets and domes you will find a finial in the shape of a crescent moon encircling a single star. Some communities choose to have their mosques reflect architecturally a particular national or regional heritage. They might hire, for example, an Egyptian architect to design in a neo-classical Egyptian style, as with the national mosque in Washington, D.C. Or they might choose to incorporate into the design some visual allusion to a particularly important mosque, the way the new Islamic Center of Cleveland aligns a large central and a smaller secondary dome, recalling the Dome of the Rock and Al-Aqsa mosque in Jerusalem. Interior decorations typically feature elegant calligraphic texts, either painted or carved in marble or other stone, of the names Allah and Muhammad, and of the Shahada and Basmallah, and possibly of any number of the Ninety-Nine Beautiful Names of God. Calligraphic

207

decoration often appears around the drum of the dome and around the niche on the wall facing Mecca. Prayer rugs or carpeting sometimes show niche designs like that of the *mihrab* (pronounced mihRAAB, niche). And somewhere in the mosque there will more than likely be a large picture of the sanctuary of the Ka'ba in Mecca, and possibly also of the Prophet's mosque in Medina.

What sorts of **signs or symbols** do Muslims use **at home**?

Many Muslim families decorate their homes with wall hangings and other small objects with religious significance. Popular items include cloth or paper panels showing beautifully written texts of the Koran. Pictures of Mecca, Medina, Jerusalem or of other important mosques or shrines are quite common. Some families prominently display a copy of the Koran, often kept in a special case or wrapping, on a book-stand or on the mantel. Shi'ite households frequently have pictures of Ali, his two sons Hasan and Husayn, and sometimes also of other Imams or their burial places. Muslim households will not own or display a picture of Muhammad or any of the other prophets. Special times and seasons often call for special religious ornament. Some families put the Koran center-stage during Ramadan, for example.

Is it true that Muslims never depict **human** or **animal figures**?

Browse the pages of virtually any publication designed for Muslim readers and you may be surprised at the number of illustrations featuring human and animal figures. Shelves of mosque bookstores are filled with books, especially those designed for children, similarly illustrated. Still, the notion persists, among Muslims and non-Muslims alike, that "Muslims don't do pictures." What most people popularly perceive as a blanket prohibition of images actually applies only to ritual settings. In other words, you will not find figural or representational imagery in a mosque. Islamic and Jewish tradition share the concern that inherent in representational visual imagery, especially of the three-dimensional sort (sculpture), is the risk of idolatry. Muslim artists throughout the ages and across the globe have produced a great deal of figural art, even including images of prophets and other holy persons. But their images are so clearly abstract and non-realistic that they can scarcely be taken as the artist's attempt to usurp God's creative power. For purposes of education and entertainment, two-dimensional images generally have been perfectly acceptable. In fact, even the prohibition on three-dimensional imagery is far from absolute, except in the context of worship. For example, Muslim children play with dolls. Devout Muslims express a preference for educationally suitable imagery that exemplifies virtue and ethical values. Under the heading "Move Over Barbie!" one company markets a doll called Razanne, dressed in white head-and-shoulder covering (the *hijab*) and green full-length gown (*jilbab*). The *hijab* is removable so that little girls can learn about donning the proper covering. Razanne's clothes are decoratively trimmed, but she wears no makeup.

What does the crescent moon and star symbol mean?

A crescent moon embracing a single star adorns the flags of a number of modern nation-states with majority Muslim populations. The sign is almost certainly not of Arab origin, and the Ottoman Turks may have appropriated the symbolism from Byzantium. At first, the symbol appeared on the flags of lands formerly under Ottoman rule, but other states with no historical connection to the Ottoman empire have also adopted the imagery. Popular understanding of the symbol usually identifies the crescent moon as the essential indicator of the beginning of Ramadan, the ninth lunar month. More generally still, the symbol reminds some of the lunar cycles that regulate Islam's religious calendar. Appearing frequently at the top of domes and minarets, the symbol has become a generic reminder of Islam, much the way the cross has for Christianity and the six-pointed star for Judaism.

What is the meaning of the **hand symbol**?

Silhouettes of a five-fingered open hand appear often as a motif in jewelry and on staffs that function as standards in some Shi'i religious rituals. Called "the five," the symbol reminds devotees of the five principal members of the Prophet's family: Muhammad, Fatima, Ali, Hasan, and Husayn. Many Shi'ite mosques display the hand as a finial on both domes and minarets in mosques of classical design. Sometimes the hand was hoisted atop a staff as a battle standard, emblazoned with prayers to Ali on the fingers and the names of all twelve Imams encircling the palm. As a symbol used by Muslims in various parts of the world by Muslims of various communities, the hand functions as a talismanic magical device, a symbol of control or power associated with Muhammad's daughter Fatima.

Is **number, letter, color, or animal symbolism** important in Islamic tradition?

These and other types of related symbolism abound. The following examples provide only a hint of the variety of symbolism. Every letter in the Arabic language has a numerical value. A common use of number symbolism involves totaling up the numerical value of all the letters in a particular phrase and then using the number as a reminder of the phrase. For example, Muslims often repeat the phrase "In the name of God, the Compassionate, the Merciful." It is called the *basmallah*, after the sound of the first three words, *Bi 'smi 'Llahi ('r-Rahmani 'r-Rahim)*. The numerical value of all the letters in the phrase is 786, and the symbol appears often, in a sort of sunburst design, in pictures of holy places such as the Ka'ba. Letter symbolism is especially prominent in classical religious poetry in languages like Persian, Urdu, and Turkish.

209

Poets love to play on meanings suggested by the shapes of the Arabic letters. As for colors, green has come to be known as the color of the prophets, and of Muhammad in particular. Animal symbols, too, have been widespread in many cultures. Muhammad's cousin and son-in-law, Ali, was known as the "Lion of God" because of his courage. Shi'i artists in particular often included images of a lion when they wanted to suggest the spiritual presence of the first Imam, Ali.

Have **relics** ever been important for Muslims?

Popular Islamic spirituality in many parts of the world has included devotional practices associated with the tombs of holy persons. People visit the shrines of the friends of God in hopes of gaining blessings and other special favors as a result of saintly intercession. Many of these shrines hold items the saint is believed to have owned, such as headgear, a special symbolic frock called the *khirqa,* walking staff, begging bowl, prayer beads, or symbolic weapon. Devotees who come to the shrines sometimes receive an object, such as a simple head wrapping or other token, that has been in contact with the holy person's tomb. Only one object has been similarly associated with Muhammad. Since the thirteenth century, Turkish Muslims believed they owned the so-called mantle of the Prophet, a green robe now in the possession of the Topkapi Museum in Istanbul. People there and in many other countries still recite a traditional poem called the *Burda* (mantle poem) during the observance of Muhammad's birthday, but the mantle itself has never been the focus of devotional practice as have the relics of many friends of God. Sacred footprints function in Islamic tradition, as in many others as well, like relics. Pilgrims to Mecca say special prayers at the "Station of Abraham" just opposite the door of the Ka'ba—a small glass and gold-colored cupola covers a small stone said to contain footprints God caused Abraham to leave in the softened stone as a proof of his prophethood. Tradition says that as Muhammad rose heavenward on his Ascension, he left still-visible prints in the large stone beneath the Dome of the Rock. Muhammad's footprints became the inspiration for several types of visual symbolism still popular in North Africa, for example. Footprints of Ali have likewise been at the devotional center of a number of shrines.

MEMBERSHIP, COMMUNITY, DIVERSITY

Where do **Muslims live** today? What are their estimated numbers?

Islam is now a truly global religious tradition. Approximately 1.2 billion Muslims live worldwide, on every continent and in most countries. In very general terms, about a third of the total live in the Middle East and North Africa. Several major ethno-linguistic groups are represented there, including Arabs, Turks, Persians, and Berbers. Many people associate Islam with Arabs even though they are now a relatively small minority of the global population. Another third live in central and southern Asia, including the southern republics of the former Soviet Union, Western China, India, Pakistan, and Bangladesh. Pakistan is the most important modern example of a nation-state established as a Muslim land. Another third are in sub-Saharan Africa, Indonesia, and in smaller concentrations in several dozen other countries. Indonesia boasts the single largest national population of Muslims, approaching two hundred million. At over a hundred million, India is home to the world's largest minority Muslim population. Muslims number from six to eight million in the United States. It may also be helpful to think in terms of religio-cultural spheres, defined by key language groups, in which Islam has been a particularly important influence. The Arabicate sphere, for example, includes all those areas in which Arabic has been the dominant vehicle of Islamic expression, namely, the central Middle East, north Africa, and east Africa. The Persianate sphere consists of Iran, Afghanistan, and all of southern Asia. Within the Malayo-Polynesian sphere are Malaysia, Indonesia, and the Philippines. Central Asia, including western China, and present-day Turkey and the Balkans comprise the Turkic sphere. Last but not least is the sub-Saharan sphere, in which Nigeria and other west African nations are most significant.

Have Muslims traditionally sent out **missionaries** to convert others?

Islam has been a missionary tradition since its earliest days. Muhammad's preaching eventually gathered a community of Meccans which in turn grew dramatically after migrating to Medina in the Hijra. Muslims believe in spreading the word whenever possible. Proselytizing is called "inviting" (*da'wa,* pronounced DA'wah) others to join the community of Islam. Many regard it as a basic religious duty, second only to their fulfillment of the five pillars. Despite perceptions to the contrary, Islam has spread far more often through peaceful means than through the sword. Among the earliest dedicated missionaries were Sufis who traveled with Muslim merchants along the trade routes to establish communities all over Asia and Africa. Some larger mission-oriented organizations have developed and moved into new territory with local or governmental sponsorship in a home country, but Muslim missionary societies are generally fewer and smaller than their Christian counterparts.

Is **Mecca** the only Islamic **holy city**?

As the birthplace of Muhammad and the site of the Ka'ba, Mecca, and its immediate environs, is naturally the holiest place on earth for Muslims. According to tradition, other prophets and important holy people passed through Mecca as well. Abraham nearly sacrificed his son Ishmael at Arafat (the valley just outside Mecca) and built the

Ka'ba. God rescued Abraham's consort, Hagar, and their son Ishmael from dying of thirst in the desert by causing the well of Zamzam to bubble forth. In 622 Muhammad traveled with his young community to Medina and there established Islam as an all-encompassing social entity. From Medina, the Prophet secured access to Mecca for Muslims and in Medina he died. Muhammad's house and earliest mosque remain a regular stop for most pilgrims who make Hajj and Umra. For these reasons and more, Medina ranks as second-holiest city for Muslims. But Muhammad and a number of the other prophets also have important connections to Jerusalem. Muslim tradition has it that God carried Muhammad from Mecca to Jerusalem, to the "farther mosque," where he met and led the other major prophets in prayer. From a spot nearby Muhammad began his Ascension or *Mi'raj* (pronounced mi'RAAJ). For a time the young Muslim community in Medina faced Jerusalem when then prayed, but the orientation for prayer changed to Mecca in connection with a falling-out with the local Jewish tribes. Nevertheless, Jerusalem has retained a special place in Muslim piety and remains politically sensitive real estate.

How does the practice of **almsgiving** express Muslims' sense of **community**?

Zakat (pronounced zaKAAT), almsgiving, is one of the five pillars. It requires all financially stable Muslims to contribute varying amounts, depending on the type of goods being taxed. For example, it comes to 10 percent of agricultural produce in general, but 2.5 percent of a person's savings or profits over and above what one needs to live. There are many ways of calculating the matter these days. What is most important to understand about religious almsgiving is that for Muslims it is an institutionalized form of social concern. Muslim authorities see to the distribution of the funds among the neediest, both at home and abroad. The United Arab Emirates, for example, might earmark charitable funds for building an airstrip for the delivery of desperately needed

Small group discussion takes place under the platform once meant for the Sultan's family, in the early seventeenth-century mosque of Sultan Ahmet in Istanbul. The group to the left is engaged in ritual prayer, facing Mecca.

supplies to the Albanian Muslim refugees from Kosovo. Devout Muslims are encouraged to give far beyond the minimum *zakat* as well. At the end of the month-long fast of Ramadan, many give generously to the *zakat al-fitr,* or alms for the breaking of the fast. Those and all other voluntary charitable donations are called *sadaqa* (pronounced SAdakah, "righteousness, uprightness"), for through these signs of social concern individual Muslims gain blessing and forgiveness. A related practice among Shi'i Muslims is the *khums* or "fifth." The tax was originally the custom of providing the Prophet a portion of the military spoils, but some Shi'ite religious authorities have collected it from their constituencies up to modern times as an offering for the Twelfth Imam expected to return at the end of time.

Do all Muslims **belong** to the same large group?

Asked whether they think of the global community of Islam as composed of various factions, most Muslims are likely to respond that all Muslims belong to the same universal *umma* or brother- and sisterhood of faith, and that any talk of sub-groups or sects is beside the point. All believe in the oneness of God, the prophetship of Muhammad, divine revelation in the Koran, the existence of angels, the ultimate accountability of all persons, and the five pillars—in short, all the fundamental items of belief and practice described earlier. But there are in fact various sub-communities within the larger *umma* (pronounced UMmah, global community), each with its unique histories

213

and contributions to the larger history of Islam. Minority communities of Muslims have often had to contend with the same problems that have beset minorities always and everywhere, regardless of the composition of the majority in which they find themselves.

Who are **Sunni Muslims**?

About 85 to 90 percent of the world's Muslims consider themselves Sunni. Their historic patrimony derives directly from the Prophet himself as institutionalized in the caliphate. Sunni tradition has been embodied in most of the regimes that have held political power from Morocco to Indonesia, since the early Middle Ages until early modern times. The ideal of the caliph, legitimate successor to Muhammad, as the spiritual as well as temporal ruler of all Muslims, has survived largely as a distant dream since the Mongols destroyed Baghdad in 1258. And since the last Ottoman sultan fell from power in the 1920s, virtually no Muslim ruler has been even nominally regarded as a universal ruler. Some Muslims still entertain the possibility of a resurgence of the caliphate, but that is definitely a minority view.

Who are **Shi'i Muslims**?

Various Shi'i communities have been identifiable since at least the eighth century. Among the principal features that distinguish Shi'i from Sunni tradition is the belief that a legitimate successor to leadership, called *imam* (pronounced eeMAAM), must be designated by his predecessor and belong to the family of the Prophet. According to ancient Shi'i belief, Muhammad did designate his cousin Ali, but Abu Bakr, Umar and Uthman managed to usurp power and prevent Ali from assuming his rightful place. Around the middle of the eighth century a split developed over who would be the seventh Imam. One group continued to pledge their loyalty to a man named Isma'il, who had just died, even though Isma'il's father, the seventh Imam Ja'far, appointed a replacement when Isma'il died. The faction that stayed with Isma'il came to be called the Isma'ilis, or Seveners, since their line of Imams ended then. There are now at least two major branches of Seveners, one of which looks to the Aga Khan as its spiritual leader. The larger group of Shi'ites in the eighth century believed the legitimate line of Imams extended to a twelfth, and ended when that Imam went into concealment until his expected return at the end of time. Twelver Shi'ites are by far the majority community, constituting nearly all of Iran's and more than half of Iraq's people.

Are the **Druze** Muslims?

During the early eleventh century a ruler, al-Hakim (d. 1021), of the Fatimid dynasty—a type of Sevener Shi'ites—did not argue when his followers began to claim that he was divine. Among al-Hakim's supporters was a Turk named Darazi. Even after

Darazi died and his former arch-rival claimed that he himself was the true spokesman of al-Hakim, the name of Darazi would live on in the word Druze. Fatimid Isma'ili doctrine had long shown very esoteric tendencies in interpreting the role of its seven Imams, and a similar esoterism remains a hallmark of Druze teaching. A collection of letters attributed to al-Hakim form the core sacred literature of the very closed and secretive communities, which now, for the most part, inhabit Lebanon, Syria, and the northern occupied West Bank of Palestine. Their esoteric teachings about al-Hakim, along with notions of reincarnation and other decidedly non-Islamic themes, leave them very much outside the fold of Islam.

What about **Baha'is** and the group called the **Ahmadiyya**?

In mid–nineteenth century Persia, a faction called the Babis (followers of the Bab, "Gateway") broke away from Twelver Shi'ism. The Bab had prophesied the coming of a promised messiah-like figure, a role claimed by a man who called himself Baha' Allah and claimed the office of prophet. Upon his death in 1892, a follower took up the claim, as did others. According to mainstream Muslim belief, there can be no prophet after Muhammad, so Baha'is are considered non-Muslims. Around the time the Baha'i movement was getting started in Iran, a group formed around a Punjabi named Mirza Ghulam Ahmad (1835–1908), who claimed to be both the Mahdi and Jesus' Second Coming. Around 1909 the Ahmadiyya (followers of Ahmad) split into two main factions. One claimed their founder was a prophet, thus meriting an official condemnation from Islamic authorities. The other Ahmadiyya faction insisted that Ahmad was only a religious reformer. From half a million to a million members live in west Africa and Pakistan. Most Muslims today consider Baha'is and Ahmadiyyas non-Muslims.

Who are the **Black Muslims** and the **Nation of Islam**?

In 1930s Detroit, W. D. Fard began teaching that the ancestors of black Americans had been Muslims. Young Elijah Poole became a devoted follower, and Fard declared Poole his successor and prophet. Elijah took the last name Muhammad and continued to develop a community called the Nation of Islam, or the Black Muslims. Two prominent young followers of Elijah Muhammad were Malcolm X and Louis Farrakhan. Malcolm X tells in his *Autobiography* how he discovered during his pilgrimage to Mecca that Elijah Muhammad's teachings of a kind of reverse racism were a lie. All human beings were brothers and sisters under God, and Malcolm returned to try to counter-teach Muhammad's misinterpretations of Islam. Malcolm was assassinated in 1965, but ten years later, when Muhammad died, Elijah's son Wallace took over and continued to pursue the reform movement Malcolm X had begun. Wallace sought to bring the Nation of Islam, newly named the World Community of Islam in the West, in line with mainstream Muslim teachings. Louis Farrakhan, on the other hand, chose to continue the separatist doctrines of Elijah Muhammad and, with his approximately fifty thousand followers, retained the name Nation of Islam.

Do Muslims allow **interfaith marriages**?

Muslims generally prefer that their sons and daughters marry members of their own faith tradition. They officially allow marriage to members of the Abrahamic faiths, Judaism and Christianity. But most still consider it acceptable only for Muslim men to marry non-Muslim women, and then it is assumed that the non-Muslim party will agree to raise the children as Muslims. Among the eight million or so Muslims living in the United States, the practice of Muslim women marrying non-Muslim men has been increasing somewhat lately.

What **gender-related issues** are important for Muslims?

Muslim tradition places great emphasis on understanding and facilitating social relations according to gender-appropriate roles and religiously acceptable behavior. In some societies, women are excluded from certain occupations, but in most instances those are cultural rather than explicitly religious norms. For example, American Muslim women participate in a wider range of professions than do their sisters in some other countries. Non-Muslim American professional women may experience the same kinds of occupational limitations as their Muslim counterparts. All societies and cultures have their gender-biases, and religious sanction and justification often becomes inextricably intertwined with them, largely because religious argument can be a useful element in social control. Gender-related restrictions by which many devout Muslims abide are largely family matters arising from the belief that God has ordained certain tasks to men and certain others to women. Gender and sex differences are real, they observe, and part of a larger plan. Traditional family life calls for a division of labor and a clear understanding of individual and collective priorities. Non-Muslims sometimes conclude that Muslim women who choose to observe a dress code are oppressed. Talk to the Muslim women, many of whom are successful physicians, lawyers, and engineers, and you get a different perspective.

How do Muslims feel when one of their members decides to **leave the faith**?

Departure from the community of believers has elicited a wide range of responses from families and society at large, depending on historical and cultural circumstances. Most of all, friends and relatives of an individual who has either simply slipped away from active involvement or made a deliberate choice to repudiate the Islamic tradition are eager to try to persuade the individual to reconsider. They will likely do whatever they can to support the individual in his or her dilemma. If they are unsuccessful, they will commend the individual to God's mercy and offer prayers on that person's behalf. Departure from a faith tradition is generally known as apostasy. Under certain social and political conditions, especially in regions where Muslims are in the majority and where the prevailing climate favors an emphasis on Islamic religious law, the response to apostasy may be more severe. This may include isolating the apostate

> ## May women attend Muslim burial services?
>
> **W**omen may attend funeral services at a mosque, though most mosques have separate sections for men and women. Sayings of the Prophet Muhammad recommend that women not attend burials because they might faint or lose control of their emotions. But the sayings stop short of barring women's attendance.

from the religous community, or, in some cases, even declaring the individual worthy of death. Such extreme behavior is increasingly rare and is generally seen in the most traditional towns and villages, though now and then a more celebrated example makes news headlines.

What does one do to **convert** to Islam?

Converting to Islam is a relatively simple matter. Interested individuals have typically already done some basic study of the tradition, but no prescribed course of religious education is required or expected. Naturally most Muslims believe that the more converts know about the tradition and its history, the more likely they can make an informed decision. Before entering into the brief ceremony that renders a candidate officially Muslim, the convert performs the major purification ritual called *ghusl*. Formal assent to the tenets of Islam entails a simple repetition of the Shahada before any two adult male witnesses.

How do Muslims view **Islam's relationship to other traditions**?

According to the Koran, the revelation delivered through Muhammad is not new, but a continuation and reaffirmation of the divine message given to all the earlier prophets acknowledged in the Jewish and Christian traditions. If prior generations of Jews and Christians had not misinterpreted or even willfully corrupted the message, subsequent corrective revelations would have been unnecessary. In other words, Muslims regard Islam's relationship to the earlier Abrahamic faiths somewhat the way Christians regard their tradition's relationship to Judaism. The later revelation completes, fulfills, corrects or abrogates the earlier one. Islamic tradition regards the "Peoples of the Book" as especially close kin. The Koran suggests that Muslims should consider Christians perhaps somewhat closer than Jews, even though there are far larger theological differences between Islam and Christianity than between Islam and Judaism. The concept of "Peoples of the Book" also came to include other minority religious communities of the Middle East, such as the Zoroastrians. In general, Muslims are inclined to regard members of other traditions, such as Hindus and Bud-

217

dhists, for example, as considerably further removed from the possibility of salvation. But views of that sort naturally vary somewhat from region to region, as for example, in India, where Muslims and Hindus often live side by side.

LEADERSHIP, AUTHORITY, ORGANIZATION

How and where do members of local Muslim communities **come together**?

When small local communities of Muslims begin to form in new locations, they typically begin by meeting in each others' homes for social and religious purposes. As their numbers grow, they need to look for a space large enough to accommodate them. In many American cities, for example, Muslims have acquired everything from former storefront buildings to former Christian churches. There they will remain until further growth and financial success permit more ambitious options, such as acquiring a piece of property, having it zoned properly, and building a dedicated facility. Whatever the venue in which they gather for prayer, Muslims call that place a *masjid,* a "place of prostration." The word "mosque" is rooted in the medieval Spanish pronunciation of *masjid.* Technically one needs no specific place for the prostration of ritual prayer—every place is a mosque, so long as one hallows the space and orients it toward Mecca. But community growth and the requirement of coming together on Fridays for a congregational prayer have made the institution known as the "mosque" a common sight all over the world, and increasingly in the United States as well—there are now more than a thousand mosques across the country. Most mosque communities eventually develop a full complement of governing, advisory, and functional committees, with emphasis on a fairly egalitarian form of governance.

Do **Sunni and Shi'i Muslims worship** in separate mosques?

That depends on a host of other social and political circumstances. In many places where Muslims are a small minority of the regional population, there are very few mosques. Most of them serve Muslims from all over the world without inquiring as to whether new members are Sunni or Shi'i. Shi'i Muslims who attend a predominantly Sunni mosque may discover that some themes they were accustomed to hearing in sermons, for example, are no longer so prominent. In some areas of countries like the United States, where there are growing numbers of immigrant and indigenous Muslims—people with ties to Iran or Iraq—for example, there might might be sufficient numbers to begin plans for a Shi'i mosque. The motivation for doing so more than likely will have a great deal to do with ties to a country of origin as well as a desire for a kind of spirituality more in keeping with distinctively Shi'ite interpretations of history and emphasis on the redemptive suffering of the Imams.

What is an **imam**?

In Arabic, the word *imam* means "one who is in front." Three distinct meanings are attached to the term. First, and most commonly, *imam* refers to the individual who leads the ritual prayer in the local mosque. Any mature adult can fulfill the role, and members of local communities frequently share this responsibility. Women may lead prayer and preach to groups of women only. Once local communities become large enough to have the necessary funds, they typically hire a religious scholar to serve as full-time spiritual leader with the more official title of Imam (with a capital I). An Imam's overall function is roughly similar to that of the pastor of a parish church. He counsels, visits the sick, performs funeral services, and generally administers the affairs of the mosque. To assist him in his work, the community often hires secretaries, directors of education and other services, and teachers, if the mosque sponsors a school. Second, important spiritual and intellectual leaders throughout Islamic history have gained the title Imam in recognition of their prominence and accomplishments. In those instances the title is honorary rather than functional. Finally, the term *imam* refers to the individuals whom the various Shi'i communities regard as special spiritual descendants of Muhammad. This narrowest of the three meanings is applied and interpreted in different ways by the major Shi'ite groups (Twelvers, Seveners, and Fivers). Most recently Twelver Shi'ites of Iran and Iraq bestowed the title on the Ayatollah Khomeini in a way that suggested a blend of the second and third meanings explained here.

What are some of the main varieties of Islamic **religious officials or specialists**?

Islamic religious specialists are a large general class of people called *'ulama,* meaning "those who possess knowledge" (*'ilm*). An *'alim* (pronounced AAHlim, commonly used singular of *'ulama,* pronounced oolaMAAH) is an individual who has done extensive study of the Koran, *tafsir* (exegetical commentary), and Hadith, for starters. Some become specialists in Koran recitation. One who memorizes the entire text and learns to "recite" it in an elaborate and demanding style called *tajwid* (pronounced tajWEED, "embellished, excellent") is called a *qari* (pronounced KAAHree, "Professional Koran reciter"). Some religious scholars further specialize in religious jurisprudence (*fiqh,* "understanding"). Such a scholar is called a *faqih* (pronounced faKEEH), "one who understands deeply," because he applies his intellect to plumb the depths of the fundamental religious sources in an effort to apply their principles to daily life. Some religious scholars routinely engage in the categorization of various acts according to

219

Visitors to the tomb-shrine of Shaykh Salim Chishti (sixteenth century), spiritual director of the Mughal Emperor Akbar, Fatehpur Sikri, India.

their relative legal and moral acceptability. In that capacity the scholar is called a *mufti* (pronounced MUFtee), "one who issues a legal advisory called a *fatwa*" (pronounced FATwah). Specialists in the religious sciences often carry the honorific title of *shaykh,* "elder," a term that was reserved for tribal leaders during pre-Islamic times. Spiritual guides of the various Sufi organizations called "orders" or "paths" (*tariqa,* pronounced taREEkah) also generally bear the title of shaykh or its Persian equivalent, *pir* (pronounced peer).

Do Muslims have a system of **religious law**?

As the young community grew and established itself in Medina, it became increasingly necessary for Muhammad to address countless questions of order and acceptable practice. Some of the later texts of the Koran deal with specific issues, such as how to pray, what foods and activities to avoid, and how to observe basic social relationships. After Muhammad died and the Arab armies expanded into new territories and encountered new cultures and religious communities, the Muslims had to confront countless problems previously unknown: How would they deal with issues that neither the Koran nor the Hadith addressed? Local Muslim leaders often had to improvise, exercising their best personal judgment and acting as they believed Muhammad would have done. They strove to perpetuate the Prophet's example, his *sunna.* But authorities and leading scholars in Medina, and later in other cities, looked for ways to standardize the proce-

> ## What is an Ayatollah?
>
> **A**yatollah is Arabic for "Sign of God," an honorific title conferred on leading Shi'ite religious scholars, especially in Iran and Iraq. In traditional Shi'ite circles, accomplished scholars can attain the rank of Ayatollah by popular acclaim and through the acknowledgment of their peers. Among those of that rank, some are also further distinguished by the title "Grand Ayatollah." Of those, in turn, a group of seven have traditionally been singled out as "Sources of Imitation" and are thereby acknowledged as the most influential teachers among Shi'ite Muslims.

dure of extending the application of Koran and Hadith to changing circumstances. They gradually agreed that one could solve problems not treated directly in Koran and Hadith by appealing to the "actual practice" of the local community or to the "consensus" (*ijma'*, pronounced ijMAA) of legal scholars. But since some questions were too new for any consensus to have developed, scholars agreed that one could apply a form of "reasoning by analogy" (*qiyas*, pronounced keeYAAS) that followed strict rules so as to keep the process as free of personal whim as possible. Leading legal scholars in different cities devised slightly different formulas for using the four "roots" of the law (Koran, Hadith, Consensus, and Analogical Reasoning), some allowing greater latitude in appealing to the third and fourth roots. Four legal methodologies dominant among Sunni Muslims came to be called the "schools" (*madhhabs*), while several other distinctively Shi'i schools eventually developed as well.

How does this system of **religious law** work?

Some legal specialists rise to greater prominence because of their erudition, earning the title *mujtahid* (pronounced MUJtahid, "one who exercises independent investigation" of the sacred sources). In Sunni tradition, the "door of independent investigation" closed by the year 900, making further bold scholarship of this level unnecessary. According to that classical view, the founders of the four major Sunni schools of legal theory were the last *mujtahids*. But in Shi'i tradition, the highest ranking ayatollahs continue to exercise the authority of mujtahids. In both traditions, it is up to scholars to offer rulings on controversial or contemporary issues. If a new ethical and legal question arises—a question of artificial life support or some other thorny biomedical matter, for example—a legal scholar would search the relevant sources to determine whether the Koran or Hadith might shed light on the precise issue at hand. If the scholar found only vague parallels that offer insufficient evidence to make a firm ruling on the new problem, he would then study further to see whether in the actual practice of Muslim communities there was an approach that might solve the problem.

Traditional Criminal Sanctions

Within the sphere of penal law, death is warranted for apostasy and for highway robbery; amputation of the hand for theft; death by stoning for sexual relations outside of marriage when the offender is married and 100 lashes if the offender is unmarried; and 80 lashes for the drinking of an intoxicant or for an unproved accusation of unchastity. Civil offenses against the person—homicide, for example, or assault—are punishable by retaliation, with the offender subjected to the same treatment as the victim. In such civil cases, only the victim or his family has the right to prosecute since the crime is not considered to be against the state. Often, the victim will choose monetary compensation (*diyah,* "blood money") in place of retaliation. Few predominantly Muslim societies today enact the traditional penalties as originally enjoined.

If the problem is too new to have any kind of useful history, the scholar might appeal to reasoning by analogy, looking for a "link" between ancient sources and practice and the new problem. Ancient sources may say nothing about artificial life support, but they have much to say about the nature of human life and about human authority to intervene. On the basis of his research, the scholar might then issue a legal advisory called a *fatwa.* In that statement he would indicate to which of five ethico-legal categories the proposed course of action (say, disconnecting life support in a particular case) belonged: forbidden, discouraged, neutral, recommended, or required. Acting upon the advisory, the parties to the case might then choose to bring the matter before a religious judge called a *qadi* (pronounced KAAdee, himself authorized as a *mufti*) to adjudicate the matter. The outcome of all this study and interpretation is called *Shari'a* (pronounced shaREE'ah), the divinely revealed law or way of life prescribed for all Muslims.

Is there a **central teaching authority** for Muslims?

No single individual or institution has universal authority over the global Islamic community. For Sunni Muslims the nearest approximation to centralized teaching authorities are religiously affiliated educational institutions in Egypt and Saudi Arabia, venerable and influential for very different reasons. Cairo's Al-Azhar, founded in 972 by the Isma'ili (Sevener Shi'ite) Fatimid dynasty, has worn the mantle of religious prestige and authoritative conservatism since it was converted by Saladin and his dynasty (after 1171) for the task of defending the cause of Sunni Islam. In Saudi Arabia, educational institutions of Mecca and Medina have come to share in Al-Azhar's prestige in modern times. Young men seeking careers in religious studies come from all over the world, looking forward to returning home with credentials from these institutions. Nowadays, a senior jurist somewhere might on very rare occasions issue a legal advisory (*fatwa*) claiming universal force, so that every Muslim ought to abide by it. The Ayatollah Khomeini, for example, delivered an order that Salman Rushdie was liable to the death penalty for blasphemy, and Usama bin Ladin has called for a *jihad* against the United States. But rare claims of that sort do not have the binding authority of a centralized institution like the papacy. In various parts of the world, religious scholars join together for consultative purposes. In the United States, for example, a Council of Imams holds regular gatherings to discuss practical and pastoral problems that arise in local communities. Elsewhere, *muftis* in a given region sometimes submit their decisions to the further judgment of a "grand mufti," who exercises special jurisdiction in religious matters.

Are there **religious hierarchical structures** in any branch of Islam?

Sunni Muslims constitute the vast majority of Islam's global membership. Since the generation that succeeded Muhammad, the dominant ideal of governance has been that a leader should be first among equals. Centuries of caliphal splendor might persuade a student of history that a type of monarchy was the preferred form of Islamic governance. In practice many of the most powerful Muslim rulers over the centuries have at least tried to call the shots religiously as well as politically. Nevertheless, Sunni Islam has never evolved quite the kind of hierarchical structure found, for example, in Roman Catholicism. Muslim authority structures in various countries and regions often take the form of councils of religious or legal scholars, or of imams. In practice, jurisdiction in matters of religious law and discipline is limited generally to the confines of modern nation-states. Following a very different model, the largest branch of Shi'i Islam, Twelver or Imami Shi'ism, has evolved a much more centralized authority structure. As a result of the Iranian revolution of 1979, the Ayatollah Khomeini and his followers sought to replace a monarchy with a theocracy. They established a pyramidal hierarchy of religious authority with Khomeini at the top. He was the most influential of a number of leading *Ayatollahs* (Sign of God) and won the title Imam by virtue of his dominance. Below him was a cluster of "grand ayatollahs" and a larger group of lesser ayatollahs. Just beneath them were two ranks of religious scholars with the title *Hujja-tolislam* (Proof of Islam), and finally the several thousand *Mullahs* (from a word that means roughly "master, reverend") who staffed the country's mosques.

Do Muslim communities run **private schools** for their children?

A tradition of Islamic religious education began many centuries ago. Younger children attended a Koran school called a *kuttab* (pronounced kutTAAB). They might progress to more advanced studies in Hadith, and eventually to the equivalent of modern-day higher education provided in institutions called *madrasas*. Students in a madrasa (pronounced maDRAsah) pursue a curriculum built around the teaching of one of the legal methodologies, *madhhabs* (pronounced MADHhab), and eventually receive credentials, a kind of license, as professional religious scholars. Many mosques in the United States are continuing that tradition by establishing primary and, increasingly, secondary schools in which religious education is prominent. Along with the regular course of studies required by state and local accreditation authorities, children study basic Koranic Arabic and related Islamic topics such as religious history and ritual practice. Students who attend public or other schools may attend special weekend religious education sessions at the local mosque.

Are there characteristically Muslim views about how **religion and political power** come together?

Muslims often describe their tradition as a "total way of life," a comprehensive approach that goes far beyond mere ritual observance or showing up at the mosque once a week. Some believe that such an all-encompassing teaching must ultimately be expressed in political terms, referring to early Muslim community life under the Prophet's leadership in Medina as the ideal. Throughout history Muslims have experimented with various models for balancing or integrating religious and civil authority. Some have worked well enough, allowing for freedom of religious practice and expression among members of religious minorities under Muslim rule. In fact, the historical record suggests that Muslims have been at least as successful as any other group at administering religiously sponsored regimes fairly and evenhandedly. Muslims in various parts of the world today continue to believe that an Islamic government represents the best hope of justice in a troubled world. But in a world where religious pluralism is increasingly evident, dividing humankind along religious lines seems a less than desirable option. The challenge now, as in the past, is to live by the Koranic dictum "There is no compulsion in religion."

What means do Muslim communities use to **engage society** at large?

In addition to the various forms of charitable giving, an important traditional device within Islamic law has had an enormous impact on life in many Islamic communities throughout history. A *waqf* is a special religious endowment by which a donor can stipulate that his or her funds be used for a particular project in perpetuity, or as long as the funds last. All over the Middle East and southern Asia, for example, scores of these dedicated trust funds established centuries ago remain in force, administered by members of particular families or by government officials entrusted with a specific mandate for the oversight of the endowments. Many endowments historically have been funded by royalty, but a significant number are supported by the generosity of other wealthy individuals or even collectives of many devout individuals. Trusts remain an important matter today, and many Muslims are devising other ways in which concerned fellow believers can contribute to endowments supporting important communal projects.

Are there any **organizations or institutions** that have their own distinctive structures of **leadership** within any of the branches of Islam?

Beginning in early medieval times, groups of Muslims throughout the Middle East coalesced informally around individuals reputed for their holiness. At first the groups typically gathered at the home of the *shaykh* (or *shakykha,* since some were women) to pray and listen to the teacher's reflections on sacred texts and topics. As they grew, these groups often found they needed larger spaces in which to meet. Some members also felt the need for a more permanent form of membership. As years went on and the central holy persons aged and died, the question of succession in leadership also arose. Eventually these groups became more highly organized and established formal courses of training. Their rules or charters often reflected highly structured membership with various ranks and offices. And they developed distinctive types of buildings combining prayer and devotional space, residences for the administrators and ordinary members, and often social services facilities as well. These organizations came to be called *Tariqas* (pronounced taREEka), analogous in some ways to the religious orders so important in the Christian, Buddhist and other traditions.

PERSONALITIES AND POWERS

What's the difference between a **prophet** and a **messenger**?

Central to Islamic tradition is the belief that God communicates ultimate truths through specially chosen persons called prophets. Without prophetic revelation, human beings would be forced to rely on intellect alone and thus could not arrive at the knowledge necessary to attain their final purpose. Every prophet (*nabi,* pronounced NAbee) passes along the divine word to a particular people and inevitably meets with tremendous resistance, at least initially. Some of these prophets receive the further designation of "messenger" or "apostle" (*rasul,* pronounced raSOOL), "one who is sent." God sends but one messenger to a given people. Prophets specified as messengers include Noah, Lot, Ishmael, Moses, Shuayb, Hud, Salih, Jesus, and of course Muhammad. Prophets preach and warn their people, but messengers are also commissioned to lead a community of faith called an *umma.* Post-Koranic tradition also teaches that Messengers function as lawgivers, whereas the other prophets do not. In short, one might say that all messengers are prophets, but not all prophets are messengers.

Do Muslims revere any **persons** as especially **gifted** with **wisdom**?

In Islamic tradition, as in Jewish and Christian, King Solomon (Sulayman) is the paradigm of wisdom. Solomon's sagacity enabled him to communicate with creatures of every kind, so that his sovereignty encompassed all of creation. Another figure from pre-Islamic history known for his wisdom is Luqman. Some traditions include him among the ranks of the prophets, but he is best understood as a prince among Muslim sages. According to the Koran, one chapter of which bears his name, Luqman was a teacher and coiner of proverbs. "Walk at a moderate pace and speak in measured tones," he advises, "for the most annoying of voices is that of the jackass" (Koran 31:19). Islamic lore describes Luqman in ways that recall the Greek sage Aesop. Wisdom did not cease with the passing of the ancients. Muslims have continued to discern in teachers, scholars, and spiritual guides the embodiment of a practical insight that goes far beyond mere intellectual understanding. God has entrusted certain individuals with the gift of wisdom, the ability to penetrate the veils of life's mystery and to untangle the snarl of daily experience.

What does **Jesus** mean to Muslims?

Jesus is the last of the prophet-messengers before Muhammad. Muslims consider him a great teacher, but not more than a human being. Jesus appears in a total of fifteen suras of the Koran. By God's direct intervention, he was the son of the virgin Mary who spoke as an infant to defend Mary from those who accused her of immorality for becoming pregnant without a legitimate husband. The Koran refers to Jesus as servant of God, spirit of God, and a word from God. God taught Jesus wisdom, gave him knowledge of the Torah, and strengthened him with the Holy Spirit (often associated with the angel Gabriel, the revealing angel). Among Jesus' special gifts were the power to raise the dead and heal the sick. Tradition says that Jesus ascended to either the second or the fourth heaven. A special element in Muslim teaching about Jesus is the belief he was not actually crucified. Instead a look-alike took his place at the last minute (Koran 4:157), but another text mentions his death and resurrection (Koran 19:33).

Is there such a thing as a **Muslim saint**?

In addition to sages and prophets, widespread Muslim tradition holds in high regard other individuals singled out for particularly intimate relationships with God. They

Dome of the Rock (692), Jerusalem, traditionally believed to be on the site of Solomon's temple, build over a large rock formation from which Muhammad is said to have experienced his Mi'raj or Ascension heavenward.

are called friends of God (*awliya,* pronounced awleeYAH, singular *wali*) and are generally analogous to what Christians and others mean when they refer to "saints." A major difference is that friends of God are popularly acclaimed as such rather than formally declared by an institutional procedure. Muslims from Muhammad's own generation are among the earliest individuals called friends of God, some so designated because of their devotion to the Prophet. Subsequent generations of Muslims have acclaimed friends of God virtually everywhere right on down to modern times, with the notable exception of Saudi Arabia and other Gulf states. There and in a few other places, modern reformers have sought to purge Islamic practice of devotional customs judged inauthentic expressions of Islam and distortions of core teachings. They have argued that beseeching friends of God for miracles is simply unnecessary, since no human being can mediate between the individual believer and his or her God. Virtually everywhere else, from Morocco's *marabouts* to Indonesia's distinctive *wali songo* (Nine Friends of God), devotion to holy persons has been an important element in the spiritual life of hundreds of millions.

What is a **Sufi**?

The word *Sufi* seems to derive from the Arabic word for "wool" (*suf,* pronounced soof). Among the first generations of Muslims Sufis were ascetics, spiritual athletes who strove to detach themselves from whatever distracted them from worshiping

A gathering of Sufis and their families in a fourteenth century *madrasa* (theological college) during a religious festival in Cairo, Egypt.

God. Garments of rough wool symbolized their desire for a simple life. Some of these early ascetics gained a reputation, often much to their personal consternation, for holiness. But some early seekers of deeper spirituality found ascetical discipline and self-denial an unsatisfactory path. A woman of Baghdad named Rabi'a (d. 801, pronounced RAAbi'ah) gave expression to a fierce longing for God in bold, shocking love poetry. How dare a mere mortal talk of a loving relationship with the infinite God! Rabi'a was the first true mystic, an inspiration to many who would risk all to communicate the unspeakable. Some, like Hallaj (d. 922), would die for their presumptuousness, accused of blasphemy and fatally misinterpreted, thus sharing the fate of mystics in many traditions. People everywhere sought out these spiritual beacons for guidance and blessing. Communities gathered around some prominent Sufis and eventually developed into formal organizations called *Tariqas* (pronounced taREEkah, meaning "path"). Over the centuries dozens of major Sufi men and women have left a legacy of poetry, arresting insight, and leadership. Jalal ad-Din Rumi (d. 1273), the original "whirling dervish," is one of the more famous classical Sufis, translations of his poetry now ranking among the best sellers in the United States. In some parts of the world, such as the Central Asian republics that made up the southern tier of the former Soviet Union, Sufi orders have been responsible in large part for the very survival of Islam through very difficult times. Many international Sufi organizations now maintain web sites. Some teach that one does not need to be a Muslim to be a Sufi, but it is nevertheless important to keep in mind that Sufism is a genuinely Islamic phenomenon.

Have **martyrs** ever been important in Islamic history?

The Arabic word *shahid* (pronounced shaHEED) means "one who testifies or witnesses," and is thus more or less equivalent to the word martyr. Since earliest times Muslim sources have referred to those who gave their lives for the cause of Islam as martyrs. Shi'i tradition has held martyrs in especially high regard. Beginning with Muhammad's grandson Husayn, killed with his small band of fighters resisting the tyranny of the Umayyads in 680 CE, the Imams have been the focus of a central belief in redemptive suffering. In this case the blood of the martyr not only assures the martyr's place in heaven but becomes a source of grace for all believers. When the Ayatollah Khomeini returned to Iran from his exile in France in 1979, he made his first major address in a cemetery called the Paradise of Martyrs, associating the revolutionary struggle of twentieth century Shi'i Iranians with that of the proto-martyr Husayn. Placing such value on martyrdom does not imply that Shi'ites or other Muslims are eager to die. It means that some Muslims, like believers in several other traditions, value their faith and are willing to give their lives for it.

Have there been any important **Muslim religious reformers**?

According to a Hadith, Muslims believe that at the beginning of each Islamic century God will raise up for the community a *mujaddid* (pronounced muJADdid), a "renewer" who calls people to a fresh awareness of their faith. Muslim tradition has identified a succession of important historical renewers. In modern times, too, a number of major reformers have taken on the daunting task of inciting their fellow religionists to adapt their ancient faith heritage to changing circumstances. Like reformers in any tradition, these Muslim pioneers have often met with resistance to the changes they proposed. Muhammad Abduh (1849–1905), for example, worked to promote reason as nearly equal with revelation as a source of knowledge. His suggestion that some elements of the Koran were not of divine origin caused considerable stir. Abduh, nevertheless, served as Grand Mufti of Egypt and was a leading influence at the al-Azhar University, a flagship institution of Islamic traditionalism.

Do Muslims believe in **angels**?

Angels function in Islamic tradition much the way they do in Christian tradition. They are beings of light and great intelligence who enjoy the presence of God and do the divine bidding throughout creation. Several angels stand above the rest. The four archangels include Gabriel, who brings revelation to the prophets; Michael, archnemesis of Satan; Israfil who will sound the final trumpet; and the angel of death, Azrael. In some important respects human beings stand above the angels. When God has Gabriel guide Muhammad through the seven heavens, Gabriel must part company with the Prophet as they approach the Throne of God, lest he be burnt to a crisp. Even the first human being, Adam, knew something to which the angels were not privy, the divinely ordained names of all things created. God assigns two guardian angels to each human being. Two especially businesslike angels called Munkar and Nakir have the unpleasant but necessary task of visiting each deceased person in the grave and administering a "final exam" about the content of the individual's beliefs. Numerous Hadiths and charming traditional stories tell of the solicitous presence of countless angelic spirits, who are ready to attend the devout at every important moment and squire them through life's most trying challenges.

What is a **jinn**?

You've probably heard stories about the magical powers of "Genies" who appear when someone rubs a magic lamp just right. The word "genie" comes from the Arabic word *jinn,* which refers to creatures of smokeless fire who inhabit a mysterious realm somewhere between the human and the divine. According to popular lore in Muhammad's time, the jinns would eavesdrop on the heavenly councils and offer to divulge their secrets to a soothsayer (called a *kahin,* pronounced KAAhin) who uttered the proper formula. Some of Muhammad's early critics charged that he was not a prophet but just another *majnun* (pronounced majNOON), one possessed by a jinn. To call someone *majnun* is to question the person's credibility as well as sanity. Countless jinns inhabit the world, some mischievous and some helpful and benevolent. King Solomon had the special gift of "taming" the jinn and enlisting them for the construction of his majestic temple. Particularly troublesome are the frighteningly ugly jinns called *ghuls* (from which we get the word "ghoul"). For those who do not know how to handle them, jinns can make life unpleasant, but their powers are limited.

Do Muslims believe in the **devil**?

Within the larger category of *jinn* are many beings who were once angels. The principal diabolical figure is called Iblis (pronounced ibLEES, from the Greek *diabolos*). God ordered him to do homage to the newly-created body of Adam, but Iblis refused, arguing that a creature of fire need not bow to one made of clay. God banished Iblis from paradise and he became the personification of the choice for evil over good. It was Iblis who tempted Adam and Eve (Koran 2:35–39, 7:19–25, 20:120–121). Tradition also names the devil Shaytan (shayTAAN) and often refers to many Satans, the lesser minions of Iblis who fan out to beset humanity with temptations of every kind. Some of Islam's mystics have focused on the story of Iblis' fall as an occasion for discussing the infinite mercy of God. As evil as the devil is, they argue, even Iblis still has hope of enjoying the transforming power of divine forgiveness at the end of time. The mystics are not suggesting that the devil is soft on sheer nastiness, only that no power in the universe can compare with God's mercy.

Are **dreams and visions** particularly important in Islamic tradition?

In the Koranic story of Joseph (Sura 12) Muslims find the paradigm of religious insight as represented by the ability to interpret dreams. Traditional Islamic sources further describe a wide range of religious and spiritual experiences, beginning of course with Muhammad's role in the unfolding revelation of the Koran. The Prophet "sees" mysterious visions as part of the divine communication. Later religious figures, especially noted spiritual guides and friends of God, have left numerous personal accounts of their dreams and interpretations of them. Muhammad himself is one of the presences they report meeting most often in dreams and visionary experiences. These reports tell of encountering various holy persons in addition to the Prophet, especially those who had in life been of particular significance to the dreamer or visionary. Sufis sometimes tell of meeting the mysterious Khizr, a figure included in many lists of prophets, who appears for the purpose of initiating the dreamer into the Sufi path through investiture with the "patched frock" (*khirqa*). Though the accounts sound as if they are reporting events as "real" as having breakfast, most are clearly talking about spiritual experiences that are well beyond the ordinary and thus are not subject to ordinary scrutiny.

HOLIDAYS AND REGULAR OBSERVANCES

What kind of **religious calendar** do Muslims observe?

Muslims follow a lunar calendar whose twelve months add up to 354 days. In a cycle of thirty lunar years, eleven are leap years, with one day added to the last month. During Muhammad's time the lunar months were associated with seasons (Ramadan means "extreme heat," Rabi' "rainy season," and Jumada "dry season," for example). As in the Jewish calendar, the pre-Islamic year maintained its connection with agricultural cycles and seasons by the intercalation of a whole month in certain years. Since the practice of intercalation ended around Muhammad's time, the Islamic lunar year rotates backwards eleven days each year in relation to the Gregorian solar year. If Ramadan, for example, begins on January 12 this year, next year it will begin on January 1, and so on. Certain practical results of this backward rotation are worth noting because of the way timing can affect religious practice. When Ramadan (the ninth month) occurs in the dead of winter, when days are shortest, the fast from sunrise to sunset is less arduous than when Ramadan falls during the height of summer. Pilgrimage to Mecca can also be more strenuous when the season of Hajj (in the twelfth month) occurs during the hottest season. Muslims the world over therefore must learn to work with two different systems of marking special times. Muslims begin their count of years with the Hijra of 622. Approximately every thirty-three years the beginnings of the Islamic lunar and Gregorian solar years roughly coincide.

What is the importance of the month of **Ramadan**?

During pre-Islamic times the month called Ramadan ("high summer") was religiously significant as a time during which the Arab tribes observed a truce from all hostilities. Of all the months the Koran mentions only Ramadan by name, identifying it as the month during which the scripture was revealed. Scripture suggests that the initial divine revelation is the reason for the practice of fasting throughout the month. Ramadan begins with the sighting of the new moon on the last night of the eighth month. Each day, from dawn until sunset, Muslims are enjoined to fast from all food and liquid, as well as from sexual activity and other forms of sensual pleasure. Fasting also means refraining from negative attitudes and complaining, and developing a sense of solidarity with those who suffer from want all year long. After Muslims break the fast with some water and dates, they eat a meal before retiring. Before dawn they may have another meal, but limit other forms of celebration during the entire month. Special prayers are scheduled in mosques, along with the recitation of one of thirty "sections" of the Koran, completing the entire sacred text over the thirty nights. A number of important dates fall during Ramadan. Most important is the "Night of Power," one of the odd-numbered nights among the last ten, usually observed on the twenty-seventh. Muslims believe that God's initial revelation to Muhammad makes this the holiest time of the entire year. Other important times during Ramadan include the birthday of the martyr Husayn (6th), death of Muhammad's first wife, Khadija (10th), the Battle of Badr (a key event in 625, the 17th), the retaking of Mecca in 630 (19th), the deaths of Ali and of the eighth Shi'i Imam, Ali Reza (21st), and Ali's birthday (22nd). Where Muslims are in the majority or a very sizable minority, the rhythm of life slows dramatically during Ramadan. At the sighting of the next new moon, all rejoice in the Feast of Fastbreaking, 'Id al-Fitr.

When do Muslims make **pilgrimage** to Mecca and what do they do there?

Formal season for the greater pilgrimage, called the Hajj, occurs between the eighth and thirteenth day of the twelfth lunar month. The journey is required of all Muslims with sufficient health and financial resources, assuming also that making the Hajj would not require them to shirk serious family responsibilities at home. As pilgrims enter a "forbidden zone" that encircles Mecca (called the *haram*), they put on the plain white wraps called the *ihram* (pronounced ihRAAM). The garb marks a transition to sacred space and time and reminds pilgrims of their simple equality before God. Though precise ritual activities depend on both variations within the four Sunni law schools as well as on whether or not pilgrims intend to combine Hajj with 'Umra (lesser pilgrimage), the following offers an idea of the major elements. On the first day (the 8th of the month) they usually circumambulate the Ka'ba seven times, pray at the Station of Abraham, pray two cycles of prostrations, and drink from the spring of Zamzam. Heading for Mina outside of Mecca, most pilgrims will stay overnight there before moving on to the plain of Arafat. They stand before the Mount of Mercy, recalling the deeds of Muhammad and Abraham here long ago. That evening they go a short distance back toward Mecca, to Muzdalifa, where on the third day they celebrate the Feast of Sacrifice ('Id al-Adha). Moving back to Mina later that day, pilgrims cast seven stones at one of three pillars, a symbolic repudiation of the temptations of Satan. After a symbolic clipping or shaving of hair, pilgrims remove the *ihram* and return to Mecca to circumambulate the Ka'ba and run seven times between the hills Safa and Marwa to commemorate Hagar's frantic search for water. During the eleventh through thirteenth days, pilgrims remain at Mina, casting the remainder of forty-nine stones collected earlier at all three of the pillars. Those who did not participate in the sacrifice on the tenth day may do so now. To end the whole event, most will again circumambulate the Ka'ba seven times. In recent years the Saudi government has expanded their pilgrimage facilities dramatically in order to accommodate annual crowds now numbering two million or more.

Are any **occasions** associated with **Muhammad** especially important?

Since medieval times Muslims in many countries have celebrated Muhammad's birthday, Mawlid an-Nabi, on the 12th of Rabi' I. Street parties and grand banquets often provide opportunity for special prayers and speeches. A very popular part of the festivities is the recitation of a poem by the thirteenth century Egyptian poet Busiri, the *Burda* (pronounced BURdah, "Mantle"). Translated into Swahili and a number of other languages, the poem sings the Prophet's praises in truly cosmic terms, attributing to his birth all manner of marvels and blessings. In some places, where festivities are minimized or forbidden altogether, even the Prophet's birthday is a kind of national holiday. On the 27th of Rajab, Muslims recall the Night Journey and Ascension (Laylat al-Isra wa-'l-Mi'raj). According to traditional accounts, the Prophet experienced this timeless mystical moment sometime during the years just before the Hijra. A major feature of the celebrations is the retelling of any of several narratives that follow Gabriel and Muhammad through the heavens, including descriptions of his meetings and conversations with the other major prophets, each associated with one of the seven celestial levels. During the course of his journey Muhammad received special instructions about instituting the five daily ritual prayers.

Do Muslims celebrate **events** in connection with any other **religious figures**?

Popular practice in many places still includes annual commemorations of birthdays and death anniversaries of various important holy persons and friends of God. Birth-   233 day celebrations of members of the Prophet's family, such as Sayyida Zaynab, remain popular in places like Egypt. Lasting for up to seven days, the festivities are like sprawling street parties. Crowds grow daily, as does the intensity of the celebration. Vendors sell food and souvenirs and Koran reciters fill the air with sacred sounds from their booths up and down the streets. Mosques within the central area of celebration can be packed to overflowing. Birthdays of famous friends of God frequently include recitation of classic poems extolling the saints' spiritual achievements and glorious intimacy with God. Anniversaries of the death of God's special friends are also important in many regions, especially those further to the east. Since holy persons are fully united with God at death, the occasions are sometimes referred to as the saint's Wedding Day (*'Urs,* pronounced OORS). On the 6th of Rajab many Indian Muslims (and members of other faiths as well) observe the *'Urs* of Mu'in ad-Din Chishti, founder of a famous Sufi order, at his tomb in the city of Ajmer.

What are some of the other **religious days** Muslims observe?

On the 15th of Sha'ban many Muslims, especially in south Asia, observe the Night of Forgiveness (*Laylat al-Bara'a,* pronounced baRAA'ah). Popular belief says that the names of all persons are written on the leaves of a great cosmic tree. On the evening of the 14th, the tree shakes and loses some of its leaves. Those whose leaves fall are destined to die during the coming year. According to a Hadith, God comes down to the lowest heaven that night and asks if anyone seeks forgiveness. That is the moment for all to wipe the slate clean, since no one knows whether his or her leaf has fallen. Celebrations of many holy persons, often centering around the individual's tomb, vary according to region. In addition to birthday (*mawlid*) and death anniversary (*'urs*) celebrations, Muslims in various places observe seasonal times (*mawsim*) with festivities connected to agricultural or other natural cycles. One such celebration is that of Nabi Musa (Prophet Moses), observed around his alleged tomb-shrine near Jericho. Its timing coincides roughly with the Orthodox Christian Holy Week, featuring elaborate processions that begin in Jerusalem.

Does the **beginning of the Muslim year** have any particular significance?

During the first ten days of the month of Muharram, Muslims reflect on a variety of spiritual themes. During Muhammad's time the community observed a one-day fast on the 10th of the month (*'Ashura,* pronounced aaSHOOrah), possibly paralleling the Jewish practice of fasting on the 10th of Tishri, generally known as Yom Kippur. Though the major fast was formally shifted to Ramadan, Muslims still observe this day, some with fasting and special prayer. Like many holy days, *'Ashura* has become associated with ancient events of great significance. This day marks the day on which Noah left the ark. Visitors to Mecca can enter the Ka'ba itself (not just the sanctuary around it) on this day alone. But the first ten days of the year are still more important for Shi'i Muslims. Some readers may recall the day in 1979 when Iranian students took over the U.S. embassy in Tehran. It occurred on the 1st of Muharram in the year 1400 after the Hijra, the beginning of the traditional period of mourning for the proto-martyr Husayn, who died at the hands of a tyrannical ruler in the year 680 CE. Observance of the sad event gains in intensity until the actual day of martyrdom, some observing a fast on the 9th day. On 'Ashura itself, some Shi'ites make pilgrimages to Karbala in Iraq, site of the martyrdom, or to the tombs of other Imams in Iran and Iraq. In more traditional Shi'i villages, people still gather to reenact the events in a "passion play" called the Ta'ziya (pronounced ta'ZEEyah). Looking at the bigger picture, a Hadith says that at the beginning of each new century (on the lunar Islamic calendar) God will raise up for the Muslim community a "renewer" who will call all believers to a fuller participation in the faith.

Procession of Shi'i Muslims carrying a model of the tomb of the proto-martyr Husayn in commemoration of his death, as they observe 'Ashura (the tenth day of the first lunar month), in Rawalpindi, Pakistan. *Courtesy of David Edwards.*

CUSTOMS AND RITUALS

Is there a standard Islamic group **liturgical worship**?

Islamic ritual prayer, performed five times daily, is called *salat* (from a root that means to make holy). Whenever Muslims gather they perform the ritual prayer together. That applies not only to the prescribed Friday midday congregational prayer but to any of

235

the set times at which two or more Muslims come together any day of the week, whether in the mosque or elsewhere. As with all Muslim ritual practice, worshipers preface this prayer with the clearly stated intention (*niyya,* pronounced NEEyah), saying "I intend to pray the dawn (for example) salat." From two to four cycles of standing, bowing to place hands on knees (*ruku',* pronounced ruKOO), sitting on the heels (*jalsa,* pronounced JALsah), stretching forward toward prostration (*sajda,* pronounced SAJdah) to place hands flat on the floor at shoulder width, and touching the forehead to the floor, make up the fundamental Salat ritual. The number of cycles (*rak'a,* pronounced RAK'ah) depends on which prescribed prayer one is performing.

Entrance to the courtyard of the Selimiya mosque, late sixteenth century, Edirne, Turkey. Centered in the courtyard before the door to the prayer hall is the ablution fountain where worshipers perform a purification ritual before prayer.

Do Muslims engage in any specific **purification rituals**?

Prior to each act of ritual prayer Muslims perform a brief purification called *wudu'* (pronounced wuDOO). Worshipers perform each of the following cleansing motions three times: rinse hands and wrists, rinse out the mouth, then the nostrils likewise, rinse the whole face, arms up to the elbows, whole head and neck, and finally toes and feet up to the ankles. Mosques today typically provide separate facilities in which men and women can perform the ablution. Older mosques often have fountains or taps running along an exterior wall, with small benches or stools for worshipers to sit on. They usually use tap water, but under peculiar circumstances even sand or earth is acceptable, in which case it is called *tayammum* (pronounced taYAMmum). Clearly the idea is to prepare oneself symbolically to enter a

236

Why do Muslims bury their dead so quickly?

Although there's no time limit, most Muslims are buried within 24 hours of their death. The tradition originated out of the practical need to keep bodies from deteriorating in the Middle Eastern heat. Although many Muslims now live in countries where technology allows bodies to be preserved, most avoid embalming, because they believe it violates the dignity of the deceased. For the very same reason, Muslims don't believe in displaying a body as is common at many Christian funerals.

special state of mindfulness. In addition to this cleansing, Muslims also regard a more thorough bathing (called *ghusl*) essential to restore the state of ritual purity after sexual intercourse, seminal discharge, or the menstrual cycle. Ghusl includes the motions of the ablution just described, but encompasses the entire body as well. The intent of these rituals is to put the individual in a state of maximum attentiveness to and spiritual worthiness for entering into the presence of God.

Do Muslims ever visit their **holy cities** outside of the formal pilgrimage season?

Hajj, or major pilgrimage, fulfills a religious duty only in connection with the formal season. But travelers to the holy city can perform the *Umra* or lesser pilgrimage any time of year. Umra is a strictly devotional activity, optional but highly recommended. Rituals include a much scaled-down version of important Hajj activities. To be more precise, Umra is actually a component of Hajj that can be performed separately. Pilgrims enter into the state of ritual consecration by donning the same seamless white cloth worn for Hajj, before entering the sacred zone surrounding Mecca. They proceed to the Ka'ba, circumambulate it seven times, perform two cycles of ritual prayer, take a drink from the well of Zamzam, and walk rapidly seven times between the small hillocks called Marwa and Safa. They conclude the lesser pilgrimage by clipping a lock of hair or shaving the head, symbolizing the spiritual change desired as a result of the pilgrimage. As at Hajj time, many pilgrims add a visit to the Prophet's Mosque in Medina, but that is a separate devotional activity.

Are there any other forms of **religious pilgrimage**?

Ziyara (pronounced zeeYAArah, meaning "visitation") is a form of minor pilgrimage still popular all over the world, with a few regional exceptions such as the Arabian peninsula. Devout Muslims travel to the tombs of holy persons to receive *baraka*, blessings, by association with the saint's power and holiness. Elaborate shrine complexes have grown up around some of these sacred sites. Since the nineteenth century especially, Muslim authorities in Saudi Arabia have sought to stamp out the practice because they have deemed the veneration of miracle-working saints a threat to pure monotheism. Ironically, Saudi Arabia remains the home of the prime example of *ziyara*. Each year millions of pilgrims to Mecca make a special trip north to Medina to visit the mosque in which Muhammad, his daughter Fatima, and the first caliph, Abu Bakr, are buried. Sunni Muslims from Morocco to Malaysia continue to visit secondary holy places, most of which are graves of Sufi shaykhs. Shi'i Muslims also visit sites connected with similar friends of God, but their devotional travel revolves more around a number of distinctively Shi'ite holy places. They are the tombs of the Imams, spiritual and biological descendants of Muhammad through his daughter Fatima. Most of the Imams' shrines are in Iran, with its overwhelmingly Shi'i population, and southern Iraq, where most of that country's slight majority of Shi'ites live.

What are **Muslim sermons** like?

An address called the *khutba* (pronounced KHUTbah) is a standard feature of every Friday congregational prayer service. Members of the congregation sit on the floor while the preacher stands near the niche (*mihrab*) or ascends a few steps of a pulpit called the *minbar* (pronounced MINbar). In larger, more established mosques, the Imam generally delivers the sermon on Fridays at the early afternoon congregational prayer. But either the Imam or some other adult might also offer some reflections at other times when smaller groups gather for salat. Speakers have a wide range of appropriate topics from which to choose. High on the list are ethical concerns such as social responsibility, the need for parents to take an active part in their children's education, and speaking out in public venues about problems that need attention from concerned citizens. Speakers might also choose any of scores of devotional themes, such as cultivating one's relationship with God, or the need to set aside time for per-

Mosaic decoration on the main dome of the Great Mosque of Cordoba, Spain, tenth century, over the *mihrab,* the niche indicating the direction of Mecca toward which Muslims face during ritual prayer.

sonal reading and reflection on the Koran. Preachers often tailor their sermons to a specific religious season, especially during Ramadan and pilgrimage season. Encouragement during the month-long fast is always helpful and welcome. Scripture naturally plays a major part in sermons, and preachers generally cite Hadiths along with Koranic texts to illustrate their themes. Sermons vary in length from five or ten minutes to perhaps a half hour for special occasions.

Do Muslims use **ritual sacrifice**?

Muslims mark the high point of the annual season of Hajj, which runs from the eight to the thirteenth day of the ninth lunar month, with the Feast of the Sacrifice. Also called "The Great Feast," the rituals on the tenth of the month include the slaughtering of an animal in memory of God providing a ram for Abraham to sacrifice in lieu of his son Ishmael. Sheep, goats, oxen or cows, and camels are traditional sacrificial animals. The person performing the sacrifice dedicates the animals to God and mentions the names of those partaking of the fruits of the sacrifice. Muslims all over the world observe the Feast of Sacrifice with special activities. Food ritually sacrificed is usually prepared in large quantities, so that as those present for the festivities share in the feast, so the abundance can be distributed to those in need. Animals ritually slaughtered during Hajj season are not sold for profit. In some parts of the world, Muslims still sacrifice a sheep in connection with an optional birth ritual. When a child is seven

239

Going to pray at the mosque, Tangier, Morocco.

days old, some families shave the baby's head, a practice dating to Muhammad's time.

Do Muslims follow specific **dietary customs or rituals**?

Muslim dietary practice is similar in many ways to Jewish traditions known as *kashrut,* or keeping *kosher.* Certain foods are forbidden altogether, except in direst need. These include intoxicating beverages, pork, blood, foods prepared or cooked with pork fat (some would include, for example, doughnuts and other fried breads), and animals that eat mainly carrion (i.e., scavengers). If non-Muslims invite Muslim friends for a celebration with a meal, it is important that they give due consideration to what they will serve. Muslims do not require the separation of meats from dairy products as do Orthodox Jews, but hosts should avoid pork of any kind if at all possible.

Meat of certain animals is acceptable only when the animal has been ritually slaughtered. As in every Muslim ritual, one begins by declaring the "intention" to perform the action religiously. After pronouncing the first part of the *basmallah* (In the name of God—leaving off the names Compassionate and Merciful) and the *takbir* (God is supreme), the butcher severs the jugular and windpipe with a single blade stroke. The idea is to drain as much of the blood as possible, for it symbolizes the life force. By custom, Muslims in various places consider certain foods traditional for special occasions, such as the meal that breaks the daily fast of Ramadan and the celebration that marks the end of that month. Many of these customs are inspired by Muhammad's own practice. For example, he is said to have broken his daily fast with a glass of water and a few dates before taking a meal, so Muslims generally try to do likewise.

Do Muslims practice **polygamy**?

Long before the beginnings of Islam plural marriage was a fairly common practice. A number of the biblical patriarchs and kings had several wives. Wealthier men of the pre-Islamic Arab tribes apparently engaged in polygamy, marrying as many wives as their wealth would allow. A major concern seems to have been that, in the inhos-

240

pitable environs of that desert world, women not attached to families had little hope of survival. As cities like Mecca developed, the practice survived in somewhat modified form. But according to a text of the Koran, polygamy in the early Muslim community was to be limited. A man could marry up to four women, provided he could treat all of his wives with complete equity ,both materially and emotionally. In modern times a number of national governments in the Middle East have outlawed the practice, arguing that modern social and economic conditions have made perfectly fair treatment all but impossible. Even where local laws allow polygamy, relatively few men marry more than one women, and those who marry four are a very small minority.

Islamic ritual and devotional objects in a mosque shop, Turkey.

What kinds of **special ritual objects** figure in Muslim worship and prayer?

By far the most important ritual object is the Koran. Since Muslims regard the sacred book as the very word of God, they try to treat the physical object with the greatest respect. Some mosques own ancient and beautifully wrought Korans, often in multiple volumes, that are used only for special occasions. The more ancient the mosque, the more likely it will also have specially crafted podiums on which to place the Koran, and possibly also storage containers. Both stand and box often feature carefully chosen inscriptions from the Koran and Hadith that remind devotees of the divine origin and power of the sacred word. One of the most important among the relatively few other items that have been a regular part of Muslim devotions is the classic prayer rug. Displaying a central shape that recalls the *mihrab* on the Mecca-ward wall of the mosque, high quality prayer rugs

241

often use geometric and floral design inspired by the Koran's "Verse of Light": "God is the light of the heavens and the earth. His light is like a niche in which is a lamp within a glass like a shining star kindled from a sacred olive tree neither of east nor west whose oil would nearly glow even if no fire touched it" (Koran 24:35). Inspired by the same verse, beautifully enameled glass lamps were once raised to a fine art and hung by the dozens in the great mosques of the Middle East. The shimmering light cast through their multicolored Koranic inscriptions and arabesque designs would have been similar to that cast through Europe's stained glass windows.

Are **music and dance** important in Islamic religious ritual?

Muslims do not incorporate either music or dance into their primary religious rituals, and they use no musical instruments as part of communal worship. Though Muslims do not as a group sing hymns or other types of vocal prayer set to music, a type of tonal recitation is very much a part of Islamic religious life. A "call to prayer" (*adhan*) broadcast from the minaret (at least in areas where Muslims are the majority population) announces each of the five daily times for *salat*. The *muezzin* (pronounced muEZzin) makes the call using a form of chanting that can strike the ear as very musical, even though it has no melody such as we generally associate with songs. Formal "recitation" of the Koran is perhaps the closest approximation to music in Muslim ritual. Specially trained reciters, who typically have memorized the entire Koran, chant texts of the scripture using either of two styles of presentation. The simpler form is called "measured" and is sung with a recurring pattern of only four or five notes. A more ornate form, called "embellished," uses a much wider tonal range, proceeds much more slowly, and punctuates the text with dramatic silences. Such recitation can be part of any religious observance in any venue. Outside of primary ritual contexts, Muslims all over the world have set religious themes and sentiments to music in countless local and regional styles and languages. Muslim musicians and singers across the globe are now producing devotional music for mass-market consumption. From Morocco to Indonesia, tapes and CDs filled with contemporary musical interpretations of classical texts and prayers are becoming increasingly popular. Dancing often accompanies popular musical performances, especially those associated with the feasts of local holy persons.

Do Muslims **pray** in any particular **language**?

Arabic is the liturgical language of Islam. All formal prayers and Koran recitation are in Arabic. Most non-Arabic speaking Muslims learn at least some texts of the scripture by heart in Arabic, along with a dozen or so other short texts that are recited regularly during ritual prayer as well as in personal devotions. Scriptural texts include, for example, Sura 1, called The Opening, a lovely prayer reminiscent of the Christian Lord's Prayer; and Sura 112, an affirmation of God's absolute oneness. In addition to the *shahada,* shorter phrases used during ritual prayer include *Allahu akbar* (God is Supreme), *Al-hamdu li-'llahi* (Praise be to God), and *Sami'a 'llahu li-man yusabbihhu* (God listens to one who praises him). Other Arabic phrases in common use all over the world include *In sha'a 'Llah* (God willing), *Wa 'Llahu a'lam*(God knows best), and *La hawla wa la quwwata illa bi 'Llah* (In God alone is power and strength). During the midday congregational prayer on Friday, the prayer leader gives an address, sometimes called a sermon. The preacher often prefaces the sermon with a series of divine praises in Arabic, and then delivers the address in the local vernacular. On special occasions, the preacher may actually deliver the entire address in Arabic and then provide a translation. Arabic is so important because it is the language of the Koran and of the Prophet, whose very sound carries great symbolic associations even for Muslims who do not speak it.

What kinds of **rituals** do Muslims engage in **privately** or alone?

Since one can perform the five daily ritual prayers anywhere, most Muslims generally pray the *salat* alone or in small groups. In mosques everywhere you can find individual Muslims praying privately outside the regular ritual prayer times as well. But Muslims also engage in a variety of other private devotions. Some are associated with local or regional custom, others practiced across the globe. Private recitation of the sacred scripture is foremost among the universal customs. Muslims who read Arabic but who are not formally trained in the refinements of performative recitation often sit alone and recite in a low voice. Meditative reading of the text in any language can nourish the spiritual life. Another popular devotion involves a prayerful consideration of the ninety-nine "Beautiful Names" of God. Many Muslims use the *tasbiha,* a set of either thirty-three or ninety-nine beads, to keep count. (These are the so-called "worry beads" people all over the world like to fidget with even when not praying.) Islamic traditions of spirituality also offer a vast array of devotional literature, from hagiography (lives of prophets and holy persons) to prayers recommended for daily use to refined religious poetry suitable for praying.

How do Muslims celebrate **birth**?

A recommended but optional ceremony called the *'Aqiqa* (pronounced aKEEkah) occurs when a baby is seven days old. In the home or in a part of the mosque outside the prayer hall, parents name their child and clip a lock of hair. Tradition suggests that parents give at least the hair's weight in silver as a charitable donation. In some places it remains customary to perform ritual animal sacrifice and distribute food to the needy. Parents can formally name their child at this time, often choosing from among the names of religiously important men and women. Sometimes also the baby's father will whisper the call to prayer (*adhan,* pronounced aTHAAN) in the infant's right ear and the invitation to begin the prayer (*iqama,* pronounced iQAAmah) in the left. Some

Muslims choose to practice a rite of circumcision on infant boys, though some prefer to postpone the practice until puberty. Depending on circumstances, some kind of reception may follow the rituals.

Are there distinctive forms of **Islamic initiation**?

Teenagers can be welcomed formally into the adult community of believers with a simple ceremony during which the young man or woman pronounces the *shahada* before two male or eight female witnesses. Sometimes the occasion is combined with a regular congregational prayer service on Friday afternoon, but the ritual can also take place in the home. The young Muslims so initiated may also recite various prayers in Arabic as part of the ceremony. There is ordinarily no reception following the ritual. As a rite of passage, the ritual itself is roughly parallel to the Jewish bar and bat mitzvah.

What are the Islamic rituals of **marriage**? Do Muslims favor "arranged" marriages?

In the United States, Muslim nuptials (called *nikah* in Arabic) can occur in the prayer hall of the local mosque in a separate ceremony not connected with the regular ritual prayer. In other places, weddings typically occur in homes or in the presence of a Muslim judge (called a *qadi*). The imam of the mosque, or the judge, presides over the ceremony and may offer religious reflections on the sacredness of the marriage contract. In some countries elaborate processions and house-warming ceremonies are part of the festivities. As in many other traditions, two witnesses attest to the agreement. Written documentation includes both mosque records and the usual license required by civil law. A reception called a *walima* (pronounced waLEEmah) follows weddings nearly everywhere. In some countries the bridal dowry remains an essential item in the social contract between families. Many Muslim families continue to prefer marriages in which the parents do the initial negotiating. They present their favored prospect to their son or daughter, but in most situations the young people have the option of declining. Many Muslims regard open dating as undesirable and believe the arranged relationship is healthier and more acceptable morally. Some parents will even take out

Muslim cemetery in Kusadasi, Turkey, showing both head and foot stones, trees painted white to a height of several feet from the ground, and stone replicas of the headgear once worn by the deceased person, indicating that person's rank in traditional Ottoman society.

ads, especially on behalf of a daughter, in the "personal" sections of Muslim publications, seeking interested parties who are well-educated and religiously committed.

How do Muslims deal ritually with **death and mourning**?

In most places Muslims retain the ancient custom of burying the unembalmed body before sundown on the day of death. Family members generally prepare the body with purification rituals similar to those used prior to prayer or to remove some ritual impurity. Sometimes mourners will say special prayers in the mosque after the regular ritual prayer, with or without the body. Basic prayers include the *takbir* (saying "Allahu akbar," pronounced takBEER) spoken four times, interspersed with longer devotional prayers calling down blessings on the deceased and on all present. In the United States, Muslim obsequies often occur in funeral homes, always with a closed casket. There the imam of the mosque leads mourners in prayer and may also deliver a brief eulogy. American funerals often do not occur immediately after death as in some other countries. At the cemetery, mourners gather around the grave and offer special burial prayers called *janaza* (pronounced jaNAAzah). Muslims do not practice cremation. Bodies are buried in such a way that if turned onto their right side, they would be facing Mecca. Following burial, mourners generally gather to express condolences either at the family home or in a space set aside specially for the purpose. Some families arrange to have a Koran reciter present or else play recorded recitation for silent reflection.

245

RELIGIOUS TRADITIONS OF SOUTH ASIAN ORIGIN

HINDUISM

HISTORY AND SOURCES

What does the term **"Hinduism"** mean?

As a standard term in religious studies, Hinduism refers to a whole family of religious traditions deeply rooted in the Indian subcontinent. "Hinduism" derives from an ancient linguistic root that means "to flow," and rivers have indeed been and have remained a central feature in the religious life of nearly a billion Indians. A bit of river imagery here will help to explain how many diverse traditions have come together to form the "greater Hinduism" of our day. Imagine an extensive network of rivers stretching across the whole of the Indian subcontinent. One major river flows from the northwest down toward the Indian heartland. Another originates in the south. Each grows as dozens of tributaries flow into it along its course. In the center of the subcontinent the two broad streams come together into one vast waterway. As it nears the sea, the great river opens again into a broad delta. The northern river, called the Aryan, carries a system of religious beliefs that came together from tributaries to the northwest of India as long as five or six millennia ago. Deities of the Aryan tradition seem to have much in common with those of the classical Greek and Roman pantheons with their lords of wind, weather, and sky. The Dravidian river to the south represents ancient indigenous traditions surrounding the forces that rule earth and fertility, mountain and valley, powers of life and death. Beyond the confluence of the two great river systems, no one remembers that the one immense flood was once many.

Did Hinduism have a **historical founder** as Christianity and Islam did?

All but two of the major religious traditions trace their origins to a specific individual teacher or foundational figure. Only Hinduism and Shinto do not—keeping in mind that the individual founders of other religious traditions identify may be impossible to pin down historically. Some people regard historical concreteness and detail as an essential feature of a religious tradition's credibility. From the Hindu perspective, it is the very uncertainty as to the tradition's origins that enhances its attractiveness. The eternal truth that Hindus call *sanatana dharma* emerges from the mists of antiquity in an aura of perfect mystery, as befits a truth of divine origin.

What are the principal historical stages in the **evolution of "greater Hinduism"**?

A stage known as the Vedic period began as early as 4000 BCE. (Some Indian scholars push the origins back as much as three or four thousand years before that.) Archaeological evidence from Harappa and Mohenjo Daro point to a highly developed civilization in the Indus river valley from around 2700 to 1500 BCE. Early texts suggest a religious culture centered on worship of numerous deities associated with forces of nature. Around 2000 BCE, there may have been a major population shift from the northwest of India to the Ganges plain as a result of the drying up of the Sarasvati river, once a prominent feature of the Indus valley. The Vedic period comes to a close around the time of that shift. The period of the Upanishadic scriptures and the Epic age, from 1500 to 500 BCE, witnessed dramatic changes and the evolution of major new forms of religious expression. During these centuries, the Upanishads developed the speculative approach now known generically as Vedanta, the "culmination of the Vedas." For the next millennium or so (500 BCE to 500 CE, sometimes referred to as the Classical Period), new post-Vedantic sacred texts, called *Sutras, Shastras, Agamas,* and earliest *Puranas,* formed the bases of a number of important schools of thought. From this period, too, came the written Epics, the *Ramayana* and *Mahabharata*. Between around 500 and 1800 CE, the so-called Medieval Period, popular devotional theism, based largely on mythic narrative texts called the Puranas, spread across most of India.

View of the seventeenth-century Temple of Minakshi, Madurai, south India. Massive royal gateways define the inner (mostly covered) courtyards, and the two spires protruding through the roof stand over the main "womb chambers." *Photo courtesy of Michael Harter, S.J.*

Beginning with the arrival of the British in the mid–eighteenth century, the Modern Period extends into the mid–twentieth century, the declaration of India's Independence, and the partition that created East and West Pakistan as separate Muslim states.

What were the earliest Hindu **sacred texts**?

A set of sacred scriptures, called the Vedas, consists of four distinct collections of texts, each with its own distinctive purpose. The name *Veda* comes from a Sanskrit root meaning "wisdom" or "vision," the same root that gives us English words like "video." According to tradition, "seers," called *rishis,* composed the texts and communicated them orally. The rishis were able to see the truths revealed to them because they were also "hearers" of the sacred word. In fact, Hindu tradition groups the most sacred of its scriptures in the category of "that which is heard" (*shruti*), to distinguish them from a secondary level of revelation called "that which is remembered" (*smriti*). The Vedas evolved over a period of centuries, and religious specialists eventually wrote them down in an ancient form of Sanskrit. The earliest and most important of the four scriptures is called the *Rig Veda,* an anthology of more than a thousand hymns to various deities. A second collection, called the *Sama Veda,* includes material from the *Rig,* edited for ease of ritual use according to melodies and poetic meters. In the *Yajur Veda,* the early priesthood gathered the most important sacred mantras. A final collection of ritual incantations makes up the *Atharva Veda.* Many of the Vedic hymns are

251

especially beautiful and offer a unique insight into how the early ritual specialists who made up the priesthood sought to understand and affect their world through contact with forces beyond human control.

How did the **Vedic scriptures** describe the **ultimate spiritual powers**?

Vedic cosmology divided the universe into three regions: sky, lower atmosphere, and earth. Eleven of the thirty-three chief deities held sway over each of the cosmic realms. A deity much like the Greek Zeus ruled the sky, but he was not the head of a divine—if often unruly—family as Zeus was. Members of the Vedic pantheon seem to have risen to prominence at different times, as reflected by the numbers of hymns devoted to several individual gods. An atmospheric wind deity called Vayu and the celestial Surya, the sun, played important but still not central roles. The celestial Varuna had once headed the pantheon and oversaw cosmic order. His main competition was the atmospheric Indra, lord of inclement weather. At some point Indra eclipsed Varuna, perhaps because Indra represented a more fearsome power and imminent danger. Only the terrestrial Agni, god of fire and thus essential to Vedic sacrifice, merited more hymns than Indra. But before long even Indra bowed to two upcoming powers, the celestial Vishnu ("all-pervading") and the atmospheric Rudra ("the howler"). Rudra eventually came to be associated with the formidable Shiva. Together, Vishnu and Shiva symbolized the global forces of sustenance and dissolution—powers that most engaged the Hindu religious imagination.

What other **early scriptures** are especially important for Hindus?

Over a span of perhaps two thousand years (c. 3000 to 1000 BCE, according to some Indian scholars), Hindu ritual specialists produced a substantial body of sacred literature by way of commentary and reflection on the Vedas. The earliest of these works were manuals for priests, or Brahmanas, each attached to one of the four Vedas. These Brahmanas elaborated on the mythic stories to which the Vedic hymns often had made only passing allusions, expanding on the tradition much as the early Jewish rabbis had developed the oral Torah. The Brahmanas served the practical purpose of recording for posterity precise directions for correct ritual performance. Still another layer of scriptural development gave rise to a series of works called *Aranyakas*, "Forest Treatises." Composed by and for hermits, these texts offered further commentary on the Vedas meant to foster the contemplative life. Aranyakas were connected with the Brahmanas much as the Brahmanas were linked to the various Vedas. With their emphasis on inward reflection, the Aranyakas signal an important turn away from the ancient Vedic and Brahmanical reliance on external ritual. Another type of sacred text called the Upanishads evolved from about 1500 to 500 BCE. The name *upa-ni-shad* means, loosely, "sitting at the feet of" a mentor. These remarkable documents, many in the form of a dialogue between teacher and student, reflect deeply on the nature of the divine and of the self. Life's true meaning rests not primarily in dealing with forces beyond human control, but in understanding both the ultimate causes of all things and the relationship of the self to those causes. The Upanishads represent major developments known collectively as Vedanta, the "end or culmination of the Vedas."

How did Hinduism become a **religion of the masses**?

For as long as several millennia, earlier forms of the greater Hinduism apparently limited direct involvement in religious ritual to a kind of religious elite. Full participation was open for many centuries only to the various ranks of priestly ritual specialists. Even after the climate began to change in the Upanishadic period, religion remained the province of professionally religious types who wrote the Upanishads, as well as independent-minded seekers who founded the early ascetic and philosophical movements. With the growth of mythic religious texts, called the *Puranas,* came parallel developments in a type of devotional theism called *bhakti* that no longer regarded the ultimate spiritual forces as fearsome and impersonal. Nor was spiritual realization reserved only for the few who had access to the lofty speculation of the Upanishads and the teachers. The Puranas talked of divine involvement in human affairs in ways that appealed to the imagination of ordinary people. Eighteen major Puranas, six dedicated to each of the three principal popular names and forms of God (Shiva, Vishnu, and the Goddess or Shakti), opened up a world in which the humblest person could approach God and be assured of acceptance. Out of that broader movement have grown the many denominations and sects that comprise popular Hinduism today. Major sub-communities are named for the principal deities they worship: devotees of Shiva are called Shaivas, devotees of Vishnu, Vaishnavas, and devotees of the female deities, Shaktas.

What **sacred sources** do the various denominations rely on?

During the so-called Classical Period (500 BCE to 500 CE) especially, various denominations developed their own distinctive sacred texts called *sutras* ("threads, aphorisms"), *shastras* ("treatise, rule"), and *agamas* ("what has come down"). Sutras often take the form of commentary on earlier major texts and are major sources for the six philosophical schools called the *darshanas.* Some philosophical texts are called shastras, but this category is best known as a vehicle for treatments of religious law. Agamas belonging to the various sects often include various types of material ranging from the mythic to the epic to the philosophical. Shaivites generally use the term *agama* to describe their twenty-eight canonical works, while Vaishnavite communities often call their unique scriptures *samhitas* ("collections") and Shakta groups prefer the term *Tantra*.

Do people actually think of all this **diversity** as part of **one religious tradition**?

Walk into the nearest institution identified as a Hindu Temple, and you know immediately that the answer to the question is yes. Especially outside of India, temples serve

253

Major Hindu Scriptures

Shruti ("heard")

    Four Vedas: Rig, Sama, Yajur, and Atharva

    Brahmanas (ritual manuals)

    Aranyakas (forest treatises)

    Upanishads (theological and philosophical reflections on the Vedas)

Smriti ("remembered")

    Epics: huge, poetic compositions still reenacted, including Ramayana (story of Rama's quest to recover his wife Sita, abducted by the demon Ravana); Mahabharata (India's national epic); and Bhagavad Gita (now part of the Mahabharata and sometimes called the Fifth Veda)

    Puranas: mythic narratives of the principal deities

    Sutras: commentary on earlier scriptures

    Shastras: treatises of religious law

    Agamas: Shaivite (*tantras*) and Vaishnavite (*samhitas*) sectarian texts

devotees from many denominations and sects and therefore include multiple images of the divine presence under one roof. Even in India, where temples typically serve constituencies somewhat less varied, most places of worship display prominent symbols of more than one denomination. Over the centuries, the many sources of religious imagery have come together to form the "greater Hinduism" as a result of several processes of integration.

How does the **Hindu pantheon of gods** fit together?

First, divine personalities that would eventually become major deities (especially Vishnu and Shiva) emerged from among the Vedic pantheon. Ancient lore from all over India contributed to the gradual "fleshing out" of stories of the major deities. Meanwhile stories of other "names and forms" of lesser divine beings continued to develop a life of their own in various regions of India. As major communities of belief formed around stories of Vishnu, Shiva, and their various female counterparts, larger mythic frameworks evolved to integrate narratives of lesser deities into those of the greater deities. For example, Vaishnavite tradition developed the structure of Vishnu's "Ten Avatars" or "descents." That mythic framework brought together an astonishing assortment of descriptions of God's involvement in human affairs. The first three avatars are non-human divine interventions in the birth of the cosmos: Matsya (the fish), Kurma (the tortoise), and Varaha (the boar). Three avatars represent divine confrontation with evil and demonic forces: Nara-simha (the man-lion), Vamana (the dwarf), and Parashurama (Rama with the Axe). The two most popular avatars are those of Rama and Krishna, heroes both on and off the field of combat, whose consorts Sita and Radha are of nearly equal importance. As a statement of its even greater inclusiveness, the list includes the Buddha himself. Avatar number ten is the dark and mysterious Kalki, the only avatar yet to come, whose task is to bring an apocalyptic end to the present age. Integrating Shaiva imagery is the concept of Shiva's "holy family." Both Vishnu and Shiva have their consorts (Lakshmi or Bhu, and Parvati, Durga, or Kali respectively). Unlike Vishnu, Shiva has children. Stories of Ganesha and Skanda brought these formerly local or regional deities into the larger structure of the divine family. Finally, a concept known as the "triple form" (*tri-murti*) unites the whole complex of images by identifying a "trinity" of divine roles. Brahma, never an object of great popular devotion, creates. Vishnu sustains. And Shiva destroys, paving the way for renewal of the endless cosmic process.

An eleventh-century CE bronze of the Goddess Parvati, consort and divine energy (*shakti*) of Shiva, Chola period (c. 900–1200 CE), Tanjore district, India. *Courtesy the St. Louis Art Museum.*

Was Hinduism ever identified with any **political regimes**?

Several important royal dynasties that identified themselves with Hindu tradition ruled various parts of India and southeast Asia over a span of about two thousand years. In some cases the dynasties bolstered their claims to political legitimacy by appealing to the concept of divine kingship. A series of fairly short-lived early Hindu dynasties, the Nanda (362–322 BCE), Maurya (322–185 BCE), and Shunga (185–73 BCE), evidently faltered as a result of their failure to keep priestly members of the royal court happy with the balance of power. The Gupta dynasty (320–647 CE) was the first major success story, taking control over the northern two-thirds of India. Promoting devotion to Vishnu especially, the Guptas oversaw what some call a renaissance of Hindu culture. After the fall of the Guptas, several Hindu dynasties ruled various segments of central and southern India. Among the most important were the Tamil kingdoms of the south—especially the Pallavas (c. 250–750 CE), Chalukyas (450–1189), and the Cholas (minor power from 100 CE, expanded 800–1300 CE)—all of which were major patrons of religious art and architecture.

Hindu kingdoms, mostly Shaivite in orientation, had significant influence on parts of southeast Asia, giving rise to the names Indo-China and Indonesia. The kingdom of Champa held sway over most of Vietnam from 150–1471 CE, while several other dynasties arose in Cambodia in the second century and expanded their control over Laos and Thailand from 800 to 1200 CE. During that same period, Hindu monarchies took root in Java and Sumatra, the principal islands of Indonesia, as well as in Malaysia. For nearly two centuries, Hinduism was a major influence throughout Indonesia, until its political patrons succumbed to Muslim invasions in the early sixteenth century. The remnants of the southeast Asian Hindu kingdoms took refuge on the island of Bali, where many still practice Hinduism.

Have there ever been any **reform movements** within Hinduism?

Since the early nineteenth century, various important reform movements have addressed the need to reinterpret ancient tradition for modern times. The Brahmo Samaj (Society of God) denounced the practice of widow suicide (*sati*) and promoted a monotheistic understanding of Hindu faith. Its successor organization, the Sadharan Brahmo Samaj (Universal Society of God), took aim at the caste system and looked for ways to update the tradition without having to resort to European ways of thinking. Some reformers, such as Ramakrishna (1836–86) and his disciple Vivekandanda (1863–1902), offered fresh interpretations of both *bhakti* and Vedanta that they hoped would appeal to the world beyond India. Twentieth-century successors to those pioneering reformers included Shri Aurobindo (1872–1950) and Mahatma Gandhi (1869–1948). Both studied in England and returned with distinctive views on how modern Hindus might revitalize their traditions. Shri Aurobindo proposed a form of "modernist" interpretation incorporating elements of European philosophy, and Gandhi emphasized simplicity of life and taught non-violent means of political protest. Both men founded *ashrams,* quiet places in which spiritual seekers could find spiritual refuge.

RELIGIOUS BELIEFS

Is there a **Hindu creed**? What are the most **basic Hindu beliefs**?

Hindu tradition has not historically developed the kinds of creedal formulations so important in some other communities of faith. But a number of important themes run like brightly colored threads through the fabric of the greater Hinduism. Bear in mind that some of the various denominations and smaller sects interpret these themes in different ways. Material and spiritual existence unfolds in a series of unimaginably long cycles governed by a cosmic Law called *Dharma* (from a root that means "to hold together"). That Law manifests itself on the level of individual beings as a potentially endless succession or cycle of birth and rebirth. The human predicament consists in getting stuck in that cycle, which is called *samsara,* "cosmic flow, endless wandering." Each being's earthly existence or lifespan comes to an end at death or dissolution, but the state of each one's soul at that moment determines whether that being remains caught in the cycle. All action *(karma)* has spiritual consequences. To break the cycle, human beings must gradually purify all actions of ego-centeredness, seeking to act only in accord with their personal dharma. According to law of cause and effect, or karma, all deeds done out of inappropriate motivation chain the individual to the wheel of samsara. Hindu tradition offers various ways of ridding one's actions of all ulterior motive and progressing toward the ultimate goal of liberation *(moksha)* from the endless cycle of rebirths. Those methods or paths include the classical mode of ritual action, the quest for knowledge and full realization of the ultimate truths of existence, and personal devotion to a manifestation of God. Beginning with the earliest scriptures, the Vedas, and extending through subsequent unfoldings of ever new sources of divine truth as explained by generations of teachers, Hindu tradition offers access to knowledge of God and hence to the hope of salvation.

Are **doctrine** and **dogma** important to Hindus?

Over the centuries many important Hindu philosophers and theologians have devised elaborate and sophisticated systems of thought. Those systems are an attempt to structure essential elements of ancient tradition so as to show their internal logic and consistency. Their teachings have had the force of doctrine for those who subscribe to the various schools of thought, but they do not constitute a body of authoritative dogma as such. The vast majority of Hindus grow up hearing about the basic themes described above. Their parents and teachers pass along the traditional stories about the forces of good and evil. But few devout Hindus think of religious belief in terms of formal assent to a body of officially defined truths. Most Hindus have a sense of great flexibility with respect to the content of the faith.

Do Hindus really believe in and worship **many gods**?

Hindu tradition uses language and symbolism that seems at first glance to suggest what is called polytheism, worship of many deities. Most Hindus, however, will tell you they believe in God, one transcendent spiritual reality. Since human beings are incapable of grasping the fullness of divine truth in anything like a comprehensive and

Revelation in Hinduism

In the Abrahamic traditions, revelation means divine truth disclosed directly to and further communicated by a human mediator, a more or less tidily packaged gift "from above." Hindu tradition describes revelation as though the divine disclosure bubbled up out of the earth itself. One can connect Jewish, Christian, and Islamic revelation with various specific individuals explicitly set aside for a prophetic vocation. In the Hindu perspective, sacred truth is entrusted to those special, generally anonymous, persons gifted with a higher sensitivity to the sound of holiness that vibrates through all creation. In other words, while revelation is more focused in the Abrahamic traditions, it is more diffuse in Hinduism.

definitive way, believers are left with a basic choice: Either they keep quiet about matters of faith and belief altogether, since the realities will forever elude ordinary language and symbolism, or they indulge in ordinary forms of expression, ever aware that those forms will never be adequate. Hindu tradition has become a monument to the second option and the world of religious belief is all the richer for that. But why not opt for mute adoration? Why choose to complicate matters by multiplying hopelessly inadequate attempts at capturing divinity? Because that is an important part of being human. People need to talk about the sources of greatest wonderment as well as about their hopes and fears and suffering. At the risk of being accused of idolatry, a charge non-Hindus often level at them, Hindus acknowledge a fundamental need for imagery. All religious traditions finally do something similar. Even the traditions that sound the loudest alarm about the dangers of idolatry, Judaism and Islam, for example, use extensive and vivid verbal imagery to say the ineffable. Most Hindus, like certain Christian and Buddhist communities, for example, include a wide array of visual expression side by side with the verbal. Words can become idols, too.

What do Hindus believe about **ultimate spiritual reality** or God?

Hindu conceptions about God are among the most expansive and arresting in the history of religion. Scores of "names and forms" make up the enormous Hindu theological lexicon. Some names and forms emphasize divine majesty and power, others divine beauty and attractiveness. For Hindus generally, the purpose of religious belief and devotion is to cultivate a relationship with the Holy, the source of benevolence and blessing as well as of death and difficulty. Most of all, God is a mystery that is willing to be unveiled. Hindu theologians define two broad ways of talking about the God, Ultimate Reality, called *Brahman* in Sanskrit. God is beyond all imagining and impossible to shoehorn into humanly devised words and concepts. But believers can still refer to the Ultimate Reality in a roundabout way, hinting at what God is by saying explicitly

Major Hindu Deities

Principal Vedic Gods
  Agni, god of fire and sacrifice
  Indra, god of sky and war
  Varuna, upholder of cosmic order
  Surya, the sun
  Vishnu, consorts and avatars

Principal consorts: Lakshmi, Shri, Bhu
  Ten Avatars: Matsya (the fish), Kurma (the tortoise), Varaha (the boar),
    Nara-simha (the man-lion), Vamana (the dwarf), Parashurama (Rama
    who wields the axe), Rama (with his consort Sita), Krishna (with his
    consort Radha), Buddha, Kalki (the dark horse who brings on the end
    of the age)

Shiva, consorts and offspring
  Principal consorts: Parvati and Uma (gracious manifestations), Kali and
    Durga (fearsome manifestations)
  Children of Shiva: Ganesha (elephant-headed deity, lord of life's transitions),
    Skanda (also known as Karttikeya and Murugan)

what God is not. From this perspective, theologians call the God "Brahman Without Qualities" *(Nir-guna Brahman)*. But the "negative way" of thinking about God can be very abstract and difficult. Human beings generally need something more concrete, something that engages the feelings and imagination as well as the logic-bound mind. Hindu tradition therefore acknowledges that one can approach the truth by considering God as "Brahman with Qualities" *(Sa-guna Brahman)*. In this approach, one has always to keep in mind that those qualities are remote approximations at best, and ultimately just a concession to the human need to imagine the unimaginable.

What are some of the principal **"names and forms"** of God?

One of the first questions non-Hindus ask about the imagery of Hinduism's deities is "Why the multiple limbs and non-human features?" Hindu tradition answers "Why not?" Since no one can know definitively and in detail what God looks like or how God operates, God sees fit to allow human beings to describe the indescribable. God is by definition beyond anything in human experience, so Hindu tradition often depicts the deity in clearly non-human form. Names of the deities always have some symbolic meaning. For example, Vishnu comes from a root that means "to pervade," alluding to the divine omnipresence. Shiva means "auspicious." Traditional sources often pun on the name,

259

suggesting that without the "i" in *Shakti* (Shiva's feminine side) Shiva would be Shava, "corpse." Ganesha's name is a compound meaning "Lord of the [attendant Vedic deities called] *ganas*." Shiva's terrifying feminine side is called Kali, "Dark." As for their multiple forms, Hindu images of deity remind believers of the infinite variety that makes God God. As a reminder of the perfect balance of energies, most male deities have a female counterpart. A popular image of Shiva in both painting and sculpture depicts the deity as "half-woman lord," one side of the body male and the other displaying the features of Shiva's consort Parvati. As a reminder of God's complete dominion over all forces and conditions, including those most of us would rather not have to deal with, Hindu deities appear in shocking and even terrible forms as well as in attractive and approachable aspects. There is a hierarchy among divine beings, a ranking that naturally develops within each denomination or sect. Among Shaivas, Shiva is the supreme deity to whom all the others defer. For Vaishnavas, Vishnu or one of the Avatars heads the list.

Are there **mythic elements** in Hindu tradition?

Hinduism's sacred texts comprise one of the world's greatest treasure troves of myth. Non-Hindus, especially "westerners" who find themselves inclined to discount Hindu tradition as "just a collection of stories," are shutting the door to that watershed of insight called the imagination. All religious traditions build on a master story composed of accounts about how the world came to be, what human beings are all about, and the relationship between humankind and the greater Being or Power responsible for the shape of things. Some traditions, such as the Abrahamic faiths, wrap themselves around narratives they call their sacred *history*. Other traditions, such as Hinduism and Buddhism, for example, consider human history much too small a stage for any drama under the direction of the Ultimate Reality. History begins, stretches out, and comes to a definitive end. But the view that history is all about what "actually happened" while myth is purely "imaginary" is seriously flawed. History and myth are two very different ways to answer the big questions about human life. Sacred history tells how God has worked in the world by identifying certain events as the result of divine intervention. Mythic narrative tells the story of the otherness of Ultimate Reality by stretching the limits of the imagination. History works from the ground up, so to speak, and turns around the power of memory, while myth starts with mystery and cultivates the human capacity for wonder. What non-Hindus may be tempted to criticize as a weakness in Hindu tradition, Hindus regard as their tradition's great strength. Both approaches yield important forms of narrative theology. Far from being simply contradictory, myth and history complement each other.

Do Hindus believe in **miracles**?

A special quality of Hindu belief generally is that all things, whether spiritual or material, result from the divine play or *lila*. God brings all things into being, sustains them for a time, then withdraws them from the realm of human experience, not by laboring, but as a kind of divine entertainment. That does not mean that God is cynical or cruel, dangling his creatures like so many marionettes. It means only that what we know as our "world" is the product of God's delight. Hindu tradition teaches that human beings are the beneficiaries of that delight. We are, in other words, invited to the party. The concept of miracle presupposes that human beings already know the limits of ordinary causality. From the Hindu perspective, that assumption is the height of arrogance because it suggests that human beings have things pretty well figured out—such as the causes and cures of disease, the roots of evil, and the wellsprings of good. One of the many aspects of the Hindu tradition's genius, and one of its major contributions to humanity, is that it refuses to close the door on surprise. All things, not merely the odd event that appears to defy the laws of nature, are cause for wonder. There is but one great miracle: God has chosen eternally to pour out the divine essence in its countless forms—and enjoys doing so. What a gift of the ultimate perspective on life, to see it all as part of one great marvel and learn not to take oneself so seriously.

How does Hindu tradition talk about the **origins of the universe**?

Early Vedic hymns as well as later sources reflect deeply and evocatively on the marvels of the world. They propose tentative possibilities as to how it came to be. Perhaps it all began as an embryo or fertile egg, out of which all the divine powers emerged from potentiality into action, separating the gold of heaven from the silver of earth. From the egg's outer membrane arose the mountains, from the inner membranes the clouds, and from its veins the rivers. Perhaps there was once, before time began, an ocean of milk on which the serpent of eternity floated in infinite silence. And as Lord Vishnu ("Pervasive") rested undisturbed in the serpent's coils, from the divine body emerged a great fecund lotus flower, unfolding to release the creative power (called Brahma). Looking in all four directions Brahma created the world, thereafter to close again with the lotus blossom, and reopen in a new cycle. Perhaps the world came to be when the gods offered sacrifice to the Ultimate Reality. From the sacred body of the Primal Person offered in sacrifice came all the elements of the universe. From his eyes the heavenly lights, from his nostrils the winds, from his mouth the priestly caste, from his arms the soldier, until all things originated from the divine body. Or perhaps the creative power was unleashed when the deity entered into ascetic meditation. Focusing the divine energy inward, he generated such spiritual fire that it could no longer be contained and burst forth in creation. But an even greater mystery than the "how" of creation is the "why." Ultimately one can only stand in awe, admitting that the mystery may forever elude the human capacity to know.

What **solutions to the human predicament** does Hindu tradition propose?

Hindus seek the ultimate spiritual goal of liberation through any of four traditional ways or paths called *margas,* "methods of seeking" or *yogas,* "joining by means of discipline." The most ancient and slowest method is that of ritual action, *karma*. Originally associated with scrupulous fulfillment of the prescriptions of Vedic ritual practice, Karma is kept within reach of contemporary Hindus by interpreting it as "unselfish service." In that sense the way of action recommends itself to all, even in the absence of a vital tradition of ritual sacrifice. The second path begins with the conviction that ignorance causes suffering. Intuitive experiential knowledge *(jñana)* is available through various intellectual and meditative disciplines associated with a variety of philosophical approaches called *darshanas* ("views"). Most of all, the way of knowledge seeks the full realization of the perfect oneness of all reality and the illusory nature of our instinctive conviction that individuality of persons and multiplicity of all things is the substance of life. It is a difficult and abstract method attractive to relatively few people. Its best known form is that of Shankara's Advaita Vedanta school. Closely associated with the way of knowledge is a path that uses the formal disciplines popularly known as "yoga." Proceeding from the conviction that suffering is the result of physical and mental distraction, meditational yoga combines various physical practices *(hatha yoga)* designed to control one's physiological states, with belief in divine assistance toward higher contemplative states *(raja yoga)*. Far more popular and accessible is the way of devotion or *bhakti* ("participation"). Whereas the way of knowledge seeks realization of a union that already exists in an impersonal Ultimate Reality, the way of devotion seeks to cultivate the union of the two distinct parties to the divine-human relationship. *Bhakti* means dedication to a personal God whose love, mercy, and grace elicit a response of complete faith and surrender. It proceeds from the conviction that suffering arises out of separation from one's divine source and goal. The devotee approaches God in full confidence of divine protection and the hope of salvation.

Do Hindus believe in the concept of **salvation**?

Most Hindus prefer the way of devotion because it is so concrete and personal. Bhakti offers the assurance of divine aid in all of life's difficulties, as well as cause for rejoicing in better times. Seekers who choose any of the classical spiritual paths are aware that human beings are ever in need of help from sources beyond themselves. But the notion of salvation assisted by divine grace is especially strong in popular theistic or devotional Hinduism. Even in the denominations that teach a modified form of predestination, such as those of Madhva and Vallabha, grace is a central feature of bhakti. Since the human soul is, so to speak, naturally divine, grace is the power that refreshes and renews the soul in its original state. Hindus, like members of various other major traditions, have held differing views as to how divine grace works. A particularly vivid pair of images characterizes one view as that of the "Cat School," another that of the "Monkey School." According to the Cat School, divine grace is all-sufficient and does not depend at all on human action. Mother cats carry their kittens around by picking them up with their teeth. According to the Monkey School, human beings must cooperate in the saving action of divine grace. Mother monkeys rescue their babies from danger, but the baby first climbs aboard and holds tight. The two schools

Hinduism's Various Spiritual Paths

Karma/Action: proper ritual and ethical action as a means to spiritual progress, including purification of one's deeds through detachment from the fruits of one's actions.

Jñana/Knowledge: attainment of intuitive or mystical understanding of the essential unity of all reality, resulting from meditative approach to the scriptures and wisdom traditions.

Bhakti/Devotion: "participation" in the divine life through devotion to a chosen manifestation of the deity, complete emotional attachment to the chosen deity, and unselfish service to God.

therefore represent different views as to the relationship between divine power and human action.

What are some basic Hindu **ethical considerations**?

Hindu tradition describes a range of morally and religiously acceptable goals or motives for action. What matters most is not the substance of the particular type of goal, but the quality of one's intentions. All good things in life are gifts of God. One has only to learn how best to use and value them. In the greater scheme of things, three of the four major goals are means rather than ends in themselves. Even so, a devout Hindu can pursue them with vigor and determination, as long as the pursuit is balanced and not obsessive. Most fundamental is the goal of *dharma,* the quest for one's own individual ethical calling in accord with the cosmic Law that holds all things together. Personal justice and righteousness are the cardinal virtues. But wealth, material success, power, and social status (*artha*) are also worthy goals, so long as one keeps them in perspective. People who use their worldly success in ethically laudable ways are exercising responsible stewardship and can make wonderful things happen for the benefit of many. In addition, a devout Hindu can enjoy to the full all of life's legitimate pleasures (*kama*) associated with culture, the arts, sexuality, and family life. This traditional teaching undercuts the common stereotype of Hinduism as world-rejecting and self-denying asceticism. On the other hand, the opposite stereotype that identifies Hinduism as the kind of wild-eyed lust sometimes associated with the *Kamasutra* is equally inappropriate. Ultimately, Hindu tradition teaches, the sincere seeker will find that none of the first three goals offers permanent satisfaction. What remains is the quest for final liberation from the enslavement that goes with even well-moderated attachments. *Moksha,* meaning "release," is the only goal worthy of being considered an end in itself. Most people will spend many lifetimes striving for it.

263

What other **ideals** does the Hindu tradition recommend?

A classical formulation of the ideal life cycle is called the "four stages of life." It applies almost exclusively to males, but the implications for women are fairly clear. The traditional system is called *varnashramadharma,* the ["law *(dharma)* of caste *(varna)* and life stage *(ashrama)."* Upper caste Hindu males begin the cycle as students, in a stage between the ages of 12 and 24. Under the tutelage of a guru young men learn the basic sacred traditions, rituals, and sacred texts. From ages 24 to 48 they become "householders," marrying and raising a family according to conventional norms. During these first two stages, men seek religious fulfillment by turning outward and engaging their world with extroverted energy and drive. At 48 a man enters into the stage of a "forest-dweller" or "senior mentor" to younger men. Some still actually move toward a life of greater solitude during this stage, even if not literally heading for a hermitage in the forest. Some men past the age of 72 enter the stage of the renunciant, or *sannyasi.* They formally set aside as many ordinary ties to their former lives as possible, leaving behind wealth as well as material responsibility in quest of self-realization. Both of the latter two stages call for increasing introspection and time for personal prayer and devotion. Though fewer individuals follow the four stages formally now than in the past, the cycle remains a traditional ideal and a useful map of spiritual progress for those who choose to pursue it.

What do Hindus believe about **life after death**?

At the heart of Hindu belief about the nature of human life is a notion called metempsychosis, also called reincarnation or transmigration of soul. Life is an infinite continuum punctuated by episodes of embodiment. Death is therefore the opposite of birth, not of life. One can escape the cycle of birth and death by liberating the soul, freeing the self from all attachments. According to the law of karma, human beings always get what they wish for—in spades: If my every effort in this life is the selfish acquisition of wealth or power or pleasure, chances are I will die wanting more. Unsatisfied desire is a form of energy so potent that it keeps the self ensnared in the bonds of attachment that ensure the soul will experience yet another embodiment in some form or another. Hindus call this potentially endless cycle of rebirths *samsara.*

Does that mean Hindus do not believe in **heaven** or **hell**?

Traditional Hindu cosmologies speak of three realms of existence or *lokas.* One scheme describes an "in-between realm" *(antarloka),* where individual souls abide both during sleep and between incarnations. This reflects the persistence of important features of ancient Vedic views of the cosmos. A version of hell called *naraka* (literally, "referring to humankind") is a thoroughly unpleasant lower part of the antarloka that functions rather like a purgatory. In any of its seven (or even as many as twenty-one) levels souls can overcome through suffering some of the effects of bad karma. A multi-levelled

> ## Is non-violence particularly important in Hindu beliefs?
>
> **R**eaders familiar with Dr. Martin Luther King Jr. may recall that he spoke of being especially influenced by Mahatma Gandhi's teachings on non-violent resistance. Concern for *ahimsa* ("non-injury"), including respect for all forms of life, seems to have become an important theme in Hindu tradition following the rise of Buddhism and Jainism in the sixth and fifth centuries BCE. Ahimsa ranks first among a list of ten spiritual qualities, called *yamas* or "restraints," in the classical system of yoga attributed to Patañjali. Avoidance of all injury in word and deed began with the rejection of Vedic sacrifice—and as a central practice of small groups of ascetics—and grew to include the practice of vegetarianism.

region called *anandloka* ("realm of bliss"), also called *svarga* ("region of light"), is roughly equivalent to a paradise or heaven. It is a temporary abode in which people who have died approaching liberation acquire knowledge that can assist them toward greater spiritual progress in their next life. Hindu cosmology includes multiple levels, both in this in-between realm and in the uppermost realms beyond that reserved for those who have achieved *moksha*. Most Hindus regard the intermediate equivalents of heaven and hell as temporary, although some smaller sects teach the existence of more or less permanent abodes of punishment in the next life.

What do Hindus think about **history** and **time**?

Imagine a bird flying past the Himalayas every hundred years, brushing the mountain peaks with the silk scarf it holds in its beak. What we call history is the time it would take that bird to wear the mountains flat. And that would be only an infinitesimal fraction of divine time. History is an infinite cycle made up of smaller, measurable cycles of creation and destruction, but even the smaller cycles are unimaginably long. Hindu myth says that God, manifested as Brahma the creator, unfolds the material world over and over. Each lifetime of Brahma lasts a hundred divine years. Each day in the life of the creator deity is called a *kalpa,* lasting four billion, three hundred twenty million years. Each kalpa, or great age (*mahayuga*), in turn is made up of four ages or aeons called *yugas.* The present cycle of human history began with the first yuga, a time of order and peace when the cosmic law (dharma) kept evil in check. During the second age disorder entered history. Dharma diminished as did the span of human life. There followed a third age, when evil gained still greater strength and dharma weakened. Social fragmentation gave rise to the caste system and attempts to gain power through ritual sacrifice. We are now in the fourth and bleakest age, a time of darkness and lawlessness destined to end in four hundred thousand years. Then, after a period of quiescence, all will begin again, another day in the life of Brahma.

Key Concepts in Hinduism

Atman: the "in-divisible" and indestructible spiritual center of each being, and the ultimate "self" underlying all reality.

Avatar(a): "crossing-over-downward," a deity's (especially Vishnu's) descent into the world of human experience.

Bhakti: "participation," devotional relationship to one's chosen deity, a major path to liberation.

Brahman: Ultimate Reality enveloping all appearances of multiplicity.

Dharma: that which holds all things together, the cosmic "law"; religio-social propriety, one's individual religious duty, and one of the four acceptable goals of life.

Jñana: "knowledge," insight into the spiritual meaning of things, one of the principal paths to liberation.

Kama: "pleasure," one of the four legitimate goals of life.

Karma: "action," ritual or ethical conduct and the consequences thereof, one of the traditional paths to liberation.

Marga: path, way, method of spiritual progress toward liberation.

Moksha: liberation from the cycle of rebirth, ultimate goal of Hindu spiritual practice.

Samsara: "journeying," the endless round of rebirth from which Hindus seek to be free.

Yoga: "joining, harnessing," system of physical and spiritual disciplines practiced by a *yogi*.

Are there Hindu **fundamentalists**?

If fundamentalism may be defined as an aggressive and intolerant religious exclusivism, there are several manifestations of it in the history of Hinduism. A nineteenth-century reformist movement called the Arya Samaj (Society of Aryans) sought to cleanse modern Hindu thought and practice of unnecessary clutter that had contaminated the tradition over the centuries. The Society condemned not only Muslims and Christians but members of various Hindu denominations as well. To its great credit, the Arya Samaj attempted to make Hindu practice more egalitarian, giving women and socially marginal groups equal access. Another fundamentalist-style force in recent times has been the political faction called Bharatiya Janata or BJP. In 1992 the party supported agitation by the militant Vishva Hindu Parishad (Universal Hindu Assembly) to destroy a sixteenth-century mosque in Ayodhya. They wanted to replace the mosque with a temple to Rama and to rededicate the site as Rama's birthplace, which Muslims had desecrated centuries before. The VHP throws its considerable weight behind political candidates who promise to do whatever is necessary to keep power in the hands of Hindus.

SIGNS AND SYMBOLS

Are there any **signs** or **symbols** that might **identify an individual** as a Hindu?

A small dot on the forehead (called a *bindu* or *bindi*) is perhaps the most common individual symbol in Hinduism. Many Indian women wear a small round red dot in the middle of the forehead to indicate that they are married, and some wear a black dot to ward off evil prior to marriage. Some regard the red dot as a generic symbol of one's Hindu faith, as worn by both men and women. Hindus in Europe and the United States sometimes have difficulty deciding whether to wear the dot in public or whether to confine its use to worship. As with so many personal religious symbols, it has become associated with issues of religious distinctiveness and cultural assimilation. Some believe the dot alludes to Shiva's third eye, a symbol of wisdom and divine power. Shaivites often wear three parallel horizontal lines on the forehead, and often on upper arms and on the chest as well. The marks are sometimes made with paint and sometimes with ash to symbolize cremation. Vaishnavites wear what appears to be a large "V" or double-V, on the forehead and sometimes on the upper arm.

What **signs** or **symbols** distinguish Hindu **religious specialists**?

Priests in most Hindu temples, whatever the denomination, generally wear a simple body wrap that covers one or both shoulders. Sometimes they will remove the upper wrap altogether. Priests may wear a white thread across the left shoulder, a symbol of initiation into the sacred scriptures. Some priests wear a set of beads (called a *mala,* or "rosary"), used to count in the repetition of sacred words or syllables, around the neck or wrist. Members of various monastic orders often wear a saffron or salmon colored robe that is the "habit" or distinctive garb of the organization. Shaivite Sadhus sometimes carry the trident, a symbol sacred to Shiva.

Do Hindus mark their **sacred spaces** with any distinctive **signs and symbols**?

Hindu temples are often very easily identified, especially if the sacred place has been built as such from the start, rather than occupying a structure originally designed for some other purpose. Two major architectural styles developed in India. The "Southern" style features three-tiered pyramidal spires (called *shikhara*) atop each of the temple's interior shrines or "womb chambers" (*garbha griha*). A monumental trapezoidal facade called a "royal gateway" (*raja gopuram*) typically rises thirty to fifty feet above the main roofline. Both the spires and the facade are nowadays generally finished in white, with small gold finials on top. Southern temples often house several shrines under a single flat roof, with the individual spires of the shrines protruding through the roof and visible to all who approach. The classic "Northern" style historically had a large outer unroofed enclosure, within which

A Hindu temple in progress, St. Louis, Missouri, 1998. A simple concrete block structure begins its transformation toward an elaborately decorated place of worship in Southern temple style, scheduled for completion in 2000. The fourth of five planned spires rises over the inner shrines or "womb chambers" (*garbha griha*) housing the principal deities. Soon the building will have a fifty-foot-high "royal gateway" (*raja gopura*).

stood a series of separate ritual spaces arranged additively along a single east-west axis. As in the southern style, the center of northern temples is always the shrine or womb chamber, typically a small dark room with only one door and a tall multi-tiered spire above. Attached to the shrine by a narrow passageway toward the east one might find a larger room for devotees to gather, and sometimes another, still larger, east of that dedicated to other ritual needs, such as ritual dancing. In other words, the various ritual functions the southern style puts together under one roof, the northern style arranges in more or less distinct spaces that look like small separate structures. Most of the Hindu temples built recently in the United States are in the southern style. The overall design is more convenient in multi-seasonal climates and allows for a variety of shrines, so that one temple can serve the needs of members of various denominations.

What sort of **symbols** and **signs** will I see in a **Hindu temple**?

First you will remove your shoes as a sign of respect for a holy place, and to help keep it clean, since worshipers often sit on the floor. Very near the door you will see an image or statue of the elephant-headed deity called Ganesha. One of Shiva's two sons, Ganesha is the guardian of openings, beginnings, and travelers, and he generally bestows blessings on worshipers as they enter. Even Vaishnavite temples usually have a Ganesha at the door. Along the side walls you may see smaller shrines containing images of deities important in one or another denomination but secondary to this particular temple's devotional focus. Straight ahead you will see the central shrine, perhaps flanked by a pair of subordinate shrines holding images of deities directly related to the one in the central shrine. For example, if the temple is primarily dedicated to a manifestation of Vishnu called Shri Venkateshvara (as are temples in Pittsburgh and St. Louis), flanking shrines might house Krishna and Radha on one side and Rama with wife Sita, brother Lakshmana, and the monkey assistant Hanuman on the other. The subordinate shrines may have prominent spires somewhat shorter than that of the central shrine. If the temple serves a large and diverse community, other side rooms may be devoted to other deities. Vishnu's consort, Lakshmi, goddess of wealth and success, often has

Two sculpture-covered "royal gateways" at the Temple of Minakshi, Madurai. *Photo courtesy of Michael Harter, S.J.*

her own shrine, sometimes with a *shikhara,* whose external elevation is slightly lower than those of the central shrine and its flanking shrines. Another room might house one large and several smaller shrines dedicated to Shiva and his "holy family." In the main Shiva shrine you will see an abstract symbol of power and blessing called the *linga-yoni,* the principal aniconic symbol of Shiva. Alongside, smaller shrines will display images of Parvati, Shiva's wife, and their two sons, Ganesha and Skanda (also known as Karttikeya and Murugan). Many, if not all, images will be elaborately clothed and festooned with floral garlands. Decorative themes on the shrines might include images of guardian figures called "doorkeepers" and other protective symbols that look like small lion faces.

269

How do Hindus use **statues** and other similar **visual imagery** in worship?

Shiva as "Man-woman Lord" (Ardhanarishwara) standing in the "triple-bend" posture, with his mount, the bull Nandi, behind him. Chola period, twelfth century. *Courtesy the St. Louis Art Museum.*

Sacred sculpture plays a central role in the overall symbolism of Hindu devotional ritual. Individual images (called *vigraha,* "something one can grasp") of each of the major deities are generally of granite or marble, though some are made of other materials. Sculptors follow principles laid down in medieval texts that stipulate in detail the proportions and features essential for each deity. Some regard dark stone as the ideal medium because it suggests infinite power and mystery. Images are not themselves deities, but merely specific places in which the deity condescends to dwell for the benefit of devotees. When devotees lavish ritual attention on the images, they acknowledge the sacred symbolized there, rather than any power inherent in the material image. Each major temple image resides in a cave-like shrine called the "womb-chamber" (*garbha griha*) that offers an essential clue to the metaphorical purpose of sacred sculpture. Images represent the dark mystery of divine fecundity from which all things emerge. Central to image-based ritual is the notion of *darshan,* seeing and being seen by the deity. In a manner analogous to Eastern Christian use of icons, Hindu practice interprets the eyes as the central visual symbol in the relationship between the devotee and the ultimate object of devotion. God sees the individual as surely as the devotee sees God. It is neither magic nor simple idolatry, but an acknowledgment of the fundamental human need to pray with all the senses. Images offer devotees something to hold on to, a way of understanding.

How the Gods Get Around

The principal "vehicles" (*vahana*) of the principal deities are as follows:

Shiva: the bull Nandi
Parvati: a lion
Durga: lion, tiger, or parrot
Ganesha: a mouse or rat
Skanda: a peacock
Brahma: a goose or swan
Vishnu: the eagle Garuda or the serpent Ananta
Lakshmi: an owl

What sort of **symbolism** is important in Hindu religious **sculpture and painting**?

Images of the deities convey their distinctive meanings through a combination of iconographic clues or themes. Here are some of the most important categories or types of imagery. Unusual physical features naturally strike the viewer immediately. They may include non-human appendages, multiple arms or faces, and stylized or highly exaggerated male or female characteristics. Features like these function as reminders of the "otherness" and mystery of the deity. Smaller distinctive bodily marks (the diamond on Vishnu's chest), along with items of clothing or ornament, are part of the standard repertoire. Posture and gesture are very important. Some deities are shown in a rigidly upright posture, but many popular images adopt the "triple bend" or S-curve posture that suggests warmth, attractiveness, and accessibility. Artists can choose from a wide range of hand gestures, but certain specific gestures are by convention associated with certain deities. They can communicate anything from reassurance to the wrath that awaits evildoers. The same is true of the various implements or devices symbolic of each deity's special prerogatives. Weapons and musical instruments are the most common items of this type. Weapons remind devotees of the deity's protective power; musical instruments, of the divine power of enchantment. Deities often appear with their consorts, or female counterparts (Shiva with Parvati, Vishnu with Lakshmi, Krishna with Radha, Rama with Sita), and with their offspring (Shiva's Ganesha and Skanda), or special assistants (Rama with Hanuman, and any number of deities with guardian figures). Finally, each of the major deities has his or her vehicle or mode of conveyance (Vishnu's eagle Garuda, for example), and these often appear in images.

What are some basic clues about the **iconography of the major deities**?

Walk through the Asian galleries of your local museum, or visit a Hindu temple, and chances are good that you will spot some of the following images. Shiva's main sym-

Hindu boy placing garlands around a linga, the principal aniconic symbol of Shiva. *Courtesy of Beata Grant.*

bol is the short pillar-like object called the *linga* which, together with the female *yoni,* represents divine creative power. But you may also find Shiva *Nataraja* ("Dance King") surrounded by a ring of fire (cosmic flux) and trouncing the demon of ignorance. His upper right hand holds the drum whose sound is that of creation, his upper left the fire of destruction. His lower left points to the earth, the lower right raised in a gesture of reassurance. From his head flows the Ganges, whose fall to earth Shiva breaks with his matted locks. You may find his beloved mount, the bull Nandi, nearby. Shiva may also appear seated with his very voluptuous wife, Parvati, and their very human looking son Skanda. There Shiva will hold an axe and a deer as symbols of his lordship over nature. You may also see the combined male and female Shiva-Parvati called "Half-woman Lord." Their other son, Ganesha, is the one with the elephant head and pot belly. He holds a bowl of sweets in one hand, and in the other one of his own tusks, which he is about to hurl at the demon who made fun of him. His vehicle is a mouse or rat, an obvious dash of humor. Vishnu may appear alone or with his wife, Lakshmi. He typically carries the conch shell (capable of making a world-shuddering sound), the discus (a weapon for cutting enemies off at the knees), and the mace, while raising a fourth hand in reassurance. Vishnu's most popular avatar, Krishna, frequently plays his world-charming flute, with his legs crossed jauntily in a dance step. His beloved Radha often appears with him. Rama is the second most important avatar, recognizable by his bow when standing alone, but usually seen in company of his wife Sita, his brother Lakshmana, and their faithful monkey assistant Hanuman.

Is **number symbolism** important in Hindu tradition?

Dozens of numbers retain traditional symbolic meanings for many Hindus. The number one recalls divine unity and the light of the sun. The number two is associated with the moon and all the dual features of ordinary human life, such as all the paired parts of the body. The number four is the number of the Vedas, 10 that of Vishnu's principal avatars, while 18 represents the number of sections in both the epic Mahabharata and the Bhagavad Gita. Perhaps the single most widely acknowledged sacred number is 108. It is arrived at by adding the seven planets to the moon's two phases and multiplying by the 12 signs of the Zodiac. The number 108 is the number of "seats of the goddess" Sati, Shiva's wife, as well as the sum of all Upanishads.

Shiva Nataraja ("Dance King"), Chola Period, twelfth century CE, South India, bronze. His upper right hand holds the drum of creation, his upper left the fire of destruction. With his lower right hand he makes a gesture of reassurance, while his lower left points to the earth where his left foot tramples on the demon of ignorance. The circle of flame recalls the world in flux. *Courtesy of the St. Louis Art Museum.*

Have **relics** ever been part of Hindu practice?

Concern over the sacred remnants of human embodiments of holiness—often called relics—does not play as important a role in Hindu tradition as in, say, Christianity or Buddhism. One reason is that Hindu myth describes the whole earth as sacred. All of creation is itself the body of God. With that kind of pervasive sense of holiness, reminders of the holiness of individual human beings are hardly necessary. Even so, Hindu popular devotional practice displays an ample array of concrete symbols that function much the way relics do in other traditions. One fine example is the use of sacred footprints called *padukas*. Footprints of Vishnu often appear in

Why are cows considered sacred in India?

Hindu tradition teaches that all living beings are sacred and inherently deserving of respect. Within that framework of reverence for nature, cows have a special place for several reasons. As far back as Vedic times, the "Mother Cow" was both source of food and material goods, and bulls and non-milking cows were the preferred sacrificial offering. When the rise of Jainism and Buddhism brought concern for non-injury to the fore, Hindu tradition began to repudiate sacrificial ritual and recommended protection for all living things. Cows still provide much in the way of food and fuel, and remind many of the all-sustaining Mother deity. Some Hindus, especially Vaishnavites, attach further meanings, since Lord Krishna was the Gopala, the Lord of Cows, whose dalliance with the Gopis (cowherd maidens) became a metaphor for the divine-human relationship. Cows are humble and ordinary and so numerous now that one wonders how people could consider them as special in any way. Perhaps it is those very qualities that so endear them to India's Hindus, for they are ever-present reminders of the divine bounty.

paintings, small items of jewelry, and metal stamps with which devotees can apply inked impressions of the deity's two feet. Especially sacred are the feet and sandals of one's guru. Devotees sometimes gather to collect the water and other materials used to bathe either the holy one's feet, or, in his absence, an image of his feet called the *shri paduka*. Devotees often convey the padukas of famous saints on wagons in procession as they sing of their desire to be at sacred feet of the holy one.

What does the symbol called the **swastika** have to do with Hinduism?

The name "swastika" comes from a Sanskrit term that means "all is well." It is a symbol of auspiciousness and good fortune. The symbol may derive from a four-spoked wheel, possibly connected with the crossed firebrands of ancient Vedic sacrifice. Originally a solar symbol, the swastika was anciently associated with Vishnu, but eventually became important in Buddhism as well. Even though Shiva has been particularly connected with lunar symbolism, the swastika has become common in the iconographic repertoire of Shaivites too. Swastikas can appear to be spinning either to the right or to the left, and have accordingly been associated with either the so-called right- or left-handed sects of Shaktism and Tantrism. The female symbolism of the left-handed swastika was generally considered inauspicious. Nazi Germany adopted the right-handed swastika because they associated it with Aryan ethnicity and thus with their pretensions to ancient racial purity. Hindus and Buddhists continue to use the symbol in many contexts.

MEMBERSHIP, COMMUNITY, DIVERSITY

Where do Hindus live today? Any estimates of numbers available?

India is home to the vast majority (about 95%) of the world's nearly one billion Hindus. Other significant minority populations have Hindu communities in more than half a dozen other lands. Almost twenty-four million Hindus are Nepalese. Over twelve million live in Bangladesh, nearly six million in Indonesia, some two million in the United States, and approaching a million and a half each in Malaysia, Pakistan, South Africa, and England. Virtually every nation on earth now has representatives of Hinduism among its citizenry. Hindus are about 200 million fewer than Muslims, half the total global population of Christians, and somewhere between two and three times that of Buddhism.

Are there any Hindu **holy cities**?

Hinduism's sacred cities far outnumber those of any other major religious tradition. All the earth is of divine origin and India stands at the center of that divinity. According to one model there are seven sacred cities, each associated with a divine event. Banaras or Kashi (City of Light) is the home of Shiva. In Ayodhya, Rama set the capital of his realm. Krishna was born in Mathura, and from Hardvar the Ganges begins its journey to the south. These (along with Kanchi, Ujjain, and Dvaraka) form the basic grid of a vast network of sacred geography in which countless other places are sacred for innumerable reasons. All important sacred places are called *tirthas,* places at which one can cross a river. Four cities function as directional *tirthas* at the four cardinal points: Badrinath in the north, Rameshwara in the south, Puri in the east, and Dvaraka in the west. According to one mythic narrative, 108 places became sacred by association with the body of Shiva's wife Sati. After she threw herself on the funeral pyre, a grieving Shiva carried her remains across India, and every place bits of her fell to earth became a "seat" of the goddess. Every denomination and sect has its favored sacred city. Perhaps the single most important city, one that most Hindus acknowledge as sacred, is Banaras. Though it is particularly holy for Shaivites, Banaras's spiritual magnetism works on all devout Hindus.

Are there anything like **denominations** or **sects** within greater Hinduism?

Mark Twain once observed that compared to India, other lands and cultures were paupers in religion. He was referring to the large number of major religious traditions that have been born in India or had a significant impact in Indian history. Hindu tradition alone accounts for an astounding diversity. Most Hindus belong to one of two major denominations (called *sampradaya* in Sanskrit, "handing down, tradition"). Devotees of Vishnu and his various manifestations or *avatars* are called

275

Shiva and consort Parvati, Basholi school painting, c. 1725 CE, India. Shiva holds the drum of creation and is dressed as an ascetic, with a serpent around his neck and his weapon, the trident, in his right hand. His third eye represents the power to destroy evil forces. *Courtesy of the St. Louis Art Museum.*

Vaishnavites (or Vaishnavas). Shaivites (or Shaivas) are those for whom Shiva and the various names and forms of divinity associated with him offer the path to salvation. Two other smaller groups within the greater Hinduism are also important. Hindus who focus on the feminine manifestations of Shiva's divine power (*shakti*) are called Shaktas. Shaktism is also sometimes called Tantrism because of its connection with a category of esoteric scriptures called Tantras. So-called "right- handed" Shaktas espouse practices very much like the other *bhakti* traditions, emphasizing worship of the goddess. Sects described as "left-handed" tend to be more secretive and esoteric. Finally, the term *Smarta* as it is commonly used now refers to Hindus for whom the path of knowledge (*jñana yoga*) represents the greatest hope of spiritual realization. Some Smartas adhere to the *advaita* or monistic philosophical teaching of Shankara. Others are devotionally and ritually eclectic, focusing on one of five names and forms of God (Vishnu, Shiva, Durga, Ganesha, and Surya) as their chosen deity. These four designations are still very broad groupings, each of which is made up of a number of sub-denominations or sects.

Who are the **Vaishnavites**?

About half the world's Hindus belong to the various sub-denominations of Vaishnavism. In general, northern Vaishnavas understand Vishnu as a form of Krishna, while most southerners think of either Rama or Krishna as forms of Vishnu. Five major Vaishnava schools trace their origins to famous founders who lived between about 1000 and 1500 CE. Different ways of describing the divine-human relationship mark the principal distinctions among the five denominations and the various sectarian divisions that have arisen from them. Ramanuja (1017–1137) was a major figure in a predominantly southern school called Shrivaishnavism, so called because of the centrality of Vishnu's consort Shri. Ramanuja taught a modified form of non-dualism (called Vishisht-advaita) according to which individual souls are aspects of the divine,

276

part of God, but retain their individuality and do not lose their identity in their union with the divine. Madhva (1197–1278) disagreed, insisting on a fuller distinction between the human and the divine. His teaching is a type of pure theism in which God freely chooses to reach with love and grace across an infinite and otherwise unbridgeable chasm. Madhva's dualist (Dvaita) branch is also primarily a southern tradition, while the remaining three are more popular in the north. Nimbarka (1125–1162) focused on the role of the guru as the central means of grace in his Minandi school. Vallabha (1475–1530) taught a form of "pure nondualism," also called "panentheism" (God in all things). His commentaries on the Bhagavata Purana detail his mystical interpretation of the so-called "Love Games of Krishna," in which the Lord's romance with the gopis becomes a model of the human quest for the divine beloved—and vice-versa. Chaitanya (1485– 1534) preached devotion to Krishna and Radha through communal dance

Krishna visiting Radha, awaiting word from her maiden, Kangra school painting, India, c. 1820–1825 CE. *Courtesy of the St. Louis Art Museum.*

and song. Of the several contemporary subsects of his Gaudiya Vaishnava group perhaps the best known is the International Society for Krishna Consciousness.

Who are the **Shaivites**?

At least six sub-denominations make up Shaiva Hinduism. As with Vaishnavism, their views on the nature of the divine-human relationship set them apart. A major sect in south and southeast Indian region called Tamilnadu is known as Shaiva Siddhanta ("Truth about Shiva"). Tracing its roots to Rishi Turmular (c. 200 CE), the group's central teaching is a blend of theism and monism: individual souls seek God, and devotees and worshipers in this life and ultimately will merge totally with Shiva. Pashupata Shavism, founded by Lakulisha (c. 200) and popular in far northeast, north, and western-central India, holds a variation on that teaching. Souls finally merge with God but maintain individuality somewhat as stars are lost as discrete bodies in the infinite night sky. Also found in the northern state of Kashmir is a distinctive Shaiva sect founded by Vasugupta (c. 800 CE). The Kashmiri school is monistic, teaching the complete and perfect oneness of all reality in Shiva. A major sect in northeast India is called Siddha Siddhanta, with roots in the teaching or Rishi Gorakshanatha (c. 950 CE). Blending theism and monism, this school says all individual things are eventually reabsorbed into Shiva as bubbles arise in water. A minor group still influential in southern India is called Shiva Advaita. Its first teacher, Shrikantha (c. 1050), preferred a qualified theism in which the worshiper participates in divinity without losing identity. Finally, a major sect in southwest Indian is known as Virashaivism. Members are sometimes referred to as Lingayats because many carry with them in a small case a miniature Shiva-linga. A major poet called Basavanna (1105–67) remains an influential source of the sect's teaching of qualified theism, according to which God is like the sun, souls its rays.

Have Hindus traditionally sent out **missionaries** to **convert** others?

Hinduism has generally not produced the kind of missionary activity characteristic of traditions like Christianity, Islam, and Buddhism. Significant traces of Hindu tradition and culture are very much in evidence all over southeast Asia, especially in parts of Indonesia. Throughout late antiquity (fourth through eighth centuries) and the middle ages (ninth through fifteenth centuries), important Hindu dynasties ruled portions of present-day Cambodia, Laos, and Vietnam. Major archaeological research attests to their splendor and power. But their trappings of Hindu symbol and ritual were less a matter of missionary zeal than of a desire to cloak themselves with the prestige of the great Indian dynasties. In addition, they sought to enhance their political legitimacy through the concept of divine kingship by identifying their monarchs as descendants of the gods. In modern times, however, a number of missionary organizations have grown from Hindu roots. In addition to the International Society for Krishna Consciousness, Vivekananda's (1863–1902) Ramakrishna Mission has made important contributions in this regard. Although its gains have been modest in terms of numbers, the Mission's members have become known for various kinds of social outreach as well as for offering lectures and spiritual guidance. In many major United States cities, branches of an organization called the Vedanta Society appeal to a well-educated public by emphasizing the traditional Way of Knowledge, rather than the Way of Devotion preferred by both Vivekananda and his teacher Ramakrishna (1834–86).

Have there ever been **schisms** or **heresies** in Hinduism?

Toward the end of the Vedic period we find the first clear references to groups called *nastikas,* "those who deny" or "nay-sayers." Early Jains and Buddhists represented the most important of the non-orthodox groups that eventually developed into distinct religious traditions. *Nastikas* are generically distinguished from the *astikas,* those who affirmed the authority of the Vedas, the existence of an indestructible soul, and the existence of God as an essential salvific power. Exponents of Brahmanic or priestly Hinduism have had a particularly large stake in combating the erosive influence of

Are Hare Krishnas Hindus?

Members of an organization known officially as the International Society for Krishna Consciousness are Vaishnavites and devotees of Krishna and his consort Radha. They are followers of the teaching of the Bengali saint Chaitanya. A former pharmaceutical salesman named A. C. Bhaktivedanta (1896–1977) was initiated by a Vaishnava guru and eventually became a sannyasi in 1959. He founded the organization in 1965 in the United States, establishing a number of temples. Membership includes both married householders and celibate members of monastic communities attached to the temples. Bhaktivedanta instilled in the organization a sense of missionary zeal, and in 1970 decided to take the movement back to India. There he established denominational temples in Vrindavan and Mayapur, the birthplaces of Krishna and Chaitanya respectively. ISKCON maintains a number of temples across North America, some supporting themselves through vegetarian restaurants attached to them. Devotees in the United States came to be popularly known as the "Hare Krishna" people because they often gathered in public to celebrate their joyous praise of God by chanting "Hare Krishna, Hare Krishna, Hare Rama, Hare Hare."

various non-conformist sectarian developments over many centuries. Some have eventually been reabsorbed into the greater Hinduism while others, such as Buddhism and Jainism, have remained distinct.

What questions does the prospect of **inter-faith marriage** raise for Hindus?

In India, with its vast Hindu majority, it is still largely taken for granted that young people will marry members of their own denomination or sect as well as of their own caste. Outside India, various external cultural pressures are changing such assumptions. Since Hindu tradition remains so intimately bound to cultural background, many traditional Hindu families would naturally prefer that their children marry other Hindus. By and large, the younger generation continuous to do so.

How do Hindus feel when one of their members decides to **leave the faith**?

Membership in most smaller local Hindu communities across India is so intimately linked with a larger network of social and economic factors that the notion of "leaving the faith" is virtually meaningless. To live in the community is to be a Hindu. In the big cosmopolitan cities like Bombay, Calcutta, and Delhi, the matter is naturally more complex. Social relations are undergoing a higher rate of change in some places, but even there most people who think of themselves as Hindu will likely continue to do so whether or not they participate regularly in traditional religious observances. When individuals make a conscious effort to forsake the tradition altogether because they find they it no longer meets their needs, their families experience a sense of loss. One fewer member of the clan participates in the family's observance of the sacred occasions that have offered a sense of togetherness and joy. Individuals who drift away from traditional practice often continue to call themselves Hindu as a cultural identifier. And among immigrant families in the United States, for example, a surprising number of younger adults find themselves going in the opposite direction. Many feel a desire to return to the tradition because of an interest in their cultural roots.

What does one do to **convert** to Hinduism?

Throughout its long history Hinduism's ranks have swelled with the addition of entire tribes and other social groups that came under the influence of Hindu kingdoms. Formal conversion to Hinduism nowadays is relatively rare in India, at least among Indian nationals. Membership in the tradition's many sub-communities is far more a matter of heredity than of deliberate choice. Some non-Indians have migrated to India out of a desire to enter Hinduism formally. They typically present themselves at the temple or ashram of their choice and ask to join. And over the past several decades small numbers of Europeans and Americans have joined various missionary-minded branches of the Hindu tradition, such as the Vedanta Society, with its associated monastic order, or the International Society for Krishna Consciousness. Some communities provide prospective new members basic instruction in the teachings of the group's founders and in the sacred texts. But membership does not depend on formal assent to a particular creed or system of doctrine. The one important and nearly universal ritual symbolizing conversion is the "naming ceremony," or *namakarana.* Taking a new name, often containing a reference to the deity one chooses to worship, symbolizes the devotee's seriousness and commitment.

How do Hindus view Hinduism's **relationships to other traditions**?

For many centuries the greater Hindu tradition has shown enormous flexibility in adapting to religious pluralism. It came to be the "greater" Hinduism, in part at least, because of that quality of expansiveness. Many Hindus regard their religious heritage as a kind of spiritual umbrella capable of sheltering all who seek refuge beneath it. Historically, different denominations have drawn once-separate traditions into their embrace. For example, Vaishnavite tradition came to incorporate Buddhism by installing the Buddha as the ninth of Vishnu's ten avatars—a hospitable gesture, perhaps, but one that Buddhists do not recognize. Some Hindus have suggested that Jesus and other foundational figures also find a place in the greater Hindu scheme of things. A major early modern movement that began as an attempt to soften the animosity between Hindus and Muslims in northwestern India especially is now known as Sikhism. The Sikh community has become largely identified with a region called the Punjab, which straddles the India-Pakistan border. Sikh separatists have continued to assert their desire for a homeland.

LEADERSHIP, AUTHORITY, ORGANIZATION

How and where do members of **local Hindu communities come together**?

Local and regional temples are the major gathering places Hindus use religiously and socially and support financially. Individual temples in India are generally dedicated predominantly to a particular deity. Most center around some aspect or manifestation of Shiva or Vishnu, or one of their major female consorts or counterparts. A temple will typically also have subordinate shrines dedicated to other names and forms of the central deity. Some smaller local temples may also belong exclusively to sects worshiping deities largely unknown outside the area. Most temples draw sectarian cliente. In many regions outside India, however, greater diversity in the makeup of local communities often requires greater flexibility in the religious orientation of temples. For example, Indian immigrants around American cities such as Pittsburgh and St. Louis come from various places in India and represent a variety of sectarian backgrounds. As a result, the temples that serve the regions are sensitive to a wider spectrum of devotional needs than might be the case at a local temple in an area where Hindus are in the majority and where one sect predominates. Large temples in both Pittsburgh and St. Louis have been funded by Indian populations largely of immigrants from south India. Both temples are therefore dedicated to a popular south Indian manifestation of Vishnu called Shri Venkateshvara (Lord of the Sin-forgiving Hill). But in order to serve the diverse local population, both temples include prominent devotional symbolism familiar both to Shaivites and to Vaishnavites.

Do Hindus have a system of **religious law**?

Surely the single most important Hindu religious concept is that of *dharma*. As a universal notion dharma is the cosmic "law" that binds all things together. Each individual person also has his or her dharma, the fundamental religious requirements and ethical expectations associated with each person's station in life. Classical Hindu sources also use the term dharma in reference to countless specific moral duties and ritual rubrics. Treatises called *shastras* are the principal repositories of the Hindu legal and ethical

281

Is there a central teaching authority for Hindus?

Since Hindu tradition is a complex of many denominations and sub-traditions, there is no central institutional structure that functions as a central teaching authority. Many of the individual denominations and sects maintain systems of checks on the integrity of the tradition in the form of teaching lineages. Instruction has historically been based on oral transmission of the basic sources, along with extensive commentary, both oral and written, on those sources. Perhaps the closest thing to centralized authority is the living master to whom disciples give their uncontested allegiance. That living master embodies both the authority of an unbroken succession of teachers and his or her personal authority as one spiritually connected to the ancient wellsprings of wisdom. Even the Vedas and the associated primary sacred texts grouped under the heading of *shruti* ("heard") do not claim the universal adherence of all Hindus.

materials. They belong to the larger category of sacred literature called *smriti* ("remembered"), revered as of divine origin, but subordinate in authority to *shruti* ("heard") scriptures. The *Dharma Shastras,* and related texts like the *Grihya Sutras* that include detailed information on every facet of "householder" life, derive ultimately from a text generally known as the Laws of Manu (dated variously from 600 BCE to 100 CE). The ancient law books have retained their authority well into modern times. Only recently have India's legislative bodies introduced serious and sweeping reforms. But the antiquity of tradition and inherent cultural resistance to change have kept many practices alive in spite of official attempts to adapt the classics to contemporary needs.

Who are the main Hindu **religious officials** or **specialists**?

Traditional Hindu vocabulary includes dozens of technical terms to designate virtually every imaginable variety of religious function or specialized qualification. Essential to every Hindu temple is its priestly staff. Larger temples often have many priests, sometimes called *pujaris*—those who engage in the daily worship called *puja*—on the staff, one of whom generally serves as chief or senior priest. People generally address priests as Shri, the equivalent of "Reverend." Frequently but not exclusively of the Brahmin caste nowadays, temple priests marry and have families. At temples that have become important pilgrimage centers, specialists called *pandas* serve as pilgrim guides and keep records of the families who make up the regular membership of the temple. Ritual specialists called *purohitas* ("those who lead") are generally Brahmins of the Smarta denominations who do mostly home ceremonies for Brahmin families. Gurus, who are generally learned Brahmins, still almost exclusively perform the various *samskaras,* or rites of passage, and tutor upper caste children in the ancient traditions.

282

Are there religious **hierarchical structures** in any branch of Hinduism?

None of Hinduism's various denominations has ever developed a formal institutional hierarchy parallel to those of, for example, Roman Catholicism or Shi'ite Islam. But there have been de facto social rankings in which some representatives of the tradition have very definite priority. In Vedic times, there were at least seven (and perhaps as many as sixteen) different types of priests, distinguished according to specific function in the Vedic sacrifice. Among them were the Brahmins, the one category of priests that has retained its influence over the centuries. Hindu religious hierarchy has generally ranked its specialists according to learning, with teachers and guardians of tradition (such as *gurus, acharyas,* and *pandits*) ranking high on the list. Historically, figures called the *purohita* served as high priests at the courts of Hindu monarchs. That individual's role was to protect his royal patron through ritual and teaching, as well as by his spiritually potent presence. In modern times the *purohita* has become the family priest charged with keeping caste and ritual practices intact. Temple priesthood staffs typically have chief priests who supervise the overall running of the temple rituals.

How are Hindu **religious leaders chosen** and **given authority**?

Priesthood is generally a hereditary office, with families often tracing their sacerdotal lineages back many generations. Priests who serve in local temples are not typically members of the Brahmin caste, but their religious roles are likewise hereditary. Spiritual guides and teachers called *gurus* are those who rise to local or wider prominence as a result of their proficiency in various facets of religious knowledge and practical wisdom. In this instance the classical system of training provides the equivalent of a license or seal of approval. But many famous teachers achieve wider notoriety as a result of popular acclaim. They set up shop initially, so to speak, with official sanction as products of the system, but their spiritual prowess spreads by word of mouth. Other religious figures gain prominence outside the system. An individual's reputation for holiness begins when those around him or her observe special powers or qualities, and grows as seekers gather in hopes of sharing in the wisdom and sanctity.

What is the **caste system**?

India's ancient Hindu social system combines several complex elements. Perhaps best known are the four principal *varnas* or "social classes." The term *varna* means "color or appearance." As early as the Vedic period, the Brahmin or priestly class rose to the top of the social ladder. They were responsible for maintaining the integrity of ritual practice and traditional teaching. Nowadays Brahmins are by no means all connected with priestly activities as such. One rung below the Brahmins are the Kshatriyas, "those who govern," traditionally called the warrior or princely class. They have been

Women's roles in Hindu tradition have varied enormously over its long history. During the Vedic period women apparently participated directly in many major rituals and exercised exclusive leadership in some. As the Brahmanic priesthood rose to prominence, women had fewer opportunities for official leadership. But women have continued to play major roles in many religious rituals outside the Brahmanic system. They often lead women's groups in communal prayer and song in gatherings connected with local observances. Some Brahmin women have functioned as itinerant preachers in rural areas. Others have become specialists, called *pandits,* in ritual and lore. Perhaps the best known are the women whose role as *gurus* has attracted seekers and devotees, often from great distances, to "take *darshan*" (that is, to be in their presence) and benefit from their counsel.

the legislators as well as enforcers of the law. On the next lower rung are the more numerous merchants, financiers, agriculturalists, and industrialists who comprise the Vaishya class. As class designations the terms Kshatriya and Vaishya are now obsolete. Most numerous of all are the Shudras, the laborers and craftspersons who perform the basic services. Varna distinctions generally cut across language, occupational and geographical barriers. In addition to the four varnas are the hundreds, perhaps even as many as four thousand, of *jatis. Jati* means "birth or species" and refers to the countless local social groups defined by occupation and language. As many as twenty-five thousand additional groupings are called "sub-castes." Members of both jatis and sub-castes generally associate themselves with one of the varnas, and many Indians still observe strict rules of purity and separation. Finally, between one and two hundred million people are considered outcastes, untouchables, or "unscheduled" classes, those who don't fit in the great system. Since India gained independence the caste system has been officially illegal, but systems of such antiquity do not yield readily to legislation passed in capital cities.

Do Hindu communities run **private schools** for their **children**?

Among more traditional upper caste Hindus, gurus still provide a special education for boys, but the practice seems to be slowly disappearing. Most active Hindu devotees tend to think of religious education as a matter of family tradition. As a result, apart from the ancient guru affiliation, Hindus generally have not developed school systems analogous to those that some Jews, Christians, and Muslims have established in order to hand on their traditions. Some organizations, such as the Vedanta society and smaller communities of devotees, offer courses of education generally for older members.

Shikhara ("mountain peak") over the womb chamber of Shiva, Temple of Minakshi, Madurai, southern India. *Photo courtesy of Michael Harter, S.J.*

Are there any organizations or institutions that have their own **distinctive structures of leadership** within any of the branches of Hinduism?

As in so many other traditions, monastic and other religious orders have played a major role in the history of the greater Hinduism. Different styles of monastic life have evolved in connection with the last two of the four traditional "life stages," namely those of "forest dweller" and "renunciant." Individual Hindu males who have arrived at the last stage, that of *sannyasi,* have been crisscrossing India on their solitary ways for millennia. Since perhaps twenty-five centuries ago, informal organizations developed as disciples gathered around renunciants renowned as spiritual teachers. These forerunners of stable monastic residences continued to welcome as occasional guests their unattached itinerant counterparts. Evidence of the earliest formal monastic organizations, from as long as eighteen hundred years ago, suggests that they followed a strictly ascetic regime. But Shankara (788–820) is the first individual credited with founding an order. The renowned philosopher and theologian organized monasteries in sacred cities marking the four cardinal directions across India. Four subsequent orders were founded by religious leaders associated with four of the five major Vaishnava denominations, Ramanuja, Nimbarka, Madhva, and Vallabha. Important orders have arisen in the nineteenth and twentieth centuries as well, such as those founded by Ramakrishna and Mahatma Gandhi. Most of the orders have offered various levels of commitment, from temporary residency, to long-term affiliation of men and women with families, to lifelong celibacy.

PERSONALITIES AND POWERS

What is a *swami*? Is that anything like a *maharishi*?

The term *swami* comes from the Sanskrit *svami,* meaning "owner, master." It was originally applied mostly to monastic *sannyasis* as an acknowledgment of their self-mastery. More recently the term has become a widely used title of reverence for a broader spectrum of religious scholars, teachers, and renunciants. One often hears Hindu religious leaders referred to as "swamiji," a term of both respect and affection. The term *maharishi,* literally "great seer," is also an honorific title with roots deep in Hindu mythology. Great seers are individuals celebrated for their profound wisdom. Popular tradition designated as "great" a number of the ancient "seers" associated with the communication of primal religious insights. But several historical persons have likewise merited the title. Ramana Maharishi (1879–1950) attracted a great following in the south of India. Maharishi Mahesh Yogi (b. c. 1911), founder of the school of Transcendental Meditation, gained fame initially as the teacher of the Beatles in Indian spirituality.

What is the difference between a *guru,* an *acharya,* and a *pandit*?

A *guru* is a religious teacher who represents a particular lineage or spiritual tradition and is authorized to initiate qualified students into the tradition. *Guru* comes from a root that means "heavy, grave" and suggests massive spiritual substance worthy of respect. Gurus have historically been distinguished according to certain specific tasks or offices. Those who perform the various rites of passage, and are particularly important in the rite of initiating young upper caste boys into Vedic tradition, are called teaching (*shiksha*) gurus. A teacher who represents a particular sect and initiates members into it is called an initiatory (*diksha*) or *mantra* guru. This guru passes along to the disciple (*chela* or *shishya*) a sacred syllable or phrase intended only for that individual. Gurus may be either male or female, and disciples often consider them direct descendants of the deity, with a claim to virtually absolute authority over their students. Many famous Hindu teachers throughout history have earned the title *acharya.* Often tacked on to a proper name as a suffix, as in Shankaracharya, the term identifies an individual who instructs others in right conduct. Many of those who have received the title have been famous philosophers and theologians. Finally, anyone who watches news coverage around election time will invariably hear commentators referred to as "political pundits." In the history of Hinduism, a *pandit* is a person "learned" especially in a broad spectrum of oral tradition and practical lore. The scope of the pundit's learning was less specialized than that of the guru, who focused on a higher wisdom aimed at liberation of the soul. Nowadays pandits are generally from families of Brahmins dedicated to transmitting knowledge of the sources from memory, much the way the ancient rabbis preserved Judaism's oral Torah. In short, these three roles complement each other. Pandits have maintained the tradition as accurately as human memory allows. Acharyas further develop the tradition, reflecting on its deeper implications. And gurus help seekers to apply the tradition's wisdom to their personal spiritual lives.

Are *sadhus, sannyasis, and yogis* all the same kinds of people?

These three common terms refer to different specific religious roles or functions, any or all of which could be exemplified in a single person. They are often used synonymously, but there are important differences. A *sadhu* is "a person of unerring trajectory" or "one who has achieved a goal" by means of a regime of spiritual practices and disciplines called collectively *sadhana.* These methods encompass a whole range of external rituals, including fasting and other austerities, and forms of meditation, and often vary from one denomination or sect to another. Sadhus pursue a highly ascetic lifestyle, live on charitable donations, and are often entirely unconnected with specific social or religious institutions—apart from the fact that sadhu-hood has become virtually an institution in itself. Some sadhus are also *sannyasis,* renunciants officially initiated into this spiritual status by a guru. Individuals may formally enter into the state of sannyasa for various reasons according to tradition: a spontaneous quest for spiritual liberation; a quest resulting from more deliberate immersion in religious studies; withdrawal as a way to cope with great loss or sadness; or the realization that one's death is imminent. Formal initiation, also conferred on women in some orders, includes vows of poverty, chastity, and obedience for those who belong to monastic communities. Sadhus and sannyasis may also engage in the disciplines of raja and hatha yoga, but a yogi is not necessarily either a sadhu or a sannyasi.

Is there such a thing as a Hindu **saint**?

Certain features of the sadhu and sannyasi are quite consistent with concepts of sainthood in various religious traditions. But individuals called *sants* add still another dimension to the Hindu tradition's complex understanding of the human embodiment of holiness. Sadhus and sannyasis may seem at first to be socially liminal characters, but they are actually very much a part of the classical socio-religious system. The term *sant* is a vernacular version of the Sanskrit *sat,* meaning "real, authentic." Ironically perhaps, the sants are genuine because they stand apart from the system and have taken up the cause of the truly marginalized, the outcastes and untouchables. Associated with bhakti movements both Shaivite and Vaishnavite, saints have often spread their message as troubadours, gathering crowds by singing at important holy places. One of the most influential of them was Kabir (c. 1440–1518), whose songs were a major influence in Guru Nanak's (1469–1538) founding of the Sikh movement. Other important Hindu sants were Jñaneshwara (1275–96), Ekanatha (1533–98) and Tukaram (1608–49).

Why was Mahatma Gandhi an important Hindu?

Mohandas Karmachand Gandhi (1869–1948) received the title Mahatma ("Great-souled One") because of his towering example of personal integrity and commitment to social justice. He was a nationalist in the sense that he sought Indian independence from British rule. But he also taught tolerance for religious diversity at a time when strident voices cried out for vengeance against members of other communities of faith. His "experiments with truth" (*satyagraha*, truth-grasping) led to his espousal of methods such as the quest for simple living and non-violent resistance to oppression. On several occasions his willingness to fast nearly unto death called attention to the evils against which he fought. Gandhi spoke out often on behalf of the socially marginalized, the untouchables—the Lord's Children he called them—and women. Human dignity and equality were the goals he pursued within the context of a vibrant religious faith. Gandhi's great-souled inclusiveness improved the lives of millions and eventually cost him his own. A militant Hindu, convinced that Gandhi was conceding far too much to the nation's Muslims, shot him on January 30, 1948.

Have there been important Hindu **mystics**?

Many of the *sants* certainly rank among India's greatest mystics. Their poems and songs represent one of the two major strands of supranormal unitive experience often described as "mystical." For the sants and other exponents of the bhakti tradition, the divine-human relationship is above all intensely personal. It is precisely the infinite chasm separating God from the human devotee that gives their conviction of the transforming love of God its immense power. This type of mysticism is often called theistic or dualistic. A number of important devotional schools trace their origins to some of the most influential theistic mystics, such as Vallabha and Chaitanya. Another stream tributary to the great river of Hindu mysticism is often referred to as cosmic or monistic. Teachers like Shankara emphasize the need to arrive through disciplined meditation at the full realization that there is no divide between what most of us perceive as the "individual" and the Ultimate Reality. That realization of the simple unity of Brahman and atman (which conventional language might call "God" and the "soul") is the essence of the monistic mystical experience.

Who are some **important women** in the history of Hindu spirituality?

Ancient tradition acknowledges that some anonymous women were among the authors of the Vedic hymns. Many other women whose names we know have made major contributions throughout the history of Hinduism. Here is a brief introduction to four of the better known women from various denominations. Antal (725–55 CE) was one of the Alvars, poet-saints in the Vaishnava tradition. She was most famous for poetry in which she described her relationship with Vishnu in the language of "bridal mysticism." Seeing herself as the spouse of Vishnu she shares the spiritual longing of women mystics in other traditions who speak of total loving union with God. Devotees still sing hymns that set her poems to music. Mahadevi was a twelfth-century devotee of Shiva and a renowned poet in the Kannada language. In the temple of her village, the principal deity was a form of Shiva called Mallikarjuna, "Lord white as jasmine." Like Antal, she thought of herself as betrothed to God alone. She was apparently forced into an unhappy marriage, and much of her poetry alludes to the suffering she experienced and her longing to be liberated and live for God alone. A late medieval holy woman named Mirabai (1498–1550) was a devotee of Krishna. She thought of herself as a gopi who had been hopelessly enam-

The god Vishnu, Chola Period, eleventh century CE, South India, bronze. Note discus in upper right hand, conch shell in upper left. Lower left once held a mace, while the lower right gestures "do not fear." *Courtesy of the St. Louis Art Museum.*

ored of the dark Lord. After extricating herself from an unsatisfactory marriage, she became a *sannyasi* and composed love songs in Hindi, a vernacular tongue in west-central India. Finally, a woman known by the honorific title Anandamayi Ma (Bliss-steeped Mother) lived in modern-day Bengal (now Bangladesh). Nirmala Sundari (1896–1982) lived a most colorful life, often flouting strict tradition in favor of sometimes highly symbolic or ecstatic behavior. In her later years she opted for a more settled life, founding an ashram and ministering to disciples who sought her out for spiritual guidance.

Do Hindus believe in **angels**?

Nothing in Hindu lore corresponds exactly to the spiritual beings known in some traditions as angels. But a host of lesser deities (called *devatas*) and spirits make up the entourages of many of the major deities. These versatile beings are often grouped in families whose mission is to do their deity's every bidding. Like the angels in some traditions, lesser deities fill the spiritual air around the major deities. In popular spiritu-

289

ality devotees often consider the need to render an account to these divine vanguards nearly equal to their duties to the central deity, for the lesser deities preside over essential areas of life such as fertility, childbirth, and disease. Those that wield more positive energies have their darker counterparts that need to be appeased in order to hold evil at bay. Among the more common beings of this rank are the "door guardians" (*dvarapalas*) who keep undesirable elements out of temples and away from the shrines of the deities to whom they are assigned. Door guardians are often depicted with iconographic clues very similar to those of their major deities. So, for example, guardians in a Vaishnavite temple typically have four arms and are equipped with Vishnu's conch shell, discus, and mace.

Do Hindus believe in **devils**?

No single personification of evil functions in Hindu tradition quite like the Satan of other traditions. Multiple embodiments of malice, perversity, and general negativity are called *asuras,* or demons. Ancient myths tell of the ongoing struggle between the *devas,* deities, and the demons for control of the cosmos. Originally the demons were not necessarily considered altogether evil. Even their generic names are ambiguous: *deva* is from the same root as "devil," while *asura* shows up in the name of the main Iranian deity, *Ahura mazda.* Both deities and demons descended from Prajapati, Lord of Living Things. Demons were at first ethically on a par with the gods. But the gods generally managed to win more battles than their siblings. Eventually the deities came to be known as more clever and more truthful. Finally, the gods achieved immortality while preventing the demons from winning that prize. Demons retained the ability to assume virtually any form in their attempts to disrupt cosmic affairs. Powerful people intent on evil could enlist the aid of demons to carry out their wicked deeds. Some demons came to represent impersonal negative qualities, such as ignorance. Lesser but still troublesome forces known as *bhutas* remain important in the lives of many villagers. Bhutas are the spirits of those who died violently, or too young, or after betrothal but before marriage, for example. Resentful and frustrated, they wander about harassing the living unless appeased by proper rituals. Hindus believe that ultimately the divine power will overcome all demonic forces.

Are **dreams** and **visions** important in Hindu tradition?

Dreams and visions are often described as the means by which particularly holy individuals receive special knowledge or responsibilities. Spiritually advanced members of different denominations describe experiences in which their particular "chosen deity" appears and manifests his or her divine form. The deity's desires for the founding of a temple in a particular place are often communicated in dreams or visions. Traditional Hindu psychology considers dreaming one of the four ordinary states of consciousness. Founders of various denominations and sects often report dreams or visions as the impetus for a personal conversion or for proclaiming a new teaching.

HOLIDAYS AND REGULAR OBSERVANCES

What kind of **religious calendar** do Hindus observe?

Combining lunar months with seasons of the solar year, the Hindu calendar functions somewhat like the Jewish. About every three years it inserts an extra month after a month with two new moons. Hindu lunar months vary from 29 to 32 days. The names of the months, with the roughly corresponding Gregorian months in parentheses, are as follows: Chaitra (March/April), Vaishakha (April/May), Jyaistha (May/June), Asadhe (June/July), Shravana (July/August), Bhadrapada (August/September), Ashvina (September/October), Karttika (October/November), Margasivsa (November/December), Pansa (December/January), Magha (January/February), and Phalguna (February/March). Leap months take the name of the month preceding them.

For ritual purposes, each month is divided into its dark and light halves, with associated celebrations, and the moment of full moon is a special time of celebration each month. And some festivals and observances fall each year on the same *solar* date. Each year is likened to a day in the life of the deities, with the solar solstices symbolizing sunrise and sundown. In addition to the complexity introduced by the blending of solar and lunar reckonings, systems vary still further from region to region in India. Historically, the greater Hindu religious calendar has been so full that virtually every day some Hindu community has celebrated something special somewhere in the subcontinent. Hinduism is not unlike Roman Catholic and Eastern Orthodox traditions in that respect, except that the majority of the Christian religious feasts are those of saints, rather than of the deity as such. All of this makes for an immensely rich sense of the intersection of sacred times and places. Every day is appropriate for religious observance, and no one day of the week is set aside as an especially sacred time.

What are some of the **regular monthly religious observances**?

The Hindu sense of sacred time presents an enormous array of possibilities, depending on various combinations of astrological phenomena, auspicious days of the week, and associations of times with particular deities. Different days in both dark and bright fortnights of each lunar month carry generic spiritual values. Most sacred is the eleventh day, while the first, fourth, ninth, and fourteenth are inauspicious. Some days are consecrated to different deities. More special occasions fall during the bright than during the dark half. During one half (both halves in some months and/or regions) the fourth day belongs to Ganesha, the eighth to Durga, the ninth and eleventh to Vishnu (a solar deity), and the thirteenth to Shiva (a lunar deity). New-moon days find some Hindus offering special meals to placate the spirits of the dead. Many of these monthly or semi-monthly occasions include a fast. Most Hindus observe only some of these special days, depending on their sectarian affiliation.

Are there other important **cyclical observances** based largely on **celestial signs**?

Every three years Hindus gather from all over India in one of four sacred cities (Hard-var, Prayaga, Ujjain, and Nasik, each on a different sacred river or confluence) for a huge religious fair called a *Kumbha-mela* ("grain-pot festival"). The mythological connection in the name is its reference to the *kumbha,* or vessel, from which drops of the nectar of immortality fell as the demons rested on their flight from the gods, making the four cities holy. Every twelve years, a series of astrological conjunctions make the gathering at Prayaga (known by Muslims as Allahabad) particularly auspicious. Since about the eighth century, travelers have made organized pilgrimages to the four cities to attain forgiveness of sins for themselves and eighty-eight generations of ancestors by bathing in their sacred waters. Four times each year, corresponding to the two solstices and two equinoxes, are particularly important events in the solar calendar. The beginning of every solar month is auspicious because of the sun's move into a new sign of the Zodiac. But the winter solstice is the most important because it signals the lengthening of days and the beginning of the solar year.

Are any **feasts** dedicated especially to the **goddesses**?

Durga Puja, also called *Navaratri* ("nine nights"), occurs at the Fall equinox in honor of Shiva's consort Durga. As the slayer of the Buffalo demon (*Durgamahishasuramardini*) Durga represents the power of good to quell all sources of evil. Devotees celebrate this deity's complete protection of her worshipers, but Durga's festival has room for other deities as well. The first day celebrates the goddess Sarasvati, patroness of learning and beauty. In some regions the fifth day belongs to a goddess called Lalita. Bengalis sometimes still sacrifice water buffalo in honor of Durga's cosmic victory over evil. Another festival, occurring at the end of winter to welcome spring, is called *Shri panchami* ("Goddess Fifth" day in the bright half of Magha). Devotees honor Sarasvati by piling up books and symbols of learning near local altars. Other days, such as several during the extended feast called Divali, also belong to the major goddesses.

What is **Holi**?

Originally a fertility festival, this late winter celebration of several days ending with the full moon of Phalguna is named after the demoness Holika. She was in the habit of

What is the celebration called Divali?

Divali is one of the most important and widely celebrated of all Hindu observances. Also called Dipavali, or "Row of Lights," this feast occurs in mid-autumn (October or November—technically from the 13th of Ashvina's dark half to the 2nd of Karttika's bright half), composed of five distinct day-long festivities devoted to such mythic events as Krishna's conquest of two demons and Shiva's reconciliation with Parvati. Shaivites and Vaishnavites alike observe the occasion, marking it as theirs by dedicating the middle night of the five to either Kali's bringing Shiva under control or Vishnu's consort Lakshmi, respectively. Socially speaking the feast belongs to the merchant castes. Divali strictly so-called occurs on the fourth day, recalling Rama's return to his royal throne in Ayodhya to end his fourteen-year exile.

eating a child each day until a holy widow summoned all the children to curse the demoness together. Amid great hubbub, participants today let out the kind of energy the children must have unleashed on Holika. They throw multi-colored powders and liquids on each other, evidently a visual remnant of the children's curses. By a fascinating process of association, the celebration has also come to embrace the mythological downfall of evil female figures. For example, Krishna destroyed the demoness Putana, whom the evil King Kamsa had sent, disguised as a wet-nurse, to kill the infant deity by poisoning him with her breast milk.

Do **Vaishnavites** have **special feasts** in honor of **Vishnu** or his avatars?

Rama Navami (Rama Ninth, during Chaitra in early spring) celebrates Rama's birthday. During a nine day festival celebrants attend a lengthy retelling of the massive epic Ramayana. A related feast occurs on the fifteenth of Shravana, a full moon celebration of Rama's crossing over to Lanka to rescue Sita. Two major feasts focus on Krishna. *Krishna Janmashtami* ("Birthday Eighth" during the dark half of Shravana) in late summer, celebrates Krishna's birthday. For a full seven days devotees reenact events from Krishna's life. The festivities culminate with a fast and midnight worship on the seventh day, the eve of the birthday. *Naga Panchami* ("Serpent Fifth," so named because it occurs on the fifth day of Shravana's bright half) comes in late summer and recalls one of Krishna's many victories over embodiments of evil, his dispatching of the serpent demon Kaliya in the river Jumna. Although the evil demon in this case is a serpent, the fast and feast celebrate the grace represented by other cosmically beneficial serpents as well. Several feasts also recall other specific avatars. For example, on the full moon of Karttika some Vaishnavites celebrate Vishnu's descent as the savior-fish Matsya.

How do **Shaivites** honor **Shiva**?

Shivaratri, "Shiva's Night" is a monthly festivity occurring on the fourteenth night of the dark half of every lunar month, just before the appearance of the new moon. Once a year devotees observe *Mahashivaratri,* "Shiva's Great Night" either during the midwinter lunar month called Magha or during the following month, Phalguna, depending on regional custom. The feast celebrates Shiva's manifestation of his power and glory to Vishnu and Brahma in the icon called the *jyotirlinga* or "fiery linga." Girls who hope to marry soon often fast during the day and keep vigil all night. Festivities in parts of India generally last all night and often include massive street parties and processions featuring elaborate floats, ecstatic dancing, and sometimes extreme demonstrations of devotion in the form of self-mutilation. A full-moon feast during Karttika, in the fall, is called *Tripuri-purnima.* It recalls how Shiva incinerated the demon Tripura's three cities, Tripuri, made of gold, silver, and iron. Meanwhile his consort Kali dispatched the demon himself, ending his partial dominion over heaven, earth, and hell (the "three cities").

What are some of the **other religious days** Hindus observe?

Many of the lesser deities have special feasts widely observed by Hindus across sectarian lines. The fourth day of the bright half of Bhadrapada in early autumn marks the birthday of Shiva's son Ganesha. This was originally a Dravidian fertility festival associated with early harvest. Another fertility feast celebrates the emergence of the Ganges from a sage's ear—one of a number of metaphors for the sacred origins of the river. Observed in early summer, the day marks a time during which devotees can cleanse themselves of ten specific evils. Some also celebrate a late summer festival called "tying the lucky threads." The day recalls how the wife of Vedic storm deity Indra saved her husband from a demon by slipping a magic string on his wrist. Sisters do the same for their brothers, and some celebrants use the occasion as a renewal of their investiture with the sacred thread of initiation.

CUSTOMS AND RITUALS

Are there **special rituals** associated with **dedicating a new temple**?

Multiple festivities typically attend the formal consecration of a new temple and its sacred icons. It begins with the careful choice of a site on which the building can be aligned on an east-west axis with all interior shrines facing east. After the structure is completed, temple staff and devotees install permanent images of the deities in an elaborate three or four day ceremony called *Kumbhabhishekam* (sprinkling of water from pots filled at sacred rivers). Rituals begin with purification of the images with various special substances (milk and clarified butter called *ghee*). Before fixing each image to its pedestal with ritually prepared adhesives, celebrants immerse it in water, grain, and flower petals. Special Vedic chants accompany an offering of ghee to a sacred fire to make up for any imperfection in the image. Then officiants pour water over the finial atop the womb chamber of each image and over the images themselves in the actual ritual called *kumbhabhishekam.* Since the images need eyes with which to "see" devotees, priests place eyes of semi-precious stones into the statues and pray that they be opened. To call the images to life they then perform a ritual that instills breath in them. Before engaging further in the ordinary forms of daily worship, officiants symbolize the great sanctity of the images so dedicated by turning their backs to the images and looking at their reflection in a mirror. Thereafter devotees may gaze directly on the images. These festivities proceed all day long for as many as four days (perhaps more in some places), giving even devotees who live at a distance plenty of opportunity to participate. It is a most joyous occasion and a celebration of community to which (in most cases) any interested party is welcome. Many temples also celebrate the anniversary of their foundations or dedications.

What **rites** do Hindus practice in the **temple**?

Puja, meaning adoration or worship, is the generic name for a range of rituals in which devotees engage in the temple. Many temples are open early in the day until early afternoon, and again in early evening. Worshipers arrive at any time during a temple's regular hours, individually or in small groups. They always remove their shoes before entering. Temple priests serve each party in turn, helping them to make their offerings to the deity or deities of their choice. Devotees' choice of dieties is based on various factors, including personal need, individual devotion, or sacred times associated with particular deities. While the priests conduct separate rituals, other parties wait their turn, sitting in the open areas of the temple and talking or praying quietly among themselves. Ritual actions emphasize the spiritual symbolism of simple ordinary elements of life such as food, water, warmth, light, and beauty, all in the context of opening oneself inwardly to a closer relationship with the source of life. Puja takes the form of visiting a royal person and offering affectionate and awe-filled gestures. Worshipers "take care" of the deity by symbolically bathing its feet and offering food and drink. Circumambulation, always to the right, around the various womb-chamber shrines in a temple are a regular part of worship. At set times during the day, the temple staff engage in other worshipful acts apart from the ongoing puja of individuals and groups. They wake, bathe, and feed the deity, and take the sacred royalty out for a walk, so to speak.

What **rites** do Hindus practice at **home**?

Protective hand-print symbols stenciled around the entrance to a Hindu home in India. *Courtesy of Beata Grant.*

In their homes many Hindus engage in a smaller-scale version of temple puja, morning, noon, and evening. Miniature shrines often occupy a special corner, where all the necessary materials and implements for worship are kept. Puja beings with entering into the proper frame of mind and with invocations. Placing flower petals on the image, along with water and other elements (ghee, honey, milk), reminds devotees of the intimacy of their relationship with God. They symbolize that intimacy with actions and materials that communicate deep affection and warmth. Both in the home and in the temple, God is the guest whom the host and hostess strive to make perfectly welcome. Making the deity beautiful often means clothing the images in elaborate garments as well. People sometimes invite a priest to come to their homes to pray, but generally the head of the household leads the home puja. Many Hindu householders regularly perform the individual morning prayer before sunrise. Facing east with the sacred thread over the left shoulder, worshipers take a sip of water, pronounce mantras over ashes, and place them on their foreheads, arms, ribs and knees. To be purified of sin, they pray the *gayatri mantra,* a lovely short hymn to the Light of the Sun. Several different forms of prayer might include facing the various cardinal directions while performing slightly different ritual actions. Other domestic rituals can include special celebrations associated with building and entering a new home for the first time. Other occasions marked with religious rituals at home include especially the various rites of passage associated with birth and early infancy.

Is there a standard **Hindu group or individual liturgical worship**?

Ordinary daily puja is often communal in the sense that a number of people, such as an extended family, might make an offering together. But puja is not strictly speaking a congregational ritual. Some sub-communities, such as those living together in ashrams or members of other exclusive groups, engage in congregational ritual as a matter of course. In general, Hindus join in larger group rituals for special occasions. These may involve congregational singing or chanting of prayers or scriptural texts, practices called *kirtana* or *bhajana*. Various forms of individual ritual prayer offer devotees opportunities to sanctify time alone wherever they may be. A form called *japa*, "muttering, recitation," is the most widespread. Devotees repeat a *mantra*, sacred syllable or phrase, and keep track of their repetitions with a string of beads (often 108 in number) called a *mala* ("garland"). Reciting names of the deity is the most popular type of personal prayer, as in the mantra "Hare Rama Hare Krishna" repeated by many devotees of Vishnu. Hindu texts distinguish fourteen kinds of japa, depending on variables such as purpose, physical posture, and method (whispered, voiced, or murmured). Processions are another important form of congregational worship. On special occasions, the priestly staffs of local temples mount a processional image of one or more deities on shoulder-borne platforms to be paraded through the streets. Worshipers often join in, or stop and catch a glimpse of the passing icon.

Does ritual **sacrifice** play a role in **Hindu ritual**?

In Vedic times animal sacrifice was a major component in many rituals. Animals as large as horses and water buffalo were offered, sometimes in great numbers, along with smaller animals such as goats. Nowadays those large Vedic sacrifices are very rare, but wealthy patrons still occasionally bankroll them. Blood sacrifice does, however, survive as a regular component of puja in some temples in India, especially those dedicated to Shiva's terrifying consort Kali. Devotees regularly offer goats and chickens in places like the Kali temple called Kalighat, after which the city of Calcutta was named. The term *yajña*, meaning worship, homage, or sacrifice in a generic or symbolic sense, still describes many different kinds of ritual that involve offering or giving up symbolic or actual goods for the benefit of another. Offerings of special oblations to the deities date from Vedic times, but many Hindus still perform personal deeds of sacrifice in which they connect spiritually with the ancient sages and ancestors, all the deities, and all of creation. Sacrifice for the benefit of living beings, human and animal, includes generosity with sustenance and charitable financial support.

What kinds of special **ritual objects** figure in Hindu worship and prayer?

Since puja involves offerings and other uses of numerous symbolic physical substances, devotees employ quite a few ritual objects. Most are made of metals such as brass, bronze, silver or silverplate. Objects owned by older temples may be ancient and precious works of art, but their purpose is to serve the larger ritual rather than to attract attention to themselves. Bells, sometimes with an image of the deity on the handle, summon devotees to attentiveness and announce their arrival to visit the deity. With a special long-handled spoon they offer water or ghee, and in a smaller cup with no handle they offer a drink of water. In a small cup-like lamp with a handle they burn cam-

Do Hindus have any special dietary concerns?

Food has always had powerful symbolic associations in Hindu tradition, beginning with the ancient Vedic sacrificial rites. Not until the rise of Jainism and Buddhism, with their emphasis on non-violence, did vegetarianism become part of mainstream Hindu practice. Brahmins have generally been more careful to observe vegetarian practice than have members of other castes. Among the various denominations, Vaishnavites have paid greater attention to dietary issues. All foods have specific effects on one of the three psycho-spiritual qualities called *gunas*—light or purity, excitement or energy, darkness or inertia. A traditional Vaishnava diet avoids foods that stir the passions (garlic, red fruits and vegetables) or incline one to negative moods (flesh and intoxicants), while emphasizing those that have a positive effect (dairy products, grains, most fruits and vegetables). Sannyasis of all denominations are usually strict vegetarians. But the majority of Hindus nowadays tend to regard all foods, taken in moderation and as part of a balanced and healthful diet, as religiously acceptable. Most believe that strict vegetarianism is required only in ritual settings and in celebration of specifically religious observances. Some Hindus still refuse to take meals in the presence of members of other castes, whether lower or higher than their own, but this is a social rather than a dietary concern.

phor and wave it before the deity, and a multi-wicked oil lampstand provides sacred illumination. A ritual plate holds offerings of food. For some rituals a brass or bronze image of a closed lotus flower can be opened like a lotus at dawn, an image of divine disclosure. In some puja ceremonies the priest briefly places a small silver crown, like that worn by the deity, on the heads of devotees, symbolizing divine blessing.

Do Hindus consider **pilgrimage** important?

In a land with countless sacred places associated with numerous divine names and forms, pilgrimage (*yatra*, "going out") remains an essential expression of religious devotion for all who can afford it. For those whose modest means prevent them from traveling distances, a pilgrimage to closer sites is always a possibility. In ancient times Hindu pilgrimages may have been related to the increasing popularity of sites associated with sacred events in the life of the Buddha. Among the most important goals of pilgrimage are the sources and confluences of major rivers. With its many important temples of Shiva and Kali, as well as the bathing and cremation *ghats* that line its Ganges banks, Banaras tops the list of pilgrimage cities. A thirty-six mile circuit around the city still attracts many travelers in search of blessing and forgiveness. Other important sites include those associated with events in the life of Krishna.

Bathing ghats (steps) along the River Ganges in Banaras (Varanasi), city of Shiva. *Courtesy of Beata Grant.*

Are **music** and **dance** important in Hindu **religious ritual**?

Ordinary daily worship is generally conducted without instrumental or vocal music, apart from the priest's chanting of Sanskrit prayers of praise and supplication. Special ceremonies, however, can include congregational chanting and singing of hymns. Many temples, especially in India, employ temple musicians to accompany certain rituals and to walk ahead of portable icons of the deity during processions outside the temple. Playing traditional instruments such as oboe-like woodwinds, drums and other percussion pieces, the musicians fill the air with auspicious sound. During medieval times troops of dancers, vocalists, and instrumentalists often performed works of classical religious poetry set to music, on the steps of the great temples. Sacred dance reenacting mythic tales of the deities remains an important cultural treasure, but nowadays it takes the form of classical performance outside the context of religious ritual. Among the most popular dances are those that tell of the timeless romance of Krishna and his beloved Radha. Hindu tradition includes a vast repertoire of devotional vocal music in dozens of major languages and regional styles. Singers pray to the various deities, often using classical poetry for their texts. Instrumental performers like the great sitar virtuoso Ravi Shankar have made classical Indian music known far beyond India in recent times. Working with the late violinist Yehudi Menuhin and the Beatles, to name only his most famous collaborators, Shankar popularized a tradition whose roots are deeply religious. Musical modes called *ragas* ("tints") play to the emotions, creating subtle "flavors" (*rasas*) with sounds and rhythms tailored to every season and time of day. God creates the world through

299

sound, and dances creation into existence. Human beings need music and dance to connect with the divine.

Do Hindus **pray** in any **particular language**?

Sanskrit remains the official sacred language of Hindu liturgical ritual. Ancestor of a number of modern Indian languages, Sanskrit is also linguistically connected with classical languages such as Latin and Greek and with modern languages such as Persian and a host of European tongues. Many Hindus still learn a little Sanskrit, not through formal language instruction, but through the use of ritual phrases and prayers. During temple rituals the priests typically recite sometimes lengthy texts from the Vedas in a chant using four or five tones. When families offer puja at home, the prayer leader often recites a number of short standard prayers in Sanskrit. Devotional hymns and prayers in a number of regional Indian vernacular languages, such as Telugu, Tamil, Kannada, and Bengali, as well as in India's "official" national language, Hindi, are standards in many ritual settings.

What are the principal Hindu **rites of passage**?

Hindu tradition includes important *samskaras,* "activators" or "impressions," for the various ages of life. Specific samskaras are associated with birth, childhood, adulthood, and older age. Connected with birth are rituals sanctifying conception, prayers for a male child, the husband's expression of love by grooming his wife between the fourth and seventh months of pregnancy, and welcoming the newborn with blessings that include placing a little ghee and honey on the child's tongue. Childhood sacraments include conferral of a name anywhere from eleven to forty one days after birth; making its first taste of solid food at around six months; piercing of the ears for gold earrings in either the first, third, or fifth year; and shaving the head any time from day thirty-one to the fourth year of life. One childhood ritual deserves special notice. Initiation into religious studies is called *upanayana,* "bringing near," in which the youngster (girls were once included, but are generally not these days) is affiliated with a guru for formal tutelage in the Vedas. Another ritual marks the completion of formal studies, celebrating an official end to childhood and entry into adulthood. Samskaras associated with adult life begin from puberty. The onset of menstruation and the shaving of a boy's beard for the first time occasion special ceremonies in the home. When young adults are engaged their families exchange gifts. Marriage ceremonies can be quite grand, including great processions in which the groom makes his entry on a white steed. Some Hindus still acknowledge the passage into older adulthood at about age forty-eight, but more widely practiced still is the moment at which an older man puts ordinary social and family concerns behind him and becomes a renunciant or *sannyasi.* Last of all come the samskaras surrounding death, cremation, and mourning.

Hindu ritual specialist performing a rite of passage or initiation for a young girl. *Courtesy of Beata Grant.*

Are there distinctive forms of **Hindu initiation**?

Boys of the "twice-born" castes are initiated into the tradition in special ceremonies called *upanayana,* which mark the beginning of formal instruction in sacred learning. The initiate receives a thread and wears it draped across the shoulder as a symbol of this "second birth." Women no longer receive the thread and only Brahmins nowadays wear it when not engaged in ritual ceremonies. Sacred threads are of white wool for Brahmins, of red hemp for Kshatriyas, and of yellow wool for Vaishyas. Tradition dictated that Brahmins be initiated at seven or eight years of age, Kshatriyas at eleven, and Vaishyas at twelve. But regardless of caste, most of those who still engage in the formal ceremony generally associate it with puberty.

How do Hindus ritualize **marriage**?

Traditional Hindu families continue the ancient practice of arranged marriage and generally do not countenance the kind of dating practices prevalent among non-Hindus in the United States. Marriage within one's caste remains a major concern for most Hindus, whether within India or abroad. An extended period of betrothal usually follows the initial arrangements between the families, and includes the exchange of gifts and chaperoned meetings of the betrothed. Ceremonies typically occur in the early evening, after sunset, in a venue chosen by the families. In the temple, the home, or at a local hotel, one or more priests preside over the ceremony, reciting set ritual texts from the scriptures. In India one priest often appears as a representative for each family. Astrological consulta-

301

Burning ghats of Manikarnika, where many families bring their dead for cremation, downstream from the bathing ghats on the River Ganges in Benares (Varanasi), city of Shiva. Note the stacks of firewood along the bank. *Courtesy of Beata Grant.*

tion still often determines the specific auspicious timing of the ceremony. Wedding ceremonies begin with the family of the bride symbolically "giving away" their daughter. After the community greets the new couple, the officiant chants special prayers while the bride and groom sit before a fire holding hands. Concluding the formal ritual, the bride and groom express consent by taking the "seven steps" symbolizing energy, vitality, success, happiness, wealth (traditionally measured in livestock), auspicious turning of the seasons, and friendship. Extended receptions generally follow the ceremonies.

What is the practice known as *sati*?

The word *sati* originally referred to a "woman of virtue," a reference to a newly widowed individual who joined her husband in death by throwing herself on his funeral pyre. The name comes from Shiva's wife Sati, who committed suicide after her father insulted her new husband. Ritual suicide by widows spread through medieval times and continued well into the early modern era. Even after the practice was outlawed in 1829, it continued in many villages. Incidents of sati still occasionally make headlines, but increasing social action on behalf of women's rights continues to improve the situation all over India.

How do Hindus deal ritually with **death and mourning**?

Hindus generally prefer cremation to burial, and most hope that their loved ones will scatter their ashes over the waters of the Ganges or one of India's many other sacred rivers. Every year many thousands of Hindu families bring the bodies of their loved ones to Banaras for cremation at the "burning *ghats* (steps)" toward the downstream side of the holy city. There (or closer to home if they cannot travel easily), led by the eldest son or an older male relative, the family completes a set of ancient rituals. They bathe and dress the body and light the pyre. The ritual leader walks four times to the left around the pyre and pours ghee over the body while the family chant divine names. For anywhere from eight days to a month the family observes a period of mourning and ritual impurity. To bring that period to a close, many families arrange a ritual meal called *shraddha*. Relatives must minister to and nourish the dead person's spirit, lest it continue to travel abroad as a restless and potentially troublesome demon. In the case of a famous Brahmin, an extended period of mourning might last a full year. Especially holy persons, such as noted gurus, are sometimes not cremated but buried, seated upright in the lotus posture. Some sects, such as the Lingayats or Virashaivas, prefer burial for all members—possibly the result of Islamic influence. Hindus in Europe and the United States generally cremate their dead within twenty-four hours of death. Mourners, wearing mostly white, gather at the home for a final viewing. Family members often arrange a memorial service in the local temple to observe the death anniversary.

BUDDHISM

HISTORY AND SOURCES

When and where did **Buddhism** begin?

Buddhism began in a region of northeast India, part of which is present-day Nepal. During the mid–sixth century BCE the kingdom of Koshala ruled the area from its capital city of Shravasti (also known as Kapilavastu). One of the realm's leading factions was the Shakya clan, traditionally identified as belonging to the Kshatriya or warrior caste. India at that time was politically fragmented into well over a dozen major regional powers. The vast majority of the population practiced forms of Hindu tradition under the leadership of a strong Brahmin priesthood. Ritual and belief centered largely on this-worldly concerns, such as managing weather to insure good harvest and curing illness. But some who had inherited the ancient tradition were beginning to question its efficacy. The famed holy city of Benares was part of the Koshala realm. There and elsewhere in the kingdom individuals and small groups of religious seekers raised issues about possible life after death, including the notion of rebirth into other modes of existence. Within the Hindu tradition the new questioning gave rise to the scriptures called the Upanishads, with their deep reflection on the nature of the self and of greater spiritual realities. Some of these new seekers parted company with mainstream Hindu tradition altogether and eventually developed into whole new communities of belief and practice. One such community is now called the Jain tradition, named after the *jinas* or "spiritual conquerors" to whom tradition attributes its founding spirit. The demanding ascetic discipline taught by Jainism's *tirthankaras* ("those who find crossing places in the river") formed one of the religious options available as early Buddhism developed. Buddhism itself would join Jainism as one of a number of splinter groups that, from a Hindu perspective, were unacceptable. These "heretics" got the name *nastika,* "those who deny" the fundamentals of Hindu belief as it was evolving then. What we now call

305

Three scenes from the life of the Buddha on wooden wall paintings, Jogye-sa Zen temple, Seoul, South Korea. They depict, from left to right, one of the "Four Passing Sights," Siddhartha Gautama's departure over the palace walls, and his quest for Enlightenment in meditation beneath the Bodhi tree.

Buddhism thus grew out of an age of political and spiritual ferment, offering seekers one of a number of significant religious options.

Who was the **Buddha** and what does tradition say about his **early life**?

According to widely accepted tradition, a child called Siddhartha ("he who has achieved his goal") Gautama was born around 563 BCE. Recent scholarship has begun to offer various views as to the chronology of the Buddha's life, but this text will retain the more traditional account since it conveys an important sense of the "feel" of Buddhist lore. Siddhartha's father, Shuddhodana, was a wealthy member of the ruling elite, a prince of sorts. When the child was born, his father consulted religious specialists to see what portents the boy's body might communicate. They told him the child was destined to become either a world-renouncer or a "wheel-turner" (*chakravartin,* an expression roughly equivalent to "mover and shaker" and sometimes extended to mean "king of all India"). Shuddhodana resolved that his son would take the path of power and influence, so he contrived to shelter the boy from any experience that might incline him another way. Gautama lived a life of ease and pleasure in his father's palace, surrounded by wealth and beauty and the trappings of authority. He married at 16 and had a son. As it turned out, Gautama's father failed to insulate his son from contact with the harsher side of life. Eventually Gautama would leave the

> ## The Buddha Up Close
>
> According to legend, the Buddha was a strikingly handsome man. One very respected Brahman leader, Canki, said of him, "the recluse Gautama is lovely, good to look upon, charming, possessed of the greatest beauty of complexion, of sublime color, a perfect stature, noble of presence." For many years Buddha's followers refused to paint the Buddha in a human form. They believed that he had moved on to a place greater than their human domain. Later, however, they began to see him and depict him as possessing the thirty-two bodily characteristics of a *mahapurusha* ("great person").

palace, as well as his own wife and child, and seek his own path. The traditional story is clearly meant to underscore certain dramatic elements in the Buddha's spiritual development. His son, Rahula, reappears later in the story as one of the early monks, and his wife is said to have become one of the first nuns.

What were the **"four passing sights"**?

On several occasions the young Gautama had to leave the confines of the palace. Although his father instructed his servants to clear the road of any unsightly reminders of human frailty, Gautama would nevertheless find himself asking the hardest questions of all. On one excursion, he saw someone bent and struggling to walk. Old age, his servants explained, a hardship many people must eventually face. Another time, Gautama spotted a leper lying by the way in pain. That was illness, his servants explained; it happened to many people. Then one day Gautama's entourage came across a funeral procession. Death, said his servants, and no one escapes that. Finally, according to the traditional account, Gautama saw by the road a young man who obviously possessed nothing and yet seemed content. That was the world-renouncer Shuddhodana so badly wanted his son not to become. The traditional account holds that all of the four experiences resulted from divine intervention, the gods assuming the roles of suffering human beings so that Gautama would be moved to take the next critical steps in ensuring the possibility of enlightenment for humankind. The clearly formulaic account admirably sums up the key issues that would eventually provide the foundations of Gautama's enlightenment and Buddhahood.

How did **Gautama** become the **Buddha**?

At the age of 29, tradition says, Gautama made the "great renunciation" of comfort and security. Borne aloft by his horse he went over the palace walls to pursue a realistic understanding of the world and the human condition. Gautama went first to learn

Buddha on the Big Screen: Some Favorite Motion Pictures

Green Snake (1993). A combonation of mysticism and action based on a Chinese fable. Green Snake (Maggie Cheung) and Son Ching (Joey Wong) are actual reptiles who have been practicing taking human form. When self-righteous Buddhist monk Fa-Hai discovers them, he thinks it's a sin to tamper with the natural order. Cantonese with English subtitles.

Kundun (1997). In 1937, in a remote area of Tibet close to the Chinese border, a two-year-old child is identified as the reincarnation of the Dalai Lama, the compassionate Buddha. He is brought to Lhasa to be schooled as a monk and as head of state. The film follows him into adulthood until his flight to India after the Chinese invasion of Tibet.

Little Buddha (1993). Tibetan Lama Norbu informs the Konrad family of Seattle that their 10-year-old son Jesse may be the reincarnation of a respected monk. Stars Keanu Reeves.

Seven Years in Tibet (1997). Heinrich Harrer (Brad Pitt) travels to the Himalayas on a mountain-climbing trip. War breaks out and he is placed in a prisoner-of-war camp. He escapes to Tibet where he befriends the young Dalai Lama and witnesses the escalation of the conflict between Tibet and China.

Temptation of a Monk (1994). Costume drama about China's seventh-century Tang Dynasty. General Shi (Wu Xin Guo) is duped into an assassination plot against the crown prince. After a massacre, the General flees and finds sanctuary with a group of Buddhist monks at a remote temple.

Why Has Bodhi-Dharma Left for the East (1989). Set in a remote monastery in the Korean mountains, the film follows an old master, close to death, who must lead his disciples in their search for spiritual freedom. Korean with English subtitles.

from two Hindu teachers, spiritual guides like those who tutor seekers in the Hindu scriptures called the Upanishads. Unsatisfied with that more philosophical approach, Gautama joined a group of ascetics in Benares, representatives of the Jain movement perhaps, and subjected himself to several years of dire austerity. When that, too, failed, he moved on and decided to meditate alone under a tree until he achieved enlightenment. During the course of seven weeks there Siddhartha went through four trance-like stages, arriving finally at the stark realization of what Buddhist tradition calls the most basic truths of human life. Siddhartha was now worthy of the name Buddha, the Enlightened One. But tradition suggests that the Buddha experienced a terrible interior struggle with the temptation to keep his newfound wisdom to himself. Mara, the demon, summoned up all his might to prevent the truths of enlightenment from spreading abroad. Overcoming all inclination to selfishness, the 35-year-old Buddha dedicated himself to teaching others the way to freedom from attachment that is the cause of all suffering. He returned to Benares, reunited with the five ascetics with whom he had parted company earlier, and preached the sermon called "Turning the Wheel of the Law." Now the Buddha was indeed a "wheel-turner," but not as his father had envisioned. For the next forty-five years, he would turn the greatest of all wheels, that of the Dharma. He died in Kushinagara at the age of 80, in about 463 BCE, of apparent food poisoning.

What were the earliest Buddhist **sacred texts**?

For several centuries the Buddhist community preserved the treasure of the Buddha's teachings orally. Monks and devout lay persons memorized increasingly formulaic versions of what the Buddha had said and the way he had behaved. As the community of monks became more stable, settling for longer periods in fixed residences, the practice of communal recitation of the sacred words became the primary mechanism for maintaining the teachings intact. Any error in recitation could be corrected immediately to ensure uniformity and, it was believed, perfect accuracy. Local communities recited the text in their own vernaculars, since no one sacred language had been decreed. Earliest texts were organized into three major groupings or "baskets" (*pitaka*). One, called the *Vinaya Pitaka,* contained all the rules of monastic discipline. Another gathered the Buddha's speeches (the *Sutra Pitaka*) and a third, much later, text included seven lengthy theoretical interpretations of the Buddha's teaching (the *Abhidharma Pitaka*). At a gathering called the Third Council in 250 BCE, members agreed on the first official formulation of all three baskets as a single scripture called the *Tripitaka* in a northeastern Indian language called Pali. Monks continued to keep the texts alive almost exclusively through memory for perhaps another century or so. Finally, the sacred texts were systematically committed to writing and became the basis of what is now known as the Pali Canon.

What other **early schools** and **scriptures** are especially important in the history of Buddhism?

A number of early Buddhist schools or denominations arose in India during the five or six centuries after the Buddha's death. One cluster, known collectively as the Hinayana ("Small Vehicle") schools, developed as a result of differing interpretations of what manner of being the Buddha was. The most important of these schools is the Theravada ("Wisdom of the Elders"), the branch largely responsible for the Pali Canon. Theravada Buddhists taught that the Buddha was a historical human being who counseled others to pursue their own path to enlightenment. But some Buddhists inclined toward more expansive, spiritual interpretation. The Mahasanghikas ("Proponents of

Four stone cosmic Buddhas of the cardinal directions flank the central Buddha, Vairocana, in a grouping especially important in the more esoteric branches of Japanese Mahayana Buddhism, at Ninnaji, a temple of the Shingon sect, in Kyoto, Japan.

the Great Assembly") taught that the Buddha's many previous lives as a Buddha-to-be, a *Bodhisattva,* prior to his birth as Siddhartha Gautama meant that the Buddha was more of a cosmic spiritual being than a mere mortal. All but one volume of their sizeable Sanskrit (called Buddhist Hybrid) scriptures have been lost. Another school, the Sarvastivadins ("Proponents of the View that All Exists"), further emphasized the importance of the bodhisattva's spiritual evolution as a model of growth in virtue. They, too, produced a body of sacred writing, but the Sanskrit originals were lost and we know of them through Chinese and Tibetan translations. Next to the Theravada school the most important of the early denominations was the Mahayana ("Great Vehicle"). So called because of its wider appeal, Mahayana teaching emphasized the larger-than-life qualities of the Buddha. More than a mere mortal, the Buddha was a saving figure whose compassion filled the universe and whose grace was available to all who asked. Mahayana scriptures in Sanskrit included *sutras* claiming to be the Buddha's own words, commentaries and treatises called *shastras,* and esoteric works called *tantras* used by smaller sects.

Was Buddhism ever identified with any **political regimes**?

Buddhism enjoyed the patronage of two very influential Indian monarchs. A ruler of the Maurya dynasty named Ashoka (r. 270–230 BCE) is credited with for the first dra-

310

> ## Buddhism in the Himalayas
>
> Like Vietnam, the Himalayan kingdoms (Tibet, Sikkim, Nepal, Bhutan) also became part of the Northern Transmission, but there the various lineages that constitute Vajrayana ("Thunderbolt Vehicle") Buddhism took hold. Tibet was the homeland of this branch of the faith, with its distinctive blend of indigenous shamanism and esoteric interpretations of the Buddha's teaching. Tibetan Buddhists also developed their own extensive scriptural canon. Of all the subdivisions of the monastic Sangha that evolved across Asia, none is more varied and colorful than that of the Vajrayana. From its most famous lineage, the Gelug-pa, comes the succession of holy men called Dalai Lamas.

matic expansion of Buddhism across much of India. He declared Buddhism the state creed and sent missionaries westward through present-day Afghanistan and south to Sri Lanka. Not until nearly four centuries later did Buddhism again profit from formal political support. A king of the Kushan dynasty named Kanishka (r. 120–162 CE) picked up where Ashoka had left off. In fact, Kanishka may have learned of Buddhism in his native land to the northwest of India as a result of Ashoka's earlier missionary endeavors. Kanishka launched a new wave of missionary activity, dispatching monks to China, Tibet, and Burma. But it was the newer Mahayana teaching that Kanishka supported. Only one other important Indian regime would give Buddhism the official seal of approval. From its capitol in Bengal to the northeast, the Pala dynasty (750–1150) supported a brand of Mahayana teaching that retained esoteric elements from Hinduism. Before the last of the Palas died, Buddhism would be nearly defunct in India. Outside of India, several Buddhist dynasties helped to establish the tradition in southeast Asia. On Indonesia's central island, Java, the Shailendras (778–864) professed a type of Mahayana teaching. Meanwhile, Buddhist monarchs helped the tradition take root in Tibet.

How was Buddhism spread through **southeast Asia**?

Buddhists call the spread of the tradition through lineages of teachers and students "Dharma transmission." Sri Lanka was one of the first regions outside of India to form a link in the "southern transmission." A lineage known as the Theravada ("Wisdom of the Elders") was introduced to Sri Lanka as early as the third century BCE. It spread into Burma and was well rooted there by about the fifth or sixth century CE. There Buddhism benefitted from the patronage of King Anawratha (1044–77), under whose dynasty Burma became almost entirely Buddhist. According to tradition, Ashoka's own missionaries brought the faith to Thailand as early as the third century BCE. The earliest solid evidence of Buddhism in Thailand is indigenous Buddhist art from eight

311

or nine centuries later. In Kampuchea (formerly called Cambodia) a blend of Mahayana and Hindu beliefs were dominant around the royal complexes of Angkor toward the end of the first millennium. Theravada teaching came to the fore after about 1200, but its institutions have just barely survived disastrous political upheavals of the late twentieth century. Vietnam seems to have participated in the Theravada transmission early on, but missionaries from China succeeded in establishing Mahayana teaching there between about 1000 and 1400.

How did Buddhism become important in **China, Korea, and Japan**?

Buddhism's spread across north and east Asia was an extended and complex process that was part of the "Northern Transmission" begun as early as the reign of Ashoka. Serious missionary efforts commenced in China sometime during the first century CE. Within a century or so, a new wave of monk-translators from India was engaged in large-scale proselytizing among the Chinese. Buddhism spread rapidly and flourished in the form of several denominations and schools. Some estimate that over half the population had accepted the new tradition by around 450 CE. A major persecution in 845 under a Daoist emperor did serious damage to all but the Pure Land and Ch'an (Zen) lineages. A Chinese missionary monk introduced Buddhism to Korea around the late fourth century. By the mid–sixth century, Buddhism enjoyed royal patronage and spread throughout the Korean peninsula. In about 552 the Korean monarch sent the Japanese emperor, as a gift, an image of the Buddha and some sacred texts. The new faith soon found itself welcome, and adapted rapidly in the Land of the Rising Sun. Monks from China and Korea continued to bring the teachings of various denominations to Japan during the seventh and eighth centuries. Those schools proved attractive to relatively small numbers of people. So during the early ninth century, three Japanese monks who had been studying in China brought back simpler teachings with greater popular appeal. Several schools based on Pure Land teaching enjoyed considerable success over the next three hundred years. Then a new wave of Buddhist growth and development washed over Japan in the late twelfth and early thirteenth centuries. Honen (1133–1212) established the Pure Land school as a distinct denomination, and two Japanese monks founded the main branches of Zen Buddhism.

How would you sum up the **history** of Buddhism?

For a quick overview, we can conveniently divide Buddhist history into four periods. 1) Foundations: A developmental period begins with the Buddha's enlightenment and early teaching and spans five centuries. During this period, Buddhists finalized their earliest scriptures in written form and spread their basic religious institutions across much of southern Asia. Several major schools of Buddhists articulated distinctive doctrinal and philosophical views and established themselves in India. 2) Spread: For about the next five or six centuries, up to around 550 CE, Buddhist missionaries carried the message and

Tibet and China

At fifteen, with his country threatened by the newly communist China, the Dalai Lama formally took charge of the Tibetan government. By 1950, peace in Tibet was destroyed as 84,000 Chinese soldiers launched an attack at six points along Tibet's border. Chinese officials claimed that communism would liberate the downtrodden Tibetan people from a feudal theocracy harshly ruled by a succession of Dalai Lamas. But many Tibetans responded that communism never was attractive for them, and that they always considered the rule of the Dalai Lama benevolent. Fearful of being captured by the Chinese and believing he would be more effective outside Tibet, the Dalai Lama fled at age twenty-four across 17,000-foot Himalayan passes into India. Together with the 70-man remnant of the Tibetan government, he was given political asylum.

Tibetans say they lived peacefully until the Chinese invaded their country. Since then, an estimated 1.2 million people—20 percent of the Tibetan population—have died in combat and through massive famines from collectivized farming and diversion of Tibetan grain to China. In addition, the Chinese gutted all but 10 of Tibet's 6,254 monasteries, and their treasure—$80 billion in jeweled, gold, silver and bronze statues and other holy items—was trucked back to China and later sold in markets in Hong Kong and Tokyo. Tibetans later rebuilt some monasteries. Still, the Dalai Lama, 1989 Nobel Peace Prize winner for his non-violent quest to free his homeland, doesn't hate the Chinese. He considers compassion as a means to regain Tibet's autonomy.

scriptures of the various Indian branches of the tradition throughout central, southeast and eastern Asia. As Buddhism's various schools traveled into new settings, still newer forms of Buddhist thought and practice evolved. 3) Inculturation and further development: From the sixth century to the eighteenth, Chinese, Korean, and Japanese cultures, as well as those in Tibet, Thailand, and Cambodia, all put their recognizable stamp on the Middle Way of the Buddha. Monks still traveled great distances and imported scriptures and artistic treasures from one culture to another. Buddhist kingdoms rose and fell in various parts of southeast Asia. During these centuries, sometimes referred to as Buddhism's medieval period, patterns of Buddhist institutional life that would endure into modern times took root all over Asia. 4) Colonialism and cultural readjustment: Sometimes called the modern period, the eighteenth through twentieth centuries have witnessed further dramatic changes, resulting from both political realignments and adaptation to accelerated intercultural communication. Buddhism is now a truly global tradition. Pilgrims have begun to return in great numbers to the sacred sites in India. Although Buddhism virtually disappeared from the land of its birth perhaps eight hundred of years ago, small Buddhist communities are again springing up on Indian soil.

RELIGIOUS BELIEFS

Is the term **revelation** useful in understanding Buddhist tradition?

Revelation, as a number of traditions use the term, presupposes that the ultimate truths remain beyond the grasp of human beings until the source or custodian of those truths chooses to make them available. By "unveiling" the mystery, the giver of truth entrusts the ultimate realities to humankind, often through a mediating figure such as a prophet. Buddhist tradition considers ultimate truths within reach of any person willing to pay attention. The truth is not, as some have always believed, "out there." It is "right in front of you and within yourself." But dealing consistently with that kind of in-your-face truth is difficult and demanding—and often lonely. As a result, Buddhists over many centuries and in many places have developed their distinctive variations on the theme of revelation, with its suggestion of privileged access to hidden truths. Buddha told his followers to be lamps unto their own feet, but there have always been Buddhist teachers and preachers to remind people what the Buddha said. Buddha told his followers the truth was not wrapped in arcane mysteries, but there have always been special, sometimes very esoteric, teachings about the secret meanings of what the Buddha said. The major difference here between Buddhism and, say, the Abrahamic faiths, is that the concept of prophetic revelation is at the heart of the Jewish, Christian, and Islamic worldviews.

Are **doctrine** and **dogma** important to Buddhists?

The Buddha emphasized that all religious and ethical teaching, dharma, is like a raft. You use a raft to get across a body of water. Once on the far shore, you would hardly choose to strap the raft to your back and trudge on under its bulky burden. Doctrine is a tool, a temporary convenience, and not an end in itself. The problem with doctrine, he taught, is that it can easily distract people from their goal. Those who ask too many questions in search of doctrinal clarity and certainty are like a person who has been shot with an arrow. Friends approach to remove the arrow but the wounded person waves them off. Not until he knows who shot the arrow and what he looked like, of what kind of wood it was made, and what kind of bird provided the feathers, will he submit to having the arrow removed. Such speculation is simply a waste of time. Pay attention to the matter at hand, Buddha counseled. Not long after the Teacher's death, followers of his dharma nevertheless developed many elaborate doctrinal frameworks with which to interpret the Buddha's teaching. Each of the various denominations has its preferred scripture and its own theoretical perspective, and some have emphasized correct belief as a criterion of membership. But no major Buddhist school has defined a large body of doctrine in the form of dogmatic pronouncements that require the explicit assent of all members. Buddhists often use the Sanskrit term *sasana* in refer-

Three Jewels and Five Vows

Perhaps the closest thing to a summary of Buddhist beliefs is the brief creedal formula of the "Three Jewels." "I take refuge in the Buddha; I take refuge in the dharma; I take refuge in the sangha." Buddhists in various places and times have interpreted those Jewels rather differently. For many the Buddha was a human teacher and an example, but no more. For many others, the Buddha represented the universal possibility of enlightenment. Still others regard the Buddha, along with countless Buddhas-to-be called Bodhisattvas, as a divine power and source of grace and salvation. Buddhist tradition retained the important Hindu term *dharma* but reinterpreted it. For Buddhists, dharma means all that the Buddha taught. They know dharma as enshrined in the sacred texts and communicated by religious teachers. The term *sangha* means "assembly" and refers to the Buddhist Order of monks and nuns and, by extension, to the whole community of believers. Along with the affirmation of the "Three Jewels," a secondary but very important affirmation of the "precepts" or vows. Members of the monastic sangha take ten vows, while devout lay persons take the first five. Many Buddhists begin their day by reciting the "Three" (refuges) and then adding the "Five" (precepts). They promise to refrain from killing, theft, unchastity, deception, and intoxication. Reaffirming one's commitment to the precepts functions not unlike a creedal statement of assent to the core beliefs of a religious tradition.

ence to the whole package of belief and practice that the Buddha taught as a way of life.

How did the Buddha reinterpret **Hindu** teaching?

Key notions Siddhartha learned as a young Hindu included those of *karma* (action), *dharma* (law), *samsara* (cycles of rebirth), and *moksha* (final liberation). Most Hindus of his day understood the concept of *karma* as external ritual action performed in the hope of tapping into divine power. Some religious thinkers were beginning to suggest that, along with ancient Vedic ritual under the direction of the priestly class, the acts of individual people might also influence their spiritual as well as material prospects. Others, like the Buddha, took their questioning of the old ways much further. They began to spiritualize the law of karma, explaining that choice and intent were more important than outward deeds. Along with their reinterpretation of karma, some contemporaries of the Buddha were also rethinking the Hindu concept of dharma. No longer merely the impersonal, inscrutable law of cosmic order, dharma now took on a personal ethical dimension. In the Buddha's view, karma included all the results of each individual's choices. He emphasized the need to purify one's intentions of all self-

315

centeredness. Perform each act purely because it is your "dharma," not because you hope to gain personally. The Hindu notion of samsara meant that the souls of individuals who died unliberated from the negative effects of their past actions would return in another form. The Buddha understood samsara to mean not only the cycle of physical rebirths, but the whole series of interior or spiritual stages the individual went through on the way to enlightenment. Finally, the Hindu idea of moksha meant the release of the indestructible soul (atman) of each individual from the cycle of samsara. The Buddha also taught the possibility of a final liberation, but he gave it an important twist. Genuine liberation meant the complete cessation of all craving—even of craving for liberation itself. He called that final freedom nirvana, "no wind," symbolizing the extinction of the flames of desire.

What is **Enlightenment**?

In Buddhist tradition the term "enlightenment" means the simple, clear realization of the most basic truths about life. It presupposes the utmost attentiveness to whatever one is experiencing as one experiences it. And for that reason it sounds too simple and ordinary to be worth pursuing. But enlightenment begins and ends precisely with the simple and the ordinary. It is the realization that the headlong pursuit of pleasure (hedonism) and the dogged avoidance of pleasure (extreme asceticism) both yield the same results: suffering. Hope fuels the one, fear the other. Both are a flight from the real as it confronts every individual in the here and now. Enlightenment means grasping the fundamental realities summed up in Buddhism's "Four Noble Truths." First, life is difficult. Look around. As the Four Passing Sights taught Siddhartha, the human condition includes some hard inescapable realities. This first truth is not as pessimistic as it might sound. It is the ultimate in realism. If human beings had the power to change the basic realities we experience, we would have done so long ago. But we can change the ways we respond to experience. Second, all that hardship and suffering comes from inappropriate attachment or grasping. Whatever I "must" either have or avoid will finally make me suffer. If I get what I want, it will soon disappoint. If I manage to avoid for a time what I fear most, something else will soon replace it. There is a solution in the third truth: to avoid suffering avoid inappropriate craving. Under ordinary circumstances no human being can stop craving altogether. The Buddha nearly killed himself with austerities before he realized the futility of such an approach. What is appropriate behavior? The fourth truth says simply, to stop inappropriate craving, and follow the Eightfold Noble Path.

What is the **Eightfold Noble Path**?

True to his hardheaded realism, the Buddha did not send his followers off on a wild goose chase. He suggested a method for achieving a balanced approach to everyday experience. Buddhists call his teaching the Middle Path because it aims at balance,

---

The Four Noble Truths

Enlightenment means grasping the fundamental realities summed up in Buddhism's Four Noble Truths:

Life is difficult.
All hardship and suffering comes from inappropriate attachment or grasping.
To avoid suffering, avoid inappropriate craving.
To stop inappropriate craving, follow the Eightfold Noble Path.

---

propriety, and equanimity. Eat what you need and use whatever is necessary for a modest style of living. The eight elements in the classical formulation of the standards for such a life are divided into three larger categories: wisdom, ethics, and concentration. Achieving wisdom requires proper belief in the form of deep understanding of the Four Noble Truths, and proper intent, which means that one performs all acts out of compassion rather than out of selfish motives. The next three steps on the Path involve ethics. Proper speech means avoiding all evils of the tongue. Proper action, expressed negatively, means refraining from inappropriate sexual relationships, killing, and stealing. And proper livelihood calls for the avoidance of occupations that cause harm, such as dealing in slavery or weapons. Training in concentration also has a triple foundation. Proper effort means perfect balance in one's attitude toward work. Proper attentiveness flows from deep reflection on the Four Noble Truths. And proper absorption, a lofty goal, means the ability to be genuinely content in equilibrium between pursuing goals and running from fears. Everything depends on carefully measured responses. That does not necessarily mean the death of spontaneity. It means a habit of discipline and keen awareness of one's personal motivations.

Could you sum up the Buddha's classical teaching on how a "good" life might unfold?

Any person who wishes to make sense of life must begin by hearing the dharma, seeking to understand the teaching of the utterly trustworthy Buddha. Translating the teaching into action means abiding by the fundamental recommendations and rules of conduct for living a moral life. Moving a step beyond the "ethical minimum" requires a person to seek greater personal discipline by guarding the senses and doing whatever is necessary to avoid the subtle corrosion of evil influences. That in turn inevitably leads to a higher level of mindfulness and awareness of each moment. This may seem at first to suggest a bland, even incredibly boring, life. But Buddhist tradition insists, paradoxically perhaps, that this alone can offer genuine appreciation and enjoyment—true bliss. Only such enlarged awareness is really worth the name "living," for everything else is life on auto-pilot, a sure recipe for stress and frustration. At some point the seeker will need to pursue serious training in meditation. Meditative discipline aims immediately to help the seeker identify and neutralize sources of anxiety and uncertainty. A kind of spiritual map for serious seekers is called the "Twelve-spoked Wheel of Conditioned Arising." It describes in schematic fashion the cycle by which ignorance gives rise to intent to act, which in turn gives rise to consciousness, awareness of name and body, capacity for sense contact, actual contact, sensation, craving, grasping, becoming, birth, old age, and death. The seeker must in effect work backward through the chain of conditions to eliminate the ignorance at the root. Those who persevere along this path hope to arrive at a genuinely contemplative approach to life and, ultimately, at spiritual liberation. This classical teaching clearly lays out a difficult and demanding path. Relatively few are able to follow it consistently. That is one of the reasons that more popular forms of Buddhist devotion and practice have had a broader appeal.

How does the Buddhist tradition describe **existence** in general?

Buddhist teaching focuses on three fundamental qualities of all things. Two are fairly obvious to anyone who cares to look, and are at the heart of the experience of enlightenment. The first is hardship or suffering, the second impermanence. Nobody is immune to sadness and disappointment. No one has a lock on success and genuine contentment. And everything comes to an end. Everything. The third quality is far from obvious even to the most careful observer, but an awareness of it does follow from the realities of suffering and impermanence. That is the notion that there is no permanent, indestructible core or "soul" at the center of any being. Hindu tradition taught Siddhartha Gautama that at the center of each individual being was a "self" or *atman* that survived physical death to be reincarnated in another life, assuming the person died still enslaved by the effects of self-centered choices. The Buddha's reinterpretation of Hindu tradition on this point was so radical that it cuts right to the psychological bone. Take away the "soul" and what remains? Nothing, apparently. But the Buddha was not attempting to empty life of its meaning. He wanted people to change their minds about what matters most. Look hard at what motivates you, what can make you nearly desperate to achieve this good or avoid that evil. Look carefully, the Buddha argued, and you will see that the qualities that attract or repel you are deceptions. Probe deeply into your choices and you will see that what you are really looking for you cannot get from this possession or that person. Each being is simply what it is and it is a serious mistake to treat your world as though it existed for you, as if what you value in each thing *is* its value. In a sense, the Buddha argued, all things are "empty," in that they simply do not possess the "soul" that a grasping, craving person invests them with. Pile all your expectations onto some person or object as though you truly hope it will deliver what you want, and you are making the fundamental mistake. The notion of non-soul (*anatman*) is difficult to understand, but it is one of the Buddha's most provocative teachings.

318

> ## Rebirth of a Non-self
>
> **B**uddhist tradition has devised various intricate ways of explaining this problem. One widely used image is that of a seal-ring. Take a pad of warm wax and press the seal-ring into it and you get a very clear impression, one that firms up as the wax cools. You've transferred "something" without actually leaving anything but an impression. The seal-ring is something like what remains when a human being dies still enslaved to inappropriate craving and desires. It represents the whole complex of psychic energies that make up a human "personality," energies so potent that most people are perfectly convinced of their individuality and separate personhood. In the cycle of death and rebirth, what transfers from one existence across the chasm of death into the "wax" of a new embodiment is precisely that incredibly powerful ego-impulse. As the Buddha saw it, no one can be finally free so long as he or she clings to the notions of "I, me, mine."

Is there a distinctively Buddhist **"ethic"**?

Compassion for all sentient beings is the overriding principle in Buddhist ethics. It was compassion (*karuna*) that urged the Buddha to share his message of enlightenment. Life's greatest challenge is to act out of genuine altruism, to be and do for others without hoping for reward. Compassion needs to be doubly disciplined. One needs to work toward the alleviation of suffering purely because that is humanity's highest calling. But it is also essential to know how best to put compassion into action. That calls for the practical wisdom that comes from a keen awareness of one's own spiritual history, including a recollection of one's previous lives. The ability to "recall one's former existences" is a mark of genuine enlightenment and a sign of profound awareness. Buddhist ethics combine the compassion of one who appreciates the pervasiveness of suffering with the practical wisdom that comes from a detailed experiential knowledge of what "works." The result is a virtue called "skill in means" (*upaya*). In other words, it is the motive for behaving ethically—compassion, the framework within which to choose a course of action—wisdom, and the resources with which to act.

What do Buddhists believe about **ultimate spiritual reality** or **God**?

One of the many issues the Buddha refused to speculate on was the existence or significance of gods. As a Hindu he naturally learned the traditional stories of the divinities. As a man of his time, with all its religious and intellectual ferment, the Buddha questioned the wisdom of reliance on ritual sacrifice. He did not deny the existence of the gods. He merely insisted that whatever power the gods might possess, it could not solve the fundamental human dilemma. That remained the sole responsibility of the individual person. Many Buddhist sacred texts talk of the gods in mythic terms. It was, for example, the gods who made sure young Siddhartha Gautama encountered the Four Passing Sights that turned his life around. But classical Buddhist teaching does not refer to an Ultimate Reality in personal terms. That changed as popular devotional forms of Buddhism developed, especially in China, Korea, and Japan. Buddha himself assumed virtually divine proportions, and the concept of the universal Buddha-nature superseded that of the Buddha as historical human teacher. Gods of ancient Hindu myth retained a place in the Buddhist spiritual cosmos but remained very much in the background.

Do Buddhists believe in **miracles**?

Popular lore about the Buddha and numerous other holy personages is bursting with accounts of miracles. Buddhist tradition attributes far more miraculous deeds to the Buddha than almost any other tradition ascribes to a foundational figure. Scores of wonders occur at the moment of the Buddha's birth, all portents of the event's cosmic significance. Lamps all across the world lit themselves at that moment, the mute sang, the lame danced, and birds were suspended in their flight. The Buddha is said to have performed dozens of fabulous feats throughout his lifetime, traveling great distances instantly, ascending into the air, subduing wild animals, and walking on water. Several of the wonders have become part of a canonical list of eight "Great Events," each associated with one of the cardinal or intermediate directions. Hardheaded realist that he was, the Buddha does not appear to have claimed miraculous powers of any sort. But within a short time of his death tales of his superhuman powers multiplied. Important tales include 547 *Jatakas,* stories of the Buddha's previous lives as the Buddha-to-be. Incarnated in myriad different forms, the Bodhisattva performs countless marvels on behalf of all suffering beings. Many other important Buddhist leaders have enjoyed similar notoriety. Founders of lineages, denominations and monasteries from Tibet to Japan are said to have performed deeds like those attributed to the Buddha himself.

Are there **"mythic" elements** in Buddhist tradition?

Mythic expression plays a far less central role in Buddhist teaching than in Hinduism. In fact, you might say one of the Buddha's main concerns was to "demythologize" Hindu tradition as he had received it. Hindu myth introduces believers to the impenetrable mystery of the divine while attempting to describe how the divine presence infuses the world of human experience. The Buddha cautioned against taking refuge in myth. However potent the divine presence may be, it does not relieve human beings of ultimate responsibility for their own choices. As in so many religious traditions, the foundational figure himself soon became the focal point of a new mythology. Even the most hardcore Theravada tradition leaves room for the Buddha to expand into a being of supramundane qualities. Wondrous tales of the Buddha's previous lives; the *Jatakas* radiate mythic energy. Some of the Mahayana denominations and sects, those of the widely popular Pure Land variety in particular, evolved their own complex descrip-

The Three Bodies of the Buddha

The concept of the "three bodies" (*trikaya*) of the Buddha evolved as a way of explaining how the spiritual entity called the Buddha-nature could transcend all earthly realities and at the same time manifest itself in the world. Pure Buddha-nature existed in the *Dharma-Body* and was personified as the Primal or Universal Buddha. Living in various heavenly abodes that made up the *Bliss-Body* were the five principal "meditational" Buddhas, one ruling the center and four ruling the paradises at the four cardinal points. Transcendent Bodhisattvas assisted the celestial Buddhas in the work of salvation through grace. Involved in earthly affairs were the Buddhas and Bodhisattvas who entered history in the *Manifestation-Body,* subjecting themselves to time and change out of compassion for all suffering beings.

tions of a multi-level cosmos ruled by multiple Buddhas and populated by countless lesser spiritual powers as well. Vajrayana Buddhism, represented especially by various Tibetan lineages, retained much of ancient Hinduism's mythic spirit and cast of characters. But the Tibetans interiorized the myth, interpreting the many spiritual beings as projections of the inner powers with which one identifies through meditative practice. Even in popular Mahayana and the more esoteric Vajrayana teachings, mythic elements never attain quite the centrality they enjoy in Hindu tradition.

Do Buddhists believe in an **afterlife**?

Although the Buddha himself emphasized the need to focus on this-worldly concerns, his followers soon developed a complex understanding of the spiritual structure of the universe. According to both Theravada and Mahayana models, all of reality is divided into three realms. The Realm of Desire (*kama-dhatu*) encompasses everything from innumerable hells through the dwelling places of animals, humans, lesser gods, and the various paradises in which good people can expect to enjoy the fruits of a good life. Each level of hell is suited to a particular kind of selfishness and evil. The heavens are similarly graded for the enjoyment of the just. A certain sexist attitude is built into the notion of paradise, since in order to gain entry into the highest heaven women must first be reborn as men. Those reborn into the next major level up, the Realm of Form (*rupa-dhatu*), leave behind the senses of taste, touch, and smell. Through hearing, sight, and mental impressions they continue the ongoing process of spiritual refinement and education. Denizens of this realm's multiple heavens (from sixteen to eighteen) progress upward through various stages of contemplative discipline, arriving finally at the third cosmic realm, that of Non-Form (*arupa-dhatu*). Dispensing with sight and hearing, dwellers in this realm progress through four additonal heavens through meditation, arriving at last at nirvana. Beyond that, according to some Mahayana schools, lie several Buddha-fields. Transcendent Buddhas, such as Amitabha (in China, Amida in Japan), reign over their individual Buddha-fields. Amitabha's is the Western Paradise called the Pure Land. Popular belief suggests that devotees can bypass the lower intermediate steps and progress directly the this final abode merely by expressing perfect faith in the transcendent Buddha.

Does **millennialism** have a place in Buddhist thinking?

Buddhist interpretations of history, like those of Hindu tradition generally, are relatively unconcerned with notions like beginnings, progress, and endings. Time is so much grander than any human mind can fathom. Unimaginably large cycles give way to more of the same. But just as Hindu explanations of cosmic cycles can include a sense of expectation, so Buddhist tradition also makes room for a kind of "adventist" thinking. Buddhists call the spiritual person or power whose future coming holds hope for all believers Maitreya, "the Benevolent One." Five thousand years after the death of this age's Historical Buddha, the one originally called Siddhartha Gautama, Maitreya will enter the world of time and change. At present Maitreya lives as a Bodhisattva in the heaven called Tushita ("contented ones," the celestial realm reserved for future Buddhas). Both Theravada and Mahayana traditions give Maitreya an important role, but devotion to this Bodhisattva is much more developed in several Mahayana denominations. Classical Chinese teachings regarded Maitreya as a savior figure, but the cult of Amitabha gradually displaced that of Maitreya. Tibetan tradition holds that Maitreya will arrive in thirty-thousand years to teach all people. This Bodhisattva has a long history of popular devotion in Korea and Japan under the name Miruk or Miroku. Colossal statues of Miruk stand on Korean hillsides and in temple compounds, some visible for several miles. And in Japan, Kyoto's ancient Koryuji temple enshrines an exquisite sixth-century statue of Miroku. Gazing down on all who enter, the beautiful and very feminine-looking Miroku radiates compassion. Moving from the sublime to the deliberately ridiculous, a comical figure called Mi-lo in China and Hotei in Japan represents another facet of Maitreya altogether. Hotei is depicted as a fat, jovial, scantily clad character. He is actually a Chinese Zen monk named P'u-t'ai who claimed to be a manifestation of Maitreya.

SIGNS AND SYMBOLS

Are there any **signs** or **symbols** that might identify an **individual** as a Buddhist?

In most parts of the world in which Buddhism remains an important presence, it is a safe bet that many people on the street have had some direct contact with Buddhist

tradition, but it is usually difficult to tell Buddhists from non-Buddhists merely by

A group of Japanese Buddhist pilgrims visiting Kyoto's Kiyomizudera on their round of sacred sites, wearing the characteristic pilgrim hat and wallet (worn around the neck) for collecting souvenir stamps at each stop on the circuit.

looking at their clothing or other personal effects. Occasionally you will spot an item of jewelry whose symbolism is more or less explicitly Buddhist. The eight-spoked Wheel of Dharma is a common symbol easily reproduced on small scale items. Buddhist pilgrims, however, often stand out because of the traditional garb and variety of symbols they wear. In Japan, for example, some pilgrims wear a large, round, pointed or bowl-like straw hat, carry pilgrim staffs, and wear around their necks a small cloth wallet in which to collect the souvenir stamps they receive from each temple they visit. Monks, nuns, and priests are surely the most obvious examples here of distinctive signs. Nearly everywhere in the world, monks and nuns shave their heads. They typically wear a distinctive habit or garb, consisting of two or three wraps—two for novices, three for senior monks and nuns. One wrap covers the lower body, another the upper. For religious rituals, monks wear a long cloth of twelve folds, sometimes called the stole, over the left shoulder. Colors vary according to region and institutional affiliation, from one branch of the monastic order or Buddhist lineage to another. Saffron is the most common color for monastic garb, but, for example, Tibetan monks often wear a dark burgundy, Japanese monks typically don darker shades of gray, brown, and violet, and Chinese nuns often wear a simple gray robe.

What **signs** or **symbols** distinguish Buddhist **ritual specialists**?

Priests who officiate in Buddhist temples that serve the public wear a variety of colors and use various implements. Priests often wear a special robe called a *kashaya* (*kesa*   323

A collection of miniature images of the Bodhisattva Jizo, patron of unborn children. Women who have had miscarriages often purchase the small statues as votive offerings and leave them at certain temples, sometimes adorning them with knit red caps or bibs, along with pinwheels and other toys.

in Japan). The vestment is unusual in that it is typically a patchwork of many colors and textures, recalling the simplicity and poverty of the Buddha's earliest disciples. An abbreviated form of the *kesa* is the *wagesa,* a simple swatch of cloth worn over the shoulders. Some monastic priests in Japan carry a staff called a *shakujo.* Six metal rings near the top make a jangling sound, alerting small defenseless creatures to remove themselves from harm's way. The Bodhisattva Jizo, usually dressed as a monk or priest, typically carries the staff. Within private or monastic settings, ritual specialists have an even greater diversity of signs and symbols, since their rituals are often more esoteric and complex. Tibetan monks, for example, don very colorful headgear distinctive of their various lineages for special rituals. Tibetans and members of other esoteric sects also use a wider variety of special ritual objects than are used in popular denominations.

Do Buddhists mark their **sacred spaces** with any distinctive signs and symbols?

Though Buddhist ritual spaces vary a great deal architecturally and decoratively from one region to another, a number of commonly used signs and symbols appear. Perhaps the single most important is the eight-spoked Wheel of the Dharma, reminder of the Four Noble Truths and the Eightfold Noble Path. Tibetan temples identify themselves with a characteristic form of the classical Indian stupa called a *chorten,* a five-level

Buddhist priest offering prayers alone in a temple near the grounds of the great Shinto shrine of Itsukushima, on Miyajima island not far from Hiroshima.

architectural form crowned with a conical shape. Chinese Buddhist temples borrowed their ground-plans from the traditional royal residence, a walled enclosure with one or more interior courtyards surrounding the main sacred structures. The principal inner structures face south and are lined up on an axis with the main gate. A multi-storied polygonal pagoda may be part of the complex. Japan largely borrowed the classical Chinese ground plan, varying the placement of the inner buildings somewhat. Always found at the back of the walled enclosure is the main image hall where central rituals occur. Three-, five- or seven-storey square pagodas are a regular feature in the main courtyard of many Japanese temples. Thai temples feature a very distinctive roof line and post very imposing guardian figures before the main door but do not generally have separate pagoda structures.

What will I see if I visit a **Buddhist temple**?

A lot depends on where you are and the size of the temple. Local or neighborhood temples are generally of simpler design than those that function like "cathedral" temples or are closely associated with the main institution of a monastic community. Larger foundations throughout Asia are often visible from a distance, punctuating the skyline with their stupa spires or lofty pagodas. Walled enclosures entered through monumental gateways surround the more important foundations. Before entering any temple, however grand or humble, you will see a rack in which to deposit your

Zen dry meditation garden in Daisen-in, one of twenty-three subtemples of Kyoto's Daitoku-ji.

footwear. Interior appointments vary somewhat according to culture and denomination. Most traditional temples are divided into two main areas. The congregational space usually has no furniture. When worshipers pause for meditation or recitation, they ordinarily either stand or sit on the floor. Some temples have individual meditation pillows stacked along the walls. But some Buddhist temples in Europe and the United States have adopted the Protestant Christian use of pews or benches without kneelers. Many such temples actually belong to denominations that call themselves "churches." Look at the back of a bench and you are likely to find hymn books in a rack. Many temples separate the sanctuary area from the body of the building with a railing or columns. A large image of the Buddha or a major Bodhisattva stands or sits atop an altar, sometimes in the company of several smaller images. Before the altar is a place for the priest or prayer leader to sit. Side altars dedicated to Bodhisattvas or holy persons, such as founders of the various lineages, are not uncommon. Some temples have meditative gardens adjacent to the formal worship space.

What's the difference between a **stupa** and a **pagoda**?

A stupa is an ancient Indian burial or reliquary monument. Its fundamental unit is a solid hemispherical earthen mound called the "egg" (*anda*) or "womb" (*garbha*). Atop the mound sits a solid square or rectangular shape, originally surrounded by a four-sided railing, called the *harmika,* that may be a remnant of the days when the village altar stood inside a fenced enclosure. Growing tree-like from that is a pillar that pierces several circular discs of decreasing diameter, usually an odd number from three to eleven. The result looks like a multi-tiered parasol. The Buddha's cremated remains are said to have been originally enshrined in a large number of stupas built all over India. Mahayana teaching developed the notion that the Buddha was a cosmic spiritual being, rather than a mere human teacher, and the architecture of the stupa evolved to reflect those changes. Stupa designers began to raise the mound off the ground by using several square bases, meanwhile stretching the mound itself upward much the way a potter turns a round lump of clay into a tall graceful vase. The "parasol" is also stretched heavenward, becoming more streamlined and adding disks. When Mahayana Buddhism moved into China, architects transformed the upper portion of the stupa into an independent structure, turning the multiple discs into roofs. The earth-hugging funerary mound was replaced by the pagoda. The new structure was derived from the stupa and still contained relics, but the pagoda symbolized transcendence rather than earthly existence. Pagodas soon added their own sets of multiple discs, leaving the stupa, so to speak, in the dust. In the Theravada lands of southeast Asia, reminders of the stupa remain in the gently tapered monuments of Burma and Thailand. Mahayana Buddhist establishments all over east Asia identify themselves with their graceful, multi-roofed pagodas. Unlike the typical stupa, the pagoda actually has interior space, sometimes on several levels.

What are some helpful clues for understanding Buddhist **iconography**?

Most important of all are images of the Buddhas and Bodhisattvas. Buddhist sculpture and painting have evolved in many different styles. Each lineage or denomination has a number of symbols and signs to which it assigns special meanings. But it is possible to suggest some general features to look for when you visit a museum's Asian galleries. As with Hindu iconography, start by noting posture, gesture, garb and other implements. Buddha images are usually seated in the lotus posture, legs crossed so that the soles of the feet face upward. Some images depict the Buddha standing or walking, but these are less numerous. Principal gestures include those that indicate blessing, teaching, or meditation. One of the most important has the left hand resting palm up in the lap and the right touching the ground just in front of the right knee, symbolizing the Buddha's conquest of Mara's temptation. Buddha images are typically clad in simple monk's garb and do not hold any specific tools or implements. Bodhisattvas sometimes appear seated in a relaxed posture called "royal ease," but standing images are more common. They ordinarily wear crowns and royal finery as symbols of the life of the Buddha-to-be prior to his renunciation. Seated Bodhisattvas often recline graciously forward and offer a gesture of kindly welcome or special attentiveness. Some Bodhisattvas have multiple arms and heads to symbolize their infinite power and ability to respond to every human need. In their many hands these potent images can carry as many as several dozen separate items, including weapons, musical instruments, and symbols of healing. Guardian figures are the most numerous subordinate images. Distant cousins of beings with similar functions in Hindu tradition, these characters glower menacingly on beings of evil intent and brandish weaponry sufficient to dispatch all undesirable elements daring to approach the holy place.

What is a **mandala**? Is it the same as a **thanka**?

Mandala is a Sanskrit word for "circle." As a two-dimensional design, a mandala is equivalent to the plan of a stupa. Viewed directly from above, a stupa reveals a series of alternating concentric square and circular shapes. From the outside in, you see the square foundation, the circular earth-mound, the square "altar" inside its square railing, and finally the circular discs mounted on the shaft of the spire. Some mandalas depict four gates on the sides of the foundation-square and add yet another outer circle symbolizing the "eight cemeteries" through which a meditator must first pass, becoming oblivious to the senses and all other distractions before entering the sacred space. Vajrayana and other esoteric Buddhist sects adapted this bird's eye perspective on the stupa and interpreted it as an image of both the macrocosm (the whole spiritual cosmos) and the microcosm (the individual meditator). Devotees meditate on the sacred design of the spiritual "city" as they move symbolically inward from the gates toward the center and enlightenment. Various "deities" and forms of Buddhas and Bodhisattvas are depicted in the different spaces of the mandala, each symbolizing some aspect of spiritual power. Tibetan monks sometimes create large mandalas using grains of colored sand. After many hours of work, they conduct rituals around it and then discard it in a river as a reminder of impermanence and non-attachment. *Thanka* is a more generic term for a Tibetan wall hanging depicting a religious theme. Some thankas depict mandalas, and some display sacred imagery of other kinds. Multiple scenes illustrating *Jataka* tales offer material designed for meditation on essential virtues modeled by the Buddha-to-be.

Have Buddhists always depicted the Buddha in **painting** and **sculpture**?

For generations after the Buddha's death his followers hesitated to depict the Teacher in human form. Perhaps they avoided direct visual representation out of respect for the Buddha, one too sacred to be so portrayed. Whatever the motivation, early Buddhist artists chose a variety of symbols to represent the Buddha. Early Christian artists likewise refrained from depicting Christ in human form, opting for symbols like the fish and the empty cross. The most important symbols for the Buddha included the riderless horse, the parasol, the tree, the empty throne, footprints, the eight-spoked wheel, and the stupa. A riderless horse recalled the Buddha's renunciation and departure from his father's palace. Parasols were symbols of royalty and represented the great honor due to an Enlightened One. Buddha reached enlightenment beneath the Bo tree, and artists often left a space before the tree to suggest the pres-

The Buddhist Rosary

Buddhists in many places have used a number of variations on the string of beads for devotional purposes. In ancient India, Buddhists used a string of 108 beads (very similar to the ancient Hindu rosary) as a symbol of the bodhisattva Avalokiteshvara. This compassionate being, whose name means, roughly, "Lord Looking Down on the World," took on 108 human characteristics in his saving descent to assume the human condition, using the beads while doing so. Chinese and Japanese images of the Buddha, as well as of various patriarchs and monastic founders, sometimes show them holding rosaries. For ritual purposes, the rosary has been particularly important in the more esoteric sects of Tibet and Japan. Tibetan rosaries have three larger beads at the end as symbols of the Three Jewels. Devotees in those sects use the beads to count repetitions of their mantras. In some more popular sects, devotees count repetitions of names of the Buddha or phrases like "Glory to Amida Buddha."

ence of the Buddha. Some scenes place an empty throne beneath the tree. Artists sometimes choose to show a pair of footprints just in front of the throne. Footprints also appear by themselves somewhere in a scene to indicate where the Buddha would have been. A wheel of eight spokes was a reminder of the Eightfold Noble Path and the Four Noble Truths. Depictions of a stupa, resting place of the Buddha's remains, frequently served as a reminder of his spiritual presence. Several other items especially popular in China among the "Eight Auspicious Signs" include a pair of fish, symbol of universal Indian monarchy; the lotus blossom of purity; and the conch shell of victory. Chinese Buddhist altars often held clay or carved wooden images of these symbols.

Do Buddhists use **special symbols** when they engage in personal or private rituals?

A number of prayer aids and other ritual accoutrements are common in many Buddhist households. Prayer wheels and prayer flags, used especially in the Himalayan nations but elsewhere as well, symbolize the belief in the ideal of continual prayer. Prayer wheels contain bits of sacred text inside a small drum fitted with an axle-like handle. A short weighted chain attached to the drum makes it easier to spin it steadily. Prayer flags are strips of cloth containing sacred text and petitions, prayers sped aloft by the winds. Many Japanese households have a small altar, called the *butsudan,* in which families keep tablets with the names of deceased relatives as well as images of the Buddha. In general, private rituals employ a scaled-down set of the same principal symbols used for temple worship.

Where do Buddhists go to get the various **signs and symbols** they use often?

Great bronze Amida Buddha, twelfth century, Kamakura, Japan. The statue is nearly forty feet tall and was once housed in a wooden temple structure. Visitors can ascend stairs inside and look out.

Wherever Buddhism has been an important part of a culture, Buddhists can easily find stores that specialize in religious goods and devotional objects. Walk down any number of streets in cities like Kyoto, Japan, or Keelung, Taiwan, for example, and you may find yourself passing such a shop. Japanese Buddhist goods stores tend to carry exclusively Buddhist items. Most prominently on display are images of the Buddha, usually of Amida, and of various Bodhisattvas. To install the images at home or the office one can buy altars and shrines built like miniature temples, with several shelves inside and doors that can be closed. In Taiwan, where Buddhism so often blends together with Daoist and popular folk traditions, items of interest to Buddhist devotees frequently appear interspersed with images of the Eight Immortals and other Chinese religious figures. Religious goods stores offer devotional items in several sizes and price ranges, small pieces suitable for homes of modest income or full-size images designed for temples with sizable congregations.

What has the **swastika** got to do with Buddhism?

A revolving cross with bent cross-beams, the swastika has been a symbol of longevity and success throughout eastern Asia for millennia. Buddhists inherited the symbol from Hindu tradition, in which it referred to different forms of cosmic energy, depending on whether the symbol rotated to the right or to the left. The symbol appears often in Chinese sculpture on the upper chest of the Buddha. There it is a reminder of the eternal validity of his teaching, a meaning attached to the Chinese use of the swastika as the number ten thousand. In some Japanese temples (such as the Asakusa Kannon temple in Tokyo) the swastika even functions as the central icon on the main altar, replacing the image of the Buddha. Zen tradition sees the swastika as a symbol of the "buddha-mind" handed down from teacher to disciple. It may have become associated with the Buddha as a result of his identification with solar imagery and power. Some suggest that the swastika symbolizes the Buddha's teaching as an abstract stylized version of the Wheel of Dharma.

Have **relics** been important in Buddhist practice?

Practically since the Buddha's final entry into Nirvana, which coincided with his physical death, Buddhists have placed

Worshipers circumambulate a large stone pagoda near Po Mun Sa temple, Seoul, Korea. Worshipers walk in a clockwise direction, past the swastika on the wall beyond the pagoda.

great importance on sacred relics. Numerous early accounts tell of the distribution of Buddha's cremated remains to political rulers so that they could enshrine them as sacred markers. One account says the great King Ashoka built 84,000 stupas as reliquaries for the Buddha's ashes. Some sources report that Buddha's followers discovered among the ashes a tooth, still intact. In Kandy, Sri Lanka, the Shrine of the Tooth claims to possess the only authentic dental relic, said to have been brought there ten days after Buddha's death. But as recently as the late 1990s, a tooth kept in Beijing made news when it was flown to Hong Kong after the Chinese takeover there, in time for a celebration of the Buddha's birthday. Meanwhile a tooth in the possession of a Tibetan monk was installed in Taipei, Taiwan, amid mainland Chinese denunciations of

331

its authenticity. Other relics of the Buddha included his staff, begging bowl, and robe. Another item that reflects the sacredness of first-class (actual bodily remains) and second-class relics (personal effects of the sacred person) and is still important throughout the Buddhist world is the Buddha's footprint. Many temples claim to possess an "actual" print, but most are highly stylized stone or metal images that devotees bathe with various liquids and adorn with flower petals. Prints frequently have various symbols of the Buddha on the sole. Most common are the Wheel of the Law and sets of either 32, 108, or 132 special marks of the Enlightened One. Footprints belong to a third category of relic, items that directly remind one of the Buddha. All images of the Buddha, as well as physical copies of the sacred texts, are therefore also a type of relic. In addition to relics of the Buddha himself, symbolic reminders of numerous other holy persons have become prominent. First and second-class relics of bodhisattvas, patriarchs, and eminent monastic founders and teachers are enshrined in stupas and pagodas throughout Asia. Miniature stupas and pagodas, made of wood, stone or metal, have often provided the visual and devotional focus in temples, monasteries, and even private dwellings.

MEMBERSHIP, COMMUNITY, DIVERSITY

Where do Buddhists live today? Are any **estimates of numbers** available?

Buddhism enjoyed much greater success in other parts of Asia than in India, the land of its birth. Estimates of the global population of Buddhists varies from about a third to half a billion. Political circumstances make statistics particularly hard to get for China and Tibet, but it is clear that Buddhists have suffered terribly in both areas during the past half-century. Meanwhile, the tradition has been enjoying modest revival elsewhere in Asia, and has become increasingly popular in Europe and North America as a result of both immigration and conversion. Nations with the highest percentage of Buddhists among the general population are Thailand (94%), Cambodia (90%), Myanmar (formerly Burma, 88%), Japan (78%), and Korea (45%). Many millions of Buddhists once lived in China, but their number dwindled dramatically with the advent of the Communist system. Buddhism has been making a comeback in China in recent years, and there are now an estimated 13,000 temples and 200,000 monks and nuns. Tibet's population was, until recently at least, almost entirely Buddhist. Between six hundred thousand and a million Buddhists, representing all major denominations, live in the United States.

Have Buddhists traditionally sent out **missionaries** to convert others?

Buddhism's vigorous missionary heritage is traditionally traced to Kings Ashoka (270–230 BCE) and Kanishka (r. c. 120–160 CE). The first is said to have converted to

Reducing Crime and Maintaining Order According to the Buddha

The Buddha believed that there is a direct correlation between crime and poverty. Because crime and immorality lead to poverty, it would be useless to suppress crime through punishment. The Buddha preached that if society were to improve the economic conditions of the poor, then crime would cease. Order could be maintained through mutual love, affection, and respect between citizens.

The Buddha not only preached these utopian ideals but also experimented with them. For example, governing the society of Buddhist monks and nuns is a strict code of vows enforcing the Buddha's vision. Every gift received is to be collectively held in the name of the group, not the individual.

Buddhism after repenting of his bloody conquests. Ashoka declared the Buddha's teaching the official creed of the realm. Tradition credits Kanishka with supplying a major impetus to Buddhism's spread into central and eastern Asia. Monks (and, to a lesser extent, nuns) have historically been the most important and effective missionaries. Wherever they traveled they carried sacred texts and art as their prime teaching tools. Buddhist missionary work continues in the form of various contemporary adaptations of traditional methods of evangelization. They call their missionary workers *dhammadutas,* those who spread the Dharma, convinced of the universal relevance of the teaching. In much of Theravada southeast Asia, missionaries continue to bring the message of Buddhism to rural areas. In Thailand, for example, teams of five travel about from March to June, then return to monasteries for the rainy season retreat. They begin by setting up a monastery and training young boys in the temple compound. Eventually they start to visit homes and ask about people's general well-being. The next step is to start elementary schools and encourage youngsters to enter the monastic life.

Are there any Buddhist **holy sites** or **cities**?

Important to Buddhists universally are the places associated with central events in the life of the Buddha. Sites identified with his birth (the Lumbini Grove), enlightenment (Bodhgaya), first sermon (the Deer Park near Benares), and entering into nirvana (Kushinagara), are at the top of the list. Pilgrims from all over the world now travel to India on pilgrimage to these and dozens of other locations of slightly lesser importance. No one city in India functions for Buddhists quite the way Mecca, Jerusalem, and Rome do for Muslims, Jews, and many Christians. Various cities have become associated with important Buddhist temples and monasteries, but they have rarely if ever attracted pilgrims precisely as cities. Instead pilgrims head for specific sites and

333

temples. Outside India, dozens of places are sacred to members of the various Buddhist denominations. Many are associated with mountains. Ancient pre-Buddhist traditions in both China and Japan, for example, attributed supreme sanctity to the high places that, according to some spiritual maps, marked the outer limits of the cosmos at the cardinal points. Different sects and lineages often chose mountains for their spiritual centers because of the centrality of Mt. Meru in ancient Hindu myth. Mountains symbolize a point of interconnection among the several levels of the cosmos. They also can be readily imagined as huge mandalas around which spiritual seekers circumambulate en route to the center.

What are the main **sub-communities** or **denominations** within Buddhism?

There are three major subdivisions of the Buddhist tradition. Theravada ("Wisdom of the Elders") Buddhism predominates in Sri Lanka and throughout most of southeast Asia, with the exception of Vietnam. Of the over half-dozen (some say as many as eighteen) so-called Hinayana ("small vehicle") schools that developed in India by the second century BCE, the Theravada alone has survived in numbers into modern times. Mahayana ("great vehicle") Buddhism in a large number of sub-denominations and schools took hold particularly in northeastern Asia—China, Korea, and Japan. Vajrayana ("thunderbolt vehicle") Buddhism consists of several schools of esoteric thought and practice. They took hold particularly in the Himalayan region, in countries such as Tibet, Nepal, Sikkim, and Bhutan.

Who are **Theravada** Buddhists?

Theravada Buddhists are members of a more or less homogeneous community of faith and worship built around the notion that the Buddha was a human being who taught by example. The historical Buddha, Siddhartha Gautama, was the last of many non-human and human reincarnations of the Buddha-to-be. A separate school from the second council on in the fourth century BCE, their main scriptures are called collectively the Pali Canon. Theravadins seek deliverance from rebirth by eliminating craving and ignorance through self-discipline. The ideal and model of the enlightened life is the *arhat*. Arhats benefit others chiefly by their example, and they possess no saving power as such. They embody primarily the virtue of wisdom. Their ultimate goal, nirvana, is a state beyond this world of samsara in which the liberated person experiences neither desire nor impressions of any kind. Theravada sources describe nirvana as a permanent pleasant state of knowledge, freedom, and peace that is largely the result of a process of personal effort. When Theravadins pray, their primary intent is more to honor the Buddha than to worship him. All good acts, including religious ritual, done with proper intent can help one gain merit toward the eradication of negative karma. For most Theravada Buddhists, the concepts of merit making and merit transfer are more basic and accessible than the kind of lofty ethical and spiritual discipline embodied in an arhat. There are, of course, some regional and cultural variations in Theravada expression and practice, but considerably less so than in the other main branches of Buddhist tradition.

Who are **Mahayana** Buddhists?

By contrast, Mahayana Buddhists belong to a wide variety of sub-communities for whom the historical Buddha called Siddhartha Gautama was one of many manifestations of enlightenment capable of saving those who ask for help. Mahayana scriptures evolved in some half-dozen languages over many centuries as the tradition moved through Asia. Mahayana teaching universalized a number of classical Buddhist concepts, broadening their popular appeal and expanding the religious options available to ordinary folk. For example, Mahayana teaching regarded the historical Buddha of this age, Siddhartha Gautama, as only one of many embodiments of enlightenment. Not merely an ethical model, the Buddha was actually a world-filling spiritual presence and power. The compassionate Bodhisattva supplanted the more self-contained arhat as a religious ideal. Bodhisattvas represented saving grace as well as a lofty goal to which any person might aspire. Mahayana teachings expanded still further by personifying wisdom as a feminine principle, attractive and accessible. At the same time, somewhat paradoxically, Mahayana tradition was also a great deal more open to the sort of speculative thinking most Theravadins considered fruitless. Mahayana philosophers developed the concept of "emptiness" (*shunyata*), for example, as a way of emphasizing the futility of clinging to anything at all, even to neat doctrinal distinctions. Of the dozen or so Mahayana schools and denominations that arose in India, China, and Japan, two deserve special mention here. First and most popular are the Pure Land communities. Amitabha (Amida in Japan), one of the five transcendent or "meditational" Buddhas, rules the western paradise called the Pure Land. Devotees seek rebirth in that heavenly realm through various spiritual means, including the simple repetition of phrases such as "Glory to Amida Buddha." In addition, several major Chan (Zen in Japan) lineages have been extraordinarily influential in eastern Asia. The Soto school emphasizes quiet, methodical meditation, while the Rinzai school uses, in addition, the mind-stopping device called the *koan* to hasten the seeker's experience of enlightenment.

Who are **Vajrayana** Buddhists?

Vajrayana Buddhism consists of a number of schools and lineages that blended Mahayana concepts with the esoteric interpretations of Hinduism's Tantric schools. Local pre-Buddhist elements of shamanism and folk religion gave further distinctiveness to the different schools. In some places, Vajrayana (also called Tantrayana, "esoteric vehicle") has blended with popular traditions. In the monasteries the monks and mystical adepts engage in arcane rituals open only to initiates, but the monks also minister to the public through more accessible teaching and worship. Monastic institutions have dominated much of everyday life in the Himalayan nations and, until recently, to a greater degree than elsewhere in Asia. Many of the largest and most powerful monasteries are perched high above cities and villages so that their physical setting is itself an unmistakable symbol of their centrality. Before the Chinese takeover of Tibet, as many as one out of five Tibetans were monks or nuns. Some half a dozen major monastic orders developed, of which the Dalai Lama's Gelug-pa Order is now the best known. Vajrayana Buddhists developed their own extensive sacred scriptures, largely by way of translation of Indian Sanskrit and Chinese texts. In 108 volumes the Kanjur ("Translation of the Word") includes monastic regulations along with philosophy. The 225 volume Tanjur ("Translation of Treatises") includes Sutras, Tantras, and commentaries on them. Perhaps most distinctive of the various Vajrayana schools is the use of special ritual symbolism and meditative techniques to achieve their spiritual objectives. Visualization techniques and highly developed forms of chanting assist the meditator toward union with the divine center. Outside Tibet and the other Himalayan nations, Vajrayana tradition exercised considerable influence on the increasingly esoteric Japanese Shingon school.

What **gender-related issues** are important for Buddhists?

Tradition has it that the Buddha rejected various forms of social discrimination deeply embedded in the Indian culture of his day. He is said to have repudiated caste distinctions altogether. The Buddha's attitudes toward the place of women in religion and society also represented a step forward in some respects, but many problems remained. When the Buddha's aunt, who had raised him after his mother died, asked to be allowed into the Sangha, the Buddha balked. Only after a prominent monk named Ananda took up the woman's cause did the Buddha relent. So began the Buddhist order of nuns, but female members of the Order have never achieved the status of their male counterparts. There has been a breakdown in the lineage of the nuns' Sangha—a complete rupture, according to some historians. Some women continue to live in community and call themselves nuns, but they lack official sanction. A sore point for many women has been that classical Buddhist teaching says that women must be reborn as men before having a chance at nirvana. Still, it appears that early Buddhist tradition did introduce significant improvements in the lot of many women in India. No longer merely the possessions of their men, women had a larger purpose than childbearing, had personal psychic lives and could seek their own spiritual goals. So much of the gender-bias that persists everywhere in our world has a great deal more to do with culture than with any one religious tradition as such. Interaction of religious tradition and culture often makes it impossible to distinguish between the two. But it is not uncommon for people in any given culture to claim religious sanction for time-honored values and practices even when the religious tradition's sources offer little support for them.

What does one do to **convert to Buddhism?**

Since Buddhist tradition generally does not emphasize doctrine, becoming a Buddhist ordinarily does not involve lengthy periods of education or examination on the teachings. Various Buddhist organizations do, however, produce catechism-like texts designed for beginners interested in joining the faith. There is no universally practiced ritual for welcoming converts. Perhaps the single most important ritual element in the process of becoming a Buddhist is the taking of the Three Refuges. Many who decide to become Buddhists seek the tutelage of a spiritual guide, especially in the various Zen and Tibetan organizations. Unlike converts to some other traditions, new Buddhists seem to be less concerned with seeking "salvation" than with finding a personally satisfying approach to everyday life. It is perhaps ironic that a tradition that de-emphasizes doctrine attracts more people committed to studying the tradition in depth than do many traditions in which doctrine plays a more central role. Above all, Buddhists almost universally agree that nothing in any religious doctrinal system leads to salvation in itself.

What are some of the main features of Buddhism's **relationships to other traditions**?

Buddhism's most important connections historically have been with Hinduism, out of which it grew, and the major indigenous traditions of the Asian lands to which it spread. Over the centuries Buddhists have therefore interacted primarily with Hindus, Daoists, Confucians, and adherents of Shinto. An earlier question outlined crucial features Buddhism's relationship to Hinduism. Here are some features of Buddhism's conceptual connections with the other traditions. China's ancient Daoist tradition made room for the Buddha among the swelling ranks of its deities, even claiming that foundational figure Lao Zi had himself become a Buddha. Dharma, some scholars argued, was the Buddhist analogy to the concept of the Way or Dao. They suggested further parallels between the Buddhist Arhat and the Daoist Immortal, and between nirvana and the concept of non-action. Confucian tradition also found ways of accommodating to the newcomer. Some scholars saw in Buddhist ethics a parallel to Confucian filial piety, even though Buddhist elevation of celibate monasticism seemed quite irreconcilable with the Confucian emphasis on family life. To Buddhism's "Five Precepts" some likened Confucianism's "Five Constant Virtues." When Buddhist missionaries brought the new teaching to Japan, the Buddha met the *kami* ("high beings") of the indigenous tradition called Shinto. As was so often the case in China and elsewhere, Buddhism's ability to survive and grow in its new environment depended a great deal on royal patronage. Imperial support gave impetus to various Buddhist-Shinto accommodations. Shinto's Sun Goddess, Amaterasu, became a counterpart to the Buddha of Infinite Light, Vairochana. Hachiman, Shinto deity of war, dressed as a Buddhist monk and became the guardian of the great Buddha. And in Mahayana teaching's multiple Buddhas and Bodhisattvas some saw parallels to Shinto's countless *kami*. Representatives of various Buddhist denominations have continued active dialogue with other traditions, especially through the monastic connection.

337

LEADERSHIP, AUTHORITY, ORGANIZATION

How and where do members of **local Buddhist communities** come together?

Temples are the focal point of Buddhist activity in most places. Many temples are free-standing institutions, while others are part of larger monastic complexes. At the heart of the temple is the primary ritual space. Some can accommodate sizable groups, but since ordinary Buddhist ritual tends to be an individual matter, central worship spaces are generally not strikingly capacious. Larger temples nowadays often have other facilities dedicated to communal functions on special occasions. People might visit their local temples individually or in smaller groups at any time on any day.

How do **monasteries** function in Buddhist life?

During the early centuries of Buddhism monks and nuns lived as itinerant beggars with no fixed abode. The practice of staying put during the monsoon season gave rise to permanent monastic institutions. Monks and nuns lived either in *viharas,* separate structures, or dwellings carved like caves into hillsides (*guhas*). Many early monasteries functioned somewhat like parishes, offering spiritual services to the local population. These smaller, more pastorally oriented monasteries were eventually replaced by larger monastic complexes with a focus on learning. Many monasteries, especially in Theravada lands, still offer educational services to the people of the area. In general, Theravada monasteries throughout southeast Asia maintain somewhat more active links with the outside community than do Mahayana monasteries. Japanese Zen monasteries, for example, still focus on a life of seclusion and solitude. Tibetan institutions have until recently been the virtual backbone of community life on the "Roof of the World" and were home to an extraordinarily large percentage of the male population. Some monasteries are now part of what one might call consortiums, with as many as two dozen individual "temple monasteries" of the same denomination clustered within one larger institution. Most classic monasteries are walled enclosures divided into private and public areas. Monks' residences and private ritual spaces are separated from the ritual and educational facilities that serve visitors.

Do Buddhists have a system of **religious law**?

A great deal of the Hindu tradition of religious law that affected the young Siddhartha's life concerned ritual stipulations and social restrictions. By fundamentally rejecting Vedic ritual practice as ineffectual and the caste system as discriminatory, the Buddha virtually wiped out at a stroke any need for much of the kind

Is there a central teaching authority for Buddhists?

No single individual or institutional center claims central authority to all Buddhists. Not long after the Buddha's death various interpretations of his teaching gave rise to distinct schools of thought, and eventually, of practice. Perhaps the closest approximation to centralized authority in the history of Buddhism are the various councils convened over many centuries. Most Buddhists concur on the authority of the first three monastic convocations, convened about a century apart, with the first only months after the Buddha's death. Members took up a range of issues, from the particulars of monastic discipline, to the shape of the canonical scriptures, to doctrinal differences. But Buddhists disagree on the number of authentic councils, and even the universally acknowledged councils have exercised limited authority. Today, many non-Buddhists think immediately of the Dalai Lama as a major Buddhist leader and authority figure. Even though the Dalai Lama has enormous moral authority and commands the respect of Buddhists in many communities, his role remains quite different from that of the Pope or the College of Cardinals in Roman Catholicism.

of legislation that is so central to religious systems such as Hinduism, Judaism, and Islam. Buddhist tradition does, however, have its own distinctive regulatory concerns. They have to do mostly with individual conduct. The eight-spoked Wheel of the Law symbolizes Buddhist ethical teaching in general. What about more specific directives? One of the earliest scriptures in the Pali Canon is the Vinaya Pitaka, the Basket of Discipline. Buddhist law generally emphasizes the "Thou shalt nots" over the "Thou shalts." On the negative side, the Vinaya lists several hundred actions considered offensive and unacceptable behavior for monks and nuns. Of those, some 250 apply to monks and 348 to nuns. Topping the list for all monks and nuns is a group of ten precepts that forbid lying, intoxicating substances, adultery, theft, killing, eating after noon, elegant beds, cosmetics, frivolous entertainment, and possession of luxuries. The first five also apply to lay persons, who might also choose to observe the next three on the four special monthly "duty days" or sabbaths. Monks and nuns are automatically expelled from the monastic community for killing a human being or an animal, grand larceny, or sexual misconduct. Other important categories in monastic law include offenses that require a community consultation, those that call for restitution of some kind (return of goods improperly received), and issues of due process in resolving problems. Apart from these specific regulations, Buddhist teaching offers a number of more general guidelines for lay people. It recommends, for example, seeking adequate income, acquiring a professional skill, frugality, freedom from debt, and giving generously to good causes.

Are there religious **hierarchical structures** in any branch of Buddhism?

Early Buddhist teaching replaced the caste system's dramatic social and religious stratification with an egalitarian ideal. "Be a lamp unto your own feet," the Buddha counseled his followers. His rejection of a mediating priesthood made the Buddha a sort of "protestant reformer." He wanted the life of the Sangha to represent a perfectly level playing field. In practice, the elevation of the monastic life over that of the laity introduced a kind of stratification into Buddhist life. Within the early monastic community seniority alone distinguished one member from another. As the Sangha expanded and the itinerant mendicants began to settle into fixed residences, monastic life became more complex and required a division of labor. Though many decisions were taken by a monastic council, a de facto hierarchy developed. At the top was the abbot, assisted by spiritual guides and preceptors chosen from among the senior monks. The majority of the community was made up of senior monks and nuns and novices. In addition, many of the denominations eventually took on a semblance of hierarchical organization. But there is a major difference between the function of such organizational structures in Buddhist institutions and parallels in traditions like Roman Catholicism and Shi'ite Islam. Buddhist hierarchies seem to evolve as a result of internal structural needs rather than as a result of doctrine. Traditions that teach the need for mediators between ordinary people and the ultimate sources of truth and spiritual power develop hierarchical structures for theoretical as well as practical reasons.

What are some of the main varieties of Buddhist **religious officials** or **specialists**?

Each of the many distinct denominations and their constituent religious institutions has its characteristic division of labor. One way to keep it all straight is to think in terms of the four functional categories of administration, instruction, pastoral care, and spiritual example. There is naturally some overlapping, but the four categories offer an idea of the kinds of responsibilities and duties Buddhists consider most important. Denominations, monastic institutions, and local temples all have administrative structures and offices. Buddhists use terms roughly equivalent to bishop, abbot, and chief priest or pastor in this regard. Teachers or preceptors are charged with instructing both monastic and lay Buddhists especially in the meditative disciplines. At the local level, priests and monks who serve the public in monastery temples and chapels fulfill the pastoral care function, offering such services as counseling and visiting the sick, as well as leadership in worship. A final category that is in many ways distinctively Buddhist and yet difficult to define is that of spiritual exemplar. Here are located all the various ranks of revered patriarchs, founders, incarnations of previous holy persons, and individuals celebrated for teaching by example. Tibetan Buddhists, for example, call such people by various titles including *lama, rinpoche,* and *tulku.*

Cave Monasteries

From as early as the second century CE, Buddhists tunneled into mountains to establish temples and even entire monasteries out of the rock. Known for their temples with internal *stupas* set in a sanctuary, many of the early cave monasteries such as Bhaja, Bhedsa, and Karli are all within reach of Bombay, India. Many others, such as those at Ellora and Ajanta, display extremely well preserved murals, statues, and other symbols of Buddhist iconography dating from the first century BCE to the ninth century CE.

What is a **monk** and how are Buddhist **monasteries** organized?

In its wider sense, "monk" refers to any male Buddhist who enters a monastic institution, whether permanently or for a short time, receiving at least the lower ordination to the status of novice (*shramanera*). Strictly speaking, a monk is a male at least twenty years old who has been in the monastery at least five years and received the higher ordination to the status of *bhikshu* ("mendicant"). Monasteries are generally independent and autonomous foundations. Rather like Benedictine monasteries in Roman Catholicism (a very loose analogy), Buddhist monasteries of the same lineage or "order" are administered separately. Each monastery's internal structure combines offices—positions assigned by a monastic council or other governing body—and ranks—distinctions often based on seniority or spiritual acumen. Offices in a Japanese Zen monastery include, for example, chief abbot (in a complex with many sub-monasteries and temples), abbot (*kancho*), Zen master (*roshi*), meditation leader and disciplinarian (*jikijitsu*) in the Zendo or meditation hall, administrator of the Zendo (*jisha*), and head cook. An important rank is that of head monk (*jushoku*), who might also hold the office of abbot in a sub-temple. Similarly, in Thai Theravada monasteries offices include abbots and meditation masters, and recognize various ranks, such as those of elder *(thera,* ten years' seniority), and great elder (*mahathera,* with twenty years' seniority).

What is a Buddhist **nun**?

The Buddha himself decided, not without hesitation, to institute a female counterpart to male membership in the monastic Sangha. Nuns, called *bhikshunis* or "female mendicants," had from the start to defer to monks and were required to abide by over a hundred additional disciplinary regulations. Many scholars note that the formal lineage of the order of Buddhist nuns has long since been disrupted. Still, groups of women throughout Asia live in community and consider themselves members of the Sangha. Most shave their heads, wear monastic garb, and live according to traditional norms and engage in practices such as scriptural recitation. Representatives of several Chinese lineages are perhaps the most numerous. Like their male counterparts, nuns also undergo a period of training as novices before they can be considered for higher ordination to full monastic membership. Once presented by her sponsor, the candidate submits to an in-depth questioning as to her suitability. If she passes, a senior nun proposes acceptance. Then the candidate is questioned again by a panel of monks. Passing that, the candidate is sent back to her sisters for further training and acceptance into the higher initiation.

Do Buddhist **communities** run **private religious schools**?

In some parts of the world traditional Buddhist religious education remains important. In southeast Asia and Sri Lanka, for example, devout Buddhists still send their children for instruction in the local monastery. Nearly half of Thailand's primary schools are those of the local *Wats* or temples, and some monks travel to other schools to teach. Adults may also attend classes, lectures, and educational sermons. Monks naturally get their core religious training within the monastery's own educational structure, but "skill-in-means" requires that an effective person know how to put that learning into action. Some Thai universities have developed special curricula designed to aid the monks in their wider ministry. They can take courses in a range of socially oriented subjects and skills, including public health and hygiene, food preparation, construction of roads and bridges, temple and village organizing, agricultural development, and conflict resolution.

PERSONALITIES AND POWERS

What is a **lama**? Is it anything like a **rinpoche** or a **tulku**?

A *lama* (Tibetan term meaning "none higher") is a teacher or guru in the tradition of Vajrayana Buddhism associated especially with Tibet. Many lamas are monks, but membership in the monastic Sangha is not a prerequisite. Whether monk or layman, a lama is one who represents the Buddha's teaching best of all. A lama's role is somewhat broader than that of the traditional Hindu guru in that lamas lead religious rituals as well as offering instruction about them. Extensive study and meditation includes a three-year period of seclusion. Some lamas, distinguished for their learning and spiritual attainment, receive the honorific title of *rinpoche,* "precious being." Some rinpoches have the further distinction of being considered reincarnations of some earlier figure. A *tulku* ("transformation body") can reincarnate the spirit of former leaders of a religious order or even be manifestations of a Buddha or Bodhisattva. In every case the individual tulku deliberately chooses to be reincarnated in a particular time and place, whereas the average person does not exercise such discretion. When certain signs appear, religious officials must investigate carefully to determine whether a possible tulku meets all the criteria. The three lamas currently most visible and influential are the Dalai Lama, symbolic leader of the Tibetan people, the Panchen Lama, generally considered the Dalai Lama's spiritual representative and associated with the Buddha Amitabha, and the Bogdo Lama who leads Mongolia's Buddhist community.

Who is the **Dalai Lama** and why is he important to so many Buddhists?

The man known the world over as the Dalai Lama is the fourteenth in a series of sacred figures believed to be reincarnations of the Bodhisattva Avalokiteshvara as well as of the preceding Dalai Lama. The original Dalai Lama was head of the Gelug-pa order on whom a Mongol leader bestowed the title, which means "teacher of ocean-wide wisdom," in 1578. Tenzin Gyatso is the current Dala Lama and a monk of the Tibetan Gelug-pa order. When the thirteenth Dalai Lama died, in 1933, officials of the order began investigations in search of his successor. They found three likely candidates, baby boys who manifested certain special signs. They chose Tenzin, born in 1935, and in 1940 brought him to the Potala Palace in Lhasa to begin his monastic life. His extensive training included studies in philosophy and the arcane scriptures of the Vajrayana tradition, as well as meditative disciplines. He learned the difficult skill of Tibetan ritual chanting, with its strikingly deep pitch and haunting overtones. Outsiders often find it difficult to understand why the monks would take a baby away from his family to sequester him for a life of spiritual discipline. Tibetans see it all as part of a much larger picture. A family could scarcely hope for a greater blessing. But the Dalai Lama's traditional role in Tibetan history has not always found him enjoying the serenity of monastic meditation. Dalai Lamas have traditionally been important political leaders in Tibet. When the Chinese invaded Tibet in 1950, they put increasing pressure on the Dalai Lama. He went into exile in India in 1959. From his headquarters in Dharmsala, His Holiness has continued to represent the cause of the oppressed Tibetan people. He has written several books that explain beautifully the genuinely open and universally tolerant teaching he espouses.

What is a **Roshi**?

The Japanese term *roshi* means "old (i.e. venerable) teacher." It is the title of the spiritual master in Zen monasteries. Monks admitted to the Zen life must submit themselves entirely to the direction of the Roshi, however harsh and unrelenting his discipline may seem. Regular activities in which Roshi and monks encounter each other include the master's instructions to the group and monks' individual sessions in the Roshi's room. A Roshi's instructions (*teisho, koza*) take place in a lecture hall. Accompanied by two assistant monks, the Roshi burns incense before the Buddha image. After the monks recite sacred texts, the Roshi assumes his teaching chair and teaches for about an hour, using short narratives and parables and concluding with a specific case of the issue he has been discussing. The monks are left to ponder the matter in depth. During the week-long retreats, called [*Dai-*]*sesshin* ([the great] "collecting thoughts"), that occur monthly during the traditional rainy season seclusion, the Roshi gives instructions daily. Ordinarily, individual monks will have the opportunity for voluntary individual sessions with the Roshi at regular intervals during the course of daily order. But during the Dai-sesshin they will each see him briefly four times daily to discuss their koan or their progress in meditation. These sessions, called *sanzen,* are not a simple chat. There is no small talk with the Roshi. In a few choice words, the monk signals to the teacher whether he is making genuine progress. If he talks nonsense, the Roshi will toss him out unceremoniously with an admonition to get serious. One of Zen's greatest teachers, Dogen (1200–53), described the ideal roshi as able to transmit the Dharma, warm but able to be harsh when necessary, standing in the Buddha's place in educating, humble enough to ask his monks' forgiveness, uninterested in fame or prestige, and concerned above all with simplicity. When it seems appropriate the monk and the Roshi might even share a hearty laugh.

Have there been important Buddhist **mystics**?

If transforming encounter with mystery and the cultivation of mental and spiritual states beyond everyday awareness counts as mysticism, then Buddhist tradition can certainly claim its mystics. But there are important differences between Buddhist mysticism and those of traditions such as Hinduism, Islam, and Christianity. All three of those traditions talk of at least two large categories of extraordinary spiritual experience. In "theistic" or "dualistic" mystical experience, the human person meets the divine "other" but retains his or her individuality. In "monistic" or "cosmic" mysticism, the human person becomes one with (or realizes the oneness that already exists in) an ultimate reality, with no trace of individuality surviving. Buddhist teaching insists that there is no "self" to begin with, so neither of those two models quite fits. True, some Buddhist schools use the language and symbolism of deity and union, but they understand those symbols as meditative aids rather than representations of metaphysical realities. So what "happens" in Buddhist mysticism? Some sources talk of realizing the "emptiness" of all things. Profound experience of the meaning of the Four Noble Truths transcends all ordinary levels of awareness. It is possible to attain nirvana in this life—"nirvana with a remainder" they call it—and that means full insight into the way things are. One who arrives at such a state of "objectless contemplation" might justifiably be called a Buddhist mystic.

Is there such a thing as a Buddhist **saint**?

Nearly all of the Mahayana denominations look to special embodiments of holiness for guidance, inspiration, and even the occasional miracle. Japanese Buddhists call some

The Ten Paramitas ("Great Virtues") of the Bodhisattva

The following ten virtues are to be attained after continuing efforts in numerous past lives as Buddha-to-be:

Charity
Morality
Renunciation
Wisdom
Effort
Patience
Truth
Determination
Universal love
Equanimity

of these figures *shonin,* an honorific designation bestowed especially on patriarchs and founders of lineages and denominations. A group called the "Eighteen Lohans" (*lohan* is derived from the Sanskrit term *arhat*) are set apart from the Buddha's earliest disciples as uniquely sacred because of their unselfish commitment to spreading the Dharma rather than retire into peaceful solitude. Theravada tradition still uses the term *arhat* ("worthy one") to refer to a living embodiment of sanctity and wisdom. But the arhat remains an ethical model only, and a rather distant ideal at that. Mahayana teaching sees the Bodhisattva as the ultimate in human potential. Some even confer the title on living individuals, such as the Dalai Lama. Bodhisattvas not only model spiritual perfection, but function as mediators as well. As emissaries of the various Buddhas, they exercise saving power and make comforting grace available to all who ask.

Have there been any important Buddhist **religious reformers***?*

Many of the various Buddhist denominations and sects are the result of attempts at reform. Some people even regard the Buddha himself as one who sought to reform Hinduism. Among the best examples of religious reformers are those who aimed to rescue Buddhist teaching from complex formulas and make it accessible to real people. Tradition calls Bodhidharma (d. 532) the first patriarch of Chinese Zen. Apparently quite a colorful character, Bodhidharma criticized several schools for getting lost in their own long-winded treatises. Toss all the superfluous verbiage, he advised, and focus on direct Dharma-transmission from master to student. About three centuries later in Japan, two other reformers set out to develop spiritual methods that would appeal to a broader public than some of the schools that had arrived in Japan during

Statue of the thousand-armed, eleven-headed bodhisattva Guan Yin, in a religious goods store, Keelung, Taiwan, the port city of the Taiwanese capital of Taipei.

the previous several centuries. Kukai (744–835) and Saicho (762–822) founded the Tendai and Shingon lineages, respectively. But eventually Tendai turned more speculative and Shingon more mystical and esoteric. Further reform developments eventually grew out of Tendai in the twelfth and thirteenth centuries. A Tendai monk, Honen (1133–1212), started a Japanese branch of Pure Land in hope of attracting people with its reliance on Amida Buddha. A successor named Nichiren (1222–82) took Honen's insights a step further, insisting that a devotee approaching in good faith had only to repeat the name of the scripture called the Lotus of the Good Law Sutra—a mantra popular singer Tina Turner recommends—to be assured of salvation.

Who is the **Bodhisattva Guan Yin**?

Next to the various Buddhas, Guan Yin is certainly one of the most important and popular sacred figures in Buddhist tradition. This Bodhisattva began life, mythically speaking, as a male guardian figure named Avalokiteshvara, the "Lord Who Looks Down." Known in China as Guan Yin and in Japan as Kannon, he was originally one of Vairochana's (the central figure among the Five Transcendent Buddhas) attendants, presiding over the cosmic northwest. Avalokiteshvara came to be particularly associated with compassion when paired with the Bodhisattva Manjushri, who represented wisdom. Boundless in his care for all, the compassionate one has appeared with multiple heads and arms—one of the few Bodhisattvas to be commonly so depicted. As Mahayana communities grew in China, Guan Yin's perfect compassion gradually transformed him into a female Bodhisattva. With a thousand arms and eleven heads,

346

The Eightfold Noble Path

Proper understanding of the Four Noble Truths

Proper intent
Proper speech
Proper action
Proper livelihood
Proper effort
Proper attentiveness
Proper absorption

Guan Yin often has a decidedly feminine countenance. But she appears more often as a kindly woman smiling gently and inclined slightly toward her devotees. In more recent times people have begun to call her more ordinary human manifestation the "Goddess of Mercy," a convenient but misleading epithet that resulted from Buddhism's interaction with Chinese popular religious lore. In Japan, the thousand-armed, eleven-headed Kannon often appears in multiple images within the same temple, sometimes even as a life-sized sculpture. Popular lore claims that each Kannon has a different face to symbolize this Bodhisattva's undivided attention to every single person on earth.

Do Buddhists believe in **angels**?

Buddhist popular belief inherited and retained many of the different types of celestial and semi-divine beings that populated Hindu myth. Nearly all Hindu deities have their personal attendants. In addition, a variety of other spiritual presences fill the heavenly and earthly realms. Artists often depict these characters as floating gracefully, but they generally lack the wings most people associate with angels. A class of being called *apsaras* (Sanskrit for "moving in water") are the most numerous of these denizens of the intermediate realm. Early Buddhist artists sometimes depicted apsaras as devotees worshiping the Buddha's footprints or gathered around the tree of enlightenment. Another group, called the *gandharvas,* were Hindu demigods who entertained the deities as musicians and dancers. Buddhist tradition retained them in that capacity. The classic angelic function of guardianship and protection resides in other classes of beings regarded as gods in some sects. *Lokapalas* ("World Guardians") are those who stand watch over the four quarters of the universe. Many Buddhist temples depict them as muscular, heavily armed gatekeepers. The *dharmapalas* ("Guardians of the Teaching") are a band of fearsome deities whose task is to guard believers (especially in Vajrayana). As a kind of personal deity assigned to each individual, these protectors can take on either benevolent or angry form, depending on whether they are dealing with a believer or with an enemy of the faith.

The monk Eisai

The Japanese Buddhist monk Eisai (1141–1215) introduced the Zen Buddhist Rinzai sect to Japan, and under him Zen first became acknowledged as an independent school of Buddhism. He is also responsible for popularizing the cultivation of tea in Japan.

Also known by his honorific title of Zenko Kokushi (national teacher), Eisai came from a family of Shinto priests in the district of Okayama. Like many famous priests in his period, he studied at the great Tendai center on Mt. Hiei. In 1168 he made his first trip to China, where he visited Zen centers, especially those flourishing on Mt. Tian Tai. He was much impressed by what he saw and felt with growing conviction that Zen could contribute greatly to a reawakening of Buddhist faith in Japan.

In 1187 he undertook a second trip to the continent for the purpose of tracing the origins of Buddhism to India. The authorities, however, refused him permission to go beyond Chinese borders. He studied on Mt. Tian Tai until 1191, where he was ordained in the Rinzai (Chinese, Lin Chi) sect and returned to Japan. He constructed the first Rinzai temple, the Shofukuji, at Hakata in Kyushu.

Eisai proclaimed the superiority of Zen mediation over other Buddhist disciplines, thus provoking the ire of the Tendai monks who sought to outlaw the new sect. However, Eisai enjoyed the protection of the shogun Minamoto Yoriie, and in 1202 he was given the direction of the Kenninji in Kyoto. Like Saicho, and particularly Nichiren, Eisai associated his type of Buddhism with national welfare and promoted Zen by publishing a tract entitled *Kozen Gokoku Ron* (The Propagation of Zen for the Protection of the Country).

Do Buddhists believe in **devils**?

Perhaps the closest thing in Buddhism to what many readers think of when they hear the word "devil" is the arch-demon Mara. As the Buddha achieved enlightenment, Mara assailed him in hopes of preventing him from sharing his new-found wisdom. Mara summoned up his own three seductive daughters as well as his hateful host of demons. Various troublesome beings, from the mildly mischievous to the viciously malevolent, haunt the Buddhist universe at every level. Unhappy spirits of the deceased pester the living. A class of characters called "earth demons" personify various powers and riches of the earth itself. Human beings who die after a particularly unethical life may be reborn as one of a class of evil beings, inherited from Hindu tradition, called *asuras*. Just as the Buddha insisted that none of the gods could rescue anyone from the human condition, so he taught that no demonic power was great enough to destroy anyone.

Still, mainstream Buddhism has allowed room for the ranks of devilish characters that are part of indigenous popular belief systems throughout Asia.

Are **dreams and visions** important to Buddhist tradition?

Important figures in Buddhist tradition are said to have learned essential truths through dreams and visions. Queen Maya dreamed that she would give birth under unusual circumstances to a child who would become the Buddha. In dreams famous people learn of the proper course of action. Buddhist sources tell, for example, of how a dream persuaded the Chinese Emperor Ming Di to send for Buddhist missionaries and scriptures. Stories of this sort are told about many holy persons throughout Buddhist history, usually as a vehicle for underscoring the individual's personal authority. Accounts of dreams and visions are by no means uniquely Buddhist, of course, and tell us more about the tone and feel of popular Buddhist lore than about the tradition's central teachings. Visionary meditative techniques, a different matter altogether, are of great importance in some Mahayana schools. Esoteric schools, such as those of Tibetan Vajrayana Buddhism, use mandalas as visual aids in complicated techniques for creating mental images. The meditator generates a visionary world patterned on the mandala, in which the divine and the human interact and all distinctions vanish. Simpler visualization techniques are used in the more popular Pure Land tradition as well. Facing west, the meditator visualizes the sun setting, and water turning into ice. Gradually, the mind fills with images of a golden land with crystalline streams, lotus-filled lakes with golden bottoms, and shores of diamond sand. As the Pure Land, with its myriad jewelled palaces, takes shape in the mind's eye, the meditator sees the Buddha Amitabha and his attendant Bodhisattvas. At length the meditator visualizes himself being reborn into that happy land enfolded in a lotus flower.

HOLIDAYS AND REGULAR OBSERVANCES

What kind of **religious calendar** do Buddhists observe?

Since Buddhism has long been identified with so many different cultural settings, there is some variation in the ways Buddhists keep track of sacred times. The basic religious calendar remains tied, at least nominally, to the ancient Hindu combination of lunar and solar reckoning, but many Buddhists now observe some festivities on fixed dates. The earliest Buddhists apparently did not concern themselves with marking special occurrences on their calendar. But within a generation or so, India's growing and spreading Buddhist communities began to incorporate religious social occasions into ordinary life. As Buddhist communities arose outside of India they naturally tended to blend religious observances imported by Buddhist missionaries with the indigenous festivities of the land. In most places where Buddhism is an important presence today, the reckoning of years begins with the date of the Buddha's entry into Nirvana (which coincided with his death). In any given year, Buddhists observe various special occasions. Some commemorate major events in the life of the Buddha, others celebrate different institutional features of the tradition, others are tied to seasonal festivities, and still others are linked to special events only in certain countries.

Are there **cyclical observances or feasts** that occur regularly but not just once a year?

During each lunar month, many Buddhists observe four special "moon" days called *uposatha.* These are the full moon and new moon days, and days mid-way between them, or the 1st, 8th, 15th, and 23rd of the month. Originally important as fast days in ancient Hindu practice, Buddhists now attach special ceremonies to them somewhat the way Christians do to Sundays, Jews to Saturdays, and Muslims to Fridays. Lay Buddhists in some countries still regularly congregate in the local temple for a time of heightened religious discipline. Rituals include listening to a monk preach, meditating, and praying as monks chant the scriptures. Some devotees seek to gain spiritual merit by observing eight, rather than the usual five, precepts during that day. Monastic life attaches special meaning to the new and full moon days. Monks assemble then to recite the rules of monastic discipline from a text called the *Pratimoksha.* They also engage in a communal confession of faults not unlike the traditional practice known as the "Chapter of Faults" in some Christian religious orders and monastic communities. After the monks recite each prohibition in the *Pratimoksha,* they pause to allow individuals to admit any transgression. Some Buddhists engage in fasting on new and full moon days, emulating the monastic practice of taking no food between noon and breakfast the following day.

Are there **days** devoted to **other aspects** of **Buddhist teaching**?

On the full-moon day of the third lunar month of Magha, some Buddhists commemorate Buddha's teaching of the monastic disciplinary code called the Vinaya. Thais celebrate by circumambulating the chaitya and listening to a sermon in the temple. Theravada Buddhists celebrate the Buddha's first sermon on the full-moon day of Asadha (eighth lunar month) by revering the scriptural text. Some schools celebrate days dedicated to their central scriptures. For example, the denomination named after the Japanese reformer Nichiren (1222–82) honors the Lotus of the Good Law Sutra, as do other groups in China and Japan. Monasteries typically celebrate anniversaries of their founding and in some countries a festive day marks the anniversary of Buddhism's arrival with the first missionaries. Members of the Jodo Shinshu (True Pure Land) sect remember their founder Shinran (1173–1262) on the 16th of each month, and with a week-long memorial every year in either January or November.

> ## Feasts of the Buddha
>
> **B**uddhists in various places commemorate three important events in the Buddha's life: his birth, his enlightenment, and his entry into nirvana. Theravada Buddhists celebrate them all on the same day, called simply Buddha Day, on the full moon day of Vaishakha (April/May). Some Mahayana groups hold separate festivities on fixed dates, with Buddha's birth observed on April 8 (called *Hanamatsuri* in Japan), his enlightenment (called Bodhi Day) on December 8, and his final entry into Nirvana on February 15. Religious activities on these occasions include special gatherings in monastery temples. Devotees bathe images of the Buddha, listen to narratives of the Buddha's life, circumambulate his relics enshrined either in large structures called *chaityas* or small stupa- or pagoda-shaped reliquaries, and water small bodhi trees. Theravadins combine the festivities because tradition says that all three events occurred on the same day in different years. In Theravada southeast Asia, Buddha Day remains associated with the onset of the monsoon rains and the planting of the rice crop.

What observances are linked with **seasonal cycles**?

The so-called Rain Retreat (*Vassa*) begins on the day after the full-moon day of the eighth lunar month, Asadha (July/August), and continues until the full-moon day of the eleventh lunar month Ashvina (September/October). Monks spend more time in meditation and study and are expected to remain in the monastery. Lay Buddhists visit temples and monasteries more frequently than usual to receive instruction, and marriages are generally not performed. Theravada Buddhists begin the season with monastic ordinations and end it with special merit-rituals said to be in memory of Buddha's emergence from heaven. Also at the end of the retreat comes the festival called *Kathina* ("cloth"). During this joyous month-long festivity, lay people give the monks new robes and other useful gifts. This is a favored time for pilgrimages to southeast Asian sites such as Rangoon's Shwe Dagon temple and Thailand's shrine of the Buddha's Footprint. In connection with the rice harvest in February or March, Theravada devotees make merit by celebrating the story of how the Buddha-to-be entered the world as Prince Vessantara in a previous incarnation.

What about **observances** related to the **locality** or **indigenous practice**?

In many parts of the world Buddhists celebrate New Year's Day on January 1. The observance is not a specifically Buddhist tradition but has become associated with it through a process of syncretism. Japanese Buddhists observe the spring and autumn equinoxes on March 21 and September 21 respectively. A festival honoring the dead,

351

Giant statue of the Bodhisattva Guan Yin, popularly known in China as the Goddess of Mercy, flanked by a pair of protective dog-like lions, at a temple on a hill overlooking the harbor of Keelung, Taiwan.

called *Obon Matsuri,* occurs between July 13 and 15. Chinese All Souls' Day, a parallel festivity, celebrated during the seventh lunar month, features offerings thought to assist seven generations of deceased relatives. A good example of an observance linked specifically to a single region is the celebration of Buddhist Churches of America Founding Day on September 1.

Do Buddhists celebrate **feast days** of any other **important religious figures**?

In China, Japan and Tibet especially, Buddhists hold feasts in honor of various Bodhisattvas and holy persons. The death anniversary of Bodhidharma, traditionally believed to be the founding patriarch of Chinese Zen, occurs on the 5th day of the tenth lunar month, Bhadrapada (August/September). Events in the life of Tibetan Buddhism's important patriarch Padmasambhava provide a kind of narrative sacred structure for the entire year with special observances occurring on the tenth day of each lunar month. Devotees celebrate his flight from the world in the first month, his taking of religious vows in the second, and his miraculous transformation of fire into water during the third, for example. One of the most widely celebrated sacred persons is the Bodhisattva Guan Yin (called Kannon in Japan). Her special day is the 19th of a given lunar month, with her birthday occurring during the second month, her enlightenment during the sixth, and her entry into Nirvana during the ninth.

CUSTOMS AND RITUALS

What **rites** do Buddhists practice in the **temple**?

Some of the ordinary ritual activity that occurs in most Buddhist temples is communal. Congregational chanting of mantras or singing of hymns occasionally plays an important role. But a great deal of Buddhist temple ritual remains relatively unscheduled and highly individualized. Worshipers in Theravada temples sit or bow before the Buddha image and recite traditional prayers in praise of the historical Buddha. Devotees often hold as an offering a candle, flower, food, or a small parasol, symbols of respect for royalty. Offerings of flowers are particularly helpful reminders of impermanence, since they invariably wither and fade. Worshipers generally regard sacred images as aids to prayer and often also as possessing certain magical powers, but the image is not itself the Buddha. Theravada ritual aims to overcome the suffering born of inappropriate craving. Some temples have wall murals depicting scenes from the *Jataka* tales, each one exemplifying one essential virtue. Worshipers can meditate on these scenes in succession and ponder the ethical implications. Since the Buddha was like an extinct fire that needs no more fuel, people do not worship him as such. Theravada temple ritual is meant to dispose the devotee for greater spiritual development. Popular Mahayana rituals are similar in some outward respects, but they focus on the Buddha and Bodhisattvas as repositories of saving grace and power. Worship is a means to assure rebirth in one of the Buddha-lands. Rituals emphasize the need to surrender entirely to saving grace and boundless compassion. Ritual helps overcome ignorance of the ultimate sources of transforming spiritual power. Mahayana temples often display multiple images, sometimes having several walls lined with statues. Devotees can pay their respects to each, waving an incense wand clasped between folded hands as a gesture of veneration.

What rites do Buddhists practice at **home**?

Many devout Buddhists pray daily at home before their domestic shrine, a miniature version of the temple or monastic oratory. They show reverence to the image of the Buddha with incense, flower offerings, and a lighted candle. All three of these simple symbols bring home the central realization of impermanence. They give pleasure to the worshiper, who should enjoy them while they last. Unburned incense is analogous a person who does not use his or her talents. A Lotus flower is a reminder of the Buddha's being rooted in the muck of real life but blossoming above it and in spite of it. These symbols also represent homage to the Buddha, not because the Buddha needs or enjoys that, but because it focuses the mind on his message. Rituals also include reciting the "Three Refuges" and reaffirming the commitment to the "Five Precepts." Prayers of petition include the same sorts of things people of many traditions ask for—happiness, success, longevity, and salvation. Mahayana devotees might wear a small rosary around a wrist, as they often do when worshiping in the temple.

Is there a standard Buddhist **liturgical worship**?

Buddhist denominations that emphasize communal worship exhibit considerable variation in their services. Recitation of sacred texts is the single most common element. One Japanese Pure Land denomination uses the following "order of service." After a call to worship expressing prayerful intent, worshipers pronounce the "Three Refuges," invoke the presence of the Buddha, praise him, make a symbolic confession of sins, and recite the name of Amida Buddha ten times. Then follows a segment of scriptural chanting, explicitly dedicated to rebirth in the Pure Land. Again invoking the name of Amida Buddha ten times, worshipers reflect on its deeper meaning. Between two further invocations of the name they recite from the teachings of founder Honen. After a recitation of the vows of the Bodhisattva the ritual concludes with the "Three Refuges" and a final prayer to send the Buddha back to his heavenly abode.

Do Buddhists engage in **ritual sacrifice**?

Sacrifice has never been part of mainstream Buddhist ritual. The Buddha himself rejected the ancient Hindu sacrificial heritage as spiritually bankrupt, as did many others among his contemporaries. Some later popular devotional Hindu sects retained animal sacrifice as an essential feature of ritual. But Theravada and Mahayana popular devotion have, in effect, spiritualized the concept of sacrifice. Traditional forms of sacrifice typically aim to appease a divine power. Buddhist tradition virtually does away with the concept. When worshipers make offerings of flowers, incense, and other symbols, they are not giving gifts to a spiritual power but offering signs of reverence and providing reminders for themselves of life's impermanence.

What is the connection between ritual and the Theravada notion of **"making merit"**?

Some actions and attitudes take on a special ritual dimension because they are associated with the two essential spiritual activities of making and transferring merit. Actions that make merit for the individual store up positive energy needed to overcome the inappropriate craving that can prevent one from achieving liberation. These actions prominently include a group of ten: proper beliefs, reverence and service of one's elders, giving generously to monks, observing the five (or eight) precepts, various forms of meditation including recitation of scriptural verses, respect for others, preaching, hearing a sermon, empathizing with merit, and transfer of merit. When lay Buddhists commit themselves temporarily to the Eight Precepts they add the monastic practices of avoiding food after the noon meal, certain forms of entertainment, and the use of cosmetics. Some lists of merit-making deeds also include building a monastery, becoming a monk or having a son do so, donating funds for the repair of a temple, and observing every *uposatha* ("sabbath"). Transfer of merit is a doubly meritorious form of altruism, since in the very intention to share, one receives back. In fact, Buddhists characteristically see a reciprocity in all ritual deeds. Devotees give generously to monks, for example, and the monks give spiritual encouragement, good example, and teaching in return.

What is the meaning of Buddhist "ordination"?

Ordination in the Buddhist tradition does not imply the same kind of conferral of spiritual power or authority that it does in many Christian denominations. A closer parallel would be the taking of religious vows. Young men and boys in many Buddhist denominations submit themselves for ordination to the monastic sangha under a variety of circumstances. In some cultures boys as young as seven can enter the monastery and receive the "lower ordination" (*parivraja*) to the rank of novice in the order. Those who choose to stay and commit themselves to the monastic life permanently can receive the "higher ordination" (*upasampada*) to full status of monk or *bhikshu*. Ordinations are often held at the start of the Rain Retreat, and it is not unusual for young ordinands to remain in the monastery only for one rainy season. Thai men sometimes still enter the monastery for a week or less after the death of a family member. In some areas ordinations occur after rice harvest, since increased revenue makes for better celebrations, but the rituals can occur anytime outside of the Rain Retreat itself. Prospective ordinands petition the abbot of a local monastery, who might then allow them in directly if they intend only a short stay. Those who propose to remain and take the full monastic ordination eventually go through a more elaborate ritual. They kneel before ten monks and the abbot, ask permission to enter, and receive the two-piece robe of the novice. After donning the garb, the candidates recite the Three Refuges and Ten Precepts. Ordination to full membership in the monastic order repeats the novitiate ritual and adds a further examination of the candidates. Each novice receives a begging-bowl and a three-piece garment.

What is a day in the life of a **Buddhist monastery** like?

Daily monastic rituals vary somewhat according to place and denomination. Theravada monasteries revolve around the chanting of scriptures from the first two "baskets," the Vinaya and Sutra Pitakas. After waking at around three a.m., members lie prostrate together in the oratory to recite the Three Refuges and chant sutras. They spend several hours in study and meditation before heading out to beg. Breakfast precedes more communal chanting and a class on the rules of discipline. Supper is scheduled before noon, after which members spend the afternoon studying scripture and resting. More chanting, study, and prayer, along with a chance to once again examine the conscience and confess faults, bring the day to a close by ten. Theravada monks in many areas engage in considerable social service activity, assisting villagers in various kinds of practical projects and in community organization. In places like Japan, monks leave

Buddhist monk performing prayer ritual for a solitary worshiper, in a small oratory-temple at Sanzen-in temple in Ohara, near Kyoto, Japan.

the monastery on a quest for alms that is more a symbolic reminder of their dependence than a substantial necessity. Daily order is strictly regulated with relatively little time for individual activities. Certain days are designated for shaving and bathing. Zen monks engage in periods of manual labor around the monastery, such as gardening, gathering fuel, and general maintenance, and place greater emphasis on silent meditation than on recitation of scriptural texts. Each month a whole week is dedicated to virtually round-the-clock *zazen*, or sitting meditation, together in the same hall where the monks sleep. Monastic life generally allows sufficient sleep and nutritious food to maintain good health, but nothing superfluous in either case. It is a physically and psychologically demanding life. In most cases, individuals can join a monastery for a time, with the understanding that they do not intend to make a lifelong commitment to it.

What kinds of special **ritual objects** figure in Buddhist worship and prayer?

Among the most common implements used in regular ritual are acoustic devices such as bells, gongs, and hollow wooden blocks. Prayer leaders will occasionally strike a large bronze bowl-shaped bell set on a pillow. As its vibrant, mellow ring decays into silence, devotees recall the universal characteristic of impermanence. When ritual leaders, sometimes accompanied by the congregation, chant sacred texts, they generally strike a hollow block of wood rhythmically to keep chanters together in their recitation. Incense burners and containers of sand into which devotees can insert their lighted incense wands are part of nearly every ritual setting. Sometimes devotees will approach a temple's large incense cauldron, waft the smoke toward them with their hands, and then rub it on various parts of their bodies for healing and general well being. Esoteric sects typically employ a larger variety of objects. Tibetans use a small scepter symbolizing the indestructibility of the thunderbolt in one hand. The other holds a small bell whose vanishing sound represents impermanence. Some groups use weapons associated with Hindu deities who became part of the Buddhist pantheon. Some also use a begging bowl, as the Buddha did, or a fly whisk, symbol of

Worshipers at Tokyo's Asakusa Kannon temple bless themselves by wafting incense smoke from the large courtyard burner toward themselves and rubbing it on their faces and bodies.

adherence to the Dharma. Most basic among the ritual objects in both home and temple are the candle holder (one for the home, two in temple), flower vase (one at home, two in temple), and small censer. Other common objects include tablets or scrolls containing sacred names or mantras, either in Sanskrit or the vernacular.

Is **meditation** important for Buddhists?

Buddhist tradition has refined a number of meditative practices. Two important aspects taught by an ancient Theravada authority named Buddhaghosa (c. 400) are called "dwelling in tranquility" (*shamatha*) and "insight" (*vipashyana*). In order to catch the "fish" of intuitive knowledge, one has first to get to the calm, clear lake. Attaining a measure of tranquility is a process of disciplined concentration in which the meditator gradually withdraws from sensory input through nineteen successive stages of attentiveness and reflection. Insight meditation involves the discipline of observing sensory input with perfect mindfulness in order to arrive at genuine wisdom. Traditional explanations typically recommend *shamatha* before *vipashyana,* but they go together and the process may actually be circular—tranquility leading to insight leading to deeper tranquility. Buddhaghosa suggests forty objects for contemplation to eliminate distraction and lead to contemplative states. Each person is characterized by tendencies to one of the three "qualities" of lust, hatred, and delusion, and must focus on counteracting that major cause of distraction. To transform lust

357

into faith, first meditate on physical impermanence and then on the virtues of the Buddha. Transform hatred into understanding by meditating first on love, compassion, and joy, and proceed to an awareness of mortality and physical dissolution. Turn delusion to deliberation by focusing on breathing as a means to calming. As for the achievement of Insight, Buddhaghosa recommends the "Seven Purities." Here the meditator focuses on the purity of virtue, of mind, of belief, of overcoming doubt, of the knowledge of right and wrong action, of insight into spiritual progress, and of knowledge and insight themselves. Mahayana tradition adapted Buddhaghosa's classical methods to its teaching about the Bodhisattva's saving role. Each dedicated seeker progresses spiritually by meditating on the "Ten Stages" of the Bodhisattva career. This is the steepest of paths, beginning with the accumulation of merit and knowledge and proceeding through multiple levels of meditative discipline.

Do Buddhists practice rituals of **exorcism**?

Since the Buddha emphasized that the individual was the only power of ultimate significance in the quest for liberation, he saw no need for formal ritual designed to do away with negative forces. Keen awareness of one's own motives and intentions would take care of all problems. Still, Buddhist practice has absorbed various indigenous forms of exorcism from virtually every culture in which the tradition has taken root. Many of the practices still in use in Japan originated in China and were brought to Japan by founders of Japan's Tendai and Shingon sects in the early ninth century. Japan's Nichiren school, a development of Tendai tradition, acknowledges four types of demonic possession. Phenomena range from pain caused by an angry spirit, to hallucinations, to possession by some animal spirit as signaled by personality changes, to severe disorders manifested in multiple personalities and voices. Priests of the Nichiren school undergo strict ascetical preparation before performing an exorcism. Someone close to the possessed person serves as a medium to the spirit world, speaking for the possessed person and delivering answers on behalf of the forces of good. In other cases the exorcist deals directly with the possessed person. Wearing white, the exorcist recites from the principal Nichiren scripture, The Lotus Sutra, makes sharp noises using a set of wooden castanets, and interrogates the one possessed. Some Buddhists prefer exorcism as an alternative to psychotherapy.

Are **music and dance** important in Buddhist religious ritual?

Formal Buddhist rituals generally do not incorporate music as such, with the exception of more recent denominations that have absorbed practices from Protestant Christianity. Chanting and rhythmic recitation use tones other than those of normal speech but are not usually done to musical accompaniment. Buddhist rituals do, however, make extensive use of a wide variety of sounds and percussive devices. Bells, gongs, drums, hollow blocks, and clappers of many sizes are standard equipment in

Buddhist Pilgrimage

Just as meditators pursue an inward path to liberation, pilgrims seek the ultimate goal using external symbolism. Sites associated with the principal events in the life of the Buddha very soon became pilgrim goals. Some texts even suggest that the Buddha directed his followers to visit the places of his birth, enlightenment, first sermon, and entry into nirvana. But Buddhists have beaten paths to hallowed places in China and Japan as well. Chinese devotees have mapped out a sacred landscape for pilgrim itineraries centered on four sacred mountains. Individual temples have also taken on a special aura, perhaps as a result of an apparition or miracle, or by association with some famous holy person. Pilgrims head for those places both on special occasions and whenever the mood strikes them. Hoped-for spiritual benefits range from grace to get through a difficult time to healing serious illnesses. Japanese Buddhists also continue to follow a pilgrim road to numerous holy places. One of the most popular circuits is that of the Eighty-eight Temples on the island of Shikoku. There pilgrims retrace the steps of the venerable monk Kukai, founder of the Shingon denomination, from temple to temple, gathering spiritual souvenirs as they travel.

different areas of temples and monasteries. Large and medium sized bells signal the beginning of worship services, and Zen masters use smaller bells to signal the end of sessions with individual monks. Large drums announce the time for certain exercises and gatherings. The most common ritual use of sound devices is that of keeping time during recitation and chanting or scriptural texts. Hollow blocks make a hypnotic "klop" to focus the attention and heavy bronze bowls emit a rich lingering note that reminds worshipers of the impermanence of all things. The combination of sustained warm bell-like tones punctuated by stark wooden percussion is very effective and surprisingly easy to listen to. Buddhists in various parts of the world sometimes use music and dance para-liturgically—that is, outside of their primary ritual settings. Zen meditative mood, for example, is often associated with the haunting sound of the bamboo flute called the *shakuhachi,* and Tibetans have traditionally used vigorous dancing in ceremonies such as exorcism and other protective rituals.

Do Buddhists **pray** in any particular language?

Even the earliest Buddhist practice apparently did not require any particular sacred or canonical language for prayer. People recited the scriptural texts and prayed in their vernaculars. Among Theravada Buddhists, the Pali tongue, distantly related to ancient Sanskrit, has functioned something like an official or canonical language, since the Pali Canon contains their full sacred text. But Theravada Buddhists across southeast

Monk of the Son (Korean for Zen) Buddhist order in front of his cell at the To Son Sa temple, in the hills overlooking Seoul, Korea.

Asia also pray in their local languages. This all seems perfectly in character for a tradition whose foundational figure taught an egalitarian way that was neither based on any one sacred source nor structured according to any ancient hierarchy. Some of the more esoteric branches of Buddhism, however, retain the practice of using archaic texts that require special education to understand fully.

How do Buddhists celebrate **birth** or **initiation** or other **rites of passage**?

Buddhist tradition generally marks fewer of life's passages than, say, Hindu tradition, and ceremonies are typically much simpler. Rites of passage also vary considerably from one region to another. Here are a couple of representative ceremonies observed by some Japanese Buddhists of one of the Pure Land groups. A special celebration marks the child's seventh day of life. On the one hundredth day, the family gathers at the temple to symbolize the baby's taking refuge in the Three Jewels and becoming a spiritual child of the Buddha. Some Pure Land Buddhists also acknowledge a variation on the theme of "coming of age" or puberty rite. The young man or woman stands before the altar and reaffirms the desire to adhere to Buddhist values. One symbol of the young person's attainment of adulthood is a white cloth inscribed "Amida Buddha." There is no set day for these ceremonies, but they sometimes occur on anniversaries or when the Chief Abbot can be present. Rituals of death and mourning are the most important rites of passage for Buddhists generally, with nuptials perhaps second in importance.

Are there Buddhist rituals of **marriage**?

Marriage has generally not been an important religious rite of passage in Buddhist tradition. Perhaps that is because of the great emphasis on the centrality of monastic life. In various regions of Asia, other religious traditions supply the devotional settings associated with new beginnings. In Japan, for example, people generally either associate marriage with Shinto or consider it a purely civil ceremony. Some do use Buddhist symbolism in their wedding ceremonies. That might include, for example, offering incense, and receiving the rosary as a reminder of a union witnessed before the Buddha. In the United States and some other regions where Buddhist missionaries have more recently introduced the tradition, Buddhists often use a modified Protestant ceremony. Held either outdoors or in a temple, the service may include brief readings from scriptures on the theme of compassion, a period of silent meditation, and a short sermon from the officiating priest or minister. An officiating monk or priest might also chant prayers from a scripture.

How do Buddhists deal ritually with **death** and **mourning**?

Practice varies according to denomination and cultural setting, but there are a number of common elements. These include prayer at the deathbed and preparation of the body; a wake that includes final viewing; funeral service typically in a mortuary or funeral home; interment, usually of cremated remains but with full burial in some circumstances; and a series of memorial services at intervals beginning immediately after death and then in anniversary years calculated in various different ways. Viewing the body at the wake is a powerful reminder of the universal fact of impermanence. Funeral ceremonies center on recitation or chanting of appropriate sacred texts chosen to help mourners to see the event in the context of the full sweep of human existence. An officiating priest, monk, or minister may offer a eulogy, and participants make offerings of incense. In some places, like Japan, families inter the cremated remains either in a columbarium connected to a temple or in a cemetery on temple grounds. Memorial services are important in virtually all Buddhist denominations, especially when Buddhism interacts with ancient traditions of ancestor veneration. Many Mahayana Buddhists observe memorials seven, thirty-five, forty-nine and one hundred days after death, and after one, three, seven, thirteen, seventeen, thirty-three, fifty and one hundred years. Some consider the forty-ninth day especially important, since at that point the soul ceases its wandering. Theravada practice often includes memorial services two days after death at the home, two or three days after that at the funeral establishment, and again seven days after interment. The object of the last ceremony is to transfer merit from the living to the dead to ensure a good rebirth. Many Buddhists also offer a meal in the home or elsewhere for mourners after funeral services or interment.

RELIGIOUS TRADITIONS OF EAST ASIAN ORIGIN

DAOISM AND CHINESE COMMUNITY TRADITIONS

HISTORY AND SOURCES

What is religious **Daoism** and what are its **origins**?

"Daoism" refers to a wide range of philosophical, religious, and magical traditions dating from perhaps the fourth century BCE in China. Here the focus will be on the specifically religious aspects of these complex and ancient developments. The most ancient roots of the tradition were in shamanistic cults dating back perhaps several millennia to prehistoric China. Legendary imperial figures of that age, Yu, Shun, and Yao, are still revered as great sages. According to legend, Daoism formally began with Lao Zi's writing of the *Dao De Jing, the Classic of the Way and Its Power* in the sixth century BCE. Scholars now believe the *Dao De Jing* actually dates from between 300 and 250 BCE. Teachings of the *Dao De Jing* came together with those of thinkers like Yang Zhu (340–266 BCE) and Zhuang Zi(369–286 BCE) to form the broad conceptual basis of a wider "Daoist" tradition that had become largely philosophical (Dao jia) by the fourth century BCE. But religious Daoism *(Dao jiao)* was still a long way off. Solid scholarly research suggests that Daoism as a religious tradition begins in the mid–second century CE. It seems a teacher named Zhang Dao Ling (34–156 CE) claimed that Lao Zi himself commissioned him to spread the teaching of the Dao. Zhang inaugurated the "Five Bushels of Rice" movement (a reference to the suggested offering for would-be members) and built a religious polity in Szechuan province. According to legend, Zhang Dao Ling's emphasis on acquiring immortality culminated in his ascension into the heavens. Out of that movement grew the first and one of the most influential branches of religious Daoism, the Celestial Masters school. Religious Daoism has since developed numerous sects and schools, each with its distinctive emphasis on various spiritual teachings and ritual practices.

What is meant by the term "Chinese Community Traditions" (CCT)?

Much more ancient than religious or even earlier philosophical Daoism are the various currents of popular religious belief and practice that together comprise what will be referred to as Chinese Community Traditions or CCT. Historians of religion suggest that most Chinese who engage in public expression of religious beliefs actually belong to this broad popular stream. Many of their beliefs have Daoist connections, but, unlike Daoism as such, CCT has not been associated with formal religious institutions such as priesthood and monastic orders, and does not possess a scriptural canon. Many beliefs and practices now widespread in popular tradition also have roots in ancient Confucian and Imperial cultic institutions, and in Buddhism as well. Countless CCT temples began to appear in towns and villages several centuries ago. Since they do not have their own resident ritual specialists, these temples often enlist the services of Daoist priests, but their day-to-day services are often handled by dedicated lay persons. Many such temples are associated with families, who maintain them as a public service and a family tradition. Some elements of CCT also appear in temples ostensibly identified as Buddhist. A Guan Yin temple in Honolulu, for example, combines Buddhist rituals with a host of other popular practices. Though the main image is that of the Buddha, numerous other icons are prominently displayed. That particular temple is run by a group of Chinese Buddhist nuns who are especially concerned with preserving the image that theirs is a purely Buddhist temple, in spite of the obvious diversity within it. Recently, when a visitor asked permission to snap a few photos inside, the nun in charge agreed. But whenever she thought his camera lens was wandering toward Confucius or another icon, she tugged his sleeve and waved a disapproving finger at him. "Only Buddha," she insisted. Just a few blocks away, above a small upholstery shop, is the Lum family temple. There, all the deities are clearly of the CCT variety, even though some are often inaccurately identified as Daoist.

What was the earliest Daoist sacred text?

First and most influential of the Daoist sacred texts is the *Dao De Jing, Classic of the Way and Its Power*. Traditionally attributed to Lao Zi, the text actually dates from between 300 and 250 BCE. Authorship and immediate historical context remain uncertain. Its attribution to the "Old Master" may have arisen out of a desire to lend the text greater legitimacy and credibility. The *Dao De Jing's* eighty-one tantalizing short poems brim with paradox as they try to describe the indescribable by saying what it is *not*. Just as the value of a cup is the emptiness within, so the Way progresses by (apparently) going backwards. As all of nature acts without conscious effort, so the person who strives in hope of gain loses all. The curiously attractive teaching of the *Dao De Jing* emphasizes the Way of utter simplicity. Divided into two parts, poems one to thirty-seven focus on the Way, poems thirty-eight to eighty-one on its Power. Some describe the Way as the passive principle and its Power as primal spiritual energy. Anyone who tries to define the Way must know that it remains indefinable. Dao is the source of all energy but eludes discovery. Impercepti-

Main altar in a family temple in Honolulu dedicated to the Empress of the West, also known as Mazu and by a variety of other names. Many such altars hold more than one image of the central deity (note the two with the fringed "mortar board" headdress) as well as images of other sacred figures. Thanks to Mrs. Au for showing the author around the temple.

ble yet irresistible, impersonal yet ever-present, the Dao's power is like that of water: the softest of all elements inevitably dissolves the hardest. Although the text may sometimes give the impression that it favors the more mysterious female Yin over the male Yang, that is perhaps a result of its need to counter prevalent social biases. In the end, life can proceed only with a perfect balance of Yin and Yang, mountain and valley, light and dark, dry and moist, evident and hidden.

Statue of Choi Bak Sing Gwan, a deity of wealth, in a family-run CCT temple, Honolulu. Thanks to Mrs. Au for allowing the author to take photos in the temple.

What other **early sacred texts** are especially important for Daoists?

A text known as the *Zhuang Zi,* named after the man whose disciples may have authored it, dates from about the fourth century BCE. The work is also known as the *Divine Classic of Nan Hua,* the town to which Zhuang Zi was believed to have retired. Zhuang Zi the Daoist philosopher (c. 389–286 BCE) remains a relatively little known figure. But the work that bears his name stands out as a foundational document in philosophical Daoism, whose interpretation of basic concepts also influenced many religious Daoists. In addition to its bold attacks on the inadequacy of Confucian teaching, the *Zhuang Zi* presents essentially the same worldview as the *Dao De Jing,* especially the importance of non-effort *(wu wei)* or "unmotivated action" and its political implications. Zhuang Zi emphasizes the concepts of longevity and immortality that would later take on great significance for many religious Daoists. Perhaps more important is the concept of mental purification called "fasting of the heart." Zhuang Zi's teaching has become an important element in Daoist mysticism, speaking often of a kind of oneness with the Dao. A Daoist philosopher named Lie Zi is likewise said to have penned a work that bears his name. That book, also known as *The True Classic of the Expanding Emptiness,* however, was almost certainly of a later time, and Lie Zi is probably a legendary figure. Containing materials of many different literary types, especially narrative forms such as anecdotes and parables, the book was probably compiled around 300 CE. Its eight chapters arrange their literarily disparate materials thematically, addressing such topics as fate and human freedom, problems in establishing ethi-

Who was Lao Zi?

Lao Zi was likely an altogether legendary figure whose "name" simply means "old teacher or master." Tradition says he was born around 604 BCE, making him a much older contemporary of Confucius (Kong Fu Zi, 551–479 BCE), who was in turn an almost exact contemporary of the Buddha. The legend says Lao Zi was a clerk in the archives of the Zhou dynasty who practiced the "Way and its power" and emphasized self-effacement and anonymity. When he became convinced that social disintegration and political corruption in the Zhou dynasty were irreversible, he decided to withdraw from society. Riding his water buffalo, the old man came to the frontier. There a customs officer besought him to write down his lofty teachings before departing. Lao Zi wrote the *Dao De Jing (The Classic of the Way and Its Power)* and disappeared, leaving a legacy of mystery. Much later stories, perhaps from a time when Daoists and Confucians were in competition for followers, tell of a meeting between Lao Zi and a youthful Confucius. No use wasting so much time studying your history, Lao Zi counseled the newcomer. Observe nature and you will see that love for the Dao is all that one needs. Popular tradition tends to identify Lao Zi as the one who first taught that ordinary folk could seek and attain immortality. Some scholars suggest that Lao Zi's legendary stature may have been enhanced as a result of his mistaken identification with the legendary Huang Di, known as the Yellow Emperor who ruled in the middle of the third millennium BCE. Lao Zi was officially declared a god around 666 CE and eventually became part of a much-expanded Daoist pan-

cal standards, and the challenge of following the Dao. Here for the first time we hear of the Isles of the Blest, home of the Immortals. Like the *Zhuang Zi,* the later work speaks at length about the complete freedom experienced in becoming one with the Dao.

Is there now an official **"canon"** of Daoist scripture?

Around 471 Lu Xiu Jing (406–77 CE) compiled the earliest formal attempt at a Daoist canon. His work only catalogued important works, but there would eventually be seven major edited collections of Daoist sacred texts. Between about 1000 and 1250 CE, five enormous collections would appear. The final product was a large anthology of separate texts organized in three sections and published in its present form in 1444 CE. The triple division of the canonical collection, called the *Dao Zang,* may have been associated with, or perhaps a response to, the Buddhist scriptural canon known as the "Three Baskets." Each is named after one of the three heavens that were the abodes of the Three Pure Ones and begins with a major text said to have been revealed by one of the Pure Ones. The *Dao Zang (jing)*'s three parts include 1,476 disparate works in over 5,000

What is the main source of information on Lao Zi's life?

The main source of information on Lao Zi's life is a biography written by the historian Si Ma Chen (145–86 B.C.E.) in his *Records of the Historian*. By this time a number of beliefs about the founder of Chinese Daoism were circulating, and Si Ma Chen himself was unsure of their authenticity. The biography, in fact, contains an account of not one, but three, men called Lao Zi. The first Lao Zi was a man named Li Er or Lao Dan who came from the village of Chu Ren in the Southern Chinese state of Chu. Li Er served as historian in charge of the official archives in the Chinese imperial capital of Loyang. He was a contemporary of Confucius and is reported to have granted an interview to the Confucian master when he came to Loyang seeking information on the Zhou ritual.

Another man identified as the founder of Daoism was Lao Lai Zi, who also came from Chu. He is designated as a contemporary of Confucius and is credited with a fifteen-chapter book expounding on the teachings of the Daoist school. Nothing more is known about him. According to a third account, the original Lao Zi lived 129 years after the death of Confucius. This man went by the name of Tan, the historian of Chou.

scroll-volumes. Every imaginable variety of text is available in the modern sixty-volume reprint of the canon. Twelve sub-divisions arrange the material as follows: primal revelations, talismans, scriptural interpretation (or exegesis), sacred diagrams, historical texts, ethical texts, ritual texts, practical techniques, biographical information, sacred songs, and memorials. Most of the various sects and schools of Daoism focus on one or a select few of the many possibilities the canon offers. As we shall see later, recitation or chanting of sacred texts forms an important part of some ritual observances.

Has Daoism ever been identified with any **political regimes**?

During several periods of Chinese history, Daoism has enjoyed the considerable benefits of imperial patronage. One Daoist emperor in particular, during the mid–ninth century, launched a devastating persecution of Buddhism that did serious damage to many of that tradition's institutions. There is a certain irony in that, given the classical Daoist teaching about law and government. According to the *Dao De Jing* and *Zhuang Zi,* the best hope for society is unobtrusive leadership that does not need to rely on law and force to lead. Governmental institutions are meddlesome and oppressive. According to early Daoist authorities, the ideal social setting is the small village in which no one carries weapons. Very unlike classical Confucian tradition in this respect, the ideal Daoist society does away with social stratification of all kinds. Where all are equal, ruling and military classes are unnecessary. Throughout Chinese history, however, Daoists and Confucians have competed with one another for imperial support and patronage. Confucianism generally has been far more closely identified with government than has Daoism. Despite classical Daoist aversion to formal structures of government, both the official and popular pantheons have retained a good deal of the imagery of imperial bureaucracy, as in the names of such deities as the Jade Emperor.

What is **Neo-Daoism**?

Neo-Daoism is a name commonly given to various developments around the third and fourth centuries CE. Some scholars suggest that there were two recognizable schools. One was called Secret Mystical Teaching (*Xuan xue*). According to some interpreters, an important theme was its emphasis on the quest for physical immortality. Earlier Daoist sources had spoken of immortality, but generally of the spiritual rather than the bodily sort. Neo-Daoism recommended exercises in breathing, diet, use of potions, elixirs, and talismans, and sexual activity reminiscent of Hindu and Buddhist Tantric practices. But perhaps more fundamental in this alchemy were intense meditative practices intended to reveal the Dao within the individual. Some scholars interpret *Xuan xue* as developing out of Confucian rather than Daoist thought.

A major feature of the second school, known as Pure Conversation (*Qing tan*), is its attempts to blend aspects of Daoist, Confucian, and Buddhist thought. Among its proponents were the so-called Seven Sages of the Bamboo Grove, whose penchant for detached philosophical discourse and the cultivation of a Daoist aesthetic were among their hallmarks. On the basis of their reading of the *Zhuang Zi and* Dao De Jing, they developed a Neo-Daoist interpretation of the so-called Confucian classics. After the fifth century, Buddhist concepts infiltrated the movement to such a degree that Neo-Daoism gradually lost its distinctiveness and identity.

Did Daoist tradition **spread beyond China**?

Daoism has exerted some influence at various times all over east and southeast Asia. Wherever Chinese have traveled, Daoism has gone and left its mark, but it rarely has made its presence felt dramatically outside of China and territories under Chinese control. Daoist teachings, however, have had a significant impact on Chinese Buddhism over the centuries. Buddhism in turn has transported those usually well-hidden contributions on its missionary road throughout Asia. In relatively recent times Daoism, and teachings that claim to be Daoist, have begun to enjoy increasing popularity in Europe and the Americas, but on a much smaller scale than other traditions of Asian origin.

In brief, what is the **history** of religious Daoism?

Religious Daoism emerged as a recognizable tradition in its own right during the latter decades of the Han dynasty (202 BCE–221 CE). Confucianism enjoyed imperial favor as

Daoist deity (no further identification available), bronze with gilding, sixteenth century (Ming Dynasty). *Courtesy the Saint Louis Art Museum.*

the official creed of the state. But when the Han dynasty disintegrated, both Daoism and Buddhism found room to grow. The early Celestial Masters school dominated the Daoist scene for the most part. Various schools teaching forms of alchemical Daoism developed early on and have continued throughout the past two thousand years. In addition, new revelations claimed by various teachers gave rise to several new schools between the third and sixth centuries, times of political fragmentation (see below for discussion of individual schools and denominations). With political reunification during the Sui (581–618) dynasty, Daoism's various schools managed to survive in spite of meager imperial support. Many monasteries flourished but remained apart from the general populace. Things improved under the Tang dynasty (618–906), when Daoists once again had friends in high places. Under the Song dynasty (960–1279), Neo-Confucianism proved a powerful rival for Daoists at court. But Daoists fared well anyway, since many Neo-Confucians gladly exchanged ideas with Daoism's leading lights. During the Southern Song dynasty (1127–1279), in spite of an almost complete lack of public imperial patronage, several new Daoist schools sprang up. Things took a turn for the worse under the Yuan dynasty (1260–1368). Daoists invited to participate in court debates suffered serious setbacks and paid dearly with the loss of monasteries and precious libraries. During the late medieval Ming dynasty (1368–1644), Daoist fortunes improved again dramatically and many Daoist masters enjoyed prominent official positions. But under the last of the imperial regimes, the Ching (or Manchu) dynasty (1644–1911), the pendulum swung the other way and religious Daoism struggled to survive the early modern period. Through the periods of the first Chinese Republic (1912–1949) and the People's Republic (1949 to present), Daoism has held on largely thanks to the establishment of several organizations designed to provide a public presence for the various orders and schools. After disastrous losses as a result of the Cultural Revolution (1966–76), Daoist religious groups are again struggling to pull themselves back together.

RELIGIOUS BELIEFS

Is there a Daoist or CCT **creed**?

Since religious Daoism and CCT emphasize practice over correct belief, they have not formulated the equivalent of creedal summaries such as those of Judaism, Islam, and even Buddhism. Daoism and CCT do, of course, presuppose certain basic beliefs and assumptions about how the world works. Most of those beliefs have to do with discerning, and understanding how to cope with and benefit from, the spiritual forces inherent in all things. All of the varieties of religious Daoism and CCT, therefore, have their core beliefs. But affirming one's assent to them pales in insignificance when compared to the importance of grasping the essential skills needed to negotiate life's daily challenges.

Is the term **"revelation"** useful in understanding Daoism or CCT?

Most Daoist sects and schools, and CCT generally, teach that religious truths are embedded in virtually all levels and facets of reality. Access to those truths is available largely through the mediation of ritual specialists and spiritual masters. Their task is not so much to disclose the mysteries as to facilitate the passage of power from the realm of gods and spirits to that of human beings. When ordinary people find themselves in the neighborhood of these spiritual powers the truth behind them remains mysterious and cloaked in ambiguity. There are, however, accounts in which famous masters and sages claim to have received explicit revelations or missions directly from a deity. When Daoists speak of the language of revelation in these relatively rare instances, they suggest that they are pointing only to the tip of the iceberg, so to speak. The whole truth remains hidden from view and available only to a select few. This contrasts markedly with the general thrust of the Abrahamic traditions, for example, where revelation implies the disclosure of the full truth insofar as human beings can fathom it. Finally, an experience called "divination writing" deserves mention here since it is occasionally described as a revelatory medium. The Shang Qing school claims to be based on a series of nocturnal revelations. Founder Yang Xi reported that heavenly beings came to him in a vision and caused his hand to write the sacred texts.

Are **doctrine** and **dogma** important to Daoism or CCT?

Most of the various schools and sects of Daoism can point to at least one source or compendium of their central teachings. In that sense, there is such a thing as Daoist "doctrine." A body of doctrine does, in effect, define the boundaries of some of the schools, especially the more esoteric ones, and sets them apart from one another. But even in those instances, the doctrinal core is largely subordinate to a given school's central rituals and practices. CCT, on the other hand, does not define itself according to any clearly articulated doctrinal system. Children learn from their parents and extended family of elders a host of convictions and practices of the sort often called "folk beliefs." Where there is no formally defined doctrine, there can be no dogma in the sense of a minimum required for membership. Of those Daoist schools and sects that have developed distinctive doctrinal tenets, only the most esoteric have even approached the kind of "official" dogmatic pronouncement one finds, for example, in Roman Catholicism.

What do Daoists believe about **ultimate spiritual reality** or **God**?

Daoists call the ultimate spiritual reality "Dao," the Way. Long before the formal beginnings of Daoism's various movements and school, Chinese tradition used the term "Dao" as a general ethical notion implying the appropriate and moral way of acting. As so often happens when a religious tradition enters a new cultural setting, Buddhism's arrival in China led some thinkers to talk of a Buddhist "Way" in contrast with which they began to define an indigenous Chinese Way in the sense of religious beliefs and values. Daoist philosophers emphasized the unfathomable mystery of the Dao, but they viewed it as non-personal power rather than a personal divine entity. The religious equivalent seems to have been a deity called the Supreme Oneness (*Tai Yi*). The *Dao De Jing's* description of how the transcendent Dao became manifest suggests a type of emanation: Dao gave rise to the One, which produced the Two, and so on. That grand and uplifting description of the ultimate mystery still remained a bit too abstract for most people. As a result, when the first schools of religious Daoism began to formulate their beliefs they naturally gravitated toward more concrete imagery. That included the deification of the individual long believed to represent the Way as an accessible teaching—namely, Lao Zi. The process also led to personification of certain essential features of the mysterious Dao in the form of the heavenly triad called the Three Pure Ones. Developments of this sort multiplied, and the deities took on life stories and personalities that invited devotional interaction. In practice, the many personifications of divinity are arrayed according to an administrative structure parallel to that of the imperial bureaucracy. Religiously speaking, of course, the *reality*

Daoism and Myth

Daoist stories of how the world came to be are full of mythic features similar to those of other cosmogonies. They tell how order overcame chaos, how the heavens and earth came to be separated, and how the innumerable deities—thirty-six thousand according to one reckoning—fit into the grand picture. What is unique and most interesting about Daoist myth is that the gods do not necessarily take an active role in cosmic affairs. They do not intervene in the unfolding cosmos, nor even nudge the process along, for that matter. Instead they allow the fundamental laws of creation itself to operate unimpeded. Indeed the gods themselves come into being as part of this whole unfolding set in motion by an impersonal power called Heaven. What good are the deities then? They, along with the spiritually accomplished ones called sages and immortals, instruct humankind in the ways to achieve salvation. A clue to the place of many of these celestial beings in the grand scheme of things is their connection with the stars. Dozens of the members of the Daoist and popular Chinese pantheons are or have been associated with specific heavenly bodies or constellations. They are thus both visible and impossibly distant.

is just the other way round: the imperial institutions imitated the heavenly order of things.

Who are some of the **chief Daoist deities**?

Bearing in mind that it is not always possible to draw neat distinctions between Daoist divinities and those of CCT, here are some of the figures that appear to have at least originated in Daoist circles. They are called the Earlier Heaven Deities. At the top of the pantheon are the Three Pure Ones (*San Qing*). They seem to have been Daoism's theological rejoinder to the Buddhist groupings in which Bodhisattvas flank Amitabha Buddha to form a celestial triad. The Three Pure Ones (or Sacred Beings) are named after the heavens in which they dwell: the heavens of the Jade, Higher, and Great Purity, respectively. This triad evidently developed out of a trio of deified human beings of history or legend. Lao Zi, known as *Tian Shang Lao Jun* (Lord of the Daoist Teaching), was the first so elevated. Later a deity called "Heavenly Venerable of the Original Beginning" (*Yuan Shi Tian Zun*) was named as chief deity. And still later a third deity, Grand Lord of the Dao (*Tai Shang Dao Jun*), leap-frogged the two others to the top of the triad. These three, often depicted as enthroned elders, came to be identified with the more transcendent and abstract Pure Ones. Many consider the deified Lao Zi still a separate deity who ranks above the Three Pure Ones. The Jade Emperor, Yu Huang Da Di, was eventually identified either as the chief deity's younger brother or as an incarnation of the Lord of the heaven of Great Purity, and became the prominent deity in

How did Lao Zi become deified?

There seem to have been a number of stages in that process. First, the legendary figure began as a teacher and writer, whose image eventually blended with that of the Yellow Emperor when Lao Zi came to be identified as a confidant of royalty. Traditional accounts, such as the life-story summarized above, transformed him into a cultural hero whose mother had conceived him virginally. By the mid–second century CE, Lao Zi had become the deity who delivered to Zhang Dao Ling the revelation of a new religious faith, giving rise to the Celestial Masters school. But his image was still not complete. Next, perhaps also around the second or third century CE, Lao Zi seems to have been identified as a creator god who also enters the world to rescue humanity from tribulation. Lao Zi was now capable of incarnating himself, almost like a Buddhist Bodhisattva. Not long thereafter he joined the triad of the Three Pure Ones, and finally Lao Zi emerged as the chief divine person. We have here one of the more interesting examples of apotheosis, or deification, in the history of religion.

some CCT cults. According to one theological model, the Three Pure Ones are manifestations of the primordial cosmic energy, *qi*.

Are there any other important Daoist **sacred figures**?

One important subordinate deity is *Xuan Tian Shang Di,* Supreme Emperor of Dark Heaven. The Jade Emperor dispatched him to earth to battle a band of renegade demon-kings. His iconography shows him enthroned and using a serpent and a turtle—leaders of the demons—as a footstool. A legendary woman named Xi Wang Mu, also known as the Queen Mother of the West, figures prominently in some Daoist writings. She is a patroness of immortality, often depicted in the company of Jade Maidens, one carrying a fan and the other a bushel of the peaches of longevity. Ruling the East is her divine consort, Dung Wang Gong, who lives in the remote magical fastness of the Kun Lun mountains. In a reversal of the more usual dynamic, a "God of walls and moats," also known as the City God, began as a popular deity and made his way into the Daoist pantheon. During certain periods in history, the Heavenly Master appointed a given city's tutelary deity. City God has the assistance of several other figures, called "spirit secretaries," in the idiom of public administration. They help the City God deliver his reports on the conduct of citizens to the authorities in Hell. A goddess named Dou Mu (Mother of the Bushel of Stars, or Northern Dipper) functions in Daoism much the way Guan Yin does in Buddhism, offering limitless compassion for the suffering. Some other potent beings are clustered in groups. The Sen Nin are a group of sacred figures who dwell in heaven or in the distant misty mountains. Among

Altar dedicated to Guan Di, whose red-faced image it enshrines. Note the scaly dragon painted behind the icon, in Pao An Kung temple, Taipei.

the Sen Nin the most important are the Eight Immortals. Originally persons either historical (three) or legendary (five), they function as guardian figures of Daoism. Although they are not officially divine, popular lore sometimes attributes divine powers to them. They are called Later Heaven Deities, as are all human figures who eventually achieved immortality.

Who are some of the **principal gods** of CCT?

Many of the popular deities play multiple roles and sometimes resemble each other enough that one has to look carefully to identify them correctly. One of the most popular and frequently depicted deities is Guan Di, often inaccurately characterized as the "war god" under the name Wu Di. He was a third-century military leader named Guan Yu who gained a kind of martyr status after he was executed. By imperial decree in 1594, the deceased general was deified and the word for deity or emperor (*di*) added to his name. By a peculiar twist, he also acquired the status of secondary God of Literature. Kui Xing is the other secondary god of literature, distinguishable by his dragonfish, writing brush and official seal, small stature, unpleasant countenance, and awkward one-legged stance. Many pray to him as they prepare for examinations. In popular belief, Kui elbowed out the principal deity of literature, Wen Chang Di Jun, who had actually begun his mythic life as a star deity who was then born as Chang Ya, a famous literary figure. Wen is generally depicted wearing a flowing robe and a large

375

hat and either enthroned or astride a mule. Kui Xing usually stands on his left while on his right stands a red-coated figure. A widely popular goddess in CCT is sometimes called "Holy Heavenly Mother." She actually lived during the tenth century and was formally deified by several emperors during the twelfth and thirteenth centuries. Originally the patroness of sailors and rescuer from storms, she soon became famous for a wider range of powers. Taiwan alone has several hundred Ma Zu temples, where she sits enthroned wearing a royal diadem.

What about lesser or subordinate **popular deities**?

Associated with Ma Zu is the Great Emperor Protecting Life *(Bao Sheng Da Di)*. A physician during medieval (Song Dynasty) times, he remains a popular healing power. Legend says that he suffered from unrequited love for Ma Zu. Shou Lao, god of longevity, appears often in Chinese art and in temple decorations. He holds a peach and a staff, walks with a crane or a deer or both, and has an exceptionally high forehead and a long white beard. Another god of longevity, Shou Xing, has the responsibility of appointing each person's time of death. Like Shou Lao, he holds a peach, but Shou Xing's companions are the stag and bat. He is sometimes depicted as one of a trinity of star gods of happiness. Dozens of other lesser gods fill out the popular pantheon. Dung Fang Shuo is the divine patron of metalsmiths, connected with the planet Venus and depicted standing on gold and silver ingots. Bian Ho is the patron deity of jewelers. Si Ming, a deity of Daoist origin, became the Kitchen God, or Director of Destinies, who oversees the fates of family members and submits reports annually to the Jade Emperor on how each person is progressing. Depicted as an elderly Mandarin, this household deity rules from his place above the family hearth.

Do Daoists and practitioners of CCT believe in **miracles**?

Devout Chinese, whether associated with Daoism or with some form of CCT, consider asking for special favors an ordinary part of being religious. In general, however, what many readers mean by the term "miraculous" would not quite describe even apparently spectacular results of supplicatory prayer and ritual in this context. A fundamental consequence of the Yin/Yang view of life is the conviction that there is an identifiable cause of everything, whether positive or negative. All evil, illness, and suffering is a result of disharmony and imbalance. It is true that ordinary people cannot always put their finger on the direct cause, but ritual specialists know about these things. More importantly, the gods and those spiritual beings who have found the secret of immortality can assist suffering humankind by bringing about needed balance and harmony of forces. A "miracle" in this context, therefore, might be a divine intervention not for the purpose of doing the impossible, but for helping the possible to happen more quickly and easily.

Daoism and Nature

According to Daoist tradition, all things naturally exist in a primordial harmony. When things go wrong, whether in nature or in human society, the cause is invariably an imbalance in the equilibrium of Yin and Yang that results in a blockage of the flow of natural energies, *qi*. Part of the problem is the human tendency to seek control. When that desire leads to ill-conceived attempts to dominate nature, the outcome can only be disastrous. Nature yields its abundance easily and graciously to all among the "ten-thousand things" (creatures) that are willing to receive without grabbing or hoarding. When human beings develop a warped notion of their place in the larger scheme of things, attempting to force their will, all of nature may suffer temporary setbacks. But in the end, nature's balance will return. Traditional Chinese landscape paintings say it much better than words can. Massive mountains loom in the upper part of a hanging scroll, their craggy peaks bathed in sunlight. From the heights a waterfall cascades into the valley below, forming a lake as the stream emerges into the plain. Tucked away in a mountain scene, a tiny human figure sits meditatively in a picturesque pavilion. Further below, an unobtrusive figure shoulders a load across a small bridge. A solitary fisherman drops a line from his slender craft. Between valley and peaks, or perhaps where the peak imperceptibly becomes valley, hangs a misty cloud of that cosmic force known as *qi*. Landscape paintings, called "mountain-water pictures," thus suggest the perfect balance between Yang and Yin.

Is there a distinctively Daoist **ethic**?

Daoism's version of the Golden Rule is this: If a person treats me well, I do so in return. If that person treats me unjustly, I nevertheless respond with goodness, like the ever-constant Dao. The central ethical principle is the enigmatic concept of *wu wei*. The term translates literally as "non-action" or "non-effort," but it means something like "acting naturally." *Wu wei* is the ultimate in "natural law." All things behave according to their inherent makeup. Human beings alone have a tendency to get it wrong by trying to take control where we have no business doing so—and where there is ultimately no good reason for doing so. Only by observing the Way of nature can people hope to grasp this elusive principle of uncontrived accomplishment. *Wu wei* is not to be confused with laziness or indifference. Observe how nature brings about whatever is needed without stratagem or artifice. Nature does act, of course, and there is no lack of struggle in its doings, but it always returns to equilibrium. The key, then, is to act spontaneously, but that is not a recommendation to act impulsively. Behind the Daoist principle is the conviction that human beings will act for the greater good so long as they are not merely reacting to unreasonable social or governmental restraints. Genuine moral leadership requires authentic altruism, the desire to lead by serving—the diametric opposite of demagoguery. Concern for effective government in a time of social and institutional disintegration seems to have given rise to the notion of *wu wei*. But Daoism's sages embodied the principle in a way that recommended it as a fundamental religious and philosophical value.

What do Daoists believe about the **goal of human life**?

Although the principal early sacred texts do not discuss prospects of life after death explicitly, the question of immortality turned into an important issue for Daoists. Archaeological evidence from well over three thousand years ago suggests that many people believed in some sort of survival after death, but that apparently meant a kind of extended earthly existence. Religious Daoism does not always make the distinction some traditions make between life here and life hereafter. Some Daoists have held views not unlike those of many Christians, believing that at death "Life is changed, not taken away." But many have argued that if indeed life is a seamless reality, it may be possible to go on indefinitely without crossing that great divide called death. Whatever specific imagery Daoists have used to describe the nature of human life, the underlying point is that the tradition has been keenly interested in promoting a sense of vitality and in helping adherents to develop a positive attitude to the human condition generally.

Is **salvation** an important concept for Daoists?

Some elements in Daoist tradition discuss at length a type of salvation from mortality itself. That is quite different from the kind of salvation Muslims and Christians look forward to, something closer to salvation in spite of mortality. For Daoists, the most spiritually accomplished individuals are capable of so purifying themselves that they can actually live on eternally in the Paradise of Immortals. They might appear to die and be buried, but only because they allowed that to happen as a concession to widespread belief and socially acceptable convention. In fact they are able to substitute something else for their body and to slip away to paradise unnoticed. What about ordinary people incapable of such lofty feats? They can still hope to receive an immortal body after resurrection, a belief with some similarity to classic Christian notions of bodily resurrection. Another important distinction between Daoist notions of salvation and, for example, Christian beliefs, is that there is no single savior figure in Daoist thought.

Do Daoists and practitioners of CCT believe in **heaven** and **hell**?

Since long before the beginnings of religious Daoism, the notion of "Heaven" (*tian*) as an impersonal transcendent reality has been very important to the Chinese. Some Daoists have identified "Heaven" as the first materialization, or a kind of emanation, of the Dao's spiritual power. In this sense, Heaven becomes an intermediary between the unmanifest Dao and all of creation, for Heaven is the source of all good things. Along with Earth and Humanity, Heaven is one of the "three powers" that bring about life as we know it. However, Daoists do not generally talk of Heaven as the eternal abode of those who lived virtuously on earth. One region beyond ordinary earthly experience is the Isles of the Blest (*Peng Lai Shan*), in the far reaches of the Eastern Sea, where the Eight Immortals dwell amid an idyllic landscape. Many Chinese express the hope of finally reaching the Isles and attain immortality there. Belief in retribution after death for a less than praiseworthy life has given rise to a wealth of imagery. But Daoism and CCT call hell a multi-storied "earthly prison." There are ten levels of hell—some prefer to talk of ten separate hells—each with its ruling deity. They function rather like the circles of hell in Dante's *Inferno,* each designated for those who commit specific sins and crimes. Presiding over the first level is a sort of chief judge who wields authority over the other nine judge-kings. Some souls never make it to their assigned hell, a difficult passageway to the hope of better things beyond that. They spend eternity wandering aimlessly and forever hungry, dependent on the kindness of the living to attend to their needs. Some sources talk of hell much as many Christians describe purgatory as temporary suffering with long-range benefits.

What does **alchemy** have to do with Daoism?

A complex system of practices known as outer (*nei dan*) and inner (*wai dan*) alchemy developed for the purpose of allowing practitioners to achieve earthly longevity and perhaps complete immortality. While the outer form works with chemicals and other substances, the inner form focuses on cultivation of the divine within each person by a variety of techniques. The goal is to transform all three of the individual vital forces into the pure spirit called *shen*. Daoist alchemy consists of countless intricate formulas and recipes involving cinnabar, jade, and gold. Initiates must virtually soak enough of these elements into their systems to render the body indestructible. A method called Gold Cinnabar Daoism spells out the details of a technique shared by various schools of alchemy. A regimen of physical exercises called *qi gong,* now even more popular than *tai ji chuan,* is historically related to classical Daoist inner alchemy. Requirements such as the consumption of specific numbers of potions and pills on devilishly difficult schedules make the goal all but impossible to reach. But if the pharmaceutical demands were not enough, there is an even more elusive ethical component. For example, a person who desires immortality must perform an uninterrupted chain of charitable acts (1200 according to one ancient source). One stumble invalidates the process and requires a fresh start. Descriptions of Daoist alchemy too often leave out this ethical component, a feature that says more about the underlying spirit of the quest than any mere list of chemicals can begin to suggest. Although it is easy enough to see how an alchemical search for immortality could easily deteriorate into a crassly magical pursuit, the classical sources still have the power to remind one that beneath it all is serious insight into the human condition.

Has Daoism ever been associated with **millennialism** or **messianic movements**?

Several major movements of a millenarian and messianic cast have been associated with Daoism. One occurred during the late second century CE under the leadership of the three Zhang brothers who claimed authority in the domains of heaven, earth and humanity. They espoused a type of Daoism called Huang Lao (possibly a combination of the first parts of the names of Huang Di, the Yellow Emperor, and Lao Zi) and claimed divine origins for their eschatologically charged sacred text, the *Highest Peace Scripture*. The brothers Zhang established a theocracy, complete with elaborate hierarchies. Toward the end of the second century the movement swelled into full-scale rebellion led by a military force called the Yellow Turbans. The rebellion fizzled even though its leaders considered 184 CE an ideal time, beginning as it did a fresh sixty-year cycle. Shortly after that ill-fated rebellion in the east, another Zhang from an unrelated family organized a theocratic state that lasted from 186–216 CE. This Zhang Lu claimed the authority of his grandfather Zhang Dao Ling (34–156 CE), tra-ditionally cited as the founder of the first Daoist religious movement, the Celestial Masters school. Both theocracies hoped to re-establish the utopian regimes they believed had existed in the past. After the fourth century, new and more powerful movements emerged, with various leaders claiming to be incarnations of a divinized Lao Zi (called Li Hung). All taught the expectation of a messiah and a final battle which only the elect would survive to live on in their religious utopia. None had long-term repercussions. Loosely related by symbolism to the Yellow Turban rebellion of 184 was the Taiping (Highest Peace) rebellion of 1850–64. It was a syncretistic move-ment that borrowed heavily from Christian millennialist imagery.

SIGNS AND SYMBOLS

What **signs or symbols** might identify someone as a Daoist or practitioner of CCT?

Symbols associated with religious beliefs and folk practices abound in societies heavily influenced by Chinese culture. Over the centuries, the major Chinese religious tradi-tions—Daoist, Confucian, Buddhist, and popular—have shared many of those symbols and signs. Overlapping of symbols of various traditions makes it difficult, if not impos-sible, to know at a glance to which tradition the owner and user of the symbols belongs. Signs and symbols generally associated with CCT include a vast range of pro-tective and magical devices, amulets and talismans. Perhaps the most widely used symbol is that of the perfect harmony of Yin and Yang. Appearing on all sorts of per-sonal items such as rings and pendants, the so-called *tai ji* (Supreme Ultimate) is a

Symbol-standards used in Daoist and popular Chinese rituals, Bao An Gong temple, Taipei, Taiwan.

circle in which two equal but opposite curving tear-shapes embrace. In other words, an S-curve line divides the circle in two equal parts. The darker half symbolizes Yin, the brighter half Yang, but the commingling of the two is symbolized by a dark dot in the larger end of the Yang shape and a corresponding bright dot in the Yin shape. Sometimes, as on the national flag of South Korea, that symbol is surrounded by the eight Trigrams (*ba gua*). The Trigrams are made up of combinations of solid Yang lines and broken Yin lines. Charm-like devices are extremely popular in Chinese societies. Textiles and other decorative items, like ceramic wares, invariably display a range of symbolic features. Symbols they show can include any of dozens of animal, plant, or inanimate objects associated with aspects of the greatest mysteries of life, of those things that human beings most hope for or fear. For example, the tortoise and crane mean long life, the dragon means protection, the phoenix warmth. The heron and countless other birds of good omen betoken happiness, while creatures of ill omen, such as the owl, portend death and bad fortune.

What **signs or symbols** distinguish Daoist **ritual specialists**?

Daoist "priests" or "masters" make extensive use of symbolic vestments in ritual settings. Apparently in imitation of the garments emperors once wore for religious rituals, Daoist specialists today wear three types of vestments in various colors, depending on sectarian affiliation. For the most sacred occasions a high priest wears a square red silk pancho-like vestment called the "garment of descent" that symbolizes earth. For   381

What are trigrams and hexagrams?

Trigrams are sets of three vertically stacked hrozontal lines made up of every possible combination of broken (— —) and solid (———) line. Solid lines stand for the solar male Yang, high, bright, active, and dry. Broken lines stand for the earthy and lunar female Yin, which is dark, moist, mysterious and associated with valleys. Combinations of Yin and Yang in varying proportions give rise to the eight essential elements in creation. Traditional presentations usually arrange the eight trigrams as an octagon at whose center stands the *tai ji* symbol for perfect Yin-Yang harmony. Each trigram is arrayed so as to face its opposite in the set. So for example, if you held a compass before you with north pointing up, Heaven's three solid lines would stand across from Earth's three broken lines at what would be north and south. At due "east" stands Water, with a solid line between a pair of broken lines, across from Fire, with its broken line sandwiched between solids in the west. At northwest, Lake's broken-solid-solid (reading from top to bottom) stands across from Mountain's solid-broken-broken. And in the northeast, Wind's solid-solid-broken balances off Thunder's broken-broken-solid. Take the eight trigrams and arrange them in all possible permutations by stacking one trigram atop another and you get sixty-four hexagrams. Pile heaven upon heaven and the result is called the "creative principle." Add earth to earth and you get the "passive principle." Earth over Heaven yields "peace," while Heaven over Earth means "stagnation." The single most important source for interpreting these arcane indicators is the *Yi Jing, The Classic of Change.* Tossing and rearranging a set of fifty sticks and then reading them as hexagrams with the help of that text remains a widely popular form of divination.

regular major rituals the celebrants might wear a red or yellow silk over-garment called the "Dao Gown" with the character for "*tai ji*" or the Eight Trigrams on front and back. Other common decorative motifs include images of the Eight Immortals, often depicted on the hems of broad, flowing sleeves. Abstract cloud designs often stand for Yin while cranes and male versions of the mythical creature called the *qi lin* (sometimes associated with the unicorn, but very different from the European unicorn) represent Yang. For penitential rites the assistants might wear the "sea-blue" vestment whose darker color accords with a darker ritual purpose. Under these garments specialists wear a square silk apron. Officiants also wear distinctive headgear, including a black skullcap under a metal five-pointed crown (recalling the five elements) bestowed in the ordination ceremony. Ritual shoes like those once worn in the imperial court bear cloud symbolism that suggests the ability to walk the very heavens as the priest delivers the prayers of the people to the deities.

Ritual specialist assists a worshiper in her prayer offering at an elaborately decorated altar in a CCT temple, Taipei, Taiwan.

What would a visitor see if he went to a **Daoist or CCT temple**?

Larger traditional Chinese temples, of whatever affiliation, are generally laid out according to the ground plan of ancient imperial residences. Like the palace, the temple enclosure and its main interior structures generally face south. Approaching the temple, the visitor first sees a monumental gateway that offers entry through the temple's surrounding outer wall. Gracefully curved roofs decorated with numerous small multi-colored glass or ceramic figures crown the gate as well as the main interior buildings. In some of the more elaborate temples, the main gateway opens into a covered forecourt, or a vestibule in which the worshiper can begin to experience the change of mind and calming of the spirit necessary for efficacious devotion. Around the perimeter of the main courtyard one might find small separate halls that function like chapels for devotion to subordinate sacred figures, as well as special features like bell towers. But the focal point of the temple, whether Daoist or CCT, is typically a free-standing structure in the middle or toward the rear of the main courtyard. A large cauldron or kettle filled with sand, into which devotees insert their offerings of incense sticks, stands ten or fifteen feet away from the main entry to the shrine.

At either end of the main building's roofline (and often on the rooflines of other structures in the temple as well) the visitor probably will encounter a curious hybrid aquatic creature, dragon-headed and fish-tailed, called the *ji wen*. Popular lore says the exuberant creature protects the building from destruction by fire. Pillars or columns decorated with deeply carved stone dragons spiraling from bottom to top often flank the

383

Central courtyard of a popular Chinese temple in Taipei. Worshipers place their incense stick offerings in the main kettle and then approach the outer doors of the central building. On the roof line are decorative symbols and a tiny pagoda at the center of the ridge beam.

entry to the main shrine. Smaller pillars, similarly decorated, sometimes protrude from the two ends of the roof peaks, columns that support the firmament. Chinese temples typically created a covered space in a portico surrounding the main courtyard and an open space in the courtyard itself. The main shrine may be a fairly large structure, but ordinary worshipers usually make their offerings standing in front of the building, while temple staff perform associated ritual actions closer to the altars within the shrine. Smaller neighborhood or family temples naturally lack the grand architectural layout; many are tucked away unobtrusively over small business storefronts, or separate single-room structures with folding doors that open the entire width across the front.

Are Daoist and CCT **sacred spaces** marked with any distinctive signs and symbols?

It is not always possible to determine from a Chinese sacred space's exterior design and decor to which of the religious traditions it belongs. Mosques (including those in Chinese settings) have their distinctive minarets, churches have their spires and crosses, and Hindu temples have their monumental facades and towers marking inner shrines. Some Chinese Buddhist temples announce their identity with pagodas or stupas, but that is not always the case. Chinese temple rooflines often display colorful small figures that appear to be engaged in vigorous action, but even these are not a reliable indicator of the holy place's specific religious affiliation. The animated figures on the rooflines are sometimes scenes taken from Chinese opera or classical novels, chosen here because they allude to certain important moral virtues. Inside the temple more specific clues are available, but even there one has to look carefully to distinguish the sacred symbols of Daoism from those of CCT. For example, a statue of the Bodhisattva Guan Yin (originally Buddhist) may appear on a small altar under the covered area toward the front of the inner courtyard, but that does not mean that this is a Buddhist temple. It does, however, indicate that this is not a Daoist temple and probably belongs to CCT, which has "borrowed" Guan Yin from Buddhism and made her an important deity. A Daoist temple's most distinctive symbol is its main altar. Although the overall setting varies from one sect to another, there are several important common features. Before the central deity on the altar stands a perpetually lit lamp symbolizing wisdom and the light of the Dao. Two candles symbolizing sun and moon flank the lamp a few inches further toward the front of the altar. Cups of water (yang), tea (yin), and uncooked rice (yang and yin united) stand before the candles. Further toward the front of the altar stand five plates of fruit, each of a different color, symbolizing the five elements in perfect proportion. Centered near the front stands an incense burner, a reminder of the heat that purifies the three vital energies symbolized by three sticks of incense. Some temporary sacred spaces are constructed of bamboo for specific seasonal Daoist rituals.

Are **statues** and other **visual imagery** important in Daoist and CCT temples?

With the notable exception of major Confucian and Imperial temples, Chinese ritual spaces are almost always filled with images of deities and other sacred figures. Principal deities occupy main altar spaces, but they often share the central spot with smaller images of other sacred figures arranged below the main image and toward the front of the altar. For many centuries Daoists and practitioners of CCT evidently felt no need for anthropomorphic depictions of their deities. The advent of Buddhism, with its growing iconographic repertoire, seems to have been an important factor in the development of Chinese religious representational imagery. Images of Daoist deities, and of those that originated outside Daoist circles but are often identified as Daoist by association, run a wide gamut. Some of the deities are of divine origin. Others began as human beings, either historical or legendary, and achieved divine status either in life or after death. In addition to statues, colorful banners, low relief in stone and other media, and mural paintings depict mythological and other scenes meant to keep the worshiper in the proper frame of mind. Even temples that began as Buddhist institutions and which still display distinctively Buddhist imagery in their main shrines and altars have often become transformed into CCT temples by accretion over the centuries. Whatever the individual deity's lifestory, anthropomorphic images abound.

What are some clues to understanding Daoist and CCT **images**?

By far the majority of Daoist and CCT images of sacred figures are portrayed with identifiably human bodies. They rarely have multiple heads or limbs, but they do have

385

various special features. Deities are more often than not somber, sometimes of downright forbidding countenance, and typically depicted in such a way that the viewer is not likely to think of them as ordinary human beings. Bright red or yellow skin, flaring nostrils, riveted gaze, and the occasional menacing gesture discourage a too-casual approach. Exceptions are some of the CCT deities who appear as gently smiling "family members," kindly aunts or grandparents, for example. But even they often have unusual skin tones, suggesting that these are not mere mortals. Some deities are recognizable, at least by association, because of the groupings in which they appear. Most important in this respect is the triad formation, generally depicting a main central figure flanked by two slightly smaller figures. Depending on the temple, these may depict any of several of the triadic variations mentioned above. Many temples install subordinate deities and semi-divine powers on side altars or in small rooms of their own along the inner perimeter of the main courtyard. Each deity has his or her distinguishing characteristics, but one generally finds fewer clear iconographic clues here than in Hindu or Buddhist art. For example, several deities may sport the same skin tones and facial expression and even carry very similar symbols. It is therefore sometimes impossible to discern individual identities of the characters without knowing in advance to whom a given temple is dedicated.

Apart from the trigrams and *tai ji,* what are some **common traditional symbols**?

Ancient lore associates fundamental features of Chinese cosmology with specific symbols. It all goes back to the "Chinese Adam," Pan Gu. In his task of imposing order on primal chaos, Pan Gu enlisted the help of five cosmic assistants: Azure Dragon, White Tiger, Phoenix, Tortoise, and Unicorn. Pan Gu assigned to each of the first four a quarter of the universe. Azure Dragon governed the East, associated with Spring, new life, benevolence and protection. White Tiger ruled the autumnal West, symbol of maturity and a life well-spent, all made possible by good government and courage. Phoenix, the ultimate solar bird, presided over the summery South with the kindly warmth and joy that arises in a world at peace. Hard-shelled and indomitable, the ageless Tortoise faced the unforgiving, wintry North. Wandering freely among them all, the rare and delicate Unicorn was commissioned to appear wherever and whenever benevolence and justice reigned on earth. It is not surprising that all five of these wondrous beings retain their appeal to the popular imagination and remain essentials of the religious symbolic repertoire. A cluster of items associated loosely with Daoism are called the "Eight Daoist Emblems." Each represents one of the Eight Immortals, a group of human beings who became immortal in various ways. They appear often as decorative motifs on all kinds of objects. The emblems are a fan, a sword, a gourd, castanets, a flower basket, a bamboo drum, a flute, and a lotus flower. This is one of several sets of eight motifs popular in Chinese art and, along with the Eight Buddhist Emblems, one that still carries specifically religious resonances.

Are **number, color, or nature symbolism** important in Daoist tradition and CCT?

Astrological calculation and cosmological imagery have long been an integral part of Chinese religious views. Hundreds of symbolic elements make up this vast system of correspondences. Zodiacal animals are associated with the twelve months. Each of the four quadrants of the universe has its seven constellations in addition to its connection with specific trigrams, all related to particular aspects of good fortune or difficulty. Each of these elements is further coordinated with one of the five symbolic colors (black, white, red, green, yellow) and elements (wood, water, earth, metal, fire) and organs of the human body. Here are some examples of popular animal symbolism. The crow, surprisingly perhaps, symbolizes the sun. The crane, guide of the Immortals, means long life, as do the dove and the hare. Fish are reminders of renewal of life and abundance. By association with plowing new fields, the ox means spring and vitality. The sharp-eyed quick-tongued parrot looks after faithfulness in marriage. Flowers, trees, and fruits almost always have some symbolic resonance. The springtime peony means tenderness and womanly beauty, as does the jasmine. The plum means winter and reminds of Lao Zi who was born beneath a plum tree. Bamboo betokens endurance, the orange benevolence. A complete listing would fill several books. Of course, not everyone thinks consciously of specific symbolic meanings upon seeing any of the hundreds of visual decorative motifs in the full catalogue. But most Chinese still grow up surrounded by countless symbolic associations of this kind.

Do Daoists and practitioners of CCT use **relics**?

Given the importance of ancestor veneration in Chinese religious traditions generally, one might expect that relics would enjoy considerable prominence. That does not appear to be the case, however. People pay homage to the dead in various ways, but rarely attribute to their mortal remains or residual personal effects the kind of miraculous power typically associated with relics in traditions like Buddhism and Christianity. Amulets of various kinds offer protection, and these may include the equivalent of second or third class relics (personal effects of a holy person, or items said to have come in contact with the holy remains).

MEMBERSHIP, COMMUNITY, DIVERSITY

Where do Daoists live today? Are any **estimates of numbers** available? How about CCT?

Until fairly recently, Daoism has been an almost exclusively Chinese phenomenon. Since the Maoist revolution of 1949, practice of Daoism in the People's Republic of China has

Children play, parents pray, at Taipei's Xing Tian temple.

diminished dramatically. Buddhism had the advantage of being an international tradition and thus of at least limited political utility. In addition, Buddhism qualified officially as a "religion" while Daoism was defined as mere superstition. Daoist temples and monasteries were shut down or destroyed and thousands of Daoist ritual specialists had to seek other means of livelihood. Things have taken a turn for the better since the 1980s. Monasteries have reopened, and as of 1995 counts, Daoist temples number over 600, with about ten times that number of nuns and priests. Some institutions have even managed to revive formal seminary training for ritual specialists. The Celestial Masters school and the monastic order of Chuan Zhen (Complete Realization school) are the liveliest Daoist organizations in the People's Republic now. Many hundreds of temples are active in Hong Kong and Taiwan, many more belonging to CCT than to specifically Daoist groups. Elsewhere in Asia, wherever significant populations of Chinese have gathered, such as Malaysia and Singapore, Daoism and CCT are growing but are still relatively small. Active Daoists may number several million, while adherents of CCT may number between one hundred and two hundred million. These numbers seem relatively small next to counts of other major traditions, but they do not include the many millions of people whose days are full of ancient symbols and small rituals even if they are not formally identified with the institutional trappings of Daoism or CCT.

What is the **Daoist Celestial Masters** school and why is it important?

Daoism's Celestial Masters school (*Tian Shi Dao,* also called *Zheng Yi,* "Correct One") stands out as the original institutional expression of religious Daoism and one of several early attempts to establish theocratic communities. It was originally known as the Five Bushels of Rice school, the "dues" expected of members, the Celestial Masters school. Founded by Zhang Dao Ling (34–156 CE) in about 142, the sect focused initially on physical, moral, and spiritual healing through ritual confession of faults and exorcism. Regular rituals included recitation from the *Dao De Jing* and communal meals, with special feasts three times annually to acknowledge the three celestial bureaucracies overseeing heaven, earth, and water. Over the centuries the Celestial

Masters school has worked to prevent the popularization of religious rituals by attempting to maintain standards in the training of ritual specialists. Two main divisions, the southern and northern schools, developed more or less independently and then merged around the fourteenth century. After losing ground to various other schools for many centuries, the school has risen to prominence in modern times and now generally dominates the formal practice of Daoism and its rituals. The school is represented officially by the sixty-third Master who lives in exile in Taiwan.

What is the **Perfect Realization** school of Daoism?

Founded by Wang Zhe (c. 1123–1170, also called Wang Chong Yang), the Perfect Realization (*Chuan Zhen*) school is among the most important Daoist monastic orders. According to legend, Wang Zhe received new revelations from one of the Eight Immortals, Lu Dong Bin. Ascetic self-denial was a central feature in the order's discipline, including meditative practices designed to maximize yang energy and minimize yin. The founder evidently insisted on the importance of studying the teachings of Buddhism and Confucianism along with those of Daoism, but focused on the characteristically Daoist spiritual goal of immortality. Of its several branches, the Lung Men ("Dragon Gate") is perhaps the most influential. Like religious orders in some other major traditions, the Perfect Realization order historically has been socially active and responsible for preserving much traditional Chinese religious culture in times of turmoil. For example, they have done extensive refugee relief work and published a major edition of the Daoist scriptural canon in 1192. From the White Cloud monastery in Beijing, the Lung Men branch of the order continues its work today.

Have there been any other **sub-communities or denominations** within Daoism?

Dozens of other schools and sects have arisen over the long history of religious Daoism. The Great Purity school (*Shang Qing*), also known as Mount Mao (*Mao Shan*) Daoism, arose during the late fourth century. The Shang Qing claims as its central revelation a set of scriptural texts in over thirty volumes. Almost contemporary in origin with that school is another called the Ling Bao. It also claims a distinctive scriptural revelation, based in part on the Shang Qing scripture. Heavenly Mind (*Tian Xin*) Daoism, emphasizing the importance of exorcism and based also on its own scriptural revelation, began in the late tenth century. The Divine Highest Heaven (*Shen Xiao*) school, dating from the twelfth century, is best known for its talismans of legendary potency and its elucidation of correspondences between the microcosm of the body and the macrocosm of the universe. Great Oneness (*Tai Yi*) Daoism, also from the twelfth century, was a celibate monastic school important for its integration of Confucian and Buddhist elements. Though none of these schools remains active today, all have made significant historical contributions to the large and complex reality called Daoism.

Fa Lun Gong (Dharma Wheel Cultivation, also called *Fa Lun Da Fa,* Dharma Wheel of the Buddha Way, was founded in 1992 by Li Hong Zhi and received official approval by China's "Research Society of Qi Gong Science." Its principal symbol is a circle with a clockwise-rotating swastika at its center. Around the central swastika are four *tai ji* symbols, at the cardinal directions, alternating with four more swastikas. The swastika is an ancient symbol of apparently south or central Asian origin that has long been associated with both Hinduism and Buddhism. The iconographic significance of the various rotating symbols is related to the concept of chakras, or energy centers, within the body. Within each person, therefore, resides a miniature of the whole spinning cosmos. This correspondence between the microcosm of the individual and the macrocosm of the universe is an important link to Daoist thought. Fa Lun Gong advertises itself as an alternative to traditional religious traditions such as Daoism and Buddhism, and to practices such as *qi gong* and *tai ji chuan.* Its spiritual leader, Li Hong Zhi, says his purpose is to bring ancient wisdom again within reach of ordinary people who find the traditional systems no longer helpful. Drawing on Daoist imagery, Fa Lun Gong's meditative method, combined with ritual movement, aims at helping practitioners to balance, maximize, and release their energies. Chinese authorities almost certainly had complex motives in attempting to suppress the sect in 1999. One concern may be the ancient connection religious Daoism had with messianic and revolutionary movements.

Have Daoists traditionally sent out **missionaries** to **convert** others?

Daoism generally has not been a mission-oriented tradition. There have been periods in the history of China during which Daoist authorities have made it clear that life would be more difficult for non-Daoists. A number of Chinese emperors espoused Daoism as the official state creed, in effect, and attempted to cleanse the realm of Buddhists. And there have been times when Daoists have been in serious competition with Confucians. But on the whole, systematic missionary activity is not the essential ingredient in Daoism that it has been in Islam, Buddhism, and Christianity. When Daoism and CCT have spread they have done so largely as a result of migration of Chinese merchant families.

Are there any Daoist **holy places**?

Mountains are the most prominent of Daoism's sacred sites, but they were sacred to the Chinese long before Daoism. Four mountains marked the cardinal directions of ancient Chinese symbolic geography, and a fifth was eventually added at the center, perhaps in connection with the notion of five elements (earth, air, water, fire, and metal). Each mountain has its chief deity who discharges his own distinctive duties. A number of individual mountains in addition to the main five also possess special properties and are connected with particular deities or Daoist sects and schools. Mount He Ming (Szechuan province) is famed as the place where Zhang Dao Ling inaugurated religious Daoism. Daoists share Mount Zhong Nan (Shensi province) with Buddhists as a sacred site. The Celestial Masters school established its center on Mount Long Hu (Kiangsi province). Hundreds of Daoist and Buddhist temples have stood on dozens of such sacred peaks. Two related features of Daoist sacred geography are the system of ten great and thirty-six lesser Grotto-Heavens and seventy-two Blessed Spots, some of which are located on famed mountains. These sites, mostly caves, are so designated

Daoist mountain deity on a mural in a side shrine at Seoul, Korea's Pong Won Sa temple.

because they are foci of sacred energy. They are often associated with religious figures believed to have found meditative solitude there and are likened to heavenly dwellings.

Do people ever decide they want to **depart** from Daoism or CCT?

Membership in Daoism and CCT has rarely, if ever, been a matter of exclusive allegiance. Members of some major religious traditions, such as Islam, Christianity, Judaism, and, to a lesser degree, Hinduism, typically regard "belonging" as a kind of all-or-nothing affair. Either you're in, or you're out. Disagree with major tenets of the tradition, or neglect consistently and willfully to fulfill the minimum ritual and ethical requirements

391

of the faith community and your membership is in question—or has lapsed altogether. Religiously involved Chinese generally do not think about membership in those terms. Belonging is deeply rooted in national and local culture, integral to the very fabric of society. Individuals who drift away from regular religious practice have not necessarily "left," so long as they have not entirely cut themselves off from family and social connections. Other family members might express regret that sons or daughters no longer find the traditional ways helpful and have chosen to delete that part of their heritage from their self-identities. And many today sense the gradual diminishment of traditional values and practices precisely because of this sort of attrition. But Chinese, whether Daoist or CCT, generally do not think in terms of "leaving the faith" unless they do so with the intention of converting to a missionary faith, such as Christianity. In those cases, people do talk of leaving behind unacceptable beliefs and practices.

Is there such a thing as **converting** to Daoism?

In relatively recent times, Daoism has attracted increasing interest among people outside China. A quick scan of Internet sites affords a fair impression of contemporary Euro-American interpretations of the ancient Chinese tradition. Many non-Chinese who are attracted to Daoism gravitate toward the philosophical rather than to the theistic or religious elements. Some proponents of "New Age" beliefs have adopted the use of Daoist divinatory techniques, especially the interpretation of the hexagrams by consulting the *Yi Jing*. But on the whole, non-Chinese who express an active interest in Daoism do not "convert" to the tradition the way one would when becoming, say, a Muslim or a Christian. Since Daoism is so intertwined with an integrated worldview that is profoundly Chinese, it is almost a contradiction in terms to talk of "becoming a Daoist."

How do Daoists view their tradition's **relationships to other traditions**?

By the beginning of the first millennium, philosophically minded Daoists had rubbed elbows for several centuries with proponents of a cultural and ethical system often identified as Confucian. Together the Confucians and the Daoists were increasingly important elements of a larger cultural matrix. "Religion," for which they had as yet no specific term, was a blend of ancient divinatory rites, ancestor veneration, exorcism, and offerings meant to secure blessings and protection from "Heaven" and several other fairly generic and non-personal divine powers. Religious Daoism evolved during the period when Buddhism was taking root in China. It was not until Chinese Buddhism was several centuries old that Chinese thinkers began to talk of "three ways" of being both Chinese and religious. It is as though the Chinese people had not thought of their ancient traditions as anything but "the way things are," rather like the air they breathed, until an imported form of thinking and acting called the Way of the Buddha entered the scene. Buddhist-Daoist relations have had a checkered history. At first many Daoists regarded Buddhism as a new Daoist school or sect, thanks to Buddhist efforts at translating key concepts into terms Daoists would understand. Before long, full scale hostility developed when Daoists began to think of the missionary-minded Buddhists as a threat. Confucians often sided with Daoists in condemning Buddhism as "un-Chinese." Periods of persecution of Buddhists alternated with rich interchange and mutual influence. Since the 1800s Daoist-Buddhist relations have been much more stable and peaceful, so that many Chinese now perceive few or no important distinctions or barriers between the two traditions. CCT has been a kind of meeting ground. As for Daoist-Confucian relations, there has been intermittent rivalry for imperial patronage. The two traditions share a great deal in the way of broad doctrinal and cultural themes, such as the so-called Yin/Yang worldview and ancestor veneration. During the Confucian revival of the twelfth and thirteenth centuries, a development often dubbed Neo-Confucianism, there was renewed positive interaction and mutual exchange of ideas. Nowadays, relations remain generally cordial, but without much substantial discussion of core belief.

LEADERSHIP, AUTHORITY, ORGANIZATION

Where do members of local **Daoist communities** and members of CCT **come together**?

By far the most important Daoist and CCT gathering places are local temples and shrines, as well as the elaborate but temporary altars set up in open spaces for the larger religious ceremonies. Temples vary in size and wealth and, naturally, the smaller the temple the more likely it is to serve a purely ritual purpose and not to have room for other activities. Community temples at the center of towns and villages often serve as multi-purpose facilities. There might be any number of functions going on at one time—classes for children, play during recess, community meetings—while worshipers attend to their devotional needs. In larger towns and cities, other organizations, such as various Daoist (and Buddhist) associations, apparently fill some of those communal functions as well. Most people still think of Daoist and CCT temples primarily as ritual facilities that also serve as centers of parish life. Temples typically govern their ordinary affairs through an elected committee entrusted with all major decisions about ritual calendar, maintenance, and finance.

Is there a **central teaching authority** for Daoists? For CCT?

Individual Daoist sects, orders, and schools have regarded—and in some cases still do regard—their teaching office as a solemn and demanding role. But on the whole, Daoists do not think of themselves as following any particular teaching or adhering to a particular orthodoxy. Even when important patriarchs, such as the living leader of the Celestial Masters school, have delivered formal pronouncements, relatively few Daoists take notice. What is true of Daoism in this respect is even truer of the much more amorphous CCT. In neither case is any specific articulation of doctrine of any particular importance. Doctrinal standards are replaced here by pure tradition—"the way we've always done things."

Is there a system of Daoist **religious law**?

Apart from the charters or disciplinary codes of Daoist organizations such as monastic orders, there is no such thing as formal Daoist religious law. The very idea goes against the grain of the concept of natural balance and harmony that is so central to Daoist thought. That is not to say that there aren't countless standard practices and expectations as to behavior. The difference between Daoism and, say, Islam or Christianity, in this respect is that the Muslim and Christian traditions have systematically codified those expectations while the Daoist has not. Every cultural and religious system has its standards and sanctions. But in the cases of both Islam and Christianity, independent legal systems became necessary largely because the religious traditions expanded into new cultural settings very different from those in which the traditions arose. In the case of Daoism, religion and culture have been much more closely and consistently identified, making a separate system of religious law largely unnecessary.

What are some of the main varieties of Daoist **officials or specialists**?

Since about the fourth century CE, religious specialists called *dao shi,* "masters of the Dao," have led Daoist communities at prayer. These leaders can be celibate monks (there are also nuns called *dao gu*) who live almost exclusively in monastic communities. Monastic priests—mostly members of the Complete Realization order—occasionally perform public rituals, but, not unlike cloistered monks in some other traditions, their principal focus is on their more private spiritual pursuits. Some ritual specialists are married family men who live near a monastery. These so-called "lay masters" (*shi gong*) make up the majority of Daoist ritual specialists. Individuals generally specialize in certain types of ritual, such as exorcism and faith-healing. Among the non-monastic, those ritualists whose functions most closely resemble those of priests in various other traditions are called the Black Hats. Many of them belong to the Celestial Masters school, perhaps the oldest of all Daoist organizations. In addition to the Black Hats, the "official" and intricately trained priests, there are the Red Turbans known as *fa shi,* specialists in the occult. Black Hats, so called because of their small mandarin cap with a gold knob on top, are authorized to perform both the greater festivals and the more ordinary ceremonies to which the Red Turbans are restricted. (The two groups are alternatively known as Blackheads and Redheads.) Specialists of earlier times called "libationers" in the Celestial Masters school had the triple duty of reli-

Images of various deities available in a popular religious goods store, Keeling, Taiwan. Here you can find everyone in the several pantheons, from the red-faced Guan Di and other Daoist figures, to Guan Yin and the jolly Buddhist figure on the right called Pu Tai.

gious instruction, local administration, and ritual leadership, not unlike the typical parish pastor in many Christian denominations.

Are there Daoist **hierarchical structures**?

Since there are many different sects and schools, there are no official and universally acknowledged hierarchical structures that unite all Daoists. But there are *de facto* hierarchies both religious, within individual Daoist organizations, and social, based on a broader kind of class-consciousness. For example, in the Celestial Masters school, the living Heavenly Master functions as a sort of archbishop, overseeing the running of the school's temples in the region. Within the administration of the school, ranks are named after those of the imperial bureaucracy, such as libationer, recorder, and director of ceremonies. The Celestial Masters school has retained much of its ancient hierarchical structure today. In addition, each of the various monastic orders is internally structured according to authority and leadership roles, with the equivalent of an abbot at the head. Hierarchical structures have also been very much a part of the several short-lived attempts to create theocratic states, but their claims to authority were naturally limited. Within their everyday lives, most Daoists would likely be aware only of the functional hierarchy inherent in the more elaborate ritual celebrations. There, a high priest presides, while subordinate priests perform much of the ceremonial action

395

Have women exercised leadership among Daoists?

One of the most famous libationers was a woman named Wei Hua Cun (251–334 CE). Her rank as libationer apparently indicates that she originally belonged to the Celestial Masters school. Some regard her as a foundational figure in the Shang Qing sect. She is perhaps most famous for having appeared posthumously on many nights over a six-year period to reveal to a certain Yang Xi the sacred texts of the Shang Qing sect. Those texts consist mainly of liturgical ritual. Throughout its long history, the Celestial Masters school has allowed women into the lower rungs of its ritual hierarchy, up to but not including that of Celestial Master itself. Another school, called "Pure Rarity" (*qing wei*), is said to have been founded by a woman named Zu Shu in the early tenth century. Centered around a thunder deity, the sect blended elements from the Ling Bao, Shang Qing, and Celestial Masters schools. There have been many priestesses over the centuries, and a celibate community of women maintain a temple in Kaoshung, Taiwan.

Hagiographical sources are extant on a number of holy women of ancient times. They make it clear that women who preferred to pursue the spiritual life rather than devote themselves to family risked almost certain disapproval. Even so, it seems that some women were associated with religious orders. Sun Bu Er (1119–1182) and her husband were both ritual specialists in the Perfect Realization order, and she founded a new division of the school dedicated to the religious education of women. A selection of her writings in translation is available in Thomas Cleary's *Immortal Sisters: Secret Teachings of Taoist Women*. A sect associated especially with the Red Turbans is popularly called San Nai, "Three Ladies," evidently so named to honor a trio of priestesses about whom little else is known. As has often been the case in other religious traditions, many Chinese women have found possibilities for active leadership and ministry more often outside the institutional structures than within.

and musical accompaniment. Other non-ordained assistants busy themselves with the overall mechanics of the ritual, keeping the action moving by making sure necessary supplies are plentiful and other practical matters are in order.

How are Daoist **leaders** chosen and given authority?

Traditional Daoist priesthood has long been a hereditary occupation, though that appears to be changing in recent times. This feature obviously applied consistently only to non-celibate branches of the priesthood. Individuals who successfully completed requisite initial training are ordained, following general patterns similar to those of Buddhist monastic practice. Ordination requires a quorum of ordained priests, and the ordinand takes "refuge" in the Dao, the canon of scripture, and the tradition's spiritual teachers, much as the Buddhist monk takes refuge in the Buddha, the Dharma, and the Sangha. Lay specialists, whether Black Hats or Red Turbans, apprentice to an authoritative master called a *dao jang*—perhaps the equivalent of "high priest." His task is to lead novices through several levels of ritual assistantship. Students begin with basic musical accompaniment, learn to watch over the incense burners, and lead group prayers. More difficult training includes learning to chant and memorizing often intricate rubrics (ritual movements). After learning to copy sacred texts and write talismans calligraphically, aspirants are ready to lead ritual. In the People's Republic of China some seminaries still provide formal doctrinal instruction, but that is generally not the case in Taiwan. Formal ordination focuses on the symbolism of the master conferring the seal of priesthood and the texts the

Women and children retrieving crescent-shaped divining blocks in Taipei's Xing Tian temple.

specialist will follow. Some scholars suggest the training of Black Hats is more rigorous and literate than that of the Red Turbans, who tend to serve less official, more "popular" functions and have much in common with the shamans of old.

Do Daoists and practitioners of CCT run private **religious schools** for their children?

People born into Chinese families with a long history of associations with Daoism or CCT, or both, grow up hearing about traditional beliefs. They participate, practically

397

from infancy, in family home, and perhaps also temple, rituals, and almost certainly learn the ways of ancestor veneration. There has been no need, generally, for an educational network designed to preserve ancient beliefs and practices. Traditional values, some believe, are being steadily eroded by the increasing pace of change the world over. It may be that if time-honored Chinese ways of being religious are to survive well past the millennium, those vitally interested in that survival will have to develop more formal, deliberate ways of instilling the tradition. Movement in that direction may already have begun with the revival of Daoist seminaries in the People's Republic of China.

Are there any organizations that have their own **distinctive structures** within Daoism?

Monastic institutions have been of great importance in the history of Daoism. Celibate monks adhere to demanding disciplinary codes. The five basic rules of Daoist monastic life are not unlike some of the essential regulations of Buddhist laity. Monks are forbidden to take life, to eat meat or drink alcohol, to lie or steal, or to engage in sexual activity including, of course, marriage. But like their Buddhist counterparts, Daoist monks face far greater demands as well. Fasting is a large element in monastic life, including ten fast days each month plus dozens of others scattered throughout the year. Historically, different orders required adherence to additional regulations varying in number from ten to several dozen. Some orders structured their membership according to levels of spiritual attainment. For example, the Realization of Truth school had three grades among its monks. "Noble transformation" characterized the "Master of Excellent Conduct" who successfully managed the first set of challenges. Abiding by a set of three hundred specific regulations brought a monk to the level of "Master of Noble Virtue." To achieve the level of "Nobility in the Dao," aspirants had to match the Immortals themselves in virtue.

PERSONALITIES AND POWERS

Who is the **Jade Emperor**?

One of the more intriguing personalities in the Daoist and CCT pantheons is the Jade Emperor, Yu Huang Da Di. His emergence as a power to be reckoned with in popular worship offers important insight into the dynamics of Chinese religion generally. During the fifth and sixth centuries Yu Huang Da Di was but one among many relatively minor deities. During the Tang dynasty of the seventh through ninth centuries he gained prominence as a result of the appearance of a new text called the *Jade Emperor Scripture* (*Yu*

Huang Jing). It tells how centuries earlier a queen had dreamt that Tai Shang Dao Jun, second of the Three Pure Ones, handed her an infant. She awoke and bore a child, who after a short time as a young prince, withdrew to mountain solitude. Lengthy spiritual discipline transformed the youth into the Jade Emperor. In the tenth century, a Song dynasty emperor named Jen Zung (r. 998–1022) chose Yu Huang Da Di as his patron deity and spread word of an expected revelation. That came in 1008 in the form of sacred scriptures, thus bolstering the weak emperor's position. Thereafter the Jade Emperor rose to the top of the popular pantheon, thus becoming the CEO of a divine bureaucracy. Stories like that of the Jade Emperor help to explain why enumerations of the Daoist and CCT pantheons are sometimes a bit confusing.

Who is **Guan Di** and why is he so important?

Like the Jade Emperor, Guan Di (also known as Guan Gong) claims a place in both Daoist and CCT pantheons. He has the additional distinction of ranking high in the upper echelons of the imperial cult, and through that channel connects with Confucian tradition as well. Guan Di was originally a military man of the third century, named Guan Yu, who was executed after enemies of the Han dynasty captured him in battle. The court funded temples in his honor and publicized his cause. Meanwhile the newly deified Guan Di was gaining popularity among practitioners of CCT as a refuge from problems as diverse as illness, bad weather, and failing business. The ever-ready all-purpose deity thus rose to such prominence that his popular cult situated him above even the Jade Emperor. In the seventeenth century a Ming dynasty emperor conferred on Guan Di the title of Grand Emperor. During the following regime, that of the Ching or Manchu, Guan Di received the title under which he is perhaps most widely known, Military Emperor or Wu Di, thus making him the official guardian of the empire. Guan Di's celebrity represents a relatively recent development. Unlike many of the older deities, whose imagery and entourage were typically patterned on those of the imperial bureaucracy, Guan Di is reminiscent of the Buddhist Bodhisattva. In fact, some scholars suggest, Guan Di also was absorbed into certain Buddhist groups after the seventh century. It seems likely that, as in the case of other indigenous Chinese deities, Guan Di was first depicted under the general influence of Buddhism's use of sculpture. He appears as a very tall man with a very long beard and a red face, sometimes accompanied by his son. Variant versions of his story give somewhat different details, as in the popular classic Chinese novel *Romance of the Three Kingdoms,* of which Guan Di is the hero. Many popular theatrical presentations based on the novel have become a major vehicle for the spread of Guan Di's popularity.

Who is the **Yellow Emperor**?

Ancient Chinese lore tells of Five August Emperors whose reigns date back to before 2500 BCE. They are sometimes called "culture heroes," in that tradition credits them with pro-

A life-sized statue of the Yellow Emperor in a glass case in Bao An Gong temple, Taipei, Taiwan.

viding humankind with a host of skills and essential practical wisdom. As guardians of the five sacred mountains, the divine quintet ruled the cardinal directions and the center. Each was associated with a color: green with the east, red with the south, white with the west, black (or "dark") with the north, and yellow with the center. By far the most famous and popular of them is Huang Di, the Yellow Emperor, giver of such arts as medicine, agriculture, weaving, pottery, silkworm culture, and domestic architecture, to name only a few. Huang Di began his life in legend as a ruler and a shaman whose magical powers allowed him to confront all manner of evil. Dated either 2697–2597 or 2674–2575 BCE, he was evidently a patron of the ancient *fang shi,* or shamans. But the Yellow Emperor went on to become one of the two patrons of an early Daoist school called Huang-Lao, perhaps a combination of the first names of Huang Di and Lao Zi. Huang-Lao Daoism may have begun as a religious movement as early as third century BCE. In any case, though the figure of Lao Zi seems to have upstaged that of Huang Di for some centuries, the Yellow Emperor made a comeback in popularity. In any number of Daoist and popular temples a visitor may encounter a statue of Huang Di prominently displayed, perhaps in his own glass case. Standing erect, the sovereign, of solemn countenance, wears elaborately embroidered robes whose main color is, of course, yellow.

Who are the **Eight Immortals**?

Three historical and five legendary persons believed to have achieved immortality figure prominently in Chinese religious lore. Daoist sources tell of many other mortals

Is there such a thing as a Daoist saint?

Perhaps the closest thing in Daoism to what many people mean by "saint" is the ideal of human development called the sage (*zhen ren*). Unlike ordinary people, the sage keeps his knowledge hidden, because there is no need to impress or persuade others. A sage is thus like the silent, unobtrusive Dao. Neither does the sage labor over the right course of action, for love is squandered when spent on specific deeds rather than lavished equally on all. The sage understands that failing to yield is not to be confused with courage. The sage knows how to give without being emptied, how to take in without being filled. Completely in harmony with nature, the sage acts without intent, learns without studying intently. Chinese religious traditions often have elevated otherwise ordinary human beings to a status above the merely human. But there is no standard formal process by which this elevation takes place. In this respect Daoism is closer to Islam than to Christianity, for example, where sainthood requires elaborate and lengthy investigation and verification. Emperors and others in authority have sometimes announced honors of this kind by decree, but sages are generally acknowledged as such as a result of grass-roots movements rather than by pronouncement from on high. There is at least one other distinctive feature of the making of a Daoist sage. Whereas saints in some other traditions arrive at a level of spiritual perfection as a result of divine grace, the Daoist sage is a product of self-help.

who have achieved immortality, but these eight are especially important. Chinese religious lore contains many sets of eight (trigrams, precious objects, cosmic directions, for example). The Immortals (*xian*) are in some ways analogous to Christianity's saints and Islam's friends of God. Lu Dong Bin, originally a patriarch of the Complete Realization school during the eighth century, generally leads the group. He usually dresses as a scholar and carries a fly-whisk. Some images show him with his magical sword, one of the Eight Daoist Emblems. Lu is patron of barbers and is celebrated for his healing powers. Li Tie Guai, a purely legendary figure whose emblems are the gourd and crutch, appears as an old crippled beggar. He champions the weak and marginalized and is a patron of pharmacists. Zhang Guo Lao lived sometime between 650 and 750 CE. Capable of making himself invisible, Zhang appears riding (often backwards!) on a white mule which he could roll up and tuck into his sleeve. His emblem is the percussion instrument made of a bamboo tube and two sticks and he is the patron of elderly men. He Xian Gu, the lone female of the group, holds a bamboo ladle, a lotus or basket of flowers, and sometimes the peach of immortality. She is said to have lived around 700 CE and is noted for her asceticism and kindness. Han Xiang Zi is the patron of musicians. He carries a flute and is known for his

Daoist female immortal He Xian Gu holding her bamboo vessel and a long-stemmed lotus, ivory with polychrome and gilt decoration, Dao Guang period 1821–1850. *Courtesy the Saint Louis Art Museum.*

spendthrift ways and delight in mountain solitude. Zhong Li Chuan is supposed to have been a soldier of old who failed in battle and became an alchemist. Apparently once a historical figure, the aging and portly fellow eventually ascended to heaven on a stork and now carries a fan. Lan Cai is a strange figure among strange figures. With one foot bare and one shod, sometimes appearing as a woman, sometimes as a boy, he carries a basket of flowers and is patron of florists. Cao Guo Jiu, patron of actors, carries a pair of castanets or, alternatively, a jade court tablet that was his entry pass and from which the image of castanets may have developed. Tradition makes this eighth Immortal the brother of a Song Dynasty empress and dresses him in royal finery. The whole octet are still widely popular and sought out for their magical powers.

Have there been any Daoist **mystics**?

Traditional accounts of many famous Daoists describe their inner experiences in terms consistent with those often associated with mysticism. A mystic, in general terms, is a human being who through a variety of ritual or devotional practices experiences spiritual transcendence. Moving out of and beyond himself or herself, the mystic abides at least temporarily in a dimension very different from what most people experience most of the time. Some refer to the great Daoist figures as "nature mystics" since they enter into that different dimension by contemplating nature. They experience oneness with the cosmos intuitively rather than by reasoning their way to an intellectual conclusion. In a trance-like state, the mystic loses all sense of selfhood and individuality becoming one with the Dao. Some have referred to the experience as the "fast of the mind" in which one listens with the ears of the spirit. What exactly the experience feels like, Daoist sources are reluctant to say, but they readily offer advice about how to cultivate the experience. By way of exception, some Daoist sources also hint that the occasional mystic has experienced a somewhat more personal form of union with the divine akin to what Hindu and other traditions call "theistic mysticism."

What has been the **shaman's role** in Daoism?

Remnants of ancient shamanism continue to color much Daoist religious thought and practice. In pre-Daoist times, shamans were tribal leaders possessed of extraordinary powers. Reports from around the third century BCE describe how these *fang shi* or "masters of prescriptions," worked their magic. They could tap natural energies, exercise control over life and death, and assume the form of various powerful creatures. Shamanic specialists included many women as well as men. With the dawn of empire and agricultural economy, shamans became part of the governmental structure. Their duties included drawing spiritual powers to themselves as they entered into trance, exorcism, explaining omens and dreams, influencing the weather for favorable harvest, curing the sick, and divining heavenly portents at the behest of the emperor. A transformed shamanism lives on in various Daoist practices that are generally divided among the Black Hat priests, Red Turban masters, and spirit mediums. Daoist ritual specialists still fend off evil spirits and perform a vestige of the ancient ceremonies symbolizing the shaman's journey to the upper and lower worlds. That spiritual journey of ascent and descent remains perhaps the most distinctive survival of shamanistic lore. It appears in various traditions in surprising forms, including, for example, Muhammad's famous Night Journey and Ascension. Daoist ritual symbolism of the journey occurs in the master's "pacing the clouds" as he prepares the sacred space for the great religious observances.

Do Daoists and practitioners of CCT believe in **angels**?

Spirits of all kinds inhabit the ordinary world of countless adherents of Daoism and CCT. But none quite fit the precise description most readers would identify as angelic. Angels are generally understood as pure immortal spirits made that way from the start. Chinese Daoist and popular beliefs include countless immortal beings, but, apart from the highest gods, most of those began as human beings and achieved immortality later. In addition, angels in other traditions typically function as messengers or guardians. A variety of spirits play those roles in Daoist and CCT lore. Perhaps the closest thing to angels in the Chinese repertoire of religious symbolism are the *apsaras* imported into China with Buddhism.

Do Daoists and practitioners of CCT believe in **demons or devils**?

Demonic forces abound in the spiritual universe of millions of Chinese. Many demons are the unsettled spirits of the dead who roam the world in search of an elusive contentment. Some demons can herald good tidings, but most are disgruntled and thirsty for vengeance. Evil spirits, or *gui,* belong to a large category distinguished from an equally large category of generally benevolent beings called *shen,* a category that includes both deities and ancestral spirits. One of the essential features of Chinese thought on these matters is the notion that there are several different kinds of soul or

403

Six of the "Twelve Nurses," divine beings assigned to look out for the welfare of infants, especially during the first year of life, each nurse associated with one of the twelve months. The other six occupy a separate small chapel in Taipei's Bao An Gong temple.

spirit. The heavenly "yang soul" (called *hun*) rises at death to become a *shen* and abides from then on in heaven and in the ancestral tablets that have a prominent place on every home altar. The earthly "yin soul" (called *po*) returns to the grave with the body. Under certain circumstances, the *po* takes a negative turn and becomes an evil spirit, a *gui*, destined to create havoc for the living. Some of these evil spirits can be particularly dangerous, but unlike the "devils" of some other traditions, the *gui* are not particularly noted for their role in tempting humans to sin.

Are **dreams and visions** significant powers in Daoism or CCT?

An ability to interpret the dreams of ordinary people has long been part of the ritual menu of Chinese religious specialists, beginning with the shamans of old. In ancient times, specialists called *zhan ren* interpreted dreams using divination and astrology as their tools. Powerful and famous people, too, report having revelatory dreams that move them toward a new course of action. Dream accounts therefore frequently function as an instrument of divine or spiritual legitimation. There is often a very fine line between dream and vision, except that one can experience a vision while awake. Religiously important visions or dreams frequently feature major deities, such as Lao Zi or the Jade Emperor, who deliver instructions or revelations to the dreamer or visionary. In addition, visualization techniques figure prominently in the meditative practice of some Daoist schools. The Shang Qing school, for example, recommends that the meditator focus imaginatively on his or her indwelling deities, a technique similar to that used by several Tibetan Buddhist schools. By conjuring up intricate detail as described in the school's sacred texts, the meditator makes the presence of the god real and can thus unite with the divine presence.

HOLIDAYS AND REGULAR OBSERVANCES

What kind of **calendar** do Daoists and practitioners of CCT observe?

Firmly anchored in traditional astrological calculations, the Chinese lunar calendar consists of twelve months of twenty-nine or thirty days, since the time between new moons is about twenty-nine and a half days. The lunar year dovetails with the solar with the intercalation of extra months at certain intervals. Reckoning began around 2637 BCE, so that the year 2000 marks the year 4637. Each of the twelve animals of the zodiac is associated with a particular quality or event and gives its name to every twelfth year, beginning with the Rat (industry and prosperity) and proceeding in order through Ox (spring planting), Tiger (valor), Hare (longevity), Dragon (power and good fortune), Snake (cunning), Horse (perseverance), Sheep (filial piety) or Goat, Monkey (health), Rooster (protection), Dog (fidelity) and Pig (home and family). The year 2000 is the Year of the Dragon, 2001 that of the Snake, 2002 that of the Horse, and so on. Five full cycles, each named after one of the five elements (wood, fire, earth, metal and water) equals sixty years, an important interval for ritual purposes. Major annual markers are the winter (maximum yin) and summer (maximum yang) solstices and vernal and autumnal equinoxes. During each month, the most important times are the moments of new and full moon. Each month is divided into ten-day periods, six of those in turn considered a special time period, and six of those in turn equaling a full year. In addition, each year is divided into twenty-four climatic periods called breaths or nodes, described by such phrases as "full of snow" or "clear and bright." Every year, month, day, and hour is further identified by a combination of ten heavenly "stems" and twelve earthly "branches" (the monthly or zodiacal symbols). Branches and stems are primarily numerical designators, but each also bears important symbolic connotations. If you match one stem with one branch for succeeding years (S1/B1, S2/B2 .... S1/B11, S2/B12, S3/B1, and so on), you end up back at the beginning after sixty years. The result is an extremely detailed system of pinpointing special times according to a host of definitive characteristics. Each event occurring on earth has its heavenly parallel. For every conceivable type of human behavior there is an auspicious moment. Thus, the calendar has been not merely a way of keeping track of times for religious observances, but a kind of temporal map for negotiating the cosmos as well.

What are the major types of Daoist **religious observance**?

Daoist sources talk about three levels of ceremony. "Great Services" called *jiao,* which occur relatively infrequently; "Ritual Gatherings" called *fan hui*; and "Feast Days" called *tan.* Two essential features of every religious celebration are the preparation and the actual event. *Zhai* refers to several types of purifying fast. Strictly speaking the *zhai* is preparatory to the main ceremonial event, the offering or *jiao,* but certain distinct actions set the purification apart. Both celebrants and their sacred space need to be prepared ritually. To purify both mind and body, participants meditate in solitude, eat vegetarian meals, fast for a time, and refrain from sex. Preparation may commence as much as three days ahead, for the major feasts, and continue through the main event itself. Celebrants prepare the sacred space through a combination of actions, including chanting and burning incense. A category of events called *jiao* includes various kinds of festivities. In ancient times the principal *jiao* were associated with planting and harvest. Eventually, various Daoist sects incorporated elements of the time-honored traditions into their liturgies, but the agricultural element became secondary. Different groups compiled extensive collections of liturgical rites in massive tomes, with specific ceremonies for a wide range of occasions.

Does Daoism have any **annual celebrations**?

For virtually every temple community, the principal deity's birthday provides the occasion for a major yearly festivity. Celebrants focus on the temple and the main icon, sprucing up the building and decking out the deity in new finery. In addition there are dozens of other special days. The New Year emphasizes fresh start, with Lao Zi's feast on the first day and special prayers to the Jade Pure One on the eighth and the Jade Emperor on the ninth day of the first month. The latter is a lengthy festivity that culminates on the fifteenth with the Lantern Festival. "Clear and Bright" falls on the first day of the third month. (In mainland China this is not lunar but occurs always on April 5.) Its main thrust is to remember the dead, maintain burial places, and offer ritual meals at the graves. Dragon Boat races on the fifth day of the fifth month commemorate the drowning of a poet of old. More important, however, is the association of that month with the need to ward off spirits of disease at a time when, with the summer solstice approaching, yin energy begins to replace yang as the dominant energy. CCT devotees celebrate Guan Yin's ascension to heaven on the nineteenth of the sixth month, during which people also mark the mid-point in the year. On the seventh day of the seventh month, people observe the only night when the Weaving Maid and the Cowherd, a celestial couple, can be together. And the fifteenth marks the birthday of a Daoist deity called the Earth Controller, known in CCT as the emperor-sage Shun. Numerous rituals acknowledging the need to placate the wandering dead occupy many during the seventh month. Most prominent is the Ghost Festival on the fifteenth day, when people seek to propitiate the spirits by leaving food out for them. Daoist masters now officiate at the occasion, which was formerly a Buddhist observance. A mid-autumn celebration of the moon goddess's birthday, once a harvest festival, occurs on the fifteenth of the eighth month. On the ninth day of the ninth month, called Double-Yang because of the auspicious nature of the number nine, people once sought protection in amulets and fled lowland evil by taking to the hills. Nowadays, most people simply go for walks in the cool fresh autumn air. On the fifteenth of month ten, worshipers mark the birthday of a Daoist deity called the Controller of the Waters, known in CCT as the sage Yu. A winter festivity marks the solstice during the eleventh month. Before the twelfth month is even half spent, planning begins for the New Year.

Why is the **Chinese New Year** so important?

Chinese New Year festivities are associated, not surprisingly, with renewal generally and with powers that hold the promise of protection for the coming year. During these celebrations, religious Chinese add to their regular roster of symbolism extra images of important figures like the Eight Immortals and the deities of happiness, success and longevity. New Year is not a specifically Daoist observance, but rather a more generic special occasion on which people are moved to intensify their awareness of essential values. Festivities begin about ten days before the actual day. It starts when families send Cao Jun, deity of the Stove, to give an account of the family's deeds over the previous year to the Jade Emperor. On New Year's day, Cao Jun returns to his kitchen throne, where the family welcomes him with a fresh picture for the wall. Most families observe a series of private rituals, including elaborate meals and reverence to the ancestors. During the following two weeks or so, people pay special homage to the god of wealth. Festivities end with the Lantern Festival at the New Year's first full moon.

What is the **most important Daoist observance**?

A grand affair called the ritual of Cosmic Renewal occurs at varying intervals in different places. It was once on a sixty-year cycle, according to the ancient calendar reckoning calculated with the "branches and stems." Some temples celebrate this way as often as every ten years now. Whenever a community erects a new temple it is time for a renewal ritual. This major festival belongs to a larger category called *jiao.* Ritual specialists from the so-called Black Hat group have exclusive rights to officiate in these events. A standard feature is recitation from the *Jade Emperor Scripture,* and the focus of prayer is on seeking blessings of all kinds for the future. Massive organizational efforts precede the larger celebrations. They include interviewing prospective high priests from whom the committee can choose a leader, who will then arrange for a full staff of ritual specialists. Full-scale festivities require extensive construction of temporary altars or shrines. Celebrations nowadays typically go on for from three to five days, though they formerly lasted as long as nearly two months.

Do Daoists and practitioners of CCT celebrate the **birthdays** of any religious figures?

Deities both great and small are generally thought to have birthdays because the vast majority of them were once human beings. CCT has transformed numerous figures originally Daoist, Buddhist, and Confucian into more comfortable characters—members of everybody's family, in effect. Other deities remain in their more exalted original Daoist forms. The following are only a few of the literally hundreds of divine birthday dates. Among the earliest in the year is the Jade Emperor, celebrated on the ninth of the first month. On the third day of the second month, CCT acknowledges Wen Chang Di Jun, the god of literature and learning. Guan Yin's birthday occurs on the nineteenth of the second month. Xuan Tian Shang Di, the Supreme Emperor of Dark Heaven, was born on the third of the third month and is celebrated in some four hundred Taiwanese temples. A quasi-Daoist deity called the Great Emperor Who Protects Life, Bao Sheng Da Di, is celebrated on the fifteenth of the third month. Ma Zu, often referred to as the Great Aunt or Grandma, has her celebration on the twenty-third of the third month. On the thirteenth day of month five the general-become-deity Guan Di gets his due. An otherwise anonymous City God's day is the fifteenth of the sixth month. Devotees of CCT observe the birthdays of Cao Jun on the third day of the eighth month, and that of Tu Di Gong on the fifteenth. Also on the third of that month Daoists celebrate the birthday of Si Ming, the Director of Destiny, known in CCT as the Kitchen God or Hearth Deity.

What are some other important **celebrations** for Daoism and CCT?

Daoists observe days special to the Three Officials (or Officers or Rulers), whom CCT call Shun, Yao, and Yu, on the fifteenth days of the first, seventh, and tenth lunar months. Their days are associated respectively with heaven, earth, and water. The Heavenly Official, Shun, ranks highest and remains very popular in Taiwan, for example. The Water Official, Yu, is celebrated for having saved the world from uncontrolled flooding. Three Daoist deities considered at the pinnacle of the pantheon are known as the Three Primordials. Their festival days coincide with those of the Three Officials, respectively, the first two of which also coincide with the CCT Lantern Festival and Ghost Festival.

CUSTOMS AND RITUALS

What **rites** do worshipers practice in Daoist and CCT temples?

One of the most important and easily observable temple rituals involves the offering of incense. Worshipers buy three slender sticks of incense at a small temple shop

Traditional Chinese grave site, with horseshoe shape sloping and opening toward the south, with memorial spirit tablet over the grave, near Malacca, Malaysia.

that supplies a variety of materials for different sorts of offerings. Devotees can make their offerings either at the main altar or at any of a number of side or subordinate altars, depending on the size of the temple and which deity they choose to address. Those who wish to worship at the main shrine may first approach the large incense kettle that normally stands in the central courtyard. Igniting their incense sticks, they hold them upright between folded hands, wave them before the deity, and bow from the waist toward the object of their devotion. After prayer they insert the handles of the burning incense wands into the sand and ashes in the kettle. On some occasions a devotee might have his or her sticks placed in a holder on an altar. Some take incense ash home for use as a curative medicine. Equally important is a more ritually generic type of devotional prayer in which devotees supplicate the various deities for favors. Worshipers generally kneel to address the chosen deity, praying either aloud or in silence, either bowing humbly or looking at the image. Offerings other than incense include a variety of foods, most commonly fruits, rice, vegetables, wine and sweets. When worshipers make such offerings, they often have a temple staff member light a candle for them on the altar. Toward the end of a typical episode of temple worship, devotees will burn symbolic imitation paper money as an offering. All temples provide one or more small furnaces in which worshipers offer gold paper to the deities and silver to ancestors. These burnt offerings symbolize personal sacrifice in hope of blessing and commitment to the ongoing well-being of departed family members.

409

Is there a standard Daoist **group liturgical worship**?

Most of the ritual activity one can observe at temples throughout the day consists of individual or family worship. At various times during the day, members of pious organizations may gather for group chanting of liturgical prayers. The priest may address a sermon to such gatherings as well. Major Daoist sects have devised their own special communal rituals, and some have survived intact into our time and are still practiced, especially in rural areas and more traditional villages. Many of these involve group chanting of sacred texts, in imitation of the chanting of the assembled gods themselves when they created the universe. One important communal ritual is that based on the teachings of the Ling Bao sect. Elaborate theatrical liturgies address issues and powers in three levels or "registers"—the celestial, the terrestrial, and the human. The Golden Register of rituals honors the family of the emperor at the celestial level. A terrestrial level called the Yellow Register is aimed at peaceful rest for the deceased. The now discontinued Jade Register once focused on securing salvation for all people. The officiants and their ritual implements mediate between the divine and human participants. Rites once dedicated to the emperor and his court are now undertaken on behalf of local or family groups known to uphold religious standards. Observances begin with an evening or vespers prayer to announce the start of the rituals and symbolically reconstruct a sacred realm in which to enact the rites. Great attention goes into setting the ritual scene, a miniature of the cosmos with gates at the four cardinal directions. Action resumes the next morning with a fast and an offering. Imitating a creative divine act, the officiant recreates the sacred space by pacing out creation and journeys symbolically to the heavens to bring down heavenly powers. As part of the ritual the master (or priest) meditates silently, focusing on visual imagery as a way of bringing health to the assembled people. The entire ritual ends on the next day with the master facing the assembly as one now returned to earth. He then dismantles the altar, burns the sacred texts, and sends the deities back to their heavenly abodes.

Is **meditation** important in Daoism or CCT?

Dominant forms of devotional expression in CCT tend to be associated with more extroverted ritual and supplicatory prayer. Classical and later Daoist sources, on the other hand, describe various meditative methods designed to help the practitioner turn inward. In fact, Chan Buddhism, the Chinese precursor to the more famous Japanese Zen, seems to have borrowed much from Daoism in this respect. The meditator "sits and forgets" in the presence of nature, engaging in the "fast of the mind." Principal stages in Daoist meditative technique are the following: First the meditator calms the body by adopting a fixed posture and slow, regular breathing. As the meditator becomes one with his or her breathing, distractions begin to dissolve. To develop greater concentration, the meditator chooses a specific symbolic focus for detailed visualization. In the next stage, the meditator moves beyond this discursive intellectu-

What is ancestor veneration and what is its connection with Daoism or CCT?

Concern over maintaining the integrity of one's connections with family lineage is one of the hallmarks of Chinese religious and social life. Members of each family line—male descendants from a shared ancestor, with wives attached to their husband's line—acknowledge both the continued spiritual presence and the sacredness of their forebears. Their reasons are many: expression of grief, assistance of the deceased in his or her struggles beyond the grave, the desire for blessings, feeling a sense of family cohesiveness, showing continued affection for the dead. Long after the funeral and an extended period of official mourning, families pay homage to the dead both at the cemetery and at the ancestral shrine in the home. There, on the altar table, the family preserves a set of tablets, each with the name of one deceased relative inscribed on it. In very wealthy families of times past the oldest son would dedicate his life to looking after the proper performance of the rites, foregoing virtually all other activities. For most families today, ongoing activities include chiefly the regular visits to the cemetery, annual refurbishment of the grave for the feast called "Clear and Bright" (*ching ming*) and daily prayers at the home shrine. At home family members make the same kinds of symbolic offerings to the ancestors as to the deities enshrined on the domestic altar. Very wealthy families have often built special ancestral temples as major monuments to the spiritual power of the dead. Few if any of these practices or specific concerns are uniquely Daoist. It is all part of the broadly Chinese religious patrimony, with some elements perhaps more closely linked to CCT than to any specific major tradition.

alizing into the "fast of the mind." Leaving behind all symbols and ideas, the meditator enters a realm where images are irrelevant. Finally, the meditator loses all sense of self and attains union with the Dao.

How do Daoists **worship at home** and throughout the day when they are not in temples?

Worshipers perform at home many of the same rituals they perform in the temple. Home shrines or family altars are miniature versions of the temple's sacred objects. Smaller images of the various deities enjoy places of honor. Before the image family members place a few apples or oranges, for example, and small incense pots hold small burning sticks just as the kettle in the temple courtyard does. Many devout Chinese begin their day by offering incense to the terrestrial deity of the home, who is sometimes depicted as five separate figures recalling the five elements. This earth deity is at

411

the bottom of an administrative "flow chart," reporting to the district deity, who in turn reports to the city god, and he to the country god. Offerings to family ancestors and consultation with an almanac as to the spiritual qualities of the particular day are other regular rituals. Many private individuals still practice *tai ji chuan,* a set of rhythmic movements designed to balance yin and yang and maximize energy.

What kinds of special **ritual objects** figure in Daoist worship and prayer?

Specific lists of objects vary somewhat among the different schools and sects. Here are the most important ritual devices of the Celestial Masters school. First and foremost are the ubiquitous talismans that consist of a written magical formula or mantra symbolizing a contract between the deities and human beings engaging in a ritual exchange. Only a qualified ritual specialist may execute a talisman, which usually includes a specially drawn Chinese character as well as other visual symbols appropriate to a particular spiritual purpose. Possessors of talismans generally think of them as guarantees of divine aid. People wear them or hang them in home or office to attract positive energies. The "Precious Sword of the Seven Stars," symbolizing the Big Dipper, appears often in blessings and exorcisms, whether for individuals or as part of Cosmic Renewal observances. As a symbolic purification to the cardinal directions, ritualists sip from a copper bowl and blow a spray through closed lips. Special stone seals of various kinds allow the specialist to make official documents such as talismans. Priests hold a stiff tablet, as if reading from a book. In exorcism rituals, Black Hats use the sword along with handbells, while Red Turbans use a horn and a whip.

Is **exorcism** important in Daoist practice?

Many Daoist rituals are designed to expel, control, or pacify troublesome spirits, or, by extension, to banish drought, famine, or outlaws who might have been plaguing the local citizenry. Daoists rarely identify individual problems as personal cases of demonic (*gui*) possession. Much more common are instances in which a specialist's skills are required to liberate temples, homes, and business establishments from evil influences. Until some thirty years ago, Roman Catholic tradition included a specific ritual to ordain young candidates for the priesthood to the Order of Exorcist, one of four so-called "minor orders." Ordination to the Daoist priesthood still includes an emphasis on the ability to perform exorcism as one of its essential features. Rare descriptions of demonic possession suggest some elements similar those described in Roman Catholic archival accounts of exorcism, including the need to have several stout attendants restrain the possessed person occasionally. After performing a variety of ritual actions, such as lighting candles and incense and burning the appropriate charm, the exorcist enjoins the spirit to depart and a contest of wills ensures. More common, indeed regularly scheduled, rites of temple purification may include dramatization of an encounter between the offending demon and the deity called Chung Kuei, dis-

Daoism and Martial Arts

Early each morning, nearly everywhere in China, people gather in public places both large and small to practice a slow graceful routine of physical movements called *tai ji chuan*. People of all ages can engage in this activity. Though it is not strenuous the way higher-speed exercises can be, *tai ji* (also commonly spelled t'ai chi) nevertheless puts noticeable demands on an astonishingly wide range of muscles all over the body. The idea is not simple physical toning, however, even though that is an obvious benefit. Its purpose is to maintain or restore one's overall sense of health and well-being through relaxed concentration. Proper practice relieves blockages of vital energy and returns the whole person to balance and harmony both physically and spiritually. *Tai ji* routines and styles are varied, with three methods called Chen, Wu, and Yang most common nowadays. Many of the underlying principles in the practice are of Daoist origin and remain a regular part of the regimen in many Daoist monasteries. But it seems more reasonable on the whole to identify *tai ji* as a more generically Chinese phenomenon, since for centuries non-Daoists have made use of it with no apparent direct connection with Daoist beliefs. As for its relationship to actual martial arts, *tai ji* movement is based on the notion that non-aggressiveness, what is called "being weak like water," is ultimately more effective than trying to overwhelm one's opponent with brute force. Hence, for example, the Japanese term *ju-do* derives from a Chinese term (*rou dao*) that means "the way of yielding."

patcher of demons. After the demon (sometimes played by a member of the temple staff or a professional actor) steals an incense burner, the priest/deity subdues the evil one and returns the stolen item to the temple gods. Only through the dominance of yang over yin can a successful exorcism be carried out. A high moment occurs as the high priest drives the evil spirit out to the accompaniment of intense sound from percussion instruments. Another method for ridding a building of an evil presence is to create billows of holy smoke by boiling oil and adding water to it.

Is **divination** important to Daoists and practitioners of CCT?

Divinatory rites are more critical to Daoism and CCT than to many other major traditions. Long before Daoism came into being as a distinct set of traditions, the Chinese practiced divination through the stars, yarrow sticks, oracle bones, and tortoise shells. Important types of divination are the celestial, the terrestrial, interpretations of events and omens, and the forecasting of individual destinies. Celestial divination, a variety of astrological interpretation, plots the locations of stars according to one of the twelve

413

Images of Guan Yin and a barrel of Joss Sticks used for divination rituals, in a CCT temple in Keelung, Taiwan.

"palaces" associated with the lunar month of one's birth in order to understand a host of factors including sickness and health, luck, family issues, and personality. Terrestrial divination uses an elaborate geomantic compass to assist practitioners in aligning their lives most effectively with the forces of nature. All ordinary events in the life of each person have their hidden meanings, and special divinatory skills allow one to interpret the nature of the energy played out in all events in relation to the specific time of day or year. Some events clearly have ominous qualities and require specialized interpretative skills. Thunder or lightning and other natural events suggest forces that set them aside from more mundane happenings. Perhaps the most important and widespread forms of divination are those that help people divine their personal destinies. Some focus on reading physical features, such as facial characteristics or palm lines. Here we are moving away from strictly Daoist teaching and into popular practice.

How do Daoists and practitioners of CCT today **determine their destinies** with divination?

Most common of the methods are those that involve the use of bamboo sticks and crescent-shaped blocks. In CCT temples, devotees approach a barrel crammed full of long sticks containing combinations of trigrams called hexagrams, or, alternatively, numbers from one to sixty-four (the total number of combinations of the eight tri-

Feng Shui and Daoism

Feng shui, a term meaning "wind and water," is a type of terrestrial divination designed to help practitioners make practical decisions about living arrangements that will be in harmony with natural energies and forces. This symbolic system coordinates critical elements of time and space to allow for maximum harmony in every conceivable human interaction with nature. All natural features, including trees, rivers, mountains, and valleys, for example, have their distinctive influences on the flow of energy. Failure to take of these forces into account can make life much more difficult than it need be. In practical terms, *Feng shui* assists people most of all in choosing the orientation and design of the "built environment"—in other words, architecture and urban planning. A geomantic compass allows people to arrange the spaces in which they live and work in accordance with the principle of the "Nine Palaces." The compass indicates where yin and yang energies flow. A grid of nine squares, each of which contains three numbers from one to nine, can be used in connection with building plans to indicate optimum placement of particular kinds of spaces within a home or office (e.g. storage, study, eating, or sleeping spaces). This ancient environmentalist system has grown from careful observation of the consequences of human interaction with the greater cosmos. Chinese tradition emphasizes the need to conform with the "way" of nature rather than attempting to dominate it.

grams). Grabbing a handful of sticks, they shake them and then let them fall back into the barrel. Invariably one stick will protrude above the rest, and it provides the critical symbol for that individual to interpret. When sticks are numbered, devotees request a corresponding slip of paper from the temple staff. On the paper they then read an often enigmatic or poetic interpretation of the corresponding hexagram. Devotees can also drop a pair of crescent-shaped blocks with one smooth side symbolizing yang and one convex side symbolizing yin. Devotees pose questions as they drop the blocks. One yang and one yin side up means "yes," while the other combinations mean "no." Worshipers unsatisfied with a particular answer may simply continue dropping blocks until they receive the desired response.

Do Daoists and practitioners of CCT make **pilgrimages**?

Pilgrimage has long been integral to most of the major Chinese religious traditions. The Chinese term typically translated as "making pilgrimage" (*chao shan jin xiang*) actually means "paying respects to a mountain by presenting incense." Beginning in at least the fourth century CE and growing dramatically from the eighth to twelfth centuries, pilgrimage practices of the various traditions came to be identified with certain specific mountains, with some mountains claimed by more than one tradition. Once identified as a particularly sacred place, a mountain became the site of one or more temples. Eventually Daoists and others developed elaborate sacred geographies mapped out with reference to the major sacred peaks or ranges. Pilgrimage to the sacred mountains thus became a symbolic journey through the universe. On some mountains, such as Wu Dang Shan, Daoists have constructed miniature versions of the macrocosm, identifying its subdivisions with such enchanting names as Jade Void, Primordial Harmony, Purple Empyrean, and Perfect Felicity. Mountains are the dwelling places of the gods and immortals and as such naturally became favorite places of retreat for Daoist scholars and masters. Mountain settings have other, more primal, symbolism for Daoists as well. They embody the perfect harmony of male Yang and female Yin. Deep within mountain caves spiritual seekers could contact the eternal feminine energies. Popular pilgrimage has generally revolved around visits to the mountain temples rather than around extended spiritual retreat. A deity called generically the Old Man of the Mountain, often depicted with his pet tiger, appears in many temples all over Asia, including Buddhist sites, making a symbolic pilgrimage possible even for those who cannot manage the actual journey. Today, various organizations arrange pilgrimage-tours to any of several dozen sacred sites in the People's Republic and in Taiwan.

Do **acupuncture and acupressure** have any Daoist connections?

Neither acupuncture nor acupressure is a specifically religious practice. They are associated with healing, but both draw on ancient Chinese principles that have found their way to the center of Daoist teaching. Illness indicates a lack of *qi,* the vital force, which courses through the body along an intricate system of meridians. Blockage of vital energy causes an imbalance of Yin and Yang. Traditional Daoist-influenced maps of the body associate particular nodes with specific symptoms and internal organs. The whole system is based on a carefully observed network of correspondences. Not only is every part of the human body connected to every other part and to the spirit, but the human microcosm parallels in every detail the macrocosm of the universe. Proper placement of acupuncture needles, or appropriate application of pressure, to the malfunctioning energy juncture along any of the meridians seeks to restore the flow and balance, and hence promotes the rise of vital energies that are the essence of health and well-being.

Is **music** important in Daoist and CCT ritual?

Music has been an essential ingredient in virtually all indigenous Chinese religious ritual for millennia. Students of Daoist masters are expected to begin their formal training by becoming accomplished in the use of a full range of string, wind, and percussion instruments. These ancient devices include not only the mysterious booming gongs and bowed or plucked strings many readers may already associate with Asian music, but the less well-known woodwinds whose high reedy voices produce an almost eerie effect. Daoist ritual music has been related to imperial court music and, somewhat more recently, Chinese opera. Ritual music aims at stirring feelings uniquely appropriate to the occasion. In these last several respects, Daoist ritual music has much in common with the music that is an essential ingredient in many Shinto ceremonies in Japan. Two percussion instruments used to keep time for chanting and recitation of scripture are virtually identical to those used for the same purpose in Buddhist ritual all over Asia. Large-scale chanting on especially solemn occasions is accompanied by an ensemble of four or more instruments of various types. Percussion instruments along with other wind and string instruments back up the lead played on oboe-like woodwinds, lutes, and bowed strings. When a single master recites a sacred text, a solo instrument is generally the only accompaniment.

What about **dance**?

Liturgical dance is just as important as music. During the festival of Cosmic Renewal, for example, the principal ritual specialist performs a dance of shamanic origin called the Steps of Yu. The dancer traces the outline of the Big Dipper to commune with the god of the Pole Star. He ascends symbolically into the heavens to visit the Three Pure Ones. Some dances engage the assembled community of worshipers, as when all gathered celebrate the new light by circumambulating the altar. Another dance functions as an offertory procession in which worshipers bring offerings to the ritual leaders who in turn present them to the gods.

Do Daoists **pray** in any **particular language**?

Since Daoism originated in China, one would naturally expect that most practitioners of the tradition pray in Chinese. That is so not because of any essential identification of Chinese as a sacred language or liturgical tongue as such. Use of the vernacular has been the general practice in Daoism, and until recently it happens that most practitioners have been Chinese-speakers. So as small pockets of Daoist practice have arisen here and there outside China, especially in recent times, practitioners have used their native tongues in ritual.

Are there any other important **Daoist ritual settings** apart from public temple and private home?

Perhaps the most common Daoist sacred space is the spectacular yet temporary structure unobtrusively called an altar (*tan*). Usually set up in large open fields or vacant lots, multi-level facades made of bamboo and covered with colorfully decorated paper simulate grand architectural spaces. These altars are the scene of the major festivals (*jiao*) that extend over several days. They enshrine such popular deities as the Jade Emperor and Zhang Dao Ling. Afterwards, the altars are taken down and the decorations burned. Several other ritual venues have been important as well, though not all intended for larger gatherings. Organizations within the various sectarian movements that have come and gone throughout the history of Daoism have typically practiced their own unique and often esoteric rituals. Always preceded by elaborate purification, these specialized rituals could take place either in natural settings, such as remote mountain retreats, or in enclosed meditative venues called "purity chambers." There initiates would closet themselves for lengthy periods of disciplined mental focusing.

How do Daoism and CCT commemorate **death and mourning** ritually?

Special rites are designed for those approaching death, for burial day and for subsequent memorials. For the elderly and terminally ill, ceremonies can include rituals related to aging and specific illnesses. Prayers for longevity might include, for example, recitation from the scripture called *The Northern Dipper's Extension of Life*. Traditional funerals conducted under Daoist auspices can be very elaborate. At many funerals, a central feature is the recitation of scripture often performed, curiously, by Buddhist monks or nuns. Many Chinese, both in China and in places like Malaysia where there are sizable Chinese communities, still choose to bury their dead in distinctive graves. A horseshoe-shaped stone or concrete enclosure is set into a gentle slope with the open side to the south and the arms of the "horseshoe" inclining toward the south. Following the principles of *feng shui,* the enclosure helps to contain the maximum positive *qi* while allowing necessary drainage. Burial ceremonies typically conclude with placing a memorial or name tablet atop the coffin during final prayers. The coffin is then buried, head to the south, within the semi-circular enclosure. Family members take the tablet home for installation on the domestic altar. Weekly rituals held from the seventh to the forty-ninth day after death may be even more complex than that of the actual burial. Salvation rituals are especially important in cases of violent or premature death. In order to liberate such unfortunate souls, a ritual of "crossing over" is designed to shatter the very portals of the underworld. The so-called Ghost Festival, held either at the end of a Cosmic Renewal or on the fifteenth day of the seventh month, placates the "hungry spirits" with often elaborate offerings and animal sacrifice presided over by seven officiants. For those who died before being able to marry, posthumous "spirit marriages" engage a living proxy to marry the deceased person symbolically, while allowing the proxy to proceed with his or her marriage plans in due course.

CONFUCIANISM, THE LITERATI, AND CHINESE IMPERIAL TRADITION

HISTORY AND SOURCES

Who was **Confucius** and what do we know about his life?

Confucius was born around 551 BCE and died in 479 BCE, making him an almost exact contemporary of the Buddha. The name by which he is most commonly known, Confucius, is a Latinized form of Kong Fu Zi, Venerable Master Kong. According to tradition, his mother, Yan Zheng Zai, had prayed on Mount Ni that she would have a child. Confucius' father, Shu Liang He, died when the child was three years old, and his mother raised him under difficult circumstances. At nineteen, Confucius married and had a son and a daughter. His marriage, which was not very happy, would end with the death of his wife, and his son died during Confucius' life. At twenty-two, he began the first of several jobs for the state of Lu. At twenty-six (some say thirty-three), Confucius went to the Zhou dynasty's imperial capital of Lu to study royal ceremony and seek a government position. There he is said to have met the aged Lao Zi. Traditional accounts of that meeting (with a decidedly Daoist slant) report that Lao Zi took Confucius to task for wasting effort on formal study and reliance on ethical absolutes. He would do far better to observe how nature accomplishes all good things without contrivance, effortlessly. Still Confucius pursued his effortful path. He spent many years teaching privately and sought to win converts to his ethical and political views. At about fifty, he won a minor governmental post. But he failed to gain the public recognition he craved. Hoping to find a willing political patron, he went into a thirteen-year self-imposed exile, wandering in and out of nine provinces. Confucius returned home at the age of sixty-eight, there to spend his last five years studying and editing the Classics. The Master had a passion for fostering the kind of order in society that he felt sure could offer genuine happiness. He sought to articulate a view of the individual who could contribute to society through self-mastery and personal responsibility.

What is **Chinese Imperial Tradition** (CIT) and when did it begin?

Long before the time of Confucius, a system of beliefs and practices had developed around the role of the emperor in cosmic affairs. The Chinese had come to regard the emperor as the Son of Heaven. He bore the awesome responsibility of securing the welfare of all his subjects by discerning and executing faithfully the Will (or Mandate) of Heaven. Though the emperor was called Son of Heaven, he was not considered a deity. He was rather one who had the ultimate sanction for exercising authority on earth, so long as he maintained contact with the heavenly mandate. Whenever a ruler failed to see that his people enjoyed universal justice, the people could justifiably conclude that Heaven's mandate had passed to a more worthy leader. Revolution was the solution. Chinese Imperial Tradition had its pantheon of deities arranged in several hierarchical levels, so that the earthly royal administration appeared to mirror the heavenly. CIT did not revolve around a sacred scripture, nor did it have a separate "ecclesiastical" structure or ordained priesthood. It did, however, have its own equivalent of religious doctrine, elaborate rituals comparable in form and content to those of many major religious traditions, and a hierarchical organization complete with ritual specialists. CIT is an integral part of the religious history of China, since it formed the broad backdrop against which nearly the whole of that history has been played out.

What is **Confucianism** and who were the **Literati**?

"Confucianism" refers to the system of social, ethical, and religious beliefs and practices associated with Confucius. The term does not imply the worship of Confucius as a supreme or central deity, but it does acknowledge his foundational and pivotal role in the cultivation of beliefs and practices that have remained important in many Asian societies for centuries. Some scholars suggest that we replace "Confucianism" with "Literati Tradition" to indicate that the complex of beliefs and practices now generally attributed to Confucius is actually part of a broader cultural phenomenon. "Literati" (the Latin for "the lettered, educated") is a name coined by non-Chinese scholars to describe the cultural elite most influential in promoting and preserving the Chinese imperial system. The Literati were the highly educated, professionally specialized bureaucrats who maintained the far-flung governmental structures of the empire. They also functioned as the ritual specialists in the many religious ceremonies performed under imperial auspices for sponsorship.

How have **Confucianism** and **Literati** traditions **interacted**?

Confucius was one of the Literati, but he and the movement that bears his name have also had a life of their own. The Literati were the social class most responsible for maintaining all the mechanisms of the imperial administration. One of their chief tools was an elaborate system of training that culminated in "civil service" examinations (the grandfather of all civil service systems) and the awarding of degrees. When the imperial examination system was abolished in 1905 in favor of more modern educational methods, the Literati began to disappear as a social class. In 1911, the last emperor was deposed, ending three millennia of Chinese imperial rule. But Confucius did not die with the Literati and the Empire, for over the centuries he had become an integral part of Chinese culture. He was both a symbol of the best in Chinese tradition and a man revered religiously as well. There is some overlapping, therefore, among these three developments—Confucianism, the Literati tradition, and the CIT—but they are not identical. Think of them as a railway that has sometimes run along a single track and sometimes branched off into two or three parallel tracks along the same broad right-of-way. In short, all Literati were Confucians, and since CIT in

Confucius in stone, Tokyo Confucius temple.

general incorporated the Confucian philosophy, the Literati became the official "staff" of CIT. But not all those who consider themselves Confucians are Literati. And with the end of the empire came the end of the Literati as a cultural/religious elite.

What were the earliest Confucian sacred texts?

A set of works called the Five Classics (*Wu Jing*) became a formal collection sometime during the Han dynasty (202 BCE–220 CE). The *Yi Jing,* or *Classic of Change,* is a manual of divination dating from the early Zhou dynasty (c. 1030–256 BCE). Based on the sixty-four hexagrams formed by combinations of the eight trigrams

421

The Tang Dynasty

The Tang (617 to 907 CE) was the sixth-to-last Chinese dynasty. It is well known because the period saw great achievements in government and business as well as in letters and the arts. Considered a golden age of Chinese civilization, the Tang was also an age of great expansion. At its height, the empire stretched from Turkmenistan in the west to Korea (which was a vassal state) in the east, and from Manchuria to northern India. One historian called the Tang "the consummate Chinese dynasty...formidable, influential, and innovative."

One of the Tang's innovations was the balance of administrative power: government was separated into three main branches: the Imperial Secretariat (which organized the emperor's directives into policies); the Imperial Chancellery (which reviewed the policies and monitored the bureaucracy); and the Department of States and Affairs (which carried out the policies through the administration of six ministries). One of the most forward-thinking developments of the Tang dynasty was the growth of a civil service. Candidates for public service were trained in the Confucian principles before they took an examination that would qualify them for official duty.

(described in the chapter on Daoism), the *Yi Jing* assists practitioners in the interpretation of fundamental life choices. Although it was originally designed as a descriptive device, popular usage over the centuries has bestowed on the book powers of prognostication. The *Classic of History (Shu Jing)* assembles historical documents from as early as 600 BCE to as late as 200 CE. An anthology of over three hundred poems, some from as early as 800 to 600 BCE, is called the *Classic of Poetry* (*Shi Jing*). Ancient tradition that Confucius himself had compiled the material from a larger collection of over three thousand pieces is probably inaccurate. But it does appear that Confucius and his disciples used the poems as sources of ethical example. Completed around 100 CE of material from much earlier times, the *Classic of Rites (Li Ji)* preserves ceremonial records that offer essential insights into ritual life. It eventually became one of three texts on "rites" known collectively (with the *Ceremonial and Ritual* or *Yi Li* and the Officials of the Zhou [dynasty] or Zhou Li) as the *Li Ching*. Finally, the *Annals of Spring and Autumn (Chun Qiu)* chronicles events in Confucius' home province of Lu from 722–481 BCE (called the period of Spring and Autumn), and the tradition that Confucius edited the text seems to be accurate. Confucius may also have authored part of an extensive commentary on the *Yi Jing*. A now-lost *Classic of Music (Yue Jing)* would have constituted the sixth "Classic." Confucius probably did not edit the last four classics as ancient tradition claims, though he certainly knew the material intimately.

What other **canonical texts** are especially important in Confucian tradition?

A second collection called the *Four Books* (*Ssu Shu*) consists of very ancient texts eventually brought together during the Song dynasty (960–1279 CE). Most famous of the four is a work commonly called the *Analects* (*Lun Yu*), a compilation of Confucius' sayings and dialogues edited by second-generation disciples around 400 BCE. The Great Learning *(Da Xue)* is a chapter excerpted from the *Classic of Rites,* singled out now as a separate Book because of its centrality to Confucian thought. Dating to about 350 BCE, this work is probably the single most important statement of Confucian views on the cultivation of the ideal human being, or "superior person," essential to a harmonious society. Another excerpt from the *Classic of Rites* is now regarded as a separate Book called the *Doctrine of the Mean* (*Zhong Yong*), traditionally attributed to Confucius' grandson Zu Ssu. Its theme is the harmonious development of human nature by means of right action and the principle of reciprocity as manifest in the five fundamental relationships. Finally the *Meng Zi* includes the largely ethical and political teachings of Meng Zi (c. 372–289 BCE), commonly known as Mencius. He was one of the foundational figures in the interpretation of the classic Literati themes expounded by Confucius. The book's seven sections emphasize the need for vigilance in cultivating virtue with the ultimate goal of living in harmony with the Will (or Mandate) of Heaven. By about 1200 CE, the complete Literati "canon" of texts included not only the Five Classics and the Four Books, but four other works considered to contain the essentials of Confucian and Literati views on all things under Heaven.

What is **Neo-Confucianism**?

During the Song dynasty (960–1279 CE), Confucian tradition underwent a kind of renaissance. Buddhism and Daoism had both developed into powerful influences at all levels of Chinese life and culture. A host of talented Confucian scholars reinterpreted their tradition in light of, and in "dialogue" with, Buddhist and Daoist concepts. Three tenth- and eleventh-century scholars pioneered what has come to be known in China as "Learning of Principle" (*li xue*) and beyond Asia as Neo-Confucianism. Sun Fu (922–1057), Shi Qia (1005–45) and Hu Yuan (933–1059) transformed and revitalized the Confucian curriculum, thus paving the way for later teachers in their movement. Zhou Dun Yi (1017–73) continued the dramatic changes by developing *li* as a spiritual or metaphysical principle rather than as simply a term for propriety in relationships and ritual. He and his successors expanded Confucian teaching into a full-scale cosmological system. Zhu Xi (1130–1200) is the "Thomas Aquinas" of the school in the sense that he synthesized the teachings of his predecessors into his own carefully coordinated system. Zhu Xi became a sort of lightning rod for subsequent generations of scholars, all of whom had to account for his pioneering thought one way or another.

The *Analects* of Confucius

Excerpts from Book II of the *Analects:*

1. The Master said, "He who exercises government by means of his virtue may be compared to the north polar star, which keeps its place and all the stars turn towards it."

3. The Master said, "If the people be led by the laws, and uniformity sought to be given them by punishments, they will try to avoid the punishment, but they have no sense of shame. If they be led by virtue, and uniformity sought to be given them by the rules of propriety, they will have the sense of shame, and moreover will become good."

4. The Master said, "At fifteen, I had my mind bent on learning. At thirty, I stood firm. At forty, I had no doubts. At fifty, I knew the decrees of Heaven. At sixty, my ear was an obedient organ for the reception of truth. At seventy, I could follow what my heart desired, without transgressing what was right."

5. Mang-I [Tzu] asked what filial piety was. The Master said, "It is not being disobedient."

Soon after, as Fan Ch'ih was driving him, the Master told him, saying, "Mang-I asked me what filial piety was, and I answered him: 'not being disobedient.'"

Fan Ch'ih said, "What did you mean?" The Master replied, "That parents, when alive, should be served according to propriety; that, when dead, they should be buried according to propriety; and that they should be sacrificed to according to propriety."

10. The Master said, "See what a man does. Mark his motives. Examine in what things he rests. How can a man conceal his character?"

20. Chi K'ang [Tzu] asked how to cause the people to reverence their ruler, to be faithful to him, and to go on to nerve themselves to virtue. The Master said, "Let him preside over them with gravity—then they will reverence to him. Let him be filial and kind to all—then they will be faithful to him. Let him advance the good and teach the incompetent—then they will eagerly seek to be virtuous."

Did **Confucian tradition** spread beyond China?

Confucian themes pervade the cultures of both Korea and Japan. Temples dedicated to Confucius have never been nearly as numerous in either country as Buddhist temples or Shinto shrines, for example, and today very few active ones remain. But the influence of the Master is still discernible everywhere. Much of that influence is due to a long history of cultural and diplomatic relations between China and Korea. As early as the seventh century, Korean rulers welcomed Confucian thought as a master plan for political administration. Under the Koryo dynasty (918–1392 CE), Confucianism took its place alongside of divination and Buddhism as the third in a triad of essential traditional teachings. Korean Confucianism reached its zenith during the long-lived Yi dynasty (1392–1910). There was a time, Koreans occasionally point out, when even the Chinese confessed that their Korean neighbors had outdone them in devotion to Confucius. In Seoul, a Confucian university called Sungkyunkwan remains an important symbol of the tradition's impact on Korea. Confucian tradition came to Japan via Korea around 400 CE, a century and a half before Buddhism. Early Confucian scholars brought Chinese ideas to the Japanese imperial court, diffusing concepts that would go on to become an integral part of Japanese culture. Today the once-elegant Confucian temple in downtown Tokyo has few visitors and is badly in need of repair. But Confucian ideals of family and social relationships are still part of the cultural air the Japanese people breathe.

Has Confucianism ever been intimately identified with specific **political regimes**?

Confucian teaching offers a great deal of reflection on the nature of an orderly society and methods of governing. It is therefore not surprising that a number of political regimes have chosen the Confucian system as their official ideology. Emperor Wu Di (r. 140–87 BCE) of the Han dynasty (202 BCE–220 CE) was the first to do so, paving the way for a long and complex association between Confucian teaching and Chinese government. In Korea, Confucianism became the official religion of Korea by decree of the Yi (1392–1910) dynasty in 1392, to Buddhism's detriment. Leaders condemned Buddhism's view of this world as illusory and argued for the more humanistic approach of Confucian tradition. Perhaps the most far-reaching result was that education toppled from its elite pedestal and became available to a wide public. Confucianism took somewhat longer to forge its links to the Japanese imperial government. During the Tokugawa period (1600–1868), after the capital had moved to Tokyo, Confucian tradition enjoyed its closest association with Japanese imperial rule. Particularly in the realm of international relations, the legacy of Confucian political thought stood out. Confucians played an important role in the Meiji Restoration of 1868, which involved a restructuring of imperial administration. As the Japanese grew to regard Confucianism as an unwelcome import, the tradition's official influence in governmental circles diminished steadily.

What is the **Forbidden City**?

A sprawling complex of over half a mile square in the heart of Beijing has been known for centuries as the Forbidden City. Some fourteen hundred royal rooms, all in single-story buildings, cover one hundred and eighty acres. Yong Le (1403–1424 CE), third emperor of the Ming dynasty (1368–1644), founded the Forbidden City as

The Ming Dynasty

The focus on Chinese culture that was the hallmark of the Ming dynasty (1368 to 1644 CE) was both its strength and its weakness. After the foreign Mongols (whose dynasty had been established by Kublai Khan in 1260) were overthrown as rulers of China in 1368, the Ming emperors returned their—and their subjects'—attention to those things that are distinctively Chinese. The focus on Chinese culture produced a brilliant flowering in the arts, evidenced by the name "Ming" itself—meaning "bright" or "brilliant." It was architects working during this period who produced the splendor of Beijing's Forbidden City.

And though the Ming rulers promoted this artistic renaissance and reinstated Confucianism and the program of civil service suspended by the Mongols, the rulers' myopia prevented them from seeing the threat of the nomadic Manchu people. In 1644, the Manchus invaded from the north and conquered China, setting up the last dynastic period in Chinese history (it lasted until 1912).

his seat of government when he moved his capital from Nanjing to Beijing. From this heart of imperial Beijing radiates a network of sacred sites toward the four directions. Aligned along the City's main north-south axis are the principal residential and ritual structures, the palaces of the inner court to the north and the halls of public ceremony forming the outer court further south. To the east and west are the dozens of subordinate residential and administrative buildings. In a massive plaza before the southernmost ritual space, the Hall of Supreme Harmony, an artificial river runs east to west. Five small bridges, symbolizing the five Confucian virtues, span it. In the various halls along the main axis all the great rituals celebrating the empire took place. In overall symbolism, the Forbidden City reproduced on earth the court from which the Heavenly emperor, Shang Di, ruled the universe. Beijing was the last of a series of walled royal capitals. Beginning as far back as 1700 BCE, cities such as Anyang, Changan, and Hangzhou all had their sacred centers. Beijing saw the abdication of its last emperor in 1912.

What is the historical and religious significance of **Tian An Men Square**?

In June of 1989, media coverage of the so-called Tian An Men Square massacre brought world prominence to one of China's most important public spaces. The huge plaza stands directly south of the Forbidden City and is named after the City's massive southern outer gate, the Gate of Heavenly Peace (Tian An Men, literally "Heaven Peace Gate"). In a matter of days the space had become a globally recognized symbol for a younger China's struggle for democracy. But Tian An Men square had been a powerful symbol for the Chinese people for some years before 1989. Early revolutionary publications spoke of the place as "the people's guiding star," the emblem of the new China. Situated just south of the ancient seat of empire, the square was created as a clear revolutionary response to imperial repression. The open "people's" square was an obvious counterpoint to the exclusivity and mystery of the Forbidden City. Its placement to the south of the palace also meant that the square overpowered the palace by virtue of its greater access to yang energy—a symbolism surely not lost on countless traditional Chinese. Mao Ze Dong and his communist colleagues preferred to play off their new symbols of power against the old. They could have chosen simply to destroy the trappings of the decadent regime, but they might thereby have risked investing the former symbols with even greater power in the popular imagination. Better to reduce them to the status of mere museums. In the square now stand Communist Beijing's Great Hall of the People and the Museums of Chinese History and of the Chinese Revolution, contemporary replacements for the old imperial symbolism. Between them and to the south stands the mausoleum of Chairman Mao (d. 1976), but facing north rather than south as the imperial centers had done for over three thousand years. The goal of countless "pilgrims" today, Mao's Memorial Hall functions as a quasi-religious monument even in its rejection of China's imperial religious tradition.

How would you sum up the **history** of Confucianism?

During the first couple of centuries after the time of Confucius, two major thinkers developed the beginnings of what we now call Confucianism. Mencius, or Meng Zi (371–289 BCE), and Xun Zi (d. 215 BCE) codified the teachings of the Master into the foundations of a political philosophy. Emperor Qin Shi Huang Di (221–210 BCE), displeased with the emerging movement, tried to suppress it by burning all the Confucian texts. Before that emperor died, in 210 BCE, he had succeeded in transforming feudal China into a centralized bureaucracy, but Confucianism survived. Under the new Han dynasty (206 BCE–220 CE), the state espoused Confucianism as its core ideology. Confucianism took institutional shape as a system for training the empire's bureaucrats and officials, thereby strengthening the cultural elite known as the Literati. For the next several centuries, Confucianism's prestige dwindled as Buddhism's star rose with increasing imperial patronage. During the Southern and Northern (265–581 CE), Sui (581–618) and Tang dynasties (618–906), Confucian ritual and Literati authority held on, criticizing Buddhism as an insidious import and enjoying sporadic periods of notoriety. Confucianism returned to prominence during the Song dynasty (960–1279) as a result of the Neo-Confucian revival. Scholars finalized the Canon of the Five Classics and Four Books, plus several subsidiary works. Official Neo-Confucian philosophies drifted away from traditional beliefs in a transcendent divine Heaven, emphasizing ethics and social responsibility. But a cult centered around Confucius survived. During the last of the Chinese dynasties, the Qing or Manchu (1644–1911), a generally strong Literati class continued to promote an increasingly static and dogmatic form of Confucian "orthodoxy." The last emperor fell with the arrival of Sun Yat Sen's new Republic

Confucians in Conflict with Their Emperor

In 213 BCE, Emperor Qin Shi Huang accepted the recommendation of his prime minister, Li Si, that all books—except the history books about Qin—be burned. Li made this recommendation to strengthen Qin's authority and to give him greater control over the scholarly class. All the books of lyrics and the writings of the various schools of thought were to be brought to governors of prefectures for burning; those who had these books and would not burn them within thirty days were to have their faces branded, then be sent to labor for four years on the Great Wall. Those who dared to talk about these books were to be executed. Those who quoted the past to criticize the present were to be killed together with their entire families. Those who knew of and did not report violations were to suffer the same punishment. The only books that were not to be burned (apart from histories of Qin) were books on medicine, divination, and tree-planting.

During the next year, 212 BCE, some Confucian scholars and magicians talked among themselves, accusing the emperor of being power hungry, prone to kill and punish, and neglectful of intellectuals. When Qin Shi Huang learned of their dissent, he ordered a thorough investigation, during which the scholars blamed each other, rather than admitting to the criticisms. Finally, it was discovered that more than 460 scholars were involved. Qin Shi Huang ordered them all buried alive in the capital.

and the Literati became functionally obsolete. Still, the leaders of the Republic held Confucius up as the epitome of Chinese culture. When Mao Ze Dong's Communist movement began its rise in the 1930s, the Chairman declared himself fed up with Confucius and the old ways. In response, the Republican-Nationalist movement insisted that Confucianism represented all genuinely Chinese values. As the Nationalists fled the mainland and established themselves in Taiwan under Zhang Gai Shek in 1949, overt acknowledgment of Confucian tradition went with them.

RELIGIOUS BELIEFS

Are Confucianism or CIT appropriately called **religious traditions**?

Some scholars argue that the teachings customarily identified as Confucianism constitute a system of ethics or political philosophy rather than a system of religious beliefs.

Imperial ritual, on the other hand, might qualify as an authentically religious phenomenon because it pays homage to deities called Heaven and Earth. Neither, however, has a distinct "ecclesiastical" structure, official ordained priesthood, or scriptures that claim the authority of divine revelation. Nevertheless, Confucian tradition has many important features that might identify it as a religious tradition, partly because it has been historically so intertwined with the Chinese imperial cult and partly because of its strong sense of the sacred in ordinary human experience. Those features include an acknowledgment of transcendent power called the Dao, manifest in Heaven and Earth, and the long-standing reverence of Confucius as a Holy One on a par with Heaven and Earth.

Inside the main memorial hall of Taipei Confucius temple is the central altar dedicated to Confucius himself, with his spirit tablet behind the table holding ritual vessels beyond the curtained arch.

Is there a Confucian or CIT **creed**?

Neither Confucianism as such nor CIT have ever formulated a specific creedal statement to which all members are expected to confess their allegiance. If asked to summarize his or her religious beliefs, a devout and well-informed Chinese man or woman of a century or two ago would likely have included a number of basic elements relating to Confucianism and CIT. Divine Heaven rules all things through a "mandate" made known to a "Son of Heaven" called the emperor. The emperor in turn governs all earthly affairs by enacting that mandate, whose hallmark is justice and equity. It is the emperor's duty to make timely and appropriate offerings to Heaven and Earth to insure the felicitous coordination of all cosmic events for the benefit of humankind. Confucius, as one of the Sages, represents a revered tradition of practical wisdom to which a sincere emperor subscribes. All good subjects, too, will acknowledge the Sage and those of his stature and will venerate them along with their own ancestors. All of this, they might add, fits into the larger picture of the ultimate harmony represented by the balance of all things under the power of the Dao, which is manifest in Heaven and Earth.

Is the term **revelation** useful in understanding Confucianism or CIT?

Confucianism is very different from traditions like the Abrahamic faiths with their scriptures believed to have been revealed by a transcendent deity through prophetic messengers. It is different from Hinduism as well, a tradition that revolves around sacred texts. But Hinduism's scriptures are not so much directly revealed as they are disclosed timelessly to those sages and seers with the sensitivity to discern the eternal truths. Confucians think of their central truths as sacred, but not as either revealed from on high or disclosed from below. They are the records of the great sages and scholars that enshrine the highest insights into human nature and preserve the bedrock of China's ritual and literary patrimony. The CIT understanding of the emperor's responsibility to maintain contact with the Will of Heaven may sound at first like a variation on the theme of revelation. But in this case the Heavenly Mandate remains rather vague and amorphous, a cosmic truth for which the Son of Heaven must cultivate a refined sensitivity.

Are **doctrine** and **dogma** important to Confucians or in CIT?

Ancient tradition gave the generic name *Ru Jia,* the "Teaching of the Scholars," to a way of thinking and performing rituals that predated Confucius. Confucius inherited the way of that imperial cult, which included elaborate sacrificial ceremonies addressed to Heaven and Earth as part of the overall world-view, described in the section on Daoism as that of "Yin and Yang." After Confucius' time, the great teacher's interpretation of that traditional heritage came to be known as the "Teaching of Confucius" (*Kong Jia*). Throughout the long histories of both Confucianism and CIT, Chinese have been aware of various elements in their teaching that in effect form a body of doctrine. Rarely, if ever, has either Confucianism or CIT shown any tendency toward dogmatic pronouncements meant to serve as a "litmus test" by which to measure the allegiance of the public. Some scholars talk of a kind of "orthodoxy" in the Neo-Confucian schools of the Song and later dynasties. But in general a broad acceptance of a core body of teachings has simply been presumed.

Are there **mythic elements** in Confucian tradition or CIT?

Confucius looked to history for lessons about life. The stories he found to have the greatest educative value were those about human beings, the truly great and the mean-spirited alike, who had shaped life in the Middle Kingdom for good or ill. The high examplars were themselves people, the rulers and sages of old. Like his Indian contemporary the Buddha, Confucius preferred not to commit his time and energy to discrediting the stories of the gods and super-human heroes of his culture. He was simply convinced that, whatever their powers and prerogatives, the subjects of China's myths could not relieve human beings of their most fundamental responsibilities. The ultimate divine favor, Confucius believed, was a climate in which people could turn their full attention to the everyday realities of family, livelihood, and the betterment of society. Still, under pressure from Daoism and Buddhism, later Confucians cloaked the birth and life of the Master in wondrous tales. A unicorn presaged Confucius' birth by presenting his mother with a tablet of announcement, a pair of dragons and five ancient men symbolizing the five directions appeared in the heavens on the day he was born, and a celestial musical ensemble provided accompaniment for his birth. CIT likewise did not revolve around mythic narratives as such. Divinely sanctioned representatives of the people under Heaven had more pressing concerns. But the emperor had the power to elevate individual heroes and gods from local to universal stature. As a result he was, ironically perhaps, China's most important myth-maker.

What do Confucians believe about **ultimate spiritual reality**?

Two of the most important concepts that define what Confucius and his followers thought about ultimate spiritual reality are the Dao and Heaven (*tian*). Confucian texts do not always make clear how the two differ, and at times it seems they are virtually interchangeable. In Confucian teaching, the Dao and Heaven are generally nonpersonal realities that are equivalent, respectively, to a primordial or eternal cosmic law (Dao) and the source of that law (Heaven). Early Confucian texts emphasize the immanent, rather than the transcendent, aspect of the Dao. For example, Confucius is reported to have observed that the Dao is very close to human beings. Dao is therefore accessible and knowable, but that does not mean the Dao is not also mysterious. Confucius did not simply deny the existence of transcendent realities. He preferred to interpret ultimate reality from the ground up, so to speak. Many of history's great theologians have constructed their systems of thought by beginning with the existence of some divine reality and working their way down. Not Confucius. He was interested primarily in the ethical implications of traditional teachings that he had inherited. He apparently thought of Heaven as the ultimate moral authority or principle. Heaven makes its "will" known to, and through, an upright sovereign. What Heaven discloses is, in turn, the Dao. Confucius reportedly described "his" Dao as consisting of two fundamental ethical components, responsibility or loyalty (*jung*) and reciprocity (*shu*). His interpretation of Dao and Heaven is therefore quite different from the traditional Daoist interpretation. In much of Daoist thought, Dao has priority and gives rise to Heaven, which in turn manifests the "ten thousand things" that many people call creation or the universe.

431

The Rise of Confucius

Very soon after after his death, the followers of Confucius initiated what would become a centuries-long process of elevating their teacher above the ranks of ordinary people. They revered him as a special ancestral figure, the pinnacle of wisdom. They built a temple in his honor in Qufu in 478 BCE and, not long after that, began to enshrine statues and paintings of the Teacher and his major disciples there. Official imperial exaltation of Confucius did not begin until nearly five centuries after his death. After Han emperor Ping proclaimed Confucius the "Exalted Mt. Ni Duke of Highest Perfection" in the year 1 CE, a dozen other sovereigns followed, bestowing similar accolades down to the at least the sixteenth century. In keeping with the hierarchy of royal titles, the emperors decreed that Confucius would be known by such titles as Duke, First Teacher, First Sage, High King of Learning, and Ultimate Sage. Around 1530 CE, emperors stopped using the language of royalty and switched to a set of titles designed to reflect wisdom rather than temporal power. As early as the mid–fifth century CE, the imperial authority dedicated a temple to Confucius, and within a century or two decreed state-sponsored offerings in the Master's honor. Though Confucians have never considered Confucius divine, he has clearly ranked at the very zenith of human perfection.

Do Confucians believe in **miracles**?

Some have described Confucian teaching as philosophical in content and religious in function. As such, Confucian tradition focuses on the role of humanity in the greater scheme of things. It does not deny the existence a divine realm or the power of beings who inhabit that realm. Instead it emphasizes the importance of each human being's full acceptance of his or her responsibility. About the rest we cannot know in detail. What we have to work with are the myriad small realities we confront every day. Countless wonders await anyone willing to observe carefully each detail of ordinary life. Confucius would not have approved of any approach to life that amounted to waiting for the gods to do what human beings alone are responsible for. As such, Confucian teaching is highly realistic. It does not deny the possibility of miracles, events beyond the ordinary. It merely suggests that people who are genuinely attentive to life as it unfolds already have more than enough to occupy them. Many devoutly religious people think of miracles as the ultimate cause for gratitude. What would Confucius have considered a cause for gratitude to Heaven? First and foremost, propriety in all of the important human relationships. In addition, he would have been grateful for the predictable workings of nature. As essential as they both are to life, neither is a sure thing. When relationships and the cosmos are as they ought to be, these are the great wonders. As for Confucius himself, though he healed no one and raised no one from the dead, he did something equally marvelous: he taught without discrimination.

Who are the **principal deities** in CIT?

CIT's formal recognition of members of its pantheon went through many changes over the course of more than three thousand years. Here are some of the principal features of this vast and rather fluid phenomenon. Deities and heavenly powers generally fit into a three-level system. At the top were the powers deemed most necessary to cosmic survival. Ancient tradition includes belief in a mysterious celestial power called Shang Di. Eventually the word *di* came to be the standard term now translated as "emperor." But *Shang Di* was still the "supreme emperor." Standard Chinese religious usage also referred to *Tian,* Heaven, as a generic term for the region in which Shang Di lived. Neither Shang Di nor Tian was a personal deity actively involved in human affairs. They were rather the generic source of all things manifest in the universe. But there was yet another power behind Shang Di and Tian. That was the Dao, whose eternal energies of Yang and Yin are manifest in the universe and made known to humanity as the Will of Heaven. Also on the top level were the royal ancestors, the spirits of earth and grain, and the Earth, sometimes referred to as "empress" to Heaven's "emperor." A notch lower came the principal heavenly bodies, Sun and Moon, and Jupiter, whose revolutions of the sun determine the ritual calendar. Rulers of earlier dynasties, patrons of farming and silk cultivation, and the spirits of Heaven and Earth round out the second level. Confucius was once a member of the second rank, but was elevated to the first in 1907. At the third level CIT begins to overlap somewhat with Daoism and CCT, with their more specialized and local deities. Here are gathered the deities of fire, literature, war, artillery, soil, mechanical arts, the hearth, the granary, and the home threshold. Along with the patron deity of Beijing are three dragon deities associated with the city. Finally, several historical heroes fit here as well. A deity called Guan Di or Guan Gong deserves special mention as a cross-over figure important in more than one pantheon listing. Guan Di is known by a wide variety of names, depending on the constituency of worshipers. Many people identify him as the God of War, though the red-faced, full-bearded deity is chiefly a paragon of civic virtue. The emperor had the authority to rearrange, shrink or expand the pantheon. He could simply decree a spirit worthy of a particular rank and eventually even declare worship of that being the practice of the realm by instituting temples in his or her honor.

Are **salvation or redemption** important concepts in Confucianism?

According to a prevailing classical Chinese view of human nature, people are naturally capable of choosing either good or evil. A central concept in Confucian teaching is that each human being has the innate capacity for moral improvement. Confucius' successor, Meng Zi, took the Master's teaching a step further, for he was convinced that human beings were essentially good and naturally inclined to ethical betterment. Even the more skeptical Xun Zi, who held that individuals were born with a proclivity for self-centeredness, allowed that proper education could turn a person around. Individuals who choose to act selfishly hurt themselves and their fellow human beings, but their choices do not in any way damage a divine-human relationship as some traditions teach. People are capable of righting the wrongs they commit if they are willing to face the responsibility of setting neglected or sabotaged relationships right. That includes all relationships. Confucian tradition therefore has no need for notions like salvation or redemption. It does not talk of savior or redeemer figures, but of moral leaders who teach by example, much the way classical Theravada Buddhism spoke of the Buddha.

What is the **nature of the human person** in Confucian tradition?

Chinese uses the word *xing* to describe human nature in its most fundamental form. The term combines the concepts of "life/progeny" with "heart/mind," the two basic constituents of the person. Confucius further described the fully developed person using the term *ren,* a Chinese word that combines the characters for "human being" and "two." A full person, therefore, is one who exists in society, in communication with others. Human beings are always works in progress, ever shaping themselves in pursuit of an elusive goal of perfection. *Ren,* sometimes translated as goodness, human-heartedness, or even love, is that which activates the other four of the so-called five great virtues—devotion, justice, wisdom, and propriety. Only in light of *ren* does law function properly, as a guide rather than as a strait-jacket. *Ren's* two components, *jung* (individual) and *shu* (the virtue of reciprocity) allow human beings to enact the principles known as the "mean," the ability to hold feelings in abeyance, and the "measure," by which one can express emotions in balance.

Is there a distinctively Confucian **ethic**?

A Confucian formulation of the universal Golden Rule at first strikes the ear as rather negative and passive: "Do not do to others what you do not want done to you." But the Confucian ethic turns out to be overwhelmingly active and positive because of its emphasis on cultivating the natural human capacity for virtue. The Master's positive approach revolves around several key concepts. First and foremost is *li,* principle or propriety, consisting of a whole range of directives for human behavior. Much of *li* arises from the customs that embody the spirit of community. When people can rely on propriety in all relationships, as enshrined in time-honored practice, they experience assurance and freedom in their relationships. Confucius gathered a huge catalogue of social rituals, not out of antiquarian curiosity, but as a way of preserving what he considered the best of tradition. Ritual propriety is not meant to confine, but to give a sense of lightness and freedom. Without *li,* he thought, there can be no justice,

Carved and painted scenes depicting the principal Confucian virtues, on the roof beams of the inner gate of the Confucian temple in Taipei, Taiwan.

no morality, for a society without propriety has no foundation in respect. Of equal importance is the notion of *shu,* reciprocity in interpersonal relationships. Reciprocity is essential to putting *li* into action, for it governs the five principal human relationships and the ten associated virtues. In the father-son relationship, the father must cultivate kindness, the son reverence. The elder brother must deal gently with his younger brother, who responds with respect. A mutuality of faithfulness and obedience should characterize husband-wife relationships. Let all elders be considerate of those younger, and expect deference in return. Finally, a ruler must strive to treat subjects with benevolence and benefit from their loyalty as a result.

What is the **principal Confucian virtue**?

Behind all the other virtues, what makes a good Confucian tick is "filial devotion" or *xiao.* The Chinese term is composed of "son" with "old" placed above it. Confucius taught that all other moral virtue, and indeed civilization itself, flows from filial devotion. As a bare minimum, one should do no harm to one's parents. Filial devotion culminates in doing one's family proud. Traditional texts go into great detail about how one ought to treat parents, summarizing ideal behavior in five duties: reverence always, joyful service, solicitude for ailing parents, sincere grief at a parent's death, and proper ritual veneration thereafter. Lack of filial devotion was a most serious offense. Individuals could be put to death for cursing their elders. Filial devotion was

435

The Superior Person as Human Ideal

Confucian teaching describes the epitome of the ideal society as the "superior person" (*jun zi*). That means an individual who arrives at a high level of personal development through self-discipline and inquiry. The superior person values justice more highly than profit, and prefers to be quiet and serene rather than vulgar and uncongenial. Cultivating a dignified manner, the superior person nevertheless avoids arrogance. Such a person looks first to his or her personal shortcomings rather than blaming others for their lack of understanding or appreciation. It is said that the way of the superior person is a lengthy journey that begins from "right here." Five "constant virtues" characterize the superior person: self-respect, generosity, sincerity, responsibility, and openness to others. Expanding on the earlier teaching of Confucius, Meng Zi taught that fully developed human life begins with four principles. Compassion leads to true humanity, shame leads to righteousness, reverence and respect to propriety, and a sense of moral value to wisdom. Behind the notion of the superior person lies a deep-seated conviction of human potential for almost unlimited moral growth.

the very bedrock of social order, a fundamental acknowledgment of authority on the family level, without which there could be no exercise of authority in society at large. Chinese tradition regards society as built on the family. Sons and daughters do not "go out" into the world as they reach maturity. Rather than "leaving the nest," they invest themselves in the family, knowing that their children will do the same. Only in that way can the foundations of society as a whole remain firm.

What is meant by the term **"rectification of names"**?

If Confucius were here today he would surely be aghast at the way inflated language seems to have taken over ordinary conversation. "I was so tired I was *literally* dead on my feet." No you weren't, he might say. Drop the "literally" and your expression will have far more impact, even though your surrounding culture insists that more is better. He would be amazed to hear restaurant staff introduce themselves as "your food and beverage counselor" or hear store cashiers and stockers identified as "sales associates" and "inventory specialists." But Confucius would worry less about such trivial matters than about the very same deep social issues he agonized over in his own time. When a man fails to show respect to his parents, do not call him a son. If he fails to guide his children, he is unworthy to be called a father. If a woman does not attend to her family faithfully, one can hardly call her a wife or mother. If a man is unfaithful to his wife, do not call him a husband. Of greatest political import is his insistence that no unjust ruler deserves the name "emperor." Beneath this apparently nit-picking criti-

A decorative and symbolic river, crossed by five bridges representing the main Confucian virtues, runs east to west in the courtyard before the Hall of Supreme Harmony, in Beijing's Forbidden City.

cism Confucius was getting at a profound truth: over the long haul, imprecise speech allows injustice to go unnoticed because it can be hidden behind acceptable names. Euphemism can erode one's sense of right and wrong and desensitize a person to violence. Eventually we persuade ourselves that "mis-speaking" is not a lie, or that stealing is nothing more than the redistribution of wealth. Confucius believed that language matters because it not only reflects, but can even change, the way we think.

What is the basic Confucian concept of **appropriate moral leadership**?

Confucius believed that order was essential for bringing out the best in human beings. He and his disciples rejected the early Daoist notions that all things work for the best if only people learn the ways of nature and that there is no need for government or military force or oppressive laws. In Confucius' view government was essential, and that almost always required bureaucratic structures. But he believed the external trappings had to be supported by a foundation of example rather than coercion. No one can bring about the good society by force of will. One can only foster appropriate government by creating an environment of propriety, reciprocity, and good music—yes, good music. Law, he believed, can erode moral values because people often prefer to act a certain way merely to escape punishment. The example of a great leader is preferable, for it instills a sense of healthy shame that leads people to seek improvement. Confucius was a realist, however, and conceded that law was often a practical

437

necessity. What he wanted for the people most of all was the sense of confidence that can grow when people feel prosperous and educated. A good leader knows how to bring out the best in his people and how to wield authority deftly. But as a concession to the vast differences among human beings, government needs levels of power—some can lead, some can support a leader, some can follow but may not understand why they ought to do so. A leader knows how to cultivate conditions conducive to the betterment of society by tapping the roots of human resources rather than waiting until the plant is fully grown and incapable of nurturance.

Is there a distinctively Confucian **interpretation of history**?

Confucius refused to think of himself as an innovator. Any individual bent on inventing his own system of thought was doomed to failure, so interdependent are we humans. His task, he believed, was what he called the "renewal of antiquity." His first step was to translate his knowledge of tradition into clearly articulated principles so that he could intelligently sort out the best of the past. Confucius discerned in the drift of history a serious problem of societal entropy—the tendency to let things unravel. Looking back to the legendary founders of Chinese society, Confucius believed the first major problem set in when the Xia dynasty (1994–1525 BCE) instituted the principle of hereditary succession. When decline in the quality of the rulers reached a disastrous low, the Shang dynasty (1525–1028 BCE) overthrew the last Xia tyrant. Unfortunately, the Shang rulers retained the hereditary throne, thus virtually sealing their own eventual demise. Sure enough, the Zhou dynasty (1028–222 BCE) was destined to be the instrument of renewal. By the Master's own time, the Zhou, too, showed signs of serious decay. The Master wondered what power under Heaven might again correct the course of history. Confucius was convinced that it was possible to imitate the eternally true in history, to avoid reliving all of the past by distinguishing the good from the evil in it. True authority arose out of the ability to blend the ancient with the new. And only through learning could a leader assimilate the eternally true to changing needs. Beginning with politics and ethics, Confucius set out to contribute to the renewal of antiquity.

Do Confucians believe in an **afterlife**?

Confucius did not focus on life after death as though it were the ultimate standard against which to measure the success of a life on earth. With the majority of his fellow Chinese, the Teacher shared the conviction that biological death did not signal a definitive end to life. Death did not mean annihilation and loss in some great void beyond the grave. Confucius clearly believed in some form of spiritual survival, and in the ongoing presence of those who have departed this life. Hence the importance of ancestor veneration. But like the Buddha, Confucius and his disciples chose not to speculate about possible celestial or infernal post-mortem scenarios. Daoism and

438

CCT would offer ample options in that regard. He neither denied nor affirmed any particular views. Confucius was convinced that human beings understood far too little of life here and now to waste it planning for a hereafter they understood even less. When classical Confucian sources talk about Heaven, therefore, they do not have in mind anything like a realm of eternal reward for those who die in a state of righteousness. Heaven is merely a name for the highest spiritual presence of which human beings are aware.

Do **millennialism or messianism** have a place in Confucian thinking?

Confucius was far more concerned about the present and its relation to the past than about possible but distant futures. He was keenly interested in offering people hope through the cultivation of a balanced society. Some have suggested that Confucius was very much a utopian, in that the society he sought to foster was destined to remain an unattainable ideal. In any case, Confucius did not envision any kind of inevitable cataclysm, an end of time at which the world of history would implode in a cosmic conflagration. Confucian thought has been intimately associated with a traditional Chinese reckoning of time that includes cycles of sixty years, but those cycles do not carry apocalyptic implications. There have been millennialist and messianic movements in Chinese history, but none of importance has arisen out of Confucian or Literati circles. However, some scholars detect in Confucian history elements that have a messianic tone. According to that view, Confucius himself may have fulfilled expectations of a messianic ruler nurtured as far back as the legendary Shang dynasty.

Is there such a thing as Confucian **fundamentalism**?

Confucian scholars have devised a wide range of methods for interpreting the classical sources. Many of the central concepts in Confucian thought are simply too large and subtle to interpret literally. Take the notion of the Mandate of Heaven, for example. Dynasties have come and gone frequently in China's long history, and many have interpreted dynastic decay as a sure indication that the emperor had lost his contact with Heaven's Will. That is an easy enough judgment to make in retrospect. But using the Mandate theory as a criterion for deciding whether the people are justified in bringing down *this* regime *now* is a much more complicated matter. Some interpreters have chosen to apply the criteria of the classical sources directly to current events. They have their Christian counterparts, for example, in those who have discerned portents of the Apocalypse in the world around them at various times in history. Some Confucian texts have lent themselves more readily to literal interpretation, so much so that their prescriptions have become the very fabric of life for countless Chinese who have never set foot in a Confucian temple. Those are books like the *Li Ji*, with its detailed descriptions of ritualized relationships across the full spectrum of human activity.

SIGNS AND SYMBOLS

Are there any **signs or symbols** that might identify an individual as a Confucian?

Confucian tradition consists far more of actions and the preservation of proper relationships than on the expression of specific doctrines. The tradition so pervades Chinese and other Asian cultures that it is like the air one breathes, rather than a distinct set of beliefs. As a result, it is virtually impossible to tell who among Chinese, Japanese, or Koreans think of themselves as Confucians. There are still some people who identify themselves as disciples of the Master, but they are relatively few in number. Since so many rituals that Chinese and other east Asians perform are common to members of various religious traditions, the fact that an individual practiced ancestor veneration, for example, offers no clues in this regard. There are, however, a number of symbols connected with daily life originally associated with Confucius that still appear in popular arts of Asia. The so-called "Four Treasures of the Literary Apartment," for example, include an ink stick, ink block, brush, and paper.

What **signs or symbols** distinguish Confucian and CIT **ritual specialists**?

Even today, leaders of Confucian rituals are typically also government officials. When they function as ritual specialists, they don the garments once worn by representatives of the imperial household and administration. As for CIT, since there is no longer any official imperial religious worship, there are no longer CIT ritual specialists. Prior to 1911, however, CIT ritualists, from the emperor on down to the humblest assistant, simply wore the garments that signified their respective bureaucratic ranks and offices. In this case, the Literati did double duty as custodians of both civil and religious ritual. For especially important events, officials wore various garments known generically as "dragon robes," each decorated with emblems of the wearer's administrative rank. Imperial robes worn by the ruler during rituals were once festooned with an array of symbolic decorative motifs known collectively as "The Twelve Ornaments (or Symbols)." Symbolizing heaven and its wisdom were the sun, shown with a three-legged raven inside its red disc; the blue or green moon surrounding a hare grinding the elixir of immortality with mortar and pestle; and the constellations. Images of mountains symbolized earth and strength. Standing for all living things, the dragon symbolized resilience; the pheasant, culture and literary accomplishment. In images of bronze ritual vessels celebrants saw filial devotion, in cereal grains abundant harvest, in flame illumination, and in the water plant purity. Along with the mountains, the latter four also corresponded with the five elements. Finally, the "fu," a geometric form meaning good fortune, and the axe, referred respectively to the imperial prerogatives of judgment and punishment. When displayed together, the twelve were

An example of Literati landscape, this meditative hanging scroll painting called "Pavilion in a Landscape" (dated 1757) shows the classic "mountain-water" imagery influenced by a Daoist world view, with nature dominating and signs of human life and habitation blending in. *Courtesy the Saint Louis Art Museum.*

done in combinations of the five symbolic colors associated with the five directions. None but the emperor's ritual vestments could depict all twelve ornaments, since they constituted a symbolic summary of the whole cosmos.

Is there such a thing as Confucian **art**?

A number of Confucian Literati have been credited with some of China's finest landscape paintings. They were particularly attracted to this artistic theme and medium because both were consistent with deep-rooted Confucian values. Images of mystic mountain settings shared scroll space with equally haunting poems that reflected on human life and the grandeur of nature. These visual and literary images were sometimes autobiographical in tone, offering insight into the creator's personal spiritual convictions. Paintings often depicted solitary scholars lost in contemplation of natural beauty, meditating on moon-rise or creating calligraphy in a mountain pavilion. Here Confucian tradition crosses paths with classic Daoist views of nature and with the

Throne room in the Forbidden City's Hall of Protecting Harmony, where the emperor performed important rituals.

spontaneous and abstract landscapes painted by Chan Buddhist monks. Painting and poetry became forms of meditation for the Literati, expressions of their holistic view of the balance and harmony of nature. Literati painting is a didactic art with ethical impact, for ideally it expresses the feelings of the superior person. Confucian theory accords visual art the ability to communicate ideas too delicate or too forceful for words. The mind of the artist takes precedence over the content of the work, for the ultimate benefit of a great work is that it offers a connection with a person who represents the highest moral values. Great art can arise only out of genuine virtue.

Are there symbolic dimensions in CIT **sacred spaces**?

Imperial temples and altars have been highly symbolic down to the smallest detail. First, their placement in relation to each other and to the royal residence was critical. In imperial Beijing, for example, the Forbidden City stood at the center of the the center of empire, which in turn was the center of the universe. Within the palace, arranged along its central north-south axis, is a succession of ceremonial halls. Beginning in the north and moving southward are the Palace of Earthly Peace, the Palace of Heavenly Brightness, the Hall of Protecting Harmony, the Hall of Middle Harmony, and the Hall of Supreme Harmony. On north-south and west-east axes stood pairs of sacred spaces balancing yin and yang forces. North of the Forbidden City was the Altar of Earth (yin), square in shape. Its counterpart due south of that below the palace was the complex centered on the round Altar of Heaven (yang) and its various related tem-

442

Circular, three-tiered Altar of Heaven in the Temple of Heaven compound, Beijing.

ple and other ritual buildings. West of the Forbidden City stood the Altar of the Moon (yin) in its square enclosure, and to the east, the Altar of the Sun (yang) in its round-edged enclosure. These four spaces are considerable distances (about two miles) from the palace. But immediately south of the palace, on either side of the north-south axis that leads out of the Forbidden City and into today's Tian An Men square, the Altar of Land and Grain stood to the west across from the imperial ancestral temple. A good example of structural symbolism is the Altar of Land and Grain's division into five sections, recalling both the directions and the five elements. Different colored earth, brought from the corners and center of the empire, filled each section: yellow in the center, black in the north, red in the south, azure or green in the east, and white in the west. That structure and its companion ancestral temple were located between the Meridian Gate, which marks the southern extremity of the Forbidden City, and Tian An Men, the Gate of Heavenly Peace, which marks the northern perimeter of the square that bears its name.

What would I see if I visited one of the surviving CIT **sacred places**?

Beijing's Temple of Heaven (*Tian Tan*) is perhaps the best example of such a site. The Chinese long ago mastered the art of creating monumental public spaces, as the Temple demonstrates admirably. From its southern gate to the northern wall the complex stretches half a mile along its main ceremonial axis. The compound covers an area larger than that of the Forbidden City about two miles to the north, and it is some 443

The Dragon and the Phoenix

One of the most important symbolic pairs is that of the dragon and the phoenix. Often depicted as though they are engaging in a heavenly ballet, they symbolize the harmonious relationship between the emperor (dragon) and empress (phoenix). The intertwined pair of celestial beings appears regularly on the interior oculus (center peak) of domes in Confucian and imperial temples especially. Dragon and phoenix also appear often on the rounded ends of roof tiles. Such symbols were not allowed as decoration on any but imperial structures. Since the emperor was considered the Son of Heaven (*Tian Zi*), you might expect various types of imagery associated with the firmament, and abstract cloud forms are among the favorites.

four times the area of its original northern Yin counterpart, the Temple of Earth. Whereas the temple compounds devoted to the feminine earth and moon are square in plan, those of heaven and sun are round-shouldered at their rear perimeters and squared off (like a large U-shape) at the opposite ends where their entry gates are located. Confucian-Literati concepts of hierarchy in authority structures and in family lineage are based on a patriarchal model, and are evident in these as well as most other traditional Chinese structures. As you enter the main southern gate of the Temple of Heaven and walk north, you come first to the Altar of Heaven. It is a square enclosure surrounding a circular terrace of three concentric tiers—round heaven surrounded by square earth, as in the overall plan of the site. The Altar's symbolism includes its use of nine courses of pavement on each of its three levels—nine being the maximum level of yang energy. The posts in its surrounding railings, numbered in multiples of nine on each level, total three hundred and sixty, recalling the totality of degrees in heaven's circle. The circular Hall of Harvest Prayer at the northern perimeter of the compound also stands within a square enclosure. Symbolizing the firmament, the triple-roofed structure stands on two concentric circles of twelve columns apiece, reminders of the months of the year and the Chinese reckoning of twelve units of time per day. Four larger central columns inside the circle symbolize the seasons. Like the Altar, the Hall sits atop a triple-tiered circular platform. Geometric and numerical symbolism abound.

If I visited a **Confucian temple**, what would I see?

Major Confucian temples are arranged along the same general lines as traditional Buddhist and many CCT temples, all influenced by the plan of the imperial residence. Simple but elegant formality sets the Confucian temples apart from the others. Most Confucian temples greet the outside world through a main gate on the south side of

Main memorial hall of Taipei Confucian temple. Note the dragon columns on the porch and dragon design on the front pedestal.

the surrounding outer walls. Here is what you would see if you visited the Confucian temple in Taipei, Taiwan, whose plan is unique by reason of local tradition. Through either the eastern or western portals, you enter a garden with a pond. The high walls recall the Master's parable comparing great teachings to unscalable ramparts that preserve the building's secrecy, so that one must work to gain entry through the door. From there you pass through doors on either side of the main gate into a forecourt that offers further opportunity to shift mental gears before approaching the heart of the temple. Local tradition has it that there the main south gate must remain closed to all but those scoring highest on imperial exams. Since no one from the region ever achieved that rank, the south gate remains closed except for special occasions. Walking northward you pass through the Gate of Rites into the main courtyard, surrounded by rooms built into the outer walls. Immediately inside the inner gate you find yourself in one or another of the temple's study rooms.

What is at the heart of the **Confucian temple**?

Looking into the courtyard you would see the main structure, the free-standing central memorial hall on a raised platform. Until the fourteenth century, most if not all Confucian temples would have had a full complement of statues of Confucius and the other major Sages. As a result of an imperial decree in 1530 (some date the change to 1382), pictures and statues of the great Teacher and his spiritual comrades were replaced by memorial "spirit-tablets" bearing the names of the sages and scholars. The

445

Roof line of the Taipei Confucius temple. Frolicking dragon and Ji Wen figures protect the holy site.

main hall's (*da zheng*) central altar houses the tablets of Confucius (named "The Most Holy Former Master, the Wise Kong") and his four most important followers, Yen Hui, Zu Si, Zeng Zi and Meng Zi. Over the central altar is a panel that reads "Teach without discrimination"; in other words, accept all sincere comers as potential students. Along the right and left walls of the main hall are side altars, each bearing six tablets commemorating the twelve Sages—eleven students of Confucius and one of the founders of the medieval development called Neo-Confucianism, Zhu Xi (1130–1200 CE). In the rooms along the right and left sides of the main courtyard you would see several more altars on which are enshrined a hundred and fifty-four more name tablets, forty Sages and thirty-seven Scholars on the east, thirty-nine Sages and thirty-eight Scholars on the west. These major historical figures represent the cream of the Literati over many centuries. Finally, behind the main memorial hall, along the north wall of the courtyard, stands a room (the *jung zheng*) enshrining tablets of five generations of Confucius' ancestors.

Do Confucians mark their **sacred spaces** with any other distinctive **signs and symbols**?

Although they are usually less flamboyant in their decor than other Chinese temples, Confucian temples typically sport a variety of intriguing iconographic details. When you enter the outer garden courtyard of the Taipei Confucian temple, you notice on its outer wall several traditional Chinese symbols: a pair of dragon-fish called *ji wen* (of which a total of fourteen protect the temple from fire—dragons bring rain, and the fish symbolizes water as well) and a pair of exuberant green dragons. On the north face of the garden's south wall is a large tile image of the Qi Lin (unicorn). Writhing dragons are the principal motif on the main hall, both on the roofline and two main front columns and around the main altar, where nine of the creatures guard the spirit tablet of the Master. A pair of carved "sky pillars" appear to protrude at either end of the main hall's central ridge beam. Some say they symbolize both Confucian ethics, which alone can support the firmament, and the chimneys in which many scholars hid their books during Qin emperor Qin Shi Huang Di's attempt to burn all the texts of the Literati. In the center of that same roof beam, a small seven-roofed pagoda may symbolize the axis of the universe, standing as it does directly over the altar dedicated to Confucius himself. In rows along the beams of the sloping eaves stand birds of prey, for according to tradition, even the fiercest raptors alighted and paused to listen when Confucius taught. Beneath the eaves of the main hall are numerous small carved figures of popular Chinese characters, such as Shou Lao, deity of longevity. Even smaller carved friezes around the upper walls of the main hall depict scenes of high virtue from popular Chinese stories. In front of the door to the Master's altar, at the base of the platform supporting the memorial hall, stands a stone carving of the dragon that symbolizes the emperor. Inside, the octagonal cupola over the main altar shows the eight trigrams arrayed around the circular symbol of Yin and Yang, the *tai ji*.

Do **colors** have symbolic meaning to Confucians? How about for CIT?

In Confucian tradition and CIT, as well as in other Chinese traditions generally, a set of five colors have special associations. Colors are paired with the five elements (wood, water, earth, metal, fire) and directions: yellow or gold in the center, black in the north, red in the south, green or azure in the east, and white in the west. Red and gold are particularly important in the decoration of the temples, reminders of the south and center. At the Temple of Heaven, the color azure and a kind of turquoise or aquamarine decorate the domical vault, suggesting an association of those colors with heaven. The Forbidden City is often described as a "purple" palace, connecting that color with royal power. Carpets spread out before the various thrones were typically yellow, the color for the center. Throughout the palace, roof tiles were yellow and columns red. Only the emperor's buildings could sport gold tiles. Red and gold were also the principal colors of royal garments, reminders of the fire at the heart of the empire.

What is a *Tao tie* mask?

One of the most common and important visual motifs in the arts associated with Confucian and CIT ritual objects is the mask known as the *"tao tie* mask." Visit your local museum's Asian galleries and head for the cases that display the Chinese bronzes. Around the main part of the body of the object you will probably see what appear to be

eyes and mouth arranged along a vertical that could very well be a nose. Look more closely and a face, like that of a large cat, will begin to emerge from the patterns of the rich design. Look again, this time examining the design on each side of the central vertical, and you may see what appear to be a pair of dragons rearing up toward each other. These mesmerizing designs have long fascinated art historians. The name *tao tie* means "ogre" or "glutton," a name given to the motif perhaps because it suggests the visage of bottomless hunger capable of devouring all in its path. This terrifying apparition probably represents a deity from the ancient Shang dynasty pantheon. Its presence on the sacred ritual vessels is a protective device to safeguard the contents of the vessel. The *tao tie* disappeared from the Chinese decorative repertoire around 1000 BCE, but its early prominence and striking visual power make it a superb example of deeprooted religious symbolism.

Shou Lao, deity of longevity, holding the peach of immortality, is depicted here on a roof beam of the main hall of Taipei, Taiwan's main Confucian temple.

Are **relics** part of Confucian tradition?

As important as ancestor veneration has been throughout Chinese history, one might expect relics to be a conspicuous feature in Confucian tradition. Confucians, along with Daoists, Chinese Buddhists, and practitioners of CCT, pay a great deal of attention to a variety of symbols associated with deceased ancestors. Those ancestors can be spiritual as well as biological forbears—people like Confucius and the other sages, for example. But here tradition emphasizes the spirit and values of the ancestor. People

448

do not focus on physical remnants of the individual as though they contained the distillate of some special power. People visit graves of outstanding figures like Confucius as well as of their departed loved ones, but they do not go in hope of a miracle as devotees of other traditions might when making pilgrimage to the site of some powerful relic. Chinese tradition reveres the simple, noble humanity and admirable personal qualities of those who have passed on.

MEMBERSHIP, COMMUNITY, DIVERSITY

Where do Confucians live today? Are any **estimates of numbers** available?

Compared to the hundreds of millions whose cultures and ways of thinking have been profoundly influenced by Confucian teaching, people who identify themselves exclusively as Confucians are relatively few in number. In China, the ancestral home of Confucianism, very few people today think of themselves as Confucians. Many Confucian temples survived the demise of imperial rule, and the founders of the original Chinese Republic in 1911 continued to hold Confucius and the sages in the highest reverence. As a result of the Maoist revolution in 1948, however, hundreds of institutions associated with Confucian tradition were destroyed, damaged severely, or shut down. Since the Cultural Revolution, which ended with Mao's death in 1976, some of those institutions have enjoyed a revival. Countless citizens of the People's Republic of China revere Confucius but are not likely to call themselves Confucians. This is also true of Koreans and Japanese, a very small minority of whom will identify Confucian tradition as their principal ethico-religious affiliation.

Are there any **contemporary remnants** of CIT?

Nearly a century has passed since the last emperor stepped down from the dragon throne, and CIT as an institution is little more than a fading memory. For many Chinese, CIT remains a historical curiosity. A large tourism industry has grown up around the preservation of major monuments such as the Forbidden City and the Temple of Heaven in Beijing. Chinese tourists flock to these great repositories of their ancient heritage. Mao Ze Dong and his political heirs considered the remnants of feudal and imperial society as reminders of a thoroughly discredited way of life. They are mere museum pieces to many, and relics of an oppressive past to others, but they remain important evidence in reconstructing the story of Chinese religion.

Temple of Heaven, Beijing, set on a circular, three-tiered platform.

Have Confucians traditionally sent out **missionaries** to convert others?

Confucius was genuinely convinced that his ethical views and integrated approach to just government under the dominion of Heaven had much to recommend them. He himself was a zealous advocate and spent much of his life trying to "convert" others to his interpretation of the human condition. When at length the Confucian system took hold as the theory behind the practice of imperial administration, the bureaucratic structure itself became the mechanism that spread Confucian thinking far and wide. Diplomatic relations with other lands became a network for the export of the Confucian way. But neither Confucius nor his most influential disciples were populists. Instead of preaching to the masses as missionary movements typically do, Confucians have espoused a "trickle-down" theory. Convince the leaders of the value of Confucianism and they in turn will spread the word to their subjects. Persuade those in authority to model the good society. Given appropriate official sanctions and incentives, the people will see the benefit of establishing proper relationships at every level.

Are there any Confucian or CIT **holy sites or cities**?

Confucian tradition spotlights a number of places associated with the lives of Confucius and other major sages and scholars. Only a year after Confucius' death the Duke of Lu dedicated a temple to him in Qufu (478 BCE). Within a few years, his tomb and temple in Qufu had become widely known holy places. As early as 195 BCE, an imperial sacrifice at the tomb further broadened Qufu's fame as a sacred site. Confucian tradition did not elevate any one city to prominence as a center of authoritative teaching, but certain cities were home to the great Confucian universities. The most important cities were always associated with the seat of imperial government, and that changed often through Chinese history, even during the tenure of a single dynasty. Beijing has been perhaps the most important Confucian city. It was the capital uninterruptedly for nearly five hundred years, and Confucianism was highly favored and influential through virtually that whole period.

Have there been any **sub-communities or denominations** within Confucianism?

An early historian of Confucian tradition, Liu Xiang (77–6 BCE), claimed that by his time the Confucians had divided into one hundred and three schools of thought, each defined by its distinctive manner of interpreting the essential texts. Whether that was literally the case or not, it is clear that during the Song and later dynasties, several important schools developed within the larger phenomenon called Neo-Confucianism. The two main branches became known as the School of Principle and the School of Mind, according to their respective theoretical points of departure. The School of Principle (*li xue*) was also called the Cheng-Zhu school, combining the first names of the men it claims as its founders, Cheng Yi (1033–1107), and his brother Cheng Hao (1032–85), and the later Zhu Xi (1130–1200). The brothers Cheng developed a sophisticated theory in which "principle" (*li*) meant not the classical Confucian rites and canons of social propriety, but an unchanging universal law inherent in all nature. Zhu Xi further refined that concept of principle, defining it as the Great Ultimate from which all forces in nature emerge. In what one might call a variety of "process theology," Zhu Xi argued that the path to ethical development was "the investigation of things." The other major branch of neo-Confucian thinking was known as the School of Mind (*xin xue*). Wang Yang Ming (1472–1529) was one of the school's leading lights. Principle, he argued, was not merely a transcendent and inaccessible cosmic force, but was one with the human mind. He taught that one could cultivate good conduct through "reverent seriousness," a type of meditative discipline through which one could realize the unity of mind and principle.

Were any other **related schools of thought** important in understanding Confucianism?

Mo Zi (468–390 BCE) started out as a Confucian but went his own way, opting for a less stratified, more egalitarian model of society. Some have characterized Mo Zi as a pragmatist because he insisted that observable improvement in the welfare of the populace was the ultimate criterion of good public policy. Confucius, he argued, put too much emphasis on ritual and filial devotion and too little on measurably advancing

451

What gender-related issues have been important in Confucianism and CIT?

Confucian tradition emphasized social order, and that called for clearly delineated gender functions. Given the conviction that only a patriarchal structure could guarantee social order, what many people today call "social equality" was simply not included in the Confucian lexicon. Confucian teaching envisioned male-female relationships according to a political model. First and foremost among questions of gender are those relating to family structure and roles. But whether within the family or in society at large, women and younger people generally shared the expectation of dutiful obedience. Women remained in the home to serve the family, which sometimes brought as many as four generations together in one household. Widows were typically expected not to remarry. When a wife produced no son, a husband could marry one or more secondary wives in the hope of securing a male heir. A telling fact is that no women are numbered among the great sages and scholars memorialized in Confucius temples. In the imperial household, there were sometimes several empresses and many royal concubines. An empress remained out of view for the most part, participating in a few affairs of state annually. Eunuchs looked after the harem, strictly organizing the lives of all women in the imperial household.

civilization. Mo Zi taught the importance of striving for a society united by a kind of mutual love that amounted to a form of enlightened self-interest. His school flourished for just over a century, but it offers a glimpse at one of several credible critiques of the classical Confucian approach. Another dissenting voice of Mo Zi's era were the Legalists (*fa jia*). They took Mo Zi's critique several steps further from Confucius' global confidence that the mere example of virtuous leadership could bring about a moral conversion in society. Governance, they argued, required clear and comprehensive legislation that capitalized on people's fear of punishment and hope of reward. Confucius and Mo Zi clearly had greater faith in human perfectibility and in a reservoir of good will at the heart of humankind.

Is there such a thing as **converting** into Confucianism?

Since Confucian tradition has been so deeply identified with Chinese culture, the notion of "converting" into the tradition is virtually meaningless. That is not to say that individuals have not been so highly attracted to the teachings of the tradition that they espoused it as a philosophy of life. But so much of Confucianism is inseparable from such practices as ancestor veneration and other culturally-rooted behavior, that the likelihood of conversion is very small. In addition, over the centuries most people one might identify as Confucian have more than likely been associated with other religious traditions as well, such as Daoism, CCT, or Buddhism. In Chinese religious history, and Japanese too, the more or less tidy distinctions many Europeans and Americans are used to making between religious communities simply have not been applicable.

How would you sum up Confucianism's **historical relationships to other traditions**?

Confucianism's most important and enduring inter-religious relations have been with Buddhism and Daoism. There have been periods during which Confucians have had more or less cordial dealings with representatives of the other two "ways" of China. But since so much has often been at stake, especially in terms of imperial patronage, Confucian scholars have frequently leveled serious criticisms at Daoist and Buddhist views. For example, Confucians have sometimes faulted Buddhism for being too other-worldly, too disconnected from the ordinary problems and needs of regular people. Confucians generally interpreted the Buddhist ideal of celibate monastic life as an abdication of filial devotion and the responsibility to perpetuate the family lineage. Daoists, on the other hand, have characteristically struck Confucians as naive in their conviction that, if left to themselves, people will naturally follow an exemplary leader. Daoism's emphasis on doing things nature's way leaves society too vulnerable to simple lawlessness. In addition, the Confucian tradition's strong emphasis on education seemed to many to be irreconcilable with Daoism's more "organic" and seemingly anti-intellectual approach to learning. When Confucian tradition began to come into prominence during Japan's Tokugawa era, it found an increasingly hostile official response from representatives of Shinto. Confucianism, Shinto authorities argued, was a non-Japanese influence and therefore undesirable. By that time, however, Confucius had already made an indelible impression on Japanese society.

LEADERSHIP, AUTHORITY, ORGANIZATION

What have been the principal venues for Confucian **communities** and CIT?

Three main kinds of sacred spaces have been at the center of activities. Several kinds of venue called "memorial halls" enshrined the spiritual presence of great Literati, beginning with Confucius himself and his ancestors. These facilities go by the generic name *wen miao,* "temple of literature/culture," while those specifically dedicated to Confucius are often called *Kong (or Kong Zi) miao.* Until at least the middle of this

453

century, Confucian temples enjoyed prestigious locations in nearly every Chinese city—as well as many Korean and some Japanese cities. In most Confucian temples one of the more important community functions has been that of a place of study. These temples tend to draw clientele from a wider area than do CCT temples, which function more like local parishes. Unlike Buddhist and CCT temples, Confucius temples do not hum with the ritual devotions of a steady stream of worshipers. There the ritual is more likely to be quiet academic work in the side rooms provided for that purpose. Once dedicated to the reading of the Confucian classics, these rooms now provide students whose homes are crowded and noisy a chance to concentrate on any academic subject. Second in importance and number are three different types of altars for the worship of agricultural deities, natural powers of mountain and river, and ancestral spirits. Generally set in a shared compound were the first two kinds of altar, twenty-foot square platforms, walled in and facing west. Temples of the imperial cult, finally, could be either of grand scale, as in Beijing's Temple of Heaven, or relatively humble, as in a local temple to the earth deity. All three venues provided a variety of circumstances under which communities have come together.

Is there a **central teaching authority** for Confucians or CIT?

One could argue that the social institution of the Literati functioned as a central teaching authority. There is no doubt that they set up the system to which any person of talent and ambition who wished to advance would have to conform. Complete with its regimen of demanding examinations, degrees, and apprenticeships, the Literati system of public service also had its religious implications, given the overall context in which traditional Chinese saw the role of the emperor. And there is no doubt that the system offered little or no flexibility—make the grade or wash out. The Literati system was, therefore, a central teaching authority for a limited segment of society. Even the ordinary people in towns and villages came under at least indirect influence of the system. But the system did not make its demands on regular people the way it did on those who aspired to rise within its ranks.

Is there a system of Confucian or CIT **religious law**?

Confucian tradition's closest analogy to the kind of religious regulation important to Jews and Muslims, for example, are the canons of ritual. It may sound at first as though Confucian law is limited to what are sometimes called "rubrics." Rubrics are instructions on how to perform a ceremony, that take their name from the Latin for "red" because the directions are printed in red ink to set them off from the liturgical text. But what Confucians mean by the canons of ritual actually includes an enormous range of human behavior. Here the Confucian scholars have codified ways of acting for every age and station in life, from members of the ordinary household, to the servant who prepares fruit for the emperor, to the emperor himself. These often elaborate and even somewhat theatrical stipulations might strike the outsider as extreme or downright compulsive. But the tradi-

454

The First Public Schools

The first public schools date back to ancient China. Confucius was among the first in China to advocate that primary school education should be available to all. He averred that "in education there should be no class distinctions." He never refused a student "even though he came to me on foot, with nothing more to offer as tuition than a package of dried meat." Confucius asserted that any man—including a peasant boy—had the potential to be a man of principle.

tional interpretation is that a person of cultivated virtue will always act in such as way as to express precisely his or her relationship to those with whom he is dealing. In this way Confucian tradition preserved a definite social hierarchy still very much reflected in the formal language usage of Korea and Japan, as well as of China. Because of its unique relationship to the civil authority represented by the emperor, Confucianism as such, with its Five Classics and Four Books, did not develop a specific code of penal law. That was still largely the province of the Literati as royal administrators, but it emanated from the imperial household and developed over many centuries.

Is **education** especially important in Confucianism?

No major religious tradition has placed greater emphasis on education than Confucianism. That is not to suggest that Confucian teaching reduces the truth to mere intellectual development. For Confucians, education goes far beyond developing mental skills and acquiring information. It means the cultivation of the whole person within the broadest possible perspective—humanism under Heaven. A number of very important Confucian institutions of higher learning have made major contributions throughout Asia over the centuries. Perhaps even more pervasive has been the Confucian influence in the development and maintenance of China's imperial civil service system, the educational system that produced and regulated the social class called the Literati.

Are there Confucian or CIT **hierarchical structures**?

Confucian thought discerns an essential need for hierarchies in all aspects of human society. It is a question of order. Human beings may be identical in essence, but they clearly differ in personal attributes, talents, knowledge, and age, to name only a few distinguishing characteristics. Confucius believed that realism required taking account of those differences. Take the challenge of living an ethical life, for example. Each stage in life has its unique problems. Young people need to conquer sensuality, adults combativeness, and the elderly greed. As for the variety of human capabilities, Confucius saw four levels: those who possess knowledge from birth, those capable of

455

becoming Superior Persons by acquiring knowledge, those who learn only with great effort, and those not at all disposed to learning. Confucian thinking has often been very class-conscious. The Master believed that society needed stratification in order to function smoothly. At the top was the scholar, supported by the farmer who produce life's basic needs, artisans who make practical items, merchants who buy and sell what others produce, and soldiers who, unfortunately, often wreck what others make. Within the highest echelons of the Confucian hierarchy there were still further distinctions. Until around 1530, those enshrined in Confucian memorial halls were ranked according to titles taken from imperial administration. Confucian greats were honored as king, duke, marquis, or earl, for example. After 1530, Confucians replaced those royal honorifics with the titles sage, correlate, especially learned one, worthy one, and scholar. Over the course of history, some individuals within the Confucian hierarchy have been promoted, others demoted in rank, and still others restored after being demoted. Such hierarchical adjustments have depended a great deal on ideological leanings within various imperial regimes, the last major rearrangement occurring around 1724. CIT was, of course, hierarchical, but with the emperor at the top and a much higher place allotted to the military.

What are some of the main of Confucian and CIT **officials or ritual specialists**?

Strictly speaking, Confucians have no separate structure of ritual officials. Bureaucrats of the imperial administration were responsible for offerings performed in Confucian memorial halls. The Emperor himself was the supreme ritual specialist in the sense that he exercised sole rights to perform certain ceremonies judged essential to the good order of life under Heaven. All subordinate, regional, and local ceremonies were delegated to the various ranks of the Literati. Today, even in the absence of imperial structures, government officials still play that role. In imperial times, the emperor's administration was divided into nine departments. Most important in this context was the Imperial Academy, whose chief officer was the Minister of Ceremonies. His function was similar to that of Chief Priest, since he was responsible for rituals performed in all imperial temples. A common ritual at local imperial altars required that a newly appointed local magistrate stay overnight, before his official installation, in the temple of the "spirit magistrate," a deity who was the earthly magistrate's celestial model.

How are Confucian or CIT **leaders** chosen and given **authority**?

Priestly orders or classes in many traditions derive their authority from either hereditary lineage or from a perceived ability to manage spiritual power, or both of these. The case of the Literati as a special class is quite different in many respects. Their role in imperial religious affairs may have originated with the office of royal astrologer, a person possessed of a special type of arcane knowledge. They had to understand all there was to know about how to plan imperial matters in perfect coordination with the rhythms of the cosmos. But the Literati's continued prestige rested on their identification with a broader range of knowledge—that of literature, history, and writing. Their privileged access to the canonical texts, the Classics and Books of Confucian tradition, gave them unquestioned authority. The Literati oversaw virtually every detail of imperial ritual and administration (so much of which was highly ritualized) and were responsible for propriety and auspiciousness in all affairs of the state under Heaven. They were, in effect, a kind of lay priesthood whose patron and model was Confucius. Prospective members of the Literati underwent extensive education designed to imbue them with the classical texts, an exquisite sensitivity to the nuances of ritual, and an appreciation of the social and political implications of the relationships implied in the great rituals. Literati achieved their various ranks within the hierarchical structure on the basis of their achievement in the imperial examinations. From about the seventh century CE on, an elaborate system of examinations could give access to any of three degrees or ranks, each requiring as many as ten different kinds of examination. The Board of Rites oversaw the examinations, and the Board of Civil Office made the final appointments. An important feature of this system was that, at least in theory, it bestowed authority on the basis of personal achievement rather than heredity or social status. The higher the rank of a local government's main official, the greater the prestige of its ancestral temple.

Have **women** exercised leadership in Confucianism or CIT?

Confucian tradition is staunchly patriarchal. Long-standing practice all over Asia, as a result of Confucian influence, has until only recently expected women to obey father before marriage, husband during marriage, and oldest son when her husband dies. Education under classical Confucian direction was limited to males. That is no longer the case in societies that still acknowledge, however indirectly, their Confucian heritage. As for CIT, a number of empresses and princesses came to prominence over the centuries, but here too the leadership was male. Empresses were generally in charge of the so-called inner court. Empress-mothers frequently had duties in matters of state and thus were often more active in the outside world. Women were never allowed in the main halls of the Forbidden City's outer court, except on the day a new empress married her emperor.

Are there any organizations or institutions that have their own distinctive **structures of leadership** within Confucianism?

Throughout history, various Confucian societies of lay persons have come and gone. Few of those have been more than local or regional. But since the Confucian community is composed exclusively of laity, there has been no Confucian priesthood, no religious orders, and no monastic life. The single most important organizational structure has been that of the Literati class with its elaborate hierarchy and system of advancement determined by examinations. Apart from that, Chinese authorities have often regarded as subversive all attempts to form separate groups within society as a whole. There have been times in Chinese history when prominent Literati have withdrawn from society, opting for the eremitical life. These reclusive types borrowed a page from the Buddhist phenomenon of the solitary monk, but the Confucian hermits were by definition loners and not at all inclined to band together.

PERSONALITIES AND POWERS

Is there such a thing as a **saint** in Confucianism?

Confucius revered the ancient kings as sages (*sheng*), figures of towering intellect and virtue who represented an ideal never again to be attained by mere mortals. Their inimitability prevented the ancients from functioning as exemplars and restricted them to the role of venerable ancestors to whom all owed a debt of gratitude. Meng Zi began to modify the role of the sage. He suggested that the sage appears in every age, not only in the distant past. And he emphasized the sage's humanity and imitability. Individuals could aspire to and cultivate the qualities of the sage through education. With the Song dynasty came Neo-Confucianism and a further expansion of the sage's role. Building on the classic text called *The Great Learning* (*Da Xue*), medieval scholars spoke of a series of stages through which an aspirant could advance toward the lofty goal of sagehood. Neo-Confucians identified the sage as the individual who had fully actualized all moral and intellectual potential and arrived at a state of oneness with the universe. Like the Daoist sage, as described in the *Dao De Jing,* the Confucian sage embodies perfect harmony with the cosmos. Unlike the Daoist sage, the Confucian puts wisdom's insights to work by active involvement in the ordinary affairs of society. A Confucian sage is like the Buddhist *bodhisattva* in that both are committed to the betterment of the human condition. The ten-stage "bodhisattva career" offers a general parallel to the Neo-Confucian system of steps toward sagehood. But whereas the bodhisattva has the power to reach down and change the plight of those who ask for help, the sage offers the hope of transformation through determination and effort. Sages model the best in Confucianism's spirituality of public service.

How do the **Sage, Correlate, Worthy One, Scholar, and Superior Person** differ?

The first four are all stages or levels in the Confucian hierarchy of human striving and perfectibility. They are the ranks of extraordinary individuals judged suitable for inclusion in the Confucian temples various memorial halls. All four are, by definition, supe-

Wang Pi and the "Mysterious Learning"

Wang Pi (also known as Wang Bi; 226–249 CE) and his patron, Ho Yen, are credited with founding the movement known in the West as "Neo-Daoism." This name is misleading, however, since the movement grew principally out of Confucianism. It began with studies of the Confucian classic the *Yi Jing,* was enthusiastically discussed with reference to the Daoist *Dao De Jing* and *Zhuang Zi* in the later third century, and in the fourth century merged into Mahayana Buddhism. The movement is probably most accurately known by its Chinese name: *xuan xue* (mysterious learning).

Wang has been accused of trying to interpret the *Yi Jing* in Daoist terms and of praising Confucius as the supreme Daoist because he refrained from saying anything about the ineffable Dao. The truth is that Wang rejected labels such as Confucian and Daoist, and instead strove to unearth the ultimate truths concealed in each.

During the waning years of the Han dynasty (207 BCE to 220 CE), various thinkers, notably the great Wang Chung (ca. 27–100 CE), had become disillusioned with standard Confucian metaphysics, which had emphasized elaborate systems of correspondences between Heaven, Earth, and Man; cycles of the so-called Five Elements; and attempts to predict the future based on these. The desire to understand the basic principles of the universe was not lost, nor were the basic ideas entirely rejected, but the simplistic excesses—the teleology and the easy belief that Heaven was regular, purposeful, and concerned with humankind—were shaved away. At the same time, the so-called "New Text" versions of the Confucian classics lost their standing and were replaced by versions of the texts purporting to be older. These "Old Texts" did not fit neatly into vast cosmological systems and left a cosmological void in Confucian thought. By the end of the Han, the great pattern of the universe had seemingly dissolved into chaos.

In the third century, *xuan xue* emerged to fill this metaphysical vacuum. *Xuan xue* is predicated on the belief that the infinite phenomena of this universe are random, transitory, and without any meaningful pattern. Yet they all must, it was reasoned, be generated by one single, eternal verity. That was the original nothingness (*ben wu*), or nonbeing (*wu*), the origin of all being.

rior persons. At the pinnacle of the pyramid stands the sage, the Confucian analogy to the saint. Confucian tradition devised the various other terms, such as "worthy one" and "correlate" to describe the historical and "spiritual" proximity of famous scholars and sages to Confucius himself. In most Confucian temples the ranks or levels in the tradition's memorial hierarchy are indicated by the relative placement of name tablets.

Those closest to the Master's tablet rank highest, and are generally called "sages" or "correlates." Those in the rooms along the side of the temple compound are the far more numerous "worthies and scholars." Scholars of sufficient prestige to have their names in the temple qualify as "superior persons," but that designation is not used in the memorial rankings.

What is the **Mandate of Heaven**?

Confucians have interpreted the concept of Mandate or Will of Heaven in various ways over the centuries. As an ingredient in Confucian political thought, the concept has functioned both as a means of legitimation of the regime in power and a justification for overthrowing an unjust regime. The notion derives from a traditional Chinese belief in an elaborate network of correspondences among all levels of existence—the heavenly, the earthly, and the human. Human beings are not the independent source of authority. They can hope for harmony only through sensitivity to the ways of Heaven above and of nature below. Order in society depends on the good faith effort of a single human being, the emperor as "Son of Heaven," to rule unselfishly by always consulting the Will of Heaven. A theory of immanent retribution holds that there is a direct connection between natural and moral evil in the world and Heaven's displeasure with any emperor who arrogantly forgets the source of his authority. When the people prosper, one can conclude with certainty that affairs of state are in order, all as a direct result of the emperor's keeping his priorities straight. Many of the great Confucian thinkers have taught that the tradition's most consistent contribution to society has been that of fearlessly holding the ruler responsible to his people. If the one on the throne presides over an unjust regime, that person is no longer worthy of the name emperor. According to Meng Zi, for example, the people have the right to remove such a fraudulent leader. Meng Zi argued that violent overthrow of an unjust ruler was not regicide but tyrannicide. The greatest sovereign, therefore, is the one who governs only after first submitting to a higher authority.

What is a **Mandarin**?

"Mandarin" comes from the Sanskrit term *mantri,* meaning "minister or counsellor." It became common especially after the sixteenth century, when Europeans came into more regular contact with Chinese culture. Europeans used the term to refer to China's social elite, so that "Mandarin" was in effect a synonym for "Literati." Technically, that meant all the bureaucrats who belonged to the nine administrative ranks of imperial government or "civil service." When the Italian Jesuit missionary Matteo Ricci (1552–1610) determined to dedicate himself to working in China, he set out to steep himself in classical Confucian learning. An important feature of his reputation is that he was so successful that he virtually became a Mandarin. In popular usage, the term Mandarin has come to refer to Asian social and cultural elites and governmental

Meng Zi and the Development of Confucian Thought

Meng Zi (also Mencius; 371–289 BCE) was a Chinese philosopher and one of the most important early Confucian thinkers. His philosophy is characterized by its idealism and the assertion that human nature is basically good.

Meng Zi was born in Tsou, a small state south of Lu, the home state of Confucius. Almost nothing is known about his early life. Like Confucius, Meng Zi apparently lost his father at an early age, and was raised by his mother. Meng Zi may have studied in one of the Confucian schools established in the Lu area, perhaps the school created by Confucius's grandson Zu Ssu. Meng Zi was trained as a scholar and teacher and received instruction in the standard Confucian texts such as the Book of Odes (*Shi Jing*) and the Book of Documents (*Shu Jing*).

Meng Zi's teachings are preserved in a book titled *Meng Zi,* a seven-chapter work of anecdotes most likely collected by his disciples. Most of the anecdotes consist of conversations between Meng Zi and his disciples or, occasionally, a ruler. His basic philosophy is an extreme idealism that views human nature as basically good and views evil as only an obfuscation of one's innate goodness. He placed great emphasis on the necessity that one try to recover his or her original goodness and, through learning, to seek what he called the "lost mind" of benevolence. Meng Zi also believed that if the government fails to maintain benevolent rule and abuses the people, then the people have a right to launch a revolution.

administrators in general. Mandarin is also the name given to one of the most important and widely spoken of the many Chinese dialects.

Has **martyrdom** ever been important in Confucian history?

Several Confucian Literati have come to be known as martyrs. They died because those in power would not countenance their calls for greater justice in the imperial regime. One such figure was Yang Ji Sheng (1516–55CE). So strong was his conviction that the imperial system would respond to good-faith Confucian criticism that he risked all to denounce a corrupt official at court. Yang meticulously crafted his case against Yen Sung and his son, fasting for three days before presenting his charges. Yen Sung managed to poison the emperor's mind against Yang, implicating him falsely in a conspiracy. Yang languished in prison for three years while fellow Literati attempted to defend him at court. All appeals lost, the heroic Yang refused to take a sedative before being tortured in prison. Before he was executed, he composed a short poem, in true Literati style. In it he expressed the hope that he would live on in spirit, still loyal to the emperor and grateful for his life of service. What is essential to note here is this martyr's dedication to advancing society through selfless commitment to justice in public administration, an outstanding feature of the Confucian spirituality of service.

Have **prophets** played a role in Confucian tradition?

Confucian tradition developed in ways very different from the so-called prophetic or Abrahamic traditions. Confucius and his disciples never claimed to have received a revelation from above. They did not consider themselves privy to divine secrets. Their job was to call people back to social responsibility, however, and in that respect they share an important characteristic with the classical "prophet" figures of other traditions. Confucius also felt himself called to speak of justice to those in power, much as Israel's prophets and Islam's Prophet Muhammad challenged the rulers of their day. But on the whole, Confucian tradition and its Literati were much too closely identified with imperial rule to function as effective critics of the system. Some scholars distinguish between prophets as "seers," and people of action, like Confucius, as "doers." One such Confucian seer came at a time when Confucianism was waning as the theory behind CIT. Liao Ping (1852–1932 CE) considered himself and Confucius prophetic figures. As it turned out, he was a minor player, known perhaps best of all for his lament over the demise of imperial Confucianism. Think of him as the exception that proves the rule.

Have there been any important Confucian **reformers**?

Wang Yang Ming (1472–1529 CE) was an outspoken government official of the Ming dynasty. He was perhaps the most influential teacher of the neo-Confucian "School of Mind," also known as the Idealists (*xin xue*). Wang believed that the teaching of his predecessors in the neo-Confucian movement had lost all credibility when Yuan dynasty bureaucrats made it the official curriculum for civil service examinations. Reduced to a fixed set of questions and answers, neo-Confucian ideas no longer required people to think independently. Wang's major work, *Investigation into the "Great Learning"*, commented on the ancient Confucian text, underscoring the need for active engagement with ideas. He condemned slavish adherence to rigid canons of ritual propriety. Wang argued for an understanding of *li* as a living universal principle rather than a list of prescribed procedures and policies. He borrowed from Daoist and Buddhist teachings, as earlier neo-Confucians had done, attempting to reinvigorate the tradition as a way of interpreting the whole of life. And Wang reintroduced a metaphysical element by speaking of a "true self" and a "heavenly principle." Above all, he insisted, one must not lose sight of the underlying challenge of human development and the struggle for moral improvement. Institutionalize what is meant to be a living tradition, Wang warned, and you create a giant fossil.

Have there been any Confucian **mystics**?

Scholars of the history of religion rarely describe the Confucian tradition as a wellspring of mystical spirituality. But several important figures, particularly among the

Matteo Ricci—a Jesuit in China

Matteo Ricci (1552–1610) was an Italian Jesuit missionary who opened China to Roman Catholic evangelization. He was the best-known Jesuit and European in China prior to the twentieth century.

Born at Macerata in 1552, Ricci went to Rome in 1568 to study law. In 1571 he entered the Society of Jesus. After studying mathematics and geography at a Roman college, he set out for Goa in 1577 and was ordained there in 1580. In 1582 he was dispatched to Macao and started to learn Chinese.

In 1601, Ricci made his way to Beijing and received a warm welcome from the Emperor. This imperial favor provided Ricci with an opportunity to meet the leading officials and Literati in Beijing, some of whom later became Christian converts. Ricci obtained a settlement with an allowance for subsistence in Beijing, after which his reputation among the Chinese increased. Besides the missionary and scientific work, from 1596 on he was also superior of the missions, which in 1605 numbered seventeen. When he died in 1610, he was granted a burial place in Beijing. Some of the outstanding Chinese Literati with whom Ricci had contact later became his converts, including the famous scholar-officials Hsu Kuang-ch'i, Li Chih-ts'ao, and Yang T'ing-yun. Ricci's writings include about twenty titles, mostly in Chinese, ranging from religious and scientific works to treatises on friendship and local memory. The most famous of these are the *Mappamondo* and the *True Idea of God*.

Neo-Confucians, spoke a language reminiscent of some of the great monistic mystics of other traditions. Zhu Xi, a leading light in the Neo-Confucian School of Principle, saw in the practice of meditation a way of becoming one with cosmic harmony. One could draw instructive parallels between traditional descriptions of this type of meditation, and of certain qualities of the sage, and characteristics of "nature mystics" in other traditions. In Zhu Xi's view, "silent sitting" promised the realistic possibility of experiencing unity with all things and all people. Wang Yang Ming, a later exponent of the Neo-Confucian School of Mind, spoke of realizing one's "true self" in a meditative quest for enlightenment. He identified cosmic principle (*li*) with the mind, so that discovery of the true self meant discovering the ultimate reality. Some discern parallels between Wang's mysticism and that of the German mystic Meister Eckhart (c. 1260–1327 CE).

Does the **shaman** have a place in Confucianism and CIT?

Shamans played an important role in Chinese religious history long before the time of Confucius. They have retained a place in Daoism and CCT, functioning as guides to the spirit world. But since Confucian teaching is far more concerned with how things are going in the "outer" world of ordinary human affairs, there have never been Confucian shamans as such. Shamans have generally been associated with folk and popular beliefs. As an important ingredient in CIT, Confucianism has often had a more aristocratic tone. However, some functions anciently connected with shamanism have had continuous importance throughout much of Chinese history for CIT as well as popular religion. Confucian Literati and their imperial patrons alike have regularly consulted diviners, specialists in *feng shui* and astrology, for help in determining auspicious times and places for momentous events and structures.

Do Confucians believe in **angels**? What about **devils**?

Confucius and his disciples preferred not to speculate about the existence of the countless beings which in popular belief animated the spirit world. If there is good in the world, human beings can take some of the credit. When evil gets the upper hand, human beings must acknowledge their responsibility and set about reestablishing a just order. Confucian tradition does not explicitly deny that spirits, both satisfied and malevolent, regularly pass unseen and generally undetected through the lives of ordinary people. In fact, its insistence on the centrality of ancestor veneration is a clear, if implicit, acknowledgment of the spirit world. But apart from that, the tradition emphasizes the need for human beings to focus on the more immediate facts of life. Follow the example of the virtuous, strive to establish justice everyday, and build all relationships on honesty. There will always be events human beings cannot explain simply, and circumstances beyond human control. Some of them may be attributable to spirits, but the important thing is not to become distracted from the ongoing demands of the call to personal virtue and responsibility.

Are **dreams and visions** important in Confucianism and CIT?

Popular and official religious practices intersect when it comes to dreams and visions. Confucian tradition as such sees little value in dreams and visions, except in so far as they reveal an individual's state of mind. But Chinese tradition generally puts considerable credence in these alternative and privileged ways of arriving at the truth. For example, emperors are often said to have dreams informing them of the proper course of action with respect to religious matters. Local CIT magistrates who experience difficulty in deciding on legal cases were instructed to stay overnight in the temple of the local "spirit magistrate," who would deliver the answer in a dream.

HOLIDAYS AND REGULAR OBSERVANCES

What kind of **calendar** do Confucians and CIT observe?

Whether Daoist, CCT, Buddhist, or Confucian, all Chinese have historically acknowledged the same overall reckoning of time. Official Confucian and CIT events were traditionally set by a Board of Astrology and promulgated by a Ministry of Rites. In overall structure, the Chinese lunar calendar consists of twelve months of twenty-nine or thirty days, since the time between new moons is about twenty-nine and a half days. The lunar year dovetails with the solar, with the intercalation of an extra month approximately every six years or when five additional days per year total thirty. Reckoning began around 2637 BCE, so that the year 2000 marks the year 4637. Each of the twelve animals of the Chinese zodiac is associated with a particular quality or event and gives its name to every twelfth year, beginning with the Rat (industry and prosperity) and proceeding in order through Ox (spring planting), Tiger (valor), Hare (longevity), Dragon (power and good fortune), Snake (cunning), Horse (perseverance), Sheep (filial piety) or Goat, Monkey (health), Rooster (protection), Dog (fidelity), and Pig (home and family). The year 2000 is the Year of the Dragon, 2001 that of the Snake, 2002 that of the Horse, and so on. Five full cycles, each named after one of the five elements (wood, fire, earth, metal and water) equals sixty years, an important interval for ritual purposes. Major annual markers are the winter (maximum yin) and summer (maximum yang) solstices and vernal and autumnal equinoxes when yin and yang are in balance. During each month, the most important times are the moments of new and full moon.

Is there any further **symbolism** attached to the **structure of the calendar**?

Each month is divided into ten-day periods, six of those in turn considered a special time period, and six of those in turn equaling a full year. In addition, each year is divided into twenty-four climatic periods called breaths or nodes, described by such phrases as "full of snow" or "clear and bright." Every year, month, day, and hour are further identified by a combination of ten heavenly "stems" and twelve earthly "branches" (the monthly or zodiacal symbols). The ten heavenly stems are associated with colors, two stems with each of the five symbolic colors (azure, red, yellow, white, black), which are in turn linked to the four directions and center as well as to the five elements. Branches and stems are both primarily numerical designators, but each also bears important symbolic connotations. If you match one stem with one branch for succeeding years (S1/B1, S2/B2 ... S1/B11, S2/B12, S3/B1, and so on), you end up back at the beginning after sixty years. In this system, only odd numbered stems combine with odd numbered branches, even numbered with even numbered. We are currently in the sixty-year cycle that began in 1984. The result of all this calculation is an extremely detailed system of pinpointing special times according to a host of definitive characteristics. Each event occurring on earth has its heavenly parallel. For every con-

Interior of the dome of the Temple of Heaven's Hall of Harvest Prayer in Beijing, showing two of the four large floor-to-dome columns (extreme right and left) representing the seasons, and several of the inner circle of twelve shorter columns symbolizing the months. At the oculus are the dragon and phoenix intertwined.

ceivable type of human behavior there is an auspicious moment. The calendar has thus been not merely a way of keeping track of times for religious observances, but a kind of temporal map for negotiating the cosmos as well. Each year, during the ninth lunar month, imperial officials set up the liturgical calendar for the year to come.

What regular or annual **observances** have been part of Confucian tradition?

For many centuries Confucians celebrated with large feasts in the Master's honor at both the vernal and autumnal equinoxes, corresponding with the second and eighth lunar months. During the fourth of the night's five watches, celebrants paid homage to Confucius' ancestors and then moved to the central memorial hall at sunrise. Arrayed carefully across the entire main courtyard were row upon row of participants, arranged according to rank, with imperial bureaucrats along the sides and six groupings of students in the center. Before and within the memorial hall the offerings and sacrificial animals were arranged. These included a roll of silk; vessels full of wine, soup and various foods; and a ritually slaughtered ox flanked by a pig and a lamb. A lengthy order of ceremony included specific offerings of each item, first to Confucius and then to the other sages enshrined in the main hall. This was accompanied by profound bowing and prostration, and songs of praise. A full classical Chinese orchestra punctuated by booming drum beats marked changes in the action. In addition to those semi-annual festivities, smaller semi-monthly observances included offerings to the spirit of Confucius at each new and full moon. In Korea, at the spring and autumn equinoxes, Confucians honor both Korean and Chinese sages at the Confucian University's shrine.

What are the **major festivities** historically associated with CIT?

Each year on the day before the winter solstice, the emperor and his retinue visited the Temple of Heaven for an elaborate event. When paying homage to Heaven and Earth, the emperor would perform special gestures of humility by kneeling three times and prostrating himself nine times. When he sacrificed to other powers, such as the sun, the moon, and the gods with power over the forces of nature, the emperor did not perform those rituals of self-abasement. At the Forbidden City's Hall of Supreme Harmony, major sacred events included the enthronement of a new emperor, royal weddings, an event held every ten years called the Great Anniversary, announcement of results of civil service examinations, and celebrations of the winter solstice and new year. In the Hall of Middle Harmony, the emperor formulated decrees to be made public in royal temples at all the various seasonal festivities. Imperial officials designated by the emperor, or local administrators in the case of smaller events, took care of the regular agriculturally-significant occasions throughout the country.

What were some of the other **regular festivals** once associated with CIT?

Many of the religiously significant times acknowledged with rituals in sacred sites affiliated with CIT overlap with popular Daoist and CCT practices. The Literati, who functioned as ritual specialists in service of the imperial house, generally looked down on Daoist and CCT devotionalism and often made fun of their beliefs. But as servants of the emperor, they could hardly afford to snub the very deities to whom the general populace prayed for success in mundane but important matters such as timely rain and abundant harvest. When the emperor's farflung political administrators entered into their roles as religious ritualists, they often found themselves crossing an imaginary line from the elite to the everyday life of the locals. Celebrating days associated with deities of purely local or regional origin and importance remained the task of Daoists and practitioners of CCT. But when they paid homage to local or regional deities whom the emperor had elevated to the CIT pantheon, the Literati were providing implicit legitimation for popular beliefs and practices. In addition to the Birthday of Confucius on the twenty-seventh day of the eighth lunar month, CIT also celebrated new and full moon occasions, some of which coincided with feasts like that of Lao Zi (second month, day fifteen) and the Hungry Ghosts (seventh month, day fifteen).

Could you describe an example of an **annual CIT ritual occasion** in greater detail?

At the Temple of Heaven in Beijing, a major event occurred at the winter solstice. Preparations commenced two months in advance. With five days to go, authorities inspected the animals to be offered. The next day they prepared the hall in which the emperor would spend a day in spiritual preparation, and the day after that the emperor began his abstinence. A procession made its way from the Forbidden City to the Temple, commoners taking care not to look at the royal person as he passed by. The emperor spent that day and night in the so-called Hall of Abstinence, a large complex to the west of the main north-south axis and about halfway between the Altar of Heaven to the south and the Hall of Harvest Prayer at the north of the compound. He bathed ritually and fasted for a day. (Later emperors often prepared in the Forbidden City itself.) Two days before the solstice, ritualists made final preparation of all ceremonial objects for the emperor's review. The day before the solstice, the emperor left the Hall of Abstinence and proceeded to the Altar of Heaven to honor Shang Di and his own royal forbears with incense and bowing, and then returned the Hall of Abstinence. Early the next day, he began a nine-part ceremony. At the round Altar of Heaven, where his ancestors' spirit tablets were arrayed, animals were sacrificed and he paid obeisance to the ancestors. Offerings included silk and jade as well as the sacrificial meats. To music and dancing, he presented wine to Shang Di and the spirits in the first of three such offerings. After the emperor bade the sacred presences farewell he withdrew to an observation dais, while officials consigned the offerings to a furnace. The ceremonies ended with the emperor exiting by the south gate and returning to the Forbidden City.

Do Confucians celebrate the **birthdays** of any religious figures?

September 28 of each year marks the birthday of Confucius in Taiwan, for example, and there it has also been declared Teachers' Day. In the People's Republic of China, celebrations of the day have been forbidden since the Maoist revolution of 1948, largely because of Confucianism's long-standing association with imperial rule. Taiwanese celebrations, however, are still elaborate and traditional, beginning at six in the morning according to ancient practice. Ceremonies commence with ritual drumming followed by a procession in which participants dressed in ancient regalia carry in special symbols to welcome the spirit of Confucius. Processional symbols include a royal canopy and fan, as well as ritual long-handled axes. In the capital city, Taipei, the celebration is modeled on the ancient pattern in which Literati bureaucrats performed the main rituals. There, the mayor presides over the various ranks of governmental employees and educational administrators, joined by ranks of students of different ages. Birthdays of particular deities or immortals do not play a role in Confucianism or CIT as they do in Daoism and CCT.

CUSTOMS AND RITUALS

How important is **ritual** in Confucianism and CIT?

There is perhaps no more fundamental notion in Chinese religious thought than that of *li,* proper ritual. The Chinese term is composed of two elements meaning sacrifice and spirit—more precisely, "contact with the upper world" combined with a character that once depicted a sacred vessel. It applies to all religious ceremony, from the most "popular" to the most official imperial cultic worship. Historically overseen by a Ministry of Rites, state rituals have generally been the most formal and precise. Pre-modern ritual practice distinguished several levels of ceremony. Supreme Offerings, performed mostly by the emperor himself, addressed Heaven, Earth, the forbears of the emperor and empress, and the deities of earth and seed. Middle Offerings propitiated sun and moon, ancestors of previous reigns, the god of agriculture called Emperor Shen Nung, and the goddess of silk production, Lei Zu. Lower Offerings occurred in local or regional state temples and revered Guan Di as deity of war, Wen Zhang as deity of literature, and Sage Emperor Fu Xi, among others. When Confucius spoke of *li,* he had in mind all of these, plus the entire range of ceremonies enacted on a smaller scale or in private. But more than that, he conceived of *li* as informing all proper human relationships.

What rituals are performed **at home**?

Confucian rituals performed in the home have historically included countless ways of expressing various levels of familial relationship. Those that most closely approximate what the majority of people would likely recognize as "religious" involve ancestor veneration (described in the section on Daoism).

What were some of the principal **CIT ritual occasions**?

Ritual responsibilities of the emperor and his official delegates, included ceremonies at various major state sacred sites: the Altar of the Spirits of Land and Grain, the Imperial Ancestral Temple, the temples of Heaven and Earth, of Sun and Moon, and within the audience halls of the Forbidden City. At the Altar of the Spirits of Land and Grain (*she ji tan*) the emperor performed sacrifices in spring for fertile fields and in the fall for plentiful harvest. At the Imperial Ancestral Temple (*tai miao*), he led ceremonies associated with the anniversaries of his own ancestors back through the history of the dynasty. There, the ancestors were said to grant audiences with their royal public much as the emperor himself did from his own audience halls. At the Temple of Heaven, the imperial officials offered harvest prayers on New Year's day, rain prayers at the onset of summer, and announced royal events, such as the designation of the heir to the throne. Within the Forbidden City, various important rituals occurred at the new year, the win-

Temple Rites

Confucian temples function principally as memorial halls. They are dedicated to the veneration and appreciation of the great sages, teachers and scholars of the tradition. Honoring the spirit and teaching of the great ones is not quite the same as praying to them in the way that some people pray to deities or to saints believed to have the power of intercession. Honoring the great Confucian figures generally lacks the kind of spontaneity one finds in the much busier Daoist and CCT temples. Confucian rituals tend to be more reserved and orderly and associated with specific occasions. Popular devotion, on the other hand, occurs virtually around the clock, seven days a week.

ter solstice, and the emperor's birthday. Subjects acknowledged the emperor's lofty authority in the various audience halls of the City's outer court, located just south of the more private palaces of the inner court. The ceremony began early in the morning outside the Meridian Gate, the southern entrance to the Forbidden City. At the sound of two drum beats, three thousand officials in nine ranks processed into the courtyard before the Hall of Supreme Harmony. Once they were arranged, three drum beats announced that the emperor would enter from the Hall of Middle Harmony, just to the north, and take his seat on the throne. Music accompanied his entry and continued as the officials paid homage. Military leaders lined up on the west and civil authorities on the east, both groups facing the central axis of the courtyard. Bird and animal symbolism was arranged on the robes so that the birds and animals of both groups were facing north, honoring the emperor as he sat on the dragon throne within the hall. All of creation was thus symbolically ordered toward the emperor, who represented Heaven. After the announcement of the specific occasion for the ritual, music resumed for another round of obeisance to the emperor. Once the emperor had departed, the ceremony ended with an exit procession of all present.

How did CIT structure its **main ritual activities**?

CIT rituals were arranged in a symbolic hierarchical order that coordinated the authority of those performing the rituals with the various ranks of the CIT pantheon. To symbolize universal dominion, the emperor would make offerings to the powers controlling all four cardinal directions, to all mountains and rivers, and to the "five domestic sacrifices." On lower levels, ritual responsibilities reflected a division of labor and authority. Imperial princes made offerings only to the power ruling their own quarters of the universe and the associated mountains and rivers, and to the five domestic sacrifices. These took place at regional sacred sites. In turn the princes' chief officers were to perform only the domestic offerings, and their subordinates only the offerings to their own ancestors.

470

These last rituals occurred in home settings and in cemeteries. Specific rituals include many of the same kinds of actions Daoists or practitioners of CCT engage in. Ritual specialists generally purified themselves for the ceremonies by fasting and ablutions. Before making offerings to divine powers of the top level in the pantheon, specialists fasted for three days, and for second level deities, two days. During times of fasting, ritualists were especially careful to avoid certain strong foods (garlic and onions) and fermented beverages. An essential ingredient in the preparatory period was avoidance of contact with death and disease. Festivities and music were put aside. Central to the actual worship ceremonies was the offering of food, wine, and incense, along with prayers of petition and physical prostration before the deities.

Stone Sage or ancestor figure on the grounds of the National Palace Museum in Seoul, South Korea.

What is the Confucian and Literati view of **ancestor veneration**?

Confucius did not invent ancestor veneration, but his teaching placed great emphasis on the practice. Already a millennium old by Confucius' time, ancestor veneration had much to do with the rather utilitarian belief that malcontent spirits of the deceased could cause great trouble. Better to attend to their needs before they became disgruntled. But Confucius stressed a more positive note of reverence for those who have gone before and of maintaining connections with one's sacred past. So much of what we are is our history. In Korea, descendants of the Yi dynasty still gather annually to perform memorial rites with full traditional costume and music. This Yi Dynasty Association maintains dynastic memorial tablets in an ancestral shrine in Seoul called Chongmyo. To each of the eighteen major Yi rulers enshrined there the worshipers offer three cups of wine and choice food. Scholars often credit Confucian influence in Japan with the continued prevalence of ancestor veneration there.

Is there a standard Confucian group **liturgical worship**?

Confucianism is surely among the most ritual-conscious traditions in history. Each day in the life of a Confucian is full of an awareness of the importance of ritualized actions and ways of thinking. But apart from the larger annual or semi-annual public

471

ceremonies, and the regular acknowledgment of revered ancestors, there is no communal Confucian liturgy as such.

Have Confucians or CIT ordinarily engaged in **ritual sacrifice**?

Sacrifice of certain animals has long been part of Confucian observances, both of the Master's birthday and of certain types of ancestor memorial. Two kinds of ritual sacrifice have also been historically associated with CIT. The *Feng* (high altar mound) and *Shan* (level ground) sacrifices were those offered to Heaven and Earth, respectively. Some emperors used the public performance of these rituals as a way of declaring and expressing gratitude for their possession of the Mandate of Heaven. History records that a number of emperors, even down to the last dynasty, engaged in the sacrifices atop or at the foot of sacred mountains. Animals sacrificed ritually most commonly included sheep and pigs, but occasionally wild game animals like deer were also sacrificed. Larger and more expensive ceremonies might feature oxen splayed across a rack after slaughtering, or the burnt offering of a whole young red bull—red is the color of *yang,* the energy needed to return warmth to the earth so that spring will renew all living things. In the Temple of Heaven complex, for example, a large slaughterhouse and "spirit kitchen" accommodated extensive sacrificial needs. Eighty butchers and two hundred-eighty cooks processed vast quantities of material. A year's worth of sacrifices, according to one record, included nearly a thousand pigs, over eight hundred sheep, over two hundred each of deer, cows, and rabbits, and over a hundred goats.

What kinds of special **ritual objects** figure in Confucian and CIT worship?

When Confucius was young he was particularly intrigued by the classic bronze vessels his ancestors had used for centuries in honoring Heaven. Most of these vessels held materials to be offered. The principal forms developed in connection with the particular types of material. A vase *(yu)* was to hold sacrificial wine; a jug *(zhue)* poured libations; and beaker *(gu)* may have been used for sharing a communion-like drink. The *ding* was a bowl for ritual foods such as cereal grains or fruit. Some of these objects apparently were designed in particularly symbolic shapes, such as the "hill-shaped" censer, whose form recalled the Five Sacred Mountains. Some bronzes bear abstract representations of the four directional creatures: the black tortoise of the wintry north, the green dragon of the vernal east, the scarlet bird of the summery south, and the white tiger of the autumnal west. Inscriptions dedicating an object to a father, for example, or expressing the hope that sons and grandsons will use the vessel for "ten thousand years," suggest that they were commonly used in ancestor veneration rituals. Even today, copies of those antique objects adorn the altars in Confucian temples and are part of the relatively infrequent offerings held there. Many of the sacred vessels were buried in tombs or even thrown into river beds during invasions to prevent

---

Exorcism

Shamans of ancient times and their Daoist successors, the Black Hat and Red Turban ritual specialists, have generally played the role of exorcists to the Chinese population at large. Confucians and members of the imperial administration might very well have enlisted the services of an exorcist in particular instances. But neither Confucianism nor CIT focuses on matters of this kind, except in relation to ancestor veneration rituals. In a way, attending to the spirits of the dead, whether of the individual family or of the imperial dynasty, seeks to obviate the need for exorcism as such. Proper, sincere, and timely acknowledgment of those spirits reduces the likelihood that frustrated souls will wander abroad with troublesome intent.

---

them from falling into the hands of barbarians. Nearly every large museum has good examples in its Asian collections, and they are well worth a visit.

Do Confucianism and CIT consider the practice of **divination** essential?

Two types of divination have been important ingredients in the ritual life of both Confucianism and CIT. As in Daoism and CCT, the practice of geomancy (earth-prognostication) called *feng shui* has always been a necessary prerequisite for the siting and planning of all structures, from the humblest home to the grandest temple or palace. Those contemplating any building project would enlist a specialist in *feng shui* for a thorough reading of the natural characteristics of the proposed site. For more detail on the practice, see the section on Daoism. In addition, people from the emperor on down regularly consulted specialists in interpreting the oracles of the *Yi Jing,* the *Classic of Change,* before undertaking any significant course of action. The imperial staff included experts in divination who could be consulted on short notice. Such specialists were not specifically members of the Literati or Confucian hierarchies, but their services were generally regarded as indispensable.

What attitudes toward **pilgrimage** are important in Confucianism and CIT?

Confucian teaching generally did not promote the popular practice of pilgrimage, associated as it was with Daoism and Buddhism. A larger concern had to do with the social and political implications of devotional travel. Many Confucians considered pilgrimage a potential threat to the stability of society. Anthropologists talk about the experience of "liminality" as an essential part of pilgrimage. Pilgrims step out of their accustomed social roles, leaving behind the rules, duties, and responsibilities of ordinary daily life. They become "liminal" in that they step across a threshold (*limen* in Latin) into another way of being and thinking, if only temporarily. For people who regard their function as maintaining social order, the prospect of throngs of pilgrims heading out across the countryside in hope of miracles or magic naturally poses a threat. Enthusiastic crowds are prey to demagogues and can turn into unruly mobs. Still, a parallel to devotional pilgrimage developed among Confucians on a smaller scale. Confucius himself became a model of the itinerant scholar, traveling from one province to another in search of disciples and patrons. Later Confucians often followed his example. Eventually the places in which these Confucian exemplars had lived and taught began to attract visitors. Not surprisingly, the tomb of Confucius in Shandung became a goal for Confucian pilgrims, who were generally in search not of miracles, but of inspiration in the struggle to live a good life. In general, it appears that the tradition of family members caring for ancestral graves may have been significant in preventing burial places from becoming pilgrimage goals. Mountains were also important destinations for China's Literati. There, one could contemplate most abundantly nature's sacred beauty. There, too, was the incomparable source of poetic inspiration.

How important is **music** in Confucian and CIT ritual?

Celebrations like that of the Master's birthday are filled with the sound of music. Confucius had always insisted that training in both music appreciation and instrumental proficiency were essential ingredients in a proper education. Many Confucian temples keep the principal musical instruments on display in the main memorial hall flanking the tablet of Confucius. Important stringed instruments include plucked cousins of the Japanese *koto* called the *jin* and *se*, which are not typically found in Daoist instrumental repertoires. Percussion pieces include a variety of bells, both individual large ones and sets of tuned smaller ones, and similar sets of metal chimes. Wind instruments include multi-tube flutes, similar to European panpipes, as well as wooden transverse flutes. A category of special decorative motifs called the "Eight Musical Instruments" appear on all sorts of fine wares, suggesting the importance of music in Chinese tradition. The eight include the musical stone, a large bell, a lute, a flute, a metal percussion instrument, a drum, a reed organ, and an ocarina. CIT rituals always included large musical ensembles that played during lengthy segments of the ceremonies, especially for the entrance and exit of the emperor and while the royal subjects were paying homage to him.

Is **dance** also a significant ingredient in Confucian and CIT ritual?

Once a central feature of many rituals in China, Confucian dance has been preserved as an art form only in Korea. During the semi-annual gathering to honor the spirits of Confucius and the sages at the Confucian University, and at the annual gathering to honor the kings of the Yi dynasty at the Royal Ancestral Shrine, dancers perform elaborate routines. Originally, Confucian dance was limited to male performers. Both military and non-military forms of dance make up the repertoire. Dancers gesture with the long pheasant feathers and small flutes they carry. Complex ritual movement was formerly integral to virtually all the major ceremonies of CIT. Whether in the courtyards of the Forbidden City or around the altars of the Temple of Heaven and other sacred imperial sites, intricately choreographed scripts called for dance on a grand scale.

Do Confucians **pray** in any particular language?

Most people who still actively pursue the teachings attributed to Confucius are of Chinese descent. Relatively small numbers of Confucians live in Korea and Japan, and the rest are scattered across the globe, mostly in communities of Chinese origin. Many dialects, some very different from each other, are spoken across China. When people gather, for example, in Taipei's Confucian temple, they naturally perform their rituals in the Taiwanese dialect. That is not to say that they all can or do read the Five Classics and Four Books themselves. Those texts are written in an archaic language difficult even for well-educated native speakers of Chinese. In Japan and Korea, Confucians who engage in ancestor veneration ceremonies at a public Confucian venue will use their vernacular languages. Japanese and Korean Confucian scholars, on the other hand, must be able to handle the sources in Chinese. In other words, although Chinese dialects are "canonical" in that the Confucian tradition's primary sources were written in them, Chinese is not a sacred liturgical language as Sanskrit and Arabic still are for Hindus and Muslims.

What are the principal Confucian and CIT **rites of passage**?

Confucian tradition prescribes a full range of very detailed ritual procedures to be observed for various family, as well as a few public, occasions. They differ from rites of passage in many other traditions in that they generally do not assume an overtly religious form. Confucian teaching places enormous emphasis on ritualized attentiveness to every detail of daily family life. All of that occurs within the larger, presumed context of life under Heaven and in a society that is at least potentially just and harmonious. In pre-modern times, many Chinese practiced rites of initiation for young women and men alike. Families conferred on young men a hat and a name symbolizing maturity. Young women received some new clothes and had their hair done specially. More recently, Chinese social custom has linked these rituals to marriage, now considered the primary sign of adulthood.

Has **meditation** been an important ritual activity for Confucians?

Confucian tradition has generally emphasized the need for a calm, contemplative approach to life. Few individuals can develop the habit of reflection without engaging deliberately in practices designed to facilitate that habit. Meditation has not occupied as prominent a position in Confucian spirituality as it has in Chinese Buddhism, but it is important nevertheless. Confucians who engage in solitary or group meditation usually sit on small stools, rather than on the floor in the lotus posture, as many Buddhists do. When Confucians meditate, they reflect on the underlying propriety and order of the universe. Cultivation of the ethical self for the purpose of contributing more conscientiously to society is the goal. Classical Confucian and Neo-Confucian writers describe meditation as "quiet-sitting" and "abiding in reverence." Unlike Zen meditation, Confucian meditation has a distinctly ethical emphasis. Some authors say the goal of meditation is to make a place in one's mind for the human beings who constitute one's own community—family, friends, associates. Not unlike a process of free-association, this form of meditation gathers whatever comes to mind and allows it all to sift and settle naturally. "Settled nature" is the goal, a state in which the meditator is free from the agitation that arises from disordered relationships. Confucian meditation may sound quite unstructured, but it requires constant mental and emotional discipline. A meditator must be alert to abstract notions that distract from concrete ethical concerns, for it is often much easier to drift off into speculation than to confront life as one is actually living it.

Are there Confucian rituals or beliefs around **marriage and family life**?

Confucian tradition—Chinese tradition in general, really—teaches that marriage is meant to perpetuate the extended family rather than to create new small social units, all going their separate ways. Marriages arranged by match-makers have long been the rule, complete with elaborate astrological calculations to assure cosmic compatibility. The equivalent of a dowry from the groom's parents means the bride has been bought from her family of origin. When young Chinese marry in the traditional way, the new couple virtually fuse with the husband's family of origin. As long as an older male survives in the groom's family, the groom and his wife own no property. Most striking of all, perhaps, is that the bride no longer makes ritual offerings to her own family, but only to her husband's ancestors. Young married couples have historically felt enormous pressure to produce a male heir for the family. Traditional Chinese marriage rituals have not generally been considered "sacramental" as in some other traditions. Nor is marriage a purely civil matter, for the family is the custodian of the sacred in Chinese tradition.

How do Confucians deal ritually with **death and mourning**?

Confucian practices associated with funerals and ancestor veneration are of a piece with those of Daoism and CCT, in that the basic elements are common to most segments of traditional Chinese societies. Confucius and his disciples did have some specific thoughts on the matter, though. Disciple Xun Zi wrote that the feelings of loss

Although much of the imagery here is Buddhist in origin, the practice of holding memorial services for deceased loved ones (note the photographs on the altar) testifies to the pervasive influence of Confucian tradition throughout Asia: Judgment Hall in a popular Buddhist temple, Pong Won Sa in Seoul, South Korea. The bodhisattava Chi Jang (not visible here, known as Jizo in Japan) rules over the realms of the next life, along with the Ten Kings of the Underworld, whose images are arranged around the right and left sides of the room and who function as judges.

and longing for a deceased person, and the ritual expression of those feelings, represented the height of human civilization and culture. In a way, one knows the humanity of others through the attachment they express for lost loved ones. Although Confucius himself declined to speculate about the experience of death or the condition of one who has died, he seems to have felt strongly that there were appropriate ritual and emotional responses. When asked whether he recommended the full three-year period of mourning, Confucius responded that if Literati who lose loved ones were to dispense with the practice, they would risk the irrevocable loss of some of society's most important rituals. He added that if the questioner felt comfortable performing only a year's grieving, he might do so. After the questioner had left, however, the Teacher commented how heartless such a person must be. Parents attend to their infants unceasingly for three years; the least their children can do is return the favor symbolically. One specific issue that has historically been very important for Confucianism and CIT is the question of monumental funereal architecture and special memorials for the great and powerful. Confucius and several of the tradition's later teachers have been remembered with fairly modest grave markers. Tombs of emperors, on the other hand, have often been grand, even extravagant, architectural works. At least one ruler even commissioned a virtual reconstruction of the royal residence underground, complete with thousands of life-size terra-cotta soldiers to protect the imperial remains.

SHINTO

HISTORY AND SOURCES

What is Shinto and what are its **origins**?

"Shinto" derives from two Chinese words—*shen,* meaning "deity," and *dao,* meaning "way." The Japanese reading of the Chinese expression comes out *kami no michi,* the "Path of the Kami." Since at least several centuries BCE, the Japanese have acknowledged the sacred presence and power of numinous beings called *kami,* "high or superior beings." Until about the middle of the sixth century CE, the Japanese people evidently did not think of their ancient religious traditions as a separate system. So organically integrated were those traditions with their entire culture and heritage that worship of the *kami* was largely assumed as *the* Japanese way. Only with the arrival of Buddhism, called in Japanese "the Way of the Buddha" (*butsu-do*), did it become necessary to give the indigenous beliefs and practices a name to distinguish them from this imported tradition. Unlike many other major traditions, Shinto had neither a founder nor a single foundational figure who represents concrete historical origins. In a sense, Shinto is as old as Japan itself, somewhat the way Hinduism is as old as India. At its core, the Way of the Kami enshrines profound insights into the sacred character of all created nature. Shinto calls people to a deep awareness of the divine presence suffusing all things, to the challenge of personal and corporate responsibility for the stewardship of the world that is home, to unending gratitude for all that is good, and to a willingness to seek purification and forgiveness for humanly inevitable but avoidable lapses. Observe worshipers at a Shinto shrine—as Buddhism has temples, Shinto has shrines—and there can be little doubt of the sincere devotion that moves so many people to prayer and ritual expression of their beliefs.

What were the earliest Shinto **sacred texts**?

Two eighth-century documents are Shinto's foundational texts. These are among the youngest of the major religious tradition's primary works. Unlike many other sacred texts, they are not considered to have been divinely written even though their subject matter is of divine origin. In other words, these scriptures are not considered divine communication as such, but communication about things divine. The Records of Ancient Matters, or *Kojiki,* dates to 712 CE. Composed by a courtier named Yasumaro, its three volumes deal with events beginning with the creation of the Japanese islands and people and continuing down to 628 CE. Exegetes have authored scores of major commentaries (called *kojikiden*) in relatively recent times. The thirty-volume Chronicles of Japan, called *Nihongi* as well as *Nihon Shoki,* was completed in 720 CE. About three times the length of the *Kojiki,* the Chronicles also recount the ancient cosmogonic myth, though in a less detailed fashion. Greater detail about subsequent imperial history includes events up to 697 CE. These two texts enjoyed special prominence after the seventeenth century, when a school of Shinto studies called "National Learning" (*kokugaku*) set out to probe the sources for the essence of being Japanese that they communicate. These primary texts are so important because they record the history of the imperial family and legitimate its authority by establishing its divine lineage.

What other **early scriptures** are especially important for Shinto practitioners? Is there a Shinto **scriptural canon**?

Scholars refer to the various sacred texts collectively as *shinten,* "texts of the deities." But although they generally agree on the importance of a certain set of works, there has never been an official process of "canonization" by which representatives of the tradition have formally declared certain texts as definitive. Here are the most important of the classical documents. From the early eighth century, the *Fudoki* ("Records of Wind and Earth") provided data about very early religious rituals from major shrines. The early ninth century *Kogo-shui* (807), or "Gleaning of Ancient Words" commented on previous documents in an attempt to legitimate the Imbe family against their enemies, the Nakatomi clan. The *Manyoshu,* "Collection of Countless Leaves," anthologizes a large selection of seventh- and eighth-century Japanese poetry of various genres. Some Shinto scholars have insisted that these poems represent the purest form of Japanese literary expression. First published in 927, the *Engi-shiki* includes a collection of more than two dozen prayer texts. A work called the *Kujiki* (also *Sendai Kuji Hongi*) or "Records of Ancient Happenings" bears the date 620 but was probably contrived as late as the ninth century to compete with the similar sounding *Kojiki* in antiquity and authority. It amounts to what some traditions might call an "apocryphal" work—not what it claims to be, but still full of valuable material. Finally, a group of thirteenth-century texts called the Five Shinto Scriptures (*Shinto gobusho*) emphasize the antiquity of Japan's Shinto heritage. Seventeenth-century

Hints for Pronouncing Japanese Words

Consonants are pronounced very much as they appear. Vowels are always "long"—e.g., a = "ah," e = "ay," i = "ee," o = "oh," u = "oo." Two items that are difficult for many people are these: the letters "ky" and "ry" followed by a vowel (kyo, ryu) are pronounced as a single syllable, so Tokyo is not To-kee-o, but To-kyo. When the letter "i" comes after "sh" and before "t" or "k," as in the company name Matsushita or the name of the Sumo champion Konishiki, the "i" is elided. So, Matsush'ta and Konish'ki. Similarly, a "u" between an "s" and another consonant (like "s," "t" or "k") is often elided, as in the name of the important Tokyo shrine, Yasukuni, pronounced Yas'kuni.

scholars who studied these texts as prime examples of Japanese culture and values went on to spearhead the National Learning school of thought.

What does the term **"Dual Shinto"** mean?

Dual (or *ryobu,* "two-sided") Shinto arose out of the early interaction between Shinto theology and Buddhist thinking newly imported from China. Some use the term *ryobu shugo,* "dual compromise," to describe the resulting syncretism. Some accounts describe the developments this way. In 715 CE a Shinto shrine annexed a Buddhist temple. Twenty years later a smallpox epidemic created a crisis, to which the emperor responded by commissioning the colossal Great Buddha (*daibutsu*) at Nara's Todaiji temple. At the same time, the ruler dispatched the Buddhist patriarch Gyogi to Ise shrine to seek the blessing of Amaterasu, the Shinto sun goddess. Gyogi secured a favorable oracle, and the next night the emperor had a dream in which Amaterasu identified herself as the Mahayana Buddha of Infinite Light, Vairocana. This laid the groundwork for further identification of the various kami as alter-egos of various Buddhas and Bodhisattvas. In 750, an image of the Shinto war kami, Hachiman, was transported from its shrine at Usa on the island of Kyushu (just south of the main Japanese island, Honshu) to Todaiji in Nara so that the kami might pay respects to the Daibutsu. Hachiman thereafter remained in a special shrine at Todaiji, where he became the guardian kami of Todaiji temple. Thus did a Shinto kami come to protect the teachings of the Buddha. This account reflects an interpretation formulated during the ninth century by teachers of a new esoteric school of Buddhism called Shingon. As always, this theological accommodation had its political implications and set the stage for many years of Buddhist growth and royal patronage. From then on until 1868, Dual Shinto was the dominant form of Shinto. With the Meiji Restoration of imperial power came increasing pressure from Shinto scholars to purge the tradition of all Chinese influences, including of course

Buddhism and Confucianism, both of which had by turns exerted considerable pull at court for many years.

How important was the school of **National Learning**?

"National Learning," or *Kokugaku,* had perhaps more to do with the modern understanding of Shinto than has any other movement within the tradition. Kada no Azumamaro (1669–1736) is generally considered the founder of the school, insisting on the need to return to the earliest genuinely and purely Japanese sources. Among those he included the Kujiki, but emphasized the Kojiki and Nihongi especially. Kamo no Mabuchi (1697–1769) continued what Kada had begun by applying philological methods to classical Japanese prayer and poetry. He considered spontaneity the native Japanese gift, without which nothing could be truly Japanese. Motoori Norinaga (1730–1801) continued the scholarly dynasty, and is still regarded by some as Shinto's best theological mind. His forty-four volume commentary on the Kojiki remains a monument of scholarship. Hirata Atsutane (1763–1843) was the latest and perhaps most influential exponent of the school, in that he implemented the thought of his predecessor Motoori. Together these four men were largely responsible for the articulation of modern Shinto's highly nationalistic and ethnocentric tone.

Was Shinto associated with the **Samurai** code?

Japan's fabled tradition of Samurai warriors did have important connections with Shinto, but it did not arise out of Shinto alone or even primarily. Some credit a seventeenth-century Japanese Confucian scholar and military theorist named Yamaga Soko

A shrine maiden called a *miko* attends to the shrine shop at Tokyo's Meiji Jingu, selling various devotional materials such as the protective arrows and cards on which worshipers can write petitions to leave on special racks at the shrine.

(1622–1685) as the originator of the "way of the warrior" (*bushi-do*). Yamaga emphasized the importance of sincerity and utter devotion to the ancestral kami as a sure road to experiencing the divine presence. Along with other thinkers of his time, he focused on the concept of Amaterasu as the ancestral kami of the imperial family. Total devotion to the ancestral kami therefore implied perfect allegiance to the person of the emperor, the shogun, and the territorial feudal lords called *daimyo*. Feudal society depended on the loyalty of its *samurai,* the knightly or military class. Even after the shogunate and the feudal system gave way to a rejuvenated imperial government under the Meiji Restoration, military supporters of the emperor turned the code of unquestioning dedication to good effect by underscoring the necessity of unstinting affection for the royal person and his household.

Has Shinto ever been identified with any **political regimes**?

What came to be known in 1945 as State (*kokka*) Shinto began as a formal development after the Meiji Restoration in 1868. The term "State Shinto" was coined in the "Shinto Directive" of 1945 to distinguish formal Japanese government involvement in religious affairs from the religious concerns of Japanese generally, which were called Sect (*shuha*) Shinto. After 1868, the Japanese government imposed a system of devotion to the emperor as a kind of state creed. Most Christians and Buddhists, as well as adherents of other traditions, considered themselves part of that system. "Shrine

483

Shinto" was another term used to refer to the system, since the government had instituted in 1868 an elaborate structure of ranks for administering the nation's shrines. Government directives regulated everything in shrine life, including specific rituals to be performed and how records were to be kept. Underlying all this was the principle of "Worship-government unity" (*saisei itchi*). Directives also set up an elaborate hierarchy of the Shinto priesthood.

One of the principal results of this extensive government control was the doctrine of absolute loyalty to the emperor and the expression of that loyalty in religious practice. A major symbol of the new way was the founding in 1869 of Tokyo's Yasukuni Shrine as a memorial to all war dead. As a way of controlling powerful symbolic expressions long connected with Shinto, the government decreed in 1884 that the *torii* gate could be used only for state shrines. In 1900, the government further ordered that Shrine Shinto was no longer to be considered a religion as such, but a universally binding attitude of reverence for the emperor, complete with appropriate rituals.

Another aspect of Shinto's relationship to the Japanese government is that long before the Meiji era, imperial palaces in the various capitals had maintained a system of three shrines within the compounds for exclusive use by the royal family. In the center, the *kashiko-dokoro* enshrined the symbols of the emperor's divinity. The *koreiden,* on the left, was dedicated to spirits of past emperors and their wives, and to the right the *shinden* enshrined all the kami of heaven and earth. These shrines remain integral to imperial ritual today. State Shinto consisted of the approximately one hundred thousand shrines held under central control between 1868 and 1945, and the Shinto rites unique to the Imperial Household. Japan's post-war Constitution guarantees freedom of religion and mandates strict separation of state and religious affairs.

What effect did the Japanese loss of **World War II** have on Shinto?

After the emperor Meiji restored imperial power when the last of the great Shoguns asked to be relieved of the burden of authority, loyalty to the emperor became a central theme. Prior to 1945, the vast majority of Japanese regarded the emperor, Hirohito, as infallible. Dedication to the imperial person and rule was perhaps the most important element in national unity. Admission of defeat in 1945 naturally struck at the heart of this central cultural institution. Since most people associated the emperor's divine descent with ancient Shinto tradition, the disastrous defeat called into question the viability of Shinto as a way of understanding the world and the place of the Japanese people within it. On December 15, 1945, the Supreme Commander of Allied Powers, General Douglas MacArthur, issued the Shinto Directive, dramatically altering the shape of Japan's indigenous religious tradition. Acknowledging the tremendous symbolic connection between Shinto and Japanese nationalism, the decree disestablished all shrines and declared them private institutions. Priests were no longer officials of the government. The Directive replaced three earlier national

Worshipers revere a large marble effigy of a sacred bull that is the symbol of the *kami* Sugawara Michizane, at Kyoto's Kitano Tenjin shrine.

structures—the National Association of Shrine Priests, Research Institute for Japanese Classics, and Supporters of the Grand Shrine (of Ise)—with the Association of Shinto Shrines. It attempted to bring as many shrines as possible into a voluntary organization whose purpose was to redefine Shinto as non-nationalistic religious tradition. Most shrines agreed to join, and most remain under local administration, entirely responsible for their own fundraising and upkeep. Longstanding tradition, however, does not yield so easily to the decrees of conquering foreigners. A number of major shrines, such as Yasukuni in Tokyo and others dedicated to Japan's war dead, still have the power to stir nationalist sentiment. Even now, politicians who want to play that card occasionally make highly publicized visits to Yasukuni.

How would you sum up the **history** of Shinto?

Beliefs now associated with the religious tradition called Shinto originated long before anyone ever referred to them as "the way of the kami." Archaeological evidence points to various forms of nature worship, ancestor veneration, shamanistic rituals and animistic beliefs in an agricultural society during the neolithic (7000–250 BCE) and bronze-iron (250 BCE–100 CE) ages. Primitive shrines dedicated to the community or clan deities called *ujigami* appeared between 100 and 552 CE. Sometime in the later sixth century CE, after the arrival of *Butsu-do* or "the way of the Buddha," Japanese distinguished indigenous beliefs from the imported tradition by inventing a name for it. During the Nara period (710–94), the Nakatomi clan served as priests of a nascent imperial Shinto whose earliest major shrines were those of Ise and Izumo. By 737 Shinto shrines numbered over three thousand, one in four enjoying direct government support.

The Fujiwara clan founded the important Kasuga shrine in Nara, the first capital. Kasuga was destined to play a critical role in the development of a hybrid of Buddhism and Shinto through its relationship with the nearby Buddhist temple of Todaiji. Throughout the Heian period (794–1185), with the capital newly established at Kyoto, Shinto's fortunes were intimately bound up with developments in Buddhism. Theologians on both sides devised theories designed to fit the two belief systems together, thereby inventing "dual Shinto," a blend of both.

The Kamakura period (1185–1333) witnessed the rise of feudal lords (*daimyo*) and a samurai warrior caste under a shogun ("throne field marshal") of the Minamoto family, which had toppled the Fujiwara clan. The Samurai code, *bushido,* was a blend of Confucian aristocratic conservatism, Buddhist mental discipline, and Shinto patriotism. Under the Minamoto the two chief kami were Sugawara Michizane, patron of literary and social concerns, and Hachiman, kami of war. Shinto grew as a popular religious tradition during the Muromachi/Ashikaga period (1333–1568, the first name referring to the capital outside Kyoto and the second to the clan in power) with imperial patronage of pilgrimage to Ise shrine.

Pre- and early modern developments during the Momoyama/Azuchi (1568–1615) and Edo/Tokugawa periods (1615–1867) included Shinto's steady ascendancy over Buddhism and identification with the political power of dictatorial shoguns. Eighteenth- and nineteenth-century Japanese isolationism went hand in hand with attempts to rid Shinto of foreign elements. That culminated in the Meiji Reform, ushering in the modern period (1868–1945) and restoring the emperor to divine status. World War II called Shinto's imperial theology into question and saw a return of popular sectarian movements.

RELIGIOUS BELIEFS

Is it appropriate to call Shinto a religious **tradition**?

Religious studies scholars have increasingly come to appreciate the genuinely religious qualities of Shinto. Every now and then criticism still surfaces that Shinto is so much a part of ordinary Japanese life that it is really a set of cultural beliefs and practices rather than a religious tradition. Some critics base their conclusion on polls of the Japanese public that seem to suggest widespread apathy about religious issues.

Decreasing numbers of people are willing to identify themselves as adherents of any religious tradition, including Shinto. Other critics note that that even Japanese who do consider themselves active participants in a Shinto-based community are likely to claim that they are Buddhist as well. Doesn't that suggests that Shinto is less than authentically religious? If it were, some argue, it hardly would tolerate multiple religious allegiances, would it? Some point to Shinto's concern with the ordinary, the everyday, the natural world that surrounds us, and its lack of interest in transcendent mystery. Shouldn't a religious tradition be more invested in turning people's attention to a world beyond this one? In fact, these and other distinctive aspects of Shinto are among its strengths and the basis for its unique contributions to our world. Shinto offers arresting insights into the inherent divine quality of the simplest things, of the beauty hidden away in life's nooks and crannies. Shinto tradition discerns innumerable causes for profound gratitude to the powers beyond the merely human that make life itself possible. Shinto may not be celebrated for producing sophisticated schools of theological speculation, but it undoubtedly possesses many characteristics that identify it as a religious tradition.

Is there a Shinto **creed**?

Shinto beliefs, like those of Daoism and the Chinese Community Traditions, have never been reduced to a concise formal summary statement. If one were to produce a brief Shinto creedal affirmation it might go something like this: I believe that sacredness surrounds me, that it pervades all things including my very self, and that the all-suffusing divine presence is ultimately benevolent and meant to assure well-being and happiness for all who acknowledge it and strive to live in harmony with it. Shortly after the Meiji Restoration in 1868, the imperial authorities formulated the rough equivalent of a brief creedal statement, called the Three Great Teachings, in an attempt to enhance the emperor's status. The three teachings included patriotism and respect for the kami, the establishment of heavenly principles in relation to human culture, and dedication to the emperor and his pronouncements. Authorities interpreted the creed in the context of worship of the sun goddess, Amaterasu, and the other chief deities in the creation myth. Although it approximated a creed in some ways, this statement was more like an acknowledgment of the importance of underlying religious conviction for the good order of Japanese society.

Is the term **revelation** useful in understanding Shinto tradition?

All religious traditions are oriented in varying degrees to two great inseparable realities—truth and power. Some, such as the Abrahamic traditions—Judaism, Christianity, and Islam—tend to tilt slightly toward truths that human beings cannot discern without direct help from the source of truth itself. Others, such as Daoism, focus more on teaching believers how to discern and benefit from the wellsprings of power.

487

Shinto is far more concerned with power than with truth. This is obviously an over-simplification, but what it means is that the power of the divine and its implications are the only important truths. Where and how do human beings have access to those truths? Preeminently through the marvels of nature, including the human. Shinto's deities do not reveal a message otherwise inaccessible to mortals, as is the case in the Abrahamic faiths, for example. They do, however, disclose to anyone who reflects on his or her life with a clear mind and heart all the truth human beings need.

Are there **creation stories** or other **mythic** elements in Shinto tradition?

Two of the earliest of Shinto's foundational documents recount the story of the divine origins of Japan and its people. In variant accounts, the *Kojiki* and *Nihon Shoki* tell of how Japan came into existence, but the myth is not so much a narrative of creation as it is of Japan's unique sacred history. The basic myth goes like this: In the beginning, heaven and earth were as one, positive and negative unseparated. In a primal egg-like mass dwelt the principles of all life. Eventually the purer, lighter element rose and became heaven, while the heavier descended to form earth. A reed-shoot grew between earth and heaven and became the "One who established the Eternal Land." After some aeons, two kami formed by spontaneous generation. Descending to earth on the Floating Bridge of Heaven, Izanagi (the Male Who Invites) and Izanami (the Female Who Invites) came into the world. In an image of sexual procreation, Izanagi stirred the ocean depths with his spear and created the first lands. On the eight Japanese islands the union of the Male and Female produced the mountains and rivers, and thirty-five other kami. Last to be born was Fire, the kami of heat, who burned his mother fatally during his birth. Izanagi slew Fire with his sword, creating numerous additional kami in the process.

The Female fled to the underworld, the Land of Darkness, desperate to prevent her husband from seeing her corrupted state. When the Male followed and lit a fire so that he could see, she chased him out and blocked the entry to the underworld. Returning to the surface, the Male immediately purified himself ritually, ridding himself of the underworld's pollution. Corruption from his left eye formed the sun goddess Amaterasu, who rules the High Plain of Heavens, and from his right, Tsukiyomi, the moon, whose province is the oceans. From his nostrils he created the storm kami, Susanowo, Withering Wind of Summer and ruler of the earth. Susanowo soon made trouble for his sister, the Sun, who took refuge in a rock cave. Needing the sun to return, the eight hundred thousand kami discussed how they might entice her from her cave. At length they resorted to enlisting the Terrible Female of Heaven to dance and shout obscenities to rouse Amaterasu's curiosity. They then offered her blue and white soft offerings, a mirror, and a bejeweled Sakaki tree. She finally came out and dispatched her grandson Ninigi to rule the world. His son in turn, Jimmu Tenno, became the first human emperor at age 45, on February 11, 660 BCE.

Are **doctrine** and **dogma** important to Shinto practitioners?

Shinto has been influential in Japanese life through a relatively small number of specific and well-defined beliefs. Ancient tradition teaches the sacredness of nature, and of the existence of specific individual and personal divine beings, including those mentioned in myths. Some of those divine beings have had universal importance throughout Japan and the history of Shinto. Others have been of more regional or local importance. The teaching with perhaps the most significant cultural implications is that of the divine ancestry of the emperor. Other important elements of the myth that one could call "doctrinal" have to do with the divine origins of Japan itself and the essential need of ritual purity. Across Japan and over the centuries, many other doctrine-like features have been important, but Shinto never has been a dogmatic tradition in that it has not explicitly made adherence to a specific set of doctrines a standard for membership in the community of believers. Far more significant has been the standard of participation in community through its vast complex of ritual practices. Those rituals are in turn deeply rooted in the primal myth.

What do Shinto practitioners believe about **ultimate spiritual reality** or God?

Kami is the most important term in Shinto theology. Its general meaning is "high or superior being," and it can be applied to a host of spiritual presences and powers. Every kami is said to emanate its own distinctive divine energy or force. Among the various specific designations are the following. Nature kami include the deities of mountain, agriculture and bestowers of sustenance, vegetation such as sacred ancient trees, and the heavenly lights. Some deities have manifested themselves as animals, such as a white bird, a deer, or a monkey. Ancestral or tutelary deities (*ujigami*) include patrons of the clans, but they can also be nature kami. These are associated especially with shrines in regions once under the political control of the powerful families. As has often happened in Chinese traditions, some of Japan's kami also originated as historical figures who became deities by dint of their leadership in a clan. Large numbers of major shrines are dedicated to such figures. Other important historical kami include literary figures as well.

Zoomorphic kami form another significant category, as represented, for example, by Inari's fox. A classification of kami connected with ancestor veneration and exorcism are wrathful deities and malcontent spirits called *goryo* or *onryo*. They reflect the moral ambivalence Japanese discern in the spirit world. Popular belief holds such evil spirits responsible for disasters from earthquake and famine to war and political failure. Many of the great sacred sites enshrine tragic heroes who suffered political downfall. Some kami function as scapegoats in that they become the focus of popular blame for all manner of unhappy events. Japanese tradition sometimes identifies kami as either *ara,* wild and natural, or *niki,* placid and cultivated. In some cases separate shrines dedicated to these aspects of the same kami are located some distance apart. Another distinction is

that between celestial deities (*amatsukami*) and the kami anciently associated with particular localities. Tradition portrays some kami as guests or visitors from a mysterious and faraway land called *tokoyo*, perhaps an acknowledgment of their origin in Buddhism and other imported traditions.

Stone statue of Daikoku, one of the seven kami of good fortune. A length of *shimenawa* girds his pedestal, where he kneels on two bales of rice, holds a sack over his left shoulder, and wields his wish-granting mallet in his right hand.

Who are some of the principal Shinto **male deities**, apart from those mentioned in the primal myth?

Hachiman, generally identified as the kami of war, is near the top of the pantheon. It is no surprise that he often appears in painting and sculpture as armed and dangerous. But some of the most famous images portray Hachiman as a meditating monk or a solicitous Bodhisattva. Almost half of all officially listed Shinto shrines—some fifty thousand or more—honor Hachiman. A curious grouping called the "Seven Gods of Good Luck" (*shichi-fuku-jin*) brings together figures of mixed background. Daikoku (sometimes called Daikoku-ten) hails from India, mythologically speaking, and probably traveled to Japan with an early influential Buddhist founder named Saicho. Daikoku is associated with accomplishment of one's goals and with wealth. Stone statues show a jovial bruiser with a sack over one shoulder, sitting on bales of rice and wielding a mallet with which he grants wishes. Also a god of prosperity, Ebisu is popular especially in fishing villages, rice farms, and local marketplaces. Ebisu is deaf and fails to hear deities being called together for his own October celebration! Like Daikoku, Bishamon (also Bishamonten) is of Indian origin. In the Hindu pantheon he was one of the four heavenly guardians, presiding over the north. In Buddhist as well as Shinto iconography, Bishamon is heavily armed and holds a miniature pagoda in his left hand as a symbol of his authority. Fuku-roku-ju, who originated in Daoism, stands for happiness, fortune, and long life, as his name indicates. When depicted in the arts he looks very much like his Chinese counterpart, Shou Lao, generally accompanied by a crane or deer. Like the next God of Good Luck, Jurojin, he also has a walking stick to which he has attached a sacred text. Jurojin is another patron of longevity of Daoist origin. Hotei, likewise drawn from the Daoist pantheon, stands for happiness and wealth. Benzaiten, also known as Benten, is the lone female of the bunch. The septet of good fortune kami have been a favorite subject for popular and charming miniature carvings called *Netsuke*. A large number of kami are associated with forces of nature. Fujin, kami of wind, carries a large bag, and his companion kami of thunder, the menacing red-faced Raijin (or Raiden), holds a massive drum. A generic group of minor deities called *dosojin* protect travelers ever since Izanagi brought them into being upon his return from the underworld. A kami called Koshin is one protector of travelers, but some also identify him with farming. His three monkey partners have become popular as "See no evil, hear no evil, do no evil." Kami keep watch over every conceivable feature of ordinary life. Suijin, a god of water, guards wells and other water sources, for water is the principal means of purification and an essential of life.

Who are some important **female deities**?

Amaterasu, the sun goddess, is the most important of the goddesses. Hundreds of shrines throughout Japan are dedicated to her. One of the most colorful goddesses is Ama no Uzume, the "terrible female of heaven," widely popular because of her identification with frivolity and dance. A kami described as both masculine and feminine is Inari. Because of her association with rice harvest, Inari is among the most important deities. Her messenger is the fox, and popular custom often refers to the fox itself as Inari. Bright reddish-orange or red torii gates, sometimes in great numbers, usually mark shrines dedicated to Inari. A pair of goddesses associated with the war kami Hachiman appear in a sculptural triad with Hachiman. One is called Nakatsu-hime, but the other remains to be identified. Seiryu Gongen was one of several goddesses adopted by Shinto in their role as protectors of Buddhist temples. Two other "imported" goddesses with Buddhist connections are Zenmyo Nyoshin and Byakuko-shin. Stories tell of how a Korean monk fell in love with Zenmyo while he was studying in China. Byakuko was once an Indian earth deity who became a Shinto kami through her associations with powers of nature. Goddesses like Kumano Fusumi Okami are often depicted round and full to suggest abundance. Goddess Tamayori-hime appears in a triad, flanked by two other goddesses, once worshiped as the "three protectresses of children." Tamayori was the daughter of Watatsumi no Kami, kami of the oceans, and Japan's first emperor's mother. Benten (also called Benzaiten) is a goddess of Indian origin. Hindus know her as Sarasvati, consort of the god Brahma and patroness of culture. She plays the Japanese lute (called the *biwa*), as Sarasvati plays the veena, and devotees beseech her for protection and for gifts of eloquence and knowledge. Numerous female kami have played important roles in Shinto life over the centuries, and some were frequently depicted in human form, but only a few remain significant in contemporary devotion.

Do practitioners of Shinto believe in **miracles**?

Check the index of almost any book about Shinto and you look in vain for the word "miracle." That does not mean the tradition is entirely without interesting analogies to what many people mean by the term. Shinto recommends regular expressions of gratitude to the kami for their inestimable bounty. It also recommends prayer of petition for whatever worshipers may need. Many people believe that one ordinary role of the kami is to make the seemingly impossible possible. In a way, that is the essence of divine power, for worshipers regard the kami as nurturing protectors who look after the best interests of their devotees.

What role do **views of the material** world play in Shinto tradition?

Shinto is one of the world's most ecologically attuned religious traditions. Divine energy suffuses all of creation and is thus cause for reverence and wonder. Very optimistic in its outlook about life in this world, Shinto teaches that when human beings are in harmony with nature, all persons and things flourish. There is therefore no serious distinction or incompatibility between the physical and the spiritual, the human and the divine. Shinto is very much what some call a world-affirming tradition. When devotees worship at a shrine the mood is generally solemn and reverent. But a sense of joy and exuberance pervades festivals. Such celebrations, which can go on for days, leave little doubt that at the heart of Shinto tradition there is a delight in the everyday world and a conviction of the inherent goodness of creation.

What is the **nature of the human person** in Shinto tradition?

Shinto tradition has not given great attention to speculation about the metaphysical aspects of the human person. Conceptions of soul or spirit at the core of human nature tend to be rather fluid, not unlike popular Chinese ideas about these things. Reflecting the various aspects of both human and divine action, soul or spirit (*tama*) can manifest itself as either rich in blessings, granting harmony and union, full of mysterious power, or "rough." Individuals take second place to the needs of society as a whole; as a result traditional Shinto thought does not reflect in depth about the self apart from the collective. Above all, human beings are children of the kami whose natural birthright is to benefit from nature's gifts. Society and family, as well as nature, are the wellsprings of life. Acknowledging and venerating one's ancestors keeps healthy the link between individual and society because it keeps alive the continuity of heritage.

Is there a distinctively Shinto **ethic**?

Some have characterized Shinto as a type of naturalistic humanism that begins with the conviction of innate human goodness. When evil gains the ascendancy, it is not because of some inherent or inherited human tendency. Evil advances whenever human beings lose their concentration on life at its simplest, most basic level. As an ethical ideal, the concept of *makoto* means something like genuineness or authenticity. An ethical person is one who characteristically makes choices unspoiled by ulterior motives. Purity of intention thus takes precedence over adherence to any specific set of commands and prohibitions. Scholars refer to an ethic of this kind as "contextual" or "situational." All acts derive their moral value from the overall setting in which people perform them. A virtuous person is one who enjoys maximum harmony with the totality of the powers of nature. How does one assess the quality of virtue? The ethical barometer is a faculty called *kokoro,* a term that suggests a union of mind and heart. What some traditions call purity of heart, Shinto tradition calls brightness (*seimei*). Purified of all ill intent, the mind and heart are illumined through intimacy with the divine. Individuals do not evaluate their actions in terms of whether they will reap reward or suffer punishment as a consequence. Rather, they think of how their actions might affect the life of the community here and now. How does one know when he or she has crossed the moral divide? Shame is a very powerful index of morality in Shinto tradition. What members of some traditions identify as moral guilt incurred objectively as a result of some specific act, Shinto tradition regards a breach of social contract for which the individual ought to be ashamed and seek forgiveness through purification.

Do adherents of Shinto believe in **salvation** and an afterlife?

Salvation is not a question of deliverance from the present human condition into a realm beyond. Shinto tradition teaches that the solution to the human predicament is just the reverse: sincere worshipers welcome the kami into the world of everyday concerns. Salvation therefore means making the ordinary sacred so that life here and now becomes the best it can be. Ancient traditions tell of another world, a realm beyond this one, called the High Plain of Heaven (*takama-no-hara*). It is a happy state, heaven (*ame*), a spiritual land connected to earth by a wondrous bridge. That mythic realm overflows with life and fecundity (*tokoyo-no-kuni*). Devout worshipers invoke the kami down, recalling how they descended before time began to bring the sacred land and its people into existence. There is also a netherworld, a most unpleasant state called the Land of Darkness (*yomi-no-kuni*). Ruled by death, that land is filled with wretched pollution and impurity. To that land worshipers dispatch troublesome spirits and hope their prayers and attentiveness to the rites of ancestor veneration will keep the negative forces at bay. Most people today do not believe that the dead end up in one or other of the realms beyond this world. Nevertheless, certain fundamental criteria determine whether an individual spirit will be content or disgruntled after death. Those include the ethical quality of one's life and one's attentiveness to avoiding the impurity attached to taboo behavior. Some speak simply of a "world beyond view" (*kakuriyo*), an otherwise non-descript state of being after this life.

Do **millennialism** or **messianism** have a place in Shinto thinking?

Mainstream Shinto thought has not developed millennialist or messianic themes of any significance. Some recent sectarian movements, however, have centered around such notions. Events surrounding and in the aftermath of World War II not surprisingly raised questions of Japan's historical destiny for many Japanese. So-called "new religions" of Japan, many with roots deep in Shinto tradition, have been fertile soil for messianic expectations. One such organization is Ananai-kyo, which teaches open relationships with and among the "five" (*nai*) religious traditions—Christianity, Islam, Buddhism, Daoism, and Confucianism. Various relatively recent Shinto-related cults and sects have centered around charismatic leaders whose teachings focus on preparation for an apocalyptic end of this world. For much of the 1990s, for example, members of a group called Aum Shinri Kyo attempted to implement the doomsday doctrine of their leader, Shoko Asahara. Conspiring to plant biological and chemical agents in Tokyo subways, they planned the final act of human history.

Children dressed in happi coats play during neighborhood Shinto street procession, in which the *mikoshi,* a portable miniature shrine, is paraded about on men's shoulders (in background).

SIGNS AND SYMBOLS

Are there any **signs or symbols** that might identify an individual as a practitioner of Shinto?

Apart from times of participation in public or private rituals, it is virtually impossible to identify practitioners of Shinto on the basis of appearances. When people join in festival processions, many don small jackets called *happi* that extend to about mid-thigh, and headbands. *Happi* sometimes bear the logo of the local association that carries the *mikoshi* portable shrine in processions. On special days, young women may dress up in their best *kimono.* Devotees sometimes return home from shrines carrying amulets or talismans, but these items are visible less often on the person than in the home.

What signs or symbols distinguish Shinto **ritual specialists**?

Shinto priests wear distinctive garb (called *shozoku*) modeled on courtly fashions from the Heian period, the days when Japan's capital was in Kyoto. Ritual robes are of several types. They wear a kimono and a kind of very full-cut pants underneath. Outer garments originally indicated courtly rank with various colors (robin's egg blue, red, purple, yellow, and light green), but now a priest's rank is indicated by either the pale

495

Shinto priest, wearing the less formal headgear called the *eboshi,* receives and arranges offerings in preparation for a shrine festival. The lanterns are decorative and symbolic items found in great numbers around most larger shrines.

blue, black, or red. Outer garments have very wide flowing sleeves and extend down to the feet. For ordinary ceremonies priests wear a white silk vestment called a *karinigu* ("hunting cloak" from medieval times). With the simpler garments for ordinary duties, priests wear a plain roundish hat called *eboshi,* reserving the taller and more elegant *kanmuri* for special ceremonies. High ranking priests wear polished wooden shoes for rituals, and their subordinates wear thong sandals of wood. During all ceremonies, officiants carry a slender, tapered slab of wood called the *shaku* in the right hand, similar to the one seen in images of Chinese ancestor figures. Since even a lay person sometimes leads rituals and wears these same garments, they do not function like a "habit" to distinguish priests from laity. When not preforming their shrine duties, Shinto priests wear ordinary street clothes. Shrine maidens (*miko*) wear a white kimono top and a vermillion or scarlet split skirt, only when they are performing shrine duties. Musicians, whether priests or not, also wear similar versions of Heian court fashion during ceremonies.

Do Shinto practitioners mark **sacred spaces** with any distinctive **signs and symbols**?

Easily the most important symbol of Shinto sacred spaces is the *torii* gate. Marking the entry and pathways to every shrine, torii typically consist of a pair of unadorned upright columns and a pair of cross beams (or lintels) at the top. The upper cross beam generally sits directly atop the column and protrudes on both sides, while the lower beam either ends at the columns or goes through and protrudes. Some torii have more elaborate uprights and cross beams, depending on local and regional architectural styles. Devotees give torii as votive offerings to some shrines, lining pathways with hundreds of them inches apart, so that the entry to the shrine feels almost like a covered walkway. According to legend, the torii recalls the perch from which birds sang to entice the sun goddess from her cave.

Most Shinto shrines use the simplest and most natural materials available, imitating nature as much as possible. Natural wood grains and the lovely green forest patina that eventually accents thatch or wood-shingled roofs gives them a rustic character and charm. Many shrine roofs still display remnants of primitive architectural elements as a reminder of antiquity. Although newer building meth-

A small side shrine at Kamakura's Zeni Arai Benten, dedicated to the one female kami among the seven gods of good fortune, shows the *shimenawa* above, the five-colored rope attached to the small bell, the offering box, and the symbolic mirror inside the doors that are usually closed in most shrines.

ods no longer require them, many shrines retain a row of logs called *katsuogi* set along the ridge beam of the roof. Older structures needed the *katsuogi* to hold the thatch roof down. Another bit of architectural nostalgia are the vertical extensions of the eave beams above the roof line. As you view a shrine from either front or rear, you notice that the roof line forms an X. Horizontally trimmed upper ends of these beams, known as *chigi,* mark the shrines of female kami, and vertically trimmed ends those of male kami. Several rather mysterious symbols adorn holy places, whether or not the site has a structure on it. Thick straw ropes called *shimenawa* mark sacred places such as trees and rocks. Outer portals of shrines, whether actual buildings or minia-

A tunnel of torii gates, votive offerings of worshipers, lines the path up from street level to the hill on which the Hie Jinja shrine rises above the bustle of Tokyo's Akasaka Mitsuke shopping district. The Hie Jinja is one of the shrines associated with a kami known as the Mountain King (*sanno*).

ture models used on home altars, also suspend shime-nawa across their facades. Attached to the rope are pieces of white paper cut in zigzag fashion symbolizing offerings to the kami. The same bits of paper are attached to a ritual wand called the *gohei*. Legend has it that the rope originated as a way of restraining the sun goddess from escaping back into her cave.

If I visited a Shinto **shrine**, what would I see?

Walk down almost any street in almost any Japanese city or town and not many blocks along you will notice a simple, unobtrusive torii gate at street side. Turning to your right to look through the gate you will be surprised to see a small grove of trees in the midst of storefronts and houses. You know from the torii that a Shinto shrine is nearby, but no structure is immediately evident. You walk through the gate and perhaps up a small hill, and as the shrine comes into view amid the trees you will pass through another torii gate. At the end of the path stands a neighborhood shrine, consisting perhaps of only a single wooden structure. Standing several feet off the ground and too small for a person to enter is the residence of one of the local kami. On the "front porch" of the shrine, or perhaps alongside the tiny steps that lead up to the porch, there are several small white ceramic foxes, messengers of the deity Inari. Also on the porch just outside the shrine door are small offerings of various kinds, including a little wooden box for donations. Uncounted thousands of these unassuming shrines are quiet testimony to the presence of the divine powers. Larger shrines are naturally fewer in numbers but still abundant. Preserving often relatively extensive tracts of forested land in burgs like Tokyo and Kyoto, the great shrines are all the more remarkable. Even in the heart of bustling Tokyo, for example, the Hie Shrine still sits atop a surprisingly high and densely wooded knoll. As you pass under one and another monumental torii along the pathway to the center of shrines like Tokyo's splendid Meiji Jingu, you will find yourself slowing down and marveling at the beauty of ancient trees. The sheer power of place here is almost overwhelming, enveloping you with a profound sense of the sacred. At the heart of the place are worshipers, perhaps in large numbers depending on the day, approaching the outer building of the sanctuary to pray and make their offerings. If your timing is right, you might witness formal ceremonies of blessing or priestly offering. Shinto shrines do not present the kind of public face that Japan's numerous Buddhist temples show. Shinto's miniature—and not so miniature—holy forests are vivid reminders of the need to acknowledge the sanctity of nature, especially when the hunger for expediency and immediate gratification compromises reflection.

What are the main **architectural** and **ritual elements** of a major Shinto **shrine**?

At the heart of a major shrine is a complex of three units called the *hongu* (for a *jingu*, *honsha* for a *jinja*). This central area, all oriented to the south as in Chinese sacred structures, houses the shrine's principal deity. Within the *hongu* are the *haiden, heiden,* and *honden* arranged front to rear along the south-north central axis. The outer and most public of the spaces is called the *haiden,* or worship hall, where devotees gather individually or in small groups for special blessings and other rituals. Most people who come to the shrine without prior arrangements for special ceremonial ministrations from the priestly staff perform their brief prayers in front of the *haiden.* But if the staff are performing rituals inside, those outside are welcome to observe. From that hall, worshipers can look across an interior courtyard to the central structure, the *heiden* or offering hall, where only the priestly staff perform more sacred rituals. From there, in turn, the celebrants can see (sometimes across yet another courtyard) the *honden,* the Shinto equivalent of the "holy of holies." There, behind closed doors and visible to no one, the kami reside. Also on the grounds of many large shrines one may find subordinate shrines called *bekku,* which house related major deities. *Massha* house lesser deities. Some shrines also have small Buddhist temples (called *jingu-ji,* "shrine-temples") on the property, remnants of the ancient connections between the two traditions.

Do Shinto practitioners use special **symbolism** in personal or private **rituals**?

Many Japanese households have a special corner dedicated to the kami. A miniature shrine building (*kamidana*) at which worshipers pray daily is placed on a shelf or table. For special occasions they will go to the actual shrine, but everyday reverence to

Is there such a thing as Shinto art or aesthetic?

Every twenty years, priests and specially skilled carpenters gather at the Grand Shrine at Ise for a ritual that says a lot about Shinto artistic sensibilities. They construct a new inner shrine on a plot left vacant for the previous twenty years. Then they dismantle the older shrine separated by only a small partition and leave its space empty until it is time to rebuild there. The carpenters use only the finest cypress, fashioned with the simplest of tools, and use no nails, adhesives, or artificially produced material of any kind. Each stroke of the plane or hammer is part of an ancient ritual that blends religious reverence and awe with the practical demands of sacred architecture. Each structure, however small and humble, is a work of sacred craftsmanship. During the Middle Ages, Shinto sculptors created anthropomorphic images of various kami, largely under the influence of Buddhism's rich iconogrpahy. Some sculptures remain important symbols in a few individual devotional cults within Shinto (such as Sanno Ichijitsu, with its images of the kami's monkey messengers). But on the whole modern Shinto worship is aniconic, focusing on the presence of symbolic objects, such as the mirror and sword, within the holy of holies. A unique and historically important art form is the so-called shrine mandala. Stylized depictions of individual shrines arrange the sacred site as a meditative device on a hanging scroll. Members of certain sects have used these mandalas as devotional focuses of esoteric contemplative rituals. Above all, shrines and their settings remain the most important visual expression of Shinto beliefs and values. Simple, natural beauty is the key.

the kami happens at home. People can purchase these charming miniature shrines, some done up in exquisitely fine architectural detail, at religious goods stores in any Japanese city or at some of the larger shrines. Worshipers who get them from shrine shops often prefer to purchase them at shrines to which their families have ancestral connections. Priests often visit parishioners to dedicate their new home shrines and sometimes make annual house visits for brief renewal ceremonies. People with more ample homes and yards might afford larger outdoor miniature shrines called *yashikigami* (kami of the home). Miniature shrines range from simple and affordable to finely wrought and costly. Business establishments, restaurants, police stations, and bridges on oceangoing ships, for example, might also have a *kamidana* to which the staff make daily offerings. Many miniature shrines have their own tiny torii gates and shimenawa. In addition, worshipers often bring small votive offerings when they visit local shrines. A popular offering is the miniature torii gate on which devotees write names and prayers of petition before hanging it on a rack along with hundreds of others like it at the shrine.

Shinto religious goods store in Tokyo displays miniature shrines for home use, as well as miniature torii gates and other ritual objects used for making offerings.

Have **relics** been important in the Shinto tradition?

Sacred objects play a very important role in Shinto ritual. Every shrine houses some small token of the deity who graciously calls this humble place home for the benefit of worshipers who come to pay their respects. These objects, called *go-shintai* or "revered kami body," are said to include such unremarkable items as a mirror, sword, comb, ball of iron, paintings, pebbles, or pieces of carefully cut paper. Worshipers generally do not get even a passing glimpse of the objects, for they remain always behind the innermost shrine's closed doors. People visit a shrine not so much because the sacred objects are there, as because the presence of the kami makes the place holy. When Christians or Buddhists, for example, make pilgrimage to a special church or stupa, they frequently do so because certain objects associated with a particular sacred person are enshrined there. They may not believe that the objects themselves contain miraculous powers, but it is the presence of the objects that makes the place worth visiting. Shinto's sacred objects play a very different role. Many worshipers may not even be aware of exactly what items a given shrine holds. In other words, the symbols of the kami are of secondary importance from the perspective of Shinto worshipers.

Shinto shrine in Honolulu, showing the *torii* gate, the *katsuogi* along the ridge beam of the roof, and the vertically cut *chigi* indicating that a male *kami* is enshrined there.

MEMBERSHIP, COMMUNITY, DIVERSITY

Where do Shinto practitioners live today? Any **estimates of numbers** available?

By far the majority of people who identify themselves with Shinto tradition still live in Japan. There are also Shinto shrines in many areas of Asia (and a few elsewhere as well) in which significant Japanese communities have developed. Honolulu's Shinto shrine, for example, is a highly visible sign of a large and prosperous Japanese community there. Accurate statistics as to membership are hard to come by, largely because an increasing number of Japanese do not identify themselves as religious at all—even if they continue to engage in some traditional Shinto practices. We do, however, have fairly reliable information about numbers of shrines and active priests from which we have some idea of the tradition's vitality today. Some twenty-thousand priests serve between eighty thousand and a hundred thousand shrines.

Have Shinto practitioners traditionally sent out **missionaries** to convert others?

Shinto has been so closely identified with Japanese culture as to be virtually inseparable from it. A desire to spread Shinto with missionary zeal would make about as much sense as wishing one could turn non-Japanese persons into Japanese. It is as unnecessary as it is impossible. Even the most devoted and active practitioners of Shinto do

Two young men seek a blessing on a new business venture at Tokyo's Meiji Jingu. At left is the principal priest, while at right the assistant priest and the *miko* (deaconess) bow.

not generally feel themselves called to spread the tradition. At the heart of Shinto is a natural wisdom that cannot be taught or spread by decree. It is as natural as breathing. Of course everyone is better off breathing, but it's not something one can teach. Since the tradition is passed on organically, so to speak, and inherited as a family and national treasure, practitioners do not think of it as something necessary for the betterment—or salvation—of humanity. At the same time, active members of local Shinto communities remain hospitable to a fault. Arrive at a shrine during a festival, and however much you may stand out from the crowd, chances are good that someone will invite you to participate in the celebration.

Are there any especially important Shinto **holy places**?

One of the most striking features of Shinto tradition is the intuition of the world's pervasive sacredness. Wherever the kami are, there is holiness—and that means just about everywhere people are willing to look carefully. Places where the kami dwell are called *otabisho,* "stages on a journey," and are not necessarily identified with shrine buildings. Certain natural settings stand out as particularly potent. Mountains, waterfalls, caves, and trees have attracted Japan's spiritual athletes (ascetics) and pilgrims over the centuries. Mount Fuji remains a revered symbol of natural perfection and beauty, and pilgrims still consider a hike to the volcano's summit spiritually uplifting. On a clear winter's day you can occasionally glimpse Fuji's symmetrical slopes and

503

The Impact of Shinto on Film-making: Jusho Toda

Jusho Toda (1928–1987) was one of the most imaginative production designers in Japanese film-making. He was first acclaimed for the ambitious set design of Masaki Kobayashi's "Seppuku" (1962), for which he created appropriately striking black-and-white backgrounds to highlight the powerful story of a struggle between samurai. The Daliesque images he created for Kobayashi's "Kwaidan" (1964), such as a pair of eyes in an orange-yellow sky and a palace floating over the smoke on colorful waters, were particularly noted for the audacious quality they gave to this anthology of ghost stories.

Nagisa Oshima invited the eccentric art director to join his film-making group, and their collaboration continued for two decades, from "Violence at Noon" (1966) to "Merry Christmas, Mr. Lawrence" (1983). Challenged by the budgetary limitations of Oshima's independent productions, Toda created ingenious settings for the spontaneous and radical ideas of this ideologically conscious director. Parts of the sets in "Death by Hanging" (1968) were made out of newspapers; similarly, many sets in other Oshima films use abstract plastic shapes to emphasize theatricality. The altars he often used in both interior and exterior scenes were similar to those of the Shinto religion, and imparted a ritualistic quality. One of the most idiosyncratic of the images he created for Oshima is the Japanese national flag whose "Rising Sun" in the center is painted in black, a symbol of the dark side of authority.

The sets Toda designed for Oshima's "In the Realm of the Senses" (1976), "Empire of Passion" (1978), and "Merry Christmas, Mr. Lawrence" are comparatively realistic but nonetheless help to create the powerful atmosphere of passionate love, violence, and abstract eroticism.

Toda was also responsible for the simple yet striking black-and-white interior settings for the gambling scenes of Masahiro Shinoda's "Pale Flower" (1963), as well as for the elaborate color schemes of the director's "The Scandalous Adventures of Buraikan" (1970). Toda was also acclaimed for the solemn interiors he created for Kobayashi's serious family drama, "The Family without a Dinner Table" (1985).

snowy cap from taller buildings in Tokyo, sixty miles away, and it is easy to see how the mountain has assumed such symbolic importance. In addition to countless holy places left as close to their natural states as possible, sacred architecture marks many others as sacred. "Founding stories" (*engi*) record how Shinto communities have chosen certain sites. These mythic tales tell how, for example, a deity went looking for a suitable dwelling and decided at last on one perfect spot. Amaterasu is said to have revealed in a dream to an imperial princess of old that she wanted her shrine built at Ise. Even into relatively recent times, Shinto tradition has considered such hierophanies (sacred manifestations) important explanations as to why certain places are high on the ladder of sanctity and power. But Shinto has not been associated with holy cities as such, as have traditions like Hinduism and Islam, for example. Shinto tradition has not associated the kami so much with urban settings as with pristine nature. Some major shrines, like Kyoto's Heian Jingu, have arisen conspicuously in the midst of bustling urban areas, showing a surprisingly public face. But most represent the cultivation of holy serenity in an increasingly disquieted world. Major publications list shrines according to their popularity and reputation for spiritual success stories, rating shrines according to particular categories of greatest interest, such as healing, help on examinations, good starts in new businesses, and fertility.

Are there any **sub-communities or denominations** within Shinto?

Numerous varieties and schools of Shinto have come and gone over the past thirteen hundred years. Here briefly are a few of the more important: An ascetical "mountain" sect called Shugendo began as early as the Nara period (710–794), and small groups remain active today. Beginning during the Middle Ages, several schools have arisen under the patronage of important members of powerful clans. Now identified by the names of those families or of the schools' individual founders, the larger groups are Urabe (also known by the later family name of Yoshida, and Yui-itsu—"unification"—Shinto), Watarai (also called Ise Shinto), the Confucian-oriented school of Yoshikawa, and Kurozumi-kyo, named after its nineteenth-century founder. Several other schools are identified by terms that suggest their principal teaching or emphases. For example, a seventeenth-century school called Suiga ("Bestowal of Blessings") Shinto laid groundwork for the growth of National Learning. Sanno-ichijitsu blended Shinto themes with esoteric teachings of Tendai Buddhism in the seventeenth century, focusing on the divine manifestation of a "mountain king." Finally, Minkan Shinko is a general designation for a host of developments called "folk" religious beliefs and practices, incorporating elements of Shinto as well as other traditions. Japanese governments have promulgated various types of legislation, especially since the late nineteenth century, aimed at keeping track of the many religious groups that have occasionally leveled severe criticism at the imperial form of governance.

What is **"sectarian"** Shinto?

Thirteen principal sects comprise what is generally referred to as "sectarian" or "sect" (*kyoha*) Shinto. Arising over the centuries and officially recognized in the early twentieth century, the thirteen cluster around five themes or emphases. First, two groups that emphasize purification are known as Misogi-kyo and Shinshu-kyo (-*kyo* means teaching or school). Fuso-kyo, Jikko-kyo, and Ontake-kyo are called "mountain sects" because they centered around cults of two sacred mountains, Fuji and Ontake. They restructured

What gender-related issues are important for Shinto practitioners?

Shinto priests (and priestesses) have almost always been married people with families. Ongoing social taboo still prohibits menstruating women from participating as official ministers in ritual activities. Contemporary custom, however, has in all likelihood loosened such restrictions. It is safe to say that in general women have historically had greater direct participation in many Shinto shrine rituals than they do presently. Only unmarried young women are eligible for the office of *miko* in shrines, and typically have access to the positions hereditarily, as a result of their families' priestly traditions.

along distinctively Shinto lines the teachings of several earlier ascetically oriented groups called Shugendo. Three more recent sects have focused on faith healing. Kurozumi-kyo, Tenri-kyo, and Konko-kyo all trace their origins to a founding figure. Two sects called Shinto Shusei-ha and Shinto Taisei-kyo have emphasized Confucian elements and have blended features of the purification and mountain sects as well. Finally among the "thirteen" are the most recent groups, whose mission has been to renew Shinto tradition. These are Izumo Oyashiro-kyo, Shinri-kyo, and Shinto Tai-kyo. The latter is an umbrella organization that was largely responsible for the official recognition of the thirteen. From these sects dozens of smaller movements have arisen in recent times.

Have there ever been Shinto **schisms** or **heresies**?

Several of Japan's so-called "new religions" have developed out of main-stream Shinto within the past two centuries or so. Some traditional Japanese may be inclined to regard them with suspicion, possibly even labeling them as dangerous "cults." Sociologically speaking, some of these groups qualify as schismatic—that is, "splinter" groups, in that they have deliberately parted company with ancient Shinto tradition. Some scholars suggest that Shinto authorities coined terms such as "The Emperor's Way" (*kodo*) and "The Kami-ordained Way" (*kannagara-no-michi*) to distinguish a type of Shinto "orthodoxy" from a host of less correct popular and folk beliefs. But since the concept of "orthodoxy" has been far less important for Shinto tradition than it has for, say, some Christian or Muslim communities, the notion of "heresy" is largely irrelevant here.

What questions does the prospect of **interfaith marriage** raise for Shinto practitioners?

Many Japanese active in Shinto communities are also active in Buddhist circles. They do not draw the kind of clear boundaries between religious traditions that many mem-

506

Shrine deaconesses (*miko*) dance together on a stage at Tokyo's Hie Jinja shrine.

bers of other faiths may be inclined to draw. Traditional Japanese are therefore far less concerned with questions of religious affiliation than with cultural and ethnic identity. Significant numbers of Japanese would like to have their sons and daughters marry in a Shinto ceremony to keep ancient tradition intact. What is more important to many, however, is that their children marry other Japanese.

Do people ever decide they want to **depart** from the Shinto community?

Membership in traditions so closely identified with ethnicity as Shinto has a great deal to do with trends in society generally. That is of course true of most religious traditions, but here there are several features about Shinto worth noting. Japanese ethnicity does not imply adherence to Shinto beliefs and practices any more than Jewish ancestry implies that an individual actively participates in Judaic religious traditions. Shinto is integral to the fabric of Japanese life. Large numbers of Japan's present population do not engage in regular Shinto rituals at all, and many others are very selective as to their involvement. But that does not imply a deliberate choice to reject the ancient traditions as such. It does, however, underscore the impact of cultural and social change on all things traditional. Shinto tradition calls people to unhurried, careful attentiveness to the mysterious details of life. In a fast-paced, often tumultuous world, the drum-beat of change can easily drown out the sound of the drums that announce the beginning of a sacred ritual.

507

Is there such a thing as **converting** into Shinto?

Since Shinto is so intimately identified with being Japanese, the concept of conversion is largely irrelevant. That does not mean that no non-Japanese has ever deliberately chosen to become a practitioner of Shinto, but such instances are very rare. The case of Judaism offers a rough parallel. Many consider membership in Judaism a matter of ethnicity, but some Jewish congregations nevertheless welcome converts into their community. Some have developed formal initiatory rites for ethnically non-Jewish individuals, but Shinto tradition does not have such a rite for non-Japanese who wish to practice and profess Shinto tradition. The difference here is that membership in Judaism presupposes assent to certain basic creedal affirmations, whereas Shinto does not.

What issues have characterized Shinto's **relationships to other traditions**?

Shinto has important connections primarily to Buddhism and Confucianism, and secondarily to the Christianity that missionaaries brought to Japan in the early modern period. During much of medieval and early modern times, Shinto and Buddhist leaders and teachers worked together at articulating points of theological cooperation between various schools of thought in the two traditions. That ongoing interaction resulted in the various types of Ryobu, or Two-sided, Shinto as well as other syncretistic denominations and sects. Such cooperation continued until the thirteenth and fourteenth centuries, when some Shinto thinkers developed belief systems in which Shinto stood at the top of a theological mountain. By the seventeenth century, the "National Learning" movement began to offer a fully articulated interpretation of Buddhist-Shinto relations. Scholars suggested that the major figures of the Buddhist pantheon were nothing more than local forms of the kami, and that the emperor descended directly from the Sun goddess, Amaterasu. Confucianism had by that time made its presence felt more vigorously than ever through its impact on courtly life and administration of the Tokugawa shogunate (1600–1867). Confucian scholars and bureaucrats also contributed significantly to the Meiji Restoration in 1868. But the more closely Shinto theology came to be identified with the Japanese throne, the more it developed into a national ideology with little room for systems of belief considered non-Japanese—Buddhism and Confucianism, first and foremost, but now missionary Christianity as well. Contemporary Shinto has once again become more open to interaction with other traditions, and Shinto leaders take it for granted that many who worship at shrines also maintain other religious affiliations. For many Japanese, the Kami Way is not a separate system of religious beliefs. It is simply what all religious persons believe underneath all their otherwise distinctive doctrines. Shinto is therefore nothing less than the very essence of acknowledging the divine in the world.

LEADERSHIP, AUTHORITY, ORGANIZATION

How and where do members of local Shinto communities **come together**?

Larger shrines provide the principal venue for Shinto community gatherings. The more elaborate shrines might have a dozen or more separate structures, each designed for a specific function. The ritual center includes facilities along the entry path for purification by water, as well as the various halls of worship and the sanctuary itself. There is often a separate facility in which the shrine ritual specialists purify themselves. Secondary shrine functions include a wide range of activities. Smaller buildings provide facilities for weddings (*gishiki-den*), sacred dance and performance of plays (*kagura-den*), and storage of the portable processional shrines called *mikoshi*. There is usually a sacred kitchen for preparing offerings and a small shop where worshipers can purchase mementoes and items such as cards on which to write petitions to be hung on special boards outside the main worship hall. Officials administer the whole operation from a shrine office, looking after all the more mundane concerns of any institution. That includes everything from scheduling of events and staff to arranging for supplies and paying bills. Smaller shrines naturally have fewer of these separate facilities, and the smallest often do not have resident priests.

Shrines are organized in a variety of ways. Some are directly managed by hereditary priestly families still connected with powerful clans of old. Committees of local elders oversee many village shrines that lack permanent priests. Trade guilds, called *za,* still worship together and manage their own shrines. Wealthy families sometimes even own and administer shrines just for their private use. Finally, some historic Buddhist temples have set up and maintained shrines in hopes of securing the protection of the kami for the temple. Some larger shrines attract worshipers from all over Japan, while most local shrines have relatively stable memberships of parishioners. But parishioners often have family or devotional ties to more than one local shrine.

Is there a central Shinto **teaching authority**?

Shinto's close identification over the centuries with Japanese culture and imperial rule has sometimes made it appear that the royal administration functioned as a central religious authority. Certain regimes have made concerted efforts to encourage uniformity of traditional thinking among the Japanese people, and that has sometimes involved "official" statements about Shinto beliefs as well as attempts to centralize the organization of large numbers of shrines. In addition, training for Shinto ritual specialists in recent times has devolved on only a select few educational institutions very much associated with "national" identity. Those academic-religious organizations have set themselves the task of clarifying and, in some cases, restructuring the count-

Is there a Shinto system of religious law?

There have been numerous bodies of legislation concerning the structure and administration of the Shinto shrine system, and about governmental controls over the spread of religious organizations in Japan generally. Laws have decreed relationships between imperial rule and religion, and between Shinto and Buddhism, and others have stipulated conditions for religious liberty. But there has never been the kind of comprehensive codification of religious law that one finds in Islam's *Shari'a,* Judaism's Rabbinical law, or Roman Catholicism's Canon Law. Virtually everything related to the regulation of conduct in Shinto tradition has been integrated into an all-encompassing and very demanding, but mostly unwritten, code of ethics. People learn what is expected of them religiously through family and local community tradition.

less elements of ancient Shinto tradition into a coherent system. Theirs has been an increasingly "theological" enterprise in modern times. Even so, Shinto tradition has remained quite fluid and inclusive, and far less identified with definitive teaching authority than, say, Roman Catholicism. Over the centuries various centralized institutions have come and gone. The "Institute of the Great Teaching" (*daikyo-in*), for example, was motivated largely by the desire to root out Buddhist and Christian influences in nineteenth-century Japan. The "Bureau of Divinity" (*Jingikan*) sought to unify the administration of shrines and the appointment of priests. It is perhaps best to think of the centralized authority as regulating matters of practice rather than of belief, setting out detailed instructions for rituals (*jinja shaishiki*) and for coordinating observances nationally.

Are there Shinto **hierarchical structures**?

Like so many other religious traditions, Shinto community structures often reflect the belief that human life mirrors divine life. Just as there is at least an implicit hierarchy among divine beings, human society needs a certain degree of structure. Long-standing Japanese tradition, much influenced and reinforced by Confucian teaching over the centuries, lays great emphasis on knowing one's place in society. Each individual stands in a relationship of higher-to-lower, or vice-versa, with his or her fellow human beings, and basic etiquette requires that one be aware of social subordination in every context. Everyday Japanese speech, with its various levels of polite address, reflects that awareness. Although contemporary Japan is a democratic society, with all the political institutions needed to support a democracy, hierarchy runs deep in the culture and so too in Shinto belief and practice. Everything, from ranks within the network of shrines to division of labor among ritual specialists, mirrors that aware-

510

ness of multi-level structure in society at large. For several centuries in the early history of Shinto, four groups were responsible for most Shinto ritual. The Nakatomi family oversaw ritual generally, the Imbe family were concerned with maintaining ritual purity, the Urabe family focused on divinatory rituals so as to know the divine intentions in all matters, and shrine musicians performed the "divine entertainments." Other powerful clans or families held and relinquished positions of power and influence over subsequent centuries.

How does the **hierarchy** among Shinto **shrines** work?

Over the centuries Shinto authorities have devised a number of structures and classifications by which to distinguish various levels and functions of shrines. The most important is called the "shrine-rank system" (*shakaku seido*) that has been in place since shortly after the Meiji Restoration of 1868. *Jingu* designates shrines of top rank under imperial auspices, such as Meiji Jingu, in Tokyo, which enshrines royal ancestors, and Ise Jingu, which is at the top of the hierarchy and is called the *Daijingu,* Grand Imperial Shrine. Next in rank are the approximately one hundred thousand *jinja,* a generic term including virtually all shrines larger than little wayside structures. About two hundred and fifty are included on a special list of highest ranking ones. Of these some two hundred were designated prior to World War II as "governmental shrines" (kansha). Many larger jinja have spawned affiliated or branch shrines called bunsha. Multiple shrines dedicated to a single kami generally constitute distinct families, with one shrine usually acknowledged as the original foundation from which branch shrines developed.

Some very important *jinja,* such as Kasuga in Nara and about a dozen others, have the honorific title *taisha,* "grand shrine," roughly equivalent to "cathedral basilica." They are also part of a cluster of twenty-two (*ni-ju-ni sha*) institutions elevated to special status, but even they are divided into three levels: seven high, seven middle ranking, and eight lower. That grouping arose out of the practice of ranking shrines within a given region according to their order of priority on pilgrimage routes, or to guide devotees intent on visiting a sequence of holy places. In various prefectures, a further ranking of area shrines simply lists them as "first, second, or third" shrine, acknowledging the three regional shrines that draw the largest crowds of worshipers. A number of *jinja* (some count 138) have been specially designated as "nation-protecting shrines" *(gokoku jinja)* because of their dedication to the souls of those who died in battle. Twenty-seven shrines within that category, also called "deceased spirit-invoking shrines" (shokonsha), have been accorded a special rank because of the importance of the heroes from all periods of Japanese history that they commemorate. Tokyo's Yasukuni Jinja ranks at the top of that category. Before 1945, countless smaller local memorials represented the bottom of this hierarchical category. The main central administration is called the Association of Shinto Shrines *(jinja honcho),* which has branches (called *jinja cho)* in each Japanese prefecture.

What are some of the main varieties of Shinto **officials or specialists**?

Shinto tradition refers to the priesthood in general as either *shinshoku* or *kannushi.* Larger shrines with full priestly staffs distinguish among a number of ranks. The chief priest is called the *Guji,* generally the highest ranking local official. Guji might have oversight of up to thirty subordinate shrines. The *Gon-guji* is second-in-command and oversees a staff of several lower ranks as well, including junior assistant chief priests (*shin-gon-guji*). Senior priests are called *negi,* assistant senior priests *gon-negi,* and regular priests (*shuten* or *kujo*) fill out the ranks of male staff. A national ranking system also distinguishes among priests by acknowledging their levels of learning with the equivalent of academic degrees, named "purity" (*jokai*), "brightness" (*meikai*), "righteousness" (*seikai*), and "uprightness" (*chokkai*).

Young unmarried women, called shrine maidens (*miko*), function rather like deaconesses. Dressed in striking vermillion skirts and white blouses, they assist in blessing rituals, run the shrine shop, and perform sacred dance. Miko traditionally begin their association with the shrine and training for service as "sacred children." Highest in rank is the unique position called *saishu,* found only at the Ise shrine and held by a woman. She is an imperial princess with the symbolic title "master of the *matsuri* (festivals)." Assisting her is a priest with the rank of *dai-guji,* "great chief priest," a function unique to Ise. In the imperial household, ritual specialists have either of two ranks. The *shoten* parallels the shrine rank of senior priest, the *shotenho* that of assistant senior priest. But the emperor himself or a personal delegate presides, much as the Chinese sovereign once did, at over two dozen annual ceremonies.

How are Shinto **leaders** chosen and given authority?

Shinto priesthood has historically been a hereditary occupation. Even after the government officially took over the appointment of chief priests after 1868, hereditary succession continued in many localities. Perhaps the most important ingredients in maintaining standards among Shinto officials are the two educational institutions now solely responsible for the training of priests. Tokyo's Kokugakuin ("national learning") University is a relatively recent development, a private university that offers general education as well as the equivalent of Shinto seminary curriculum. It supplies research for the present centralized shrine authority, the *Jinja Honcho.* The Kogakkan ("Imperial hall of learning") University near Ise was originally a public institution that closed after World War II and then reopened in 1952 as a private university. Priests-to-be study Japanese history and literature, but focus on Shinto studies, especially ritual and theology. Shinto priests are not ordained clergy, strictly speaking. They are lay persons granted certification or licensure upon satisfactory completion of the seminary curriculum and its qualifying exams.

Have **women** exercised leadership among Shinto practitioners?

In ancient times, women played an indispensable role as shamans in countless Shinto shrines. Even after imperial decrees reduced women's roles in shrine life, giving precedence to a male priesthood, women continued to fill some key positions. Well into the sixteenth century, for example, women functioned as priestesses in some shrines. The last of the priestesses was a young woman serving the Suwa Shrine in Nagasaki. Women have long acted as spirit mediums consulted by many a priest over the centuries, as well as by individual worshipers. Restrictive legislation arising from the Meiji Restoration in 1868 dramatically curtailed women's official participation in shrine staff ministries. Only at the Ise Grand Shrine, sacred to the sun goddess Amaterasu, does a woman currently hold the position of high priestess. During the Second World War, many women took over priestly functions when their husbands departed for military service.

Do Shinto practitioners run **private schools** for their children?

Private schools equivalent to parochial educational systems in some other traditions have not been institutionally significant in the history of Shinto. Perhaps the closest thing to structured education in Shinto beliefs and values have been occasional government attempts to insert components of Shinto—i.e. traditional or national Japanese—ethics into school curricula. In 1937, for example, the Ministry of Education incorporated themes from an 1890 imperial document on education into a new ethics curriculum called "Principles of the National Entity" (*Kokutai no hongi*). Meant to implement the concept of "State Shinto," the document emphasizes the historicity of the classic mythical narratives concerning the emperor's divine descent. It praises unquestioning dedication to the corporate good of the Japanese people under the virtuous rule of the emperor. These pre-war governmental actions, however, are entirely different from the grass-roots impulses that gave rise to private religious schools in traditions such as Islam and Christianity. There is really no Shinto parallel. In fact, the Meiji and subsequent regimes' attempt to teach ethics from on high, so to speak, explicitly forbade religious education on the local or shrine level. Since World War II, however, numerous shrines throughout Japan have developed programs for children and young people, including nursery schools and kindergartens. But these are exclusively social and cultural, rather than religiously educational, developments.

Are there any organizations or institutions that have their own distinctive structures of **leadership** within Shinto?

An important organization in Shinto is the shrine guild (*miya-za*), composed of village elders who share responsibility for their local clan or parish shrine. Each man agrees to oversee shrine affairs for a full year. Other organizations called *kosha* have occasionally sought to raise funds to send members on pilgrimage or to galvanize public support for a particular project such as shrine renovation. Some of those groups eventually grew into the various Shinto sects of modern times. Various groups known as *sodai-kai, ujiko-kai,* and *ujiko-sodai* (loose synonyms for "associations of parishioners/worshipers") have sprung up all over Japan for the purpose of gathering donations and sponsoring festivals. Unlike some other traditions, Shinto is not famous for developing major internal organizations such as religious or monastic orders. That may connect to the fact that the Shinto priesthood itself is historically associated with heredity and clan and has never been an ordained clergy as such. There are, however, exceptions, such as the monastic order that grew out of a sectarian lineage called Yui-itsu Shinto.

PERSONALITIES AND POWERS

Have the Japanese ever worshiped the **emperor**? And is the emperor still a **religiously important** figure?

In early modern times, especially since the Meiji Restoration of 1868, Japanese governmental policy included the veneration of the divine Emperor as a central element. Major institutions enshrine twenty of the total number of one hundred and twenty-four emperors, as well as eleven princes, and focus on their worship. Seven of the imperial shrines are dedicated to honoring the spirits of rulers who died unfortunate deaths. Since the end of World War II, the role of Japan's imperial family has undergone dramatic changes from its former centrality to culture and religion. People still revere the emperor and his household as noble people who continue to represent and uphold ancient Japanese tradition. Many venerable and arcane Shinto rituals still occur only behind the walls of the imperial palace. But fewer and fewer Japanese have much interest in those ceremonies, and the emperor no longer has the national priestly status he once enjoyed. Still, many hope a royal son will continue the imperial line long into the future, and some even dream nostalgically of an eventual return to the days when the emperor wielded considerable political power. On the whole, though, it is safe to say that most Japanese no longer regard the emperor as divine and do not think of him or his family as significant religious symbols.

Have there been any Shinto **mystics**?

Mainstream Shinto tradition has not been particularly noted for producing important mystical figures. That is not to say that there have been no Shinto mystics. But talk of mystical union with the divine has come more from various syncretic schools and

The Imperial Oath

The following oath is taken from the 1889 Constitution of the Empire of Japan. It was spoken by the emperor in the sanctuary of the Imperial Palace:

We, the Successor to the prosperous Throne of Our Predecessors, do humbly and solemnly swear to the Imperial Founder of Our House and to Our other Imperial Ancestors that, in pursuance of a great policy co-extensive with the Heavens and with the Earth, We shall maintain and secure from decline the ancient form of government. In consideration of the progressive tendency of the course of human affairs and in parallel with the advance of civilization, We deem it expedient, in order to give clearness and distinctness to the instructions bequeathed by the Imperial Founder of Our House and by Our other Imperial Ancestors, to establish fundamental laws formulated into express provisions of law, so that, on the one hand, Our Imperial posterity may possess an express guide for the course they are to follow, and that, on the other, Our subjects shall thereby be enabled to enjoy a wider range of action in giving Us their support, and that the observance of Our laws shall continue to the remotest ages of time. We will thereby give greater firmness to the stability of Our country and promote the welfare of all the people within the boundaries of Our dominions; and We now establish the Imperial House Law and the Constitution. These Laws come to only an exposition of grand precepts for the conduct of the government, bequeathed by the Imperial Founder of Our House and by Our other Imperial Ancestors. That we have been so fortunate in Our reign, in keeping with the tendency of the times, as to accomplish this work, We owe to the glorious Spirits of the Imperial Founder of Our House and of Our other Imperial Ancestors. We now reverently make Our prayer to Them and to Our Illustrious Father, and implore the help of Their Sacred Spirits, and make to Them solemn oath never at this time nor in the future to fail to be an example to Our subjects in the observance of the Laws hereby established. May the heavenly Spirits witness this Our solemn Oath.

sects, especially those heavily influenced by non-Japanese schools of religious thought. Kurozumi Munetada, founder of the Kurozumi sect with a distinctively neo-Confucian tilt, taught the importance of the deliberate quest to become a kami. He himself is said to have experienced oneness with the sun goddess Amaterasu when she suffused his body.

Has **martyrdom** ever been important in Shinto history?

Shinto tradition reveres many religious heroes who died defending their emperor and homeland. They are martyrs in the broadest sense of the term. They died not for a religious creed narrowly defined, but out of allegiance to the larger complex of beliefs

"**D**ivine Storm Blast" roughly translates the term *kami-kaze* that so many World War II films brought into relatively common English usage. Japanese began to use the term during the middle ages in reference to how the gods fended off the Mongol invaders led by Kublai Khan in 1280, a descendant of Ghengis Khan. During World War II, the Japanese air force resorted to a desperate tactic when the tide began to turn against Japan. Pilots willing to commit suicide for their nation's honor aimed their explosive-laden dive bombers at enemy warships and went down with them. Ever since then, popular usage has referred to any self-immolating tactic or maneuver born of desperation as a "kamikaze mission." However, to identify Shinto narrowly with war or with desperate acts such as those associated with kamikaze pilots is to miss out entirely on an overwhelmingly peaceful and beautiful tradition at whose core is the celebration of life and the sacred riches of creation.

that has been integral to Japanese history and culture. People like the cultural icon Sugawara Michizane, who is said to have perished as a result of his convictions, take their place alongside the royal heroes, the princes who died in defense of the imperial house. Shrines designated as "nation-protecting" shrines are dedicated to the memory of war dead. They enshrine as kami the souls of all who gave their lives out of conviction. Yasukuni Jinja in Tokyo is a fine example of such a martyr memorial.

Do Shinto practitioners revere any persons as especially **gifted with wisdom**?

Japanese tradition generally has held teachers in high regard. But, in the words of one famous Japanese scholar, Shinto is "caught" rather than "taught." As a result, sages, scholars, and teachers do not occupy the place of honor in Shinto tradition to which, for example, Confucianism has elevated them. Human beings are made to worship the divine in all things and to respond in gratitude for countless gifts. Thanksgiving is the wisdom of Shinto. One can encourage it, but most of all it is a gift in itself. Shinto tradition emphasizes first-hand experience of the world and of one's place in it.

Is there such a thing as a Shinto **saint**?

Many exemplary human beings have been identified and revered as *kami* after their deaths. Since the category of *kami* is an all-inclusive grouping of forces and persons considered "above" the merely human, Shinto tradition has no need of an intermediary category such as that of "saint." Most traditions that discuss sainthood in one form or another do so out of one of two convictions. In some traditions the deity is so exalted and transcendent that ordinary human beings can scarcely imagine approaching it directly. Saints function as intermediaries because they share the humanity of devotees and are thus more approachable. Other traditions, however, elevate certain persons not as intermediaries or intercessors, but as examples of lofty yet attainable perfection. Shinto stands alone here in the sense that the kami are everywhere and thus perfectly accessible, and that certain human beings are themselves kami.

Have **prophets** played a role in Shinto tradition?

Shinto tradition does not revolve around a revealed truth or set of beliefs considered inaccessible without divine intervention; therefore, prophets have not figured prominently in its history. Arguably Shinto's closest functional analogy to the classic prophet are the various founders of sectarian groups who criticized the imperial system. Not unlike the prophets of the Semitic traditions, some of them have played the role of an accusatory conscience, especially in modern times.

How do **trials** or **ordeals** function in Shinto ritual?

Remnants of ancient practices reminiscent of "trial by fire" survive in several Shinto ceremonies, most of which are still practiced, in relatively few locations. Unique to the Suwa shrine in Nagasaki is a frightening ritual called *yutate-sai*. At the end of the purification and exorcism rituals, the chief priest of the shrine thrusts his hand into a kettle of boiling water. This rite dates back to the Shugendo sect of late medieval times. Now it represents not the ascetic or magical power of ancient practitioners, or the power to banish spirits possessing an unfortunate soul, but the need for radical purification. Some sects use a variation on this ritual, with a priest scattering scalding water on the main participant with a bamboo stick. A related ritual of trial involves walking over burning coals. Called *chinka shiki* ("taming the fire"), the ceremony involves circumambulating the bed of embers before walking across it. Anyone present may participate after the principal ritualists complete the ordeal. Again the purpose is purification, and prayers may include petitioning the kami of the moon to exert his influence on the fire kami.

Does the **shaman** have a place in Shinto?

In ancient times shamanesses were very important in Shinto circles. Today the shrine maidens, miko, may represent a vestige of that ritual specialization of long ago. Blind female shamans called *itako* still ply their trade in various parts of Japan. Strict asceticism marks the apprenticeship of young blind girls to older teachers. After lengthy training the aspirant marries a kami symbolically to secure spiritual power and protection. Shamanesses perform the service of connecting with the kami world, sometimes functioning as spirit-mediums. Some of the so-called "New Religions" with Shinto roots give prominent roles to shamanesses. Ancient Shinto tradition associates certain forms of spirit possession with shamanesses, explaining their extraordinary powers in special circumstances. Newer sects such as Tenri-kyo acknowledge that male or female shamans experience a "kami descent" (*kami-gakari*) in which the deity totally takes over the human being.

Do adherents of Shinto believe in **angels**?

Perhaps the closest formal analogy to the angel in Shinto tradition are the *tennin,* the Japanese version of Buddhism's celestial nymphs called *apsaras.* They are spirits, but other than that, they do not function quite the way angels do in other traditions. Lovely celestial beings have sometimes been said to

Solitary worshiper pays respects to the kami at a small local wayside shrine, Kyoto, Japan.

descend and dance in response to divinely beautiful music. If we focus on the functional parallels—on angels as messengers of the divine world—Shinto offers a number of analogies. But they don't "look" at all like angels. These messengers are, for example, Inari's fox and the monkey assistant of *Sanno,* "the mountain king." Another functional aspect of angels is that of protection and generally mediating peace and blessing. Shinto psychology divides "soul" or "spirit" into two main types—positive and negative. *Nigimitama* are the benign spirits that either bestow blessing on or effect spiritual changes in people or natural objects. In that sense, they function somewhat like angelic spirits, but they were not necessarily created as spirits as angels are. They can be the spirits of the deceased that continue to roam the cosmos. A post-war sect called Byakko Shinko-kai, however, focused on a modified version of the "guardian angel" as an essential spiritual power.

What about **devils** or **demons**?

Numerous demons (*oni*) inhabit the cosmos of popular Shinto belief, but their particular province is the north. They are associated with negative forces generally and bad luck. "Rough spirits" (*aramitama*) are among the larger category of generic spirits or souls. A category of beings called *onryo* consists of angry spirits. Other beings called *goryo,* or "august spirits," are also generally troublesome but deserving of respect for their power. Some of Shinto's most important shrines are known as *goryo* shrines, because the kami dwelling there was once a human being who died under inauspicious circumstances. Another large category of evil spirits is that of *bakemono,* a term that refers to several specific groups of beings especially prevalent in folklore.

Have **dreams and visions** or other spirit manifestations been important in Shinto tradition?

Shinto legends are full of famous figures who have enjoyed—or barely survived—encounters with the spirit world. Many religiously prominent individuals have claimed to receive divine visitations and privileged communications in dreams. Various spirits, even evil ones, *goryo,* are capable of making their presence known for the purpose of delivering a message. These spirits, also called "living human kami" (*arahitogami*), can return in their human form to make things both positive and negative happen in the land of the living. Certain famous people, like Prince Shotoku Taishi (574–622) and poet-calligrapher Sugawara Michizane (845–903), to whom over ten thousand shrines are dedicated, who died untimely or violent deaths later became kami, but could also exert unhappy influence if not dealt with properly. This is a striking amalgam of positive and negative powers in one spirit. Such a spirit can manifest itself in frightening apparitions as well as in blessings.

HOLIDAYS AND REGULAR OBSERVANCES

What kind of **calendar** do Shinto practitioners observe?

Shinto reckoning of ritual time has been much influenced by Chinese traditions. As early as 675 CE, religious Daoism had made a significant impact on the Japanese imperial court, which formally adopted many Daoist practices. Most importantly, the court set up a special bureau of divination, called the Onmyoryo ("Office of Yin-yang"), based

What does the term *matsuri* mean?

Matsuri is the inclusive word for virtually all Shinto-inspired communal celebrations. The term derives from a root that can mean "to deify or enshrine." These festivities generally celebrate manifestations of the kami who have a special relationship to a region or town, though some celebrate kami of more widespread significance as well. They acknowledge the inseparable link among the kami, the land, and the community of people living there. Since it emphasizes the seamless interrelationships among these three elements, Shinto tradition makes no distinction between sacred and profane time. All of creation, time and space, is sacred. *Matsuri* mark those times and places that are more than ordinarily sacred. Just when divine energy appears on the wane, a *matsuri* occurs and renews that spiritual potency. Festivities periodically restore the ancient cosmic order of nature.

Japanese often celebrate *matsuri* with an enormous vigor, an almost uncontrolled energy. Bands of young men undertake strenuous feats of lifting and hauling enormous loads, competing with other groups to deliver their sacred burdens to the shrine or another ritual destination. That feeling of wild unpredictability offers an important insight into the Shinto sense of the divine as both benevolent and dangerous. Some *matsuri* are explicitly identified as non-religious civic events, but even today the majority are of religious origin and reflect classical Shinto or folk beliefs, or both. Most also retain their ancient associations with seasonal and agricultural concerns. *Matsuri* typically include both processions and activities within a shrine compound. Special offerings and prayers, plays and dancing and other entertainments, and communal meals are features of all the great festivities.

on Daoist principles. One of the Onmyoryo's chief functions was to establish a liturgical calendar that patterned earthly life on the rhythms of the cosmos. This lunar calendar retains all the main features of its Chinese model, including the cycles of sixty years based on the combinations of twelve "branches" and ten "stems" (see the sections on Daoism and Confucianism). The Japanese call their Chinese version of the lunar calendar *Kyureki,* as distinct from the modern solar calendar adopted in 1872, the *Shinreki.* An early formal cycle of annual observance, called the *nenchu gyoji,* literally "year-round-discipline-rituals," developed as early as the tenth century CE. Imperial authorities promulgated it in a vast historical record called the *Engi-shiki* ("Institutes of the Engi Era," 901–23 CE), an essential source of information about Shinto ritual in general. Japan's lunar calendar needs to tuck in an extra month every three years or so.

Prior to the nineteenth century, many Shinto shrines maintained their own calendars of events, including uniquely regional and local festivities. Today some major

A senior priest serves his fellow priests a symbolic communion sip of sake at the conclusion of a new moon ceremony at Itsukushima Jinja, on an island near Hiroshima. He kneels before each in turn until all have been served, then they file out and return to the priests' quarters. The priest on the far left holds a symbol of ancient courtly authority called the *shaku*.

events still take place according to various ways of adapting the lunar calendar to fit the solar. For example, some festivals now occur on the same numbered day within the same numbered month, but transferred to the solar reckoning. In other words, a festival that fell on the seventh day of the seventh lunar month now falls on July 7. Some festivals are now dated by keeping the day date but adding a solar month, so that a celebration once held on the seventh day of the seventh month now occurs on August 7. Finally, and more rarely, a few special days retain their lunar dating completely, so that they rotate backwards against the solar year. From the solar point of view, therefore, these are moveable feasts. Since the late nineteenth century, the timing of the major festivals has been coordinated so that all the larger shrines observe them at the same time. But there are still many distinctive local and regional festivities attached to individual shrines, such as the rituals dedicated to the patron deities of particular places. In addition to the liturgical calendar, an important related feature is the Japanese custom of dividing history according to imperial reigns or epochs. Emperor Hirohito died in 1989, ending the Showa era, and his son Akihito's accession inaugurated the Heisei epoch.

How does the Shinto tradition determine specific days for **festivities**?

Carrying on the Chinese custom, Shinto tradition has designated certain days each month auspicious and certain others inauspicious for religious celebrations. The days most favored include the four each lunar month that correspond with the new and full moons (the first and fifteenth) and waxing and waning half moons (around the seventh/eighth and twenty-second/third). Since solar months are longer than lunar months, festivals that retain the same day- and month-numbers they once had in the lunar calendar (e.g. seventh of the seventh) do not always correspond perfectly with the lunar event that originally made certain days auspicious and others not. Calculation of the beginning of a festival day begins with the eve of the feast (*yoi-matsuri*). Special days begin at sunset on the eve and last through sunset of the actual festival day (*hon-matsuri*). Japanese call the actual day of a feast *saijitsu*. Large scale annual *matsuri* associated with a particular shrine, such as observance of the anniversary of the shrine's founding, are called *reisai*, "regular festivals." These are distinguished from lesser festivals or national occasions such as those associated with the imperial household.

What **annual festivities** do Shinto practitioners celebrate?

"Five seasonal days" (*gosekku*) celebrate simple but essential blessings. Timing of the five seasonal days is still based on the lunar calendar, but transferred to the solar months. For example, the days were originally observed on the third day of the third lunar month, the fifth of the fifth, the seventh of the seventh, and the ninth of the ninth. The days now retain the same position, but in solar months of the same numbers. Seven Herbs Day now falls on January 7, when people greet the spring with a specially seasoned soup. For Hina-matsuri, or Doll Festival (nowadays called Girls' Day) on March 3, many people reenact the ancient practice of floating clay or paper dolls on a river or the sea to ensure the health of their daughters. Boys' Day (*kodomo-no-hi*) falls on May 5, when little boys receive dolls of heroic figures who model valor and loyalty. On July 7, *Tanabata*, or "Seventh Night," recalls the Chinese story of the celestial cowboy and the weaver maid, condemned to be distant stars forever because their romance caused them to slacken their labors. On this night the two reunite briefly on the bridge of the Milky Way. Farmers and textile workers take the opportunity to pray for success in their occupations. Finally, Chrysanthemum Day (*kiku no sekku*) falls on the ninth of September. Many still go to local shrines to appreciate the beautifully cultivated flower, which became the official symbol of the emperor during the Meiji era in the mid–nineteenth century. One curious period calculated by the lunar calendar (equivalent to October usually) sees all shrines sending off their kami to the Izumo Taisha, where they stay together for a spell before moving for similar brief visits to two other shrines. At their home shrines, worshipers observe "a month without kami" (*kami-na-zuki*).

How does the **agricultural cycle** affect Shinto-related ritual celebrations?

Many festivities are still tied to various agricultural occasions. Spring and autumn festivals correspond with planting and harvesting. A large cluster of so-called spring festivals (*haru-matsuri*) covers events that run generally from January to May, though some areas stretch the season into July. In late March or April people celebrate Cherry

Blossom festival, one of nature's sublime but fleeting glories. On May 5 (fifth of the fifth in some places, other days elsewhere) many people observe a special Rice Planting day. Two of Kyoto's larger shrines, Kamigamo and Shimogamo in the north of the city, celebrate a prayer for good harvest called Hollyhock Festival (*aoi-matsuri*), complete with elaborate processions and reenactments of ancient imperial events. With countless regional variations, the planting (or transplanting) rites occur generally during May, June, and July, stretching well into the summer season. This seasonal overlap is a result of using more than one system for converting special occasions from the lunar to the solar calendar. Some shrines host enormous gatherings centered around processions and contests of various kinds.

Autumn festivals (*aki-matsuri*) include a similar grouping of celebrations that begin even before the summer festival season has ended and extend into October. At the beginning of each imperial era, the new emperor performs an Autumn celebration called the "Great Feast of New Food" (*daijosai*), offering rice to the Sun Goddess and imperial forbears. Whether in the imperial palace or at local shrines, these are all occasions for gratitude to the kami for bountiful harvest. Between planting and harvest are a host of generally smaller summer festivals (*natsu-matsuri*), during which people pray for a healthy crop. Some shrines, however, still host major celebrations during July, August, and September. Many of these are occasions for teams of younger men and boys especially to engage in spirited competition, vying to get their *mikoshi* along the procession route faster and arrive at the shrine first.

Winter festivals (*fuyu no matsuri*) revolve largely around preparations for the end of the year and New Year's celebrations (*shogatsu*). Calculated on the solar calendar, the winter solstice heralds the new year, so many people begin them with ceremonial cleaning and wrap up the old year by laying old sewing needles to rest at a local shrine. Honor for all things that contribute to human civilization—not for human beings alone—that have come to the end of their lives is essential. Seven days during a period called the "great cold" (*daikan,* generally between January sixth and twenty-first) retain some of their ancient associations. People gather at shrines to enjoy the return of the sun in lengthening days that portend spring, and to pray for good fortune in general.

Are there **cyclical Shinto observances**, such as feasts that happen regularly but not annually?

Some gatherings still take place on set days in certain odd-numbered months, but not monthly. For example, a practice called Waiting for the Sun (*himachi*) finds people gathered private residences on the fifteenth day of the first, fifth, and ninth lunar months to keep vigil until dawn. A Shinto priest is often among the celebrants. During the same months, but on the odd-numbered nights of the third week, people come together in "Groups Awaiting the Moon" (*tsukimachi*). September's full moon is especially beautiful, for it falls in the ninth month and is known as the harvest moon. Participants celebrate the lunar beauty with special songs and food. These gatherings occur only in homes. Some people still make special arrangements to observe their "unlucky year"—age forty-two for men and thirty-three for women—with rites at a shrine to ward off misfortune. They may take precautions by means of extra rituals of purification on that day. Some regard certain days each month as "fortuitous connection days" because they associate them with particular kami, and such days often occasion shrine visitation.

Do Shinto practitioners celebrate **sacred birthdays** or **honor particular figures**?

Many shrines hold special festivities in connection with dates important in the lives of enshrined kami who were historical figures prior to their deification. For example, the Akama Jingu enshrines the child Emperor Antoku (1178–85) who reigned for the final five years of his very brief life. From April 23 to 25, celebrants recall his untimely death and the reign of his predecessor, Emperor Gotoba. *Tenjin Matsuri,* from July 24 to 25, celebrates the deified scholar and court minister Sugawara Michizane (845–903). Over ten thousand branch shrines ritualize the deity who is mythically associated with oxen and cattle. According to tradition, Sugawara was born and came of age in the year of the ox and was saved from his enemy by a bull who miraculously appeared to kill his would-be assassins. Ironically, it was members of that same enemy clan, the Fujiwara, who had Sugawara enshrined some fifty years after his death. He received the name *Tenjin* ("celestial kami") and has remained popular as the kami of learning. Large numbers of worshipers still go to his shrines on the twenty-fifth (both his birth and death day) of each month to reverence statues of reclining bulls, rubbing them and then rubbing the blessing onto themselves or their children. Birthdays are not as important on the whole as are death anniversaries and seasonal associations with the deified figures.

What are some of the **other days** Shinto practitioners celebrate?

O-Bon matsuri is one of those feasts whose timing is determined by adding a solar month to the lunar reckoning. Hence a feast formerly celebrated during the middle (i.e., full moon) of the seventh month now occurs during the middle of August, the eighth. On November 23 and 24 falls the "New Food" festival (*nii-name-sai*). Acting as high priest, the emperor himself leads the ceremonies. When a newly enthroned emperor presides, the feast is called "Great Food" festival (*daijosai*), and the ritual seals and formalizes the new ruler's accession. This is one of some thirty regular imperial ceremonies (*koshitsu saishi*) that occur through the year, most conducted privately within the palace. The Autumnal Equinox still calls for quite elaborate observances in some places. Suwa shrine in Nagasaki, for example, holds its annual *Okunchi* for three full rousing days and nights. Involving a full range of activities, from raucous processions to solemn pre-dawn purifications conducted in almost total silence, the festival engages large numbers of worshipers actively. Festivities begin and end with more private rituals designed to bring the kami into the ceremony and see them back to their places of repose.

Some ceremonies occur often but on a more ad hoc basis than the regularly scheduled festivals. Nearly every new architectural venture occasions special religiously inspired observances. "Earth Sanctification" (*Jichin-sai*) is a ritual of Daoist origin conducted by a Shinto priest to prepare the ground for new construction. Participants call on the kami of the place for protection. These ceremonies are roughly analogous to the American practice of hoisting a small evergreen to the top of a newly completed structure—perhaps religious in origin, but now purely customary. A rite called *senza-sai* or *sengu* can occur on any number of occasions. In the ritual a kami is relocated, either permanently to a new shrine or temporarily, such as during repairs, or for a matsuri, or for a time of repose in one of several of the deity's regular abodes. In the case of Ise shrine, for example, the ceremony happens every twenty years, when a new shrine is constructed on the grounds.

CUSTOMS AND RITUALS

What place does **purification** occupy in Shinto ritual?

Few traditions place greater emphasis on the need to purify both participants in ceremonies and the place designated for the rites. Just as the primordial deity, Izanagi, purified himself upon exiting from the underworld, so must all worshipers before engaging in sacred rituals. The contrasting states of pollution or spiritual alienation (*kegare*) and ritual-moral purity (*harae*) encompass a great deal of what Shinto tradition considers important. Purification with water is a prerequisite to even the simplest acts of worship. As an ordinary part of rituals performed by priests and shrine staff, purification requires waving a special wand over the individuals or their offerings, and sometimes involves sprinkling salt water or salt. Watch a Sumo wrestling match and you will see the behemoth contestants liberally scattering fistfuls of salt across the ring as they enter to confront each other—a clue to the ancient religious associations of the sport. More elaborate purification involves ceremonial bathing to cleanse the individual of pollution and sin. Priests sometimes purify by immersion before major rites. Some adepts seek out sacred mountain waterfalls and stand beneath their frigid cataracts in winter as an especially potent form of purification. Most important is the ceremony called "great purification," in which priests of the imperial household as

Japanese boy prepares to offer the author a ladle of water for purification at a small Shinto shrine in Tokyo.

well as throughout the country symbolically purify the whole nation—the whole world, according to some interpretations. Reciting special prayers, they mark the middle and end of the year with cleansing. Before a given shrine's major festivals, shrine priests put considerable time and effort into preparing themselves and the site. Officiants enter seclusion the day before the festival, bathe several times, and follow strict rules with respect to clothing, food, and abstinence from sexual activity.

What **rites** do Shinto practitioners perform in their **shrines**?

When worshipers go to their local or larger regional shrines, they may engage in several types of ritual called "worship gestures" (*omairi*), depending on the occasion. A simple list of "Four P's" sums up the essential ingredients of Shinto ritual: purification, presentation (of offerings), petition (or prayers for blessing), and participation (of the assembled worshipers). For ordinary, everyday prayers, in which they express a whole range of needs and concerns, worshipers typically perform a simple offering before the sacred presence. Alone or in small groups, they enter the shrine precinct and proceed along the path, passing beneath perhaps several torii gates, to the purification font. There they take some water to cleanse the mouth and hands as necessary preparation (a ritual action called *misogi*) for approaching the holy place. Moving to the front of the shrine, worshipers announce their arrival by ringing a bell that hangs over the threshold of many shrines. Ringing the bell may be either for quieting the mind or summoning the kami. With or without the bell, all toss a coin in the offering box, then bow and clap their hands twice to summon the deity. After making a brief prayer, they bow twice (one deep and one slight bow) and then depart.

For special occasions, individuals or small groups can arrange for the services of the priestly staff. Rites that last from ten to fifteen minutes take place inside the front worship hall (*haiden*). Various spiritual purposes of the rituals include divine blessing and protection, the opportunity to communicate with the kami about countless daily happenings and concerns, and expressions of personal dedication to the divine beings. These services are available most days in shrines with larger staffs, for the tradition has set aside no one day of the week as a canonical day of worship. In larger shrines, the priestly staff also make daily morning and evening offerings to the kami. In addition to the various daily rites, shrines host numerous events throughout the year for special occasions, as described above (*matsuri*).

What are the basic features of the more **elaborate shrine rituals**?

Larger rituals typically include four features. Before beginning any sacred act, including the simplest ones, celebrants purify themselves with water or salt. Welcoming the kami (*kami-mukae*) is among the first acts of the presiding priest. The invocation is necessary because many *matsuri* begin away from the shrine in places where the kami does not ordinarily reside. Next is the offering to the kami (and that includes ancestors, as in Chinese traditions). In addition to responding to the obvious requirement of funds to maintain the thousands of shrines great and small all over the country, people make symbolic offerings and the priests in turn formally present them to the deities. Flowers, food and drink, beautiful textiles or jewelry, and even the performance of traditional art forms or sport can be included among offerings. Entertainment arranged in connection with a religious festival is known as "divine amusement" (*kan-nigiwai*).

When the priestly staff perform elaborate offerings, the chief priest opens the doors of the innermost sanctuary. The priests pass the offerings among themselves and finally the assistant chief priest places the offerings before the sanctuary doors. Ritual specialists then recite prayers—many of ancient origin and some more recently composed—of praise, thanksgiving, historical recollection about the meaning of the particular occasion, all concluded with appropriately humble leave-taking of the kami with a gesture called "Sending the kami away" (*kami-okuri*). Ceremonies conclude with a kind of communion rite in which the chief priest serves the other members of the ritual staff a symbolic sip of sake. The priests walk in procession from the inner worship hall to the outer hall for this rite, which is usually brief, depending on the number of officiants participating. When large crowds are in attendance for a particularly festive occasion, the closing meal can be quite elaborate, and include a share in some of the food just offered to the kami. One ritual element notably lacking in Shinto worship is preaching. Since worship is entirely focused on relating ritually to the deities, Shinto tradition does not regard persuasive religious rhetoric a necessary tool.

What does Shinto home worship entail?

Religiously committed Japanese families still maintain regular daily home rituals centered around the *kamidana,* and perhaps also around the *butsudan* or miniature Buddhist temple. Home shrines are dedicated and put into service when family members invite a priest over to install a talisman from the local shrine on which is written the name of the kami to be honored in the home. Worshipers perform a brief purification ritual and then do before the miniature shrine much the same thing they would do at an actual shrine. These rituals, often observed morning and evening, are generally very brief, lasting perhaps three to five minutes. Some families still ritually incorporate in the evening meal food offered to the kami.

Is there a regular, standard Shinto **group liturgical worship**?

Communal worship is not a regular feature of Shinto liturgical practice. People may arrive at a shrine in large numbers, but they generally do not gather to worship as a large congregation. Individual and small group worship is the norm, whether for brief impromptu visits made outside the shrine or for more elaborate priestly rituals in the worship hall. A distinctive feature of Shinto architecture is the absence of worship spaces large enough to accommodate sizeable congregations. By contrast, the bigger Japanese Buddhist temples accomodate sizable groups in a single worship space. Even in larger Shinto shrines, the parts of the worship facility open to the public are in any case not fully enclosed. Being very much at the mercy of cold weather is the price of wanting a sacred space to be as much in tune with nature as possible. This also reflects the underlying sense that people build community through other activities, but perform their most intimate spiritual duties as individuals or families.

Is **ritual sacrifice** part of Shinto tradition?

According to Shinto tradition the kami neither require nor ask for sacrificial offerings. Sacrifices in many traditions imply the need to assuage guilt or undo an evil action. Shinto tradition focuses on impurities that one can overcome merely by sincere purification. Some rituals in Shinto history have included animal sacrifice, perhaps under the influence of imported Chinese practices. But that did not become a regular feature of Shinto worship.

What kinds of special **ritual objects** figure in Shinto worship and prayer?

Shinto tradition refers to all of its "ritual furniture and utensils" with the term *saikigu.* It includes several items used on every altar during offering ceremonies. The priest carries the offerings (*heihaku*) and gifts of food (*shinsen*) on a tray (*sambo*), which he sets upon an eight-legged table (*hassoku-an*) made of a special reddish cypress wood (*hinoki,* "fire tree"). Priestly staff remove these objects after worship ends. Objects used regularly in nearly all rituals include several items that ritual specialists wave over those to whom they are ministering. Branches of the *sakaki* (combining characters for "tree" and "kami") provide a splash of greenery and association with living nature. A wand used for purification, either in place of or in conjunction with the *sakaki* branch, is called *haraigushi*—a thick cluster of white paper streamers attached to a long stick. Another stick with a set of zigzag-cut white (and sometimes of other colors) paper symbolizes the kami's presence in the holy place. All three objects are mounted on stands and displayed when not in use by one of the priests or a miko. Miko also use a set of five bells (*suzu*) for their sacred dances.

Several larger implements play a central role in the great public festivals called *matsuri*. Most important is the portable shrine called the *mikoshi*. Celebrants carry this miniature, but still often very heavy, four-sided model of a shrine sanctuary in procession, shouldering long beams that hold the shrine aloft. Larger mikoshi can weigh up to several tons and require a large crew of strong bearers. In some places large wagons called *yatai* and *dashi* rumble through the streets on massive wheels, carrying groups of musicians and revelers. Built like mobile shrines, the hefty wooden wagons range in height from just over thirty feet to about sixty-five feet.

Is **exorcism** important in Shinto practice?

Demons and assorted evil influences miss no opportunity to make nuisances of themselves, especially at times when human beings and natural processes are most vulnerable. Beginnings, such as planting time or the birth of an infant, can be particularly difficult in this respect. Shinto tradition includes various understandings of how evil forces work and several methods for contending with them. Most undesirable forces are associated with impurity and pollution. Some evil spirits will depart in a ritual that designates as a scapegoat any animal or object capable of taking on the negative forces. Emperors of old rubbed a human effigy over their bodies, leaving all personal impurity on the image, which officials of the "Bureau of Yin and Yang" then ritually consigned to a river. Other rituals use a weapon such as a sword to attack the evil power as though it were a physical presence. Some rituals assume the evil forces have taken on demonic bodies and must be pursued and expelled from a locality. In one rite, people throw soybeans in unlucky directions and command the demons to depart, an important part of the Spring Setsubun ("season change") Matsuri.

Some large festivals are entirely dedicated to a type of communal exorcism. An originally Buddhist rite called *Goryo-e* ("meeting with august spirits") has been associated with Kyoto's famous Gion Matsuri, for example. That festival arose out of a need to banish the spirits of disease, and eventually grew into a full-scale Shinto celebration. Another important interpretation of spirit possession has been traditionally asso-

A couple consult the divining arrows they have purchased at the Shinto Shrine shop, Meiji Jingu, Tokyo.

ciated with the belief that the fox is capable of changing shapes. Extraordinary spiritual states were therefore sometimes explained as a type of "fox-possession." Some popular traditions identify various psycho-somatic illnesses as forms of possession. "Soul pacification" (*Tama-shizume*) is a kind of reverse exorcism in which ritualists seek to make a spirit content to remain in the body of a person suffering from illness.

Are there any Shinto **divination rituals**?

Bokusen is the Japanese term for the complex process of divining auspicious times for agriculturalists. Divination encompasses a variety of specific devices. As in Chinese Community Traditions, people often draw lots—the Chinese shake bundles of numbered sticks and pull the one left protruding, and Shinto worshipers draw numbered bits of paper. Sometimes they will read the angle at which an arrow sticks in its target, or read the designs on a turtle shell, or hold a deer's shoulder blade in a flame and observe how it cracks. (A similar ritual uses arrows for slightly different purposes. People purchase white arrows at shrine shops, especially around the New Year, and use them as amulets, protective devices, at home throughout the year.) Divination is required for setting the dates for many major festivals. Ritual leaders invite certain divinatory kami to be in attendance as the diviner kindles a sacred fire on which to heat a turtle shell. Specialists then read the relationship of the cracks to lines and characters pre-drawn on the shell. A ritual cousin of Chinese *feng shui* is called *kaso*. It involves a set of geomantic calculations to establish optimal conditions for all sorts of human habitations. Another type of divination has wor-

Does Shinto tradition include pilgrimage?

Pilgrimages of various kinds have long been important to Japanese in connection with both Buddhism and Shinto. Sacred natural objects and shrines are of course the most common goals of Shinto pilgrims, but people do not always make neat distinctions between Buddhist and Shinto sacred sites. What is most significant is that the place has been hallowed by some event or person of great influence in Japanese history, or by natural qualities that betoken beauty and perfection. A distinctive aspect of Japanese pilgrimage is the formation of pilgrimage circuits (*junpai*) that encompass multiple stops at sacred groves, mountains, caves, waterfalls, shrines or temples, in all imaginable combinations. Most common are circuits of either thirty-three or eighty-eight sites set up in relatively recent times by railway and other transportation companies. In medieval times there was even talk of "thousand-shrine pilgrimages" (*senja mairi*), with multiple visits motivated by desire for greater spiritual merit. Some pilgrims undertake their journeys as acts of asceticism or spiritual discipline, but most seem to regard pilgrimage as an opportunity for reflection and spiritual renewal. A type of pilgrimage to Shinto's most sacred site, the Ise shrine, has come to be known as the "blessing visit" (*okage-mairi*). Another popular pilgrimage circuit leaves by rail from Osaka and takes in sites associated with the "seven gods of good luck," including both Shinto shrines and Buddhist temples. Over four hundred traditional pilgrimage routes still attract Japanese Buddhist and Shinto devotees.

shipers write on small pieces of paper their various options as they prepare to make a major decision. In what may be a variation on a contemporary popular Chinese practice, people typically pull a stick from a bundle, read its number, and take a piece of prewritten advice from a correspondingly numbered drawer. Numerous Shinto shrines provide racks where people who find the advice unpalatable can tie their paper to be rid of the effects of the bad news.

How is **music** important in Shinto ritual?

Gagaku, "refined music," is ancient courtly music originating in China as early as the Han dynasty and cultivated by the Japanese in Heian imperial circles. Often associated with dance, the fourteen-member instrumental ensemble consists of percussion and reeds. But it also includes the stringed instrument similar to the Hawaiian guitar called the *so,* cousin of the larger *koto,* identifiable by its frequent use of the technique of note-bending. A plucked string called the *biwa* is also part of the ensemble. Woodwinds are the "three reeds" (*sankan*), short, piccolo-like six- and nine-hole flutes, a primitive oboe-like woodwind that produces a sharp, edgy sound, and a cluster of seventeen bam-

531

boo pipes called the *sho* that is in fact a tiny pipe organ for the mouth. Slow stately rhythms beat out by the percussion underlie the haunting, almost plaintive sounds of the high-pitched reeds. Few sounds are a more apt musical communication of the sense of solemnity and perfect "otherness" of the deities the music addresses in Shinto shrines. Most non-Japanese who encounter music identified as Japanese are likely to associate that musical tradition with the sound of plucked strings, such as the koto and shamisen. In Shinto shrine ritual, however, stringed instruments do not play the major role they play in Chinese ritual. Percussion and woodwinds make up the bulk of the typical ceremonial ensemble. Percussion instruments include the massive *taiko,* a large barrel with two skin heads that sits sideways on an elevated stand just inside the outer ritual hall of larger shrines. A shrine ritualist, often one of the *miko* ("deaconesses"), announces the beginning of ceremonies by a pulse-pounding crescendo-decrescendo on the great drum. Various smaller drums keep time for dances.

Are **dance** and **drama** equally important?

Bugaku, "refined dance" in 160 different styles, is often performed to the accompaniment of a gagaku ensemble and sometimes occurs in Buddhist temples as well as Shinto shrines. It is somewhat more formal and classical than *Kagura,* a uniquely Shinto form of liturgical dance with musical accompaniment. The name apparently derives from a term that means "temporary abode of the kami," a place on earth to which worshipers summon the deities. Kagura has its mythic roots in the dance of the Terrible Female of Heaven that lured the sun goddess to emerge from her cave. Unlike the more staid classical version danced for the emperor on December's full-moon night, shrine (or village) kagura now reenacts often raucous scenes from mythological narratives. Several of the great shrines, such as those of Izumo, Kasuga, and Ise, are especially known for their long-standing traditions of kagura performance. Some shrines have special structures dedicated to kagura, but many still stage the dance in the large open space in front of the worship hall. *Bon odori* is a popular form of folk dancing performed at festivals on shrine grounds. Celebrants dance around a large, raised, scaffold-like platform on which drummers and other musicians perch to play their popular *hayashi* style music. Perhaps the best known of Shinto-related dances is the Dragon dance often associated with festival parades. In shrine dances, the dragon begins by bowing to the kami and the chief priest before writhing its way across the sacred precincts. The ancient Japanese theater form called *No* also has roots in the re-enactment of Shinto myths.

Do Shinto practitioners **pray** in any particular language?

Since Shinto has been an exclusively Japanese phenomenon, it will come as no surprise that Shinto prayers have almost always been expressed in Japanese. That does not necessarily mean that Japanese functions as a liturgical or canonical language, as Sanskrit does in Hindu tradition or as Latin once did in Roman Catholic tradition. The role of

A Japanese Wedding

Contemporary Japanese weddings are celebrated in many ways, often combining traditional Japanese and Western elements side by side. Typically, a religious wedding ceremony is performed in Shinto style at a shrine located inside the hotel where the wedding celebration occurs. The ceremony is conducted by a Shinto priest and is attended only by the couple's closest family members. The couple is purified, drinks sake, and the groom reads a statement of commitment. The ceremony ends with symbolic offerings to the kami. The couple wears traditional Japanese garb.

A reception is usually held after the ceremony. The wedding couple might welcome anywhere from 15 to 250 guests: relatives, friends, and co-workers. After the bride and groom are introduced, a meal is served and brief speeches are delivered. At the end of the party, the couple thank their guests for joining them on this important day.

In recent years, many Japanese couples have incorporated traditionally Western elements into their weddings—for example, brides wearing white, Christian-style dresses. Sometimes the entire ceremony takes place in a Christian church and according to a Christian-like ritual, even when the couple is not Christian. Many couples also perform other Western-style rituals, including cake-cutting, an exchange of rings, and elaborate honeymoons.

Japanese in Shinto practice is a purely functional one—it's the vernacular language of virtually everyone associated with Shinto. There is, however, one important respect in which Japanese usage in Shinto ritual does retain the flavor of a sacred tongue. Many Shinto prayers that priests recite in shrines are quite ancient. The language and vocabulary are so archaic that only the most learned and specially trained Japanese fully understand what is being said. In that sense, the continued use of the classical language has the feel of, say, the Catholic Church's use of Latin well into the twentieth century.

Does the sport of **Sumo wrestling** have any Shinto connections?

Japan's ancient and still wildly popular sport of Sumo wrestling is not itself a religious ritual, but it has surrounded itself with rituals associated with Shinto tradition. Once, these matches occurred on shrine grounds as part of the larger category of activities called "divine entertainment." Today the bigger matches take place in specially decked out arenas, and are scheduled in fortnightly tournaments at set times of the year. Action occurs under a shrine-like roof suspended high above the floor. Two enormous wrestlers—the heavier the better, in general—confront each other in a raised circle of well-tamped earth bounded by the heavy braided ceremonial rope called the *shimenawa*.

As they enter the ring, the giants sprinkle handfuls of salt to purify the space. They squat and spread their arms in an ancient Samurai gesture designed to assure opponents that they carry no weapons. A referee dressed in ancient ceremonial garb signals the beginning and end of a match and declares a winner, using deliberate, archaic gestures. Sumo champions are among Japan's highest paid and most popular athletes. The best of them do countless product endorsements, and parades of Sumo greats led Olympians into the arena when Japan hosted the games at Nagano in 1998. Complex as the phenomenon has become in Japanese society today, Sumo has its roots in the same simplicity and basic feeling for nature that pervades so much of Shinto tradition.

Does the form of **ritual suicide** called "**hara-kiri**" or "**seppuku**" have Shinto connections?

Ritual suicide has sometimes been associated with Shinto by way of the Samurai code of honor. The principle behind taking one's life has been that one can be cleansed of shame incurred through bad judgment or ill will by means of suicide. *Hara-kiri* means literally "belly cutting," a grim ritual in which the subject disembowels himself with a short blade while kneeling. His "second" then dispatches the subject by decapitating him with the longer samurai sword. There have been few publicized instances of the ritual, also called by the preferred and more polite term *seppuku,* in recent times. Surely the most famous such act was that of celebrated novelist Yukio Mishima in 1970. Most people no longer consider ritual suicide in any way laudable or virtuous and certainly do not think of it as part of Shinto religious belief.

How do Shinto practitioners celebrate **birth**?

Not long after a couple have a baby—traditionally about thirty days—they take the child to the shrine for a natal blessing. This is consistent with the belief that all new ventures and beginnings will fare better if brought before the kami. In addition, the symbolism includes the belief that the infant thus becomes a child of the family's protector kami. Parents arrange with shrine staff for a standard ceremony that takes place inside the *haiden,* or outer worship hall. At larger shrines a senior priest, assistant priest, and miko typically perform the ceremony. Pronouncing solemn prayers in an archaic Japanese, the priests then perform blessings over the young family by waving the *haraigushi.* The miko may also participate by blessing the worshipers with a green sakaki branch. Ancient Shinto tradition retains a class of divine beings called "kami of birth or beginnings" (*musubi no kami*). They include kami of fire, youth, plenty, and the creator divinities who brought all things to birth.

Are there other distinctive Shinto **rites of passage or initiation**?

Several types of ceremony and celebration are associated with various stages in life. Tradition recommends that parents (formerly the grandmother, since mothers remained

A young couple bring their new baby for a special blessing at Tokyo's Meiji Jingu. The officiating priest waves over them the purifying wand called the *haraigushi*. In the background is the courtyard that separates the Hall of Worship (*haiden*) from the Hall of Offerings (*heiden*) where the priestly staff perform more exclusive rituals. Yet another, smaller courtyard stands between that and the holy of holies (*honden*).

impure for a time after childbirth) bring thirty-two day old boys or thirty-three day old girls to the shrine for a special blessing. This "first shrine visit" (*hatsu-miya-mairi*) functioned as the infant's initiation into the Shinto shrine community. Older children also have their days. Each November 15, a festival called *Shichi-go-san* ("Seven-five-three") marks a rite of passage for both boys and girls. Three- and seven-year-old girls and five-year-old boys don their fanciest dress-up outfits for a shrine visit to pray for a safe and happy future. Putting on special clothes is a major ingredient in rites of initiation. Young people reach the age of adulthood at twenty. On "coming of age day" (*seijin-no-hi*), January 15 each year, young adults, especially women, visit shrines in formal attire for a blessing. Other coming-of-age observances identify manhood with age seventeen and womanhood with nineteen, acknowledging the difficulty of life's changes with the bestowal of protective talismans. Many older Japanese still observe rites of passage that acknowledge the challenges of aging. They may visit shrines when they reach the ages of 61, 70, 77, 88, and 99, to ask for protection and blessings.

Are there Shinto **rituals of marriage**?

Weddings in Japan have traditionally followed Shinto ritual, and the vast majority still include Shinto elements even when performed in connection with other traditions, such as Christianity. Until recent times, however, weddings occurred in homes and

535

Young Japanese women walking along the main path of one of Tokyo's major Shinto shrines after celebrating the annual Coming of Age Day (*seijin no hi*), for which they are decked out in their fanciest traditional dress.

were performed by lay persons only. Since the mid–nineteenth century, shrine nuptials performed by Shinto priests have been more common. A ceremony called *shinzen-kekkon* (nuptials in the presence of kami) may take place in a wedding hall on shrine grounds or in other public spaces. According to some, a marriage deity called *musubi no kami* ("the god who ties the knot") is a Japanese counterpart to the moon-dwelling Daoist, Yue Lao, who bound together the feet of marriage partners. Many Japanese continue the ancient practice of arranged marriage, and some young couples still live with the groom's family, following Confucian traditions. At the heart of the wedding ceremony is a shared drink of sake (rice wine). Many Japanese families still value elaborate ritual as a form of social communication, and some will even have two ceremonies, one Shinto and one Christian, for example. Daoist-influenced traditions still recommend that couples be wed only on days determined to be auspicious.

How do Shinto practitioners deal ritually with **death and mourning**?

According to a saying, "Shinto marries, Buddhism buries." During the Tokugawa era (1600–1868) an imperial decree stipulated that only Buddhist priests should conduct funeral rites. Most cemeteries in Japan are connected to Buddhist temples rather than Shinto shrines. But there are exceptions to that general rule, and practitioners of Shinto have important beliefs and rituals concerning death and mourning. A major difference between Buddhist and Shinto practices is that Shinto rites never occur in shrines, for shrines are strictly dedicated to the kami. Shinto tradition regards death as a form of evil and a serious source of pollution. Shinto belief and practice has been profoundly influenced by certain Confucian attitudes toward departed ancestors, and large numbers of Japanese still perform rites of ancestor veneration. Some Japanese families still follow the practice of enshrining a deceased person's symbols in a "spirit house" (*tama-ya*), placed beneath the home's *kamidana,* seven weeks after a funeral. Some of Japan's largest shrines are dedicated to memorializing the spirits of great human beings elevated to the status of kami. Grief (*kibuku*) is associated with a prescribed period during which the experience of death renders family members impure. The bereaved family should stay away from shrines and refrain from Shinto ritual generally during that interval. In pre-Buddhist times, the Japanese sometimes constructed monumental memorials to the dead. Historically, lay people performed Shinto funeral rituals, with main participants wearing white. Today, Shinto rites, led by priests, occur in homes or funeral establishments. Some shrines continue to perform memorial rites for those who have died in battle.

Resources

General Introduction and Comparative Works

Armstrong, Karen. *Jerusalem: One City, Three Faiths*. New York: Ballantine Books, 1997.

Bell, Catherine. *Ritual: Perspectives and Dimensions*. New York: Oxford University, 1997.

Bowker, John. *The Oxford Dictionary of World Religions*. New York: Oxford University, 1997.

Carman, John B. *Majesty and Meekness*. Grand Rapids, MI: Eerdmans, 1994.

Carmody, Denise Lardner and John Tully Carmody. *Eastern Ways to the Center*. Belmont, CA: Wadsworth, 1983.

———. *Western Ways to the Center*. Belmont, CA: Wadsworth, 1983.

Coleman, Simon and John Elsner. *Pilgrimage: Past and Present in the World Religions*. Cambridge, MA: Harvard University, 1995.

Corrigan, John et al. *Jews, Christians, Muslims: A Comparative Introduction to Monotheistic Religions*. Upper Saddle River, NJ: Prentice Hall, 1998.

Covell, Ralph R. *Confucius, the Buddha, and the Christ: A History of the Gospel in Chinese*. Maryknoll, NY: Orbis, 1986.

Eliade, Mircea, ed. *Encyclopedia of Religion*. New York: Macmillan, 1987.

Fischer-Schreiber, Ingrid et al. *The Encyclopedia of Eastern Philosophy and Religion*. Boston: Shambhala, 1989.

Gimbutas, Marija. *The Goddesses and Gods of Old Europe: 6500–3500 BC*. Berkeley: University of California, 1982.

Graham, W. A. *Beyond the Written Word: Oral Aspects of Scripture in the History of Religion*. Cambridge: Cambridge University Press, 1993.

Hawley, John Stratton, ed. *Saints and Virtues*. Berkeley: University of California, 1987.

Humphrey, Caroline and Piers Vitebsky. *Sacred Architecture*. Boston: Little, Brown, 1997.

Kieckhefer, Richard and George D. Bond, eds. *Sainthood: Its Manifestations in World Religions*. Berkeley: University of California, 1990.

Magida, Arthur, ed. *How to Be a Perfect Stranger: A Guide to Etiquette in Other People's Religious Ceremonies.* Woodstock, VT: Jewish Light, 1996.

Nielsen, Niels C. et al. *Religions of the World.* Third edition. New York: St. Martin's, 1993.

Noss, David S. and John B. Noss, eds. *A History of the World's Religions.* Ninth edition. Upper Saddle River, NJ: Prentice Hall, 1994.

Peters, F. E. *Judaism, Christianity, and Islam.* 3 vols. Princeton: Princeton University, 1986.

Rice, Edward. *Eastern Definitions.* Garden City, NY: Anchor, 1980.

Smart, N. and Hecht, R. D., eds. *Sacred Texts of the World: A Universal Anthology.* New York: Macmillan, 1982.

Smart, Ninian. *The World's Religions.* Second edition. Cambridge: Cambridge University, 1998.

————, ed. *Oxford Atlas of the World's Religions.* New York: Oxford University, 1999.

Sharma, Arvind. *Women in World Religions.* Albany: State University of New York, 1987.

Wilson, A. *World Scripture: A Comparative Anthology of Sacred Texts.* New York: Paragon, 1991.

Judaism

Amaru, Betsy Halpern. *Rewriting the Bible.* Valley Forge: Trinity International, 1994.

Bradshaw, Paul F. and Lawrence A. Hoffman. *The Making of Jewish and Christian Worship.* Notre Dame: University of Notre Dame, 1991.

Charlesworth, James H. et al. *The Messiah.* Minneapolis: Fortress, 1992.

Cheyette, Brian and Laura Marcus, eds. *Modernity, Culture, and the Jew.* Stanford: Stanford University, 1998.

Davies, W. D. and Louis Finkelstein. *The Cambridge History of Judaism.* Cambridge, NY: Cambridge University, 1984.

Donfried, Karl P. and Peter Richardson, eds. *Judaism and Christianity in Rome in the First Century.* Grand Rapids: Eerdmans, 1998.

Friedlander, Albert H. *The Five Scrolls: Hebrew Texts.* New York: CCAR, 1984.

Frank, Daniel. *The Jews of Medieval Islam.* Leiden: E. J. Brill, 1995.

Glick, Leonard B. *Abraham's Heirs: Jews and Christians in Medieval Europe.* Syracuse: Syracuse University, 1999.

Goldenberg, Robert. *The Nations That Know Thee Not: Ancient Jewish Attitudes towards Other Religions.* New York: New York University, 1998.

Grabbe, Lester L. *An Introduction to First Century Judaism.* Edinburgh: T&T Clark, 1996.

Liebes, Yehuda. *Studies in the Zohar.* Albany: State University of New York, 1993.

Lipsitz, Edmond Y. *6400 Questions about Judaism and the Jewish People.* Downsview: J. E. S. Educational Products in cooperation with Canadian Jewish Congress, 1986.

MacLennan, Robert S. *Early Christian Texts on Jews and Judaism*. Atlanta: Scholars, 1989.

Marcus, Ivan G. *Rituals of Childhood*. New Haven: Yale University, 1996

Neusner, Jacob. *Ancient Judaism: Debates and Disputes: Second Series*. Atlanta: Scholars, 1990.

————. *Dictionary of Judaism in the Biblical Period: 450 BCE to 600 CE*. New York: Macmillan Library Reference, 1996.

————. *Formative Judaism: Religious, Historical, and Literary Studies*. Chico: Scholars, 1992.

————. *An Introduction to Judaism: A Textbook and Reader*. Louisville: Westminster/John Knox, 1991.

Shermis, Michael and Arthur E. Zannoni, eds. *Introduction to Jewish–Christian Relations*. New York: Paulist, 1991.

Waskaw, Arthur O. *Down-to-Earth Judaism*. New York: W. Morrow, 1995.

Wasserstrom, Steven M. *Between Muslim and Jew Islam*. Princeton: Princeton University, 1995.

Werblowsky, R. J. Zwi and Geoffrey Wigoder, eds. *The Oxford Dictionary of the Jewish Religion*. New York: Oxford University, 1997.

Wolpe, David J. *In Speech and in Silence: Jewish Quest for God*. New York: H. Holt, 1992.

Christianity

Bernadino, Angelo di. *Encyclopedia of the Early Church*. Cambridge: James Clark, 1992.

Bettenson, H. *Documents of the Christian Church*. London: Oxford University, 1977.

Bouwsma, W. J. *John Calvin: A Sixteenth Century Portrait*. New York: Oxford University, 1989.

Brown, David. *The Christian Scriptures*. London: Sheldon, 1968.

Brown, Peter. *The Cult of Saints: Its Rise and Function in Classical Antiquity*. London, 1981.

Bruce, F. F. *New Testament History*. Revised edition. London: Pickering and Inglis, 1982.

Cameron, E. *The European Reformation*. Oxford: Clarendon, 1991.

Chadwick, Henry and G. R. Evans. *Atlas of the Christian Church*. Oxford: Phaidon, 1987.

Carmody, Denise Lardner. *Christianity: An Introduction*. Belmont, CA: Wadsworth, 1983.

Close, B. E. and M. Smith. *A Student's Approach to World Religions: Christianity*. London: Holder and Stoughton, 1995.

Colliander, T. *The Way of Ascetics*. Crestwood: St. Vladimir Seminary, 1989.

Cross, F. L. and E. A. Livingstone. *The Oxford Dictionary of the Christian Church*. Oxford: Oxford University, 1997.

Davies, R. E. *Methodism*. London: Penguin, 1985.

Edward, D. L. *What Is Catholicism?* London: Mowbray, 1994.

Evans, Alice F. *Introduction to Christianity*. Atlanta: John Knox, 1980.

Fredericks, James L. *Faith among Faiths*. Mahwah, NJ: Paulist, 1999.

Helm, Thomas Eugene. *The Christian Religion*. Englewood Cliffs: Prentice Hall, 1991.

Hessert, Paul, *Introduction to Christianity*. Englewood Cliffs: Prentice Hall, 1958.

Johnson, P. *A History of Christianity*. Harmondsworth: Penguin, 1990.

Livingstone, E. A. *Concise Dictionary of the Christian Church*. London: Omega, 1977.

Lossky, N. *The New Jerusalem Bible*. London: Darton, Longman & Todd and Doubleday, 1985.

McGrath, Alister E. *An Introduction to Christianity*. Cambridge: Blackwell, 1997.

McManners, J. *The Oxford Illustrated History of Christianity*. Oxford: Oxford University, 1992.

Pelikan, Jaroslav. *The Christian Tradition: A History of the Development of Doctrine*. 5 vols. Chicago: University of Chicago, 1971–.

Phipps, William E. *Muhammad and Jesus: A Comparison of the Prophets and Their Teachings*. New York: Continuum, 1996.

Rahner, Karl. *Foundations of Christian Faith*. New York: Seabury, 1978.

Robinson, Neal. *Christ in Islam and Christianity*. Albany: State University of New York, 1991.

Islam

Amin, Sayyed Hassan. *Islamic Law in the Contemporary World*. Glasgow/Tehran: Vahid, 1985.

Armstrong, Karen. *Muhammad: An Introduction*. Albany: State University of New York, 1992.

Ayoub, Mahmoud. *The Qur'an and Its Interpreters*. Albany: State University of New York, 1984.

Baldick, Julian. *Mystical Islam: An Introduction to Sufism*. London: I. B. Tauris, 1989.

Barboza, Steven, et al. *American Jihad: Islam after Malcolm X*. New York: Doubleday, 1994.

Blair, Sheila S. and Jonathan M. Bloom. *Islamic Art*. London: Phaidon, 1997.

Cragg, Kenneth and R. Marston Speight, eds. *Islam from Within: Anthology of a Religion*. Belmont, CA: Wadsworth, 1980.

Denny, Frederick M. *An Introduction to Islam*. Second edition. New York: Macmillan, 1994.

Esposito, John L. *Islam and Development*. Syracuse: Syracuse University, 1980.

———. *Islam: The Straight Path*. New York: Oxford University, 1996.

———. *Women in Muslim Family Law*. Syracuse: Syracuse University, 1982.

Glasse, Cyril. *The Concise Encyclopedia of Islam.* San Francisco: Harper and Row, 1989.

Haddad, Yvonne Y. and Adair T. Lummis. *Islamic Values in the United States.* New York: Oxford University, 1987.

———, ed. *The Muslims of America.* New York: Oxford University, 1991.

Lapidus, Ira M. *A History of Islamic Societies.* Cambridge: Cambridge University, 1988.

Lee, Martha F. *The Nation of Islam: An American Millenarian Movement.* Syracuse: Syracuse University, 1996.

Lings, M. *Muhammad: His Life Based on the Earliest Sources.* Cambridge: Islamic Texts Society, 1992.

Lippman, Thomas W. *Understanding Islam.* New York: Meridian, 1995.

Mitchell, G. *The Society of the Muslim Brothers.* London: Oxford University, 1993.

Momen, Moojan. *An Introduction to Shi'a Islam.* Yale: Yale University, 1985.

Murata, Sachiko and William C. Chittick. *The Vision of Islam.* New York: Paragon, 1994.

Netton, I. R. *A Popular Dictionary of Islam.* London: Curzon/Atlantic Highlands, N.J: Humanities, 1992.

Rahman, Fazlur. *Major Themes of the Quran.* Minneapolis and Chicago: Bibliotheca Islamica, 1980.

Renard, John. *Seven Doors to Islam: Spirituality and the Religious Life of Muslims.* Berkeley: University of California, 1996.

———. *Windows on the House of Islam: Muslim Sources on Spirituality and Religious Life.* Berkeley: University of California, 1998.

———. *Responses to 101 Questions on Islam.* Mahwah, NJ: Paulist, 1998.

———. *In the Footsteps of Muhammad.* Mahwah, NJ: Paulist, 1992.

Robinson, Neal. *Islam: A Concise Introduction.* Washington, DC: Georgetown University, 1999.

Ruthven, Malise. *Islam: A Very Short Introduction.* Oxford; New York: Oxford University, 1999.

Schimmel, Annemarie. *Islam: An Introduction.* Albany: State University of New York, 1992.

———. *Deciphering the Signs of God: A Phenomenological Approach to Islam.* Albany: State University of New York, 1994.

Sells, Michael A., ed. and trans. *Early Islamic Mysticism.* New York: Paulist, 1996.

Hinduism

Basham, A. L. *The Origins and Development of Classical Hinduism.* Boston: Beacon, 1989.

Bhattacharya, Narendra Nath. *A Glossary of Indian Religious Terms and Concepts.* Columbia, MO: South Asia Publications, 1990.

Blurton, T. Richard. *Hindu Art.* Cambridge, MA: Harvard University, 1993.

Clooney, Francis X., S.J. *Hindu Wisdom for All God's Children.* Maryknoll, NY: Orbis, 1998.

Doniger, W. and B. K. Smith. *The Laws of Manu.* Harmondsworth: Penguin, 1991.

Doniger, Wendy, trans. *Hindu Myths: A Sourcebook.* New York: Crossroad, 1981.

———. *Shiva: The Erotic Ascetic.* New York: Oxford University, 1983.

———. *Textual Sources for the Study of Hinduism.* Manchester: Manchester University, 1988.

Eck, Diana L. *Banaras, City of Light.* New York: Alfred A. Knopf, 1982.

———. *Darshan: Seeing the Divine Image in India.* Second edition. Chambersburg, PA: Anima, 1985.

Flood, Gavin D. *An Introduction to Hinduism.* New York: Cambridge University, 1996.

Hawley, John Stratton and Donna Marie Wulff, eds. *Devi: Goddesses of India.* Berkeley: University of California, 1996.

Hawley, John Stratton, ed. *Sati, the Blessing and the Curse.* New York: Oxford University, 1994.

Herman, A. L. *A Brief Introduction to Hinduism.* Boulder: Westview, 1991.

Hopkins, Thomas J. *The Hindu Religious Tradition.* Belmont, CA: Wadsworth, 1971.

Huyler, Stephen P. *Meeting God: Elements of Hindu Devotion.* Yale: Yale University, 1999.

Kinsley, David. *Hindu Goddesses.* Berkeley: University of California, 1986.

———. *Hinduism: A Cultural Perspective.* Englewood Cliffs, NJ: Prentice Hall, 1993.

Klostermaier, Klaus K. *A Short Introduction to Hinduism.* Oxford: Oneworld, 1998.

———. *A Concise Encyclopedia of Hinduism.* Oxford: Oneworld, 1998.

Knott, Kim. *Hinduism.* Oxford and New York: Oxford University, 1998.

Kramrisch, Stella. *The Presence of Siva.* Princeton: Princeton University, 1981.

———. *Manifestations of Shiva.* Philadelphia: Philadelphia Museum of Art, 1981.

Mahony, William K. *The Artful Universe: An Introduction to the Vedic Religious Imagination.* Albany: State University of New York, 1998.

Michell, George. *The Hindu Temple: An Introduction to Its Meaning and Form.* London: Paul Elek, 1977.

Mitter, Sara S. *Dharma's Daughters: Contemporary Indian Women and Hindu Culture.* New Brunswick, NJ: Rutgers University, 1996.

Olivelle, Patrick, trans. *Upanishads.* Oxford: Oxford University, 1996.

Renard, John. *Responses to 101 Questions on Hinduism.* New York/Mahwah: Paulist, 1999.

Sullivan, Bruce M. *Historical Dictionary of Hinduism.* Lanham and London: Scarecrow, 1997.

Walker, Benjamin. *The Hindu World.* 2 vols. New York: Praeger, 1968.

Werner, Karel. *A Popular Dictionary of Hinduism.* Chicago: NTC Publishing Group, 1997.

Zaehner, R. C. *Hindu Scriptures.* London, New York: Dent, 1992.

Buddhism

Boucher, Sandy. *Turning the Wheel: American Women Creating the New Buddhism.* Boston: Beacon, 1993.

———. *Opening the Lotus: A Woman's Guide to Buddhism.* Boston: Beacon, 1997.

Ch'en, Kenneth. *The Chinese Transformation of Buddhism.* Princeton, NJ: Princeton University, 1973.

Dumoulin, Heinrich, S.J. *A History of Zen Buddhism.* Trans. Paul Peachey. Boston: Beacon, 1963.

Fisher, Robert E. *Buddhist Art and Architecture.* London: Thames and Hudson, 1993.

Frederic, Louis. *Buddhism.* Flammarion Iconographic Guides. Paris: Flammarion, 1995.

Humphreys, Christmas. *A Popular Dictionary of Buddhism.* Chicago: NTC Publishing Group, 1997.

Keown, Damien, *Buddhism: A Very Short Introduction.* Oxford: New York: Oxford University, 1996.

King, Sallie B. *Buddha Nature.* Albany: State University of New York, 1991.

Lopez, Donald S. *Buddhism in Practice.* Princeton: Princeton University, 1995.

Lopez, Donald S. *Curators of the Buddha: The Study of Buddhism under Colonialism.* Chicago: University of Chicago, 1995.

Morreale, Don, ed. *The Complete Guide to Buddhist America.* Boston: Shambhala Publications, 1998.

Paul, Diana. *Women in Buddhism.* Berkeley, CA: Asian Humanities, 1980.

Prebish, Charles S. *Historical Dictionary of Buddhism.* Lanham, MD and London: The Scarecrow, 1993.

Renard, John. *Responses to 101 Questions on Buddhism.* Mahwah, NJ: Paulist, 1999.

Robinson, Richard H. and Johnson, Willard L. *The Buddhist Religion: A Historical Introduction.* Third edition. Belmont: Wadsworth Publishing Co., 1982.

Sangharakshita. *The Three Jewels: An Introduction to Buddhism.* Glasgow: Windhorse, 1991.

Stevens, John. *Marathon Monks of Mt. Hiei.* Boston: Beacon, 1988.

Swearer, Donald K. *Buddhism and Society in Southeast Asia.* Anima Books, 1981.

Tucci, Giuseppe. *The Religions of Tibet.* trans. Godfrey Samuel. Berkeley: University of California, 1980.

Daoism and Chinese Community Traditions

Bokenkamp, Stephen R. *Early Daoist Scripture.* Berkeley: University of California, 1997.

Chappell, David. W. *Buddhist and Taoist Practice in Medieval Chinese Society.* Honolulu: University of Hawaii, 1987.

Cleary, Thomas. *Immortal Sisters: Secret Teachings of Taoist Women.* Berkeley, CA: North Atlantic Books, 1996.

Dean, Kenneth. *Taoist Ritual and Popular Cults of Southeast China.* Princeton: Princeton University, 1993.

———. *Lord of the Three in One: The Spread of a Cult in Southeast China.* Princeton: Princeton University, 1998.

Khn, Livia, ed. *Taoist Meditation and Longevity Technique.* Ann Arbor: University of Michigan, 1989.

———, ed. *The Taoist Experience: An Anthology.* Albany: State University of New York, 1993.

———. *God of the Dao: Lord Lao in History and Myth.* Ann Arbor: Center for Chinese Studies, University of Michigan, 1998.

Lagerwey, John. *Taoist Ritual in Chinese Society and History.* New York: Macmillan, 1987.

Little, Stephen et al. *Daoism and the Arts of China.* Berkeley: University of California, 1999.

Naquin, Susan and Chun-Fang Yu, eds. *Pilgrims and Sacred Sites in China.* Berkeley: University of California, 1992.

Mair, Victor H., trans. *Tao Te Ching.* New York: Bantam Books, 1990.

Maspero, Henri. *Taoism and Chinese Religion.* Amherst, MA: University of Massachusetts, 1981.

Palmer, Martin. *The Elements of Taoism.* New York: Barnes and Noble, 1991.

Pas, Julian F. *Historical Dictionary of Taoism.* Lanham and London: The Scarecrow, 1998.

Robinet, Isabelle. *Taoism: Growth of a Religion.* Stanford: Stanford University, 1997.

Saso, Michael R. *Blue Dragon, White Tiger: Taoist Rites of Passage.* Washington, DC: Taoist Center 1990.

———. *The Gold Pavilion: Taoist Ways to Peace, Healing, and Long Life.* Boston: Tuttle, 1995.

Van Over, Raymond, ed. *Taoist Tales.* New York: New American Library, 1973.

———, ed. *Chinese Mystics.* New York: Harper and Row, 1973.

Wong, Eva. *The Shambhala Guide to Taoism.* Boston: Shambhala, 1997.

———. *Feng-shui: The Ancient Wisdom of Harmonious Living for Modern Times.* Boston: Shambhala, 1996.

———. *Seven Taoist Masters.* Boston: Shambhala, 1990.

Confucianism and Chinese Imperial Tradition

Beguin, Gilles and Dominique Morel. *The Forbidden City: Center of Imperial China.* New York: Abrams, 1997.

Berthrong, John H. *All under Heaven: Transforming Paradigms in Confucian–Christian Relations.* Albany: State University of New York, 1998.

———. *Transformations of the Confucian Way.* Boulder: Westview, 1998.

Chen, Li-fu. *The Confucian Way: A New and Systematic Study of "The Four Books."* London: New York: Routledge & Kegan Paul, 1986.

Ching, Julia. *Chinese Religions.* London: Macmillan Ltd., 1993.

DeBary, William T. *The Unfolding of Neo-Confucianism.* New York: Columbia University, 1975.

Eber, Irene. *Confucianism: The Dynamics of Tradition.* New York: Macmillan, 1986.

Eno, Robert. *The Confucian Creation of Heaven: Philosophy and the Defense of Ritual Mastery.* Albany: State University of New York, 1990.

Feuchtwang, S. *The Imperial Metaphor.* New York: Routledge, 1992.

Holdsworth, May. *The Forbidden City.* Oxford: Oxford University, 1998.

Meyer, Jeffrey F. *The Dragons of Tiananmen: Beijing as a Sacred City.* Columbia, SC: University of South Carolina, 1991.

Nivison, David S. *The Ways of Confucianism.* Chicago: Open Court, 1996.

Raguin, Yves. *Ways of Contemplation East and West.* Taipei, Taiwan: Ricci Institute for Chinese Studies, 1997.

Taylor, Rodney L. *The Confucian Way of Contemplation.* Columbia, SC: University of South Carolina, 1988.

Thomson, Laurence. *Chinese Religion: An Introduction.* Fourth edition. Belmont, CA: Wadsworth, 1989.

Tu, Weiming. *Confucian Traditions in East Asian Modernity.* Cambridge, MA: Harvard University, 1996.

Yao, Hsin-chung. *Confucius and Christianity: A Comparative Study of Jen and Agape.* Brighton, UK: Sussex Academic; Portland, OR: International Specialized Book Services, 1997.

Yu, David C. *Guide to Chinese Religion.* Boston, MA: G. K. Hall, 1985.

Shinto

Ashkenazi, Michael. *Matsuri: Festivals of a Japanese Town.* Honolulu: University of Hawaii, 1993.

Bocking, Brian. *A Popular Dictionary of Shinto.* Chicago: NTC Publishing, 1997.

Grapard, Alan. *The Protocol of the Gods: A Study of the Kasuga Cult in Japanese History.* Berkeley: University of California, 1992.

Hardacre, Helen. *Kurozumikyo and the New Religions of Japan.* Princeton: Princeton University, 1986.

Kageyama, Haruki. *The Arts of Shinto.* New York: Weatherhill, 1973.

Kanda, Christine Guth. *Shinzo: Hachiman Imagery and Its Development.* Cambridge, MA: Harvard University, 1985.

Nelson, John K. *A Year in the Life of a Shinto Shrine.* Seattle: University of Washington, 1996.

Ono, Sokyo. *Shinto: The Kami Way.* Rutland, VT: Charles E. Tuttle, 1998.

Picken, Stuart D. B. *Essentials of Shinto.* Westport, CT: Greenwood, 1994.

———. *Shinto: Japan's Spiritual Roots.* Tokyo: Kodansha International, 1980.

Plutschow, Herbert E. *Matsuri: The Festivals of Japan.* Surrey: Japan Library, 1996.

Reader, Ian. *Religion in Contemporary Japan.* London: Macmillan, 1991.

Ross, Floyd H. *Shinto: The Way of Japan.* Boston: Beacon, 1965.

Tanabe, George J. *Religions of Japan in Practice.* Princeton, NJ: Princeton University, 1999.

Tyler, Royal. *The Miracles of the Kasuga Deity.* New York: Columbia University, 1990.

Yamashita, Hideo. *Competitiveness and the Kami Way.* Brookfield, VT: Avebury, 1996.

Index

549

554

562

571

574

575

581